D0066548

UNDERSTANDING SOCIETY

A Survey of Modern Social Theory

Douglas Mann

OXFORD
UNIVERSITY PRESS

OXFORD
UNIVERSITY PRESS

70 Wynford Drive, Don Mills, Ontario M3C 1J9
www.oup.com/ca

Oxford University Press is a department of the University of Oxford.
It furthers the University's objective of excellence in research, scholarship,
and education by publishing worldwide in

Oxford New York
Auckland   Cape Town   Dar es Salaam   Hong Kong   Karachi
Kuala Lumpur   Madrid   Melbourne   Mexico City   Nairobi
New Delhi   Shanghai   Taipei   Toronto

With offices in
Argentina   Austria   Brazil   Chile   Czech Republic   France   Greece
Guatemala   Hungary   Italy   Japan   Poland   Portugal   Singapore
South Korea   Switzerland   Thailand   Turkey   Ukraine   Vietnam

Oxford is a trade mark of Oxford University Press
in the UK and in certain other countries

Published in Canada by Oxford University Press

Copyright © Oxford University Press Canada 2008

The moral rights of the author have been asserted

Database right Oxford University Press (maker)

First published 2008

All rights reserved. No part of this publication may be reproduced,
stored in a retrieval system, or transmitted, in any form or by any means,
without the prior permission in writing of Oxford University Press,
or as expressly permitted by law, or under terms agreed with the appropriate
reprographics rights organization. Enquiries concerning reproduction
outside the scope of the above should be sent to the Rights Department,
Oxford University Press, at the address above.

You must not circulate this book in any other binding or cover
and you must impose this same condition on any acquirer.

Library and Archives Canada Cataloguing in Publication
Mann, Doug
Understanding society : a survey of modern social theory / Douglas Mann.

Includes bibliographical references and index.

ISBN 978-0-19-542184-2

1. Social sciences—Philosophy. 2. Social sciences—Philosophy—History. I. Title.

H61.M4228 2007   300.1   C2007-901765-7

Cover Image: ©2007 Jupiter Images Corporation
Cover Design: Sherill Chapman

2 3 4 – 11 10 09 08
This book is printed on permanent (acid-free) paper ∞.
Printed in Canada

CONTENTS

PREFACE

The central question in this book is, 'What does it take to understand society?', a question that all good social theorists have tried to answer. The great classical theorists—Durkheim, Marx, and Weber—provide comprehensive answers to this question, answers which I've sketched out in the introductions to Chapters 2, 3, and 5. Modern theorists are no different—they provide an almost bewildering variety of answers to this question. Thus my first task in writing this book was to edit down this vast variety of answers into a manageable number, and then to group these into readable topical chapters.

This leads directly to another question, that of style. Too many textbooks are written in a style that Thomas Carlyle would have called 'dryasdust': humourless, pedantic, and free of metaphor. I have tried here to make the dust of social theory a bit less dry than usual, to be less humourless, less pedantic, and to inject the odd metaphor into my writing. The short stories I've included in about half of the 12 chapters are meant to spark students' interest in the subject at hand, to get them thinking about *why* the problems outlined in the chapter are important to their own lives, to bring social theory home to living human beings.

So why 'modern' and why 'social' theory? I sort out the various meanings of 'modern' and 'modernity' in my opening chapter, but suffice it to say here that I follow the tradition of dividing sociological theory into 'classical' and 'modern' periods, the former ending roughly with the deaths of Durkheim in 1917 and Weber in 1920. A few 'bridge' theorists are discussed in the book, for example, Sigmund Freud and G.H. Mead, but for the most part I've given considerable space only to theorists writing from the 1930s to the present. Social theory is any attempt to understand society in a systematic and abstract way. Within this broader circle one finds sociological theory, the theorizing done by professional sociologists. All sociological theorists are also social theorists, yet not all social theory is done by sociologists. In fact, about half of the theorists outlined in this book have no connection with professional sociology at all. Thus this book is about modern 'social theory', that is, any significant attempt to understand social life, whatever the academic affiliation or status of the inquirer, thus avoiding the rigidity of formal disciplinary boundaries.

As for the question of what to include and what to exclude, I wrote this book from the perspective of a contemporary Canadian interested in the great social changes brought about by modern technology and communications and by a globalization process that has greatly accelerated since the end of the Cold War in 1989. In this sense, *Understanding Society* is very much about the state of social theory at the turn of the millennium—though it by no means ignores the leading theoretical schools of the mid-twentieth century, notably functionalism, Marxism, and symbolic interactionism. In the second half of the book especially, I focus on the shape of the technological, economic, cultural, and social worlds of the last few decades with the hopes of making this text relevant to its readers. The emphasis placed on European and Canadian theorists corrects a fault found in many American-authored social theory texts, which often spend more time on minor American theorists and schools of thought—one text devotes 70 dense pages to rational choice theory—than on more important 'foreign' movements such as post-structuralism and communications theory.

As for the structure of the book, it's organized into topical chapters on major schools of thought such as functionalism or major social issues such as globalization. The order of the chapters reflects the rough chronological order in which these schools of thought or social issues were dominant. So I start with functionalism, dominant from the late 1930s to the 1950s, and then move on to the debate surrounding materialism and critical theory, dominant in the mid-twentieth century. In mid-text comes a chapter on symbolic interactionism, appropriate since Goffman's and Blumer's glory days were the 1960s and 1970s. Later come the chapters on postmodernism, which really only gets started with Foucault and Derrida in the mid-1960s and was at the forefront of social theory at least until the early 1990s. Finally I discuss globalization and corporatism, burning issues still with us today.

Another fault of social theory texts that I have tried to correct here lies in the skewed balances between biography and theoretical content and between primary and secondary sources they offer. In each case I opted for a 'back to basics' approach. Given the constraints of publishing space and readers' time, instead of spending several pages outlining the lives of the great modern theorists (which can be found in other textbooks and on web pages), I usually offer just a brief bio-graphical sketch before leaping into each of their theoretical pools. Finally, many texts try to jam into 10 or so pages a summary of all the major works of an important theorist like Herbert Blumer or Erving Goffman, along with an account of scholarly reaction to those works. This is a mistake. Although a number of broad overviews of theorists or schools of thought are included in the chapters that follow, in many cases I focus on one work alone, in the above examples Blumer's *Symbolic Interactionism* and Goffman's *The Presentation of Self in Everyday Life*. In a few cases I have even written short sections concentrating on a single article by a prominent theorist—Ralf Dahrendorf and Terry Eagleton being cases in point. Generally speaking, it's wiser to give students of social theory a detailed account of a major theoretical work than to spread their understanding thinly over a theorist's long career, leaving them befuddled as to how that theorist's major ideas fit together. It's better to light one big bright bonfire in the darkness than to demand that readers peer through a murky twilight illuminated by a dozen dull flames. I hope my readers find their understanding of modern social theory sufficiently illuminated by these bonfires that they will light paths to more in-depth explorations of the field later on.

Douglas Mann
London, Ontario
February 2007

CHAPTER 1 AN INTRODUCTION TO SOCIAL THEORY

We begin our journey through modern social theory with some philosophical and historical basics. This introduction will serve three purposes. First, it will deal with some basic issues in the philosophy of social science. Second, it will offer three distinct though related answers to the question, 'What is modernity?' (1) Modernity is a process of intellectual change starting with the Enlightenment; (2) modernity is a collection of political, social, and economic changes that include the Industrial Revolution, capitalism, democracy, and imperialism; and (3) modernism is a movement in the arts and letters featuring such luminaries as Picasso, Marinetti, Munch, and Stravinsky. Third, it will define what Thomas Kuhn means by a paradigm and lay out the basic paradigms of social theory that allow us to classify individual theorists into a discrete number of camps.

THE BASICS: WHAT IS SOCIETY?

Before we delve too deeply into some of the more complex issues surrounding the nature of social science, we must deal with the most basic question—what is a 'society'? Well, the first ingredient in our recipe is obviously people. But how many? A couple of people *could* be a society. Yet it would seem odd to use the term to describe a pair of friends or a married couple, so it looks like we need a minimum of three. Second, these three or more people have to be connected in some way, either by living in the same place and interacting with each other, or by communicating with each other over a distance. One useful way of defining this connection between people is by saying that

our three or more people have to *exchange* something in order to be considered a society. This exchange could involve money, information, services, commands and acts of obedience, symbolic gestures like greetings or signs of respect, ceremonial or celebratory acts, a mutual agreement to laws or religious principles, or simple conversation. Naturally, in real societies *all* of these things are exchanged at some time, and there's a lot more than three people involved. Yet without some form of exchange, it's difficult to see a group of people as a 'society', even if they happen to coexist in the same time and space.

Social science is, of course, the scientific study of human life. In modern universities the social sciences include sociology, which studies society as a whole; psychology, which studies the human mind; anthropology, which studies human beings as cultural groups; economics, which studies the economy; and political science, which studies power relationships and forms of government. Sometimes the list includes geography, which studies both the physical environment and the human relation to that environment, and history, which studies human actions in the past. All of these disciplines claim to be scientific because they claim to be able to understand and explain the phenomena they are interested in.

To 'understand' something is not the same thing as 'explaining' it. *Understanding* a phenomenon is to grasp its meaning and significance; to understand a person might also mean that we sympathize with that person. To *explain* something might parallel understanding it: it might involve making that thing comprehensible. Yet in social science it also means to offer a reason or cause for something's existence. For example, one might explain the occurrence of the US Civil War by saying it was caused by a dispute over the moral and legal rightness of slavery. Now sociology obviously tries to understand society; the real question is whether it also has to *explain* the nature and structure of society to be considered scientific.

Commonsensical people, and those addicted to statistics or empirical research, sometimes think that facts 'speak for themselves', or that we had better accumulate some good hard data before we start forming theories about society. Yet just what do these facts describe, e.g., the fact that there is an unemployment rate of 7 per cent in our country? First of all, facts are expressed in one or another language, which is one step removed from the world of hard physical objects. Yet even assuming everyone speaks the same language and understands the meanings expressed by that language perfectly, descriptions of society still use concepts like 'unemployment'. We can't even *think* about social life until we introduce some concepts: all social scientific thinking involves theory by its very nature. In social theory we think in terms of such concepts as 'power', 'gender', 'class', 'property', 'unemployment', 'family life', and 'alienation'. When statisticians measure things, outside of a few strictly physical qualities such as age or place of residence, they are usually measuring things defined by concepts. And all models of society involve concepts, and thus theories. Without theoretical concepts, there would be no social science at all.

SCIENCE AND VALUES

The branch of philosophy to do with how we know things, the theory of knowledge, is called epistemology. This is the subject of the first half of this introduction—specifically, the question how we can have knowledge about society. A basic question in epistemology is what do we mean when we say that a proposition or item of knowledge is 'scientific'? Reams of papers and books have been written on the nature and status of science, so we'll

only cover the tip of the iceberg here. There are two basic ways of defining science: (1) the way we usually do so in the English-speaking world, as the study of nature with the aim of explaining and predicting events, and (2) the European way, as any organized and systematic body of knowledge. Under the former definition, physics and chemistry qualify as sciences, whereas history and philosophy do not; under the latter, all academic disciplines can be said to be 'scientific'.

At least in the Western world, scientists are expected to be 'objective'. This means seeing the objects they're studying free from personal bias and independent of moral, political, or other values. So if a medical researcher discovers that a given drug has dangerous side effects, he or she would be expected to report these in published form and not ignore them because the researcher (or the drug company paying the researcher) doesn't like the results. Similarly, if a physicist puts forward a hypothesis and then does experiments showing that this hypothesis is false, he or she is expected to admit this. Only under this model of value-free objectivity can we expect science to produce valid results, to give us principles and theories that allow us to predict how nature will behave.

The problem with objectivity in social science is that it involves treating *people* as objects. Yet people obviously have hopes and fears, reason and emotions, unlike rocks and trees and earthworms. In short, the *objects* of social science, unlike those of physical science, are at the same time *subjects* both to themselves and to their families and friends. Once a researcher begins to probe into their lives, they are able to react to that intervention in various ways—people do not always remain passive objects of contemplation to sociologists. Further, some social theorists say that not only is scientific objectivity difficult to achieve because people react to being studied, but it may not even be desirable in and of itself: the point of social theory, to paraphrase Marx, is not just to understand the world, but also to change it.

So the first basic distinction between types of social theory is that between descriptive or explanatory theory, which describes and explains the nature of a given society, and normative theory, which also suggests what is right and wrong about that society and what needs to be done to change it. We can also call the latter critical theory insofar as it criticizes aspects of a given society, though the term also refers more specifically to a group of German social theorists who started their careers at the University of Frankfurt in the 1920s. Normative or critical theorists often accuse descriptive theorists of smuggling in moral and political values by the back door: this was famously the case in the 1950s and 1960s when critical theorists argued that functionalism tended to buttress the status quo by offering a model of society that always returns to a state of equilibrium.

The distinction between descriptive and normative theory remains a useful one, despite the fact that descriptive theorists obviously do import values into their work. The distinction is based on the fact that normative theorists are making a conscious effort to criticize and reform society, while descriptive theorists are, at least on the conscious level, trying to avoid basing their conclusions on values. So on the level of intentions, the distinction holds up. Yet whether descriptive theorists are actually able to keep their descriptions of society free of all values is a much more dubious question. It's unlikely that we can actually achieve a full-fledged scientific objectivity in social theory, however noble this may be as a goal. As to whether social theory *should* critique society, the answer is obviously yes, though the critic should always have a good knowledge of the past and present nature of the society before leaping from the descriptive to the normative.

CAUSALITY AND LAWS

When we try to *explain* social life, we encounter new problems. The core of social scientific explanation is the discovery of one or more causes of social actions or social facts. Explanation involves moving from an observable phenomenon back to some event or situation that explains the existence of that phenomenon:

Phenomenon (e.g., drug addition)	←	Cause (e.g., poverty, alienation)

If we want to explain drug addiction, we might think that it is caused by poverty, dysfunctional family lives, urban alienation, or the decline of religion in modern life. Naturally, we'll have to do some empirical investigation to see exactly which item from this list accounts for actual cases of drug addiction. Yet if we believe that we can explain a given phenomenon, we must believe that *something* accounts for its presence. It's not very satisfying to say that drug addiction comes from nowhere!

Causality is important when science seeks to predict how things will behave in the future. To predict the future we must (1) assume the uniformity of nature (and, to some degree, of human nature in the social sciences), and (2) identify and explain the causes of the phenomenon we wish to predict. David Hume (1711–76), a leading thinker of the Enlightenment, argued that to say event Alpha causes event Beta, Alpha must be spatially close or 'contiguous' with Beta, Alpha must be temporally prior to Beta (they cannot happen at the same time), and there must be a 'necessary connection' between the two—the presence of Beta cannot be accidentally connected with the presence of Alpha (e.g., I drop a pencil on the floor at 2:30, and the fire alarm bell goes off two seconds later—these two events are obviously not connected). Yet Hume thought that the real reason we believe that Alpha causes Beta is our psychological habit of seeing events of the type Alpha always followed by events of type Beta. He called this connection 'constant conjunction': when we see an Alpha, we expect to see a Beta, since we have always seen them conjoined in the past. So causality is a psychological feeling in our minds, not something in the quality of Alpha and Beta themselves. Hume's problem—how can we offer a scientific explanation of a phenomenon if causal connection is just a psychological tendency and not part of the structure of the universe—later became known as 'the problem of induction'. Needless to say, scientists tend to see more going on in causal relationships than this mere psychological habit of constant conjunction. Yet constant conjunction is the ground zero of causality, the minimum condition of scientific explanation.

This leads some sociologists to use laws to explain social phenomena, just as physicists and chemists use laws of nature to describe the physical world. A law usually connects distinct types of phenomena so that one type of thing leads to another type of thing in a regular way. A law links causes to effects. For example, the law of gravity connects a 'falling thing' (effect) to the cause of the planet's gravitational force. Also, scientific laws have a wide general validity: they apply over a wide area of space and time, if not universally. For example, gravity operates everywhere on the planet Earth.

For the most part, laws are able to predict what will happen in the future when the first type of phenomenon and the relevant cause or causes are present: this power of prediction is part of what makes them scientific laws. Scientific laws also assume the regularity of nature: the same causes operate in the same way everywhere, all other things being equal. And there must be some evidence that these causes actually exist for us to speak of scientific laws. For example, if I claimed that the sun will rise tomorrow due to an operation of certain astrophysical forces, this prediction could be seen as scientific; yet if I claimed that the sun will rise tomorrow because Apollo's chariot will draw it across the sky, this would not be scientific, as there is no evidence of Apollo's existence, nor can we assume, even if he did exist, that he will behave in a consistent manner. Similarly, social scientific laws must assume, at least in the short term, some sort of regularity of human nature for human acts to be predictable.

Philosophically speaking, we can have two basic types of law. First, deductive laws argue that given cause(s) X, phenomenon Y will *always* happen (assuming a number of background conditions). We see such laws in logic, e.g. 'Socrates is a man; all men are mortal; therefore Socrates is mortal': such a relationship must be true. Also, we see it in physics, as in the law of gravity: things don't just hang in the air from time to time when

we release them from our grip. They always fall down unless their path is blocked by some countervailing force, e.g., a gust of wind catches a piece of paper and causes it to float away.

On the other side of the coin, inductive laws tend to be used more in biology and social science. These express statistical regularities between groups of phenomena or between a group of phenomena and their supposed causes. Another way of defining inductive laws is when a scientist moves from a few cases (e.g., 10 smokers getting lung cancer) to all cases or a general rule or principle (e.g., smoking causes lung cancer). Most of social science is by this definition inductive—we can never be 100 per cent sure of the laws we pronounce to be true, just as we can rarely if ever examine all possible cases of a given cause. So inductive generalizations tend to be expressed as statistics, e.g., '40 per cent of long-time smokers will get lung cancer.'

For example, the French sociologist Émile Durkheim found that suicide rates tended to be higher in Protestant countries than in Catholic countries, which he explained by the greater social solidarity created by Catholicism (based on tighter family structures). This doesn't mean that no Catholics committed suicide, nor that all Protestants are constantly thinking about how empty their lives are; nor is it a matter of *all* Protestant countries having higher suicide rates than *all* Catholic countries. For example, Denmark might have a lower suicide rate than Spain. He's just saying that there's a greater likelihood that a Protestant country will have a high suicide rate than a Catholic country.

Now the problem with inductive laws is, given the fact that they only express statistical regularities, how do we know whether the proposed cause for the social phenomenon in question is the real one? If Lars the Dane kills himself, is it because he is Protestant, or because his wife left him? In Durkheim's discussion of suicide, how do we know it's not the colder climates and longer winters of Protestant countries like Germany, England, or Sweden that cause higher suicide rates, and not religion?

This leads us to the problem of falsifiability, a major issue in the philosophy of social science. Karl Popper (1902–94), a philosopher of social science, argued that the real point of science is not to prove things true, but to prove extravagant and ungrounded claims to be false. This allowed him to ignore the problem of induction. Most theorists would say that all scientific claims, especially laws, have to be falsifiable to be taken seriously: one must be able to think of circumstances that at least in theory would prove them false. If this weren't true, tests of their validity would be meaningless. So the claim that 'there is life on Mars' is falsifiable, at least in theory, by means of a space mission to Mars. But the claim that 'modern Western society is more corrupt than that of ancient Egypt' is probably impossible to prove either way, so it could be treated as an unscientific claim.

A last requirement of a law is that it has to be interesting, to tell us something that seems relevant and non-trivial (in philosophical terms, to not put forward a *tautology*). So if I became very excited with my new discovery, my Iron Law of Shoes that 'students at this university show a definite shoe-wearing tendency during fall and winter terms', I don't think you'd be too impressed with the predictive power of my new law. My law certainly seems to hold true. Yet what it tells us is not terribly interesting. This is why it's important not to put forward theories that merely redefine the basic concept or concepts being used, e.g., 'workers are alienated from their labour because they don't feel part of the labouring process.' This is not an explanation, merely a redefinition of terms.

To finish this discussion of causality and laws in social science, we must touch on a powerful rejection of the very notion of sociological laws. Some sociologists, such as Max Weber and the symbolic interactionists, claim that since social actors are active and creative individuals, it is not possible to predict their behaviour consistently. Unlike rocks and trees, people attribute meaning to their acts, and the social theorist has to understand that meaning to explain human action. They claim that this makes it impossible to transfer the idea of scientific laws from physical nature to human social action: there are no social equivalents to the laws of chemistry and physics. If we try to make general laws of society, we miss most of the *individual reasons* that actors have for acting as they do. So social explanation is giving an account of these reasons, and not trying to classify social phenomena into causes and effects.

As we have seen already, there are real problems associated with assuming that sociology is a science that can draw causal connections between types of events, never mind establishing laws governing these connections.

MODERNITY AND THE ENLIGHTENMENT

When we use the term 'modern' we mean three distinct though related things. First, in an intellectual sense, the modern age starts roughly with the Enlightenment of the eighteenth century and ends either in the present or with the development of postmodernism in the 1960s. Second, 'modern' encompasses the social, economic, and political world that came out of the American and French Revolutions (which helped to spread liberal democracy throughout much of the Western world), the Industrial Revolution, and the flourishing of capitalism. Third, 'modern' is connected to *modernism*, a movement in the arts and letters between roughly 1880 and 1960 that had far-reaching implications for Western culture. We'll deal with each of these three senses of the term 'modern', all of them important for social theory, starting with modernity as shaped by the Enlightenment.

We can loosely define the intellectual space occupied by the modern era, from the Enlightenment to the present day, as one that has occupied itself with Reason, Science, and Progress (including political progress towards liberty, technological progress, and progress in happiness). Tied to all of this is a sense that knowledge is ceaselessly advancing. The Enlightenment was centred in France, with strong secondary movements in Scotland and England (and to an extent Germany), taking place roughly speaking between two revolutions, the Glorious Revolution of 1688 in England and the end of the French Revolution in 1799. These dates also roughly coincide with John Locke's major works on epistemology and political theory at the start of the Enlightenment and Immanuel Kant's last critique at its end. The philosophers and scientists of the Enlightenment elevated Reason to the leading idea of the age, yet they were very much attached to experiment and observation in their scientific work. Most Enlightenment thinkers were empiricists who followed the great seventeenth-century English thinkers Francis Bacon and Locke: they believed that knowledge came to us through the senses, not from pure logical and mathematical thinking, as true rationalists such as René Descartes (1596–1650) thought. Yet in their writings many of them attacked theology and traditional religious beliefs as irrational, making Reason their prime weapon in their attack on tradition. Hence the age was called 'the Age of Reason' since Enlightenment thinkers used reason to attack religious and political oppression. But it was much more an age of *reasonableness*, which demanded that all beliefs be grounded in reasonable claims or proofs.

There is perhaps no better definition of the age than the one put forward by the great German thinker Kant in his essay 'What Is Enlightenment?': one must *dare to know.* In other words, use your reason and your common sense to figure things out for yourself, check to see if your ideas are supported by experience, and refuse to accept traditional beliefs simply because others have accepted them in the past. Kant further said that enlightenment was the liberation of humanity from its self-incurred state of tutelage. So it was not just a matter of thinking for yourself, but of achieving social and political freedom for the human race as a whole.

Philosophically and scientifically, the Enlightenment can be said to start at the end of the 1680s with Isaac Newton's espousal of a system of physical laws based on a mechanical picture of the universe, including his famous law of gravity, in his book *Principia Mathematica*. John Locke (1632–1704) joined to Newton's mechanical cosmos his empiricist picture of perception and the mind, as outlined in his 1690 *Essay Concerning*

Human Understanding. He argued, against Descartes, that all knowledge came from experience, thus paving the way for modern social science, with its emphasis on observation. Also important was Locke's defence of liberalism, as laid out in his 1690 *Second Treatise on Government.* In it he defended the human rights to life, liberty, and property, and a limited right of a people to rebel against tyrannical governments (which the Americans picked up on in 1776 in their revolution). In other words, he argued for the right of people of property to change their political structures when that property was threatened by kings or autocrats governing outside the law.

The Enlightenment was one of those rare historical movements which in fact named itself. Certain thinkers and writers, primarily in Paris, Edinburgh, and London, believed that they were more enlightened than their compatriots, who they set out to enlighten. They believed that human reason could be used to combat ignorance, superstition, and tyranny and to build a better world. Their principal targets were religious superstition (embodied in France in the Catholic Church) and the domination of society by a hereditary aristocracy. The most famous philosophers of the period, after Locke, were the great Scottish thinker David Hume, with his skepticism and interest in a science of human nature, and Immanuel Kant (1724–1804), with his synthesis of empiricism and rationalism in his *Critique of Pure Reason* (1781).

But also important were a large group of French philosophers, writers, and scientists generally referred to by the French term *philosophes.* Most of them advocated a middle-class optimism based on a mechanical and materialist view of science, combined with a trust in a nebulous but benevolent God. They enthroned reason in politics and reasonableness in morals, and equated virtue and progress with intellectual culture. But they also advocated a fierce anticlericalism—being profoundly suspicious of the priesthood—and natural religion, the idea that religion should be 'naturalized', freed of absurd stories about miracles and other supernatural events. Connected to this for many of them was deism, the idea of a 'watchmaker' god who got the universe started, then stepped aside to let natural laws and human beings run things. This was not the god of the Old Testament, but an abstract, impersonal deity. They thus tried to clear the intellectual decks of religious ideas to allow for a scientific study of human nature in the psychological, moral, and social spheres. And they wrote down many of their ideas in an encyclopedia entitled, appropriately enough, *The Encyclopaedia*.

The *philosophes* included the philosophers Voltaire (1694–1778), Dennis Diderot (1713–84) (the founder of the *Encyclopaedia)*, Jean-Jacques Rousseau (1712–78), the Baron de Montesquieu (1689–1755), and the Marquis de Condorcet (1743–94). Allied to this group were many others, including the scientist Buffon and the economists Quesnay and Turgot. They all believed in progress through intellectual development. More specifically, they believed that ignorance and superstition were the great enemies of human happiness, enemies that could be defeated by scientific progress and sound political thought. So they tied social and political progress to Enlightenment, to freeing people from ignorance and educating them in modern science and philosophy. This was especially Condorcet's basic position: that social progress depended on enlightenment.

There were a few exceptions to this general belief. Rousseau believed that the modern arts and science had corrupted the human race, which was better off in its primitive stage, as 'noble savages', when it was organically connected to nature. The modern arts and sciences only made human beings unhappy. Rousseau's idea that maybe society just wasn't worth the bother would haunt social theory right up to this day, as found in anarchism, the Luddite fear of technology, and Freud's doubts about the value of civilization and the repression it fosters.

Montesquieu's Spirit of the Laws

Some claim that sociology starts in 1748 with Montesquieu's book *The Spirit of the Laws*. Montesquieu was a *philosophe* and Encyclopedist. He was a progressive aristocrat who wanted to reform the Old Regime in France along the lines of the English political system, which he saw as preserving liberty by means of a balance of powers between the King, Parliament, and the legal system. He saw this separation of powers as fundamental to the preservation of liberty. The American Constitution to this day reflects Montesquieu's ideas on politics. He was generally tied into the empiricist trend of Enlightenment thought: if you want to understand how something works, you have to observe it, and, if possible, perform experiments on it.

His great work *The Spirit of the Laws*—14 years in the writing—is a comparative study of law and government and of how these are related to social and environmental factors. Montesquieu combines philosophy of history, political and legal analysis, and sociological survey in this work, and relates the laws and character of a people to their form of government, to climate and terrain, and, to a limited degree, to the economic conditions of the country. What he's doing in the book could be best described as political theory with a touch of political sociology: of his 31 chapters, all have to do with law or government; of these, four are on the effect of climate on the laws, one on the effect of the soil, and only three bear directly on economic causes.

He starts by observing that the history of human beings presents a diversity of manners, customs, ideas, laws, and institutions. But Montesquieu finds general causes underneath this diversity that help us to understand it, a very important first step in the history of social theory. His second major contribution to social theory is his reduction of the diversity of all the laws, governments, and customs in the world to a small number of types. These are ideal only: they exist in mixed forms in real cases. Real societies are imperfect embodiments of these 'ideal' types (he thus anticipates Max Weber's notion of ideal types). Montesquieu thought that there were three types of government, each with its own 'animating principle', as shown in Table 1.1.

He found that the laws in a country were relative to the principle and form of its government.

Table 1.1 Montesquieu's Forms of Government

Type of Government	Animating Principle
Republic	Civic Virtue
Monarchy	Honour
Despotism	Fear

So fearful despotic states might have laws that protect the leader against popular dissent, republics have laws that encourage individual initiative, and so on. Yet even within one form of state we can find some cases of the animating principle of other forms, e.g., virtue in a despotism.

Further, Montesquieu believed that a wise legislator should make laws that conform to a country's climate and to its people's character, even though these do not determine the nature of the laws. Yet he was no relativist. In addition to being an empirical and inductive scientist, he believed in natural moral laws that transcended individual political societies. Specifically, he believed in political liberty, which should be enshrined in a liberal constitution that separates the powers within the state into three branches: the executive, the legislative, and the judicial.

The Scottish Enlightenment

Despite Montesquieu's modest innovations, it is undoubtedly the case that the origins of both sociology and social theory as branches of inquiry separate from philosophy can be traced back to the Scottish Enlightenment of roughly 1740–1820. Scotland in the eighteenth century was a divided society. The southern lowlanders were largely Presbyterian Protestants, English-speaking, and modernizing; the northern highlanders were a mixture of Catholic and Protestant Gaelic-speaking (or bilingual) semi-feudal clansmen. The Highlands represented a sort of anthropological museum at the Scottish thinkers' back door, allowing the Scots to go back in time, sociologically speaking, several centuries by travelling a hundred miles or so due north from Edinburgh.[1]

The Highlands saw two struggles between tradition and modernity in this period, both of them bloody. In the first half of the eighteenth century Jacobitism kept the region in ferment. The Jacobites were the followers of the old Stewart line of kings of Scotland (and of England, too, for most of the seventeenth century), who were ousted in the Glorious Revolution of 1688. The followers of these Catholic autocrats staged a number of plots and revolts against the British Crown from 1689 to 1745. The most vigorous of these were the 1715 rebellion of the 'Old Pretender', James Stuart, and the much more successful 1745–6 revolt led by his son Charles Stuart (Bonny Prince Charlie), whose Highland army marched into the heart of England before retreating north and being slaughtered at the Battle of Culloden in April 1746. The aftermath of Culloden was a repression of Highland culture by the government of King George II, including executions and banishments of the Jacobite soldiers and their leaders, a ban on tartans and kilts (later rescinded), a disarming of the clans, and the end of the duty of military service of the clansman to his chief. It also led to a wave of emigration of Highlanders to the colonies in North America and Australia.

The second struggle between tradition and modernity in the Highlands resulted from the clearances of poor tenant farmers by 'improving' landlords wanting to raise rents or to turn the land over to sheep and cattle. These landlords were often clan chiefs and lords related to the very farmers being evicted, so it was not so much a clash of Lowland (or English) and Highland cultures as a battle between a modern profit-oriented economic system and a semi-feudal one where laird and crofter, chief and clansmen, owed each other mutual loyalties. The clearances started in the 1760s, but didn't really kick into high gear until the first two decades of the nineteenth century. They were cruel affairs. The most notorious of these were perpetrated by the Duke of Sutherland and his wife Elizabeth Gordon between 1811 and 1820, during which the houses of those being cleared were burnt to the ground as their inhabitants fled in fear. Some 15,000 were evicted by the Sutherlands in this period. The clearances led to more emigration, many of the Highlanders winding up in Canada, where a Gaelic-speaking community still exists on Cape Breton Island.

In any case, the Scottish Enlightenment was almost an entirely Lowland affair. It was centred in the university towns of Edinburgh, Glasgow, and Aberdeen, especially the former, aided by the independent Scottish legal system (in those days lawyers had a philosophical bent) and by a fairly liberal Scottish national church, the Presbyterian Kirk. Added to this mix were a soaring rate of literacy and a sense of intellectual and economic competition with their southern English neighbours.[2]

The Scottish thinkers of the day took a dynamic and historical approach to their examination of social phenomena. The five main Scottish literati were David Hume, a philosopher, historian, and literary essayist; Adam Smith (1723–90), who founded the theory of capitalist economics in *The Wealth of Nations* (1776) and was a respected philosopher to boot; Adam Ferguson (1723–1816), a philosopher, political theorist, and in my view the first sociologist; John Millar (1735–1801), whose book *The Origin of the Distinction of Ranks* (1771) ties together economic development and the growth of social stratification (or 'distinction of ranks'); and William Robertson (1721–93), a minister and writer of histories of Scotland, America, and of the Hapsburg King Charles V, who argued along with the other Scots that economics is the foundation of social stratification and political hierarchies in all societies. These men lived in a pre-specialist age: they had wide interests, not confining themselves to any single narrow field.

The first premise of the thinkers of the Scottish Enlightenment is that man is a social animal: there is no pre-social state where people lived in brutish, nasty isolation before signing a social contract, as Thomas Hobbes thought. The glue of society is a sense of moral sympathy, a theme that Adam Smith emphasized. Hume said in his essay 'Of Original Contract' that although there *may* have been something like a social contract in the 'most ancient rude combinations of mankind', this original agreement had been wiped out long ago by a thousand changes of governments and princes. All modern states, according to Hume, are based on war and violence, and held together by feelings of sympathy and habit.

The Scots thought that we can best understand our present social condition by introducing principles of order into the welter of historical, social, and economic facts they had in front of them. Their main assumption was that focusing on forms of property was the key to understanding society. The economic system in a given society tells us what type of society it is: from property came distinctions of rank, dignity, and power. Like Karl Marx, Adam Smith thought that the purpose of government was to defend the rich from the poor, to protect the ruling class. Yet unlike Marx, the Scots saw the rise of the middle class under early capitalism as, for the most part, a good thing, for the middle ranks would act as the best bulwark against tyranny.

This view that economics was the key to understanding politics led Smith and Millar to outline four stages of history based on four distinct types of property (all the other literati agreed, except for Ferguson):

- *Primitive:* This is a hunting and fishing economy, where blood and kinship provide social ties. Property comes in the form of a communal sharing of goods; it is not a basis for social stratification or dependence because of its shared nature. Personal strength, physical skills, or cunning determines who rules the tribe.
- *Pastoral:* Here we see the domestication of animals. Wealth accumulates in the hands of a few chieftains and lords, and social stratification becomes more distinct, as property becomes the basis for political power.
- *Agrarian:* In agricultural societies wealth becomes inheritable. The landowners rule, make themselves lords, and employ vassals to maintain their control of the land. Slavery and serfdom become common as sources of cheap labour. This form of economic organization came to an end with the development of trade and manufactures. Smith talks about how agricultural surpluses led to the concentration of 'artificers', i.e., blacksmiths, armourers, butchers, bakers, etc., in the towns, leading to the commercial stage.

- *Exchange/commercial:* Here we see a growing division between manufacturers and agricultural workers. Instead of peasants serving lords in the countryside as part of a feudal obligation, we now see the development of wage labour, as the central nexus of power becomes that between worker and owner. Cash payment for mass-produced goods drives this form of society: economic development depends on a demand for commodities expressed in money terms.

The Scots also emphasized the role of the division of labour in shaping social structure, seeing it as a natural development over time that was for the most part progressive. Modern commercial societies, with high divisions of labour, were superior to traditional tribal ones, with little division of labour. Yet there were drawbacks to specialization: Smith, Ferguson, and Millar all thought that it led to social fragmentation, a lack of community spirit, and in the worst cases stupidity and drunkenness. Their treatment of the ill effects of the modern division of labour is a remarkable anticipation of Marx's theory of alienation (see Chapter 3).

If one wants to pin down the exact moment when sociology was born, 1767 is the most reasonable guess one could make. This is the publication date of Adam Ferguson's *An Essay on the History of Civil Society*. Ferguson was a Highlander who knew both English and Gaelic, a chaplain in the famous Black Watch regiment, and later a professor at the University of Edinburgh. Ferguson's *Essay* not only grounds the nature of a society in economics, unlike Montesquieu, but hints at a number of distinctly modern sociological ideas. He says that his book will deal with people in 'troops and companies', not as isolated individuals. His central metaphor for history and society is that of a passing stream: things are always changing. Society is not made up of fixed entities, but fluid combinations of people and things. The foundation of all societies is the form of property that dominates in them, which is intimately connected to the level the division of labour has achieved in the society in question.

Ferguson argued that there were three distinct types of societies in history:

- *Savage societies:* Tribal societies, where hunting, fishing, and gathering provide sustenance. These tribes pay little attention to property and have minimal social stratification. This is the stage the other Scots called 'primitive society'. Ferguson called both this type of society and the next one in his tripartite division 'rude', meaning lacking refinement.
- *Barbarian societies:* These are mostly pastoral societies where herds of animals have been domesticated. There are servants and masters, rich and poor, in these societies. Barbarians own and care for property, even though it isn't protected by regular laws. This is roughly the pastoral societies of the other Scots.
- *Polished societies:* These are modern societies where property rights have been clearly established. This includes the agricultural and commercial societies of the other Scottish thinkers, and of course modern society.

The interesting thing about Ferguson's treatment of the first two stages of history is that he analyzes them in depth, describing the savages and barbarians in a mixed light, using North American Indians as his main contemporary case of a 'savage' society. For example, he condemned the savages for being superstitious, yet commended them for their courage, martial spirit, and disdain of filthy lucre. In fact, he argued the repetitive, mechanical labour demanded in modern industrial societies makes men stupid:

> Manufactures . . . prosper most where the mind is least consulted, and where the workshop may, without any great effort of the imagination, be considered as an engine, the parts of which are men. (Ferguson, *Essay*, Part 4, Section 1)

This is what Marx would later call the alienation of labour, and is still a problem in contemporary society.

One other key sociological idea that Ferguson emphasized is what later became known as 'unintended consequences':

Every step and every movement of the multitude, even in what are termed enlightened ages, are made with equal blindness to the future; and nations stumble upon establishments, which are indeed the result of human action, but not the execution of any human design. (Ferguson, *Essay*, Part 3, Section 2)

In a word, society is not the product of the thought-out plans of wise elites, but of a long series of experiments tried out by countless individuals and groups, many of them motivated by self-interest and passion, not reason.

So sociology, like the steam engine (James Watt), the historical romance novel (Sir Walter Scott), the telephone (Alexander Graham Bell), and television (John Logie Baird), was a Scottish invention.[3] The Scots' contribution to the invention of the modern world was far in excess of the size of their relatively tiny nation. Yet we have to travel once more eastward across the North Sea to pick up the story of the early development of sociology, to the France of the Great Revolution.

Condorcet's Idea of Progress

Antoine Nicholas de Condorcet was a mathematician, philosopher, social theorist, and politician during the French Revolution of 1789–99. He wrote a constitution for the new French Republic during the height of the Revolution and allied himself with the Girondins, the liberal republicans in the French National Convention. They voted against the execution of the King in 1792 and fell out with the radical Jacobins over a number of political and economic issues, leading to the Jacobins' purging of the Girondins from the Convention in 1794. Condorcet escaped and went into hiding, where he wrote his most famous work, *Sketch for a Historical Picture of the Progress of the Human Race* in 1794. It was meant to be a sketch of a much longer work, which was never finished since Condorcet was captured by the police and thrown in jail. He was found dead the next day, probably having taken his own life.

Condorcet wanted to apply the new mathematical and scientific methods being discovered in his age to social and political issues to produce a 'social mathematics' that would help an enlightened government rule society. His *Sketch* is the long story of human progress from primitive times to the present age, and focuses on how advances in science, technology, and philosophy have driven the human race forward, despite occasional setbacks like the Dark Ages. Condorcet's aim was to demonstrate the progressive emancipation of the human race from the arbitrary domination of physical nature and from bondage of our own making, and:

. . . to show by appeal to reason and fact that nature has set no term to the perfection of human faculties; that the perfectibility of man is truly indefinite; and that the progress of this perfectibility, from now onwards independent of any power that might wish to halt it, has no other limit than the duration of the globe upon which nature has cast us. This progress will doubtless vary in speed, but it will never be reversed as long as the earth occupies its present place in the system of the universe, and as long as the general laws of this system produce neither a general cataclysm nor such changes as will deprive the human race of its present faculties and its present resources. (Condorcet, 1955 [1794]: 4)

His general historical principle, despite his occasional attention to economic matters, is that intellectual changes lead to social and political changes. The main obstacles to the progress of the human race are religious superstition and political tyranny, as one would expect from the only *philosophe* to actively participate in the French Revolution. He hoped that one day 'the sun will shine only on free men who know no other master but their reason', though we have a way to go before achieving such a blissful state.

Condorcet argued that there were 10 stages in history, though he didn't date them as precisely as I have in some cases below:

1. Tribal society, with hunters and gatherers. This is a violent and superstitious stage of history.

2. From pastoral to agricultural peoples, where priests use their special knowledge of medicine and astronomy to dupe the masses.

3. Agricultural societies up to the invention of the alphabet. Here we see the beginning of economic classes, the limited power of chieftains, and the continuing power of priests and sorcerers.

4. Ancient Greece up until the death of Alexander the Great (323 BC). Here philosophy, in the persons of Socrates, Plato, and other Greek thinkers, battled it out with superstition, and political tyranny was partially checked by early notions of human rights.

5. From the Hellenistic Age to the end of the Roman Empire (about 323 BC–AD 476). Philosophy, dependent on the relative political freedom of the Greek city states, declined under the Roman boot. Condorcet condemns the fantastic ceremonies and idols of the paganism of the day as retarding human progress.

6. The Dark Ages up to the Crusades (about 476–1096 AD). This was a disastrous stage of history full of stupidity and cruelty where people suffered under the triple tyranny of kings, warriors, and priests. Theological daydreaming was the order of the day.

7. The Middle Ages up to the invention of printing (1092–1452). The sciences began to recover thanks in part to the discovery by the Europeans of Arab mathematics, science, and philosophy during the Crusades. The invention of the compass aided navigation, while that of gunpowder brought the rule of the knight on horseback to an end. Chivalry moderated the mistreatment of women.

8. The Renaissance (about 1452–1650). The invention of the printing press allowed for the wide dissemination of books and thus created an educated public opinion. Scientists such as Galileo and Copernicus questioned age-old wisdom about the structure of the universe, disrupting the authority of the ancients.

9. From Descartes (mid-1600s) to the French Republic (1792). This was the Enlightenment, where new ideas like the social contract, the natural rights of man, liberty of thought and writing, and the hatred of fanaticism and hypocrisy led philosophers such as Condorcet to hope for the indefinite perfectibility of the human race.

10. The future. Condorcet hoped this would bring three things: (a) an abolition of inequalities between nations and thus the end of war; (b) greater equality within each nation thanks to improved education and freedom of trade; (c) the continued perfection of humanity in both the physical and mental senses.

Condorcet's picture of human history is painted on a huge canvas, encompassing political events, economic changes, scientific revolutions, new technologies, and advances in philosophical and political ideas. Although his hopes for the future may have been far too optimistic, his general picture of history as the story of human progress is a core element in the first sense of the modern.

Comte's Three Stages

Auguste Comte (1798–1857) invented the term 'sociology', though by no means did he invent the discipline. Comte was a positivist, someone who saw the future of the human race as best guided by physical science.[4] Specifically, he thought that society operates according to social laws just as physical objects, plants, and animals operate according to physical laws. Just as in physical science, we can figure out these laws by means of observation, experiment, and comparison. His general conclusion was that societies are like biological organisms with various types of pathological phenomena present in them, just as individual people can have various diseases. He was an early forerunner of functionalism in that he saw people and groups as organs in the social body, each performing a given function. His prescription for the present social body was a strong dose of rule by a scientific elite whose understanding of social laws would allow them to cure the evils of society.

Comte agreed with Condorcet that intellectual development is the primary cause of social change. He saw human history as going through three stages:

- *Theological:* Everything is explained by divine powers or supernatural beings, which are given concrete shape through the symbolism and magic of the priestly caste. This period is dominated by priests and military leaders.
- *Metaphysical:* The divine powers become abstract essences or forces. This was, roughly speaking, the early modern period, when religious leaders and lawyers dominated.
- *Positive:* Only empirical facts and scientific laws are used to explain all phenomena. In this stage industrial administrators and scientific moral guides will dominate.

As with Condorcet's account of the progress of human mind, Comte saw social institutions and the material conditions of life as paralleling these intellectual stages. Yet he was much less concerned with political tyranny than Condorcet, who lived and died in a time of revolution, choosing to centre his account of history on the progress of science alone.

So the first sense of modernity is that embodied by the Enlightenment, especially the social theory of Smith, Ferguson, Condorcet, Comte, and other key thinkers of the age. It centres on the general idea of historical progress connected to either changes in property forms or the advance of science, technology, and ideas. The second sense of the modern has to do with the social and economic conditions of the late eighteenth and early nineteenth centuries, the age of the industrial and democratic revolutions.

MODERN HISTORICAL TRENDS

The Industrial Revolution

The second sense of the term 'modern' we'll explore here is in terms of social modernity, a complex series of events from the eighteenth to the twentieth centuries that gave shape to the world as we know it today. The first aspect of this modernity is the Industrial Revolution of the late eighteenth and early nineteenth centuries, itself predated by the agricultural revolution of the eighteenth century. The general result of the Industrial Revolution was that human beings went from the small-scale production of things by hand to the mass-scale production of things by machines. As a result of this modernizing process between roughly 1760 and 1850, town and country were radically reshaped.

Starting in the early eighteenth century in England and elsewhere in Western Europe, landlords began to improve their lands by various means, looking for greater agricultural profits. This was the agricultural revolution, which generated greater agricultural surpluses and thus extra cash, allowing for investment in trade and manufactures and creating the beginnings of a consumer economy. These improving landlords began to enclose their lands, putting walls or hedges around plots of land (as opposed to using open pastures); to evict non-rent-paying tenants; to rotate their crops to allow the soil to enrich itself, and to use specialty crops such as water-meadows, clover, and turnips to keep cattle alive during the winter. In the case of England, where this revolution was seen in its strongest form, some of the money for these improvements came from colonial landlords who had gotten rich off of sugar plantations and slaves in the West Indies.

Eventually these improving landlords started to make profits, and looked for things to spend these on, including what we would call 'consumer goods' today—fine pottery, furniture, clothes, household ornaments, boots, and carriages. As demand rose for these goods even among the more well-off peasant farmers, and as the population began to rapidly rise around 1740 (the so-called 'demographic revolution'), English towns grew larger and industry prospered. Thus the agricultural revolution, combined with a series of important technological innovations, led to the Industrial Revolution.

The second foundation of the Industrial Revolution was a series of inventions that created the technologies needed for modern industry and transportation:

1769: Josiah Wedgwood opens a pottery factory in England.

1769: Richard Arkwright invents the water-powered spinning frame.

1770: James Hargreaves patents the spinning jenny.

1775: James Watt perfects the first useful steam engine.

1784: James Watt patents a locomotive.

1785: Edmund Cartwright patents a power loom.

1793: Eli Whitney invents the cotton gin.

1829: George Stephenson perfects the steam locomotive.

By 1800, all the necessary techniques for the mass production of cotton and other fabrics, the driving force in the early Industrial Revolution, were in place in England. By 1830 the means for the fast transport of bulk goods—the railway—arrived (though canals predated it by several decades). Without the right technology, the social and economic changes brought about by the Industrial Revolution would not have been possible.

England was the first real industrial power because it was the first country to mass-produce textiles, to mine coal as a fuel on a large scale, to advance iron manufacture and use, and to develop the steam locomotive as the primary mode of transportation. But even before the steam engine, England gets the whole ball rolling in the mid-eighteenth century when the Protestant Dissenters like the Methodists and Baptists, who were excluded from universities, the army, and political office, decided to make their way in life as merchants and industrialists. To move their coal, iron, and other bulk goods, they needed something better than the old trails and Roman roads, so they built roads and a whole network of canals, especially around the new industrial centres of Birmingham, Newcastle, and Manchester in the north.

This canal network, the wealth produced by the agricultural revolution, the creation of the Bank of England in 1694, the rise of new banks like Lloyds and Barclays that served the English provinces, and Dissenter entrepreneurial energy all combined to kick-start the Industrial Revolution in England. Soon factories were being built all over Britain, especially in the north of England; by 1800 iron, cotton, and manufactured goods of all sorts were being produced around the clock in British factories.

The factory system, the core of the Industrial Revolution, was as much the result of changes in industrial organization as of the introduction of new machines (Bronowski and Mazlish, 1960: 307–22). Between 1760 and 1820 in England, small-scale village production of goods shifted almost entirely to large-scale urban production. The first bottleneck in mass production broken was the spinning of cloth, which steam engines and mechanical looms solved. The new factories had several advantages. They allowed the capitalist to:

- control materials, working hours, and the workforce itself;
- rationalize production, making it reliable and predictable;
- introduce new machines that even unskilled women and children could operate;
- centralize production near the power sources needed by the new machines—at first, water power provided by fast-moving rivers; later, steam power fuelled by coal.

The key to factory production was a consistent source of power, which was first reliably provided by James Watt's steam engine. Watt did not invent the first steam engine, but he produced the first one to effectively turn a machine using cylinders, pistons, and cranks. From then on coal and iron became the backbone of the Industrial Revolution: the former to power the steam engines, the latter to build new engines with. Especially after the development of the railways, coal mining and the iron industry entered into a symbiotic relationship, each fuelling (in one way literally) the other's growth. But two related ingredients were needed: the habit by the upper classes of investing excess capital in industry, and the availability of credit to entrepreneurs through the banks and joint stock companies. These factors, along with the complex of iron, coal, steam power, and wool and cotton textiles, drove the changes in production in England and eventually in all of Western Europe and North America, bringing the factory and the industrial city in their wake.

The other important social product was the industrial working class, Marx's proletariat. Human beings—including women and children—were pressed by industrialists bent on making their fortunes into working long hours, often in dirty and unsafe conditions, for little pay. Eventually, after the workers developed a class identity and banded together into unions, they forced their employers to increase their pay and better their conditions. But this split between owner and worker, capital and labour, is still with us today. For much of the twentieth century it was dramatized in the world struggle between capitalism and communism, notably during the Cold War of 1947–89, which pitted the Soviet Empire against the West.

Political Revolutions

Another aspect of social modernity was introduced by the democratic revolutions of the eighteenth and nineteenth centuries, notably the American Revolution of 1775–83 and the French Revolution of 1789–99. In 1775 the colonists of America revolted against King George III and the British Empire, and after a war of several years won their independence. Among other things, the revolution was started by the American colonists' feeling that it was unjust to be taxed by the Crown without having representatives in Parliament. Their Declaration of Independence enunciates principles that evoke the liberal ideas of John Locke (1643–1704):

> We hold these truths to be self-evident, that all men are created equal, that they are endowed by their Creator with certain inalienable Rights, that among these are Life, Liberty, and the pursuit of happiness.

But more important to world history was the French Revolution, probably the most important event (or set of events) in modern Western history until World War I given its influence on rebels throughout the world up to the Russian revolutionaries of 1917. The whole thing got started when a financial crisis in the French monarchical government of Louis XVI forced him to recall the Estates General, the ancient French parliament, which was divided into three estates (the clergy, the nobles, and the middle class). They met in May 1789.

On 17 June the Third Estate—the representatives of the propertied middle class—declared itself a 'National Assembly'; they were locked out of their meeting hall, so on 20 June they assembled in a tennis court and took an oath to stick together come hell or high water. The King wanted them to dissolve, but the Paris mob stormed the Bastille, a royal prison in Paris, on 14 July, which started the violent phase of the revolution. Peasants burned the chateaus of their lords throughout the provinces, and the Paris mob armed and organized itself. The three estates joined together, and in a set of laws passed in early August abolished feudal rights and dues. On 26 August the Assembly passed the famous Declaration of the Rights of Man, which summarized the political ideals of the Enlightenment, with a decidedly bourgeois and libertarian flavour (note the proclamation of negative liberty, the separation of church and state, and the right to property being sacred). Here are some of its articles:

> I. Men are born, and always continue, free and equal with respect to their rights. Civil distinctions, therefore, can be founded only on public utility.
> II. The end of all political associations is the preservation of the natural and imprescriptible rights of man; and these rights are Liberty, Property, Security, and Resistance of Oppression.
> V. The law ought to prohibit only actions hurtful to society. What is not prohibited by the law should not be hindered; nor should any one be compelled to that which the law does not require.
> VI. The law is the expression of the will of the community. . . . It should be the same to all . . . and all being equal in its sight, are equally eligible to all honours, places, and enjoyments, according to their different abilities, without any other distinction than that created by their virtues and talents.
> IX. Every man is presumed innocent till he has been convicted. . . .
> X. No man ought to be molested on account of his opinions, not even on account of his religious

opinions, provided his avowal of them does not disturb the public order established by law. XVII. The right to property being inviolable and sacred, no one ought to be deprived of it, except in cases of evident public necessity. . . .

The rest of the history of the French Revolution involves a complex series of events dominated by a struggle between political factions—the monarchists, constitutional democrats, Girondins, Jacobins, and *enragés* or radicals—which led in 1792 to the execution of King Louis XVI and the declaration of the first French Republic, and in 1793–4 to the Reign of Terror and daily visits to Madame Guillotine by the French aristocracy for a 'shave' from the 'national razor'. Despite the excesses of the French Revolution, we can credit it with a number of largely positive achievements: the destruction of feudalism; the introduction of the democratic ideals of liberty, equality, and fraternity into mainstream European thought; the notion that all men have certain basic rights that the governing powers cannot ignore (including equality before the law and freedom of the press); and the sense that a people has the right (if not a duty) to overthrow a despotic government. Over the next century and a half many revolutions followed, inspired in part by the French. The most important of these was no doubt the Russian Revolution of 1917, which overthrew the Czar and created the Soviet Union.

The Industrial Revolution created a modern industrial society; the political revolutions in America and France led to the modern liberal democratic state. These two developments are the core elements of what we mean by 'social modernity'.

MODERNISM IN THE ARTS, LETTERS, AND SCIENCES

A third and final way of looking at the 'modern' is related to 'modernism', a movement in the arts and letters that dominated Europe and America from roughly 1880 to 1960. Ironically, though it affected modern social theory less than the first two senses of modernity, it parallels the rise of modern social theory in a chronological sense fairly closely. Modernism has two broad streams:

- *Triumphant modernism:* This stream of modernism wants us to embrace modern science, technology, and political life, even though it recognizes that there is a void in modern life. It worships the machine and the machine aesthetic, and the power of the masses.
- *Alienated modernism:* This stream sees modern humanity as fragmented and cut off from some inner or natural essence by the advances of modern life. Progress is put in question. The power of mass democracy and of technology is seen as morally ambiguous. The artist is seen as alienated from society at large, so he or she celebrates this feeling of isolation, of being an 'outsider'.

Both streams, however, call for a new art; both follow the poet Ezra Pound's advice to 'make it new.' Just as the beginning of modernism in philosophy can be traced to Friedrich Nietzsche's pronouncements of the will to power and the death of God in the 1880s, the beginning of modernism in the arts can be traced to Norwegian painter Edvard Munch's *The Scream* (1893). Here is modern alienation in a nutshell. A figure on a steep bridge holds his head and screams: the landscape around him is a swirl of colours. There is an intensity of feeling, but this feeling is undirected, or is directed towards immoral ends. Everything is unstable and fragmented, as William Butler Yeats describes in his poem 'The Second Coming' (1921):

> Things fall apart; the centre cannot hold;
> Mere anarchy is loosed upon the world,
> The blood-dimmed tide is loosed, and
>   everywhere
> The ceremony of innocence is drowned;
> The best lack all conviction, while the worst
> Are full of passionate intensity.

The intellectual, artistic, and political work of the modernists is varied. Yet we can find three common factors that most of it shares:

1. *Avant-gardism:* There is an immense self-awareness of the artist as part of an aesthetic elite, an avant-garde. This causes a celebration of revolutionary aesthetic or moral values. The modernists felt they were ahead of the masses, and thus accelerated the split between high and popular culture.
2. *Shock:* The modernists wanted to shock mainstream society by unconventional behaviour, aesthetic representation, or scientific theorization. There is a strangeness and opacity in modernist works. They seem to violate common sense in some cases. Part of the reason was that modernists sought to shock the public out of their aesthetic complacencies.
3. *Epistemological shift:* Modernist works abandon the idea that there is only one objective reality and replace it with humanly derived structures that are self-consciously arbitrary and/or transitory. The truth is no longer out there, but inside the human observer's mind.

There are a wide variety of examples of how these three themes play out in the two streams of modernism. First, a few examples of triumphant modernism. In political life we see shock in the rejection of Christian morality and democratic values in the various fascist movements in Europe in the 1920s and 1930s, notably in Nazism. The Nazis preached a religion of the master race and of the glories of modern warfare, defending mass exterminations of peoples at the altar of their new faith. Yet years before the rise of fascism in Europe, in 1909, F.T. Marinetti (1876–1944) wrote *The Futurist Manifesto*, which celebrates modern technology (Marinetti calls his car 'my beautiful shark'), speed, war, courage, audacity, and revolt. In these few lines from his manifesto the influence futurism had on fascism should be obvious:

4. We affirm that the world's magnificence has been enriched by a new beauty: the beauty of speed. A racing car whose hood is adorned with great pipes, like serpents of explosive breath— a roaring car that seems to ride on grapeshot is more beautiful than the Victory of Samothrace.

5. We want to hymn the man at the wheel, who hurls the lance of his spirit across the Earth, along the circle of its orbit.
7. Except in struggle, there is no more beauty. No work without an aggressive character can be a masterpiece. Poetry must be conceived as a violent attack on unknown forces, to reduce and prostrate them before man.
9. We will glorify war—the world's only hygiene—militarism, patriotism, the destructive gesture of freedom-bringers, beautiful ideas worth dying for, and scorn for woman. (Marinetti, 1909)

Marinetti's futurism glorified struggle and war, revelling in the beauty of the new age heralded by such modern technologies as electricity, automobiles, railways, and airplanes. All of this appealed very much to the Italian Fascists, who turned Marinetti into an intellectual hero.

Even though few people still read Marinetti, futurism is alive and well in our own day. We see it in the love of technology, speed, blood, and war in contemporary media and culture. These are especially celebrated by the American media: witness CNN's fascination with the technology of death during the two Gulf Wars—from stealth fighters to smart bombs being manoeuvred down Iraqi chimneys—and Hollywood's fascination with the American war machine. Watch Francis Ford Coppola's bitterly ironic *Apocalypse Now* (1979), notably the attack on a Vietnamese village by helicopter gunships to the tune of Wagner's 'Ride of the Valkyries', and Ridley Scott's *Black Hawk Down* (2001), where a new generation of helicopters have become the stars and death is slowed down to a symphony of splattered blood and ultra-realism. Or consider the many dozens of violent video games, from fantasy role-playing games to first-person shooters such as the top-selling *Grand Theft Auto* and its sequels. Marinetti's adoration of his beautiful shark has led to North America's unholy love of the automobile, which has turned most of our cities into conglomerations of expressways, parking lots, and drive-through fast-food joints. David Cronenberg's film *Crash*

(1996) presents the unconscious foundation of this unholy love in all its mangled glory, while the more recent *The Fast and the Furious* films present its papered-over Disney version, where fast cars and hot guys and gals stick together like super-magnets. North America's romance with the automobile has lasted far longer than even the best of marriages. The price we pay for this love affair in North America is about 46,000 deaths in car accidents per year. The death toll in the 11 September 2001 al-Qaeda attacks was 2,986, only 6.5 per cent of the annual car accident total. Yet we hear no hysterical CNN or Fox News reporters attacking GM, Ford, and Toyota as auto-terrorists.

Modernist architecture also celebrated the new. It's noted for its cool functional buildings, which are in effect huge blocks of steel, glass, and concrete. We see these in the city cores of all modern metropolises. Le Corbusier (1887–1965) said that modern architecture had to destroy the past by making buildings 'machines for living in' made up of pure mathematical forms—squares, pyramids, and cubes. They would be free from frivolous ornamentation, a paean to functionality. A main player in the 'International School' of architecture, Ludwig Mies van der Rohe (1886–1969), designed some of the more famous glass and steel boxes that populate urban landscapes in North America using the same functional logic Le Corbusier used. Modernist architecture is an example of misguided avant-gardism: they saw themselves as creating a new public space, one that would be efficient and functional, representing a clear break from the classical and gothic styles, with their use of columns, statues, colour, and ornamentation.

Our third case of triumphal modernism was seen in physics, notably in Albert Einstein's theory of relativity and Werner Heisenberg's uncertainty principle. Both ask us to make a fundamental epistemological shift, from the view that time and space are objective and movement through them continuous to the idea that space and time are relative phenomena—they depend on the position of the observer.

Alienated modernism dominated the world of the arts and letters. We've already had a glimpse of Yeats's vision, with its bleak nihilism about the current state of things, a 'centre [that] cannot hold', and a twisted, apocalyptic second coming of Christ as a 'rough beast slouching towards Bethlehem to be born'. Yet the best-known modernist poem is undoubtedly 'The Wasteland' (1922) by T.S. Eliot (1888–1965), an experimental and fragmented poem full of literary, historical, and mythological tidbits depicting a soul and society in fragmentation and despair seeking a new sense of integration and authenticity, a new centre of things. Here's how it starts:

> April is the cruelest month, breeding
> Lilacs out of the dead land, mixing
> Memory and desire, stirring
> Dull roots with spring rain.

Eliot was an avant-gardist who tried to shock his readers with the loose structure and obscure subject matter of his work. His works painted a picture of the modern world as one where decline and decay dominated—it was a wasteland, a not unreasonable conclusion to the generation who survived the carnage of World War I. For Eliot the world ends not with a bang, but a whimper: for his world-weary soul *all* months were cruel Aprils.

We see this same desire to create an artistic avant-garde and to shock in modernist music. Igor Stravinsky (1882–1971) wrote jarring unmelodic works such as *The Rite of Spring* (1913), which caused its original audience to riot. Arthur Schoenberg (1874–1951) went one step further, composing atonally using a 12-tone series, producing almost unlistenable music. In both cases their motivation was to shock their audiences with an epistemological shift in the way we listen to music, a music produced not for the masses but for an artistic avant-garde.

As for modernist prose, we see in the works of the Czech writer Franz Kafka (1883–1924) an attempt to shock and disorient the reader with such strange stories as the one about Gregor Samsa, a man who slowly turns into a bug ('Metamorphosis', 1915), and another of a certain Mr K. who is lost in a labyrinthine legal bureaucracy he can never understand after he is put on trial for

Picasso's *Les Demoiselles d'Avignon* (1907). (Picasso, Pablo (1881-1973) © ARS, NY. Les Demoiselles d'Avignon. Paris, June-July 1907. Oil on canvas, 8' × 7' 8". Acquired through the Lille P. Bliss Bequest. (333.1939). Location: The Museum of Modern Art, New York, NY, USA. Digital Image © The Museum of Modern Art/Licensed by SCALA/Art Resource, NY. (Art 162072) © Picasso Estate/SODRAC (2007).)

some unknown reason (*The Trial*, 1925). The great Irish modernist James Joyce (1882–1941) wrote stories about ordinary Dubliners in a 'stream of consciousness' form: we hear stories of ordinary life, literary allusions (notably to Homer), word games, and elaborate puns in his novels and stories. His massive novel *Ulysses* (1922) is still a challenge to students of literature to read cover to cover, even though it encompasses only one day in the life of the Bloom family in 1904. Modernist literature as a whole seeks to shock the reader with fragmented tales of souls lost in confusion while appealing to an avant-garde that understands both its difficult technique and its mythological, historical, and literary allusions.

Yet modernism really cut its teeth in the world of visual art. All three elements of modernism are there in abundance: avant-gardism, shock, and an epistemological shift. Pablo Picasso (1881–1973) was one of the founders of cubism, which reduced three-dimensional organic figures to the solid two-dimensional geometry of cubes, spheres, and cones. His goal was to reorient the way we looked at the world by allowing us to see all sides of an object at once, thus giving us multiple viewpoints on the same thing. His painting *Les Demoiselles d'Avignon* (1907), only in part cubist, features five women, probably prostitutes, painted in a very angular way in pinks, oranges and blues. Two of the heads of the women have strange mask-like faces suggesting African masks; one of them has rectangular breasts. Picasso is clearly moving painting away from representation of any external reality in this work. Rather, he's showing us his inner vision of the world, a vision that certainly shocked the ordinary patron of the arts when first put on display. This lack of faith in the power of art to realistically represent the world is another theme that would connect modernist art to postmodernist theory, which among other things disputes the power of social theory to represent the social world.

Marcel Duchamp (1887–1968) was a cubist painter who was also a key player in the 'Dada' movement, which started in Switzerland during World War I. The Dadaists tried to destroy traditional notions of beauty by writing random poetry (e.g., by cutting up newspaper headlines and picking random words out of a sack), by creating collages out of everyday objects like train tickets, bits of wood, and buttons glued onto a board, and by holding public meetings where they gave nonsensical speeches. This anti-art tried to show how art, morality, and civilization were absurd nonsense. Duchamp's most famous effort in this regard was *Fountain* (1917), which was simply a urinal signed R. Mutt and put on display in a museum. Duchamp both challenged the artistic establishment to redefine what they meant by art and shocked the viewer into making an epistemological shift into a new sense of anti-beauty

A third artistic movement, surrealism, borrowed from Sigmund Freud and Carl Jung the idea that in dreams and semi-conscious states the mind is freed from the tyranny of the rational ego and can produce images of the unconscious that are illuminating and fresh. The surrealists tried to paint their dreams. Salvador Dali (1904–89), the grand master of surrealist painting, included melting clocks, burning giraffes, and tigers leaping from the

mouths of fishes in his work, all meant to defy traditional images of waking rational reality. A fourth
artistic movement worth mentioning is abstract
expressionism. One of the major figures, American
artist Jackson Pollock (1912–56), spattered and
poured paint onto his huge canvasses to express in
abstract form his feelings, and not to represent
reality. His splatter paintings were seen by many as
a truly American movement in art, distinct from the
socialist realism promoted by Soviet Russia and the
neo-classical works promoted by Nazi Germany. All
four of these movements in art—cubism, Dadaism,
surrealism, and abstract expressionism—painted a
picture of the modern world as one of shock, alienation, and fragmentation.

Modernism profoundly influenced culture in
the early and mid-twentieth century with its various attempts to embrace modernity as a series of
technological, political, and artistic currents, from
Marinetti's sleek automobiles and van der Rohe's
functional black boxes to Eliot's wasteland and
Dali's dreams. It also contributed to the rise of
postmodernism in the last third of the century,
which fed on the modernist themes of shock,
fragmentation, avant-gardism, and fundamental
shifts in the way we see the world. This is the third
sense of what we mean by the 'modern', after the
intellectual modernity of the Enlightenment and
the social modernity of the democratic and industrial revolutions.[5]

PARADIGMS OF SOCIAL THEORY

This final section of the introduction will sketch
out a trail map that will help to guide us through
the tangled forest of modern social theory. Social
theorists make certain basic choices about the way
they see society before getting into the nitty-gritty
details of their theories. These choices parallel
what Thomas Kuhn (1922–96), a prominent
philosopher of science, called 'paradigms'—
patterns or models of how a whole field of
research should see the world. As Kuhn explained,
'These I take to be universally recognized scientific achievements that for a time provide model
problems and solutions to a community of practitioners' (Kuhn, 1970: viii).

Kuhn argues that most of the time scientific
researchers work within one or another paradigm,
a process he calls 'normal science'. Only once this
paradigm is challenged by anomalous experimental results do people rethink their basic assumptions. He calls this period a scientific revolution,
when the accepted paradigm for a field of research
changes.[6] A famous example of such a paradigm
shift came during the sixteenth century when
thanks to Copernicus's astronomical work, scientists gave up the geocentric view of the solar
system—the view that the sun and planets
revolved around the earth—and adopted a helio-
centric view with the sun at the centre of everything. This was the Copernican Revolution in
astronomy, one that took the human race and our
little blue globe out of the cosmic centre of things.

Paradigms help us to order the endless field
of data before us and to give direction to our
thinking—this is just as true in social science as
in astronomy, physics, or chemistry. In fact, they
are often about things that cannot be clearly supported or refuted by empirical evidence, e.g., like
the belief in God, or the idea that someone loves
you. Yet they involve powerful beliefs such as
those concerning religion, love, and the nature of
reality that structure and dominate our thinking
all the same.

How does Kuhn's idea of a paradigm apply to
social theory? All important social theorists make
some general assumptions about the nature of society. Some theorists claim that we can only understand social life by looking at the big picture and
considering such mass phenomena as revolutions,
unemployment rates, or rates of suicide. These theorists engage in macro-sociology, with the focus on
large-scale phenomena that admit of exceptions in
individual cases. Philosophical analysis and statistics are two of their favourite methods. Macro-
sociologists tend to focus on mass human action
rather than the individual meanings that social
actors attribute to their acts.

On the other side are micro-sociologists, who
argue that we can only really understand social life
on the individual level. Such theorists might suggest that to understand a social problem we should
interview individual actors or become participant

observers in the appropriate field of social life. For example, if a micro-sociologist wanted to understand the culture surrounding drug addiction, he or she might find a number of drug addicts and spend time with them, seeing how they live and what meanings they attribute to their actions.

Parallel to this distinction between micro- and macro-sociology is another distinction between a focus on individual human agency and that on social structure as the core of theoretical analysis. Those who focus on human agency take into account the specific reasons and emotions that go into the individual actor's decisions, while those who focus on social structure argue that interpersonal structures cause or determine social actions independent of the wills of those actors.

We can make a second basic distinction in the understanding of society based on whether the theorist sees consensus or conflict as the core of social life. Some theorists, such as Émile Durkheim and the functionalists, see society as an organism that requires certain functions to be fulfilled for it to remain healthy. They imply that the healthy functioning of the social organism is the 'normal' state of affairs and see disruptive factors such as crime, dissent, and revolution as social diseases. These theorists emphasize social consensus and tend to support the status quo: they see society as a social body whose normal state is health, an analogy for social peace and the absence of conflict.

On the other hand are conflict theorists, including Karl Marx, Max Weber, and Herbert Marcuse, who see society as full of disputes and struggles between social groups or classes with different interests. Since these interests conflict with each other (especially under conditions of economic scarcity where everyone can't get what they want), the major elements of society fight with each other to grab their slice of the pie, whether the pie is money, jobs, social status, or political power. So conflict theorists see social conflict as the norm, not social peace.

Table 1.2 lists the basic starting paradigms of many of the major classical and modern social theorists. Although this oversimplifies their ideas somewhat, we can separate social theorists into at least four camps based on whether they place the greatest emphasis on individual agency or social structure, and on whether they emphasize social

Table 1.2 Mapping Social Theory

Explanatory Emphasis	Individual Agency (Micro-sociology)	Social Structure (Macro-sociology)
Social Consensus	Herbert Blumer and symbolic interactionism	Émile Durkheim on social facts and forms of solidarity
	Erving Goffman's dramaturgy (tending towards conflict)	Talcott Parsons's functionalism
	Phenomenology	
Social Conflict	Max Weber's *Verstehen* sociology	Marx and Engels's dialectical materialism (and later Marxism)
	Anthony Giddens's structuration theory (tending towards macro)	C. Wright Mills
	Christopher Lasch (tending towards macro)	Frankfurt School (Adorno, Marcuse)
	Naomi Wolf and liberal feminism	Birmingham School of Cultural Studies (Hall, Hebdige)
	John Ralston Saul (roughly)	Shulamith Firestone and radical feminism
	Most postmodern theory	Situationists
		Jean Baudrillard

consensus or social conflict in their works. So Karl Marx is basically a conflict theorist who emphasizes social structure, while the symbolic interactionists are basically consensus theorists who focus on human agency.

As we consider the various social theorists in this book it might help to flip back to this chart from time to time to remind yourself of the basic paradigms each begins with. Our first entry into the dense forest of modern social theory brings us to functionalism, the dominant paradigm in American social theory from the 1930s to the 1950s. Yet before we encounter Talcott Parsons, the dominant functionalist thinker, we must first visit a darker and more dangerous place, Thomas Hobbes's state of nature.

STUDY QUESTIONS

1. Define 'society'. Give examples of something that is a society and something that is not a society.
2. What is the difference between understanding a social phenomenon and explaining it?
3. What is objectivity in social science? Can social science really be objective?
4. What is the difference between descriptive and normative social theory? Which path do you think social theory should take?
5. What is causality? How is it connected to explanation? Why is it important in social science? What was David Hume's skeptical approach to the analysis of causality?
6. What are the two types of scientific laws? Which applies to social science? Why?
7. What is falsifiability? How does it apply to social scientific laws?
8. What are the general principles of the Enlightenment? More specifically, what were the principles of the French *philosophes*?
9. What three types of government did Montesquieu outline, and what spirit did he find in each? Do these types of government still exist today? Where? Do they still match up with the same animating principles Montesquieu outlined?
10. What were the Scottish Enlightenment's basic ideas about the nature of society? In what sense could we call these 'modern'?
11. What four stages did the Scots see in history? What were they based on?
12. Why can we call Adam Ferguson the first sociologist?
13. What were Condorcet's basic notions about the nature of historical progress? What were his hopes for the future? Did these hopes come to fruition in the 200 years after his death?
14. What was Comte's basic view of society? How did he differ from Condorcet's view of history, if at all?
15. What were the basic social and economic preconditions of the Industrial Revolution? What important social effects did it have?
16. What were the main social and political effects on Western society of the French Revolution? Why is it a key event in defining modernity?
17. What were the two main streams of modernism? Give two examples of each from the arts, letters, or political life.
18. How is Marinetti's futurism connected to fascism? Do we see any evidence of futurist ideas in modern life?
19. Discuss how the writings of Yeats, Eliot, Kafka, and Joyce evoke alienated modernism.
20. How do cubism, Dadaism, surrealism, and abstract expressionism express the three basic factors found in modernism in general?
21. What is a 'paradigm'? Give an example from science or social science.
22. What are the two basic paradigmatic choices social theorists make that allow us to divide them into four camps? Give examples of two theorists, showing what camps they fit into.

Short Bibliography

[*Internet versions of original Enlightenment texts have been included in some cases to make research easier. Modern book editions of these works are also available.*]

Bronowksi, J., and Bruce Mazlish. 1960. *The Western Intellectual Tradition*. New York: Harper.

Burke, James. 1985. *The Day the Universe Changed*. BBC TV series.

Chitnis, Anand. 1976. *The Scottish Enlightenment: A Social History*. London: Croom Helm.

Condorcet, Marquis de. 1955 [1794]. *Sketch for a Historical Picture of the Progress of the Human Race*, trans. Jane Barraclough. Westport, Conn.: Greenwood Press.

Ferguson, Adam. 1767. *An Essay on the History of Civil Society*. Available at: <www.constitution.org/af/civil.htm>.

Glover, Janet R. 1960. *The Story of Scotland*. London: Faber & Faber.

Hume, David. 1739/1740. *A Treatise of Human Nature*. Available at: <socserv2.socsci.mcmaster.ca/~econ/ugcm/3ll3/hume/treat.html>.

Kuhn, Thomas. 1970. *The Structure of Scientific Revolutions*, 2nd edn. Chicago: University of Chicago Press.

Lehmann, John C. 1960. *John Millar of Glasgow: His Life and Thought and Contribution to Sociological Analysis*. Cambridge: Cambridge University Press.

Mackie, J.D. 1969. *A History of Scotland*. Harmondsworth: Penguin.

Marinetti, F.T. 1909. *The Founding and Manifesto of Futurism*. Available at: <www.unknown.nu/futurism/manifesto.html>.

Montesquieu, Baron de. 1914 [1752]. *The Spirit of the Laws*, trans. Thomas Nugent. London: G. Bell and Sons. Available at: <www.constitution.org/cm/sol.htm>.

Swingewood, Alan. 1970. 'The Origins of Sociology: The Case of the Scottish Enlightenment', *British Journal of Sociology* 21: 164–80.

CHAPTER 2 | FUNCTIONALISM AND ITS CRITICS

HOBBES'S QUESTION: WHY HAVE A SOCIETY AT ALL?

We start our exploration of modern social theory with the most basic question imaginable—why have a society at all? Thomas Hobbes (1588–1679), a classical political philosopher, helped to answer this question in a way that provided the grounding for functionalist theory. In his masterwork *Leviathan* (1651), itself indirectly a product of the chaos and violence of the English Civil War of the 1640s, Hobbes paints his reader a picture of a 'state of nature' where there is no law or government, where life is 'solitary, poor, nasty, brutish, and short'. Life is a war of each against all, where the weakest can kill the strongest, and property is not secure.

Thankfully, the denizens of this dark place have their reason and their self-interests, so they (or so Hobbes argues) agree to a social contract to establish peace. The signing of the peace treaty between the inhabitants of the state of nature is Hobbes's first 'law of nature': seek peace if you can get it, and defend yourself by any and all means if you can't. Following hotfoot from the first law is the second, which is the necessity to lay aside as much natural freedom towards others as they're willing to give up for you. This allows for the citizens of this newly formed community to secure their property and their person, which is for Hobbes a sort of property. Third is the promise made by one and all to keep any contracts made. After a whole slew of more laws of nature comes Hobbes's final gambit: the contract signers agree to give up their freedom to a powerful Sovereign, who is given broad powers to create laws and enforce them. This could be either a king or a parliament, as long as the institution has teeth.

Hobbes's basic question 'why have a society at all?' was very much on the minds of functionalist thinkers. They also asked, more specifically, what the point was of such social institutions as churches, the police, the courts, schools, the family, and, in the twentieth century, the mass media. Their basic answer is that each of these institutions performs a vital 'function' within a wider social organism. The first thinker to give this sort of answer was Émile Durkheim.

DURKHEIM ON SOCIETY AS A FUNCTIONAL ORGANISM

Émile Durkheim (1858–1917) was a French/Jewish academic sociologist whose father, grandfather, and great-grandfather all were rabbis. Durkheim taught at the University of Bordeaux from 1887 to 1902 and from 1902 until his death at the University of Paris. He funded the first French sociology journal, *L'Année Sociologique*, and was the first professor of sociology at the Sorbonne. He was very patriotic during World War I. Tragically, his son André died during this conflict in 1916. This, along with overwork, led to a heart attack that killed Durkheim the next year. His main works were *The Division of Labour in Society* (1893), *The Rules of Sociological Method* (1895), *Suicide* (1897), and *The Elementary Forms of the Religious Life* (1912). He was very much interested in the effects of moral norms on social solidarity, especially those emanating from the division of labour and religion.

Durkheim was influenced by the French sociological tradition going back to Auguste Comte and by the philosophy of Immanuel Kant (1724–1804). He was a student of Kant's philosophy during his youth, and never forgot Kant's notion that our minds organize experience through ideas. He took this aspect of idealist thought and applied it to sociology—he saw society as constituted by our ideas and values, our norms. His general goal was to establish sociology as a science distinct from psychology and biology, with which it had traditionally been mixed up. To do so he tried to show that sociology dealt with something other than human thoughts, feelings, and physiology, with something he called 'social facts'.

Social Facts

Durkheim was a macroscopic theorist who emphasized the power of society over the individual. He focused on the way individuals are integrated into society, and how society maintains its social equilibrium. Durkheim wanted sociology to be a science of society. We have to focus on social facts as the core of such a scientific understanding of society. A social fact is something having a general existence over all of society, independent of our individual wills and situations:

> A social fact is every way of acting, fixed or not, capable of exercising on the individual an external constraint; or again, every way of acting which is general throughout a society, while at the same time existing in its own right independent of its individual manifestations. (Durkheim, 1964 [1895]: 13)

A social fact constrains our behaviour from the outside. It makes us do some things and not do others, and is general in nature, existing independently of this or that case of it.

An example is the way people dress. In theory, you could come to class dressed like a Renaissance courtier wearing a cape and a big-brimmed hat with a red feather in it, but no one actually does this due to the social ridicule it would bring. In fact, few would even consider it in the first place. So fashion is a case of a social fact. Laws, moral norms, strongly held beliefs, and general statistical rates of things like unemployment and suicide are also social facts. Social facts are objectively true for some collectivity of people. They're not merely in your head—they're objectively out there.

As scientific sociologists, according to Durkheim, we must be detached from the social facts we study. Durkheim said we must 'consider social facts as things.' By doing so he believed that sociology could be a science just like physics or chemistry (yet if social rules and norms were simply ideas in our heads, this wouldn't be possible). People are moulded and constrained by social facts, especially those of a moral nature. Durkheim thought that moral rules are shaped by society, not by philosophical debates between individuals. Moral rules and connections between people were the core of what he meant by 'social facts', which he thought he could scientifically observe, describe, and classify.

The Social Organism and Functionalism

At least when talking about modern, complex societies with high divisions of labour, Durkheim was more or less a functionalist: he focused on the functions that each element of the social system played within a greater social body. Institutions and norms serve the general needs of the social organism; the function of religion is to reinforce moral rules, while that of the police is to catch criminals.

He compares the functions of social institutions to the functions of organs in our body: our heart pumps blood, our kidney filters alcohol and other poisons, our eyes allow us to see, and so on. Yet he avoids an error common among later functionalists. The function a thing performs is separate from its cause, even though these can interact. A social fact may have been caused by something totally unconnected to the function it performs. For example, the function of punishing criminals is to reinforce social rules and to reawaken a sense of moral order in the minds of the average citizens, even though the actual cause of crime might be poverty.

This led Durkheim to borrow another concept from biology: pathology. Just as when I have the flu my body is in a pathological state, when a society isn't functioning properly we can say that it's in a pathological state and look for a cure. His definition of a 'normal' social state of affairs was simple enough: if this state of affairs is typical of such a society at its current stage of evolution, it is 'normal'. In other words, a phenomenon is normal if it's common. This idea of normal and pathological states of the social organism led Durkheim's critics to accuse him of being a conservative too much in love with the status quo—after all, aren't 'normal' societies better than pathological ones?

Collective Conscience and the Organic Analogy

For Durkheim the principal factors holding society together are shared ideas, values, and norms. He argued that societies have a *conscience collective*, a French expression that can mean either a collective conscience, where we share basic moral values, or a collective consciousness, where we agree on basic ideas about time, space, and reality as whole. In either case, these ideas and norms regulate our thinking and our lives independent of our individual decisions or reasoning.

He was arguing against utilitarians such as Herbert Spencer (1820–1903), who saw humans as rational beings who entered society in order to maximize their utility or self-interest, and thus their individual chances at happiness. The utilitarians say that it's in our self-interest to keep our agreements—morality can be explained by a rational human choice to protect our persons and our property in order to promote both our own and the general happiness.

Durkheim saw social norms as a social product. Society is more than a collection of disjointed contract signers or utility maximizers who rationally agree to social peace as Hobbes suggested: even to respect a contract, we must have in place some sort of collective norms in the first place.

This is found in the collective conscience. Durkheim argued that the collective conscience was stronger in traditional societies, where the division of labour was less striking. It is the metaphysical and moral glue holding society together.

Mechanical vs Organic Solidarity

Durkheim saw the division of labour as a key element in understanding a society. He argued, against Marx, that the separation of trades and professions characteristic of advanced industrial societies need not be alienating—in fact, since such societies obviously function to some degree, they must have some form of social solidarity at work in them.

Solidarity in a society comes from two things: the division of labour and a similarity in beliefs. He distinguished two types of solidarity:

Table 2.1 Durkheim's Forms of Solidarity

Form of Solidarity	Characteristic Society	Description
Mechanical	Primitive tribal	Rigid social norms enforced
Organic	Modern industrial	Interdependence of roles

In primitive tribal societies, mechanical solidarity was at work: pretty well everyone totally accepted the norms and laws of the tribe and followed them in their day-to-day lives. Moral and other values were clearly established and mechanically followed. There were no debates over the moral constitution of society. These primitive societies had a strong collective conscience, as Durkheim described in *The Division of Labour in Society*:

> The social molecules that cohere in this way can act together only in so far as they have no action of their own, as with the molecules of inorganic bodies. That is why we propose to call this form of solidarity 'mechanical'. (Durkheim, 1972 [1893]: 139)

In societies with mechanical solidarity, people were similar and performed similar tasks. All men might be hunters, while all women reared children and gathered berries and root crops.

But more advanced societies resemble a complex organism, where no one clear set of norms governs all people. Instead, different norms seem to govern each class, professional group, and so on. Yet they still seem to hang together, like the bones, muscles, and sinews in a body. People's occupations are more specialized in such societies: one person might serve coffee all day (but have no idea where the coffee comes from); another might repeat over and over a single operation on an assembly line in a car factory. Such specialization leads to a more limited social horizon for each member of modern society.

Durkheim calls this looser sense of solidarity 'organic'. We see this form of solidarity in societies held together not by rigid traditional customs but by an interdependence of roles. In other words, economic ties based on our functional place in the modern division of labour replace those provided by religion and tribal solidarity. Organic solidarity takes the place of a strong collective conscience in modern societies. Society is no longer just a collection of similar atoms mechanically glued together in a primal horde, but is more like a body where each person is part of a group, an organ performing a given function within the overall social organism. One person picks the coffee beans in some distant field, another puts them in the hold of a ship to sail to North America, a third drives the beans to a distribution centre, and another unpacks them and sends them to the local coffee shop, where finally they are brewed into coffee.

Durkheim's point that organic solidarity holds modern society together quite well is easy enough to understand: in such a complicated division of labour, if one 'organ' of the social body fails to do its job, the whole process collapses—for example, if your kidneys failed, you would eventually die, and if the truck driver failed to drive the coffee to a local distribution centre, you wouldn't be drinking your morning coffee, even if the others in the chain did their jobs. In modern urban societies we depend on this complex form of solidarity for our very survival (and for a lot more too), just as we depend on the major organs in our body to survive as a whole person. Organic solidarity is dualistic: it separates us into our little work cubicles (either metaphorically or really) while simultaneously making us more and more dependent on the work of others to get through the day. We see examples of how this organic solidarity segments and isolates people yet keeps them socially integrated at the same time: waiters bring us food without lecturing us on the evils of the class system, while lawyers give us legal advice without discussing in detail their favourite films of the year. People do their jobs in isolation from other aspects of their lives.

But just to be clear, Durkheim felt that the real achievement of the modern division of labour was its moral effect, its creation of a feeling of social solidarity, not the economic efficiency it promoted. In modern societies the cult of personality would take over totally if the ties that bind a person to his or her society did not increase. Organic solidarity is the firm structure that holds the loose moral bits of modern society together, preventing them from falling apart as each person pursues his or her own interests. In Durkheim's words:

> This is what gives moral value to the division of labor. Through it, the individual becomes cognizant of his dependence upon society; from it come the forces which keep him in check and restrain him. In short, since the division of labor becomes the chief source of social solidarity, it becomes, at the same time, the foundation of the moral order. (Durkheim, 1933 [1893]: 400–1)

The Division of Labour

Durkheim has a somewhat odd but commonsensical argument for the increased division of labour in advanced societies. He says that the division of labour of a society varies with its degree of 'dynamic density', or frequency of contact between people. So the size and density of a society are the key factors in advancing the division of labour.

In tribal or primitive societies, people might live far away from each other and not engage in a lot of interaction—think of the pioneer homestead on the western plains in nineteenth-century America. Here one had to fend for oneself: grow food, hunt, fix fences, defend one's family against marauders (though, of course, nineteenth-century America as a whole was still a very modern society).

But in modern industrial societies people group together in cities, often living cheek by jowl in crowded neighbourhoods or apartment houses. Here individualism rules and everyone is more able to do his or her own thing, economically speaking at least. To use Durkheim's own examples, the soldier can seek military glory, the priest moral authority, and the industrialist wealth. Think of the difference between a small village and a modern mega-city today—the village might have one general store or market; the city might have stores devoted exclusively to South American knick-knacks, electric lamps, or rubber stamps. This level of specialization is largely the result of the size and concentration of the population in the city in question.

Alongside the growth of the division of labour in modern societies goes an increase in personal autonomy and the cult of the individual. The individual is seen as more important than the collectivity as people's interests and values become distinct from those of their neighbours. People leave farms and small towns, moving to cities, free from the moral regulation of their parents and the snooping of neighbours into their private affairs. In the city people tend to mind their own business, averting the gaze of strangers. This leads to anomie.

Anomie

In modern societies with high divisions of labour and organic solidarity, a sense of rootlessness and a lack of values grips many people. In them, as Yeats wrote, 'Things fall apart; the centre cannot hold.' Moral values are confused or not there at all. Social bonds weaken as the power of the family and religion decline. As Durkheim put it, 'Man

is the more vulnerable to self-destruction the more he is detached from any collectivity, that is to say, the more he lives as an egoist' (Durkheim, 1972: 113). We can see this every day of our lives: we travel by jet planes around the world, and thus are less attached to where we live; we move from city to city to take up new jobs, seeing money as more important than community; religion and traditional moral values erode, causing the decline of the family structure and more and more short-term relationships; and many people become cynical, narcissistic, or depressed.

Durkheim called this general state of malaise anomie. It's characteristic of modern industrial societies where there are no clear social values, and where we are, in effect, offered infinite goals, whether these are defined as pursuing a career, wealth, happiness, or consumer goods. Naturally, notes Durkheim, if we accept infinite goals in life, these goals cannot be reached, leading to our perpetual unhappiness.

He distinguished two basic types of anomie. *Acute* anomie is the result of a sudden change in a person's life such as the death of a spouse or the loss of job. *Chronic* anomie is caused by the long-term effects of modern industrial society on the individual, e.g., through its erosion of religious certitudes and the migration of large numbers of people from rural villages to large, alienating cities.

Suicide

In his landmark study *Suicide* (1897), Durkheim argued that suicide can be studied as a social fact and can be classified into a number of general types. He thought there were four basic types of suicide based on the degrees of moral regulation and social integration present in a given society (Table 2.2).

The basic problem with modern societies is their weak levels of moral regulation, their lack of norms. As we have seen, Durkheim called this anomie. So his first form of suicide, and obviously the key one for modern societies, is anomic suicide, when a person takes his or her own life due to a lack of emotional support from the family, or

Table 2.2 Durkheim's Forms of Suicide

Type of Suicide	Society and Situation	Cause
Anomic	Modern—weak moral rules	Normlessness: few or no moral rules.
Fatalistic	Traditional—strong moral rules	The downtrodden abandon themselves to fate.
Egotistical	Modern—weak social integration	The cult of the individual leads to too much focus on personal dramas.
Altruistic	Traditional—strong social integration	The sacrifice of the self for the tribe or nation.

because the person's life is seen as empty and religion offers little or no moral guidance. The opposite situation is a traditional society where there are too many moral rules. Here the slave gives up the struggle against these rules and ends it all with a fatalistic suicide.

The third and fourth forms have to do with degrees of social integration. In most modern societies this integration is weak: we are left to our own devices to chart our course in life. Individualism, narcissism, and egoism rule the day, especially under consumer capitalism. Yet some individuals lose their way when crossing this sea of egoism and allow the personal drama of their lives to dominate their emotions. They engage in an egotistical suicide, thinking that if their girlfriend has left them or they didn't get that all-important promotion, then life must not be worth living.

Lastly, in more rigidly ordered societies and in subcultures like the military, individuals' identities can be submerged in that of the collectivity. They become willing to sacrifice their lives for the greater good of the tribe or nation. They commit altruistic suicide. Examples include Japanese kamikaze pilots plunging their airplanes into the decks of American aircraft carriers in World War II or terrorist suicide bombers blowing themselves up to strike a blow for whatever cause they happen to champion.

Religion

Durkheim thought religion was a very important moral force in society regardless of whether or not religious beliefs are literally true. The core of a religion isn't its rites, priests, and temples, but the collective beliefs and practices it endorses. Religion encourages social cohesion by underwriting certain moral values as divinely inspired (for example, the Ten Commandments). Even if religion is a metaphysical illusion, the moral force it creates is quite real (Durkheim, 1973: 160). This moral force has the key function of helping to maintain social cohesion, especially in more primitive societies. In *The Elementary Forms of Religious Life* (1912), a study of the Australian aborigines based purely on secondary research, Durkheim showed how in primitive tribes religion provided a large degree of social integration by giving the tribe common values and a god or gods to identify with. Religion was the collective conscience of the tribe. This was symbolized in the totem, the emblem of the god. Through the totem all members of the tribe or clan saw themselves as connected together, if not related.

Durkheim makes a basic distinction between the sacred and the profane. Things having to do with religion or spirituality are sacred, while everything else is profane. The sacred and the profane interact and depend on each other, yet remain separate. He defines religion as 'a system of beliefs and practices relative to sacred things, that is to say, things set apart and forbidden' (Thompson, 1982: 129). The sacred symbolizes a community's values. The great moral power religious beliefs exercise is due to the fact that these beliefs are collective representations of the tribe's beliefs and values. These collective representations of the tribe are reinforced by means of such religious ceremonies as sacrifice. In modern societies, religion still functions as a way of integrating people into society, though it is in decline. Durkheim hoped that the public school system would act as a modern alternative to religion as a source of moral integration for children, which it has to some degree. It would perform the same 'function' fulfilled by religion as the key source of social integration.

TALCOTT PARSONS AND STRUCTURAL FUNCTIONALISM

America in the late 1940s and 1950s was a forward-looking place of social stability and political conformity where most people wore the rose-coloured glasses of cultural confidence rather than the dark sunglasses of pessimism. It was where the consumer society was born. At least for the middle class, there was a car in every garage and a spanking new TV set in every living room. The nuclear family ruled supreme (until Betty Friedan showed up), and solid and reliable Dwight D. Eisenhower was in the White House. It was an age of social consensus. And sociology provided the perfect social theory for such an age: Talcott Parsons's structural functionalism.

Of course, even if this social consensus was one part reality, it contained equal portions of illusion and coercion. America was (and in many ways still is) a racially divided society: segregation was official policy, especially in the South, where Klan crosses still burned bright. The post-war nuclear family stripped even middle-class women of careers and political power, leaving them stranded in suburban golden cages with their shiny new kitchen gadgets. To fight the Soviet menace, the American military stockpiled atomic bombs and the jet bombers to deliver them to their targets, leading to the development of a huge military-industrial complex, as Eisenhower warned of in his 1961 farewell address. The battle for world supremacy between America and Russia led to a hot war in Korea in the early fifties and to American interventions all across the globe to prop up friendly regimes and to bring down independent-thinking leaders such as those in Iran, Guatemala, and Cuba (it didn't work in the third case). The Cold War led to repression at home, as seen in the witch hunts for domestic Communists and 'fellow travellers' by Senator Joe McCarthy

and his Senate committee. Parsons's picture of functional unity was more of a social *myth* than a reflection of American social reality. Yet it was a powerful myth all the same.

Background on Functionalism and Parsons

Functionalism dates back to Auguste Comte, who saw society as an interdependent organism where each element played the role of a given function. As we've seen, Durkheim was also a functionalist, loosely speaking. A functionalist is someone who explains the existence and actions of individuals and institutions in terms of the functions they perform for the social organism or system. Functionalism is also known as structural functionalism, which emphasizes the role of social structure in functionalist theory. They are more or less the same, though structural functionalism tends to focus on how the needs of the social system are met by various social structures, as opposed to specific individuals or small groups. In either case, functionalists see society as a system of interrelated parts that has a normal state of affairs—or equilibrium—which it tends to return to when it's disrupted. As Durkheim pointed out, functionalists also argue that the social system is held together by norms and values.

Functionalism was the reigning paradigm in American sociology during the 1940s and 1950s. It went into decline in 1960s and 1970s and was pronounced dead when Talcott Parsons died in 1979. It went out of favour for a number of reasons, the chief of which was that the reality of social conflict in the 1960s (the anti-war movement, the civil rights movement, and feminism) offered a real-world critique of the functionalists' emphasis on social consensus and of their advocacy of equilibrium as a natural social state.

Talcott Parsons, the most famous American sociologist of the twentieth century, was born in 1902 in Colorado. He attended Amherst College, studying biology at first, which would seriously affect his later social theory. He attended the London School of Economics for a year and read Durkheim in French. He also studied at the University of Heidelberg, concentrating on economics and Weber; he later translated Weber's *The Protestant Ethic and the Spirit of Capitalism* into English. He saw his functionalist system as an attempt to combine the best elements of Durkheim and Weber.

Parsons came back to the US after his graduate work and taught at Harvard from 1927 until his retirement in 1973 (for three years in economics, then in sociology proper). He became chair of the new Department of Social Relations at Harvard in 1946 and dominated American sociology from around then until the early 1960s. He was in effect the King of Sociological Theory in America during this period. His functionalism was so dominant in the 1940s and 1950s that many American textbooks defined sociology in purely functionalist terms, ignoring Marxism and other forms of critical theory.

The Theory of Action

In 1937 Parsons published his first important work, *The Structure of Social Action*. In it he laid out a 'voluntaristic' theory of social action, arguing that action theory cannot explain social structure or institutions, but only deal with the most elementary forms of social life (Parsons's later theory would abandon this position). This theory was voluntaristic because he saw human action as voluntary and at least potentially rational. Parsons was steeped in the sociology of Comte, Durkheim, and Weber, and downplayed the view that human beings acted according to their self-interest alone. Instead, he argued that people pursue goals rooted in the norms and bounded by the values of their cultural system. Motivated actors create goals and use various means at their disposal to achieve these goals. But they are constrained by two things: the normative standards of the social system and situational conditions beyond their control.

So he saw four basic components to social action: (1) an actor seeking a goal; (2) the means the actor uses to achieve this goal; (3) situational conditions the actor cannot control; and (4) and the norms and values of the society. A well-integrated actor does not ignore the normative rules of the game: these have been internalized by actors who have been successfully socialized. Parsons's action theory, as applied to university students, is shown in Figure 2.1.

The Social System

Parsons saw society as a system with a series of subsystems. Each of these systems performs one or more basic functions, and each has its limits. For example, if we see the university as an educational system, its basic function is to teach students and

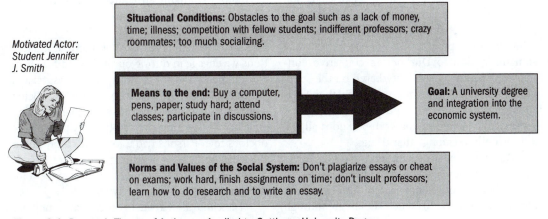

Figure 2.1 Parsons's Theory of Action, as Applied to Getting a University Degree

do research; its limits are its geographical boundaries, the limited power it has over students' lives, and the limited time in a person's life during which he or she attends the university.

One can imagine the social system as a whole as a Chinese box that contains a series of smaller boxes within it. Within Canadian society we have educational systems; within the system of higher education is a specific university; within each university there are departments, staff organizations, and a student body; within each department are a number of faculty; each faculty member has a body, a personality, and a set of values.

So what holds society together? What prevents it from falling apart? Parsons calls this 'the Hobbesian problem of order'. Hobbes, as we've seen, argued that prior to laws and government we lived in a state of nature, where life was poor, nasty, brutish, and short. Everyone could kill everyone else, and property wasn't secure. So, at a certain point, according to Hobbes, people had to lay aside their natural freedom and choose a strong Sovereign to rule them. Parsons wanted to figure out how we manage to avoid Hobbes's state of nature. He laid out his lengthy answer to the Hobbesian problem in his 1951 opus, *The Social System*, the major concern of which is social integration.

He viewed society as a system containing subsystems that always return to a state of equilibrium by reacting against disruptive forces with counteractions. The most compact system is the individual human being, a system his theory of action covers. The largest system is an entire society, or perhaps the global community of nations. His solution to the problem of order is to postulate something akin to Durkheim's collective conscience, a feeling of solidarity based on the set of norms and values that hold society together. Society inculcates norms and values into us through a process of socialization: that's why we don't all just kill each other, among other things.

Parsons turned to Freud and psychoanalysis to explain the power the value system has over us: the collective conscience is reproduced in our individual conscience, Freud's super-ego, through the socialization provided by our parents. We learn further respect for authority by the commands and punishments of the educational system, the legal system, and our superiors at work. Here Parsons uses psychology working through what he called 'the personality system' to explain how the social system maintains equilibrium.

So, how does social order work? Here the influence of biology came into play. A body is made up of parts that fulfill various functions to make the whole body function: the liver filters poisons, the heart pumps blood, our eyes see, etc. Society is like a body: it contains a number of subsystems that fulfill various functions, like organs in the body. Similarly, Parsons explained, human life is made up of four subsystems of action, each with its own function: the cultural, social, psychological, and behavioural systems. Parsons agued that the cause of social structure and social stability is found in the interrelation of these four types of systems, not just in the acts of individuals by themselves (as Max Weber argued). Table 2.3 outlines these systems.

The social system. This is the most far-reaching system for Parsons. Here's how he defines it:

> A social system is a plurality of individual actors interacting with each other in a situation which has at least a physical or environmental aspect, actors who are motivated in terms of a tendency to the 'optimization of gratification' and whose relation to their situations, including each other, is defined and mediated in terms of a system of culturally structured and shared symbols. (Parsons, 1951: 5–6)

The social system consists of all the role interactions we engage in during our lives within a given environment, and the various statuses associated with these roles (the 'status-role complex'). Being a respected doctor is a type of status, while giving checkups or writing prescriptions is part of the doctor's role. Parsons had a lot more to say about the social system as a distinct unit: after all, his 593-page mature statement of his system of thought is called *The Social System*.

The cultural system. Cultural traditions are shared systems of symbols, e.g., in religions, languages, national values, or moral and intellectual

Table 2.3 Parsons's Four General Systems

Social System	The patterns and units of social interaction—social status and social roles—in a given situation and physical environment.
Cultural System	The symbolic aspects of action learned through socialization—ideas, norms, and values.
Personality System	The needs, motives, attitudes, and quirks of the individual actor—his or her individual psychology (especially how the individual processes socially created drives).
Behavioral/Organic System	The human being as a biological being—our bodies and their physical environments.

life. These shared symbols make up the cultural system. For example, a cross has a powerful meaning to Christians but little to Buddhists. The words of the English language have meaning to us, but not to monolingual New Guinea tribal warriors. Our cultural ideas and values are internalized through socialization, thus allowing for social integration.

The personality system. This is the personality of the actor, including needs, motives, and attitudes. Parsons thought that actors are generally motivated towards gratification, but are limited by the norms and values of their society. So he only half agreed with the utilitarians. The personality system is the person's individual identity, his or her quirks.

The behavioural system. This is our body and its physical environment, which Parsons saw as a biological system. As we shall see, these four systems interact in various ways.

The Pattern Variables

In his theory of action, Parsons looked at the sort of decisions we must all make before acting in the social realm. He argued that we could break these down into general 'dilemmas of orientation', and classified these dilemmas into five basic questions or sets of questions we in essence ask ourselves before acting. He called the answers to these questions pattern variables, that is, the fundamental and basic choices people need to make when they encounter or interact with other people.

Parsons used Ferdinand Tönnies's (1855–1936) distinction between a *Gemeinschaft* or traditional community, held together by close personal bonds and kinship, which Parsons saw as characterized by 'expressive' relationships with a sense of community loyalty; and a *Gesellschaft* or modern society, which he saw as characterized by goal-oriented or 'instrumental' action that is more impersonal and business-like. He argued that these two models of social life generate distinct answers to the five questions posed by the dilemmas of orientation (Table 2.4).

Ascription/achievement. The first choice we have to make is between treating people according to their ascribed nature—their social status, gender, ethnicity, race, or economic background—or in terms of what they've done, their achievements or performance. The former is more characteristic of traditional societies, the latter of modern ones. For example, it would be morally inexcusable for a modern corporation to hire someone because of that person's sex or race (except in cases of affirmative action), yet there is no problem in not hiring someone because of a weak resumé. In modern societies, then, performance or achievement is supposed to trump ascription. Of course, things don't always work out that way in the real world.

Diffuseness/specificity. This is a choice between wide, undefined relationships, like that with a wife, husband, or friend, and relationships with functional limits that serve a specific purpose, like those with a server at a fast-food outlet or a bureaucrat in a government office. Specific relationships strictly limit the type of interactions you have with other people: for example, you wouldn't tell your dentist about your love life (besides, he or she probably couldn't understand you in the first place with all that dental technology in your mouth!).

Affectivity/neutrality. Next we have to choose between a connection with someone from which we expect significant emotional gratification and a neutral attitude to the interaction. It's the difference

Table 2.4 The Pattern Variables

(dilemmas of orientation faced by social actors when making a decision how to act)

Expressive Action/Relationships	Instrumental Action/Relationships
(*Gemeinschaft:* Traditional community with strong ties of kinship and place, low division of labour, strong collective conscience. Parsons is following Tönnies's distinction.)	(*Gesellschaft:* Modern society with higher degree of urbanization, high mobility, looser communal ties, higher division of labour. Action is goal-oriented.)

1. Is your orientation towards others based on who they are (their status, sex, race, ethnicity, age, etc.) or on what they have done, their performance?

Ascription (who they are)	**Achievement** (what they have done)

2. What is the range of demands on the relationship? How far-reaching are the obligations in the interaction situation?

Diffuseness (wide demands, e.g., spouse)	**Specificity** (specific demands, e.g., dentist)

3. Can an actor expect emotional gratification from the interaction? Do we see people as valuable in themselves or as means to our ends?

Affectivity (strong emotions, e.g., lover)	**Neutrality** (coolness, e.g., bureaucrat)

4. Should the same standard be used to evaluate all actors in interaction situations? Should action be based on a particular relationship or a general norm?

Particularism (unique standards)	**Universalism** (general standards)

5. Is action oriented towards the individual or the group? Is the obligation collective or private? [Later dropped by Parsons as belonging to another theoretical level.]

Collectivity (altruism or sacrifice for the group)	**Self** (pursuing self-interest)

between interacting with a lover and a bank teller (unless your lover is also a bank teller, of course). We treat the bank teller in an instrumental way, as someone who helps us conduct our business with the bank. Some interactions are in the grey area between affectivity and neutrality, though it's fair to assume that most economic interactions are much closer to the 'neutrality' side of the dualism.

Particularism/universalism. Here it's a question of whether we treat all people the same, according to a general or universal norm (e.g., all late essays will have the same marks deducted), or according to some particular criteria (e.g., doing favours for your friends but not for strangers). Modern society usually expects people to treat each other according to universal norms, for example, not to discriminate against a given group of people in hiring.

Collectivity/self. Although Parsons dropped this distinction from his list of pattern variables after 1953 because he saw it as connected to

another level of meaning, this problem has to do with whether one's actions are oriented towards the collectivity or the self. It's a matter of where one's obligations are aimed, at one's individual interests or at the well-being of some larger group of people. In a traditional society (*Gemeinschaft*) the collectivity is supreme, while in modern society (*Gesellschaft*) we're primarily concerned with looking out for ourselves.

In general, the pattern variables lay out the differences in relationships between traditional and modern societies, and how certain traditional elements have survived into modern social action. In modern societies, most people are individualists, and see their social roles as instrumental means to the end of individual achievement and happiness. This is a reflection of Durkheim's idea of organic solidarity. In traditional societies we see a greater willingness to sacrifice one's interest for those of the collectivity. In general, the pattern variables lay out the differences in relationships between traditional and modern societies, and how certain traditional elements have survived into modern social action.

Parsons's Four-Function Paradigm and Social Equilibrium

We've seen above that Parsons also set out a detailed model of how the four types of general systems outlined above are related, and the functions of each of them in relation to each other. The result of this interaction, he believed, was social equilibrium. The key factor in this integration is the way that most people internalize values that integrate them into the social system. He studied the interaction of small groups of Harvard undergraduates and from his findings concluded that certain categories of action can be applied to *all* systems of action. The fact that these college students were all young white men put into question the objectivity of his functionalism as a general model of society, especially in the eyes of feminist critics.

Parsons identified problems that all organizations or social systems must solve if they're going to survive:

- They must *adapt* to their environment.
- They must achieve *goals*.
- They must get actors to commit to *shared values*.
- They must *integrate* actors into the system, if necessary by coercion.

These four functions are essential to all systems.

Parsons defines a function as 'a complex of activities directed towards meeting a need or needs of the system' (Ritzer, 1992: 240). We can tell whether a function is significant by looking at a case where the input of the subsystem has failed. For example, if our lungs failed and we couldn't breath, we would die, so we can be pretty sure that functioning lungs are essential to our physical survival and thus our organic system.

All systems must perform these four functions in order to survive: this includes not only the social system as whole, but smaller subsystems within it, such as a family, a charity organization, or a university. To return to a previous example, a university must adapt to its environment, set itself goals, maintain a minimum of shared values, and integrate its students into a common system. This is where Parsons got himself into trouble: he argued that within a family, the father fulfills the functions of adaptation to the environment (he is the breadwinner), attaining goals (he is the boss), and to some degree value maintenance. The mother's main role is to integrate children into society by socializing them, along with managing tensions within the family. Needless to say, few people today would accept this rigid division of familial functions.

In any case, Parsons argued that each of these four functions of the social system is fulfilled by distinct, though interrelated, subsystems. This generates a two-by-two matrix of functions and the social institutions that perform them, as shown in Figure 2.2.

Adaptation (to environment)	Goal Attainment
Economic System (finds and allocates resources)	Political System (sets goals, makes decisions)
Family, Religion, Educational System, Media (create and renew values)	Legal System and Police Force (adjust and regulate human relationships)
Latent Pattern Maintenance–Tension Management	**Integration**

Figure 2.2 Parsons's AGIL Four-Function Paradigm and the Social System

Adaptation. A system must contend with external situations, adapt to its external environment, and make that environment fulfill its needs. It has to get resources from the environment and distribute these throughout the social system. This is done through the economy, whose primary institutions are the contract and property.

Goal attainment. The social system must define and achieve its primary goals, set up priorities between competing goals, and mobilize resources and human energies to achieve these goals. It does this mainly by means of political institutions.

Integration. A system must co-ordinate, adjust, and regulate the relationships of actors and institutions within the social system, maintaining a level of harmony and non-interference between them. This leads to social cohesion and control. In human societies this is done mainly by means of the police and legal institutions, though the family, the schools, and churches also help to adjust and regulate human relationships.

Latent pattern maintenance–tension management. A social system must create, maintain, and renew the dominant patterns of values in the system in question and manage the system's internal tensions. Actors must be encouraged or coerced into conforming to the system's social values. Actors transmit values maintaining basic cultural patterns through educational and religious institutions, the family, and the media, the primary units of socialization.

If these functions are all being fulfilled effectively, then actors have a *complementarity of expectations.* When they interact with others, they can expect these others to share the same basic cultural values and use the same normative rules of the game. Only deviants and criminals will upset this social equilibrium, but not for long: Parsons believed that in the long run social consensus was natural.

Further, if socialization works, social norms are internalized, and when we pursue what we see as our private interests, e.g., spending the best part of a decade in university to become a doctor or professor, we serve the needs of the social system at the same time. A well-socialized and successful person fulfills some vital function for the system as a whole, whether or not they know they're doing it.

If we return to Parsons's four general types of systems, we can see how they can be roughly integrated with his AGIL paradigm. Figure 2.3 shows how the social system is surrounded by the three other types of general systems he envisioned.

Parsons's four basic types of systems—social, cultural, organic, and personality—roughly parallel his AGIL four-function paradigm of the functions of systems *within* the social system. In other words, not only are there four *general* types of systems on the 'meta' level, there are also four types of functions performed by systems *within* each society, and thus four types of subsystems within each larger social system (remember the Chinese box). So within society there are organic systems (the economy), cultural systems (institutions like the church, the university, and scientific research institutes), and personality systems (the roles we play, political leadership).

Further, these systems and functions interpenetrate each other, interfacing through media of interchange. For example, the organic system interfaces with the social system through money, which is a sort of code or language that allows us to exchange goods and to measure the value of services. Social roles connect the individual personality to the social system in that they define a 'collectivity' of people with the same expectations as a group. The political system operates according to the medium of power, which allows it to command actors and institutions to do its bidding. The cultural system interfaces with the social system by the medium of commitments—people's acceptance of value patterns created by cultural institutions. Parsons also talks about how the social system interfaces with its environment through the technological system, which also interpenetrates with the economic system. Technology protects us against nature (buildings and heating systems) and allows us to exploit that nature more effectively (think of the various harvesting and reaping machines used by farmers, of the invention of plastics, or of factory production as a whole, among many other things).

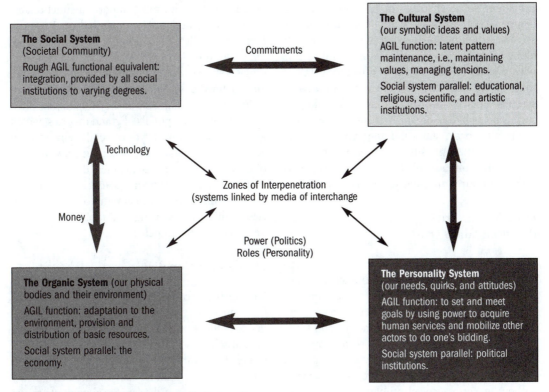

The Social System
(Societal Community)
Rough AGIL functional equivalent: integration, provided by all social institutions to varying degrees.

Commitments

The Cultural System
(our symbolic ideas and values)
AGIL function: latent pattern maintenance, i.e., maintaining values, managing tensions.
Social system parallel: educational, religious, scientific, and artistic institutions.

Technology

Zones of Interpenetration
(systems linked by media of interchange

Money

Power (Politics)
Roles (Personality)

The Organic System (our physical bodies and their environment)
AGIL function: adaptation to the environment, provision and distribution of basic resources.
Social system parallel: the economy.

The Personality System
(our needs, quirks, and attitudes)
AGIL function: to set and meet goals by using power to acquire human services and mobilize other actors to do one's bidding.
Social system parallel: political institutions.

Figure 2.3 The Social System and Its Environment
Source: Adapted from Parsons (1968).

Criticisms of Parsons and Functionalism

Is Everything a Function?

It seems as though functionalists have an easy explanation for everything in terms of its social function, even seemingly negative things like crime, the function of which might be to reassert social values by punishing criminals. But does everything have a social function? Aren't there some things, such as stamp collecting, that don't really have a function? More seriously, does it make sense to say that negative things like crime really provide a function for society? Crime may reinforce social values, as Durkheim says. Yet if we stretch the notion of function this far, we can dream up a significant function for almost anything, no matter how negative or trivial it is.

Does Parsons's System Predict Actual Events?

Parsons has established his four types of system, his pattern variables, and his AGIL four-function paradigm in the name of social science. But do his models allow us actually to predict how actors and social institutions will act? Aren't these merely descriptions of things after the fact? Although we may find his models historically interesting, that doesn't make them good science.

How Is Equilibrium Restored?
Where Does Change Come From?

Parsons talks about disequilibrium and deviance as disruptions of social norms, but is vague when it comes to explaining where deviance comes from. On a broader scale, he's not very good at explaining social change, unlike Marx's material-ism or Weber's account of the Protestant ethic. It seems as though his social system trots merrily along its way, always reinstating equilibrium whenever it's disturbed. But real history isn't like this: fundamental changes take place; new social systems replace old ones. Perhaps his analogy of society being like an organism is false: societies *can* change their basic values and rules, while our bod-ies can't just stop using their basic organs or change the function of these organs—we can't think with our kidneys or see with our toes.

Does Parsons Privilege the Social Status Quo?

Last but not least, Parsons has been severely crit-icized for creating a theoretical model that sup-ports the social status quo. He argues that the normal state of affairs is for the actors in a system to be morally committed to the norms and func-tions of their society. He clearly seems to prefer equilibrium to deviance, stability to change. Yet American society in the 1940s and 1950s was not without its serious social problems: overt racism against blacks, especially in the South, an inferior social and economic status for women, not to mention foreign imperialism and the militarism and sabre-rattling related to the Cold War. Why should we prefer a stable equilibrium to social change if the current system contains serious injustices? In the 1960s many Americans rejected the status quo and worked to change their society in the civil rights and feminist movements and in the domestic struggle to end the war in Vietnam.

ROBERT MERTON

Robert K. Merton (1910–2003) was a graduate student of Parsons at Harvard who grabbed the baton from his mentor's hand, and tried to mod-ify functionalism in order to save it from the slings and arrows of outraged critics. The son of a work-ing-class immigrant family in Philadelphia, he joined the sociology faculty at Columbia Univer-sity in 1947, where he worked until his death. He

became the second most important functionalist theorist in America. He expanded on Parsons's ideas and dealt with a number of obvious prob-lems with functionalism. Merton argued that soci-ologists should work on middle-range theories, as Durkheim did in *Suicide* and Weber did in *The Protestant Ethic and the Spirit of Capitalism*. Such theories avoid the pitfalls of grand theories, which are too far removed from social behaviour to account for what actually occurs in society, while offering more than just detailed descriptions of empirical facts (Merton, 1968: 39). Merton sketched out a series of such middle-range theo-ries in his own writings, notably a theory of deviance, discussed below.

Fixing Functionalism

Merton tried to deal with the basic problem of functionalism, the myth of coherence—the ten-dency of functionalism to see society as one whole unit in which social actors conform to dominant values. He outlined three more specific fallacies of functionalism, which he called postulates.

The postulate of the functional unity of society. This 'article of faith' of functionalist thinkers is the idea that societies have a sort of functional unity, leading to social harmony. Standard beliefs and practices all contribute to the well-being not only of the social body as a whole but to each member of this body (ibid., 80). Yet why should we assume that all societies are integrated, coherent, happy systems? Some clearly are not—for example, countries where civil wars are taking place between ethnic or religious groups, or where some oppressed minority (e.g., American blacks in the 1950s or South African blacks during the apartheid regime) feels short-changed by the social system and rejects its basic values.

Merton agrees that the functional unity of a given society is a question of fact, not a matter of opinion that requires no empirical data to prove. In many individual cases there is no such unity (ibid., 81, 84). Further, we should specify *which* institutions and beliefs are functional for *which* individuals, groups, or societies as a whole, and not make sweeping claims about the functionality of a given social or cultural 'item' for all systems (ibid., 84). For example, religion may pack some integrative wallop for pre-literate societies; yet in modern ones, where some people are atheists and several religions may prosper within a given nation, it's by no means obvious that religion always contributes to social integration. In short, Merton concedes this point to the critics of functionalism: there's no reason a social theorist needs to assume that social harmony is *always* present in social systems.

The postulate of universal functionalism. We have already mentioned the notion that all social forms and actions have positive functions. Yet this is far from obvious. Aren't some things just mindless fun, like collecting stamps or going for a walk? And aren't other things truly negative, such as violent crime? Merton got around this problem by distinguishing normal functions from dysfunctions. Dysfunctions (e.g., deviance, crime) make a negative contribution to the operation of the social system: they break up the universal functionality of social institutions. They throw a monkey wrench into the works. This led Merton to ask of a given social practice, 'functional for whom?' Poverty may be functional to rich people in that it creates a class willing to do their dirty work for low wages; but from the point of view of that class, it's quite dysfunctional to be poor.

The postulate of indispensability. This begs the question of the social purpose of a custom or institution. Functionalists say that to understand a given custom or institution, we have to assume that it has a function—or why would it be there in the first place? So merely by existing, all cultural and social institutions are assumed to have some vital function. They are seen as indispensable to the operation of the social system. What customs and institutions are not vital to the social system? Those that don't exist. This, needless to say, sounds fishy.

Merton challenged this postulate by noting that the same social function can be fulfilled by more than one institution. For example, although religion can help to control people's values and

behaviour, other social institutions can step in and play this role if systems of supernatural belief decline in popularity. There are several 'functional alternatives' for every important social task. A given institution is not necessarily vital to a given function—in other words, there's more than one way to skin a functionalist cat.

The chapter in *Social Theory and Social Structure* in which Merton discusses these three postulates also contains an important amendment to functionalist theory that he hoped would end the confusion between the motivation for an action and its objective consequences, or between an account of the *cause* of an action and its social *function*. This was Merton's famous distinction between manifest and latent functions. This paralleled Freud's distinction between the manifest and latent content of dreams, and has been hinted at many times in the history of social theory. Manifest functions are the consequences actors intend and overtly recognize, e.g., the Catholic Church supports the institution of marriage by refusing to recognize divorce. Latent functions are results that are either not intended or not recognized: they are the unintended consequences of human action. The difference, then, is between an actor's conscious motivations and the objective consequences of those actions (ibid., 114). Merton illustrates this distinction with the Hopi rain ceremonies: from a meteorological point of view, Indian dances don't increase rainfall (their manifest function); yet they *do* bring the tribe together in the same place, increasing group solidarity (their latent function). So they make sense from a latent point of view. Merton (ibid., 118–22) argues that focusing on latent functions helps the sociologist in three ways:

- It helps us avoid quick and easy moral judgements of the seemingly irrational practices of so-called 'primitive' peoples, which to the modern mind seem pointless failures. Looking at their latent functions helps us understand them.
- It guides us to theoretically fruitful avenues of inquiry, avoiding having sociology degenerate into the keeping of a scorecard on the

successes and failures of the actions of 'practical men of affairs' (i.e., the manifest functions of their policies).

- It adds significantly to sociological knowledge by going beyond common-sense knowledge to a deeper understanding of things.

Yet the sociologist who goes looking for the latent function of seemingly crazy or destructive practices might get stuck in the quicksand of relativism. For example, it's no doubt true that human sacrifice helped to unify the ancient Mayan society of Central America, yet we would still feel horrified if a Mertonian functionalist suggested we adopt such a practice to help unite contemporary society.

Having said this, Merton's introduction of latent functions certainly corrected a major flaw in functionalist theory by reminding the theorist that social practices can be explained without relying entirely on the explicit, conscious aims of the actors involved. In general, he softened Parsons's functionalism in order to defend it against its critics, to the point where one wonders whether he was still a functionalist. For one thing, he recognized the reality of social conflict, opening the door for a group of more intense critics of functionalism to enter the fray.

CONFLICT THEORY

The Basic Assumptions of Conflict Theory

'Conflict theory' is, generally speaking, any social theory that emphasizes the importance of conflict over consensus in understanding society. The term is somewhat confusing since Marxism and its progeny are by definition all conflict theories (remember the class struggle?). Yet in a narrower sense we can use the term to refer to a group of non-Marxist theorists writing mainly in the 1950s and 1960s who criticized the obsession of functionalists with social consensus. These conflict theorists borrowed from both Marx's idea of the class struggle and Weber's discussion of forms of power and authority to criticize some of the main tenets of functionalism. The basic assumptions of this narrower school of conflict theory are as follows:

- *Competition and conflict are natural.* Human beings are rational animals who pursue their interests, which are for the most part economic resources, political power, and social status. Since all real societies have a limited amount of these things, people compete for them. Especially when formed into groups and classes, this competition leads to social conflict. Such conflict is not an aberration, as the functionalists claim, but a natural part of social life.
- *Hierarchy is inevitable.* As a result of this social conflict, hierarchies of wealth, power, and status are formed in all societies. Contrary to Marx's vision of a classless society, conflict theorists see some type of social hierarchy as inevitable.
- *Ideas and values are used as weapons.* Contrary to the functionalist view that norms and values glue the social fabric together, conflict theory sees ideas and values as weapons used by the various parties in social conflicts. This notion dates back to Machiavelli (1469–1527), who in *The Prince* argued that wise rulers should appear to be sincere, merciful, humane, and religious, but act in the opposite manner if necessary. This is what Marx meant by ideology, though in the case of conflict theory all ideas and values are not merely reflections of economic structures.
- *Revolutionary change is possible.* Radical or abrupt changes can occur from time to time in a given society, changes that are not just rumbles in the belly of the social system that then returns to a state of equilibrium. These changes are the products of the very social conflicts that drive all societies.

We'll now look briefly at two of the conflict theorists who helped to bring about the decline and fall of the functionalist empire in the 1950s, Lewis Coser and Ralf Dahrendorf.

Lewis Coser

Lewis Coser (1913–2003) was born in Germany, studied at Columbia, and taught most of his career at Brandeis University and the State University of New York (Stony Brook). His best-known work is *The Functions of Social Conflict* (1956). Coser tried to show how social conflict can be functional for maintaining, adjusting, or adapting social structures, so his view is really a hybrid of functionalism and conflict theory. His general position is that in all social systems there will be conflict since individuals and groups from time to time stake rival claims to scarce resources, prestige, or power positions (Coser, 1956: 152). Coser's book lays out 16 specific propositions, each a variation on ideas introduced by Georg Simmel (1858–1918). Here are a few of them (I'm paraphrasing a bit):

- *Proposition 1.* Conflict can bind a society together, especially in a hierarchically organized structure like the Indian caste system, where it establishes group boundaries and keeps the various classes separate from each other (ibid., 33).
- *Proposition 2.* Conflict can act as a safety valve, allowing us to express our opposition to injustice, tyranny, or mere moodiness without attacking society as a whole (ibid., 39). It does this by providing 'substitute' objects for our hostility such as scapegoats. The more rigid a social structure is, the more such objects are needed, since the social system is unable to absorb this hostility by adapting its institutions.
- *Proposition 6.* The closer the relationship, the more intense the conflict (ibid., 67). When a group is very closely knit, conflicts involve the individual's total personality: for example, heretics within a given religion are hated more than adherents of unrelated faiths.
- *Proposition 9.* Conflicts with external groups help to unify the group (ibid., 87). The notorious example here is how a nation can be unified by war, no matter how dubious the purpose of the war is—think of Germany under the Nazis.

- *Proposition 11.* Groups seek enemies to help unify themselves (ibid., 104). A recent example here is the position of America in the world after the Cold War: it took only a few years in the 1990s before the Soviet enemy was replaced by new foreign foes.
- *Proposition 15.* Conflict establishes and maintains a balance of power within a social system (ibid., 133). Often the only way of figuring out the strength of rival people or groups is by allowing them to play out their conflict, assuming they adhere to some sort of rules of the game. They can let off some steam in such a conflict, and will probably come to accept their place in the order of things more willingly than if, over a period of time, they nursed a feeling of being cheated of power unfairly by a rival group.
- *Proposition 16.* Conflict also calls for allies (ibid., 139). Just as a group is unified within itself by conflict, its struggle with external enemies will often lead it to seek out new friends, new associations, and coalitions to aid it in its struggle.

We can see how, in general, Coser argues that conflict can actually stabilize a social system by reinforcing a sense of group identity, often at the expense of external enemies or by scapegoating an internal one. It can also reinforce social solidarity within a society, as long as the conflict doesn't concern the basic values of the society in question: for one thing, it can help to sort out the relative levels of power and access to resources of competing groups (Proposition 15). Think of an industrial strike. The union demands a wage of $15 per hour for its members, while management offers $13. After a few weeks of negotiation, posturing in the media, and name-calling from both sides, they settle for $14 per hour and the union goes back to work. This is presumably better for all concerned than a violent confrontation or the intervention of some external authority forcing a settlement on both sides. The conflict has actually increased social solidarity since it was played out within established norms concerning collective bargaining, and wasn't about core social values, just money. From this viewpoint social conflict can actually be *good* for a society, as paradoxical as this may sound.

Ralf Dahrendorf

Ralf Dahrendorf (1929–) was born in Hamburg, Germany, and studied both philosophy and sociology in Hamburg and London. He taught in several German universities in the 1960s and served in the West German parliament in 1969–70. From 1974 to 1984 he was the director of the London School of Economics, from 1987 to 1997 a dean at Oxford University. Queen Elizabeth knighted him Sir Ralf in 1993.

Starting in the late 1950s Dahrendorf, like Coser, argued for a conflict theory approach to sociology. His main intellectual conversation was not so much with Talcott Parsons as with the ghost of Marx, yet his work was very much a critique of functionalism. In his 1958 article 'Out of Utopia: Toward a Reorientation of Social Analysis', he lays out the elements of literary utopias and dystopias, such as Plato's *Republic*, Aldous Huxley's *Brave New World*, and George Orwell's *1984*:

1. Utopias have a nebulous past and no future: they exist outside of time (Dahrendorf, 1958: 116).
2. They assume a universal consensus on values and the nature of institutions.
3. There is social harmony in utopias: they have no strikes or revolutions or other violent conflicts, since there is really nothing to quarrel about.
4. They feature recurrent patterns of behaviour in things like sex, the education of children, and the division of labour (ibid., 117).
5. They're isolated both in time and in space: they're shut off from the outside world.[1]

Dahrendorf's point in discussing these literary utopias is to show that the structural-functionalist picture of the social system is itself utopian as it exhibits all of these characteristics. It sees the social system as mostly harmonious, disrupted from time to time by 'deviants' whose origins Parsons never really explained. It claims a general consensus on values, which Dahrendorf sees no evidence for in real societies. It exists outside of time and space, as a series of concepts in the minds of functionalist theorists who wind up defending the status quo insofar as they picture society as a homeostatic, stable system. Dahrendorf describes the Parsonian social system with some sarcasm:

> What a peaceful, what an idyllic, world this system is! Of course, it is not static in the sense of being dead; things happen all the time; but— alas!—they are under control, and they all help to maintain that precious equilibrium of the whole. Things not only happen, but they function, and so long as this is the case, all is well. (Ibid., 121)

Such utopias don't exist in reality. Society is in a constant state of change, unless some force arrests that change. In the end Dahrendorf calls for the recognition that conflict is just as natural to a society as consensus—no society in history has been free of strife. It's the absence of conflict that is abnormal (ibid., 126).

In *Class and Class Conflict in Industrial Society* (1959), Dahrendorf takes up his conversation with the shade of Karl Marx on the question of whether we live in a class-based society. He agrees with Marx that authority, in the nineteenth century, was based on income, and thus the rich bourgeoisie ruled the state. The workers were excluded from upward social mobility and political power until greater democracy opened up government structures to their participation, and they had no way of legitimately fighting for their economic demands so they dreamed of a revolutionary overturning of the state. Money, political power, and social status were all controlled by the same group—the capitalists—which gave the workers little incentive to accept the status quo.

Yet things have changed since then. The workers formed trade unions, which allowed them to negotiate with the capitalists. The widening of the franchise allowed them to vote for political parties more sympathetic to their plight. And social mobility opened up somewhat, allowing some workers to become capitalists. Dahrendorf even argues that these changes allow us to see some parts of the industrial world as 'post-capitalist'. He defines classes in the post-capitalist societies of Western Europe not in economic terms, like Marx, but as 'conflict groups that are generated by differential distribution of authority in imperatively coordinated associations' (Dahrendorf, 1959: 204). He sees the main conflict in such societies as that between those who can exercise authority and those who cannot. Since post-capitalist societies still have interest groups, such as trade unions and political parties, and 'quasi-groups', such as factories, churches, and government, that are 'imperatively coordinated' (i.e., are hierarchically organized with leaders, followers, and those in between), we can conclude that we still live in a class society (ibid., 246–7). Differentials of authority lead to class structure. This supports his general thesis that conflict is natural in all societies but the imaginary ones of a Plato or an Orwell, since the various classes will battle over the means of authority, just as Marx saw them as battling over the means of production.

C. WRIGHT MILLS

The Sociological Imagination

C. Wright Mills (1916–62) was an unruly Texan who in the 1950s drew his theoretical six-gun and took deadly aim at the conservative world view he saw all around him in American intellectual life. He fired off four rounds that disrupted the calm complacency of functionalist social theory: *White Collar* (1951), *The Power Elite* (1956), *The Causes of World War Three* (1958), and *The Sociological Imagination* (1959). He was born and raised in Texas, and spent most of his academic career at Columbia, dying of a heart condition while still in his forties. His sociology was quite critical of power structures in America during the heyday of

the Cold War. He saw himself as a lone wolf, attacking the American corporate and military elites, along with his fellow intellectuals for abdicating their political responsibilities in accepting the injustices of the American society of his day. He was certainly a conflict theorist, linking him to Coser and Dahrendorf, but was also a critical theorist, seeing one of the key roles of social theory the criticism of current social arrangements and government policies and actions.

He starts *The Sociological Imagination* by noting how much modern people feel unable to control their lives: they feel trapped in their private orbits by forces beyond their control. People in the mid-twentieth century have witnessed great changes: industrialization and capitalism have transformed huge parts of the world from a feudal to modern state, changing our lives in a profound way. Yet all of this has eaten away at our most cherished values. To help overcome this, modern journalists, theorists, scientists, and artists need to understand the interplay of humanity and society, of biography and history, to overcome this feeling of impotence and alienation. They need a sociological imagination that is able to use reason to give us 'lucid summations of the world' that can help individuals to understand their place in history and society (Mills, 1959: 3). Mills argues that the best sociology allows us to grasp the relations between the history of a society and the biographies of the actors within it, mediated by social structure. Imaginative sociologists have asked three sorts of questions:

- What is the *structure* of the particular society being studied?
- Where does that society *stand in history*? What is its place in and meaning for the development of humanity?
- What type of men and women, what type of *human nature*, dominates here? (Ibid., 6–7)

Connected to this triple task is a basic distinction, that between *personal troubles*, which have to do with the character of an individual and his or her immediate relations to others, and *public issues*, which take place on a larger scale, transcending a single individual's life (ibid., 8). This is the difference between biography and social structure. Mills gives several examples: a single unemployed man has a personal trouble; but if there are 15 million unemployed, it is also a public issue. Trying to survive a war is a personal trouble, while the causes and political effects of a war are public issues. A single marriage breakdown is a personal trouble, while a divorce rate of 45 per cent is a public issue. Mills critiqued the family arrangements of the 1950s, which turned women into 'darling little slaves', and hinted that marriage requires structural changes to survive as a social institution. Lastly, individuals can escape a dirty, noisy, ugly city if they can afford a quiet country home, but this doesn't solve the structural problem of a degraded city life. The moral of the story here is that we need to use our sociological imagination to move from fretting over our personal troubles to understanding our problems in structural terms, as public issues.

Mills noted how one style of reflection tends to dominate an era. For modern times this style is obviously that of physical and biological science. Yet the value of science was being questioned more and more, especially given the power of nuclear weapons to destroy the world. Science raised more problems than it solved. It conquered nature, and thus was seen as footloose and aimless. Scientists, according to Mills, were no longer able to provide a true outline of human destiny. Science had become a 'false and pretentious Messiah', its practitioners becoming more and more technocrats at the beck and call of the military and corporate elites (ibid., 16). Mills described how the grim realities of twentieth-century war and history in general had made people hungry for social and historical reality, and for values adequate to deal with that reality. Science can't do it, so people turn to poetry, plays, and novels.

He opposed social science that focused too much on bureaucratic techniques and methodological pretensions, that used obscure concepts, or that lost itself in research into trivial minor problems. Classic social analysis paid attention to historical social structures, and thus connected personal troubles to urgent public issues. But many contemporary American social scientists, such as Parsons, had been reluctant to meet the political and intellectual challenges of the day. Especially, they tended to get lost in working on empirical studies that wind up accumulating a jumble of meaningless facts that only serve to scatter the researchers' attention. Mills was clear that social research 'is advanced by ideas; it is only disciplined by fact' (ibid., 71).

We should also try to avoid arbitrary academic specialization in terms of departments, but specialize only according to topic and draw on whatever ideas and studies can help us to understand human actors in their historical time and place. Social scientists should not bureaucratize their research and reason, but try to show how reason operates in human affairs. This did not mean they have to run for office, set up a soap box in the park and make speeches, or give alms to the poor (ibid., 192). But it does mean they have to be politically critical, to make democratic reason relevant to human affairs in a free society.

Sadly, Mills saw specialization in university life as deadening the minds of college professors (Mills, 1951: 39). Further, academic freedom is restricted by the influence of wealthy foundations and military and corporate elites on the content of research as well as by the intimidation academics impose upon themselves that 'eventually becomes so habitual that the scholar is unaware of it' (ibid., 151–2). Little has changed in this regard over the past half-century. Leagues of academic gentlemen (and one might add, of late, gentlewomen, too) use manipulation and prodding and selective hiring to dispose of potential insurgents and thus reduce the flow of free thought in the universities to a mere trickle.

Yet the availability of a vigorous and critical intelligentsia is absolutely necessary to a democracy, Mills argues. It also requires an active and informed public, nationally responsible political parties, a skilled and independent civil service, mass media that can mediate between peoples' private troubles and public issues, and free associations of families and communities with the state, the military, and the corporate elites (Mills, 1958: 121–3). Sadly, none of these bulwarks of democracy existed in a healthy form in America, nor, one might add, in present-day North America.

White Collar: Rationalization and Alienation in the Workplace

Mills argues that there are three forms of power: coercion or physical force; authority, where people obey because they believe that the power being exercised is legitimate; and manipulation, where people are tricked and duped into obeying (ibid., 41). Since our society is becoming more and more centralized and our economy structured according to principles of impersonal rationality, manipulation has replaced coercion and authority as the main means by which power is exercised. Mills agrees with Weber that Western society is firmly in the grips of the iron cage of bureaucratic rationality, of the 'calculating hierarchies of department store and industrial corporation, of rationalized office and government bureau', which 'lay out the gray ways of work and stereotype the permitted initiatives' (Mills, 1951: xvii). These seek to rationalize government administration and economic production to encourage efficiency to the point where we have a society that has so much 'rationality' but so little reason (Mills, 1959: 170), leading to a psychological alienation that Mills sees as part and parcel of white-collar work.

But don't imagine that such a society is in any danger of falling apart. It has no need of the consensus on values so dear to the functionalists. Instead, all we need is a network of 'expediences and conventions', a framework of semi-legitimate power and material comfort for the masses to hold the whole system together (Mills, 1951: 350).

Mills argues that the material hardships of factory workers find their modern equivalent in white-collar workers' psychological alienation both from what they 'make' and from themselves. White-collar workers are tools in a bureaucratic machine that routinizes and specializes their labour into narrow niches. As a result, they become apathetic, frightened, and estranged from their jobs. They help to create profits for others during their dull daily routine, yet get little intellectual stimulation from their work. The loss of traditional values and self-esteem embroils bureaucrats and other office workers in a 'status panic': they are oppressed, but can't identify their oppressors since their plight is the product of a general system and way of thinking, not a result of the actions of a few individuals.

All of this isn't merely the fault of capitalism per se, as Marx thought, but of the very division of labour itself (ibid., 225), which encourages the rationalization and specialization of work. Mills also disagrees with Marx that work is an essential expression of our lives. But he does see modern bureaucrats and other white-collar workers as alienated from their work and thus their lives. Salespeople sell their personalities like commodities, as part of the personality market. Their personalities become part of the means of production: as the old saying goes, they have to 'sell themselves'. They are thus alienated from themselves as products. They have to pretend to be interested in others to sell them their wares, making manipulation a key aspect of human contact (ibid., 187–8). So they are also alienated from their customers. This is just as true today as it was in the 1950s: visit a shopping mall or a fast-food outlet for some empirical proof.

Mass Markets, Mass Media, Mass Society

Following from his criticism of the alienation of white-collar work, Mills is also suspicious of the value of mass markets and the mass media. In the following passage he presages the coming of suburban shopping malls and big-box stores, criticizing the Big Bazaar of consumer society as a replacement for the family:

Do you think the family is important to society? But the Big Bazaar feeds, clothes, amuses; it replaces families, in every respect but the single one of biological reproduction. From womb to grave, it watches over you, supplying the necessities and creating the unmet need. . . . it is also a factory of smiles and visions, of faces and dreams of life, surrounding people with the commodities for which they live, holding out to them the goals for which they struggle. . . . Measured by space or measured by money, it is the greatest emporium in the world: it *is* a world— dedicated to commodities, run by committees and paced by floor-walkers. (Ibid., 167)

The Big Bazaar contributes to our self-alienation by erecting a temple to salesmanship: its very existence depends on manipulating people into buying things they do not especially need, as the Frankfurt School also pointed out.

Mills argues that Marx was wrong in thinking that the material life of human beings determines their ideas in modern society. Between our consciousness and our material existence stand the forms of mass communication dominant in our society, and Marx couldn't foresee the role of media in the formation of consciousness. He had no radio, no movies, no TV (ibid., 333–4). Our class consciousness is no longer a product merely of our experience of social and economic life, but also of our exposure to mass media, which gives us our standard of reality—and, in Marxist terms, a false consciousness in regard to whose interests the current socio-economic order serves. The slant the media give our perceptions of our material life goes a long way towards determining what we think about that life. Images and sounds from the mass media seep into our consciousness from an early age and help to shape our view of ourselves. Ironically, Mills thought that the most skilled media types don't concern themselves with politics, but with the worlds of sports and entertainment.

Our world of mechanical communication makes the individual a passive spectator of everything and an active human witness of nothing, a point that many media and social critics were to make in the 1960s and later. The moral springs of revolt tend to dry up, as there are no longer any plain targets for this revolt. Mills even saw mass communication as making our souls cold, private, and blasé due to a lack of human interaction

(Mills, 1958: 83). This leads to the dire consequence of a mass indifference that rules Western societies, where being a spectator is almost always preferable to being a participant in political life.

The Power Elite

Mills's most famous and most polemical book is undoubtedly *The Power Elite* (1956), where he seems to lay out a conspiracy theory that sees American society as run by a self-perpetuating elite of corporate chiefs, politicians, and generals, despite the fact that Mills was adamant that he wasn't a conspiracy theorist. Yet he does so with such verve and conviction that it's hard not to be convinced of its truthfulness.

Mills begins with some general remarks on history (Mills, 1956: 3–29), arguing that in primitive societies the means of power are simpler and decentralized, and thus historical change tends to be a local product. But in modern societies there has been a great increase in the scope and centralization of the means of power. A few strategically located individuals with institutional power can now make key decisions that change the structural conditions under which we live. This centralization has enlarged the history-making power of elites.

Mills isn't saying that a small creative minority or ruling class has run things in all epochs of human history. In fact, for most of history—e.g., in ancient Egypt or Mesopotamia—historical changes were invisible, even to social leaders. They took hundreds of years to happen. Now, the pace of change is much more rapid. Fate, fortune, or the unseen hand cannot be blamed for major events and changes, as it could be in earlier, simpler times. Human changes are no longer the result of innumerable individual decisions taking place over a long period of time, but of the decisions of a few key elites.

This was especially the case in international politics. The power elites of great nations, notably the leaders in the Cold War of the day, the Soviet Union and the United States, could not blame their struggle on impersonal forces beyond their control. This struggle was their fault, as Mills would say that war and peace are the fault of power elites today. Moral responsibility is increased when small elites can make major decisions. It's now 'sociologically realistic', morally fair, and politically realistic to hold the powerful responsible for the fate of the world (Mills, 1958: 100). They can't cop out of this. It's nonsense to think that all groups are equal in the making of history. Each is limited by the technical and institutional means of power. The means of power, organization, and violence have greatly increased in modern times, at least for elites. The leaders of a nuclear power like the US can wipe out whole cities in minutes, something that Caesar or Napoleon could not even dream of doing.

Mills's basic argument in *The Power Elite* is quite simple—the economic, political, and military elites in America in his day formed an interlocking structure that made many of the key decisions determining the fate of both the average person and the country:

For they are in command of the major hierarchies and organizations of modern society. They rule the big corporations. They run the machinery of the state and claim its prerogatives. They run the military establishment. They occupy the strategic command posts of the social structure, in which are now centered the effective means of the power and the wealth and the celebrity which they enjoy. (Mills, 1956: 4)

He defines the power elite as those political, economic, and military circles that act as a series of overlapping cliques sharing decisions with national consequences. Their ability to make these decisions is greatly aided by the centralization of the means of power in the country. Understanding how this triangle of power works is the sociological key to understanding the higher circles in America. And since the corporate chieftains, warlords, and political party chiefs run the country, Mills implies that American democracy is largely a sham (Figure 2.4).

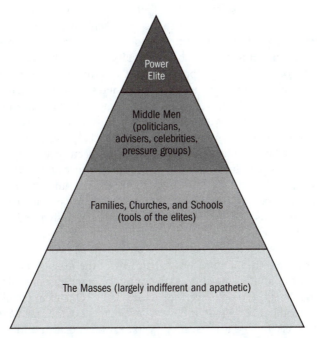

Figure 2.4 Mills's Picture of the Structure of American Society

The elites are not solitary, however, for they have advisers, consultants, media representatives, and public relations people. Right below them are the middle levels of power, e.g., professional politicians, pressure groups, and full-time celebrities with connections to political and economic chieftains who the masses usually take as the real foci of power. Far underneath the power elite are the institutions of the family, the church, and the school. These institutions adapt to modern life—they don't make it. Rather, they are increasingly shaped by the power of the big-three elites—think of the corporatization of education today and of how children are raised in front of television sets that bombard them with advertising and other consumer propaganda.

These elites have gone through a fundamental historical shift over the previous century. The economy was no longer a mass of small companies, but effectively operated through 200–300 giant corporations. The American government was no longer a confederation of states but had become a powerful federal establishment through the course of two world wars and the Great Depression. The military was no longer a collection of state militias, but a massive complex with a sprawling bureaucratic organization to run it (ibid., 7). Thanks to modern bureaucracy, communications, and 'fabulous technology', power had been centralized in each of these domains. We can only wonder how much more Mills would see this to be the case today, with new media and high-speed Internet communications, economic and cultural globalization, and the stumbling attempts by America to be the world's policeman.

Further, Mills notes that these three elites were no longer separate but interlocking. The political economy was linked in a thousand ways to military institutions (ibid., 8). The state managed the economy through corporate subsidies, tax policies, trade treaties with other countries, and so on. It also massively funded the military machine (at least in the US), bankrolling the development of new military hardware without corporations having to worry about the risks inherent in creating new technologies. The same, of course, is true

today. President Dwight Eisenhower warned Americans of the power of the 'military-industrial complex' as he left office in January 1961. This complex is alive and well in the twenty-first century, as witnessed in the Gulf War of 1991 and the Iraq War of 2003 to the present day.

The leaders of each elite can shift from one to the other with ease: generals become politicians, corporate chiefs enter politics, ex-politicians join boards of directors. The elites intermingle like guests at some swanky cocktail party. We have seen this in America when General Eisenhower became the President in the 1950s, and much more recently when General Colin Powell entered George W. Bush's cabinet and General Wesley Clark threw his hat into the ring as a candidate for the leadership of the Democratic Party in 2004. And more notoriously we've seen some serious intermingling of the entertainment and political elites in the last two decades of the twentieth century, a phenomenon that Mills discusses in *The Power Elite*. Hollywood B-actor Ronald Reagan became President in 1980, leading the 'forces of freedom' in the final years of their ideological battle with the 'evil empire' of the Soviet Union, while action hero Arnold Schwarzenegger entered the governor's office in California in 2004, with what results only the future will tell (unless you're a time traveller, of course). Many other entertainment and sports figures have been elected to local, state, and national office in the United States in the past several decades.

Especially important in this interlocking of elites has been their support for a continual war economy, especially during the Cold War. This allows the state to pay for costly and risky private research—corporate interests are being served by the continual design and production of weapons that are obsolete in a decade or two.[2] This war economy is allowed to operate due to the political apathy of the masses and the inactivity and abdication of moral responsibility by leading intellectual circles. One example of this is the attempted development of the Star Wars missile defence program under Reagan and later George W. Bush, despite the claims of leading scientists that it couldn't work. Mills saw the war economy not as a question of strategic defence, but as the product of the elite's self-interest, which intellectuals are morally bound to criticize but for the most part remain silent about or actively support. The problem is that this silence or support could lead America down the road to a civilization-killing World War III, which is bad for everyone's health.

Power is the ability of a person to realize his or her will against the resistance of others. The source of the power of these elites lies in their control of key institutions such as large corporations or government bureaucracies, not their wealth or individual status. (In fact, very rich families today are all closely connected to one or more mega-corporations—their wealth comes from this connection, either through direct ownership or executive control.) Social prestige is connected to such institutions, aided by their publicity machines (e.g., advertising agencies and political spin doctors). The fact that the elites are interchangeable is linked to the cumulative nature of prestige: the more you have, the easier it is to get more, as with money at a bank. For example, if you make your name in the military, you can translate this into political or economic prestige (ibid., 10). To be celebrated, wealthy, or to have power involves having access to key institutional positions, and not just money or special social status.

In addition to looking at the institutional position of the power elite, we can also describe its members in terms of the values they share, in terms of the social class they occupy, or in terms of their psychology. Values, psychology, and class are indicators of the power elite's distinctiveness. They accept and marry each other, understand each other, and think and work alike (ibid., 11). The elite selects and forms certain personality types for power in its institutional hierarchies. They train them for these roles. They share the values of other elite members and are able to make impersonal decisions for large bodies of people.[3]

Mills emphasized that his theory was not just a sophisticated form of paranoia. On one side, we shouldn't take the view that there is an omnipotent elite, like the Nazis' worldwide Jewish conspiracy or vulgar Marxism's capitalist ruling class, running the show. This is to reduce the power elite to a secular substitute for God. On the other hand, Mills thought, we should not take the liberal pluralist view that modern bureaucracy, technology, institutions, and special interests checkmate the power of the ruling elite, severely restricting their ability to make decisions. In this view they are forced to go along with standard operating procedures, being handicapped by myriad rules and regulations made by others. The power elite is neither omnipotent nor impotent. Yet it is quite powerful all the same, aided by the centralization and bureaucratic rationality that govern all modern societies.

Mills's theory of the power elite is a critique of the functionalists' emphasis on social equilibrium and their ignorance of the exploitive hierarchies that exist underneath their neatly diagrammed elements of the social system. It is also a muckraking attack on the elites who ran American society in the 1950s, and still run it today. We'll pick up this critical strain of thinking over the next two chapters, but before we do we need to look at sociobiology, which can be taken as either a criticism or a defence of functionalism, depending on how one looks at it.

SOCIOBIOLOGY: AN EVOLUTIONARY FUNCTIONALISM?

The Genetic Basis of Human Behaviour

Imagine yourself a caveman or woman huddling in your rocky home, cowering before the bellowing of the woolly mammoths and the growls of the sabre-toothed tigers in the valley below. Your needs are simple: food, water, shelter, and companionship. You need to find a mate to reproduce the species and, more specifically, your genes. You need to defend yourself against thieves and aggressors, so you make stone clubs and axes. And you need to cook your meat, so you invent fire and cut down wood for your outdoor oven. If you're a bit more advanced, you might also herd a few goats or cattle, make pots and baskets, or paint pictures of antelopes and bears on your cave wall.

Edward O. Wilson (1926–), the coiner of the term 'sociobiology', argues that this picture of a primitive human being applies to the vast majority of human history. To be specific, Wilson points out that most of human evolution took place during the five million years prior to the advent of civilization when hunter-gatherer societies dominated, not in the 10,000 years of relative civilization our species has enjoyed (Wilson, 1978: 34). For 99 per cent of human biological evolution, hunter-gatherer societies have ruled supreme. Thus, it should not be surprising if we have inherited some important traits from our primitive ancestors.

Wilson has published a dozen books and over 400 articles on a variety of biological and philosophical issues. He is an ecologist, a champion of biodiversity (the saving of as many species of plant and animal life as possible from extinction), and invented the notion of 'biophilia', our genetic tendency to bond with other parts of nature. In his Pulitzer Prize-winning 1978 book *On Human Nature*, which I'll focus on in this section, Wilson argues that sociobiology is the best way to understand human social behaviour. Sociobiology is 'the systematic study of the biological basis of all forms of social behaviour' (ibid., 16). In other words, biological principles derived from the study of animal behaviour can be applied to human societies. Specifically, Wilson wants to apply Darwin's theory of evolution to the humanities and the social sciences. He argues that human nature is made up of a great number of evolutionary traits, and that we cannot base explanations of social behaviour solely on cultural factors. Biology is the key to understanding human nature, and social scientists have to pay attention to it to enrich their understanding of society.

This is a radical view. Many theories of human nature today, including those based on feminism, Marxism, and liberalism, are social constructionist: they argue that human psychological traits and behaviour are socially constructed. Wilson is saying that this view is both false and unscientific to boot. We are in part products of our environ-ments. But we are also, to a large degree, products of our genes, which have resulted from millennia of evolutionary adaptations. Culture, according to Wilson, isn't all-powerful, and social behaviour can't be shaped into almost any form, as is politically fashionable to think today. Wilson claims there is hard evidence for the genetic determination of *some* human social behaviour, although he admits that culture can shape the pathways that specific cases of behaviour take.

Our genes give us the *capacity* to develop one set of traits over another. It is not simply a matter of nature ruling over nurture. Wilson asks us to think of ourselves at birth as a ball at the top of a mountain. Below us is a landscape of ridges, hills, river valleys, and marshes. As we roll down the mountain (i.e., grow up), our culture determines to some degree which valleys we wind up in, but our genes determine the topography of the valleys, ridges, and rivers before us (ibid., 60). When it comes to heavily cultural things such as language and forms of dress, the landscape of our genetic determination is like a low-lying delta with lots of rivulets and marshes (ibid., 63). Yet to get to the lowlands which represent these mostly cultural things, we had to roll down the genetic mountain in the first place.

Wilson thinks that most of the behavioural changes we went through from the dawn of civilization in Mesopotamia to now are the result of cultural evolution. Yet most of our biological characteristics were shaped in hunter-gatherer days. He makes a powerful argument for the validity of sociobiology here: as different societies went through the stages of hunter-gatherer bands, tribes, chiefdoms, and states, the same social institutions were invented in roughly the same order— male leaders, religious rituals, the division of labour, elites, codified religion and law, irrigation, and monumental building. We see this process at work in all the early civilizations: Egypt, Babylon, India, China, and the Mayan empire of Central America. They parallel each other: the Egyptians and Mayans even both built pyramids, without any real possibility of having copied each other (ibid., 88–9). If this is the case, then it's difficult to see how independent civilizations somehow created the same institutions and practices in the same sequence if these are all cultural constructions. Nature must have had a hand in things.

If culture rules nature, then we would expect the people in modern hunter-gatherer societies to differ significantly from modern industrial societies. Yet in really basic ways, they differ very little, at least when we compare human beings to all other animal species. Wilson cites an anthropologist's long list of the human traits and practices that can be found in *all* human cultures. These include, among other things, bodily adornment, dancing, education, ethics, hair styles, hygiene, incest taboos, jokes, magic, medicine, marriage, property, religious rituals, soul concepts, sports, and tool-making (ibid., 22). This suggests that the social constructionist view of human social behaviour is just plain wrong: if a practice is found in *all* societies, even in societies totally ignorant of each other's existence, how can we say it is socially constructed? Wilson compares this with a list of social behaviours that would come out of a society of ants—his particular specialty in biology. In some cases ants' list of behaviours repeats the human list, but adds a number of odd things like co-operative labour, larval care, sterile workers, and metamorphosis rites. The point is that the list of practices common to all human societies is idiosyncratic to our biological *species*, not to this or that specific culture.

Sociobiologists believe that if people were raised in total isolation, they would still develop many of these traits—a language (though it might be totally different from any existing ones), rules about incest, taboos, property rights, courtship practices, bodily adornment, myths and legends, dancing, murder, suicide, bodily adornment, etc. Human behaviour is stubbornly idiosyncratic, and not just cultural.

Some human-like behaviours, such as smiling and laughing, can be seen in our nearest cousins in the animal world, monkeys and apes. Wilson compares us to chimpanzees, arguing that we are different from chimps to the same degree that some fruit-fly species are different from each other. Chimps will stare at mirrors, indicating some sense of self; they form troops that are hostile when meeting outsiders; they can be territorial; they use co-operative strategies in the hunt; they have primitive technology, using sticks to dig up termites and stones to defend themselves; they can be taught sign language; and they even show some altruism, giving strips of meat from a kill to chimp beggars. So basic human behaviour is mammalian and primate-like—in many ways we are merely overdeveloped chimps. We can see how human behaviour rests on a genetic foundation every time we go to the zoo and visit our banana-eating distant relatives.

Many of the main traits of human nature were adaptations to the environment created during the millions of years of human evolution. We now have predispositions to develop these traits. An adaptation is simply a trait that gives the individual a better chance of having his/her genes passed down to his or her children. Wilson calls this genetic fitness, which increases the chances of our personal survival, of our successfully mating, and of producing fit children.

The behaviours most likely to be explained by sociobiology are those that are the least rational and the most innately biological, e.g., mating, territoriality, and aggression. If a decision has to be made quickly and irrationally, then it's more likely that the brain will fall back on inherited traits located in the pleasure and pain centres of the brain. Our unconscious, emotional decisions are more likely to be influenced by genetic evolution—Wilson cites the case of phobias against spiders, snakes, and rats (ibid., 68). Another obvious example is the universality of incest taboos in all human societies. Unrelated children who grew up on Israeli kibbutzim never marry each other, even though there is no cultural taboo against it. Wilson explains that this is a genetic predisposition to avoid sexual contact with those one grows up with (ibid., 36). Thus, the incest taboo is a case where evolutionary adaptation carried culture along with it. This taboo is unconscious and irrational, not the product of reasoned debate. Its ultimate cause is the need to maximize genetic fitness, a hard lesson which it probably took many generations of malformed children for human beings to learn.

A simple test of Wilson's hypothesis of the genetic foundation of much of human behaviour can be made by comparing fraternal twins with identical twins, the latter being the product of the same fertilized ovum. If social constructionism is right, and both sets of twins are raised together, then there should be no variation of behaviour between the fraternal and identical sets of twins. Yet if sociobiology is right, the identical twins should be closer in their behaviours than the fraternal ones, being the product of the same egg. And lo and behold, the identical twins are closer in learning ability, memory, perceptual skills, tendencies towards mental illness, and other factors. So it would appear that genetic identity trumps cultural construction.

Sociobiology can be seen as an ally of functionalism in that it lays out a series of social 'functions' common to all societies, from territoriality and reproduction rituals to dancing and art. Its list of attributes common to all human societies, borrowed from anthropology, is quite long, longer even than most functionalists would make it. Yet sociobiology is also an implied critique of functionalism, since it links these functions not, for the most part, to social structure or cultural constructions but to our genetic structure as it has evolved over the millennia. This is why we can see it at best as an evolutionary functionalism. Let's now look at two of Wilson's specific applications of sociobiological principles in *On Human Nature*.

Aggression

Wilson claims that aggression is tied to human evolutionary development, disagreeing with Sigmund Freud's theory that aggression is one of our two basic psychic instincts (the other being sex). He sees aggression as an innate genetic trait of all mammals, including human beings. As proof of this claim, Wilson argues that warfare is endemic to all human societies in history. All societies have laws against murder, rape, and blackmail. So humans have a hereditary predisposition to violence and war. Yes, there are a few pacific societies—but innateness only means that it's very *likely* that a given society will have some mode of aggression and warfare, not that it's absolutely guaranteed to be continually fighting actual wars.

Aggression is a set of responses to various environmental factors that can be broken down into a series of categories, each with a wide variety of manifestations. Wilson proposed seven categories of aggression, each of which can be altered by genetic evolution:

- defence and conquest of territory;
- assertion of dominance;
- sexual aggression;
- acts of hostility associated with the end of weaning;
- aggression against prey;
- defensive attacks against predators;
- disciplinary aggression to enforce social rules (ibid., 101–2).

Human aggressiveness, as Wilson describes it, is the product of an interaction between genes and environment. Its mere presence is genetic, but which aggressive behaviour we choose is based on a menu of possibilities given to us by our culture. We have an innate tendency to manufacture some cultural apparatus of aggression, but its exact nature is left up to each culture to decide. The cultural evolution of aggression is guided by three factors: (1) our genetic predisposition to communal violence; (2) the necessities imposed by the environment; and (3) the previous history of the group, which offers a series of aggressive responses to external challenges or threats (ibid., 114). For example, animal aggression is often related to territoriality and is a response to a crowded environment. Territoriality prevents animal populations from crashing, as it spreads out a species over a given space. Yet humans, too, have definite rituals with regard to property and space—we defend our territory against outsiders, whether our country or our backyard. We're no different from bears and baboons in this respect.

War is a violent rupture of taboos of territory, usually caused by tribal loyalties. This is true even today: nation-states lay claim to patches of ground that they will usually defend against all aggressors. The cultural traditions of primitive warfare evolved through the selective retention of certain traits that led to greater genetic fitness for the individual and the community, including bravery and self-sacrifice. Like animals, we tend to defend territory that we see as economically useful. Most wars are connected to tribalism, to the division of the world into 'us' (i.e., our home, village, kin, friends, or nation) and 'them' (i.e., everyone else). And when fighting these wars, we often reduce our enemies to frightful or subhuman status.[4]

War also has a sexual side to it. Wilson notes that surviving hunter-gatherer warriors are wildly successful in the game of reproduction—every woman loves a man in uniform, even if it is only body paint and a spear! Wilson cites the case of one hunter-gather warrior who had 45 children (ibid., 115). Those who were feared and were willing to aggress against strangers had a clear biological advantage, so they won out in the Darwinian struggle for survival.

Sex

Wilson notes that sex permeates every part of our lives, yet it is not designed specifically for reproduction. Sex is, in fact, a rather inefficient way of creating new members of our species: bacteria's use of asexual reproductive splitting is far more effective. The evolutionary point of sex is not giving or receiving pleasure. Most animal species have sex very quickly, without any prolonging of pleasure (never mind bouquets of flowers or boxes of chocolate). Pleasure is at best a bonus paid to animals to induce them to invest the time and energy required for courtship, intercourse, and being a parent. In addition, sex is risky business, opening up the partners to attacks from predators, and it guarantees that half of the parents' genes are lost. Sexual reproduction makes no sense from a Darwinian point of view. So why sex? First, it increases genetic diversity and thus allows for greater adaptability to a changing environment; second, it stimulates pair bonds by the pleasure associated with it. Sex is only secondarily about reproduction, which does not in itself require an exclusive pairing off of a man and a woman.

Human beings have the most intense and varied sex lives of all primates. We are connoisseurs of sexual pleasure, celebrating it in song, anticipating it in fantasies, and encouraging it through flirtation (ibid., 141). Love and sex go together in cementing the family pair bond. Human females don't go into heat like dogs and cats, but stay sexually receptive most of the time. The female provides the eggs, the male the sperm. The human female can be expected to provide only about 400 eggs in her lifetime, while the male can produce millions of sperm. So the female makes a much greater investment in her sex cells (ibid., 124). Males, having lots of sperm to waste, are aggressive and assertive, hasty and undiscriminating. Females are the opposite, being genetically jostled to be more choosy. It is important for females to choose male partners who will stay with them through the child-rearing process, not to mention young, healthy, strong hunters and providers to defend them and provide fit genes. Some males are big winners in the courtship stakes, while others are absolute losers; but virtually all females will be fertilized eventually (think of a singles' bar at closing time).

On the question of sexual differences, Wilson says that men have inherited greater muscular mass and running and throwing skills from our hunter-gatherer days. Top male athletes can defeat their female counterparts in most sports— the best female marathoner couldn't break into the top 700 in the US. Even steroid-driven East German women athletes couldn't break male records in the glory days of Eastern European communism (ibid., 127). Women are less assertive and aggressive than men, though this depends in part on culture. Yet history records *no* society where women dominate men economically and politically: men have traditionally been the warriors, kings, shamans, and judges, and such exceptions as Elizabeth I and Margaret Thatcher only prove the rule. Young girls are more sociable and less adventurous. Boys are the opposite, engaging in rough-and-tumble play, threats, and physical attacks. Admittedly, these modest genetic differences between the sexes are often exaggerated by cultural training. A social constructionist would say that this is all the product of cultural training creating stereotyped gender roles, but Wilson notes that this would have to be a worldwide conspiracy unconsciously carried out by parents everywhere for this to be true (ibid., 130). It seems more likely that a genetic explanation of sexual difference accounts for these differences. Physical and character traits that survive as relics of our genetic history are often senseless, yet real all the same. One of these is the predisposition to specific sex roles.

Wilson returns to his favourite hunter-gatherer societies for evidence of the genetic foundation of sex roles. In almost all of the currently existing ones, the men hunt and the women gather, along with making clothes and sometimes building shelters. The hunter-gatherer female wants to bond with a male who will hunt and help with child-rearing, while the male wants exclusive sexual and economic rights to his woman. Sexual love and the joys of family life are enabling mechanisms in the brain that promote a compromise between the sexes.

One might take the decline of the so-called nuclear family as evidence of the triumph of culture over nature in the creation of sex roles. Divorce rates are in the 40–50 per cent range in many Western countries, and higher than this if the breakups of cohabiting couples are factored in. Birth rates are also down. But Wilson feels that the family—a universal form of social organization—is under no threat of dissolution. He gives a number of examples of how it survives even under stress: in slave families in the US before the Civil War, in hippie communes in the 1960s and 1970s, and among inmates in prisons. The nuclear family reasserted itself in the hippie communes even though the ethics of these mini-societies promoted communal child-rearing.

Critiques of Sociobiology

Criticisms of Wilson's sociobiological perspective are not hard to come by. Insofar as Wilson bases his discussion of human traits on genetic structures, he has been accused of being sexist and racist. For one thing, the Nazis also based psychological characteristics on genetic structures, though in their case differentiated by race. But to be fair, Wilson is clear that the genetic differences between the various human cultures are so slight that one can't define them as distinct races, as we would define gorillas, chimps, and baboons as separate species (ibid., 48). As for the charge of sexism based on his claim of a mild genetic determination of sexual roles, Wilson would probably say that ideology and science don't mix: if the facts support the existence of a limited sort of sexual differentiation, we cannot simply ignore this because it offends us politically.

Second, Wilson has been accused of being a biological determinist in that he ignores human agency and robs us of our free will. Yet once again, this is only partly fair: he says that although the general forms of societies are largely the product of genetics, specific cultural developments are not. The fact that we wear clothes may be the dim echo of some ancient genetic adaptation to the environment. But the fact that we wear blue jeans and not seal-skin skirts is the result of a cultural decision.

Third, contemporary constructionists argue that human cultures are so diverse that it's hard to believe that human social action isn't almost entirely the product of cultural constructions. Wilson's imaginary answer to this critique would be something like the following: human cultures are diverse in their superficial aspects, in things such as their forms of dress, music, art, and language. But in their most basic characteristics human cultures are much more like *each other* than they are like any animal 'society', whether imagined or real. They each share a long list of practices and institutions that are the products of parallel genetic adaptations to primal environments.

So Wilson's sociobiology remains a serious challenge to the autonomy of social theory, despite these criticisms. His claim that human behaviour, in its broadest outline, is the product of a long evolutionary process compels us to understand society in a way quite different from that of pretty well all of the other theorists discussed in this book.

CONCLUSION

Functionalism claims that societies are best understood as systems whose elements perform a set of discrete functions leading to social equilibrium. Conflict theorists argue that this is largely a myth, that social life is as much about conflict as consensus, while sociobiology argues that both conflict and consensus are the result of a long series of evolutionary adaptations of the human organism to its environment. In the next chapter we'll explore a rich vein of conflict theory—materialism—based on the notion that society is best understood in economic terms.

STUDY QUESTIONS

1. What was Hobbes's basic question? How did he answer it? Was this a good answer?
2. What did Durkheim mean by a 'social fact'? Do social facts really exist? What are a couple of social facts that directly affect your own life?
3. What two types of solidarity did Durkheim see as dominating society? What type of solidarity rules today? What problems with this form of solidarity did Durkheim outline?
4. What were Durkheim's four types of suicide? Which types are more relevant to modern society? Why?
5. Outline Parsons's theory of action and apply it to a major goal in your own life. Does the model accurately describe the process you have to go through to achieve this goal?
6. What are Parsons's pattern variables? Give an example of types of relationships that apply to each pair of variables. Did Parsons miss anything when setting up his pattern variables?
7. What is the AGIL paradigm? Apply it to either your university or your place of work, showing how different people or institutions perform each of the four functions.
8. Outline the basic criticisms of functionalism, offering counter-arguments where you can.
9. Outline the main moves Merton makes in his strategy to defend functionalism. Is his strategy successful? Why or why not?
10. What are five of the functions of social conflict for Coser? Give a historical or current example of each function.
11. How and why does Dahrendorf compare functionalism to utopian thinking? Is he right?
12. What are the main elements of Mills's sociological imagination? How is it a criticism of functionalism?
13. How does Mills connect rationalization, alienation, and mass societies?
14. What does Mills mean by the 'power elite'? How does it operate? Does it still rule your country today?
15. What is Wilson's basic argument about the basis of human social behaviour? How can one criticize this view?
16. What types of aggression does Wilson outline? How are these types found in the world around you today, if at all?
17. What does Wilson say the evolutionary point of sex is? What are some of the examples he uses to defend his position? Critically evaluate his sociobiological view of sex.

SHORT BIBLIOGRAPHY

Collins, Randall. 1975. *Conflict Sociology: Toward an Explanatory Science*. New York: Academic Press.

Coser, Lewis. 1956. *The Functions of Social Conflict*. Glencoe, Ill.: Free Press.

Craib, Ian. 1997. *Classical Social Theory*. Oxford: Oxford University Press.

Dahrendorf, Ralf. 1958. 'Out of Utopia: Toward a Reorientation of Sociological Analysis', *American Journal of Sociology* 64, 2: 115–27.

———. 1959. *Class and Class Conflict in Industrial Society*. Stanford, Calif.: Stanford University Press.

Durkheim, Émile. 1933 [1893]. *The Division of Labor in Society*, trans. George Simpson. New York: Free Press.

———. 1964 [1895]. *The Rules of Sociological Method*, trans. Sarah A. Solovay and John H. Mueller. New York: Free Press.

———. 1972. *Emile Durkheim: Selected Writings*, ed. Anthony Giddens. London: Cambridge University Press.

———. 1973. *Émile Durkheim: On Morality and Society, Selected Writings*, ed. Robert N. Bellah. Chicago: University of Chicago Press.

Hobbes, Thomas. 1981 [1651]. *Leviathan*, ed. C.B. Macpherson. Harmondsworth: Penguin.

Merton, Robert. 1968. *Social Theory and Social Structure*, enlarged edn. New York: Free Press.

Mills, C. Wright. 1951. *White Collar: The American Middle Class*. New York: Oxford University Press.

———. 1956. *The Power Elite*. New York: Oxford University Press.

———. 1958. *The Causes of World War Three*. London: Secker and Warburg.

———. 1959. *The Sociological Imagination*. New York: Oxford University Press.

Parsons, Talcott. 1937. *The Structure of Social Action*. New York: Free Press.

———. 1951. *The Social System*. New York: Free Press.

———. 1968. 'Social Systems', in Parsons, *Social Systems and the Evolution of Action Theory*. New York: Free Press, 177–203.

——— and Neil J. Smelser. 1956. *Economy and Society*. Glencoe, Ill.: Free Press.

Ritzer, George. 1992. *Sociological Theory*, 3rd edn. New York: McGraw-Hill.

Thompson, Kenneth. 1982. *Émile Durkheim*. London: Tavistock.

Wilson, Edward O. 1975. *Sociobiology: The New Synthesis*. Cambridge, Mass.: Belknap Press.

———. 1978. *On Human Nature*. Cambridge Mass.: Harvard University Press.

MARX'S MAIN IDEAS

What Is Materialism?

'Materialism' is a loose term to be sure. In philosophy, materialism is the idea of the primacy of matter over mind—as opposed to idealism, which says that ideas rule the world, or religions like Christianity, Judaism, and Islam, which tell us that we have an immortal non-physical soul and that the physical world was created and is maintained by an immaterial divine being. In social and political theory, a materialist says that we can best understand the structure of society by looking at the material life of the people within it—the way they eat, drink, sleep, have sex, produce offspring, and make things from the raw materials provided by nature. In short, a materialist says that we must look at the economic structure of a society to understand it. This is sensible enough. Even today, the status, financial well-being, and physical surroundings of factory workers are quite different from those of bank managers; certainly, the material life of a medieval peasant was dreary, bleak, and disease-ridden as compared to that of even the most humble office paper-pusher at the turn of the twenty-first century. How we work, exchange goods, and turn money into power over others is obviously of tremendous importance in understanding society. Marx was such a materialist—he said our economic life determines our ideas. This position has been the subject of much debate among social theorists in the twentieth century, as we shall see in this chapter.

The Factory

Let's go back to Manchester, England, in 1844 and visit Polly Prole.[1] Polly is 30 years old but looks much older, burdened by a lifetime of hardship. She works in J. Uppington Pennypincher's textile mill, a loud and dirty place powered by two massive steam engines that clank away around the clock. The factory employs 200 souls, mostly women and children. Polly works 12-hour shifts to make enough to feed her four children and her husband Bill, who has been thrown into the 'reserve army of the unemployed' by an oversupply of the tin pots made by the factory he used to work at (not to mention the fact that he lost two of his fingers when he wasn't quick enough to remove his hand from the automatic stamping machine). Polly's immediate boss is the foreman Dan McDuff, a rough-and-ready fellow who is a bit too friendly with his favourite female underlings and all too ready to fire those who don't succumb to his shenanigans.

Polly hates her job. All day long she does the same thing over and over—she makes sure that endless spools of cotton are fed into the power loom, clearing away any jams before they clog up the machine. And needless to say, the end products—sheets of cotton fabric—are not her property. In fact, if she tried to take some home, she would be fired or jailed. So she feels alienated from both her work and the product of her labours.

On top of that, she is forced to compete with her fellow workers for her job—just last week her best friend, Charlotte, was laid off due to a lack of work. And she's unhappy working all day long in a sweaty, grimy workshop when her children are outside playing in the warm sunshine. 'This isn't natural', she says to herself. So she is alienated from her fellow workers and from her human essence. She's only at home when she's not working and not at home when she's working. Finally, Polly can't help but notice that the factory owner, Mr Pennypincher, drives about in a fancy carriage, wears the finest clothes, yet never does any real work himself. This hardly seems fair. Sure, he pays Polly and the other workers, buys the machines and raw materials they work on, and owns the land where the mill was built. Yet even given all of this, he makes a hefty sum each month for doing nothing. He gets lots of 'surplus value' out of his investments in men and machines.

Polly's story illustrates a number of key points made by Marx. His basic point about the capitalist system is that under it the workers—the proletariat—are exploited by the bourgeoisie—the capitalists. The bourgeoisie use capital, which includes money, stocks, and machines, to control the means of production of modern industrial society for their benefit. After they have paid for the raw materials they need for their factories, for the wages of their workers, and for other expenses, they make a profit, which Marx called surplus value, from their investments. This was despite the fact that, according to Marx, a commodity is given its *real* value by the work put into it (hence this is called 'the labour theory of value'). More specifically, in his *Economic and Philosophical Manuscripts of 1844* (not published until 1932 in German), Marx argues that workers under capitalism are alienated in four ways—from their work, from the products they make, from each other, and from their *species being,* their human nature. Indeed, alienation is a basic quality of life under capitalism, an insight that would greatly influence later theorists such as the Frankfurt School and the Situationists.

Marx's Life and Influences

Karl Marx was born in 1818 in Trier, in the Rhineland region of Germany. It was under Pruss-

ian rule at the time, but during the Napoleonic Wars had absorbed the rationalism and other new ideas of the French Enlightenment. Marx's father converted from Judaism to Christianity for practical reasons before Karl was born. Marx attended first the University of Bonn, then later Berlin, where he became attached to the Young Hegelians, a group of radical thinkers who used G.W.F. Hegel's ideas about human perfectibility to criticize religion and the Prussian state.

Marx worked off and on as a journalist in the 1840s and 1850s, getting his start editing and writing for the *Rheinische Zeitung* (*Rhineland Times*) in 1843. He started his career as a socialist writer and pamphleteer in the 1840s. He met his long-time colleague and sometimes bankroller Friedrich Engels in this period. In 1845 they wrote *The German Ideology* together, sketching out what would later be termed historical materialism. Marx spent most of the 1840s on the run from various governments and police forces who did not appreciated his radicalism. While in London a workers' organization asked him and Engels to write a socialist tract, which appeared in 1848 as *The Communist Manifesto*, just in time for the liberal and socialist uprisings that swept across mainland Europe that same year. By the early 1850s Marx had settled in London permanently, taking a regular seat in the British Museum like a good graduate student studying government reports, economic statistics, and political economy. The result of these research efforts was his monumental critique of capitalism, *Capital*, the first volume of which appeared in 1867 (the second and third volumes appeared after his death).

Marx had three major influences. First and foremost was the idealism of Hegel. Hegel saw all of history (not to mention philosophy and nature itself) as propelled forward by a dialectical conflict between a long stream of opposing ideas embodied in a variety social forms. History for Hegel was this dramatic struggle between opposing ideas during which Spirit attempts to become conscious of its inner essence, freedom. Marx took from Hegel the notion of this dialectical struggle, but replaced Hegel's Spirit with economic classes. For Marx history became a series of class struggles, culminating in the current battle between the bourgeoisie and the proletariat.

Second, Marx was influenced by fellow materialist, Ludwig Feuerbach. Feuerbach's 1841 book *The Essence of Christianity* argued that God was just a human invention. When we put our faith in Him, we are alienating our human essence into a fiction of our own creation. If only we could abandon our religious beliefs, we would cease to be caught up in this alienation and more fully realize ourselves as *human* beings. Marx agreed, though he thought Feuerbach's materialism failed to go far enough. He said in his 1845 *Theses on Feuerbach* that we need a sensuous, practical view of human life. We have to see human beings as active creators, not as static objects of contemplation, as he accused Feuerbach of believing.

Third, and less well known, came the influence of the political economy of the late Enlightenment, especially that produced by the Scottish Enlightenment of the second half of the eighteenth century. Most of its leading figures—Adam Smith, Adam Ferguson, John Millar, and William Robertson—wrote philosophical histories where they understood social relationships in a given society in terms of the form of property dominant in that society, not in terms of its political structure or dominant ideas. Smith and Millar saw four types of property and thus four types of society in history: primitive hunting and fishing communities, where property is largely communal; pastoral societies, which lived off cattle, sheep, and other domesticated animals, where property was concentrated in the hands of tribal chieftains; agricultural societies, where great landowners dominate; and modern commercial societies, where manufacturers and wage labourers spearhead the economy. As we saw in Chapter 1, Ferguson, probably the most interesting of this group for Marx, narrowed this down to three types of society: savage (hunting and fishing), barbarous (pastoral), and polished (agricultural or commercial with clear property rights). He said in his *Essay on the History of Civil Society* (1767) that law is a sort of treaty that members of a community sign to protect their property, and just as prophetically, writing at the very beginning of the Industrial Revolution, he noted that:

Many mechanical arts, indeed, require no capacity; they succeed best under a total suppression of sentiment and reason; and ignorance is the mother of industry as well as of superstition. . . . Manufactures, accordingly, prosper most, where the mind is least consulted, and where the workshop may, without any great effort of the imagination, be considered as an engine, the parts of which are men. (Ferguson, 1767: 182–3)

Here we see Marx's theory of alienation foreshadowed by an eighteenth-century Scot. The origins of materialist social theory can be traced most definitively back to the Scottish Enlightenment—in it we find the first clear exposition of the idea that the structure of a society can be understood best in terms of the type of property that dominates it.

Historical Materialism

Marx called his social theory 'the materialist conception of history'. Thanks largely to Engels it later became known as 'historical materialism' in order to emphasize the fact that Marx understood human beings not only in terms of their present material conditions, but also in terms of how these conditions gave rise to social structures that changed over time. His view is also called dialectical materialism because he saw history as driven forward by a dialectic of class struggle. In *The German Ideology*, Marx and Engels stated the basic premise of their materialism quite clearly: the 'nature of individuals . . . depends on the material conditions determining their production' (Marx and Engels, 1978 [1845]: 150). The 'phantoms formed in the human brain'—our ideas about religion, philosophy, and politics—are nothing more than the 'ideological reflexes and echoes' of human beings' material life processes (ibid., 154). Our ideas depend on our relationship to the means of production. Ironically, though he wrote great reams of essays, books, and newspaper articles, after *The German Ideology* Marx never again outlined what he meant in a general way by the 'materialist conception of history' except in a brief preface to his *Contribution to a Critique of Political Economy* (1859). In it he lays out the famous Marxist distinction between a society's super-structure—its ideas and political relations—and its economic foundation:

> In the social production of their existence, men inevitably enter into definite relations, which are independent of their will, namely relations of production appropriate to a given stage in the development of their material forces of produc-tion. The totality of these relations of production constitutes the economic structure of society, the real foundation, on which arises a legal and polit-ical superstructure and to which correspond def-inite forms of social consciousness. The mode of production of material life conditions the general process of social, political and intellectual life. It is not the consciousness of men that determines their existence, but their social existence that determines their consciousness. (Marx, 1859)

For Marx the really important part of society is its economic substructure, which determines the nature of the ideas and the legal and political rela-tions that dominate it. Our legal, political, reli-gious, artistic, and philosophical ideas reflect the economic class we belong to.[2] They are *determined* by our economic role in society. This is what Marx means when he says that our social existence deter-mines our consciousness. This economic deter-minist element in Marxism will become the subject of much discussion in materialist social theory in the twentieth century, as we shall see over the course of the next few sections of this chapter.[3]

The Marxist view of society is summarized in Table 3.1.

Revolutionary change happens when the property relations (which are legal and political) in a given society get seriously out of whack with the forms of economic production and division of labour. For example, feudal societies emphasized landownership as their primary form of property, along with the legal and political domination of the aristocracy over the peasants in the countryside and the merchants in the towns. When industrial capitalism started to grow in the eighteenth cen-tury, the rising capitalist class was no longer happy with their lack of political power and freedom, and was frustrated with the feudal ties binding the lower classes to the aristocrats' land when they could be much more profitably exploited in their own shiny new steam-driven factories. Feudal rela-tions of production, along with feudal politics and law, became what Marx called a 'fetter' on society, which was removed by a violent revolution in France in 1789 and by a more peaceful series of reforms in Britain and continental Europe in the late eighteenth and early nineteenth centuries.

One last key point that Marx makes in this preface is that no social order ever goes under until the 'material conditions' of the coming order have sufficiently matured within its bosom. Thus, for the capitalists to overcome the feudal order they first had to build networks of factories, canals, railways, and banks, a market economy, significant interna-tional trade, and a large urban working class. Fur-ther, for the workers to seize control of bourgeois society, that society first had to have in place a fully developed industrial economy that could generate a surplus of goods, thus eliminating the struggle for bare survival. By the early twentieth century, this *had* happened in Britain, France, Germany, and America, but it *had not* occurred in Russia or China,

Table 3.1 The Historical Materialist View of the Structure of Society

Element of Society	Composition
Superstructure	Ideology—art, religion, philosophy (including social and political thought)
	Non-economic social relations—political and legal institutions
Substructure/Foundation/Base (economic life)	Social relations of production—specific jobs, power structure of the workplace, classes
	Forces of production—machines, railways, workers
	Means of production—raw materials, land, water

the two major sites of Communist revolutions. This problem in Marx's historical materialism would be a thorn in Lenin and Trotsky's side leading up to the Russian Revolution of 1917.

Class Struggle and the Stages of History

Marx and Engels appropriated Hegel's notion of dialectical struggle, wrenching it from the realm of philosophical ideas and applying it to the material side of history. The opening salvo from their 1848 *Communist Manifesto* makes their position clear:

> The history of all hitherto existing society is the history of class struggles. Freeman and slave, patrician and plebian, lord and serf, guildmaster and journeyman, in a word, oppressor and oppressed, stood in constant opposition to one another, carried on an uninterrupted, now hidden, now open fight, a fight that each time ended, either in a revolutionary reconstitution of society at large, or in the common ruin of the contending classes. (Marx and Engels, 1848)

They saw six basic stages in history, a division that roughly parallels that made by the political econ-omists of the Scottish Enlightenment (if we ignore Marx and Engels's Asiatic stage). These stages, along with the dominant forms of property and class structure of each of them, are summarized in Table 3.2.

For Marx's purposes the key stage of history was capitalism, our present stage. In it the bourgeoisie revolutionized the means of production, building factories powered by steam engines in urban centres whose population of proletarians skyrocketed in the early nineteenth century as more and more workers were drawn to work for wages in the factories. To feed their factories, the capitalists invested in mines from which they drew coal and iron, and built first canals and later railways to carry both raw materials and finished goods. Feudal ties between lord and peasant melted into air, being replaced by liberal ideas of political freedom and individual rights. The contract and the corporation became the new legal fictions of choice for capitalist society.

Marx argued that capitalism would develop its powers of production while keeping wages down, leading to falling rates of profit and a series of crises of overproduction. The capitalists would accumulate too many goods in their warehouses,

Table 3.2 Marx and Engels's Stages of History

Stage of History	Dominant Form of Property	Class Structure
Primitive Communism	Hunter-gatherers: property shared	Tribal: no economic classes to speak of.
Asiatic Mode of Production	Property communal; surplus goes to despot	Oriental despotism: a king unrestrained by law rules over a society linked by kinship; land held in trust from the despot.
Ancient Mode of Production	Mixed private and state ownership of land; slaves	The city is the centre of the ancient world; peasants control their own land, but only as citizens of the city state (e.g., ancient Greece).
Feudalism	Land	Countryside: the nobility own landed estates, peasants grow food and create agricultural surplus to support the nobility. Towns: craftsmen work in guilds, merchants sell goods, lend money. The king rules everyone, the clergy extracts tithes.
Capitalism	Capital	Bourgeoisie (capitalists) own industries, proletariat (wage workers) work in factories. Minor classes: petite bourgeoisie run shops and engage in craft trades in towns; the aristocracy own land; peasant farmers grow food.
Communism	Social (shared)	Class structure abolished (in theory): 'From each according to his abilities, to each according to his needs.' Wage labour ends, people work for their own benefit.

so they would try to reduce costs by reducing wages and laying off workers, throwing more and more of them into the reserve army of the unemployed. This series of bursts of growth and depression would build up resentment and political awareness of the pitfalls of capitalism within the working class, who would create its own political organs. The final stage of history would be announced by a workers' revolution led by the Communist Party and its allies. After the revolution, bourgeois property relations would be dissolved, the state as an organ of class domination would wither away, and human beings would be liberated so they might hunt in the morning, fish in the afternoon, and write literary criticism at night (as Marx and Engels stated hopefully in *The German Ideology*). History has been less than kind to Marxists on this issue.[4] What really happened after the Bolshevik Revolution in Russia was a massive *strengthening* of the state apparatus, with no visible opening up of the division of labour. Twentieth-century Marxists had yet another important question to come to grips with: Is a state with coercive powers perhaps a permanent fixture in social life, independent of the form of economic organization existing in a given society?

Ideology and Religion

For Marx, ideology is any systematic view of things distorted by class interests. This distortion ranges from partial and imaginary views of reality to false consciousness or outright illusions (Craib, 1997). Marx believed that many of our political and philosophical ideas are ideological reflections of our class interests. They are phantoms of the material conditions we live in. Thus, the bourgeois liberal ideas of individual freedom and rights, as noble as they might sound, are really just ideological justifications for the oppression of the workers by the capitalists. After all, individual freedom means little if one has neither money nor a job; and from the point of view of factory owners, a free market where one can buy raw materials and labour power cheaply and sell finished products at a healthy profit is a lucrative situation.

Further, Marx believed that the ruling ideas of a given age are the ideas of its ruling class (Marx and Engels, 1848). Aristocrats favour loyalty and honour as ideals to tie peasants and servants to their rule; the bourgeoisie favour freedom and equality to open up the market to their manufactures and trade. One doesn't have to believe in the coming of a Communist revolution in the Western world to take this aspect of Marx's historical materialism seriously today.

In addition, Marx saw religion as the opium of the people. It drugged the masses into acceptance of the social order with promises of a glorious afterlife in the Christian heaven. This is why the European bourgeoisie took over Christianity from its feudal predecessors, even though the Enlightenment of the eighteenth century was in many ways a great age of religious skepticism: they knew a good tool when they saw one. Not surprisingly, most materialist theorists are either skeptics or atheists concerning the question of God's existence.

Use Value, Exchange Value, and Commodity Fetishism

Several issues discussed in Marx's *Capital* continue to be important to materialist social theory. First his theory of value. Marx argued that most things have use value, that is, utility—a hammer can help one build a bookcase; a bicycle can transport one across town. Most of these useful things can be bought and sold in the marketplace. As such they also have an exchange value expressed in money terms: they become commodities. Marx argued that under capitalism things are seen more and more purely in terms of their exchange value— even human beings, whose labour power is bought and sold for wages.

Along the way a 'fetishism' of commodities kicks in. Commodities, he argues in *Capital*, have the mysterious imprint of human labour power stamped on them. Relations between people become relations between things. Commodities assume a life all of their own, like the fantastic beings and relics given credence by religion. They become fetishes, like the bones of long-dead martyrs. We do not see the social relationships embodied in the production of the item we buy, just its cost and the pleasure and status its purchase will bring us. Under his labour theory of value, Marx refused to believe that commodities have any real value independent of the work put into them.[5] The fact that a hammer costs ten dollars isn't as important as the fact that it can usefully hammer nails. Yet to the hardware store owner, its value is precisely the profit he can make from selling it— it's unlikely he ever uses any of the tools he sells. His relation to his customers is *through* the commodities he sells them, as it is with any capitalist. And buyers adopt this mindset, seeing the commodities they buy as the real purpose of their labour and lives. This is another of Marx's precepts that survives, even prospers, in twentieth-century social theory. If you're skeptical, think about all the times you see people relating to each other through the commodities they possess—their cars, stereos, clothes, computers, cellphones. If anything, commodity fetishism has increased exponentially in the advertising-driven consumer economy of the post-World War II era. This point would be picked up in the late 1960s when Jean Baudrillard turned his attention to the structure of the consumer 'society of objects' he saw all around him.

TWO MARXISTS WHO SHOOK THE WORLD: LENIN AND TROTSKY

Lenin the Revolutionary

The basic problem faced by all revolutionary intellectuals in the Europe of the 1880s and 1890s, Lenin's formative period, was a simple one—why hadn't the revolution against capitalism predicted by Marx several decades ago already happened? Marx had claimed that capitalism would go through a series of crises causing workers' wages to drop, making more of them unemployed, throwing the proletariat into turmoil. Soon working-class revolutions would break out across the developed world. Yet by and large this just hadn't happened in either Europe or America. There had

been the liberal democratic revolutions of 1848 and then the bloody Paris Commune of 1871, a rising confined to the capital that took place in the wake of the French defeat in the Franco-Prussian War. But no where else did a workers' revolt take place on the scale imagined by Marx and Engels in their *Manifesto*.

Vladimir Ilyich Ulyanov (1870–1924), a.k.a. Lenin, was born to a Russian father and a Volga German mother in the southern town of Simbirsk. His brother Alexander became involved with the Narodniks (Populists), a group of pro-peasant revolutionaries who on occasion resorted to terrorism. They assassinated Czar Alexander II in 1881 and tried again with his successor, Czar Alexander III, in 1887. Alexander Ulyanov was executed for his part in the plot. This personal loss, along with his reading of Chernyshevsky's *What Is To Be Done?*, a mediocre political novel about dedicated revolutionaries fighting the Czarist regime in Russia, propelled Lenin into a career as a professional revolutionary. Lenin joined the Russian Social-Democratic Labour Party in 1893 and spent much of his adult life in both legally imposed and self-exile, living in Siberia from 1895 until 1900. From 1893 to 1917 Lenin fought many factional battles—both over theory and political tactics—with members of the Russian Social-Democratic Labour Party and with foreign socialists such as Karl Kautsky in Germany. His most famous dispute within the Russian party was with Georgi Plekhanov, the elder statesman of Russian Marxism, which started with Plekhanov's removal of Lenin from control of RSDLP's newspaper, *Iskra* (*Spark*), when Lenin returned from Siberia after 1900. His aims in these battles differed, though his central goal was to establish a cadre of professional revolutionaries committed to bringing about a proletarian revolution in Russia with himself as their leader. During this turbulent period party members representing different shades of socialist thought hurled insults like 'opportunist' or 'revisionist' at each other, often over minor differences of political strategy or theory.

In 1903 the RSDLP split in two during a party congress. The more moderate faction was dubbed the 'Mensheviks' (from the Russian for 'minority') because they lost a vote for control of the editorial board of *Iskra (Spark)*, the RSDLP's newspaper, though they represented a majority of party members. Their leader was Julius Martov. Lenin's Bolsheviks (from the Russian for 'majority') controlled *Iskra* but were a minority within the party. The issue that caused the split was a difference over revolutionary strategy: the Mensheviks favoured a broad-based working-class party open to all, while the Bolsheviks wanted a party run by a centralized cadre of professional revolutionaries surrounded by a greater mass of supporters who would be called on to take up arms in the decisive hour. Two years later, in 1905, a short-lived revolution broke out after Russia's defeat in the Russo-Japanese War. Czar Nicholas II was forced to concede reforms, and the Duma, a parliament with limited powers, was elected in 1906. It was at first dominated by moderate parties such as the Constitutional Democrats (Cadets), but by the fourth Duma of 1912 many Social-Revolutionaries, the party of peasant revolution, and Mensheviks were elected. Lenin despised both parties.

Lenin spent much of his life in the two decades before the Revolution of 1917 in Switzerland and elsewhere. Russia was drawn into World War I (1914–18) by its support of Serbian independence against Austrian threats and by its part in a complex structure of alliances that pitted Britain, France, and Russia against Germany, Austria-Hungary, and Turkey. The Russian army suffered a number of defeats along a wide front at the hands of the Germans, being poorly led and chronically undersupplied. From 1914 to 1917 they had lost around 1.3 million dead, but held on despite ammunition and food shortages. By 1917 the situation at the front and back at home was becoming desperate—rampant inflation caused the peasants to hoard their grain, which resulted in massive food shortages in the cities. A revolution broke out in March, with the Czar abdicating by mid-month. A coalition government of conservatives and liberals declared themselves the provisional government. Their wobbly control over the Russian state led to a game of musical chairs in the cabinet, with Alexander Kerensky, ironically a moderate socialist from the same hometown as Lenin, becoming Prime Minister in July. The Bolsheviks supported an abortive coup by soldiers and workers in August, and then waited in the wings for another attempt to seize power.

In the period leading up to 1917 Lenin agreed with the Mensheviks that even after a revolution against the Czar the socialist parties would have to allow bourgeois capitalism to develop the Russian economy before a full-fledged socialist system could be put in place. But he disagreed with them how this would be accomplished: Lenin wanted the coming revolution to be spearheaded by a democratic dictatorship of the proletariat and peasantry led by a party of revolutionary vanguard—namely his own Bolsheviks. The Russian bourgeoisie was relatively small and weak politically, while the Russian working class was concentrated in a few major cities. The key to the coming revolution for Lenin would be an alliance between the proletarians of Petrograd and Moscow and the peasants scattered across the great Russian hinterlands. Lenin aimed to bring this alliance into effect by revolutionary agitation and military discipline within his party.

He did precisely this. He returned to Russia from his long exile in April, passing through Germany in the famous sealed train that the Germans provided in the hopes that Lenin would disrupt the Russian government and their war effort. Lenin's Bolsheviks tried to create their own revolution by agitating against the Kerensky government among the soldiers and workers, especially in Petrograd, the capital. The key to Bolshevik power was the Petrograd Soviet, a council of workers' and soldiers' deputies that, by the fall of 1917, had more control over Peter the Great's old capital than the central government. It was led by Leon Trotsky, a former Menshevik who came over to the Bolsheviks in 1917. After the unsuccessful August rising, Lenin went into exile once again, returning from Finland in October. He appealed to soldiers and peasants alike with his slogan 'Peace, Land, Bread'.[6] The Bolsheviks seized power in Petrograd with military precision on

6 and 7 November (26 and 27 October by the old Russian calendar), calling on the Soviets of other cities to follow suit immediately afterward.

After the November revolution came several bloody years of civil war (1918–21) between the Communist Red and Czarist White armies, the latter at first supported by contingents of foreign troops. Trotsky steamed from front to front in an armoured train, building a huge Red Army that defeated the revolution's enemies one by one. These years also witnessed Lenin's harsh policy of War Communism, which saw the freshly minted Soviet government nationalizing major industries and 'expropriating' (i.e., stealing) set quotas of grain and other foodstuffs from the peasantry. Lenin quickly eliminated the other socialist parties and factionalism within his own Communist Party (as the Bolsheviks were known from 1918 on), setting the stage for the totalitarianism of Stalin's USSR. Along the way Lenin approved the formation of the Cheka, the secret police, whose Red Terror hardly gave evidence of the withering away of the state Marx had predicted would follow quickly upon the dictatorship of the proletariat. These policies caused great unrest, not to mention crippling the economy. Lenin admitted his economic mistake in 1921 when he announced the New Economic Policy, a loosening of state controls on the economy that he termed 'state capitalism'. He suffered from a number of debilitating strokes starting in 1922, finally dying in 1924. His body remains on display in Red Square in Moscow, embalmed like some pharaoh of a lost proletarian age.

Imperialism

Lenin made two theoretical attempts to modernize Marxism. His first, *Imperialism, the Highest Stage of Capitalism* (1917), explained that there were no successful revolutions in advanced capitalist countries like Britain, France, and Germany because these powers bought off their workers with 'super profits' from their imperial adventures. They seized huge colonial empires in Africa, Asia, and the Pacific between 1870 and 1910, then used these empires as sources of cheap raw materials and as secondary markets for their finished products. Lenin drew many of his ideas for this book from J.A. Hobson's *Imperialism: A Study* (1902), which argued that the 'economic taproot' of British and other imperialisms was the search for these very raw materials and markets, not the blood, land, and glory publicly proclaimed by the more energetic defenders of European colonialism.

The real striking change that Lenin noted taking place around the end of the nineteenth century was the decline of market capitalism and its replacement by monopoly or finance capitalism. Capitalists in the great imperial countries formed cartels and monopolies in steel, shipping, railways, oil, electricity, and other basic goods and necessities. This was especially true in England, Germany, and the United States, where vast industrial empires regulated production, in effect 'socializing' it. Industrial production was becoming concentrated in larger and larger monopolies like Standard Oil in the US and AEG (General Electric Company) in Germany. In addition, these industrial capitalists became more and more dependent on the banks to fund their activities, which were concentrated into fewer and larger enterprises like their industrial counterparts. Industrial and financial capital merged into one great behemoth. Britain, France, and other imperial powers lent large sums of money to debtor nations like Russia, turning them into political satellites. The stock market flourished, with up to one million Britons becoming 'rentiers' (i.e., people living purely off their investments) by the early twentieth century (Lenin, 1975 [1917]: 126).

Lenin's explanation of European and other colonialism was that the great industrial nations could no longer effectively invest their capital at home, so they looked abroad to more fertile fields for their excess pounds, francs, marks, and dollars. They exported investment capital that could not be profitably invested domestically to other countries—both to their own colonies and to more developed regions of the world such as Russia, South America, and the Far East. Imperialism was caused by the 'overripe' state of monopoly capitalism. The purpose of colonies was to:

- absorb this surplus capital in profitable investments;
- lock up secure sources of raw materials for industry at home;
- provide cheap labour;
- create new markets for exports (ibid., 73).

In fact, according to Lenin, the more developed capitalism becomes, the more acutely it feels a shortage of raw materials and the greater the competition for them among the great industrial nations (ibid., 98).

The imperial carousel could not spin forever—by 1914 unclaimed territory had pretty well run out. The imperial powers had carved up the whole world between them. A 'fierce struggle' for the last scraps of undivided territory broke out (ibid., 100). Now war was the only way to win a bigger piece of the colonial pie.

When war did break out in 1914, Lenin was shocked to see parliamentary socialist parties across Europe voting for war subsidies. They lined up like good soldiers behind their kings and generals, ready to fight for the glory of their nations. He saw the pro-war policy of the German Social-Democratic Party as especially troubling, reserving his most venomous invective for its leaders, notably Karl Kautsky. Why did these workers' parties support an imperialist war? Part of the answer for Lenin was that the upper echelons of the British, German, and other working classes actually benefited from their countries' colonial policies, winning steady employment and higher wages. They were in effect bribed by their national bourgeoisies to support their colonial policies. As Cecil Rhodes said, imperialism was a 'bread and butter issue' (ibid., 94), and British and other workers in the imperial powers knew which side their economic bread was buttered on.

For Lenin, the military and political side of imperialist expansion was directly caused by the predatory nature of world capitalism at the turn of the twentieth century. In this sense he could be seen as hewing closely to Marx's economic determinism while introducing an important new element to Marx's analysis of contemporary capitalism. Lenin's theory of imperialism is a mixture of sound analysis and dubious propaganda. It seemed to explain the connection between the failure of socialist revolutions in the West, the carving up of the world by colonial powers over the 1880–1914 period, and the outbreak of the Great War in 1914 in largely economic terms. Certainly European imperialism was motivated in part by economics, but the Asian and African colonies were hardly beehives of industrial activity. In fact, the French colonies of the early twentieth century imported more than they exported (Conquest, 1972: 75), while colonial investment for the great cartels was a risky enterprise at best. Even today, most African countries still lag far behind European levels of industrial production and standards of living, for which most leftist writers blame colonialism.

Lenin's view of imperialism was tremendously influential in socialist circles for at least a half-century after he put it forward. As late as the 1960s Marxist writers such as Paul Sweezy and Paul A. Baran were describing the American involvement in the Vietnam War as a search for fresh markets for US goods and capital, not as an overreaction to the fear of Soviet and Chinese expansionism, despite the meagre economic pickings that Vietnam represented in the world economy at the time. Similar analyses were applied to American and European 'neo-colonialism' even after the European empires dissolved in the 1950s and 1960s—now imperialism was conducted indirectly, by multinational corporations, the Central Intelligence Agency (CIA), undercover arms deals, and the control of puppet regimes in the Third World. The materialist account of imperialism—that it has an economic taproot—is still dominant today, for which we have Lenin to thank in part. The reaction of some critics to the Gulf wars of 1991 and 2003 merely underscores the fact that many clear-headed people understand empire-building not in terms of ideological battles or military adventurism, but as attempts to control basic resources like oil.

State and Revolution

Lenin's other important contribution to the debate over materialism was his attempt to remind readers of what he saw as Marx and Engels's view of the role of the state before and after the proletarian revolution in *State and Revolution* (written just before the Russian Revolution in 1917, published in 1918). Much of the book is taken up with invective against his fellow socialists (notably Kautsky and Plekhanov), the anarchists, and bourgeois democrats. Lenin aims to get at the true teachings of Marx and Engels on the role of the state under capitalism and communism. Yet interestingly, his interpretation of the Marxist canon leads Lenin to a view of the relation of the state to the proletarian revolution very much at odds with the way things actually worked out in the state he himself help to found, the Soviet Union.

Marx and Engels's basic claim was that the state was the 'ruling committee' of a society's dominant class, a way of using the army, police, and bureaucracy to keep the lower classes in their place. Lenin agreed that the state is an 'organ of class domination' (Lenin, 1932 [1918]: 9), with democracy being the organized use of violence by one class against another (ibid., 68). Lenin sneered that the essence of parliamentary democracy was just a choice every few years by the people of which members of the ruling class would repress them (ibid., 40). Democracy under capitalism was just democracy for the rich, for wage slavery prevented the worker from any meaningful participation in political life.

Early in the book Lenin refers to a key quote from Engels on the role of the state after the workers' revolution. The proletariat seizes control of the bourgeois state and centralizes the means of production in the state's last independent act: 'Government over persons is replaced by the administration of things and the direction of the processes of production. The state is not abolished, *it withers away*' (ibid., 16). For Engels, the post-revolutionary state is put in the museum of antiquities besides the spinning wheel and bronze axe. Yet Lenin notes that before it becomes an

antiquity, the state must become a dictatorship of the proletariat during the first or 'socialist' stage of communist society. During this stage the revolutionary proletariat must organize itself as an armed mass and crush the resistance of the bourgeoisie to the new order of things, since they will be reluctant to give up their control over the economy and the state (ibid., 23). The bourgeois state must be smashed and replaced by new bureaucratic machinery responsive to working-class rule. Society must be radically cleansed of 'all the hideousness and foulness of capitalist exploitation' (ibid., 84). This cleansing, however, will not be nearly as bloody as when a minority (such as the capitalists) oppresses a majority (such as the workers), which requires 'seas of blood' (ibid., 74). After all, the rule of the lower classes will be that of the vast majority of humanity over a small cadre of exploiters. After this transitional stage of socialism, true communism can be attained. Here, according to Marx, each works according to his ability, and each takes from society in return what they need. This becomes possible once the last vestiges of capitalist exploitation are removed, and after the new socialist quasi-state has developed the forces of production to a massive degree, as Lenin predicted it would.

As to how revolutionary socialists could run the supposedly complicated bureaucratic machinery of the modern bourgeois state, Lenin argued that modern capitalism had so simplified the systems of accounting and control that an ordinary worker, with a little extra training, could step into these positions immediately after the revolution. He thought that the average literate person who knows a smattering of arithmetic could manage modern factories, railways, postal services, and telephone exchanges, working for workingman's wages (ibid., 38, 84). Yet he or she wouldn't become a bureaucrat in the ordinary sense word, except insofar as everyone had become a bureaucrat (ibid., 92). And they would do so for equal wages.

In the end, in the final stage of communism, there would no longer be any need for the state as an organization that uses violence to protect the power of the ruling class. It would truly wither away, as Engels predicted. In the most utopian passages in the book, Lenin describes how social order under communism would no longer need to be reinforced by the coercive power of the state. All need for force would vanish, as people become accustomed to following the basic rules of social life. It would be just like a crowd spontaneously separating a pair of combatants or defending a woman against an attacker (ibid., 68, 75). Only in an exploitive society does social order have to be founded on the organized use of violence by the state. Once this exploitation ends, he reasons, the vast majority of people will spontaneously treat each other fairly. The police and the army will presumably be sent home, no longer necessary.

Needless to say, this never happened in the Soviet Union, which developed one of the strongest and most enduring totalitarian state systems in history. To be fair, the USSR was always surrounded by foreign enemies that forced it to maintain at least a sizable military establishment (as became quite clear when the Nazis invaded in 1941), if not a massive bureaucracy and internal security apparatus. Yet one can critique Lenin on grounds other than the seeming hypocrisy of the picture of a repression-free communist society he paints in his book. Does he carry his materialism too far, grounding the need for state coercion exclusively in the class struggle? Is perhaps Hobbes closer to the mark in saying that human nature itself seems to require at least the fear of a coercive power to make people behave in a civilized manner? If Lenin had lived another decade or so, he might not have been so optimistic that the higher stage of communism would in fact cause the state to wither away.

Lenin thought that a socialist party should be run on the principle of 'democratic centralism'. In theory this means that the individual party members should vote for members of a party congress or central committee, which in turn elects an executive (in the Soviet Union, the Politburo) whose decisions are binding upon the membership. In practice the Soviet Communist Party was more centralist than democratic during Stalin's absolute rule (roughly 1928 to his death in 1953), becoming in effect a one-man dictatorship. Unlike the theory of the state laid out in *State and Revolution*, one can clearly trace the totalitarian aspect of Soviet communism to Lenin's theory of how a revolutionary party can best seize control of the state.

Trotsky and Permanent Revolution

Lev Davidovich Bronstein (1879–1940), better known as Leon Trotsky, is historically important for the role he played as a fiery orator during the 1917 revolution and for his later role in forming the Red Army and winning the Russian Civil War for the Communists. Yet from 1903 to 1914 Trotsky had a tempestuous relationship with the Bolsheviks and Lenin, going so far as to write in *Our Political Tasks* that the latter's view of the party would lead to a personal dictatorship of the party chief. After the revolution, he quarrelled with other Bolsheviks, including Stalin, in whom he saw the very potential for tyranny that would emerge in all its bloody horror in the 1930s. Between 1923 and 1927 he was associated with the left-wing opposition in the Soviet Communist Party who wanted more democracy for the workers (it was *their* revolution after all!) and opposed Stalin's bureaucratic view of the state. Yet he did not have Stalin's skill at manipulation and stacking party committees, so was forced into exile from the Soviet Union in 1929, eventually finding refuge in Mexico. Trotsky spent the late 1920s and 1930s writing a history of the Russian Revolution, defining his own view of socialism, and describing how Stalin had betrayed the proletarian cause in the USSR. Stalin paid him back in 1940 by sending a henchman to kill him with an ice pick to the head.

Trotsky was associated with the Mensheviks in the period before the revolution, but had no sympathy for their view that Russia had to go through a capitalist phase before achieving socialism. He argued instead that with the help of the peasants, the Russian proletariat could use a liberal democratic revolution as a sort of springboard to jump right over the liberal capitalist stage of history directly into socialism. In an appendix to his history of the Russian Revolution he argued:

In a country economically more backward the proletariat may come to power sooner than in a country capitalistically advanced. The idea of some sort of automatic dependence of the proletarian dictatorship upon the technical forces and resources of a country is a prejudice derived from an extremely over-simplified 'economic' determinism. Such a view has nothing in common with Marxism. (Trotsky, 1932)

He goes on to note that the size, weight, and culture of the proletariat have something to do with the level of capitalist development in their country, yet this relation isn't a direct one. Various 'socio-political factors' intervene between the economic structure of a society and the political force of each of its classes, including the proletariat. He cites the difference between the revolutionary mood of the Russian proletariat of the day and the much more conservative stance of the American working class. This point is a key one for modern Marxists who actually wanted to *make* a revolution. Lenin and Trotsky did not think it necessary to wait decades for Russian capitalism to slowly develop, nurturing a larger and larger urban working class, Marx's 'gravediggers' of the bourgeois order. This sort of economic determinism ignores the power of active political agents to change the structure of their society right now, whether or not the material conditions for that change—in this case from capitalism to socialism—actually exist.

Trotsky laid out his full theory of the permanent revolution as early as 1906 in *Results and Prospects*. His logic was clear enough:

1. Capitalism in its imperialist stage has created a world economy, which even backward Russia is part of.
2. A democratic bourgeois revolution could bring a number of positive things to Russia: the elimination of the last scraps of feudalism in the countryside, an elected parliament, freedom of the press and speech, and individual rights.
3. Yet the Russian bourgeoisie is too weak and dependent on foreign money to stage such a

revolution, while the peasantry is too dispersed and unmotivated.
4. So the workers must lead the way. Yet if they win power, they won't accept simply handing it over to bourgeois liberals, as the Mensheviks suggested they do in 1917.
5. So the democratic revolution in Russia will almost immediately morph into a socialist revolution led by the proletariat and aided by the peasants.
6. Yet the relatively backward Russian economy and state cannot support socialism by itself for long. A socialist Russia will have to pursue a policy of permanent revolution—of encouraging revolution in the advanced capitalist countries of Europe, notably Germany, France, and Britain—to protect its own revolution.

Years later, in *The Permanent Revolution* (1930, translated into English in 1931), Trotsky reiterated his main ideas. The three main social forces desiring change in Russia in 1917 were the liberal bourgeoisie, the urban proletariat, and the peasantry. He argues that upon staging a democratic revolution, as happened in Russia in March 1917, the workers must fight for control of the state in order to establish a dictatorship of the proletariat. They must lead the disorganized peasant masses while doing so, and make the democratic revolution grow into a socialist one, therefore becoming a permanent revolution. Its permanence, according to Trotsky, was necessary because the full realization of socialism within one country was 'unthinkable': capitalism had created a world market and division of labour, thus preparing the world as a whole for 'socialist transformation' (Trotsky, 1931). Without the permanent revolution, a socialist country would have to cut itself off from world trade, reverting to a primitive economic state while remaining constantly under threat of being invaded by the imperialist powers. In fact, this is more or less what happened in the Soviet Union between the 1930s and 1980s.

This notion of a permanent revolution radiating out from Soviet Russia to light revolutionary fires around the rest of the world was the central bone of contention between the exiled Trotsky and the brutal master of the Kremlin in the late 1920s and 1930s, Joseph Stalin. By then Stalin had given up on world revolution, being satisfied with building 'socialism in one country'. He controlled that country through a massive bureaucracy that by 1930 was both cowed and conservative. Stalin's first five-year plan, initiated in 1928, attempted to force-feed industrialization and collectivization to the reluctant Soviet peoples, resulting in mass famine and millions of deaths. Even if we can see Stalin's modernization of the Soviet Union as a partial success by the 1950s, the enormous price in the loss of life and in restrictions on political freedom paid by the citizens of the USSR makes one wonder whether Trotsky was right all along.

ANTONIO GRAMSCI AND HEGEMONY

Antonio Gramsci (1891–1937) was an Italian journalist, thinker, and activist who wrote for socialist newspapers and helped form the Italian Communist Party in 1921. He was arrested for his efforts by Mussolini's Fascist government and spent the years 1926–37 in a prison cell. Here he wrote his *Prison Notebooks* (first published in 1947), smuggled out of the prison by his sister-in-law, Tatiana Schucht. He had to write in a rather obscure manner to get his work passed by the prison censors, so he is known today more through his interpreters than by a direct reading of this work. Gramsci saw himself as an 'organic intellectual' with deep ties to working-class activism, not just as an abstract theorist. He was very much concerned, like Lenin, with making a revolution, not merely thinking about one. Much of his fame came long after his death when his ideas were taken up by materialist cultural and social theorists who found them invaluable in explaining how modern capitalism was able to sign a truce with its proletarians.

Gramsci had one very good idea that helped to explain why a workers' revolution never happened in the advanced capitalist countries of Western Europe and North America—his theory of hegemony. Remember that Marx and Engels saw the state as the organ of the ruling class. It uses the army and the police to repress the lower classes by direct force, along with ideology to indoctrinate the lower classes into accepting their rule, thus avoiding a continual recourse to brute force to keep them down. This was part of Marx's larger 'base/superstructure' model of society: culture, ideas, politics, and the law are superstructural elements of society dependent for their existence on their economic base. Gramsci argued that ideas and culture weren't just a pale reflection of the economic or class structure of a society; rather, they are in part autonomous and just as important as economics in influencing the political relations between classes.

For Gramsci, the modern capitalist ruling class uses its control of education, religion, culture, and the mass media—in his day, the press, radio, and film—to make its ideology appear to be common sense to the masses. What Marx called the 'superstructure' of society—its ideas, culture, and legal/political relations—was for Gramsci crucial in explaining how the capitalist class was able to maintain its rule over the workers and put off a proletarian revolution throughout most of Europe in the early twentieth century. He called this use of culture and ideas to win the spontaneous consent of the lower classes hegemony, which he saw as more diffuse and widespread than Marx's notion of ideological control. Gramsci made a basic distinction between *direct coercive control* of the lower classes through the law, the police, and the army and the *ideological control* of the workers exercised through the agencies of 'civil society' (the family, religion, education, and the media). Civil society was the province of hegemony—its ideological institutions were called into service by the ruling classes and their minions to buttress their rule. So, for Gramsci, the success of capitalist societies in forestalling revolution wasn't just a matter of having large police forces and jails; it was also due to their use of ideology to convince the lower classes to accept their lot in life.

Yet the workers were not merely ignorant dupes of this control—the ruling class had to negotiate its hegemony over them with concessions such as higher pay, leisure time, and mass entertainment relevant to their interests. By giving the workers a bit of sweetness and light in their lives, the fire of revolution could be dampened. Gramsci argued that its hegemonic position in society could not be taken for granted by the ruling class; it had to be constantly pursued, reinforced, and renegotiated. The capitalist class had to exercise moral and intellectual leadership to maintain its dominance. The task of the organic socialist intellectual was to convince the masses that this leadership was *not* effective, to dispel the cloud of illusion spun by the ruling class and its functionaries.

We can compare Gramsci's hegemony to the relationship between a labour union and management in a modern industry. Most weeks in the year the workers punch the clock, work, and collect their pay without seriously disputing the 'hegemony' of the owners of the factory and their appointed managers. Yet from time to time industrial disputes break out, especially when the union goes on strike and management has to negotiate a fresh contract with its workers. Then management must make some concessions: higher pay, more holidays, and better working conditions. At this point the capitalists must negotiate the consent of the workers or the strike will continue. As with the overall hegemony of the capitalist class, management has to work at throwing an ideological blanket over the discontent of the workers, trying to convince them they're working in their best interests, even though this isn't true. Sometimes it works, sometimes it doesn't.

For Gramsci there were two basic strategies by which the proletarian revolution could be pursued, depending on the type of society where the struggle is taking place:

1. *War of manoeuvre:* In countries with weak civil societies and a strong state, such as Russia in 1917, the party of the proletariat is best advised to attack the state directly, as the Bolsheviks did in their revolution. We can compare this to the German blitzkrieg strategy in World War II, where columns of panzers struck deep into enemy territory to overwhelm their opponents quickly.

2. *War of position:* In advanced liberal democratic societies where the institutions of civil society—religion, education, and the media—are strong, Gramsci advised a strategy akin to the trench warfare of World War I (Gramsci, 1971: 235). In such warfare, a defender has several trenches to retreat to, and a quick assault might take only the first of these defensive lines. Similarly, a revolutionary party must build up its forces slowly and engage in a prolonged assault on the old order. Part of this buildup was the equivalent of the classic creeping artillery barrage in trench warfare: the winning over one by one of the institutions of civil society to socialist ideas preceding the final call to the foot soldiers of the proletarian revolution to go 'over the top'.

This distinction explains how a socialist revolution can succeed in a backward country like Russia in the early twentieth century, yet fails at the same time in a more advanced country like Germany— the German state, even in the chaos of defeat in 1918, could call on the institutions of civil society to defend itself, unlike the Russian Czar.

Gramsci's theory of hegemony remains a seductive one to socialist intellectuals interpreting society and culture. For one thing, it avoids a strict economic determinism where human agency is swallowed up in omnipresent material structures. Gramsci thought that what individuals did mattered. Second, it claims that our ideas and culture *do* have an effect in questioning the power of the capitalist ruling class—so much so that Gramsci believed that unions and working-class political parties should work to establish a counter-hegemony as part of their struggle to build socialism in Western liberal states. Third, the theory provides Western intellectuals with a useful task which doesn't require them getting their hands dirty—that of criticizing capitalist hegemony in speech and print, a task that a more determinist view of Marxism would consider as of marginal utility only.

So is Gramsci a materialist? He certainly accepted the notion that our ideological notions were connected to the economic base and relations of production dominant in our society, as Marx and Engels argued, and thus he accepted some form of the Marxist base/superstructure model. And he also clearly believed that class struggle was a key element in modern society. On the other hand, insofar as he argued that ideology has an independent causal role of its own in determining the political relations between classes in a given society, he abandoned materialism as an explanation for all the wrongs of capitalist society. This is one major reason why cultural theorists find Gramsci's ideas so seductive, as we'll see when we examine subcultural theory in Chapter 7. Now popular culture—music, movies, television, fashion—can be seen as a way of actively opposing the hegemony of the ruling class, not as mere smoke spewing from the engines regulating our relation to the means of production. Our tastes and ideas are more than epiphenomena of the class struggle. This ambiguous relation to materialism would be repeated by a number of other important twentieth-century social theorists, including Louis Althusser.

LOUIS ALTHUSSER ON IDEOLOGY

Althusser and Marxism as a Science

Louis Althusser (1918–90) was a prominent French Marxist whose work was much admired in the 1960s and 1970s as an attempt to reread Marx for a new age. His conclusions were published in two main works, *For Marx* and *Reading Capital*, both of which appeared in 1965 in French. His fall from intellectual grace came in 1980, when he killed his wife, spending three years in an insane asylum as a result. Althusser was a committed Communist, though like many of his comrades he was critical of Stalin's barbarities. Yet he thought that the best way to fight Stalinism was not through moral condemnation but by a theoretical attack.

Althusser saw Marxism as a science, one of history and 'social formations'. Dialectical materialism explains in a rigorous way how societies work and historically change. Yet he was also an anti-humanist: he was distressed that so many of

his Marxist colleagues centred their understanding of Marxism on the writings of the young Marx of the 1840–5 period and not the mature Marx, the creator of dialectical materialism. This 'humanist' Marx was sentimental and unscientific, still too much under the influence of Hegel and Feuerbach (as seen in his theory of alienation in the *1844 Manuscripts*). In fact, Althusser argued that in 1845 Marx went through an 'epistemological break' from his humanist phase, leading him to embrace a scientific view of history that only reached its fruition after 1857, especially in *Capital* (Althusser, 1977 [1965]: 32–4).

Yet having said this, Althusser thought one of the major problems with Marxism was its economic determinism. At times, Marx and Engels seemed to believe that the historical shifts from feudalism to capitalism and then to communism were the inevitable results of technological and economic forces beyond the control of individual human beings. It didn't matter how a few individuals acted or what they thought. The way Althusser got around this deterministic implication of classical Marxism, which he called 'economism', was by emphasizing the role of ideology in structuring society.

In the glossary to *For Marx*, Althusser defines ideology as 'the "lived" relation between men and their world, or a reflected form of this unconscious relation, for instance a "philosophy"' (ibid., 252). Ideology is the way that an individual consciousness becomes a social subject. Althusser makes a basic distinction between the almost endless collection of ideologies that have existed throughout history and ideology in general, which he says has no history. In its general sense, ideology is eternal. He compares it to Freud's picture of the unconscious: this is an abstract transhistorical structure of the human mind whose content is an infinite variety of dream images, phobias, neuroses, and childhood sexual traumas, depending on the individual's personal history. Our mind is deeply structured by ideology—we always act according to one or another ideology. We can never escape its influence. And we can only recognize ideology in others: we take our own beliefs for truth, just as a Christian might laugh at the Hindu gods yet fervently believe in the Christian God, oblivious to the ideological nature of religion.

Althusser is also often seen as a structuralist, despite the fact that he denied being one. A structuralist, as we shall see in greater detail in Chapter 7, is someone who understands language, myth, popular culture, or society as systems containing structures that constitute the phenomenon in question (e.g., the general structure of a language makes specific sentences and words meaningful; the cultural codes found in music and fashion allow us to understand these as more than random choices). These structures are often hidden to the casual observer yet causally powerful all the same—'deep structures', like the massive block of ice hidden below the surface of the water in an iceberg that keeps it afloat. Some structuralists also claim that what makes the structures work is the fact that they are imprinted on our unconscious minds—thus they influence our thinking and acting without us being consciously aware of them (at least most of the time). One of the main critiques of structuralism is that it tends to be static and anti-historical—for example, structuralist theorists of language are more interested in the structure of meaning or grammar at a given point in time (i.e., its synchronic nature), and not how the language they're studying evolved to become what it is over time (its diachronic nature). Althusser can be seen as a structuralist in that he emphasizes the study of complex wholes and often speaks of the social 'function' played by ideology in turning individuals into social subjects, a process most people are not aware of. However, Marxism itself is not as clearly structuralist in the sense outlined above, since Marx fervently believed that social structures change over time thanks to the class struggle. For Marx, there are no static, transhistorical systems keeping everything stable.

Althusser's most important work for our purposes is his essay 'Ideology and Ideological State Apparatuses' in *Lenin and Philosophy*. In it he claims to be rereading the 'Marxist classics' for a modern age, plugging up a few holes in the otherwise solid wall of Marxist theory with his own

ideas. His basic interest in the essay is how a society reproduces its relations of production, notably how a society makes sure that each new generation submits to the rules of the social order. The answer is, of course, through ideology, which for Althusser comes very close to what modern sociologists call 'socialization'. To escape from economism, he argues that ideology is relatively autonomous from the economic base of society, being determined by it only 'in the last instance' (Althusser, 1971: 135). Like Gramsci, Althusser thought our social, political, and philosophical ideas have some freedom from the economic base, which in some less than clear manner brings them into existence.

Marx tended to see ideology as a distortion of the world that alienated the lower classes from the reality of their exploitation. In his first 'thesis' in this essay, Althusser argues that ideology is a representation of our *imaginary* relationship to our real conditions of existence (ibid., 162–4). It is not our 'real world' that we imagine in a deluded fashion, but our relation to it that becomes distorted, a subtle but significant distinction. Our relation to the world is always imaginary—we can never get at the way our world *really* is because we only see that world through ideology. This is reminiscent of the German philosopher, Immanuel Kant, who said that we always perceive the world through the pure mental forms of space and time and through such mental categories as unity, multiplicity, and causality.

His second thesis is that ideology has a 'material existence', that is, our ideas cause us to act in certain ways, and our actions are part of material practices governed by material rituals. These rituals are created and protected by ideological apparatuses such as the church and the schools. There are no practices without an ideology, just as there is no ideology outside of social subjects (ibid., 170). So we become social actors thanks to ideology, while there's no such thing as an ideology without someone thinking it as they act. Althusser's model of the subject, ideology, and society is shown in Figure 3.1, using his own example of belonging to the Catholic Church.

Althusser may be playing a bit with the meaning of the world 'material' here—he uses it in more than the economic sense—but what he means is plain enough. As members of a society we are subject to a set of concrete rules about how we should act. These rules often take the form of standard rituals backed up by organized bodies, such as the church, the education system, and the law, each with its own set ideologies.

Just as Gramsci distinguished between the direct coercive control exercised by the police and legal system and the hegemonic control exercised by the institutions of civil society, Althusser distinguished between two agencies of control in modern societies:

- *Repressive state apparatuses (RSAs):* These are the military, the police, the courts, and the army. Their power comes *mostly* from the threat or use of violence.
- *Ideological state apparatuses (ISAs):* These are the family, religion, the schools, the trade unions, forms of communication (the mass media), forms of culture and entertainment, and the political and legal systems in their non-repressive modes. These function 'massively and predominantly' through ideology (ibid., 143–5).

Althusser argues that no class can control a society without controlling its ISAs most of the time. Yet like Gramsci's institutions of civil society, Althusser's ISAs are the site of a bitter class strug-

gle (ibid., 147). Here the bourgeoisie and the proletarians duke it out in modern societies. The difference between Gramsci and Althusser on this point is that Gramsci seems far more optimistic that the oppressed classes can escape the ideological control of the ruling class and negotiate some cultural space and a bigger slice of the economic pie for themselves. For Althusser, ideology seems omnipresent and inescapable.

Althusser argues that one specific way in which ideology is inscribed on individuals, transforming them from unformed into subjects with a given place in society, is through *interpellation*, or in ordinary English, hailing. We can see this happening when a person hails another in a way the other is expected to recognize, as when a cop hails a scruffy looking teenager on the street with a 'Hey you!', thus asserting his authority over the potential miscreant, or a professor hails an inattentive student with a 'Hey you, the student in the fifth row reading the newspaper!', thus identifying bored Beth as a student with a poor attention span not interested in learning. In a broader sense, hailing can 'recruit' an individual into membership in a social group based on job, class, age, sex, criminality, etc. Advertising does this too—think of all those television commercials that seem to be speaking to you directly, imploring you to buy a new car so you will have power, prestige, and sex appeal or to try the latest shampoo that will give your hair an unbelievable sheen. In fact, advertising only works if its customers accept the hail being made as relevant to them.

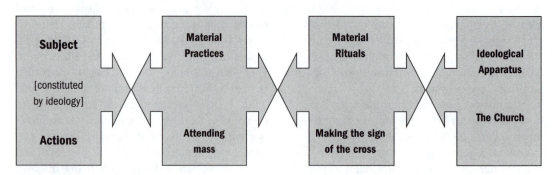

Figure 3.1 Althusser's Model of Society

Certainly interpellation is *one* way in which we become members of social groups. Yet whether this provides Althusser with a general theory of how we absorb ideological notions about our place in society is dubious—we can also think for ourselves about such things, mulling over our social role with a Hamlet-like 'to work or not to work, that is the question', not to mention the fact that we absorb many indirect messages from the ISAs we encounter in our lives that are not explicit hails. For example, a lawyer might watch a film about a courageous fictional attorney fighting injustice and take the main character as a model for her own life. Of course, Althusser could claim that this is a form of *indirect* hailing, but it is far easier to assume that an element of human agency enters the equation at some points in the process whereby we become social subjects.

For most of modern human history, the most important ISA was obviously the church. It performed many roles now done by secular institutions. Today, however, the educational system has taken over from the church the role of chief dispenser of ideology. Althusser saw the schools as absolutely vital in reproducing the relations of production in capitalist societies. The schools teach their students a bit of know-how, yet inside the silvery wrapper of technical knowledge they find the real sweet, the ruling ideology, which is drummed into them either directly in ethics and political philosophy, or indirectly through languages, literature, and the sciences (ibid., 155). These students are 'ejected' into society in several stages: 16-year-olds as workers and peasants, secondary-school graduates as technicians and clerks, university graduates as intellectuals, capitalists, police, or professional ideologists. In short, the educational system tries to make sure that by the time a young man or woman reaches early adulthood, they have accepted capitalism as common sense.

Insofar as ideology helps to structure our view of society and our relation to the material world, it can be seen as performing the function of socialization. In fact, Althusser doesn't shy away from using the word 'function' in his essay on the ide-ological state apparatuses to describe the purpose of ideology. This comes dangerously close to Parsons's functionalism, where one of the basic functions of what Althusser calls the ideological state apparatuses—the family, the church, education, and the media—is 'latent pattern maintenance', that is, inculcating a society's dominant values in each fresh generation. Unlike Gramsci's theory of hegemony, with its tie to political activism, Althusser's view of ideology leaves less room for political change, since it is not clear how an ideology critical of the ruling class can actually arise (despite the fact that it obviously exists in Marxism itself). If the economic base of society causes the ideological state apparatuses to drum the ruling ideology into kids' heads in the family, the schools, and the mass media, where is there room for freedom of thought, or at least a counter-hegemonic set of ideas? Once again we run up against a main problem in materialist accounts of society: Do an individual's ideas and human agency in general count for anything in shaping our actions, or are we just passive products of our economic circumstances? Althusser's theory of ideology restricts human agency to a great degree, even though the class struggle is always lurking in the background. The French writer Jean-Paul Sartre started from the opposite position—not from economic determinism, but from a philosophy of human freedom, existentialism.

JEAN-PAUL SARTRE'S SEARCH FOR A METHOD

Jean-Paul Sartre (1905–80) was the most important existentialist philosopher of the twentieth century. He had a troubled early life: his father died a year after his birth, and he was raised by his mother and a grandfather he came to hate, Charles Schweitzer. As a child he was a lonely and isolated bookworm. Sartre decided to become a writer as a young boy, and stuck to his guns. He taught in secondary schools from 1931 to 1945, interrupted in 1939 by the German invasion of France and his military service. He was a prisoner of war from 1940 to 1941 and worked for the French Resistance during the rest of World War II.

His war experiences were largely responsible for his greater commitment to socialist politics from the late 1940s onward, although he had always been contemptuous of the French bourgeoisie and of capitalism as a whole. He had a lifelong friendship and on-again, off-again romance with Simone de Beauvoir (1908–86), a fellow existentialist writer and pioneering feminist, though both asserted their fundamental human freedom by sleeping with other people.

In a nutshell, existentialism is the philosophy that claims that as conscious beings with individual life projects we are condemned to be free, though we often deny that freedom by denying the reality and necessity of human choice. Sartre was influenced in the 1930s by two German phenomenologists,[7] Edmund Husserl (1859–1938) and Martin Heidegger (1889–1976). Heidegger's *Being and Time* (1927) argued that human beings are 'thrown' into this world and experience anguish at the prospect of their mortal existences, which he called in German *Dasein* ('being there'). Sartre expounded at great length on his own brand of phenomenological existentialism in *Being and Time* (1943), in which he argued that the world consists of two types of being—*in-itself being* (physical things like rocks and trees and blood and bones), which obeys physical laws but doesn't think, and *for-itself being*, thinking conscious beings—human beings. We are free, even though we have bodies, drives, and emotions that push us this way and that, seemingly denying our freedom. Sartre argued in his important 1946 essay 'Existentialism Is a Humanism' that we are 'condemned to be free': even though we like to deny this fact, we are responsible for everything we do. Life is a series of projects we create for ourselves, a portrait we are continuously revising until that last moment when we die and become lifeless flesh and bones, in-itself things. We *are* what we *do*—the ideas we have of ourselves are mere delusions unless we manifest them in action. At least up to the 1950s and his attempt to reconcile existentialism with Marxism, Sartre thought that all forms of determinism were just excuses we use to deny any responsibility for what we have done or what we are.

The trick is that too often we for-itself beings treat ourselves and others as in-itself things. We pretend that God, our family history, or impersonal social forces are responsible for our failures or for our refusal to take a political stance. For Sartre, existentialism spells out the logical consequences of atheism—if there is no God, we are entirely responsible for our own lives. This is part of what he meant when he said that 'existence precedes essence': we have no set human nature, no essence, only the things we do in our lives. When we make excuses and pretend we're not responsible for our actions we're living in what Sartre calls 'bad faith'. This is when we take our 'facticity', the physical facts about our current and past existence, as the sum total of our reality. Many of Sartre's novels, stories, and plays are populated with characters living in bad faith. For example, in 'Intimacy' from his 1939 collection of short stories *The Wall*, the main character, Lucienne, wants to leave her uncaring and sexually inactive husband Henri for her lover Pierre. But when she does so, she goes to a part of Paris where Henri will discover them, not being able to bear full responsibility for her infidelity. In Sartre's most famous play *No Exit* (1944), three characters are stuck in a room they cannot leave. They bemoan their inauthentic lives, Garcin making excuses for his cowardly acts, Inez for being a lesbian, and the coquettish Estelle for killing a child. At the end we discover that in fact they're dead and in hell, except in this case (as Garcin proclaims) 'Hell is other people!' The triad of characters in Sartre's inferno is essential to proving his point about bad faith. With only two people alone, they can indulge each other's illusions about their personal failures. But a third person can judge the others' mutual illusions, cutting through their bad faith. *No Exit* illustrates another couple of key points in Sartre's existentialism—the idea that to strive to live freely leads to anguish, and how the 'look' of the other can objectify us, turning us from thinking beings into rock-like objects.

The relevance of Sartre's existentialism to the debate over materialism in social theory should be clear by now—insofar as we're living human beings, we are free to make choices. In fact, we're condemned to choose whether we want to or not. The younger Sartre believed in freedom so radically that he even thought we choose our passions—when we're overcome by love or hate, anger or joy, these are all choices. Sartre's existentialism would seem to be at odds with the notion that our lives are determined by material forces. Indeed, it's hard to see how we can get social theory out of Sartre's existentialism at all, given its focus on individual freedom. Yet surprisingly, Sartre became very sympathetic to Marxism after 1946, coming to see it as the great philosophy of the age. Socialism, for him, was the political form of society most likely to bring freedom to the great mass of people. He couldn't just stand on the political sidelines during the struggle against fascism in the 1940s, the revolts against European colonialism in the 1950s, and the Vietnam War and student revolts of the 1960s. He took sides.

Dirty Hands

A new Sartre emerged from World War II. In *What Is Literature?* (1947) and in his review *Les Temps Modernes*, begun in 1945, Sartre laid out his theory of the committed writer against the idea of art for art's sake. In his case he was committed to socialism and, at least until invasion of Hungary by the Red Army in 1956, the French Communist Party (though he was never a formal member). In the 1950s he opposed French colonialism in Indochina and Algeria; in the 1960s and early 1970s he argued against American neo-colonialism in Vietnam. He was also critical of Stalin's reign of terror in the USSR and of the Soviet invasions of Hungary in 1956 and Czechoslovakia in 1968.

In 1947 Sartre published a play called *Dirty Hands*, which takes place during World War II in a fictional Eastern European country called Illyria. The main character, Hugo Barine, is in the 'Proletarian Party' and works for the local resistance against the Germans. He is ordered by Moscow to befriend and then assassinate Hoederer, a moderate party leader who favours co-operation with other parties against the Nazis. Hugo gets to know

Hoederer as a compassionate human being, and can't do the deed until he discovers Hoederer dallying with his wife Jessica. He's captured and thrown in jail. Meanwhile Moscow has changed its mind, and adopted Hoederer's old policy of co-operation. After trying to kill Hugo, the party offers to rehabilitate him if he agrees that the murder of Hoederer was a crime of passion. He refuses, takes responsibility for his political act, and is shot by a party assassin. This play is a sort of allegory for the engaged intellectual, for Sartre himself. The intellectual must get his or her hands politically dirty to be a real writer. Ideological purity is less important than achieving concrete political goals, which sometimes requires co-operation between diverse political groups. In acting, politically committed actors must assert their responsibility for their actions, and not hide behind personal passions when working for the cause of socialism against fascist or bourgeois enemies.

The Progressive-Regressive Method

Sartre's *Search for a Method* (originally 1957), meant as a sort of extended postscript for his much longer and quite convoluted *Critique of Dialectical Reason* (1960), wound up being printed separately as an extended introduction to the latter. Together these works represent Sartre's attempt to wed Marxism to existentialism. He lays out his method in *Search for a Method*, his basic question being how the social and economic structure of a society and an individual's biographical details interact to produce a life.

In his *Critique*, Sartre argues that the basic fact about society is *scarcity*—there isn't enough stuff to go around. Hence societies create hierarchical structures where people give up their individual sovereignty (his new term for freedom) to authority figures to organize the distribution of goods within a system of scarcity, thus creating a situation of non-reciprocal sovereignty. Like Marx, Sartre argues that only under conditions of plenty can full freedom be won. Our freedom is embodied in praxis, or voluntary purposeful action in the material world, which is restricted not only by scarcity but also by the *practico-inert*, a complex term that includes not only brute matter and our general physical environment but also the unintended consequences of human social actions that accumulate in structures such as property relationships, set social roles, and traditional social institutions. Even though human beings make their own world, they store up this making in the objects produced by labour. Sometimes these inert objects and structures work against us as *counter-finalities*, as when industrialization creates wealth and reduces poverty, yet pollutes the environment and warms up the planet. Sartre's point here is that the best laid plans of social actors often go astray when looked at from a longer historical perspective. Sartre's new categories—praxis and the practico-inert—parallel very roughly his old distinction between for-itself and in-itself being. Although we're free in the abstract, each day of our lives we face the practico-inert world, which we and others have built up over time, as a challenge to our free pursuit of ends of our own choosing.

Sartre's *Search for a Method* is his attempt to lay out a method that combines the Marxist belief that economics underlies human action and thought with the existentialist belief that human freedom can be expressed in the praxis of individual actors. He needs a link between economic determinism and human freedom, which he finds in *mediations* and in the progressive-regressive method. He starts off by agreeing with Marx and Engels's general proposition that human beings make their own history on the basis of real prior conditions, among which economics is decisive (Sartre, 1963: 31), and with Marx's general base/superstructure model whereby our ideas are based on our relation to the means of production. Indeed, Sartre sees Marxism as 'the one philosophy of our time', with existentialism now only an enclave within it, a parasite living off the body of true knowledge (ibid., xxxiv, 8). Yet existentialism, starting with Søren Kierkegaard (1813–55), reminds social theorists not to absorb the individual into a system of abstract concepts, as Hegel and too many contemporary Marxists are wont to do. In fact, Sartre's *Search for a Method* is full of stinging attacks on the frozen Marxism he saw as

dominant in the Europe of his day. As Marxism became the state ideology of the USSR, it caused people and things to yield to abstract ideas, with the Communists making up their mind about events like the Hungarian Revolution of 1956 in advance of the facts, always ready to ignore experience if this served the interests of the Party (ibid., 22). At its heart Marxism should teach, not dictate; its principles are regulative, helping us to understand the relation of social phenomena to each other and to their economic base. Against the scholastic and a priori nature of modern Marxism, we still need the corrective of the existentialist emphasis on individual freedom and the reality of our subjective lives. Sartre concludes 'Marxism and Existentialism', the first of three essays in *Search for a Method*, by repeating Marx's idea that the realm of freedom will be achieved only once a society overcomes scarcity. Then, and only then, can a full-fledged philosophy of freedom take its place (ibid., 34).

In the second essay Sartre explores in some depth the materials that will go into the bridge he wants to build between Marxism and existentialism. These are 'mediations' and the use of auxiliary disciplines such as psychoanalysis (the existentialist, not the Freudian, variety) and sociology. If we are to understand the motivations of the leaders of world-historical events like the French Revolution and the meaning of their actions, it does us no good to simply slot them into such prefabricated Marxist categories as 'mercantile bourgeoisie' or 'petite bourgeoisie'. Sometimes their actions can be explained as the product of economic contradictions; at other times, 'superstructural motives' dominate (ibid., 42). Sartre gives the example of how the ambitious and flamboyant Girondins led France into war with Austria in 1792 not because it would benefit shipbuilders and speculators, but to save the Revolution, to expose the treachery of Louis XVI, and to keep their faction in a position of leadership in the National Assembly. These were purely *political* motives. In addition, the consequences of our actions often escape us: even if we *wanted* to aggressively pursue our economic interests on a daily basis, our actions become entwined with those of all others, often frustrating our plans (ibid., 47).

Lazy Marxism turns 'real men into the symbols of its myths', refusing to see them as individuals with real subjective depth (ibid., 53). The works of the human mind are complex and cannot be reduced to the product of a single class ideology (ibid., 116). We might choose to situate a writer like Paul Valéry as a 'petite bourgeois intellectual', yet not all petite bourgeois intellectuals wrote Valéry's poems. To understand his life, we need a hierarchy of mediations, a series of bridges between the life of the individual and the social-economic structure of his or her society. These mediations help the individual to emerge from the background of the relations of production (ibid., 56–7). The first and greatest mediation in our lives is that between our family and society as a whole. Marxists seem to think that we become human beings only after picking up our first paycheque. Yet we experience childhood as an all-encompassing experience that is unique to each of us, even though during this time we take our place in the hierarchy of classes. Sartre also mentions residential groups as another mediation. His general point in this second essay is that there are only real living individuals and relations between them. Engels is wrong to speak of the biographical details of the life of a historical figure like Napoleon being a product of mere 'chance': his place in history isn't assured by iron laws but by the concrete conditions he found himself in and how he tried to shape those conditions to his liking.

In the third and final essay in *Search for a Method* Sartre lays out his progressive-regressive method. Sartre reads Marx as saying that 'man in a period of exploitation is *at once both* the product of his own product a historical agent' (ibid., 87). The structures of a society are the starting point of all human action—our material conditions set definite limits to what we can do in our lives (ibid., 93). Peasants are unlikely to become bank presidents. Yet insofar as we set ourselves *projects*—to become a doctor, write a book, or build a log cabin—we use our praxis to create something new, to go beyond our present situation and project into the future some goal. Like for-itself consciousness, we transcend inert matter

and practico-inert social relationships to inscribe our individual being onto an indifferent cosmos.

Every act has a hierarchical multiplicity of meanings. Sartre compares it to a pyramid—at its base are more general meanings (for example, the connection of an act to the class one belongs to), higher up more concrete and individual meanings (for example, one's resentment for an uncaring and domineering father). Although the base of the pyramid supports its upper layers, we cannot logically deduce the content of the individual meanings (e.g., the uncaring father) from the more general ones (e.g., one's being a member of the working class) (ibid., 102). As existentialism recognizes, the subjective qualities of an individual's life aren't just by-products of their economic situation—they are more unique than that.

Sartre's method, as shown in Figure 3.2, aims to understand a person's place in society and thus in history. It contains two 'moments': an analytic/ regressive one, where the social theorist breaks down a person's life into its discrete biographical complexities, and a synthetic/progressive one, where the theorist looks at the person's project and tries to comprehend how it relates to the overall social structure he or she is working within.

This method describes an enriching reciprocal movement between the object being studied and its epoch, between the biography of an individual and the times the person lives in. We define ourselves by our projects. But these projects always take place in a society where *need* is a fundamental existential category, and therefore where we find ourselves slotted into a specific class position. So our projects are coloured by the social and economic structures we find around us, by the previous acts of other projecting beings. Sartre's method avoids economic determinism by holding fast to the freedom of the individual to express his or her ends in a given project, even if that project is distorted or halted by the projects of others congealed in the great existential blob that is the practico-inert. Yet he believes to the end in the freedom of the cultural order from nature. For this reason, Marxism requires an injection of existentialism to prevent it from becoming a living corpse. It needs to integrate an appreciation of the

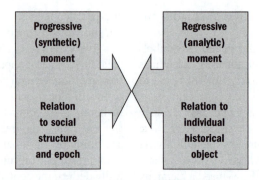

Figure 3.2 Sartre's Progressive-Regressive Method

'unsurpassable singularity of the human adventure' (ibid., 176) into its tendency to deal with individual actions as the products of abstract economic structures. After all, labour itself, the foundation of Marxist materialism, has as its basic structure the human need to project goals into the future.

Whether or not Sartre is successful in marrying his philosophy of human freedom, existentialism, to Marxist materialism must remain an open question. It certainly makes sense to say that in the *abstract* human beings are free, yet our lives are conditioned in a thousand ways by the class we were born into and by scarcity or the absence thereof in our lives. Yet in the end we have to return to the beginning of Sartre's career to understand how the roots of individual freedom can grow in the soil provided by a philosophy of economic necessity—to see this freedom as a *nothingness*, an absence of determination, a mysterious ghost in the machine. With Karl Mannheim we return to Sartre's home territory, the relation of consciousness to material life, though this time without any early notions of absolute individual freedom to throw a monkey wrench into the deterministic works.

KARL MANNHEIM'S SOCIOLOGY OF KNOWLEDGE

Mannheim's Methodology

Karl Mannheim (1893–1947) was born in Budapest to a Hungarian father and a German mother. He was a sickly lad, and died at the rela-

tively young age of 53 due to a heart condition. He studied at the universities of Budapest, Paris, Freiberg, and Berlin, getting his doctorate in philosophy in 1918, the year of the German defeat in World War I. He fled Hungary and the fascist and anti-Semitic regime of Admiral Horthy in 1920 to work at the University of Heidelberg. In 1921 Mannheim married Juliska Lang, who had a doctorate in psychology herself and got her husband interested in psychoanalysis. In 1930 he became a professor at the Goethe University in Frankfurt, working in the same building as the soon-to-become-famous Frankfurt School theorists (they squabbled over Mannheim's lack of interest in leftist politics). He became a refugee once again in 1933, after Hitler's rise to power, moving to London to take up a position at the London School of Economics in 1933. For the rest of his life Mannheim lived in England, working until 1945 in a series of temporary teaching jobs.

Mannheim's best-known work is *Ideology and Utopia* (1968 [1936]), which we'll concentrate on here. It puts forward a theory of the sociology of knowledge. This is the notion that knowledge is not objectively true or false, but *related to* or *dependent on* (depending on how strong one's sociology of knowledge is) the knower's social-economic-historical location. In the Marxist theory of ideology, this location is usually the knower's class: bourgeois thinkers have bourgeois ideas, while proletarians have proletarian ideas, unless tricked by the capitalists into a false consciousness of their own interests. Mannheim was not a Marxist, though he was influenced by both Marx and Weber.

His work is in essence a synthesis of materialism and idealism, idealism in social theory being the notion that ideas (as opposed to material forces) shape social structure and cause historical change. For this reasons I've placed him *after* Sartre, who at least claims to be a Marxist, even though chronologically speaking most of Mannheim's work predates Sartre's major forays into social theory.

For Mannheim, all knowledge is situationally dependent, related to the thinker's social and historical situation. Marx saw ideology as a biased or distorted picture of the world whose purpose was to serve class interests. Mannheim argues that this encompasses only the first and lowest type of ideology: that of conscious trickery. There's also a middle type, 'cant', where a person is committed to an idea for deep emotional reasons but could *in theory* come to realize its ideological character, and the more comprehensive type of ideology where the individual has absorbed the ideas of some class or other social group to such a degree that he or she is self-deceived about their truth (ibid., 41). For Mannheim, even after all distortions are removed, knowledge still reveals traces of its origins, the situation and interests of an age, class, generation, status group, sect, or group of people doing the same job. Notice that Mannheim's list of the social foundations of knowledge is much longer than Marx's list of the economic foundation of ideology, which contains essentially only one item, class.

The job of the sociology of knowledge is to obtain a 'systematic comprehension of the relationship between social existence and thought', it being a theory of the 'social or existential determination of actual thinking' (ibid., 309, 267). For Mannheim, all knowledge comes out of purposeful human thinking, which by its very nature is tied to human intentions and thus to acting in a given social world. The idea that there is a pure realm of Truth free of all social influences is an illusion. New types of knowledge grow out of new forms of life—what we consider to be 'truth' always depends on the *Weltanschauung* (world view) of our age. Compare the way that a modern scientist might investigate some phenomenon in

nature—e.g., the cure of a given disease—with the way that a medieval monk might investigate the same phenomenon. It isn't just a matter of having more advanced technological equipment today. It's also a matter of what counts as good research technique—consulting the ancient writings of Hippocrates or Aristotle or Christian theology would be seen as a waste of time by modern doctors, though not by medieval physicians. Yet to understand *why* these strange medieval men saw God in all natural events, including disease, we have to understand the general nature of their society and how it was shaped by its Christian world view.

In fact, Mannheim applies his sociology of knowledge to his own ideas. Only in an age like his own, when social classes started to mix with each other and this vertical mobility exposed social groups to significantly different ideas, can one begin to see how knowledge in general depends on one's social situation. It was only appropriate that psychoanalysis, with its theory of the unconscious mind destroying any last vestiges of our faith in human rationality, arose at the same time. As long as social groups can manifest their values in splendid isolation from each other, such a theory is unlikely to arise. But in the age of uncertainty that Mannheim lived through between the First and Second World Wars, this isolation came to an end, giving birth to the sociology of knowledge.

The Pitfalls of Relativism

Mannheim made a crucial distinction between *relativism* and *relationism* to save his sociology of knowledge from losing all pretenses to being objective. Relativism says that all knowledge is relative to the social and historical position of the knower, and thus there is no way of judging one person's ideas against those of another. Knowledge in this case becomes a sophisticated version of the old adage 'beauty is in the eye of the beholder.' Relationism is the notion that all knowledge is related to the social and historical position of the knower, although we can evaluate one person's views against those of another. It says 'there are spheres of thought in which it is impossible to conceive of absolute truth existing independently of the values and positions of the subject and unrelated to social context' (ibid., 78). Mannheim argues that those who charge his sociology of knowledge with being a form of relativism believe in the false notion that there are eternal, objective, static truths independent of any colouring by the subjective position of the knower, while his relationism accepts that there are no such eternal truths and instead tries to distinguish between well and poorly justified knowledge. Once we give up any notion of an ethereal realm of Truth independent of any influence by the social position of the knower, we'll see how all knowledge is in fact conditioned by one's social-historical location and learn to live with it. We'll come to a point where we dispense with the 'impersonal point of view' and replace it with a human point of view that admits its flaws but tries to constantly enlarge itself (ibid., 297).

But it's hard to say whether this distinction holds up in practice. The problems of relativism and relationism may be the same: does truth not entirely disappear if we say that knowledge is *in some basic way* related to our social-economic circumstances? How can we know whether or not our ideas are just reflections of our class interests? Isn't there a difference between the way that concepts of physical science, e.g., Einstein's theory of relativity, and those of political theory, e.g., John Stuart Mill's defence of individual liberty, are related to the social backgrounds of their originators? Mannheim hints that we have to make such distinctions, yet he refuses to exempt any type of knowledge from social conditioning. Whether we see our ideas as *relative to* or merely *related to* our social circumstances is a thin distinction, though softened by giving up on abstract notions of truth that are in turn destroyed by claims that knowledge is socially conditioned.

Objectivity becomes a key issue for Mannheim's sociology of knowledge. If all knowledge is situationally related, and truth is always truth for a given person in a given place and time, how can a researcher claim to be objec-

tive? Mannheim admits that concepts of truth change over time (ibid., 291). Yet we can compare different perspectives on a problem within our own day and age and choose the perspective that 'gives evidence of the greatest comprehensiveness and the greatest fruitfulness in dealing with empirical materials' (ibid., 301). Mannheim argues that because we always see a physical object from a limited, specific perspective, therefore all these perspectives are false. The trick is to compare as many perspectives as possible to build up a complete view of the object. Detachment can also result from a number of social changes: (1) when a person shifts social groups; (2) when a group alters its way of living and thus its values; and (3) when two or more social views conflict with each other and illustrate each other's shortcomings (ibid., 282). Mannheim held out his greatest hope of objectivity for modern intellectuals, who as a group are free floaters socially, attached to no specific class.

Two major criticisms of Mannheim's sociology of knowledge come immediately to mind (Robert Merton, the functionalist theorist who we visited in Chapter 2, made similar criticisms). First, an issue raised above, isn't Mannheim's 'relationism' just a watered-down version of relativism? Don't both theories stop us from believing in the truth of our own ideas and those of others? Second, what exactly is the relationship between (A) knowledge and (B) the knower's social-historical situation? Does B *cause* or *determine* A, or merely influence or condition it? Or do A and B travel along parallel roads, only from time to time influencing each other? In some instances Mannheim uses strong language, claiming, for example, that a group's social location *determines* its ideas, but at other times he remains nebulous, suggesting, for example, that thinking is 'bound up with' the concrete position of the thinker (ibid., 78–9). The problem here is like that found in a drink recipe where a Bloody Mary is described as 'part tomato juice and part vodka'. The budding bartender would surely want to know, how much juice, how much vodka? Similarly, one might ask Mannheim just how much freedom can a thinker have from his or her social-historical position. The devil is in the details.

Ideologies and Utopias

Mannheim makes some less disputable theoretical points in *Ideology and Utopia* concerning the nature of social thought. He argues that we should make a distinction between two ways of looking at ideology:

- *The particular conception:* The purpose of ideology is to manipulate others or to deceive oneself, as Marx suggested. It is a series of *particular* hidden facts, half truths, or lies, whether conscious or unconscious, intentional or unintentional.
- *The total conception:* Here ideology expresses the total structure of the mind of a social group or the spirit of the age. In this sense, the term has no moral intent: the total conception of ideology merely aims to establish how knowledge is tied to social and historical locations (ibid., 265–6).

By 'ideology' specifically Mannheim meant systems of thought that distort the real conditions of people's lives in order to maintain the present social order. Ideologies obscure the real conditions of society in order to keep things stable (ibid., 40). Utopian thought, on the other hand, is a system of thinking maintained by an oppressed group that points towards a better world, and thus to social change. Utopias point out the negative aspects of current social conditions in order to transform them so that the oppressed group can feel at home. They are the explosive materials that burst the old order asunder (ibid., 199). Naturally, one person's utopia is another person's dangerous illusion: defenders of the status quo will see the key elements of utopian thought as hopeless and unrealizable dreams. Yet without these dreams, human beings will become mere creatures of impulse and society will freeze into its present form (ibid., 262–3).

Mannheim discusses four types of utopian thinking in modern history:

- *Orgiastic chiliasm:* In early modern Europe, Christian religious sects like the Anabaptists looked forward to the establishment of the kingdom of God here on earth. Politics is spiritualized by the dispossessed of the world.
- *Liberal humanitarianism:* This is the thought of the 'progressive' bourgeoisie emerging from the battle against the aristocracy in the French Revolution. It advocated a moderate view of progress and intellectual cultivation.
- *Conservative mode:* Conservatives favour keeping things the way they are to oppose the changes fought for by anarchists and communists. This is only in part a utopian way of thinking, since it doesn't seek to transform society. Yet it can look back to a past golden age. This is the utopia of aristocrats or the upper bourgeoisie.
- *Socialist-communist mode:* This mode argues that a utopia where everyone is equal is just around the corner if only we could dispense with capitalism and its inherently exploitative nature. It is the utopia of the working class.

Mannheim's typology of utopian modes of thinking echoes Weber's notion of ideal types. In real life, most people won't hold on to one mode exclusively. Also, we can see from the list above that each of the four types of utopian thought echoes the hopes and fears of a given social stratum or class—the workers dream of a more equal, less stratified society, while the wealthy dream of an unchanging, stable society where the lower classes know their place. Certainly, the notion that each social group has its own way of seeing the future of society follows from Mannheim's sociology of knowledge: our existential situation determines what form of change (or lack of change) we hope for.

Rationality, Industrial Society, and Democratic Planning

In his later 'English' period, Mannheim became more interested in concrete empirical issues and in how sociology could actually improve the world. This was no doubt due to the twin facts of the rise of Nazism in Germany and its threat to world peace and Western democracy, and his residence in England, where sociology was more practically oriented. A key work in this period was his *Man and Society in an Age of Reconstruction* (1940 [1935]). In it he lays out a basic distinction between substantial and functional rationality. Substantial rationality has to do with thinking with intelligent insight about something, free from emotional distortion. Thus, 'substantial irrationality' is being dominated by one's feelings, drives, and whims. Functional rationality has to do with action, not thought, as when we arrange our actions, and those of others, to contribute in a functional way to some predefined goal. This is close to what some theorists call 'instrumental' rationality, that is, thinking in terms of using the most efficient means to achieve a given goal.

A third level of rationality Mannheim discusses in *Man and Society* is self-rationalization, the 'systematic control' of one's impulses (ibid., 55), as when we bite our lips because the social function we're performing calls for it, for example, an angry bureaucrat controlling herself and not yelling at a boss she hates, or a waiter forcing himself to be polite to an abusive customer in his restaurant. When we take self-rationalization so seriously that we constantly observe our inner and outer selves for failures to live up to its dictate to think and act rationally, we enter Mannheim's fourth level of rationality, self-observation. Here we transform ourselves into rational beings not just in our actions, but in our inner lives as well. These four kinds of rationality are outlined in Table 3.3.

Modern industrial societies are more and more trapped in Max Weber's iron cage of ration-

ality, or what Mannheim calls functional rationality. Means are streamlined and maximized to more effectively produce the ends they are aimed at. Yet these ends may not be substantially rational—a functionally rational society may pursue insane goals, as did Hitler's Germany (even though the trains did run on time). Further, waves of substantial irrationality sweep through mass societies more quickly than they do in traditional ones. Think of the consumer crazes of the last few decades—Cabbage Patch dolls, pop stars whose music has a shelf life of two or three years, or such 'fashion' items as tattoos and baseball caps. These burn brightly for a short period of time, consuming a whole culture like fire consumes dry prairie grassland, and then are as quickly forgotten. Indeed, one could argue that modern means of communication actually *accelerate* the spread of waves of substantial irrationality.

Mannheim's solution to the problem of modern substantial irrationality is rational democratic planning. He saw how in the 1920s and the Great Depression of the 1930s laissez-faire capitalism couldn't be trusted to maintain a prosperous and stable economy—it crashed and burned, causing social chaos for many. Similarly, fascism shows the dangers of political irrationality sweeping through a country. So some 'planning for freedom', to eliminate extremes of poverty and wealth by promoting full employment, would be a good idea. Mannheim was sensitive to the issue of the tyranny of the majority in a democracy, and thus he wanted to be sure that even in his planned society criticism and the charm of a limited irrationality would still be allowed. He wanted a balance between an overly centralized and an unplanned, chaotic society. In the end he was a

Table 3.3 Mannheim's Forms of Rationality

Form of Rationality	Description
Substantial	Thinking with intelligent insight (as opposed to drives, wishes, impulses, and feelings)
Functional	Actions efficiently aimed at some predefined goal (instrumental)
Self-rationalization	The systematic control of one's impulses
Self-observation	Transforming the self to act in a rational manner

democrat who didn't trust capitalism to create stability without some strong degree of regulation. In this sense, he was very modern.

PIERRE BOURDIEU AND THE VARIETIES OF CAPITAL

Pierre Bourdieu (1930–2002) was until his recent death arguably the most important social theorist and cultural anthropologist in his native France. He was born in a small town in the southwest near the Pyrenees and was educated at the École normale supérieure in Paris alongside the prominent philosopher, Jacques Derrida. Bourdieu spent two years in Algeria in the mid-fifties with the French Army as part of the French campaign to suppress the Algerian independence movement. He stayed in the country to do anthropological studies on the Kabyle and other local cultures, teaching at the University of Algiers in 1959–60. After a couple of short stints elsewhere, he became the director of the prestigious Centre of European Sociology in Paris in 1968, where he taught for many years.

Bourdieu was not an engaged intellectual like Sartre until late in life, in the 1990s taking up the fight against globalization and 'neo-liberalism' (the conservative right) in France. His main contribution to the debate over materialism in social theory is to broaden the notion of 'capital' to include not only economic resources but cultural and social resources also. The dominating class in modern society rules not only by its control of the economy and state, as Marx thought, or by its control of ideas, as Gramsci and Althusser added, but by its comprehensive control of cultural tastes and how these are manifested in the unconscious dispositions of each and every individual. Class structure isn't found just in economic life or ideas but also in our very bodies, in the way we engage in the practices of everyday life. In fact, in his most important theoretical work, *Outline of a Theory of Practice* (1977), he argues that the notion that only economic capital exists, and that things like art, literature, and abstract ideas are part of a realm free of the rules of exchange, is not surprising in an era ruled by the bourgeois class, the very class that more or less

monopolizes the cultural objects we find in this 'realm of freedom'. This idea that high culture is part of a realm of freedom helps to legitimate the rule of the bourgeoisie: only they, or so they imagine, can really appreciate the higher things like Picasso's paintings, Schubert's symphonies, or Sartre's novels and plays. Hence they are 'worthy' to rule.

Overall one could characterize Bourdieu's social theory as an attempt to reconcile the subjective emphasis on individual human consciousness typical of existentialism with the structuralist or Marxist emphasis on how social structures dominate our lives. Yet he doesn't see the social actor as an active subject confronting society, but as under the sway of objective social structures that incorporate themselves into the actor's very physical being and way of speaking and acting through what Bourdieu calls 'habitus' (more on this later).

Forms of Capital

Marx thought that capital was economic—money, stocks, and other material resources. Bourdieu argues that there are in fact *three* types of capital, plus a fourth general type that stands in opposition to economic capital:

1. Economic capital, i.e., money and things that can be directly transformed into money.
2. Social capital, i.e., connections to durable networks or groups of people such as a family, a social club, the alumni of a prominent school, the aristocracy, an ethnic or tribal group, etc.
3. Cultural capital, i.e., all forms of cultural know-how. Cultural capital is usually the product of education, whether during childhood in the home or later in schools and universities. Naturally, the more economic capital a family has, the longer its children can stay at home or in school, and thus the longer they can accumulate cultural capital. One can see this process operating on pretty well all college and university campuses: working-class students have to spend their summers and evenings working to earn their way through school, while the children of upper-class

families have their education paid for by their families, own their own cars, and spend their summers learning French or Italian or German in Europe. Needless to say, the upper-class students have an inherent advantage in this regard. This is in addition to the fact that the 'educational market' tends to favour the linguistic products (ways of writing and speaking) of the dominant class, thus erecting barriers to higher education for the lower classes (Bourdieu 1991: 62). This is probably somewhat less true for North America than for France, and does not account for the majority of students from middle-class families.

4. Symbolic capital, i.e., forms of capital that aren't recognized as such. Thus, when social capital and cultural capital are *misrecognized* as individual merit or good taste, as good breeding, or as a group's inherent worthiness, we see symbolic capital at play. This is when a form of capital other than money is seen as legitimate competence on the part of its holder. For example, a person who speaks well, free from grammatical errors or swearing, exhibits a form of symbolic capital that we can't slap a specific price tag on, yet that will enhance his or her entry into a variety of institutions. It has a symbolic, as opposed to a financial, value. When the upper classes use symbolic capital to arbitrarily impose their own cultural and social values as universal and natural, and thus dominating the lower classes, they are engaging in what Bourdieu calls 'symbolic violence'. This comes close to what Gramsci meant by 'hegemony'.

Bourdieu makes it clear that even though cultural and social capital can never be entirely reduced to money, economic capital is at their root (Bourdieu, 1986: 252). In this sense he is an oblique materialist. Traditional Marxism says that classes differentiate themselves in terms of their control of economic capital. Bourdieu argues that this is too simple—classes reproduce themselves not only in terms of their money but also in terms of their social connections (i.e., their social capi-

tal) and their cultural know-how (i.e., their cultural capital). He sees social life as a series of fields where individuals compete for a variety of forms of capital. Marx saw the capitalist economy as a field where capitalists compete for profits, while Bourdieu adds that in cultural fields people compete for the 'symbolic profits' of greater prestige or power. Obviously, social capital in the form of family connections, old boys' clubs, fraternities and sororities, or political party or tribal connections can be vital in helping one get a head start in life. These 'relationships of mutual acquaintance and recognition' are consecrated in ceremonies and reinforced by the exchange of gifts, words, or, in less enlightened societies, women (ibid., 248–50).

Bourdieu's real innovation in social theory is his discussion of the importance of cultural capital. He argues that there are three general types of cultural capital: *embodied capital*, which involves dispositions of the body to behave in certain ways, including the body's repression over a long period of time during formal education; *objectified capital*, including cultural objects such as paintings, recorded music, and machines that distinguish their owner as a member of a given class; and *institutionalized capital*, mainly academic qualifications such as university degrees—informally acquired knowledge isn't as valuable as that degree from Harvard or Yale on one's office wall (ibid., 243). Yet simply owning cultural objects isn't good enough—one must know how to use and appreciate them. Buying a recording of 'Mozart's Greatest Hits' doesn't make one a classical music buff: one must be able to distinguish a concerto from a symphony, not to mention Mozart from Vivaldi. Further, both social and cultural capital can be converted into money. For example, academic qualifications can be transformed back into economic capital, though the rate of exchange fluctuates considerably as the value of these qualifications enters a deflationary spiral in the modern world. If a member of the upper class thought that a graduate degree had no economic value, its pursuit would lose some of its rationale. Yet the more idealized and concealed the social or cultural capital is, the greater the risk that it won't 'pay off' in cash terms (ibid., 253).

Habitus and Doxa

A key term for Bourdieu is habitus, 'an acquired system of generative schemes objectively adjusted to the particular conditions in which it is constituted', engendering 'all the thoughts, all the perceptions, and all the actions consistent with those conditions, and no others' (Bourdieu, 1977: 95). In other words, habitus is thinking and acting according to a code of behaviour accepted as proper for one's class or class fraction at a given time. The habitus is not a set of rules one consciously learns. Instead, it is inscribed unconsciously through breeding and education, leading each individual to stand, speak, feel, and think in a given way. Biological individuals carry around their position in the social structure 'at all times and places, in the form of dispositions which are so many marks of *social position* and hence of the social distance between objective positions' (ibid., 82).

The habitus shares a loose connection with Marx's notion of ideology and Gramsci's notion of hegemony, yet is closer to Althusser's roughly structuralist view of the way that class ideas are brought to the lives of individuals. Bourdieu's innovation was to see habitus not just as a set of ideas, however deeply held, but also as a series of bodily dispositions to speak, act, and even move in certain ways. One can see it as a very embodied and unconscious version of ideology. Its brilliance lies in the fact that it's transmitted mostly by the suggestions of everyday life, not by means of conscious communication and language. This leads to a form of symbolic domination of those higher in the social pyramid over the lower classes (Bourdieu, 1990 [1980]: 51). Their superiority is taken as common sense because their habitus, their way of thinking, looking, and acting, is seen as an ideal to which all should aspire.

As for ideas proper, Bourdieu defines doxa as the belief that the social world as it stands is natural. All social systems try to naturalize their own arbitrary structures. The systems of classification doxa uses to justify divisions between classes, sexes, age groups, and types of work arbitrarily reproduce relations of power, but they are taken for granted insofar as people see them as natural and not imposed by the powerful (Bourdieu, 1977: 164). Doxic thinking misrecognizes the arbitrary nature of the social power of the upper class as legitimate, so the upper class has a vested interest in the integrity of doxa. When it fails in part, doxa is exposed as *orthodoxy*, ideas that purposefully defend the status quo, with *heterodoxy* being the ideas that challenge it.

Consumption, Distinction, and Symbolic Capital

Bourdieu's notion of habitus plays into his broader analysis of how modern culture helps to reproduce class membership from generation to generation. His general point is that social distinctions are created and reinforced by different levels of cultural competence. There are three broad classes in modern society: the bourgeoisie (the upper class), the petite bourgeoisie (pretenders to upper-class membership whose economic capital is limited), and the working class. Each has its own set of distinct tastes in material culture—food, clothing, and consumer objects such as cars and furnishings—and non-material culture—books, music, and art.[8] Bourdieu argues that habitus helps to transmit the distinct culture of each broad class to the individuals in that class, and thus to reproduce the objective structure of society as it stands. In this sense he is a structuralist, although he speaks of struggles and battles for symbolic capital within the upper class at least. Bourdieu argues in his magnum opus, *Distinction* (1984 [1979]), that the working class tends to favour more earthy, concrete cultural objects and practices connected to physical survival: fast cars, fatty foods, beer, pop music, and paintings of sunsets. The economic necessity driving their lives has become ingrained into their habitus as a taste for functional and sensuous things. The bourgeois prefers more abstract and formal culture that is less connected to physical survival: modern art, wine, classical music, and lean meats and vegetables. They have a disgust for the vulgar taste of the masses, for things that force enjoyment on their consumers (think of romance novels or catchy pop tunes). The petite bourgeois is somewhere in between, aspiring to bourgeois formality but never quite pulling it off (in part due to a lack of economic capital). Naturally, commentators have criticized Bourdieu for characterizing the working class as somewhat simple, if not animalistic.

In such cultural practices each class is able to both *distinguish* itself from others and to reproduce its members from within. In Bourdieu's universe, when Jacques the worker shows up to a glitzy art gallery opening with a hot dog in one hand and a beer in another, he is shooed out the front door, lacking not economic capital—he may actually have that—but cultural capital. Jacques goes home cap in hand, denied entry to the social field he was never suited for in the first place. How is this reproduction accomplished in the first place? Mainly through education. The young bourgeois is sent to elite schools, learns to speak the language of the elite, to dress as they dress, to move as they move. The cultural capital they get from an elite education is almost inevitably translated into economic capital as they enter the worlds of business or politics. And it can go the other way too: money can be used to buy the objects (jewellery, cars, watches, art) that give their owners objectified cultural capital. The *nouveaux riches* can become an accepted social elite if they are willing to open up their wallets and purses a metre or two.

Critiques of Bourdieu

Bourdieu is not without his critics. First of all, his emphasis on the powerful ways in which habitus reproduces social structure in the lives of individuals contains more than a whiff of determinism. He says in *Distinction* (ibid., 474) that taste is '*amor fati* [love of fate], the choice of destiny, but a forced choice, produced by conditions of existence which rule out all alternatives as mere daydreams

and leave no choice but for the necessary.' Workers cannot help but love beer and football matches, the bourgeois Picasso and Puccini. Yet even though class is an important conditioning factor in all societies, it is obviously the case, especially in North America, that from time to time people break through class barriers despite such early disadvantages as lowly family origins or difficulties at school. Even if most workers do not appreciate Wordsworth's poetry or classical music, the odd son or daughter of the working class can come to appreciate these things. Classes reproduce themselves, but with some individuals slipping through the cracks. Bourdieu's habitus seems to ignore this fact.

Connected to this critique is the sense that Bourdieu's concept of habitus is too broad, vague, and all-encompassing. In accounting for all our feelings, thoughts, bodily deportment, and ways of speaking, it leaves very little outside of the process of socialization. In explaining *everything* in terms of competitions over various forms of capital, it makes all of social life a series of either self-deceptions or cynical calculations.[9]

Third, we can criticize Bourdieu for offering us a plate of warmed-over Gramscian and Althusserian social theory dressed up with a few new concepts. To be fair, though, his emphasis on how differences in cultural capital actually take hold of our bodies and not just our minds takes some of the sting out of this criticism.

Fourth, Bourdieu's use of nineteenth-century Marxist terms to distinguish classes, while a commonplace in Britain and Continental Europe, simply doesn't wash with many North Americans, who see everyone except the homeless and filthy rich as 'middle class'. The sort of fine distinction Bourdieu makes between 'petite bourgeois' posers and the upper bourgeoisie is lost on a society of suburbanites who buy most of their culture at shopping malls.

Finally, the evidence for real and deep distinctions between the cultural interests of the bourgeoisie and the working class is ambiguous at best. Certainly the bourgeoisie in Western countries is more likely to take an interest in classical music, 'serious' literature, and high art than the working class. But both ends of the social spectrum consume popular culture—Hollywood films, popular music, and television—while the differences between class tastes in material culture like food, dress, and consumer goods are slight at best (Gartman, 1991: 430–2). In material culture class distinctions are based more on income than taste: well-paid workers can buy minivans, snow-blowers, and big-screen televisions just as easily as the suburban middle class. In a word, well-off workers and the bourgeoisie can both 'talk the common language of consumerism' at least within the realm of material culture (ibid., 445).

This leads us finally to Jean Baudrillard, who in his early works uses Marxism and structuralism to analyze consumer society.

JEAN BAUDRILLARD ON CONSUMER CULTURE

Jean Baudrillard (1929–2007) went through at least two fairly distinct phases in his long career as a social theorist and cultural analyst. In the first, which we'll concern ourselves with here, he was a Marxist sociologist who used some of the ideas of French structuralism to help understand modern consumer culture. In the second he turned toward postmodernism, seeing modern society as a media-saturated culture that has lost its grounding in reality. His early works were published in the years following the failure of the student and working-class revolt in May 1968 against the ruling Gaullist regime in France, a key event for all French intellectuals of the day. Some of them, namely the Situationists, saw the principal problem with contemporary society not as the need for greater political rights for the down-trodden masses, but as the boredom, alienation, and commodity fetishism of consumer society. Baudrillard took up the Situationists' challenge, trying in his early work to spell out the structure of that society. Baudrillard's first four books, combined, present a post-Marxist mediation on the nature of consumer society today. We'll return to Baudrillard's ideas later when we discuss postmodernism.

The System of Objects

In *The System of Objects* (1968),[10] Baudrillard argues that advertising tries to sell us consumer goods by paradoxically suggesting that a particular product will make us unique even though its uniqueness involves everyone else buying it at the same time (Baudrillard, 2001: 15). The purpose of consumer society isn't to satisfy our needs; rather, consumption is *the virtual totality of all objects and messages presently constituted in a more or less coherent discourse . . . a systematic act of the manipulation of signs* (ibid., 25). Here we see Baudrillard's structuralist influences. Consumer society seems to promote a 'new humanism' where its shimmering products offer us total fulfillment and liberation, but never (of course) an end state of complete happiness, since that would stop us consuming. This society is no longer a productive one driven by a Protestant work ethic, but a consuming one driven by a hedonistic ethic. It is ruled by a code that forcefully integrates a whole system of needs—not individual ones like a need for a new coat or pair of shoes, but needs in general—into its matrix or system of products. It connects categories of objects to categories of persons in what market researchers call 'demographics'.

The system of objects is at best an impoverished form of language. It speaks through brand names and images—these signals impose their meanings by means of the conditioned reflexes created by advertising (ibid., 20–1). He agrees with the Frankfurt School theorists that consumerism does not offer us true freedom from repression, but just a new set of gratifications and frustrations. The point of what Baudrillard refers to mysteriously as 'the code' is to use consumer objects to indicate social standing in a way similar to Bourdieu's notion of cultural capital. All desires, plans, and passions are turned into signs related to consumer objects that must be bought and consumed—even marriages are symbolized by consumer objects (hence the soaring divorce rate!) (ibid., 26). In the end, consumer society cannot be seen as aiming at satisfying needs, for such a goal is in theory realizable, thus sounding its death knell. In fact, there are no limits to consumption (ibid., 28).

The Consumer Society

Baudrillard's second book, *The Consumer Society* (1970), offers both concrete and theoretical pictures of the society we live in. Concretely, consumer society represents 'a fundamental mutation in the ecology of the human species' (ibid., 32). We live in a world of objects, and not surprisingly have become object-people. Our shopping malls show that we have conquered scarcity, with consumer goods being displayed in endless variety in their shop windows. The malls are climate-controlled, their cultural diversity homogenized into networks of consumer objects. The old anarchic cities of Europe and North America have become domesticated into places where work, leisure, culture, and perpetual shopping can coexist under one roof.

Baudrillard also presents a theory of consumption in this book. He argues that our 'affluent society' (to borrow the title of John Kenneth Galbraith's book) creates a fable in which people are naturally endowed with needs that push them towards objects to satisfy those needs (ibid., 39). This consumerism has been criticized by social theorists like Galbraith, who argue that what really happens is that needs are conditioned by the corporate economy, and that people are persuaded by advertising to accept the dominant lifestyle of the day (ibid., 40–1). Consumers aren't in any sense free agents choosing which products to satisfy their needs with—since cars are easier to make than to sell, General Motors and Ford have to convince consumers that they really *need* the newest Chevrolet or Mustang. Baudrillard agrees that needs are created by manufacturers, but he disagrees that we can distinguish between these artificial and more natural needs—my second computer might be just as much a need to me as your second pair of socks. Yet more fundamentally, he disagrees with Galbraith that the need for specific products is created by the consumer economy. Instead, whole systems of needs

are created by the system of modern production (ibid., 45). Consumption is not about pleasure, but about a need for social difference that can never be satisfied. What he calls the 'fun-system' compels the citizen, as a duty, to consume, and thus to be happy, in love, adored, or seduced (ibid., 51).[11] This new 'fun morality' replaces the old ethic, which told us to work hard to get ahead; now all the possibilities of being thrilled and excited have to be tried out or we'll be afraid that we've missed something.

The great shift of the modern age from production to consumption parallels the great trek in the nineteenth century of rural peasants and farmers from agriculture to industrial labour (ibid., 53). Yet for Baudrillard both industrialism and consumerism are part of the same great logical process, that of the expansion and control of productive forces (in this sense he's trying to update Marx's materialism). What the system now needs are consumers, not workers. So it seeks to turn the consumer into the image of the universal person and make consumption the only real path to human liberation (ibid., 56).

The Political Economy of the Sign

For a Critique of the Political Economy of the Sign (1972) contains a quite complex criticism of Marx's theory of value in the light of the modern consumer economy. Marx argued that all objects have a natural use value, which is assigned a monetary or exchange value by the market—hammers nail things, and cost, say, $10 in the hardware store. Baudrillard expands this basic theory of values into a fourfold typology:

- *Use value* is the object's functional value.
- *Exchange value* is what the object costs as a commodity.
- *Sign exchange value* is the object's value as a sign that distinguishes its owner from other people within the system of signs found in consumer societies. The rich businessman wears a Rolex not because it works better than other watches, but to show off his status to others.

• *Symbolic exchange* is not really a type of value at all, but the type of exchanges made outside of the consumer society per se. The main exchange here is a gift from which no value is expected in return (though Bourdieu might point out that even gifts give one social capital). A wedding ring symbolizes a marriage, yet doesn't have any real function. Once given, it's no longer a commodity and doesn't especially act as a social sign differentiating its wearer from others.

Baudrillard's main claim in this book is that Marx was wrong to see use value as natural and exchange value as artificial. For exchange value to work, it must take use value as a foundation or 'alibi': if the hammer had no use at all, why charge $10 for it? To be exchangeable, products must be rationalized in terms of their utility. But in fact, says Baudrillard, both sides of the equation 'use value/exchange value' are linguistic signs that depend on each other to mean anything at all. The fact that the hammer's exchange or market value is $10 is based on its utility as a tool, but its utility as a tool is tied to its place in a 'system of needs' created by the consumer economy. All our instincts are rationalized and objectified as consumer needs (ibid., 71). These needs are massaged and manipulated by advertising to such a degree that it makes no sense for us to say that we can distinguish 'real' needs from 'artificial' ones; indeed, at times Baudrillard seems to be denying that we ever had real needs.[12] So the hammer's utility is just as much a cultural construction as is its price at the hardware store.

Why does Marx see use value as more 'real' than the artificial prices assigned commodities by the marketplace? Because, according to Baudrillard, seeing use value as a real-world referent or foundation for the exchange values of products gives us 'the promise of a resurgence beyond the market economy, money and exchange value, in the glorious autonomy of the simple relation of people to their work and their products' (ibid., 67). It allows Marx to promise us some sort of escape from the callous cash nexus of capitalism into a world where we work only when we want to, and only for things we truly need, not for wages used to buy the useless trinkets sold us by the consumer economy. This leads Baudrillard to Daniel Defoe's *Robinson Crusoe* (1719), about a man shipwrecked on a desert island with only his servant Friday to help him—this represents the myth of a man with natural 'needs' that he works on nature to fulfill. Both the bourgeois economists and Marx used this story to illustrate their own ideas about the way capitalism works. At the heart of the Crusoe story is the notion that when we labour to fulfill our needs, we're trying to create something we value because it's useful. Baudrillard replies that it's circular to say that people labour to acquire objects because they 'need' them, as though the object's utility is the cause and our 'needing' it is the effect. In fact, he says, an object's use value is created by its exchange value as much as its price depends on its utility.

Of course, an obvious criticism of Baudrillard's claim about the equal artificiality of use and exchange value is that some objects have little or no economic value, yet in certain situations they can be very useful. An old stick of wood could be quite useful in propping up a window or kindling a fire, but is not worth even 50 cents at a garage sale. Yet this leaves Baudrillard's point intact for *most* of the consumer economy—the cost of consumer goods is justified by their supposed utility, the image of this utility being largely a creation of the mass media.

The Mirror of Production

The fourth of Baudrillard's mediations on the consumer society, *The Mirror of Production* (1973), more or less ends the early period of his thought as he shifts from an interest in consumerism as mainly an economic phenomenon to an attempt to explain the influence of mass media and electronic communications on our sense of reality. Just as *For a Critique of the Political Economy of the Sign* criticizes Marx's belief that the exchange value of an object is grounded in its more 'real' use value, *The Mirror of Production* criticizes Marx's labour theory of value, specifically, his idea that the core of our human nature is to work to transform nature into useful objects. This is tied to Baudrillard's broader criticism of Marxism as a philosophy of production—in this sense he says that Marxism is in cahoots with capitalism, as they both believe in using science and technology to increase the productive forces of society (although for different goals). Marxism is tied to the Protestant work ethic as much as capitalism is—work is good in itself. It confuses the liberation of productive forces (i.e., the economy) with the liberation of human beings as a whole (Baudrillard, 2001: 101). Baudrillard argues that we must break this 'mirror of production' in which both the bourgeois political economists and Marx saw their society reflected, a mirror that reflects back all human efforts as the production of values (whether in terms of useful objects or objects for sale in the marketplace).

Even when Marx talks about the coming of the realm of freedom under communism, he sees play and the end of alienated labour as possible only once the realm of necessity has been overcome by the full development of productive forces in a society. In other words, work first, play later. Baudrillard says this is a fatal flaw in all revolutionary imaginations based on Marxism: work is sanctified to such a degree that non-work or play can only be seen as 'the end of work', its dialectical fulfillment (ibid., 110–12). Marxism tries to convince us that only under capitalism is industrial labour alienated. The darker truth, the more 'radical hypothesis', says Baudrillard, is that workers are alienated *as workers*: there's no such thing as non-alienated labour insofar as work aims to produce value (ibid., 107). The solution to the problem of alienated labour is not the Communist revolution, but a shift of human efforts from the production of value to symbolic exchange.

In the end Baudrillard sees Marxism as an imperialistic attempt to impose a scientific code on all societies at all times. He argues that Marxism's critique of political economy has gone as far as it can, opening the door for post-materialist philosophies. Not surprisingly, he wrote this in the years immediately after the failure of the May 1968 revolt in France and the broader fading of the counterculture of the 1960s across the West.

THE END OF THE LEFT?

By the first decade of the twenty-first century the question of a socialist revolution against capitalism is for most of us in the post-industrial West a dead issue.[13] Enthusiastic university students no longer wear T-shirts emblazoned with romantic pictures of Che Guevera, the Argentinian revolutionary hero of the 1960s,[14] or debate the relative merits of Lenin, Trotksy, and Mao in their spare time. Capitalism has won, at least for the time being. The first sounding of the death knell of socialism as a mass movement came in Paris in May–June 1968, when students and workers rebelled against the Gaullist regime in their country. Student radicals, including the Situationists (who we'll visit in the following chapter), dreamed of proletarian revolution or of a smashing of the consumer society and its replacement by a society that celebrates everyday life as the place where equality and love rule. Yet their rebellion failed, and by the late 1970s leftist radicalism began to slip from popularity not only in France (though it never entirely disappeared there), but in Britain and North America as well. The dreary authoritarian regimes of the Communist bloc in Eastern Europe and the Soviet Union did little to keep alive either the theory or practice of left-wing materialism in the West. By the 1980s Ronald Reagan was in the White House in Washington, with his voodoo 'trickle-down' economics, which claimed that it's good that there are lots of rich people in America, since their ceaseless accumulation of capital would somehow trickle down into more jobs for the lower classes. Prime Ministers Margaret Thatcher in Britain and Brian Mulroney in Canada held similar, though perhaps more moderate, conservative views in the same decade.

Yet the real death knell of European socialism sounded in 1989, with the fall of the Berlin Wall and the start of a surprisingly rapid disappearance of Communist regimes throughout the Soviet

Empire. In 1991 Boris Yeltsin, President of the Russian Federation, stood atop a tank in front of the Russian White House, defying a military coup led by old Communist Party bureaucrats and generals with the aid of a mob of Muscovites (the coup plotters had already put Soviet General Secretary Mikhail Gorbachev under house arrest while he was on vacation in the Crimea). When the old Communists backed down, this led to the dissolution of the Soviet Union and a quick slide into gangster capitalism in Russia.

So is the left dead? Yes and no. The authoritarian communism of Lenin, Stalin, and their successors would seem to have gone the way of the dodo and other extinct species—too much history has accumulated for most people to believe that a state exercising massive state control over the economy, aided by a ruthless secret police apparatus, protected from enemies by a massive military machine, can sustain itself or provide the average worker or farmer with a happy life. Yet all is not well with capitalism—from the end of the 1990s until recently, major demonstrations have disrupted meetings of the International Monetary Fund, the World Bank, and other international economic organizations, notably at the Battle in Seattle in 1999, where a coalition of anarchists, socialists, and disenchanted youth disrupted the meeting of the World Trade Organization. As we'll see in the final chapter, a serious and well-respected critique of globalized capitalism has emerged in a variety of works written in the 1990s and later, including George Ritzer's *McDonaldization* and Naomi Klein's *No Logo*. European communism may be dead, but we should not infer from that fact that we have arrived at the end of history and a capitalist paradise.

Further, materialist social theory itself is alive and well, though not all of it is coming from the pens or word processors of socialist thinkers. Remember that I defined materialism as the notion that economics is the key to understanding society. As Francis Fukuyama has noted, right-wing materialism of the *Wall Street Journal* variety does just this, interpreting politics, social problems, and ideas in general in economic terms. In fact, neo-conservative supporters of an unencumbered free market, such as the noted American economist Milton Friedman (1912–2006), who was an adviser to the Reagan administration in the 1980s, argue vehemently that if only we let people buy and sell what they want at whatever price they want, with as few as possible government restrictions in place, our political and social problems would solve themselves. Whether or not this dubious claim is true, the basic claim of materialist social theory—that how we eat, drink, work, and consume determines both who we are and the nature of the society we live in—is alive and well.

STUDY QUESTIONS

1. What is materialism in social theory? What can we contrast it with? Outline some of the problems you see with materialism in general.
2. What did you learn about Marxism from the story of Polly Prole? Do these ideas still apply today?
3. What is Marx's model of base and superstructure? What does this have to do with his historical materialism?
4. How does Marx outline the stages of history? What basic force drives historical change for him?
5. What is 'commodity fetishism'? Give an example from everyday life of how it works.
6. What was Lenin's solution to the problem of the failure of the workers to revolt in capitalist countries? What effect did this solution have on events in Russia from 1917 on?
7. Was Lenin's theory of imperialism a materialist theory? Does it apply to contemporary international politics?
8. How did Lenin interpret Marx's theory of the role of the state after the Communist revolution?
9. What was the logic behind Trotsky's advocacy of the permanent revolution?

10. What does Gramsci's theory of hegemony say about how the ruling class maintains its power over the workers? Does this theory move Gramsci away from a strictly materialist position?

11. What is the role of ideology in Althusser's account of modern capitalist societies? Compare and contrast his ideas on the stability of modern capitalism with Gramsci's.

12. What are the basic premises of Sartre's existentialism? Can we derive a social theory from it?

13. What was Sartre trying to do with his progressive-regressive method? Was he successful?

14. What is the basic claim Mannheim makes in his sociology of knowledge? How does this lead to relativism? Does Mannheim adequately deal with the demon of relativism?

15. How does Mannheim define 'ideology' and 'utopia'? Give some examples of utopian thinking.

16. According to Bourdieu, how do social capital and cultural capital help to reinforce class distinctions?

17. What role does education play in Bourdieu's analysis of the various types of capital?

18. In what sense is Baudrillard's analysis of consumer society a critique of that society? Is consumption really based on a code that helps maintain differences in social classes?

19. According to Baudrillard, what are the various ways that an object can have value? Is he right that Marx's theory of value has serious gaps that he fills in?

20. Does the decline of the political left herald a similar decline of materialism in social theory?

Short Bibliography

Ali, Tariq, and Phil Evans. 1998. *Trotsky for Beginners*. Cambridge: Icon Books.

Althusser, Louis. 1971. 'Ideology and Ideological State Apparatuses', in Althusser, *Lenin and Philosophy and Other Essays*, trans. Ben Brewster. New York: Monthly Review Press.

———. 1977 [1965]. *For Marx*, trans. Ben Brewster. Old Woking, Surrey: NLB.

Assiter, Alison. 1984. 'Althusser and Structuralism', *British Journal of Sociology* 35, 2: 272–96.

Baudrillard, Jean. 2001. *Jean Baudrillard: Selected Writings*, ed. Mark Poster. Stanford, Calif.: Stanford University Press.

Bourdieu, Pierre. 1977. *Outline of a Theory of Practice*, trans. Richard Nice. Cambridge: Cambridge University Press.

———. 1984 [1979]. *Distinction: A Social Critique of the Judgment of Taste*, trans. Richard Nice. Cambridge, Mass.: Harvard University Press.

———. 1986. 'The Forms of Capital', trans. Richard Nice, in John G. Richardson, ed., *Handbook of Theory and Research for the Sociology of Education*.New York: Greenwood Press.

———. 1990 [1980]. *The Logic of Practice*, trans. Richard Nice. Cambridge: Polity.

Conquest, Robert. 1972. *Lenin*. London: Fontana.

Craib, Ian. 1997. *Classical Social Theory*. Oxford: Oxford University Press.

Ferguson, Adam. 1980 [1767]. *An Essay on the History of Civil Society*, ed. Louis Schneider. New Brunswick, NJ: Transaction Books.

Flynn, Thomas R. 1979. 'L'imagination au pouvoir: The Evolution of Sartre's Political and Social Thought', *Political Theory* 7, 2: 157–80.

Gartman, David. 1991. 'Culture as Class Symbolization or Mass Reification? A Critique of Bourdieu's *Distinction*', *American Journal of Sociology* 97, 2: 421–47.

Gramsci, Antonio. 1971. *Selections from the Prison Notebooks*, ed. and trans. Quinton Hoare and Geoffrey Nowell Smith. London: Lawrence and Wishart.

Laing, R.D., and D.G. Cooper. 1964. *Reason and Violence: A Decade of Sartre's Philosophy 1950–1960*. New York: Humanities Press.

Lenin, Vladimir Illyich. 1932 [1918]. *State and Revolution*. New York: International Publishers.

———. 1975 [1917]. *Imperialism, the Highest Stage of Capitalism*. Peking: Foreign Languages Press. Reprinted from 1952 Moscow edition of Lenin's *Selected Works*.

Mannheim, Karl. 1940 [1935]. *Man and Society in an Age of Reconstruction*. New York: Harcourt, Brace and World.

———. 1968 [1936]. *Ideology and Utopia*, trans. Louis Wirth and Edward Shils. New York: Harcourt, Brace and World.

Marx, Karl. 1859. Preface to *A Contribution to the Critique of Political Economy*. Available at: <www.marxists.org/archive/marx/works/1859/critique-pol-economy/preface.htm>.

——— and Friedrich Engels. 1848. *The Communist Manifesto*. Many editions.

——— and ———. 1978. *The Marx-Engels Reader*, 2nd edn, ed. Robert C. Tucker. New York: Norton.

Powell, Jim, and Joe Lee. 1998. *Postmodernism for Beginners*. London: Writers and Readers.

Sartre, Jean-Paul. 1963. *Search for a Method*, trans. Hazel E. Barnes. New York: Vintage Books.

———. 1975. 'Existentialism Is a Humanism', trans. Philip Mairet, in Walter Kaufmann, ed., *Existentialism from Dostoevsky to Sartre*. New York: Meridian Books.

Stillo, Monica. 2004. 'Antonio Gramsci', at: <www.theory.org>.

Storey, John. 2001. *Cultural Theory and Popular Culture: An Introduction*, 3rd edn. Harlow, UK: Prentice-Hall.

Strinati, Dominic. 1995. *An Introduction to Theories of Popular Culture*. London: Routledge.

Trotksy, Leon. 1930–1. *The Permanent Revolution*, trans. John G. Wright. Available at the Trotsky Internet Archive: <www.marxists.org/archive/trotsky/works/1931-tpv/index.htm>.

———. 1932. *The History of the Russian Revolution*, trans. Max Eastman. Volume 3: *The Triumph of the Soviets*, Appendix 3. Available at the Trotsky Internet Archive: <www.marxists.org/archive/trotsky/works/1930-hrr/index.htm>.

Wolfreys, Jim. 2000. 'In Perspective: Pierre Bourdieu', *International Socialism Journal* 87. At: <pubs.socialistreviewindex.org.uk/isj87/wolfreys.htm>.

CHAPTER 4

SLAMMING SOCIETY: CRITICAL THEORY AND SITUATIONISM

THE PHILOSOPHICAL FOUNDATIONS OF CRITICAL REASON: HEGEL AND NIETZSCHE

At its most basic, critical theory is any theory that criticizes society. Yet in the twentieth century it took on a more specific meaning, referring to a group of German theorists working for a time in the 1920s and early 1930s at the University of Frankfurt, hence called the Frankfurt School. These theorists included Theodor Adorno (1903–69), Max Horkheimer (1895–1973), Walter Benjamin (1882–1940), Herbert Marcuse (1898–1979), and Erich Fromm (1900–80). They were inspired not only by Marxism but also by G.W.F. Hegel's idealism and Sigmund Freud's psychoanalysis. The rising storm of Nazism in the mid-thirties blew these radical theorists from their native Germany to various places, most of them fleeing to America. The Frankfurt School inspired a number of other critical theorists, including Jürgen Habermas (1929–), considered a second-generation Frankfurter, the American Christopher Lasch (1932–94), the Situationist theorists Guy Debord (1932–94) and Raoul Vaneigem (1934–), and the cultural critic Kalle Lasn. We'll deal with most of these thinkers in greater detail below.

Critical theory in the more specific sense used in this chapter is basically Marxist, with a few other theoretical elements mixed in. Yet the Marx who influenced critical theory the most was not the older, 'scientific' Marx who spent endless hours in the British Museum in the 1860s and 1870s writing *Capital* but the young romantic Marx who described the alienated worker in the *Economic and Philosophical Manuscripts of 1844*

and who spoke in *The German Ideology* (1845), with Engels, of the end of dreary wage labour and of a communist society where one could hunt in the morning, fish in the afternoon, tend to cattle in the evening, and write literary criticism at night. Significantly, these works were first published by a Soviet press in the 1930s, alerting critical theorists to a side of Marxism that excited them more than the often sober economic analysis of *Capital*.

To the ideas of the young Marx, critical theorists added Hegel's expanded notion of reason and of the dialectic as a negation of the status quo, a bit of Nietzsche's genealogy of morals, and, perhaps most importantly, Freud's insights into the unconscious mind, his theory of instincts, and his picture of civilization as organized repression.

Hegel: The Journey of Reason

G.W.F. Hegel (1770–1831) published four massive tomes in his lifetime: *The Phenomenology of Mind* (1807), *The Science of Logic* (1812–16), *The Encyclopedia of the Philosophical Sciences* (1817), and *The Philosophy of Right* (1821). These taken together, along with a series of lecture notes written down by his students and edited into book form after his death (the most important of these is *The Philosophy of History*) added to the mix, form a complex philosophical system that stands at the summit of German idealism. We're looking at it here both because it forms the starting point of Marxist thought, as described in the last chapter, and because some of Hegel's ideas inspired a revision of classical Marxism in the twentieth century that morphed into the post-Marxist hybrid theoretical beast called critical theory.

Although he rarely used the term, Hegel called his philosophy Absolute Idealism. His view of the world was definitely metaphysical, yet there is much debate among scholars over exactly what this means in Hegel's case. The idealists of the eighteenth century, notably George Berkeley, thought that ideas are what define reality: only ideas in human minds (and ultimately in God's mind) truly exist. This is not quite what Hegel meant by idealism. He was a 'conceptual idealist' (Wartenberg, 1993: 103). All things are defined by concepts, which as they develop together make up the 'Absolute Idea,' or simply the 'Idea'. Hegel saw the world in organic terms: everything is connected to everything else, just as the plants, insects, and animal life in a given ecosystem depend on each other for survival. This was just as true for human history and for the development of philosophical thought as it was for nature. The concepts behind individual things within these fields—specific historical events and thinkers—are linked together not only logically, but also in terms of how they develop over time. What drives nature, history, and thought to develop? Hegel borrowed from the ancient Greek philosopher Aristotle the notion of the 'final cause' or teleology (from the Greek word *telos*, for goal or purpose). Just as the final cause or purpose of the chestnut is to grow into a chestnut tree, that of philosophical thinking is rational truth, while the final cause of human history is the self-consciousness of freedom. Hegel's idealism thus saw all things in the realms of logic, nature (the physical world), and spirit (the human world) as connected together by their final causes. Yet as Frederick Beiser observes (2005: 68), the purpose 'that governs the world is only its inherent form or structure, and it does not necessarily imply the intention of some agent.' God's purpose doesn't especially govern the world, even though Hegel sometimes uses very religious language to describe the nature of reality. This teleology, which allows Hegel to see the world as a rational whole, is one of the most controversial aspects of his philosophy. Modern analytic philosophers such as Bertrand Russell (1872–1970) have either entirely rejected Hegel's thought as utter nonsense or tried to interpret it in such a fashion as to remove offending metaphysical elements such as final causes and the Absolute Idea.

One of Hegel's most famous claims, taken from the Preface to his *Philosophy of Right* (his book on political philosophy), is that 'What is rational is actual and what is actual is rational' (Hegel, 1991 [1821]: 10).[1] In this same Preface Hegel rejects any supernatural interpretation of reality: by 'actual' he means living human beings and actual historical events. His famous aphorism means that just as the world develops according to rational concepts, the things that exist do so by necessity: they make sense within their own environment and historical milieu. When we look upon the actual world we live in:

> the great thing is to apprehend in the show of the temporal and transient the substance which is immanent and the eternal which is present. For since rationality (which is synonymous with the Idea) enters upon external existence simultaneously with its actualization, it emerges with an infinite wealth of forms, shapes and appearances. (Ibid.)

In other words, the Idea is present in all things despite the endless variety they seem to display. Since reality is rational, the concept (in German, *Begriff*) of each thing ties it to all the other things in the same system. To use a post-Hegelian example, the burning of fossil fuels by the billions of individuals making up the population of planet Earth has led to the buildup of greenhouse gases in the atmosphere and to a greater concern with ecological issues—the individual wills of the fuel burners were rationally tied together by nature to produce a collective effect, a new actuality: the threat of global climate change. The rational progress of science and technology has led to actual environmental problems, just as these problems are rationally connected to human decisions and actions.[2]

Other than this 'ontological' concept of reason, Hegel's other major contribution to critical theory is his notion of the dialectic. The simple version of the dialectic, the one found in most textbooks, sees both history and thought as progressing by a series of conflicts of opposing ideas—a starting idea, the thesis, and its opposite, the antithesis, struggle in military, political, economic, and philosophical arenas to produce a synthesis combining elements of both thesis and antithesis while subsuming both. The synthesis becomes a new thesis from which the dialectic starts again:

Thesis 1 ← → Antithesis 1 → Synthesis 1 = Thesis 2

Thesis 2 ← → Antithesis 2 → Synthesis 2 = Thesis 3

Thesis 3 ← → Antithesis 3 → Synthesis 3
(and onward to the Idea)

The problem with this model is that Hegel explicitly referred to it only once, and it is thus something of an oversimplification of his dialectic. It was invented by nineteenth-century commentators to make sense of some of Hegel's complex system of thought. What we *can* say with certainty is that Hegel saw development within the three realms of reality—logic, nature, and spirit (human affairs)—as taking place by a process of contradictions and negations that *usually* had a triadic structure. The opposing ideas or historical forces destroy each other while preserving elements of each in their offspring (Hegel's word for this process is *aufgehoben*). So the dialectical process is also an evolutionary one. In the realm of politics we might start with an abstract or formal view of rights and duties, e.g., 'all people must obey the law.' At the other extreme we have particular wills or decisions: for example, whether a given citizen decides to break the law in a specific instance. These two extremes come together in the Idea in its concrete instance, in what Hegel calls 'ethical life'—structures like the family, civil society, and the state (ibid., 35–6). In these structures individuals obey the law as a regular duty, thus combining abstract principles with specific cases.

It is important to recognize the fact that Hegel's dialectic is not an abstract form of logic that he tried to impose upon reality but a description of a process that he saw as emerging from the inner movement of a given subject matter (Beiser, 2005: 160). By their very nature, things progress by a process of dialectical change. Think of how the conflicts in your own life with friends, family, teachers, co-workers, and bosses change you, helping you to realize certain things about both yourself and the social, economic, and political worlds you live in. Unless you're run over by a truck or struck by lightning, you take these conflicts into your psyche and thus your character, changing you so that you approach new conflicts differently (or so one hopes). In other words, life itself is dialectical. Each category or concept, according to Hegel, contains a contradiction that drives it forward until we reach the Absolute Idea. Truth isn't a matter of asserting individual well-grounded propositions such as 'the rain in Spain falls mainly in the plain' and leaving things at that. Instead, it emerges from a dialectical opposition of ideas.

Thought, by its very nature, is historical. For instance, one of the most basic of Hegel's philosophical oppositions is that between Being, all that exists, and Nothing:

Being ← → Nothing → Becoming

We can see here why Hegel thought that the dialectic tends to drive itself forward to embrace more complete or holistic notions. The idea of Being encompasses everything. It excludes nothing. Its opposite, Nothing, is empty. Neither is very helpful to understand reality: both concepts are too broad and empty, and besides, even the simplest child knows that things grow, change, and die. The dialectical opposition of Being and Nothing pushes us to develop the notion of Becoming, of things changing. So although the thesis–antithesis–synthesis model simplifies the Hegelian dialectic, in the end we can agree with Thomas Wartenberg (1993: 131) that the model captures Hegel's method reasonably well.

Marx took up the basic structure of Hegel's dialectic, but replaced concepts with economic formations, mainly classes. In an Afterword to *Capital* he briefly discusses his relation to Hegel. He thought that for Hegel the real world was only a mirror image or external form of the Idea, while for him the ideal is the material world reflected in thought (Marx and Engels, 1978: 301). Hegel had stood the dialectic on its head: to understand human life, Marx's job was to turn it right-side up, to move from idealism to materialism, from abstract philosophical concepts to forms of property and work. Marx saw modern society as propelled at its core by a basic contradiction:

Bourgeoisie ← → Proletariat → Communism

The bourgeois capitalist class finds itself in opposition to the developing industrial working class, the proletariat, who will overthrow its rule when the time is ripe and create a communist society. We should keep in mind that at least for some commentators, Marx's attack on Hegel's idealism was an attack on a bogeyman—like Marx, Hegel also believed that religious, philosophical, and literary ideas had their origins in social and political conditions (Beiser, 1993: 278). According to this line of thought, which certainly has some merit, both Hegel and Marx were historicists; they both believed that historical societies created ideas, not the other way around. The big difference with Marx is that he did not talk about the Absolute Idea or final causes being inherent in all things; his class struggle was more down to earth, not motivated by the universal self-realization of freedom.

One of the key aspects of Hegel's dialectic, especially for the Frankfurt School, is its power of negation, its power to deny that which exists. This is clear enough in Marx's use of it to describe the class struggle: he predicted that the proletariat would one day 'negate' the capitalist system. This idea of the power of theory to negate the status quo is at the heart of critical theory, which saw itself not just as an abstract philosophy but as an attempt to change the world (as Marx said in his *Theses on Feuerbach*, this should be the business of all philosophers). Herbert Marcuse begins his *Reason and Revolution* (1960 [1941]: xxii), on Hegel and the rise of social theory, with a short note on dialectic. He praises dialectical thinking for its power to negate the status quo:

> Dialectical logic is critical logic: it reveals modes and contents of thought which transcend the codified use and validation. . . . Dialectical analysis . . . recovers tabooed meanings and thus appears almost as a return, or rather a conscious liberation, of the repressed.

Marcuse notes that this liberation of tabooed meanings from repression is still only in thought or theory. Yet to separate the world of theory from that of action is to negate our freedom, which Hegel saw as expressed both in our ideas and in our actions. Hence Marcuse uses Hegel's notion of the unity of thought and action to show how critical theory was itself a type of practice (or 'praxis').

A key term for Hegel is *Geist*, translated as either 'mind' or 'spirit' though usually the latter. Hegel argued that human psychology, or 'Subjective Spirit', moves from a bare sensory awareness of the things around us through self-consciousness to an awareness of one's place in the development of history. On the other side, 'Objective Spirit', which has to do with the family, morality, and political life, also goes through a series of dialectical conflicts until we arrive at the end point of a nation that becomes aware of itself as expressing an ethical will in the state.[3] When our Subjective and Objective Spirits conflict, we are driven from individual consciousness, on the one hand, and social and political life, on the other, to the Absolute Spirit, which Hegel saw as expressed in art, religion, and philosophy. This is where reason comes to recognize itself in the structure of reality, which is at the same time a reflection of our reason.

Looking back over the past, Hegel concluded that history is a rational process where Spirit attempts to become self-aware, to realize its own nature, which is freedom. In his words:

It is only an inference from the history of the World, that its development has been a rational process; that the history in question has constituted the rational necessary course of the World-Spirit—that Spirit whose nature is always one and the same, but which unfolds its nature in the phenomena of the World's existence. . . . The History of the world is none other than the progress of the consciousness of Freedom . . . . (Hegel, 1956 [1822–30]: 10, 19)

The essence of Spirit is freedom—this is its final cause, its *telos*. All nations strive to become conscious of this freedom. Yet for most of history this potential for freedom isn't actualized and often seems to be buried deep beneath the rocks of caprice and tyranny. Hegel, however, is an optimist on this point. This Spirit never entirely dies, for it is immortal and 'comprehends within it all earlier steps' each time it consumes itself and is reborn like the phoenix of myth (ibid., 79). The progress of Spirit towards freedom is a long and winding road comprised of all human history.

Even though history as a whole is a rational process, Spirit has to manifest itself in individual human wills. Most people are driven to act out of their interests, needs, characters, and passions. The *Weltgeist* or World-Spirit must use these passions to drive history towards its inherent goal of freedom whether or not human actors are aware they are being so used. In Hegel's words, 'we may affirm absolutely that *nothing great in the World* has been accomplished without *passion*' (ibid., 23). The Idea and passions depend on each other, like cars and gasoline or computers and software. This 'cunning of reason' sets the passions to work for rational goals, most importantly the progress of Spirit towards freedom. Hegel saw this cunning at work in his own day during the French Revolution, whose bloodthirsty Reign of Terror helped to institutionalize the revolutionary goals of liberty and equality and a liberal constitutional state. This notion that the World-Spirit uses human passions to advance its rational purpose is one of Hegel's more contentious points: it smacks of a fuzzy spiritualistic determinism and

has been attacked for this reason by a number of philosophical critics.[4]

In any case, Hegel saw three rather huge historical stages in the progress of Spirit towards freedom. In the ancient world of Oriental despotism, only one man in a given society was free, the despot, whether King Tut on the throne of Egypt or Xerxes on that of Persia. In the ancient Greek and Roman world some men were free: the male citizen, but not foreigners, women, and slaves. In the modern 'Germanic' world of Hegel's time, a consciousness of freedom had become more general so that man *as such* is free (ibid., 18). If we take out the metaphysical language and see Hegel's story of the development of the spirit of freedom as solely a reflection on the past, and not a description of how things *had* to turn out from the very beginning, then this is a fair description of history. Certainly the idea that history could be understood as a process of dialectical development would have a major influence on Marx and his followers.

Nietzsche: The Genealogy of Morals

A second, less significant influence on twentieth-century critical theory was the philosopher Friedrich Nietzsche (1844–1900). Nietzsche had many things to say on a wide variety of subjects. What concerns us here is his critique of conventional morality, especially that of Christian Europe. Nietzsche saw in history two basic types of morality: master morality, best represented by the ancient Greeks and Romans, and slave morality, which he associated with Judaism and Christianity. Master morality revels in struggle, war, self-overcoming, and a vigorous acceptance of the pleasures of the flesh. Slave morality emphasizes pity, humility, and asceticism, hoping against hope that the meek shall inherit the earth, as Jesus said in the Sermon on the Mount. Yet it's also clever and full of *ressentiment* (resentment) against its masters, so it invents self-denying religious codes like Christianity to keep the strong at bay. Nietzsche links the genealogy of these two broad types of morality to psychological and physiological differences between their holders: the holders of slave morality tend to be sicker, weaker, and psychically unhealthy as compared to the defenders of master morality. The slave moralists are the herd, the great mass of modern human beings who accept their own mediocrity and distrust those who don't.

Nietzsche saw all moralities as reflections of various levels of will to power, which he thought dominated all of organic life. All human beings are driven to seek power, whether over others or themselves. This was the basic drive he found in all human life, especially in religion and moral codes. In *On the Genealogy of Morals* Essay I, Nietzsche tells the parable of the sheep and the birds of prey to illustrate the difference between master and slave morality. The sheep say to themselves that the birds of prey are evil, while all those with lamb-like qualities are good; but the birds of prey saw 'we don't dislike them at all, these good little lambs; we even love them: nothing is more tasty than a tender lamb' (Mann and Dann, 2005: 441). The sheep are the slave moralists, resentful of the predatory birds; the birds of prey the masters, ever on watch for a good meal.

In the end, Nietzsche thought that 'There are no moral phenomena at all, but only a moral interpretation of phenomena' (Nietzsche, 1967 [1886]: 108; Mann and Dann, 2005: 434). This view of moral life is called perspectivism: our moral values are the product of this or that perspective. Nothing in the nature of the world rationally compels us to accept one moral set of rules over another. Nietzsche's notions of morality, the will to power, and perspectivism were based on his sense that human life is driven as much by the unconscious as the conscious mind, which heavily influenced Freud.

Nietzsche had many other things to say, proclaiming that 'God is dead' and forecasting the coming of a Superman who would go beyond good and evil to drag Europe out of nihilism. The Nazis thought that he meant Adolf Hitler, though it is highly doubtful that Nietzsche would have had much respect for the little Austrian corporal. His main influence on critical theory was the notion that moral and religious codes are not in any sense 'natural', but the product of historical circumstances and the peculiarities of human diet, health, and psychology, notably the way we express our wills to power.

FREUD ON CIVILIZATION AND ITS DISCONTENTS

Freud's Theory of the Human Mind

Sigmund Freud (1856–1939), the main figure in the development of psychoanalysis, has with some exaggeration been called the discoverer of the unconscious mind. In fact, the Romantics in the early nineteenth century, along with Nietzsche, both explored how human decisions are not always the product of conscious thought. Freud, however, developed a sophisticated theoretical picture of the human mind that emphasized the power of the unconscious, and applied that theory to the workings of human society.

Like Arthur Conan Doyle's detective Sherlock Holmes, created at about the same time that Freud was developing his psychoanalytic approach to the mind, Freud looked for clues of hidden mental process in dreams, slips of the tongue, jokes, and other paraphernalia of everyday life. For Freud, dreams were dramas of wish fulfillment, where the dreamer acts out unconsciously his or her hidden wishes while the moral guardians of the conscious mind slumber. His major discovery in the 1890s, while working with Dr Joseph Breuer on hysteria, was that his patients' neuroses could usually be explained as repressions of some childhood sexual trauma, whether this trauma was a real seduction or merely a fantasy. Freud called this the seduction theory of psychological development. The king of all such wishes was the desire of a young boy to have sex with his mother, which is considered a tad immoral in Western society and thus has to be 'repressed' by the conscious mind. Freud christened this youthful dilemma the 'Oedipus complex' after the ancient Greek myth of King Oedipus, who killed his father and slept with his mother. The notion that even children had strong sexual feelings certainly shocked the Viennese bourgeoisie, and led to a split between Freud and Breuer (but not before they published *Studies on Hysteria* in 1895).

By the time of his *The Interpretation of Dreams* (1900) and *The Psychopathology of Everyday Life* (1901), Freud had come to the conclusion that the human mind was divided into conscious, unconscious, and preconscious levels. The preconscious involves thoughts that you *can* bring to consciousness by an act of attention—for example, if I asked you, 'Does your toenail need clipping?', you could have a look and answer my question, even though it's highly unlikely you were meditating on the state of your toenail a few seconds ago. Unconscious thoughts and feelings are more deeply buried and only come out in dreams, jokes, and slips of the tongue. They have been repressed by our psychic censor, which he later came to call the superego. The conscious mind refuses under normal conditions to deal with that which is unconscious.

Freud had also come to the conclusion that the human mind could be seen as a complex of warring forces, echoing Hegel's and Nietzsche's general view of reality as one where ideal or psychological forces struggle. He thought at first that the basic force driving us is sexual energy, which he called the libido. Yet our sexuality by itself doesn't explain the phenomenon of repression: if we were truly libidinous beings, why aren't we all having sex right now? His explanation was that a second instinct is at work in the human mind and thus in human societies, the death instinct (later called Thanatos by Freud's followers, after another Greek god). The death instinct provides aggressive energy to our psychic sensor that causes us to repress our sexual drive in a variety of productive or unhealthy ways. So the human mind is driven by a dialectic of Eros and Thanatos, sex and death. Freud also concluded that human civilization itself is driven by these two forces writ large.

For example, he argued in *Group Psychology and the Analysis of Ego* (1921) that crowds represent a partial return to the primal horde, a band of uncivilized barbarians. A crowd is a suggestible mass (witness Hitler's speeches, lynch mobs, and crowds at sporting events) where emotions are passed contagiously from one person to another. This is possible because the underlying source of the crowd's sense of solidarity is 'aim-inhibited' erotic love, which can turn very quickly into hatred for a scapegoated individual or group, e.g., the Jews in Nazi Germany. Love holds a nation together, yet this erotic bond is enhanced by a feeling of aggression towards an enemy. Not surprisingly, Freud saw the carnage of World War I as strong evidence of a death instinct gotten out of hand.

By the time of his 1920 work *The Ego and the Id*, Freud saw the human mind as having three aspects. The id is the unconscious source of our sexual and aggressive drives. It operates by the Pleasure Principle: it wants to have some fun, and have it right now. The ego is our primarily conscious self, which is aware of the world around us and acts as a mediator between that world and the demands of the id. It's our psychic referee, and is anchored in the Reality Principle. The superego is our psychic censor, fuelled by aggressive energy from the id. It's an internalized father figure that represses unacceptable or unrealizable wishes from the id back into the nether regions of our unconscious. Yet when we sleeps, so does the superego, so our repressed wishes are free to swim about in the pool of our unconscious mind as coded stories, which the psychoanalyst can use talk therapy to unravel and thus understand the foundation of the patient's neuroses.

Civilization and Its Discontents

Freud's key work in social theory is his short but striking *Civilization and Its Discontents* (1930), which would influence the Frankfurt School, especially Herbert Marcuse, to a great degree. The basic assumption of Freud's social theory was that he could apply his model of the human mind to society as a whole and make some sense of it. In the book he pictures human civilization as a battleground between Eros and Death, a battle that makes it difficult for human beings to be happy. Thus the book is also about the most basic question in social theory: is civilization worth all the bother? Would we be happier as uncivilized barbarians? Freud's basic answer is that we would be, though life would be considerably nastier, brutish, and short, so we shouldn't get rid of civilization too quickly.

Freud discusses the sources of suffering in human life and the various ways we deal with it. He argues that there are three basic sources of suffering in our lives:

1. that caused by our own *body*, including illness, pain, and growing old;
2. that caused by the *external world*, especially nature in general;
3. that caused by *other people*, which we feel most acutely today since nature has for the most part been conquered and pain and death are seen as inevitable.

Most people moderate their claims to happiness to overcome suffering. In fact, if we are hedonists and spend all our time pursuing pleasure, life will punish us. Human beings deal with suffering in three general ways: (1) powerful deflections like hobbies; (2) substitutive satisfactions like art; and (3) intoxicating substances like alcohol and drugs. Freud fleshes out the specific forms these general categories could take, arguing that none of them is entirely successful.

1. *Isolation*. We can avoid the pain caused by other people by isolating ourselves from others, avoiding relationships as much as we can. This is the happiness of quietness. Its extreme form is the life of the hermit, who has turned his back on the world. Freud argues that it's better to join a human community and to aid it in subjugating nature than to live in a cave like the hermit.

2. *Intoxication*. Obviously, we can dull the pain of existence with a pint in the pub or some less legal substance. Things often seem much rosier in altered states. Since suffering is just a feeling, we can alter our bodily states with chemicals and thereby make ourselves incapable of feeling unpleasurable impulses. We can thus remove ourselves from the pressure of reality. Yet this solution is foolish: it has wasted a huge amount of energy that could have been used to improve human life.

3. *Meditation or yoga*. Another way to deal with suffering is to use meditation or yoga to limit or kill off our instincts. That way we don't feel as disappointed if they can't be satisfied. Yet this kills our pleasures too—satisfying a mild impulse is much less pleasurable than the happiness one feels from satisfying a wild instinctual impulse that hasn't been tamed by the superego, e.g., a wild and crazy night of love.

4. *Work (including science and art)*. Some solutions involve displacing our instincts into socially acceptable activities—this involves sublimating our drives into work, such as the artist's joy in creating or the scientist's pleasure in solving problems. Freud thinks that these activities stand a greater chance of success than other methods. But they are of use only to a few people with special abilities, and cannot deal with the suffering given to us by our own bodies. Freud notes that work is tied firmly to the Reality Principle and offers an excellent way of displacing our sexual and aggressive drives into a useful direction. Most people, however, don't prize work and prefer to avoid it whenever they can. This is a big social problem, since they will likely take out their instincts in other less productive ways.

5. *Art (from the spectator's point of view)*. Art is also important as a way for the imagination to indulge in harmless fantasies. The enjoyment of art creates a mild sense of narcotic pleasure, but it can only last for a short while, after which our vital needs return.

6. *Religion*. One way to deal with the world's pains is to transform the world through some form of mass delusional remoulding of reality, as religions do. Naturally, religious followers do not recognize their religion as a delusion. Freud compares the mass delusion of religion to the delusions of a madman: in both cases, reality is too strong for the deluded ones. Religion depresses the value of life and distorts the nature of the world (here Freud borrows heavily from Nietzsche). This intimidation of our intelligence saves many from neurosis. In the end, though, all that is left to the believer is a blind acceptance of God's inscrutable decrees, which isn't much of a guarantee of happiness.

Freud sees religious feeling as based on the idea of God as a caring and watchful father with enormous powers, who can understand the needs of his children and who can be made happy with prayers. He says that the whole thing is 'patently infantile' and that anyone friendly to the human race would be humiliated by so many people still sympathetic to religion, including philosophers who attempt to turn God into an impersonal, abstract principle and thereby attempt to defend religion by a series of 'pitiful rearguard actions' (Freud, 1961 [1930]: 21). For Freud, religion is a childish illusion that the human race would be better off without.

7. *Erotic love*. The opposite path to a removal from reality is one that passionately clings to the reality of sexual love. Here we find one of the most intense pleasures of human life. But we are never more open to suffering than when we have lost the object of our love. Eros is a fickle god.

8. *The love of beauty (the aesthetic life)*. Some people seek relief from suffering in finding pleasure in beauty, including that of the human form, natural objects, landscapes, art, and science. The enjoyment of beauty is mildly intoxicating, yet even it cannot protect us from suffering. Freud admits that psychoanalysis has little to say about beauty, other than that it's derived from sexual feeling in some general way.

9. *Neurosis or psychosis*. A final technique of avoiding suffering is the flight into mental illness. This is the worst solution.

We shouldn't tie up all our psychic capital into one solution; rather, but mix together a few of the healthier ones, such as love, work, and art, if we want a healthy and happy life. This leads Freud into the larger question regarding whether civilization itself is responsible for our misery, and whether primitive human beings weren't better off than we civilized types. For Freud, 'civilization' (in German *Kultur*) is the totality of achievements and rules that distinguish us from animals. Its purpose is to protect us against nature and to adjust human relations (Freud, 1962 [1927]: 36).

Freud's balance sheet contains a number of entries in both the credit and debit columns. Our power over nature hasn't made us happier, though things like modern medicine certainly lighten our load. Technology is also a mixed blessing—we can communicate with people in foreign countries and travel to distant lands, but railways and ships take our loved ones away from us. Yet beauty, cleanliness, order, philosophy, moral values, and freedom from brute force are all marks of civilized life, things most of us would be reluctant to give up.

Civilization and the Instincts

In the second half of *Civilization and Its Discontents* Freud applies his theory of instincts to society as a whole. The sexual instinct, Eros, seeks to preserve living things and to build larger units. The death instinct seeks to return us to primeval, inorganic, dead matter. Eros combines people into bigger and bigger social units, while Death tears these units apart. For Freud:

> the meaning of the evolution of civilization is no longer obscure to us. It must present the struggle between Eros and Death, between the instinct of life and the instinct of destruction, as it works itself out in the human species. This struggle is what all life essentially consists of, and the evolution of civilization may therefore be simply described as the struggle for life of the human species. And it is this battle of the giants that our nurse-maids try to appease with their lullaby about Heaven. (Freud, 1961 [1930]: 69)

The price we pay for civilization is the renunciation of our instincts. Both Eros and Thanatos are restricted by all modern culture; the civilized person trades freedom for security. But if an instinct cannot be satisfied directly and its loss isn't compensated for, it will result in mental illness. In fact, at the end of *Civilization and Its Discontents* Freud muses whether it's possible to call our whole civilization 'neurotic'. Freud speculates that early humans found genital love to be one of their greatest delights. Over time, however, this was repressed in the service of the social needs of organized societies. Added to this problem of repression was the fact that too much faith in Eros could lead to great unhappiness if one's love object is unfaithful or dies.

Freud argues that too much attention paid to erotic love has another important consequence: it removes energy from work, which civilization needs to build itself. So civilization slowly but surely withdraws psychic energy from sexuality in order to develop. It acts towards sexuality like a ruling class towards a dangerous, discontented populace. The fear of revolt leads the civilized ruling class to develop defences against the erotic mob such as the curbing of sexual life in children and monogamous marriage. It only tolerates sexuality because it needs it to propagate the human race.

The second of our primal instincts is aggression, the death instinct. Freud mocks the Christian commandment to 'love thy neighbour': what if my neighbour jeers, insults, or robs me? Our neighbour might be someone who will exploit us, seize our goods, sexually use us, cause us pain, or kill us. We don't have that much love energy to waste it on our enemies. Men are not gentle creatures who only defend themselves, but aggressive beings willing to attack others. Freud argues that 'Man is a wolf to man.' Human beings tend to wait around for some provocation to aggression; when we get such a provocation and our instinctual defences are down, we become savage beasts—witness the ancient Huns, the Crusaders, or the great European nations during World War I. Our aggressive instinct acts against civilization, perpetually threatening it with disintegration. So civilization has to think up psychical defences against the beast within us all. One is by focusing our aggressive impulses on an external enemy, preferably one nearby. Freud repeats a point that David Hume made 150 years earlier—close neighbours are more likely to feel hostility to each other (e.g., the French and Germans, English and Scots, etc.) than towards distant nations. In other words, we need enemies, and the closer they are the better.

Another important way we cope with our aggressive drive is to internalize it into our superego, which directs this aggression against our own ego. This internalized aggression becomes guilt. Through the superego, civilization sets up its own psychic garrison in our minds to control our nastier impulses. The superego torments the sinful ego with anxiety, replacing the need for punishment from parents and schoolmasters with a sense of guilt. The superego is always on guard for bad thoughts. It's easy to see why Talcott Parsons and the early functionalists turned to Freud to help understand the process of socialization.

Freud concludes that we pay for each advance in civilization with a loss of happiness and a heightened sense of guilt. Conscience makes cowards of us all. Things were so bad in Freud's day that parents and authority figures hid from the young the dominant role sexuality and aggression would play in their lives—it was like equipping an expedition to the North Pole with summer clothes and maps of the Italian lakes (ibid., 81). It could be argued that this repression of our sexual drive slackened thanks to the consumer society and the sexual revolution of the late 1960s and 1970s, yet it remains a central concern of critical theory, as we shall see when we look at Herbert Marcuse.

Freud ties his analysis of the individual person's psychic development to the moral and libidinal structure of society. He argues that the community develops its moral rules, its superego, out of the personalities of great leaders, men with a powerful force of mind, just as the individual superego comes from the internalization of the father. These forceful men may even be mocked and maltreated in their lifetime, as Jesus was. Yet they are revered by future generations. Freud sees the development of the cultural superego as coinciding with the development of our individual superegos. In fact, we can usually see how our cultural superego works more easily than our own individual, unconscious superego—the moral demands of our community are usually clearer to us than the hidden demands of our own conscience.

Freud concludes *Civilization and Its Discontents* with a prophetic quandary. The problem today is that we have gained enormous control over nature and have the power to obliterate all human beings. So the question is whether our instincts to communal life can overcome the death instinct, which seeks aggression against others and self-destruction. Who will win—Eros or Thanatos? This question became even more serious during the Cold War, when two giant nuclear-armed behemoths threatened the world with atomic incineration. These arsenals remain largely intact today, while other nations have joined the nuclear club, perhaps proof that Freud was right that our civilization harbours a deep death instinct it can't seem to shake off.

THEODOR ADORNO ON CULTURE

What Was the Frankfurt School?

Starting with Marx's early historical materialism, adding touches of Freud's psychoanalysis and Hegel's dialectical reason, the Frankfurt School offered a powerful critique of popular culture in the mid-twentieth century. As we have seen, it numbered among its members at various times Herbert Marcuse, Theodor Adorno, Max Horkheimer, and Erich Fromm. They aimed to update Marx for the modern age, and in many cases turned to the insights of psychoanalysis to do so. They got their name from the fact that most of them worked in the Institute for Social Research at the University of Frankfurt from its founding in 1923 to the exodus of most of its leading lights to America in the mid-1930s due to fear of Nazi persecution (most of them were Jewish, and the Nazis were rabid anti-Semites). After World War II, Marcuse and Fromm stayed in America, while Adorno and Horkheimer returned to Germany. Walter Benjamin, a loose associate of the school, fled the Nazis in the 1930s to France. In 1940 he tried to go into Spain and killed himself in a border town when he was denied entry.

The Frankfurt School felt that intellectuals should try to fight the cultural power of consumer capitalism by adopting a ruthlessly critical attitude in their work, even though they did not really believe, as Marx did, that a workers' revolution would mark the end of the capitalist system. Their central concern was the danger of totalitarianism, the first instance of which was European fascism, which dominated the continent from the mid-1930s until the defeat of Germany in 1945, and then in a diluted form consumer capitalism, which they saw as colonizing human hopes and desires with false needs. Their ideas, especially Marcuse's vision of a non-repressive society, were highly influential in the radical student movements of the 1960s.

The Frankfurters doubted the possibilities of objective social knowledge held out by positivists and functionalists. After all, the idea that social facts can be kept separate from social values just winds up supporting the status quo. Despite this, however, they believed in the power of critical reason and in a robust notion of truth, unlike the later postmodernists. They believed that the free development of human reason was critical to the development of free societies.

The Dialectic of Enlightenment

Theodor Adorno and Max Horkheimer were leading lights at the Institute for Social Research until its closure in 1934. Once Hitler was established in power, Adorno and Horkheimer left their native land for the much friendlier intellectual and political climate of America, where they absorbed the popular culture they found all around them—jazz music, Hollywood films, radio, and advertising—and developed a critique of modern mass culture that stands as one of the grand gestures of twentieth-century social theory. They called the enterprises producing popular culture the 'culture industry' and saw in this industry an insidious form of totalitarianism.

In 1944 Adorno and Horkheimer published *The Dialectic of Enlightenment*. The key essay in this collection was 'The Culture Industry: Enlightenment as Mass Deception', in which they criticized popular culture (including music, movies, and radio) as the product of a culture industry whose goal was to stupefy the masses with endless mass-produced copies of the same thing. Adorno and

Horkheimer argued that the content of films, hit songs, and radio only appears to change; their reproduction of the same patterns over and over again is linked to their central message, the necessity of obedience of the masses to the social hierarchy in place in advanced capitalist societies. Cultural products are standardized to help these masses understand and appreciate them without too much effort or attention. Society is anaesthetized by popular culture. The goal of the industry is to encourage conformity in its buyers, both to keep them consuming the culture industry's products and to keep capitalism as a whole in power.

At the same time, a pseudo-individuality is encouraged in these products to keep the customers coming back for more. A bit of deviation is fine, as long as it can be absorbed into the product as a cog in the engine of mass conformity. The culture industry encourages connoisseurs of small differences in cars, gadgets, films, music, and other products to perpetuate the illusion of competition. However, its products are predictable. As soon as a film begins, we know how it will end. They even predicted, a few years before it took off as a mass medium, that television would intensify the aesthetic impoverishment of popular culture so much that the thinly veiled identity of all industrial culture would come out into the open. The producer and consumer are caught in a feedback loop of the selling and buying of standardized products:

> By craftily sanctioning the demand for rubbish it inaugurates total harmony. The connoisseur and the expert are despised for their pretentious claim to know better than the others, even though culture is democratic and distributes its privileges to all. In view of the ideological truce, the conformism of the buyers and the effrontery of the producers who supply them prevail. The result is a constant reproduction of the same thing. (Adorno and Horkheimer, 1993 [1944])

The culture industry's products obey a logic of domination, suppressing any mental effort

among the masses with catchy tunes and glamorous movie stars, thus turning the populace into its eternal consumers. Consumers are categorized and labelled to better manage their needs, to provide them with a smooth supply of mass-produced goods, using what is now called 'demographics'. These needs are predetermined so people will be eternal consumers: the producers, not the buyers, determine what the masses want.

It may sound like Adorno and Horkheimer aren't much fun, but they have an answer to this critique. Insofar as amusement takes the place of higher things as the goal of life, we defend the social order. To be amused is to say 'Yes' to that order. Pleasure means emptying your mind of suffering, taking flight from any idea of resistance. 'The liberation which amusement promises is freedom from thought and negation' (ibid.). As our consumer society has become more and more sophisticated over the last half-century at supplying us with amusements, it is easy to understand why Adorno and Horkheimer were worried that the culture industry floods our brains with so many idle pleasures that social critique is the last thing to come to mind.

In other early works, Adorno attacked jazz for its standardization and for distracting people and making them passive consumers, thus alienating them. He also attacked the astrology column of the *Los Angeles Times* for using occult mumbo-jumbo to assure people that their lives can be made whole, thus supporting the current social structure. Many of these columns told people to work hard and to get on with their chores, thus championing the drudgery of their work lives. Even today psychics, astrology columns, and other occult practices offer us the false hope that things will change in our humdrum lives without us doing much about them.

Adorno's 'Culture Industry Reconsidered' and Popular Culture Today

Adorno's short essay 'Culture Industry Reconsidered' appeared in 1975, after his death. In it he reflects on his general thesis about the culture industry in a way that can be applied to issues in contemporary popular culture. Adorno sticks to his theoretical guns: the culture industry produces vacuous commodities, banal trash that encourages shamelessly conformist behaviour among consumers. These cultural commodities are fetishes that exude a false individuality, disguising their role as political pacifiers of the masses. He thinks that the products of consumer capitalism are mass-produced things tailored to suit these masses. But the consumer isn't king, as the advertisers would have us believe. Instead, the consumer is the object, not the subject, of capitalism.

Under consumerism, high art is cheapened by the methods of mass production. Walter Benjamin argues in 'The Work of Art in the Age of Mechanical Reproduction' that mass production of copies of famous paintings, sculptures, and other works of art had served to make art less authentic, causing the originals to lose their 'aura'—why line up at the Louvre to see the *Mona Lisa* if you can go to the local art store and buy a good copy for $10? Art was once autonomous, but is now totally under the control of the culture industry, whose main goal is to make a profit. It is a commodity, like soap, bacon, or shampoo.[5]

Adorno feels that culture once had a critical role to play with respect to capitalism and its social relations. Now culture has been absorbed totally into these relations. Art and music are commodities through and through. The products produced by the culture industry become their own advertisements. In the decade after the essay appeared, music videos added fuel to Adorno's fire. The consumers in the music shop must ask themselves what are they buying: the music itself, the singer or band's persona, or some remembered image from a video?

As in his earlier work, Adorno's major critique of the culture industry here is the sameness of the products it produces. He talks about how the film industry seems to retain a sense of individual artistry, yet is industrial in the way it is organized. Adorno dismisses the creation of stars and heartthrobs by the film industry as a false individualism. This sameness extends to popular music as well. Today there is evidence both for and against Adorno's thesis: boy bands all sound the same, Hollywood movies usually have happy endings, and rap and hip-hop artists repeat the same beat and lyrical themes—sex, violence, and getting rich—over and over. Much of American television recycles the same tired formulas. On the other side of the coin, we can point to alternative and roots music, even if it's not as popular as its more standardized cousins, as an attempt to break the mould of sameness. We can also point to films from independent studios and Europe that use innovative cinematic techniques and morally ambiguous characters. Yet the music and films that draw the biggest audiences are still the most formulaic and trite, as Adorno predicted.

A case in point: as I write this, on 23 February 2005, the two biggest films at the box office in America were *Hitch* (with a gross of $37 million US on the previous weekend), a formulaic romance film starring Will Smith, and *Constantine* ($34 million), a horror/sci-fi film in which Keanu Reeves battles evil spirits from Hell. Both films received an average critical rating of C+ on the Yahoo movies website.[6] The second-place film the previous weekend (after *Hitch*) was *Bogeyman*, a formulaic horror film geared towards teens that received positive ratings from only 12 per cent of critics on a website that collects reviews from throughout North America.[7] Yet the excellent film *Sideways*, with multiple Oscar nominations and a collective rating of 'A' from the critics, did only $4.5 million business the same weekend. This temporal snapshot of the gap between critical and mass tastes in film would apply pretty well any weekend in any recent year, and could no doubt be extended to other parts of the cultural industry, including music and TV. When Adorno and Horkheimer (1944) took the film industry to task for 'the rubbish they deliberately produce', they were not just speaking of their own day. If anything, the production of cinematic rubbish has accelerated today as the film industry caters more to the tastes of affluent teens with spare change in their pockets.

Adorno notes that some critics warn about being too snobbish and against underestimating the importance of the culture industry. He admits that it is tremendously important in the spiritual life of the masses. But we cannot be duped by the deceptive glitter or be afraid of the monopolistic power of the culture industry; we have to treat it critically, to challenge it on both the aesthetic and social levels. We might ask ourselves today, is life really like that pictured on TV sitcoms? Are pop icons like Britney Spears really creative artists? Are Hollywood films really the best we can expect from an industry that is willing to spend $100 million on one picture and pay its stars multi-million dollar paycheques?

Adorno says that some intellectuals praise the democratic nature of the culture industry, or its ability to disseminate information or relieve stress. He replies that this information is of poor quality (thus anticipating Noam Chomsky's critique of the media), the advice it offers empty and banal, and the patterns of behaviour shamelessly conformist. At least legitimate culture attempted, by picturing suffering and the contradictions of life, to imagine the good life. The culture industry evades responsibility for failing to do this by claiming not to be art at all. It always hammers into us the idea that the best social order is the status quo. 'You shall conform!' its says. Yet social order is not good in itself. The heroes of films, TV shows, and pulp fiction get into false conflicts, only to be rescued by representatives of the social order. We know as soon as we take our seats in the theatre, or switch on our televisions, that the bad guy in a crime film is not going to get away with it, that the unhappy singles will wind up as a happy couple, that the terrorists will be hunted down and eliminated by the police. Adorno offers a couple of specific observations: American film producers appeal to 11-year-olds in making movies (a fact that has not changed in most cases). Also, the seemingly benign case of reading an astrology column in fact stupefies its readers into thinking that their daily lives are best led with approval of the stars.

The consuming masses are split between accepting the prescribed fun and doubting its value. Yet most people want to be deceived and fall for the swindle. They crave delusion, but won't admit that if they were to give up the satisfactions of the culture industry their lives would become intolerable. 'They force their eyes shut and voice approval, in a kind of self-loathing, for what is meted out to them, knowing fully the purpose for which it is manufactured' (Adorno, 1975: 89).

The cultural industry is an agency of anti-enlightenment, engaging in a mass deception of its consumers. It prevents them from becoming the autonomous independent individuals that the reason of the Enlightenment promised them they could be. In short, the culture industry aims to keep its consumers irrational children (ibid., 92).

Adorno on Popular Music

Adorno, a student and composer of music, had some specific things to say about popular music. He saw pop music in the middle of the twentieth century as having a *standardized core* that was designed to appeal to the conformist masses, with that core surrounded by the *pseudo-individuality* of peripheral frills and variations. This standardized core is what hooks the consumer. Popular music is mass-produced by the culture industry just like all other forms of popular culture under modern capitalism. Its purpose is to soothe the stresses felt by the masses created by their dull and repetitive jobs. Unlike classical or avant-garde music, pop music lacks originality, authenticity, and intellectual stimulation. Of course, this standardization and lack of originality have to be hidden, so music producers add a pseudo-individuality to musical genres. Then the listener has the delusion of making a free choice in choosing Artist A over Artist B, Pearl Jam over Nirvana, N'Sync over the Backstreet Boys (to use more recent examples), even though the core of the songs is basically the same.

Adorno called pop fans 'regressive listeners' with infantile tastes. Yet this wasn't entirely their fault. Their dull, mechanized jobs created the need for some distraction and inattention in their leisure hours, which the standardized and repetitive nature of pop music amply provided. The standardized, repetitive nature of their work is reflected in the standardized, repetitive nature of the cultural commodities they consume, notably music. The dullness and repetitiveness of work has been expanded today—it applies not only to industrial labour, but also to clerical work involving computers and to jobs in the service industry, especially fast-food restaurants and stores in shopping malls.

Adorno saw the lives of most working people as impoverished and unhappy, even if this is covered up some of the time with consumer goods. Pop music and Hollywood films offer them fantasies and catharsis, reconciling them to their lot. The culture industry helps to keep capitalism in place by feeding the workers the sugar-coated sentimentality and escapism of pop music and films (and later TV, although Adorno had less to say about this). This allows them a vision of a better life that most of them will never actually experience.

Some Critiques of Adorno

Perhaps Adorno's view of popular culture was a bit elitist. Yet we need to remember the cultural context in which Adorno and Horkheimer were writing in the early 1940s. This was the era of the big band led by the likes of Tommy Dorsey and Glenn Miller. Their music was sweet jazz and swing; their purpose to get people to dance and romance, not to think about the injustices of capitalism. The Justin Timberlake of the day was Frank Sinatra, godfather of a gang of crooners swooned over by teenaged girls as demigods of song. Hollywood churned out predictable romance, crime, and propaganda films for the war effort that did nothing to challenge official or mainstream ideologies. To transplanted Europeans, American pop must have looked like a cultural wasteland.

Having said this, Adorno's theory of pop music is open to at least four fairly obvious criticisms. (1) As Dominic Strinati (1995: 77) suggests, we can see standardized genres as positive things— as *organizations of pleasure*. We can take pleasure in a simple, repetitive musical beat or in a formulaic Hollywood action film, knowing what to expect in each. Even high culture—opera, symphonies, and literature—has genre-specific expectations, e.g., a classical symphony never features a 10-minute

drum solo, yet will feature masses of violins playing in harmony or counterpoint. (2) Genres in pop music *do* change fundamentally. They are not standardized, except perhaps within themselves. Think of the history of pop music from the postwar period until today—it includes jazz, swing, early blues-based rock and roll, country influences, doo-wop, surf music, the British sound of the sixties, Jimi Hendrix, Bob Dylan's folk rock, the progressive rock of the seventies (Yes, ELP), punk and New Wave in the late 1970s and 1980s, the Britpop of the 1980s (New Order, Duran Duran), reggae, the Seattle sound of the early 1990s, dance and techno, boy bands, rap and hip-hop. Imagine the reaction that a performance of gangster rap would have produced at a 1950s high school dance—it would have sounded like music from another planet![8] (3) Popular music, even if mass-produced by powerful corporations to earn a profit, can be repossessed by anti-status quo youth subcultures and used to critique society. This definitely seems to have happened during the hippie counterculture of the late 1960s and early 1970s, and again during the punk subculture of the late 1970s and 1980s. Pop culture is not inherently conservative, even if it often seems that way. (4) Popular culture can also be seen as innocent fun, as a temporary harmless diversion, not preventing critical thought after its consumption.

The question of fun leads us to Herbert Marcuse, who was more concerned with countering social repression than critiquing popular culture.

HERBERT MARCUSE ON MODERN INDUSTRIAL SOCIETY

Herbert Marcuse was the most influential of the Frankfurt School critical theorists on North American intellectual culture for two main reasons. (1) He stayed in America after the defeat of Nazism in 1945 and wrote his major works in English. (2) He engaged with the student and countercultural movements of the 1960s in his work, taking some sting out of the charge of elitism often levelled against the Frankfurters. He offers a powerful critique of modern industrial societies and the material and entertainment cultures they manufacture, arguing that they use new forms of social control to dupe the masses into accepting the way things are. His first foray into critical theory, his 1941 work *Reason and Revolution*, discusses how Hegel's dialectic, with its spirit of negation, should act as the basis of critical thinking about society. Yet his two most telling works of social theory are *Eros and Civilization* (1955) and *One-Dimensional Man* (1964).

Eros and Civilization

In *Eros and Civilization* (1955) Marcuse attempted to reconcile Marx and Freud, arguing that under capitalism our basic instincts are excessively frustrated. He looked forward to a non-repressive civilization where work would become play and where our sexuality could be freely expressed. Marcuse says that modern civilization imposes on us a 'surplus repression' of our instincts in order to maintain social control and high levels of productivity in the masses. This surplus repression exceeds the normal sort of repression of our sexual and aggressive instincts that Freud argued was necessary for all civilizations. Marcuse wanted to try to reduce this surplus repression and free people to explore their sexual and play instincts.

Much of the book is taken up with a review of Freud's theory of the instincts and how these apply to modern industrial societies. Marcuse sees modern society as focused on the Reality Principle, which is tied to our obsession with productivity. Technology and efficiency are our civilization's watchwords. Yet given modern technology, increased productivity should *reduce* the need for social repression, since modern industrial societies produce more than enough goods to give everyone a decent life. So productivity is turned against people, keeping repression in place by manipulating our basic needs. The many choices and gadgets produced by our society hide from us the fact that we could work less and 'determine our own needs and satisfactions' (Marcuse, 1955: 91). The continual upping of the social definition of a healthy standard of living only serves to jus-

tify the perpetuation of the repression of our sexual and aggressive drives because we feel we have to work so hard to continue to afford to buy the products that make up this standard (ibid., 139).

Marcuse admits that sexual repression has slackened in part in modern societies. It has been 'desublimated', but mainly in the interests of selling more products to the masses. Sexual energy, Freud's libido, has been concentrated in one part of the body—the genitals—leaving the rest of the body free to act as an instrument of labour (ibid., 44). The relaxed sexual morality of the day winds up plugging into a 'profitable conformity', as sex and romance become products sold by the cultural industries (ibid., 86). Marcuse's vision of a non-repressed future sees human bodies eroticized as a whole, becoming instruments of pleasure in a society where work would be much less important in our lives. This would necessitate a disintegration of certain key institutions, notably the monogamous and patriarchal family (ibid., 184). This is one of Marcuse's more utopian hopes, though it seemed much more of a possibility during the sexual revolution of the late 1960s and 1970s.

One of Marcuse's solutions to the repression of modern industrial society is art:

> Art challenges the prevailing principle of reason: in representing the order of sensuousness, it invokes a tabooed object—the logic of gratification as against that of repression. Behind the sublimated aesthetic form, the unsublimated content shows forth: the commitment of art to the pleasure principle. (Ibid., 168)

Art serves Eros, sexuality. Yet it must struggle against the drive to industrial productivity.

In *Eros and Civilization*, then, Marcuse extends into the consumer age Freud's analysis of modern society as the battlefield between Eros and Thanatos, seeing the struggle today as one between the parallel pleasure and reality principles. As we'll see in the next section, the reality or productivity principle is propped up by the creation of a bevy of false needs that keep us working as hard as our grandparents.

One-Dimensional Man

In the opening chapter of his 1964 book, *One-Dimensional Man*, Marcuse argues that modern industrial society is obsessed with mass production governed by a technological logic, and it keeps its members committed to its goals by creating a distorted consciousness of false needs through new forms of social control. Liberal capitalism trumpets freedom, but the freedoms of modern capitalist societies are phony freedoms. They include: the freedom to choose from among a bevy of unneeded brand-name goods and gadgets; the freedom of a competition among goods sold at artificial prices; the freedom of a variety of press and media outlets that regurgitate the same news and information; the freedom to choose between a bunch of politicians who are all saying more or less the same thing; the freedom to pursue modes of relaxation whose real purpose is to soothe us enough to allow us to return to our stupefying job on Monday morning so that the whole cycle of work and consumption can start all over again (Marcuse, 1964: 7). For Marcuse, all this is extremely wasteful and destructive.

We seem to have a reasonable, smooth, democratic freedom in Western societies. Yet the rights and freedoms of earlier stages of Western societies—critical ideas like freedom of thought, speech, conscience, even free enterprise—are losing their traditional rationale, being squashed by the logic of domination of advanced technological societies. Instead, our advanced economies have become totalitarian—they impose limits on our free time by expanding labour, convincing us to accept the widespread economic-technical co-ordination of our lives by manipulating our sense of what counts as our basic needs.

Our societies may seem open and pluralistic, but our governments actually aid in mobilizing and organizing the scientific and technological productivity of the masses. They help to make our societies *machine* societies (even though this machine productivity is the potential basis for a free society). Real freedom is freedom from the economy, from the daily struggle to make a living.

The same goes for intellectual freedom, which would be freedom from the 'public opinion' created by the mass media, replacing this with individual thought. These freedoms are killed by the implanting of false material and intellectual needs by industrial society (ibid., 4).

Marcuse argues that human needs, beyond the biological level, have always been preconditioned. Thus we can distinguish between our 'true' and our 'false' needs. Our false needs are superimposed on us to repress us, to perpetuate toil, misery, and injustice. These involve us consuming, relaxing, having fun, all in accordance with how everyone else relaxes and has fun, as prescribed by ads. Our true needs are food, clothing, and shelter. Marcuse thinks that the true or false nature of our needs is objective, and that the satisfaction of our vital needs (and thus an end to poverty and toil) is a universally valid moral goal. He's no relativist, and thus even today serves as a viable antidote to postmodern social theory.

Just because we can choose between a wide variety of goods does not mean we are free if we have to work long hours at a job we hate to buy those goods. The free election of our masters does not make us free. The media offer us the false freedom of the same news repeated on a dozen different channels (at least on cable). Further, simply because different classes read the same newspaper or own the same car, this doesn't mean that class has disappeared. In fact, social needs have been transformed into individual needs so effectively that we cannot tell the difference between the mass media as instruments of information and entertainment and as agents of manipulation and indoctrination. We have been colonized.

Even the old alienation that Marx talked about is in decline, buried by commodity fetishism on a mass scale. We are now tied to society through our manufactured needs:

> The people recognize themselves in their commodities; they find their soul in their automobile, hi-fi set, split-level home, kitchen equipment. The very mechanism which ties the individual to this society has changed, and

social control is anchored in the new needs which it has produced. (Ibid., 9)

We have become, as later critical theorists have pointed out, 'commodity people'. We've internalized our social controls so much that the intellectual and emotional refusal to 'go with the flow' is seen as a waste of time, if not neurotic.

Marcuse argues that in theory we have an inner consciousness separate from public opinion and behaviour—a private space where we have 'inner freedom'. Today this private space has been invaded by technological reality and the economy of mass production. The fact that this inner realm has been whittled down makes the individual identify thoroughly with society and the false needs it propagates. This inner realm is the home of critical reason, which depends on the power of negative thinking, saying No to the way things are. Yet it has been polluted by the smog of advertising and other seductive images from the mass media.

Marcuse is skeptical that we have entered a period when ideology is ending—quite the opposite. The new ideology of our day is the process of production itself, with its technological rationality. Our means of communication and transportation, the commodities we consume, and the entertainment and information industries all impose specific ways of thinking upon us. They bind us to their producers, indoctrinating us into a false consciousness of our needs. The goodness of our way of life creates one-dimensional thought and behaviour where ideas that transcend or critique the way things are tend to be repelled or reduced to terms the system can deal with (ibid., 12).

Marcuse sees this one-dimensionality in the domination of an extreme empiricism in the sciences, including psychology and philosophy. All valid knowledge is now seen as based on the senses, on experience; hence, only empirical methods are valid. All ideas are reduced to their operational definitions—how they can be carried out in practice. In both Communist and capitalist countries (remember, the Soviet Union was alive and well in 1964) only operational ideas—ones that fit in with the logic of technological mass production—are taken seriously, despite the fact that these ideologies fight over the question whether public or private enterprise is the best way to organize production.

In other words, the empiricist or operational point of view supports the established universe of discourse and action. We have to transcend empiricism to be able to rationally criticize our society. To accept this empiricism is to accept the logic of technological domination, with its alienation of our true needs into manufactured ones and its repression of what Freud called Eros in favour of the death instinct, symbolized for Marcuse by empty and meaningless work.

Marcuse suggests that the way out of this dilemma is not to satisfy more false needs, but to use modern technology to reduce necessary labour time to the minimum needed to fulfill our vital needs. In this manner work might be moved from what Marx called the realm of necessity to the realm of freedom. This could be accomplished in part through automation (ibid., 16). Unfortunately, it looks like the more technology is perfected, the more the system of production resists the freedoms it might offer us. Our industrial society uses technology and science for greater and greater domination of humanity and nature. Marcuse agrees with Marx that before human freedom is realized, the technical means of production must be advanced and labour made productive. But Marcuse thinks that this has largely already happened in the century between himself and Marx.

Technological rationality dominates industrial societies today. Our minds and our bodies are slaves to its logic. It integrates all authentic opposition. In the age of Microsoft's dream of a world communications network running whatever version of Windows happens to be the cutting edge that year, we can certainly appreciate as much today as many did in the 1960s Marcuse's point that our society is run by a technological rationality. Yet can we ever escape that rationality into a realm of freedom? A difficult question to be sure.

Later in *One-Dimensional Man*, Marcuse argues that high culture, especially art, was traditionally part of a 'Great Refusal' of the status quo, part of a refusal to behave. It transcended everyday experience. Now this Great Refusal has been absorbed by our technological society, by social reality. Images from high culture become TV commercials used to comfort and excite us, to sell us things.

Marcuse even had an answer for those who pointed out that in modern culture we can more freely express our sexuality and have therefore escaped some of the old repressions. As he already outlined in *Eros and Civilization*, Marcuse sees the freer sexuality of the modern age as part of a 'repressive desublimation'. Now sexuality is channelled by mechanisms of social control into 'socially constructive forms' (ibid., 72). He argues that traditional societies had wider universes of erotic pleasures—their members derived pleasure from handicrafts, from making and eating homemade bread, and from direct contact with wild nature. Now our erotic experience has been reduced to sexual satisfaction, images of which bombard us in ads, television shows, and films.

Sex has been desublimated. But in the process it becomes a new form of social control, a new way of hooking us into the system of production and consumption. Marcuse compares making love in the backseat of a car with making love in a meadow: in the latter the natural environment invites us to participate in it erotically, while the mechanical nature of the former blocks this participation, separating the sex act from its environment (ibid., 73). He criticizes modern literature along the same lines. Classical literature shows us a sublimated, hidden, taboo sexuality. In this context, sex was still exciting. Sex in modern literature is more explicit, more daring, more immoral, and therefore harmless. Now that Eros is out in the open, sexuality has become 'a vehicle for the bestsellers of oppression' (ibid., 77). Sex has been re-engineered by consumerism to keep its workers happy at home and to sell them products at the shopping mall.

SOME CRITICISMS OF THE FRANKFURT SCHOOL

The Frankfurt School is open to a number of serious criticisms (see, e.g., Strinati, 1995: 74–81). Among these, five stand out.

(1) As noted earlier, Adorno and Horkheimer's critique of the culture industry is from the point of view of elite intellectuals who lack sufficient sympathy for the cultural plight of the average working person. Not everyone prefers Beethoven to rock or pop music, and it's unfair to criticize the tastes of ordinary people with such stringent standards.

(2) Popular culture doesn't really buttress social conformity and stabilize capitalism as much as the Frankfurt School thinks—after all, capitalist countries have had strong movements of discontent, some of it tied to pop culture itself.

(3) Adorno attacked popular culture as banal and standardized, yet much of elite and folk culture is also standardized. People like standardization, but mixed in with an element of surprise. In reality, popular music, cinema, and television are mixtures of new ideas and standard themes.

(4) Audiences are partly critical and discriminating. They aren't all cultural dopes who will buy any old trash (though the choices of products they *can* choose between are largely decided by the culture industry).

(5) Marcuse's distinction between true and false needs is tricky. Do we have a true need for freedom, autonomy, or a classless society? If everyone stopped watching TV, would they do anything useful? Aren't all needs historically conditioned—so maybe having a TV has become a 'true' need, just as a wig was a true need for an eighteenth-century gentleman?

These are telling criticisms. Nonetheless, the Frankfurt School's original critique of modern industrial society is a striking one and looms large in modern social theory. We now turn to an American theorist, Christopher Lasch, who picked up the baton of their critical spirit and carried it past the turbulent 1960s to the end of the century.

CHRISTOPHER LASCH ON THE CULTURE OF NARCISSISM

Christopher Lasch (1932–94) was a unique figure in American social theory. He was neither a functionalist, nor a symbolic interactionist, nor a postmodernist, and thus stood outside the major trends in American theory in the last century. His major works include *The Minimal Self* (1985), *The True and Only Heaven* (1991), and *The Revolt of the Elites* (1994). Yet his most read work is *The Culture of Narcissism: American Life in an Age of Diminishing Expectations* (1978), in which he attacked the American culture of the post-war period as a whole. He is considered by some as a backward-looking conservative, given his nostalgia for religion and for earlier forms of family life, by others as a Marxist critic of consumer society. However one reads him, Lasch can definitely be loosely categorized as a comrade-in-arms of the Frankfurt School, given his free use of economic analysis tied to psychoanalysis, and thus his evocation of both Marx and Freud.

The Culture of Narcissism

Lasch begins *The Culture of Narcissism* by suggesting that American liberalism is bankrupt, partly because there has been a collapse of the historical faith that formerly surrounded public events with an aura of moral dignity and patriotism. He sees the American bourgeoisie as in crisis. Capitalism and modern bureaucracy have undermined the tradition of local action, 'the revival and extension of which holds out the only hope that a decent society will emerge from the wreckage of capitalism' (Lasch, 1978: xv). To Lasch, we no longer do anything for ourselves, but have our entire lives managed by forces outside of our control. His book describes the dying culture of competitive individualism where a Hobbesian war of each against all leads from the pursuit of happiness to the dead end of a narcissistic preoccupation with the self (ibid., xvii). He sees us as having moved from a historical to a therapeutic culture, one that depends on the constant intervention of specialists into our personal lives (e.g., psychiatrists, marriage counsellors, social workers, New Age teachers).

Lasch means by narcissism the same thing as Freud did. A narcissist is someone who is in love with him(her)self, who, like the Narcissus of Greek legend, loves to look at his or her own reflection in a pool of water, or in modern terms a mirror and other people's eyes. Freud defined narcissism as when the ego (the conscious part of the mind) takes itself as a love object, when a person lavishes on his or her own body caresses usually reserved for another person. Lasch sees narcissism as a very general social phenomenon. The narcissist seeks an immediate gratification and 'lives in a state of restless, perpetually unsatisfied desire' (ibid., xvi). Economic man—the devotee of the Protestant ethic—has given way to psychological man, the final product of bourgeois individualism, haunted by anxiety, seeking meaning in life, yet finding this meaning all too elusive.

Many radical movements have drawn their strength from imagined or real golden ages (for example, the Diggers and Levellers in the English Civil War, or the Jacobins during the French Revolution). The past is a political and psychological treasury from which we draw indispensable psychic reserves of loving memories to help us cope with the future, but when we lose this past we lose these valuable memories. Our culture's indifference to the past comes from a narcissistic impoverishment of the psyche, of our inner life. The denial of the past by the culture of narcissism embodies the despair of a society that cannot face the future. Nostalgia has become a commodity, and we learn our history from Hollywood films.

Lasch argues that the pathological narcissism found in the character disorders of individual patients tells us something about narcissism as a social phenomenon. In other words, if the fringe of our society is haunted by severe narcissism, then we can guess that our whole society is to a lesser though significant degree narcissistic. Lasch lists the psychological traits of the narcissist, a list echoing in the *Diagnostic and Statistical Manual of Mental Disorders*. He or she:

- is protectively shallow;
- charming, but lacking in curiosity about others;
- lacking in real intellectual engagement with the world;
- has a ravenous need for admiration and for emotional experiences with which to fill an inner void and to fight feelings of emptiness and inauthenticity;

- has little capacity for sublimation or sustained work and is parasitically dependent on infusions of admiration from others;
- is sexually promiscuous;
- is chronically bored and in search of instant intimacy (ibid., 39–40).

Lasch sees the narcissist's fear of dependence and manipulative and exploitive approach to personal relations as bland and superficial. His or her perfect relationship would be two months, and then it is time to move on to greener pastures. The narcissist cannot afford to invest his or her love objects with too much emotion—significant emotional commitments are out of the question.

Aging holds a special terror for the narcissist, who lacks the usual defences against the fear of growing old. As youth, celebrity, and charm fade, there's little left to prop up a fading ego. Lasch connects this to the fact that the narcissist cannot sublimate or re-channel erotic energy into non-sexual activities or thoughts, such as work, family, or religion.

The Propaganda of Commodities

In *The Culture of Narcissism*, Lasch claims that consumer capitalism—the economic system in place at least since the 1950s, which emphasizes the mass production of consumer goods—has significantly altered how we live our everyday lives. The modern manufacturer must educate the masses in the culture of consumption because the mass production of commodities demands a mass market to absorb them. Advertising now manufactures a product of its own:

> the consumer [is] perpetually unsatisfied, restless, anxious, bored. Advertising serves not so much to advertise products as to promote consumption as a way of life. It 'educates' the masses into an unappeasable appetite not only for goods but for new experiences and personal fulfilment. (Ibid., 72)

The propaganda of commodities, the name Lasch gives to mass market advertising, does two things: (1) it upholds consumption as an alternative to rebellion; (2) it proposes consumption as a cure to spiritual desolation and alienation (ibid., 73). Thus advertising tells us that our feelings of rebellion or alienation can be drugged into submission by more and more consumption, but it winds up making consumers increasingly alienated, wanting to consume more and more. That's the whole point of advertising: after all, happy consumers don't want to buy more products.

The mass production of luxury items extends aristocratic habits to the masses: it attacks ideologies based on postponement of gratification, allying itself to the sexual revolution, women, and the young. Women and children emancipated from patriarchal authority fall prey to the new paternalism of the corporation and advertising. Lasch's keen analysis of the youth culture of the 1960s and 1970s shows how corporations learned to give up their old inhibitions and target young people with massive advertising, a trend that dominates most of the brand-conscious consumer market today.

Now truth is replaced by credibility in advertising and politics. In political propaganda and advertising, objectivity is not as important as whether the information 'sounds true', i.e., is credible. Lasch refers to Richard Nixon's many distortions of the truth during the Vietnam War and Watergate scandal. More recently, we can think of Bill Clinton's grammatical quibbles over what his claim that 'I did not have sexual relations with that woman, Miss Lewinsky' meant during the 1998 Monica Lewinsky scandal, and George W. Bush's deception of the public concerning the weapons of mass destruction supposedly held by Saddam Hussein prior to the invasion of Iraq in 2003. Both claims sounded credible to the public and a substantial portion of the media, yet both were lies.

The Theatre of Everyday Life

Lasch sees everyday life in our culture of narcissism as like a theatre. He uses the Canadian Erving Goffman's idea of the dramaturgical self, as found in Goffman's *The Presentation of Self in Every-*

day Life, to illustrate this. We perform in this theatre, and we suffer from an escalating cycle of self-consciousness. Goffman says that we must engage in a 'bureaucratization of the spirit' to make all our actions conform to some preconceived model of our selves. To the performing self, reality is constructed out of materials from advertising, film, and popular fiction, all of them torn from a vast range of cultural traditions understood as a series of present-tense events. Lasch echoes Fredric Jameson in this regard (see Chapter 9).

We live surrounded by mirrors (both real and virtual), looking in them for approval and blemishes. Advertising sees the creation of the self as the highest form of creativity, yet creates a society that is imprisoned in self-awareness. Modern man seeks the lost innocence of spontaneity, but cannot find it due to this gnawing anxiety that he is missing something, a something that consumer products can fleetingly give him.

Consumer society and the theatre of everyday life create a sense of ironic detachment as an escape from the dull, routine nature of everyday life (ibid., 94). Anxious self-scrutiny establishes ironic distance from the deadly routine of daily life as the norm. Cynical detachment results from doing jobs below one's ability, and leisure becomes more and more like work. These are meant as antidotes to the boredom and despair of everyday life. We can see this in the case of the donut shop or burger joint employees who cynically do the job without seeing themselves as part of the 'company'. A decade and half after Lasch's book appeared, we saw this mindset celebrated even more strongly in the stereotypical picture of the Generation X slacker as presented in Douglas Coupland's novels and parodied on television shows like *The Simpsons*: the cynical knowingness, the lack of engagement with art, work, and love objects, the sense of not having a worthwhile future. When rock star Kurt Cobain committed suicide in 1994, he could have left behind a few pages from this chapter of Lasch's book as his suicide note (ironically, the celebrator and critic of narcissism both died in the same year).

The mass culture of romantic escape, by filling our heads with visions of experience beyond most of our means, further devalues routine. The romance/reality split leads to an ironic detachment that cripples the will to social change, to restore meaning and reality to everyday life (ibid., 96). We can see this in the ceaseless urge to travel, in soap opera fanatics, in beauty magazine readers, in entertainment shows about celebrities' love affairs, and in the crowds of strangers who wept for Lady Diana's death.

Distancing oneself from the world and others around us becomes a routine in itself. An escalating cycle of self-consciousness inhibits spontaneous action and makes people resent more and more what for most of them are the meaningless roles prescribed by modern industry. In a society without illusions, the ultimate illusions of art and religion have *no future*, to paraphrase the Sex Pistols.

Education as Commodity

Lasch thinks that the democratization of education has failed to improve the popular understanding of society, to raise the quality of popular culture, or to reduce the gap between wealth and poverty. Yet it has contributed to the decline of critical thought and the erosion of intellectual standards. With the rise of the multiversity, the university that attempts to cater to all tastes, the decision to combine professional and liberal education in the same institution made the faculty incapable of addressing larger issues of academic policy. Administrative bureaucracies grew up to manage the sprawling complex of institutions that contain within their ivy walls graduate schools, professional and vocational schools, academic institutes, semi-pro athletics, hospitals, real estate operations, and innumerable other enterprises:

> Under these conditions, the university remains a diffuse, shapeless, and permissive institution that has absorbed the major currents of cultural modernism and reduced them to a watery blend, a mind-emptying ideology of cultural revolution, personal fulfilment, and creative alienation. (Ibid., 151)

Although the university has become less of a breeding ground for cultural revolution of late, the themes of personal fulfillment and creative alienation are as strong as ever.

For Lasch, the university has boiled down all experience to courses of study, 'a culinary image appropriate to the underlying ideal of enlightened consumption', like menus of knowledge (ibid., 153). More controversially, Lasch feels that higher education destroys the students' minds and incapacitates them emotionally, making them unable to confront experience without texts, without pre-digested points of view, leaving them unable to perform the simplest task—making a meal, going to a party, or jumping into bed with someone—without elaborate academic instruction. Perhaps he exaggerates on this point.

The Sex War

In *The Culture of Narcissism* Lasch also deals with the sociopsychology of the sex war, which he feels has trivialized personal relations. The motto today is to do what you want as long as no one else gets hurt. Lasch argues, with some merit, that Americans now invest personal relationships with overweening importance. Sex is free from procreation thanks to the birth control pill, allowing erotic life to be valued for its own sake. There is a growing determination to live for the moment, yet the cult of intimacy conceals a growing despair of finding it (ibid., 187–8). Lasch sees personal relations as crumbling under the great emotional weight that they're burdened with now that religion, family, and education have been devalued by our culture.

If we look at the social history of the battle of the sexes, we can see a recent intensification of sexual combat as modern feminists demanded social, economic, and political equality for women. This intensification has accompanied the transformation of capitalism into a managerial, corporate, and bureaucratic system. The sex war has been accelerated by at least five specific causes:

- the collapse of chivalry;
- the liberation of sex from moral or religious constraints;
- the pursuit of sex as an end in itself;
- the emotional overloading of personal relations;
- the irrational male response to the liberated woman (ibid., 189–91).

In the 'good old days', the tradition of gallantry masked and mitigated the oppression of women. Men saw themselves as the protectors of women, of the so-called 'weaker sex', saving them from unlimited, forceful exploitation by men in a patriarchal society (ibid., 190). But women connected men's sentimental exaltation of the 'fairer sex' to its oppression, rejecting the pedestal of male adoration and demanding a demystification of female sexuality. Democracy and feminism stripped the veil of courtly convention, revealing the contradictions under the feminine mystique, making friendship and love more difficult. Without the mystique of female sexuality, men no longer put women on emotional pedestals, no longer see them as special. Now women are compelled to share both the burdens and the benefits of liberation, whether they like it or not. Lasch summarizes this by saying that men no longer treat women as ladies (ibid., 191).

Thanks to the sexual revolution, there is now a desublimation of sexuality. Its aura and mystery are gone. Contraceptives, abortion, and the weakened links between sex, love, marriage, and procreation all contribute to this. Sexual pleasure is pursued as an end in itself, unmediated by romance. Lasch feels that sex valued for its own sake brings no hope of permanent relations (ibid.). Lovers give up the right to be jealous or to insist on fidelity as a condition of erotic union. Easygoing promiscuity has become the norm. As they used to say in the 1960s, everybody does their own thing (though the AIDS crisis of the 1980s dampened some people's enthusiasm about their things).

Now that the veil of secrecy has been lifted from female sexuality, men fear women's greater sexual response. Without the old sexual reserve, sexual performance and its measurement are exploited by women in the sex war. As both sexologists and feminists point out, women can have an almost unlimited number of consecutive orgasms.

The pseudo-liberated woman of *Cosmopolitan* exploits sex in a calculating way because she avoids emotional entanglements. Have a look at any recent cover of the magazine to see that this is still true today—witness the many articles on how to get, keep, and control men, to use sex as a weapon, or on how to have an endless series of orgasms.

Let's pause in our account of *The Culture of Narcissism* to offer a counterpoint to Lasch. Freud said that one of the great prices we pay in moving from barbarian societies to civilized ones is the repression of our sexual and aggressive drives, that it's easy for a barbarian to be happy but much harder for a civilized person. He thought that repression allowed social peace and the sublimation of our basic drives into work, art, and science. Perhaps the liberation of sex from love, procreation, and marriage is a liberation of our natural sexual drives from the constraints of culture. After all, aren't sexual feelings natural? Isn't our sexual attraction to other human beings a healthy thing? On this point Marcuse and Lasch part company.

Lasch argues that in manipulating others and avoiding emotional injury, both sexes now cultivate a protective shallowness and cynical detachment, which become habitual and embitter personal relations. After the degradation of work and communal life, people turn to sex to satisfy emotional needs. There was an easygoing contempt for the other sex in folk wisdom; but feminism and the ideology of intimacy now bring sexual antagonism to the level of all-out warfare. There is an acceptance of sexual friction only in the working-class now. This has become even truer in 1990s and beyond thanks to the hypersensitivity of the 'political correctness' movement, with its attempt to purge all humour from comments about the sexes (or at least from men commenting on women). We can see this clearly in university life, where many people willingly censor themselves on sexual matters and gender differences.

Lasch is critical not only of consumer capitalism, but also of the radical feminism that dominated public discourse in the 1970s and later. The cult of companionship and feminism make new demands on men, who are hated when they fail. Younger women want sex, compassion, and intelligent understanding, but they are disappointed by men not being able to provide all three at the same time (ibid., 196). Men cannot meet the erotic needs of women under the present sexual arrangements, yet feminism itself gives these demands the strongest ideological support. Feminists say that men oppress women, yet they urge women to approach men as friends and lovers. This is a contradiction (ibid., 198). If men aren't the oppressors, who is?

Capitalism, Consumers, and Communities of Competence

Lasch argues that we face a new type of capitalism today, one that Marx didn't foresee. The therapeutic elite of doctors, psychiatrists, social workers, and so on, which has replaced the nineteenth-century utilitarian elite, serves not only their own professional class interests but also those of monopoly capitalism as a whole. Modern capitalism tries to create new demands and new discontents 'that can be assuaged only by the consumption of commodities. . . . The same historical development that turned the citizen into a client transformed the worker into a consumer' (ibid., 234–5). As we shall see in the final chapter, this relates to John Ralston Saul's idea that our society tries to turn the democratic citizen into a 'client' for government social services on the model of clients of corporate services. Thus we 'consume' government services just like we consume Big Macs, hopefully with a smile on our faces.

Lasch sees the growth of management and the proliferation of the professions as representing new forms of capitalist control, spreading out from the factory: the 'struggle against bureaucracy therefore requires a struggle against capitalism' (ibid., 235). Ordinary citizens must try to control production and the technical knowledge on which modern production rests, to take solutions to problems into their own hands—they have to create what he calls 'communities of competence'. 'Only then will the productive capacities of modern capitalism, together with the scientific knowledge that now serves it, come to serve the interests of humanity instead' (ibid.).

Lasch concludes that in a dying culture, narcissism appears to embody—in terms of such things as 'personal growth' and 'self-awareness'—the highest attainment of spiritual enlightenment. Obviously, this is hardly a very enlightened state. His critique of the general structure of modern capitalist culture along psychoanalytic lines aligns him with Adorno, Marcuse, and other Frankfurt School critical theorists, whatever differences they might have over the details of his critique.

JÜRGEN HABERMAS ON CAPITALISM AND COMMUNICATIVE ACTION

Jürgen Habermas (1929–) studied philosophy at the universities of Göttingen and Bonn, and mixes his sociology with a hefty dose of philosophical analysis. He worked under Adorno at the University of Frankfurt in the late 1950s, left at a young age for a professorship at Heidelberg in 1961, and then returned to Frankfurt in 1964. He became director of the Max Planck Institute near Munich in 1971 and then returned to Frankfurt once more in 1983. He is a prolific writer, and far too complex to deal with in detail here. He offers no grand vision or critique as do the earlier critical theorists, and due to its difficulty and obscurity his work is read for the most part only in academic circles. We'll take a look here at a few snapshots of his more important ideas as they apply to modern capitalism and critical theory.

Capitalism and Legitimation

Habermas was influenced mainly by Marx and the Frankfurt School, but he also took Max Weber's analysis of modern rationality as the key to capitalism seriously and was influenced by Talcott Parsons's systems theory and the analytic philosophy of John Austin and John Searle, with its focus on the analysis of speech acts. Habermas saw himself as updating Marx's historical materialism for the modern age and at the same time trying to find a way out of Max Weber's 'iron cage of rationality'. Like the earlier Frankfurt School theorists, he saw no proletarian revolution on the horizon in advanced capitalist societies. Although modern capitalism still produces a class society, class conflict no longer drives it. Instead, capital and labour have reached a compromise by means of the welfare state, which regulates both the marketplace and the nature of work through laws enforcing a minimum wage, allowing collective bargaining, and prohibiting dangerous workplaces, child labour, and excessive industrial pollution.

In *Legitimation Crisis* (1975) and *Communication and the Evolution of Society* (1979), Habermas reworks Marx's philosophy of history based on his interest in communication as the foundation of social order. Oddly, the nature of legitimacy in each of his three main stages of history, as shown in Table 4.1, roughly parallels Auguste Comte's account of the intellectual development of civilization.

Primitive societies rely on myths to understand their world. Traditional societies translated myths into organized systems of religion, for example, Greek paganism and Christian monotheism, to legitimate themselves. But modern societies rely on market exchanges as the basis of their legitimacy. As Weber pointed out, these exchanges are most successful where they're organized in terms

Table 4.1 Habermas's Stages of History

Type of Society	Basis of Communication and Legitimacy	Historical Period
1. Primitive	Mythology	Tribal societies
2. Traditional	Religion and metaphysics	Ancient and feudal societies
3. Modern	Rationality (the market)	Capitalism
a. Liberal capitalist		Nineteenth-century capitalism
b. Organized capitalist		Welfare-state capitalism
c. Post-capitalist		State socialism (e.g., USSR)

of instrumental rationality, which is based on economic efficiency—the cheapest and quickest means are chosen to achieve a specific goal.

Twentieth-century capitalism is distinct from the liberal capitalism of the nineteenth century due both to the dominance of huge multinational corporations and to the increased level of government control of the economy. Habermas calls twentieth-century capitalism 'organized' capitalism. Labour unions and pro-labour parties have won concessions from capitalist interests in terms of higher wages and government-sponsored welfare schemes such as unemployment insurance. In addition, governments directly invest in education, infrastructure (e.g., roads, public transit systems, electricity transmission, telecommunications), and resource management, along with regulating markets and currency exchanges with both laws and national banks. Lastly, Habermas called the state-socialist regimes of Eastern Europe and the Soviet Union 'post-capitalist' rather than socialist because he was dubious they represented an entirely new stage of history—after all, they still emphasized productivity and rationality, just like their capitalist cousins.

Capitalist societies believe that market exchanges are just. Like Weber, Habermas saw the essence of capitalism as instrumental rationality. Under organized capitalism, governments become the managers of healthy economies. Since they take a technocratic and practical approach to managing the affairs of state, Habermas says that this can lead to a legitimation crisis when they fail in their role as economic managers if the economy suffers a downturn. Once traditional loyalties have disappeared, it is hard to feel any loyalty to the state as a group of incompetent money managers. Habermas echoes here Marx's comment that once feudal bonds are dissolved by the callous cash nexus of capitalism, 'all that's solid melts into air': notions of loyalty and honour as the basis for legitimating the state are replaced by a simple desire for cold cash. Habermas argues that a second crisis, a crisis of motivation, arises in organized capitalist societies. Once the Protestant work ethic is dead and the worker has the welfare state to rely on when unemployed, why work hard?

Unlike Marx, Habermas does not think that there is only one way of understanding social life. In his earlier work, *Knowledge and Human Interests* (1972), he argues that there are three distinct aspects of human society, each with certain 'knowledge constitutive interests' and certain intellectual disciplines associated with them:

- *Labour* (material production and interchanges with nature). The interest here is prediction and control, and the most relevant disciplines are the empirical sciences.
- *Symbolic interaction.* The interest here is the understanding of people's meanings. The most relevant disciplines are hermeneutical ones like history and sociology.
- *Power/domination.* Here the knowledge-constitutive interest is emancipation (i.e., freedom from domination), which is accomplished through critical theory (Giddens, 1985: 127).

Habermas also believed that critical theory operates at three distinct levels: the socialization of the individual, the way culture transmits knowledge, and the social system's ability to socially integrate its members. Interestingly, these parallel three of Parsons's four types of systems: the personality, cultural, and social systems.

Communicative Action

Habermas is best known for his theory of communicative action, which he lays out in a massive two-volume study on the subject (1984 and 1988) and in earlier works such as *Communication and the Evolution of Society* (1979). In the latter work he argues that there are universal conditions for the possibility of understanding each other, and these are grounded in an 'ideal speech situation' where communication is clear and undistorted. Such a situation is one where people can communicate openly in an uncoerced, free, and equal way, using sound arguments and evidence to convince one another.

Habermas (1979: 1–2) argues that all speech acts have a basic telos or goal: mutual understanding. Dialogue is the key to this mutual understanding, and thus to rational communication. For us to understand one another in a rational way, a communicative or speech act must fulfill four requirements. It must be:

1. Intelligible: we can understand what is being said.
2. True: it corresponds with some fact or other set of valid ideas.
3. Sincere or truthful: the speaker really means what he or she says.
4. Justified: the speaker speaks with some authority or within a situation grounded on well-established norms (Giddens, 1985: 128; Habermas, 1979: 2–3).

Thus, if I say, 'Your essays are due next Tuesday', my proposition is clear and meaningful to others if the class understands my words, if it corresponds to what the course outline says is the real due date, if I'm being serious and not making a joke, and if I am indeed the instructor in the class and have the right to make this pronouncement. If I wandered into a geography class and made a similar pronouncement, it would fulfill the first condition, perhaps the second and third, but not the fourth since I'm not a geography professor and thus would not be justified to give the class a due date (leaving aside the fact that it may not be true or sincere).

Habermas hoped that the proliferation of ideal speech situations would lead to freer, more open societies. The revolution in organized capitalist societies would not come from class warfare but communicative action. Yet an old-style Marxist would offer an obvious criticism of Habermas on this point: the problem is not so much our lack of freedom to communicate, but instead the very social and economic structures that block this freedom in the first place. If I can't speak freely in my institution, the nature of the institution is at fault, not the speech situation. In other words, Habermas places too much emphasis on language and not enough on concrete social and economic hierarchies that block human freedom.

In any case, Habermas sees communicative action as the process where all social actors interact and socialize with each other. This leads him to distinguish the sort of communicative rationality outlined above from the instrumental rationality that Weber saw as the iron cage of modernity. Instrumental or 'strategic' rationality is based on the idea of trying to use the best means to achieve a given end. We can see it embodied in the notion of economic efficiency. Habermas sees communicative rationality as a way out of Weber's iron cage since it is not locked into a given purpose or goal, nor is it grounded in the nature of the universe (like the rationality of such early thinkers as Plato and St Thomas Aquinas). Instead, it seeks only mutual understanding, and is thus freer from material self-interests.

Habermas borrowed the notion of the 'lifeworld' from Edmund Husserl (1859–1938), a pioneering German phenomenologist. 'Lifeworld' is yet another in a long train of fuzzy concepts in the history of German philosophy, but it means basically the background psychological and intellectual tone of a person's life, including the largely unconscious moral and metaphysical assumptions that guide this life. Habermas thought that all our lifeworlds are rationalized by modern capitalism. Our modern social system operates according to instrumental rationality, based on the model of the market. But our lifeworld is also based in communicative rationality, since we attempt to mutually understand one another. Under capitalism the system and our lifeworld are uncoupled as our lives become more and more rationalized, and people interact in the marketplace without sharing meanings or inhabiting the same lifeworld (Wallace and Wolf, 1999: 176). The logic of the social system supplants that of the lifeworld, which is grounded only in part on instrumental rationality. On this point Habermas seems to be pointing towards Marx's notion of alienation, where workers become estranged from their labour, what they make, one another, and nature itself. Today we are alienated from our communicative rationality by the instrumental (goal-oriented) reason of the market.

Undistorted communication is the key to human liberation for Habermas. He hopes that we can come to understand one another's lifeworlds and thus pierce the veil of instrumental reason, just as Weber hoped the social theorist could understand other social actors' subjective meanings. Habermas compares this process to that of a psychoanalyst who tries to strip away a patient's repressions to achieve an understanding of the individual's neurosis. In this sense Habermas sees critical theory as more concerned with therapy than with social and political change.

We end with a criticism of Habermas's theory of communicative action. What if our economic or political interests conflict—can't we have undistorted and well-grounded communication where we still disagree? For example, two candidates apply for a job. One is young and inexperienced, the other older and more experienced. The young person argues that her youthful enthusiasm will serve her well in the position, while the older fellow argues that his experience better qualifies him for the job. How can rational communication settle this sort of debate, where there is a fundamental conflict of interest and sound arguments on either side? There is no obvious answer.

We now take a sharp left turn away from the critical theory of the Frankfurt School to a related though distinct form of critical theory born and reared in France, Situationism.

SITUATIONISM

What Is Situationism?

Situationism is an important but often overlooked movement in critical theory centred in France in the 1950s and 1960s that acted as a non-academic parallel to the work of the Frankfurt School. The Situationist International (SI) was formed in 1957 when two avant-garde artistic groups, Guy Debord's Lettrist International and Asger Jorn's International Movement for Imaginist Bauhaus, merged. Debord was the spiritual centre of the SI until it broke up in 1972 after many internal squabbles. The Situationists published the journal *L'Internationale Situationniste* between 1958 and 1969, using it as a forum for their critique of modern culture. At first they tended to promote various strange artistic events, but in the 1960s the Situationist International become more political in tone.

Their moments of glory came in 1967 and 1968. In 1967, Guy Debord published his important short book, *The Society of the Spectacle*. His comrade, Raoul Vaneigem, published the more poetically phrased *The Revolution of Everyday Life* the same year. In May 1968 students and workers in Paris revolted against the Gaullist regime. The Situationists were at the centre of the rebellion, with their slogans scrawled on Paris walls. This political agitation, along with their theoretical works, influenced not only such French theorists as Jean Baudrillard, but the pioneers of punk rock, such as Malcolm McLaren and the Sex Pistols and, more broadly, the worlds of avant-garde art, music, and advertising from the 1980s on.

Situationism is a mixture of Dadaism, surrealism, anarchism, Marxism, and existentialism. Dada was an early twentieth-century artistic movement that wanted to shock the art world by writing nonsense poems, gluing together pieces of wood, train tickets, and other debris into collages, and holding events that turned into riots. The Situationists were sympathetic to the Dadaist idea of a 'happening', an event deliberately planned to shock our complacent view of art. A good example of such a happening was Yves Klein's 1960 Monotone Symphony, when 10 musicians gathered in a museum played a single note as nude women covered in blue paint rolled their bodies against blank canvases mounted on the wall. Klein finished the performance with the remark 'the myth is in the art.'

Their debt to surrealism could be seen in their concept of art. They took a piece of art or some element of popular culture and diverted it from its original meaning, just as Salvador Dali mocked the pretensions of high art with both his persona and his pictures of melting clocks and burning giraffes. Unlike the postmodernists, who ironically quote past art forms, the Situationists wanted to subvert art and culture as part of a political program to undermine that culture. We see this in the punk style of the late 1970s in Britain and North America—the use and abuse of the swastika, the safety pin, ransom note typography, and pictures and text cut-and-pasted from one source to another, a technique pioneered in punk 'zines and borrowed by the contemporary magazine *Adbusters*. The core of the SI-influenced punk style is do-it-yourself (DIY), the making of things by hand, as opposed to the mass production of slickly engineered commodities.

The Situationists were also deeply sympathetic to Marxism, especially the work of the young Marx, who emphasized the alienation created by capitalist societies. Marx argued that capitalism alienates us from our work (since we work for wages), from the objects we make, from human nature (which is to be creative, not to engage in mindlessly repetitive work), and from other people (since we compete against them). The SI argued that boredom, passivity, isolation, and alienation were at the core of everyday life in consumer society, but in a way Marx didn't entirely envisage.

They also took Marx's idea of commodity fetishism seriously—the idea that capitalism turns useful things into commodities for sale in the marketplace that become like religious icons or fetishes to which we ascribe an almost religious status. Instead of seeing commodities as merely useful tools, we turn them into fetishes into which we pour our spirituality. Relationships between people become relationships between things. Related to this is the Marxist idea of reification, turning real structures and relations into abstract ideals. For the Situationists, consumerism reifies our relations to work, leisure, commodities, and the marketplace, freezing them in place like immovable blocks of ice.

They borrowed the idea of the need to live an authentic existence from the existentialists. Sartre thought that we shouldn't live in bad faith, by which he meant allowing our physical situation and other people to control our lives and then blaming them for our lack of freedom and our unhappiness or immoral acts. We are always free,

he said, even when we feel constrained by material forces. The key to an authentic life was to realize this freedom in action. Consumer society attempts to compel us to flee our authenticity into a circus of false needs.

The basic historical fact that the Situationists faced in the mid-1950s was the shift in Western societies from a society of production, which attempts to plug up holes in the dike of scarcity by increases in industrial output, to a society of consumption, where the chief problem is unloading goods that the masses don't really need. Debord, in *The Society of the Spectacle*, argued that the first phase in the domination of the economy over social life turned 'being' into 'having' (i.e., early capitalism), while now we live in a society where 'having' is sliding into 'appearing' (i.e., consumer capitalism) (Debord, 1967: 17).[9] This hints at the key Situationist concept, the *spectacle*, which is the way the commodity appears under modern capitalism, along with being a way people relate to each other in our society of material abundance and mass-produced consumer goods.

> The commodity used to be a material thing; now it is a spectacular event. The *spectacle* is the commodity that has left its material body on earth and risen to a new ethereal presence. One does not buy objects; one buys images connected to them. One does not buy the utility of goods; one buys the evanescent experience of ownership. Everywhere, one buys the spectacle. (Ball, 1987: 28)

The Situationists were hostile to modern consumer culture, which they felt falsifies our lives, turning them into spectacles full of commodified images and brands. Modern society emphasizes not only conformity to corporate and media control, but also boredom. The Situationists fought boredom as their mortal enemy, seeing it as one head of the hydra of consumerism. On its other heads they saw atomization, alienation, loneliness, and passivity.

Our leisure hours are filled with preprogrammed shows and spectacles. People are trained to become alienated from and bored with past acts of consumption, pushing them to consume more. More deeply, we are trained to equate fun with consumption and feel bored when not being fed some consumer spectacle. The Situationists even criticized vacations as part of a loop of alienation and getting away from it all. These sanity-savers are necessary because our lives are so empty—why get away from it all if your life is so good in the first place? The result is wasted human potential. Ivan Chtcheglov put the Situationist case against contemporary culture poignantly in his 1953 pre-SI essay, 'Formulary for a New Urbanism':

> A mental disease has swept the planet: banalization. Everyone is hypnotized by production and conveniences: by the sewage system, by the elevator, by the bathroom, by the washing machine.
>
> This state of affairs, arising out of a struggle against poverty, has overshot its ultimate goal—the liberation of man from material cares—and become an obsessive image hanging over the present. Presented with the alternative of love or a garbage disposal unit, young people of all countries have chosen the garbage disposal unit. It has become essential to bring about a complete spiritual transformation by bringing to light forgotten desires and by creating entirely new ones. And by carrying out an *intensive propaganda* in favor of these desires. (Chtcheglov, 1953)

The Situationists' solution was to take back the show, to make your own show, to de-commodify our social relations. Chtcheglov hoped that everyone could live in his/her own cathedral where there will be rooms 'more conducive to dreams than any drug, and houses where one cannot help but fall in love'. The SI developed a number of concepts and strategies to help erect this cathedral.

The Situation

The situation is their key concept. They wanted to break through the boredom and alienation of modern life by emphasizing the situation, the event that breaks through consumerist conformity and our addiction to spectacles. In order to overcome boredom and alienation, the Situationists thought they had to construct 'situations' to change everyday life to something made up of endless moments of love, hate, delight, humiliation, and surrender—a sort of anarchic street theatre. By spontaneously creating a situation, you can live your own life, be a little risky and wild, instead of simply acting out the roles prescribed by our society.

And they practised what they preached. One of their most legendary situations was in the 1950s, when the Lettrists gagged and bound a priest at Notre Dame Cathedral, then had one of their members put on the priest's vestments and preach to the congregation on the subject of Nietzsche's idea of the death of God. The Christians attending this Easter Mass chased the pranksters out of the church into the arms of a police officer.

Détournement

This means to divert or turn aside a prefabricated aesthetic construction. The Situationists turned aside cultural objects or ideas into a path other than that which they were intended to follow, thus turning the aesthetic system against itself.

This was the same sort of thing that the Dada artist Marcel Duchamp did earlier when he painted a moustache on a copy of the *Mona Lisa*, and later when the punks cut and pasted letters from newspapers and magazines onto posters and 'zines. The Situationists used *détournement* in films, posters, graphics, and comics. Debord's 1957 book *Mémoires*, illustrated by Asger Jorn, was made up entirely of pirated elements, with pieces of text running off in all directions. It contained comic strips with the cartoon bubbles replaced by Situationist slogans, and was bound in sandpaper to destroy whatever other books were shelved next to it.

Dérive and Psychogeography

To *dérive* is to drift. The Situationists wanted to aimlessly drift around a city, imbibing its psychological atmospheres. Debord laid out his theory of the *dérive* in a 1958 essay printed in the second issue of the SI journal:

> One of the basic situationist practices is the *dérive*, a technique of rapid passage through varied ambiances. *Dérives* involve playful-constructive behaviour and awareness of psychogeographical effects, and are thus quite different from the classic notions of journey or stroll.
>
> In a *dérive* one or more persons during a certain period drop their relations, their work and leisure activities, and all their other usual motives for movement and action, and let themselves be drawn by the attractions of the terrain and the encounters they find there. (Debord, 1958)

The Situationists argued for 'unitary urbanism' where cities could be treated as places where people could drift about in play, seeking to fulfill their desires. This was seen as an affront to mainstream society, as most people walk or drive to 'go somewhere'. Debord mentions that a good *dérive* in the heyday of the SI might involved slipping into houses about to be demolished, hitchhiking non-stop, or sneaking into the parts of the Parisian catacombs prohibited to the public (ibid.).

Psychogeography is the study of the effects of a *dérive*. Some English Situationists actually wandered around London conducting acts of psychogeography, which involved soaking up the emotional and historical connotations of various buildings and giving sensational names like 'the dangerous quarter' or 'the fun quarter' to neighbourhoods. This echoed the urban wanderings of nineteenth-century writers like Thomas de Quincey, Charles Baudelaire, and Charles Dickens. Its point is to reinvigorate everyday life in the urban metropolises where so many of us live. This idea of drifting was tied to the Situationists' desire to avoid going to work or consuming. They rejected the idea that time is money—Guy Debord never had a proper job in his life. One of their mottos was *ne travaillez jamais*—never work. Naturally, they hated shopping malls as destructions of living communities.

The Situationists shared with anarchism a hostile attitude towards authority. They pursued spontaneous moments of truth with the banality of everyday life, seeking the rocky island of an authentic life amid the placid seas of a false life governed by consumer spectacles.

The Society of the Spectacle

The bible of Situationism is undoubtedly Debord's *The Society of the Spectacle*, so it behooves us to look closely at its first three chapters where the core of the Situationist critique of modern culture is outlined. In general Debord argues that we live in a society where real human relationships have been replaced by relationships between commodities. Yet our society manufactures not only commodities, but also dissatisfaction and boredom. Everything that used to be experienced directly has been turned into a spectacular show. Real life is replaced by pre-packaged experiences, immediacy by mediacy, togetherness by separation.

Debord (1967: 1) says that in modern societies life has become an 'immense accumulation of spectacles'. A continuous stream of images from magazines, advertising, television, and film prevents us from living our lives as free and autonomous beings. Yet the society of the spectacle isn't simply a society where images are everywhere; rather, our social relations are dominated by images (ibid., 4). When we talk and act, we think in terms of spectacular images, not creative or authentic pictures we make ourselves.

The spectacle is the affirmation of a life lived in mere appearances, so in this sense it's a negation of life (ibid., 10). To copy the hair of a film star or to buy some new gadget because a TV commercial associates it with coolness or sexiness is to alienate oneself from what one is into someone else's picture of a real or meaningful life. Even modern technology winds up turning into a religious fetish—it separates us inside ourselves, splitting us up into authentic and mediated beings, the former independent and creative, the latter pathetically dependent on pieces of consumer technology (think of the many cellphone addicts around us today). Debord says dramatically that the spectacle is the sun that never sets on the modern empire of passivity (ibid., 13). If you think he's exaggerating, imagine your current life and subtract all TV, all video, all films, all mass-produced music, the Internet, shopping malls, and all other consumer spectacles. What would be left? The agencies of pacification are everywhere.

Debord says the spectacle imprisons society by putting it to sleep (ibid., 21). The spectacle is the guardian of sleep, just like Freud's superego, censoring out feelings that there is anything more to life than consumerism. He agrees with Marshall McLuhan that the mass media are not just neutral tools. They mediate our social needs for us, shaping and defining them (ibid., 24). Our society discourages direct personal communication (ibid., 26). Technology isolates us—TV and cars help to perfect our separation, turning us into (to use David Reisman's term) 'lonely crowds' (ibid., 28). The key to the process is alienation—Debord sees the consumer losing him or herself in images of need projected by the mass media, in the process losing an authentic sense of self (ibid., 30). Interestingly, he uses the same image that Baudrillard would use 15 or so years later in his essay on simulacra: in modern society we more and more lose touch with reality, so that if we see the spectacle as a map that covers the whole world, we believe in the reality of the map more than the territory it covers (ibid., 31). The main task of the society of the spectacle is to manufacture alienation and thus turn us all into endless consumers. It does this by turning capital into a massive series of images (ibid., 34).

Marx saw capitalist commodities as things that are bought and sold. To Debord, the commodity has become a spectacle, and the market spreads these spectacles throughout the world. In the early stages of capitalism, the production of goods was aimed at ensuring people's survival (along with a profit for the capitalist, of course). But now, with the question of physical survival more or less settled, the definition of survival had to be altered to keep pace with the mass production of commodities. New needs had to be stimulated. The notion of 'privation' had to be fattened up. Automation eliminates the amount of human labour that industry must use to produce a given object, so to keep consumers employed and consuming, new jobs had to be created in the service sector. Artificial needs were created to preserve labour as the core commodity in our culture, to keep everyone working busy as bees (ibid., 45). With the endless economic development of modern industrial societies, 'the satisfaction of primary human needs is replaced by an uninterrupted fabrication of pseudo-needs' (ibid., 51). An economy of abundance must spin a web of illusion to keep consumers pinned to these pseudo-needs.

Thanks to this 'second industrial revolution', the masses must put up not only with the alienated labour that Marx described, but with alienated consumption, too (ibid., 42). Capital expands to dominate not only the worker's productive activities but his or her leisure. The spectacle is the Trojan Horse of capital, as the consumer becomes no longer merely a consumer of things but also a consumer of illusions (ibid., 47). The spectacle makes war on use value, turning everything into a commodity, into an exchange value, so that people will identify useful goods with commodities and happiness with economic 'survival', or well-being as it is currently defined (ibid., 44).

Debord describes a global division of labour where the First World dominates the Third not just through economics, but also through the export of shimmering spectacles (ibid., 57). Hollywood conquers as effectively as US military forces, presenting its pseudo-goods to the masses in poorer countries. The society of the spectacle makes life banal and empty, draining the moral repression out of the family and religion. It even encourages rebellion, as long as that rebellion can be commodified, that is, turned into a product, as with youth fashions and the acceptance (after a decade or so) of rock music by capitalism (ibid., 59). It turns rebellion into money. Debord goes on to discuss how the celebrity embodies the banality of life by dramatizing magically the shimmering products that hard work can give us. Celebrities typify different types of personality to make it appear that mass consumption is available to any of us. But underneath slight differences, the stars are all the same—or they wouldn't be stars (ibid., 60, 61).

He agrees with the Frankfurt School that the consumer economy offers 'false choice in spectacular abundance', where a 'struggle of vaporous qualities' stimulates people to be loyal to trivial differences between spectacles in sports, elections, and consumer choices (ibid., 62). An endless series of trivial confrontations is set up—between football teams, liberals and conservatives, Pepsi and Coke, and so on. Debord sees each commodity as justified as part of the whole spectacle of consumer society, even if they compete. We cannot consume the whole, or buy all the cars or computers or clothes offered by the system, so we can only touch fragments of the happiness that commodities bring us (ibid., 65). We can never have the total happiness supposedly offered by the total system.

Commodities now fight it out for our attention—the spectacle is not of arms and men, as it was in Homer's *Iliad,* but of products and their passions (ibid., 66). As commodities change, the world becomes more like one big product. Debord argues that consumers get enjoyment out of commodities purely as commodities, being filled with religious fervour to own them. Waves of enthusiasm for new products are spread with lightning speed by the media. He even thinks that our fetishistic feelings for commodities reach the levels of exaltation found in the ecstasies surrounding religious miracles (ibid., 67).

The pseudo-needs propagated by consumerism, according to Debord, have squashed our genuine needs and desires. Social needs are now artificially defined. This building up of the power of artificiality falsifies our social life (ibid., 68). As each new product comes out, it's celebrated as a 'dazzling shortcut' to total consumption and thus happiness—think of the media-impelled rushes to purchase the latest and hottest video-game machines. But once we've got it home, it soon loses the glamour it was given by the spectacle that made us buy it. We get bored

with the latest video game, glossy black shoes, or computer gadget. They reveal their poverty, and boredom comes flooding back in. But then along comes another product to lure us back into the spectacle (ibid., 69). The fraud of satisfaction is revealed by this feeling of disappointment and the obsolescence with products (ibid., 70). Every new lie of advertising is a sort of admission that all those past sales pitches were also lies: 'Sure, your old brand of jeans are out of style, but buy these and you'll be in style again!' Of course, your new jeans will be out of date soon too.

Thus, Debord sees consumerism as a series of falsifications and lies concerning our basic feelings, values, and social relations. He believes that the society of the spectacle turns us into inauthentic 'commodity people' too easily programmed by the mass media, especially advertising.

The Revolution of Everyday Life

The Situationists aimed to revolutionize everyday life, and Raoul Vaneigem's *The Revolution of Everyday Life* (1967) gives us some ideas about how to accomplish this. Vaneigem's work is more poetic than Debord's tersely worded *The Society of the Spectacle,* though he agrees with the main lines of Debord's critique of consumer society. It is a society where spectacles dominate life. Production and consumption are the drugs of modern society, which has become a dictatorship of consumer goods. As we consume more and more, we're inundated with a waterfall of gadgets, an avalanche of consumer goods. This avalanche turns human beings into consumers of empty, fictitious values, of commodities that provide us with no lasting fulfillment. Vaneigem mocks the worker who sees freedom as sitting in his air-conditioned apartment watching TV: surely this isn't what the radicals of the nineteenth century fought for (Vaneigem, 1967: ch. 7).[10] Yet consumer society contains the seeds of its own destruction in the fact that the consumer can't be allowed satisfaction or he or she would stop consuming. New false needs have to be created on a continuous basis. This impoverishes our lives as authentic experiences, replacing them with things. At the same time, we can't become attached to these things—we consume them and they either disappear or become trivialized. This leads to continual discontent (ibid., ch. 17). Vaneigem identifies the main problem with consumer society in his introduction: he does not want to buy freedom from starvation at the cost of being bored to death. Consumerism, however, does precisely this to keep itself alive—only bored, alienated people feel the need to consume commodities to cheer up their empty lives.

Three concepts are central to Vaneigem's version of the Situationist critique of modern society—survival, sacrifice, and exchange. In feudal society and early capitalism, the struggle for physical survival was serious business, which led to social and political hierarchies being created. Now survival is much easier—it has grown fat (ibid., ch. 11). The very meaning of survival has changed. Capitalism has demystified it. Now survival 'is life reduced to bare essentials, to life's abstract form, to the minimum of activity required to ensure people's participation in production and consumption' (ibid., ch. 17). More simply put, survival is life reduced to what can be consumed, to economics (ibid., ch. 18). We work to survive, we survive by being consumers, and we survive only to consume more and more things. In fact, Vaneigem relates consumption to political and social status by suggesting that our ability to consume cars, alcohol, TV sets, and girlfriends faster and faster indicates one's lofty place in the hierarchy. He echoes the distinction between societies of production and consumption made by the Frankfurt School and Debord. The proletarians of Marx's day sold their labour power to survive, passing their leisure time drinking, arguing, rioting, and making love; but the proletarians of our day sell their labour to consume, and spend their leisure hours hooked into the society of the spectacle, consuming the products of its cultural industries (ibid., ch. 7).

Workers today sacrifice lived time and authentic lives to the imperatives of consumerism. Every aspect of life today is dominated by quantitative measures, time being the mother of all such measures. Our lives are filled with empty, mechanical gestures; we worship the quantitative Eros of speed and novelty and make love against the clock of our busy days (ibid., ch. 10). We sacrifice our authenticity to the reign of things, of commodities. Like Marx, Vaneigem sees capitalism as converting all use values into exchange values: everything is for sale. Yet he argues we should refuse this sacrifice, this exchange of real life for consumption. Human beings are not exchangeable: there is nothing equivalent to the individual living, breathing person (ibid., ch. 12). To sacrifice a human life to meaningless work, to exchange it for mere things, distorts the value of that life.

Vaneigem also picks up on Marx's critique of alienation by recasting it in terms of social roles. We are constantly being caught like dull fish in nets of received ideas, buying willy-nilly prepackaged ideologies so we do not have to think for ourselves. The old natural alienation felt by earlier cultures struggling to survive against droughts, earthquakes, and wild animals becomes social in our culture as we become slaves of class oppression or the psychological manipulation of consumerism. One way social alienation operates is by enforcing roles, which Vaneigem sees as soaking into the individual, being 'the nuclei of alienation embedded in the flesh of everyday experience' (ibid., ch. 14).

In his discussion of roles (ibid., ch. 15), Vaneigem argues that stereotypes act as the models of roles, just as roles model behaviour. We act out the various roles we play in our lives—father, boss, worker, teacher, student, girlfriend, sales clerk—like actors in a play that, vampire-like, sucks the lifeblood out of our spontaneous, authentic selves. These roles are the 'bloodsuckers of the will to live'. Vaneigem echoes Herbert Marcuse's notion of repressive sublimation in saying that the aim of roles is to 'absorb vital energies, to reduce erotic energy by ensuring its permanent sublimation. The less erotic reality there is, the more the sexualized forms appearing in the spectacle' (ibid.). In this Vaneigem proved to be something of a prophet, as sex is used today even more than it was in the 1960s to sell everything from blue jeans to power tools without especially improving our erotic lives one bit.

Roles also determine the rank we have in the society of the spectacle, for by playing a role we can consume some small measure of power. Roles obscure us from our real lives—to play them, we have to sacrifice any sense of self-realization. They are both a threat and a protective shield; they impoverish our experience, but stop us from becoming conscious of this. Vaneigem compares them to a suit of heavy medieval armour that reduces our freedom of movement, but deadens the blows of our enemies. Within this suit we can stay polite, continue consuming, and keep a low profile. He speaks of the 'pathetic sequence of clichés' found in the life of a typical 35-year-old who gets up in the morning, drives to work, pushes papers, comes home at night, kisses his kids, eats dinner in front of the TV, goes to bed, and then repeats the whole process the next day. Our entire society is a series of such preprogrammed roles that stultify any sense of creativity and joy we might feel.

Consumer society develops 'decoding centres' to create profiles of consumers, the better to sell them things. As Lasch also noted a decade later, consumer society needs to alienate people from their desires to keep them consuming and thus penned up in the spectacle. Vaneigem even sees age as a role, as the teenager is turned into a marketing demographic, doomed to premature senility by consumer society. The teen is consumed by inauthenticity, killed by the dead things he or she consumes (ibid., ch. 16). What Vaneigem calls 'survival sickness' (i.e., the false need for commodities and the need to work to earn money to buy them) turns young men into haggard old Fausts, into consumers who sell their lived experience to the devils of capitalism for a few shiny baubles. They become part of the market's trivial glory, exchanging the freedom and subjective wealth of childhood for the society of the spectacle (ibid., ch. 22). Yet despite all this, no one is ever completely swallowed up by roles: we have within us a core of creativity, poetry, and love that cannot be entirely silenced by the society of the spectacle.

For the Situationists the revolution to come can't be just a shuffling of the means of production from one class to another. It must be a revolution of everyday life powered by a subversive love and a refusal of constraints (ibid., ch. 1). 'Revolutionary movements are carnivals in which the individual life celebrates its unification with a regenerated society.' Yet we fear this regeneration, this freedom (ibid., ch. 12). We like our consumer goods, our suburban houses, our visits to the shopping mall. The reconstruction of everyday life requires a struggle against the empty commodity form, that old vampire at the throat of human authenticity. Vaneigem hopes that the boredom of consumerism will breed a rejection of uniformity and an embracing of revolutionary poetry. As we all know, however, the shopping mall has defeated revolutionary poetry, at least for now—whether this is a telling critique of Situationism or simply a historical fact, I leave to the reader's judgement.

Vaneigem sees three forms of repressive power at work in modern society: coercion, seduction, and mediation (ibid., ch. 23). The state coerces us, advertising seduces us, and the mass media mediate our relations to each other. The non-repressive equivalents of these forms of power are self-realization, communication, and participation, the triad of hopeful goals for the revolution of everyday life. To achieve these goals, we must return to the triad of basic human needs that Vaneigem sees as just as vital to life as food and shelter are to survival: the desires to create, to love, and to play. The attempt to realize ourselves requires creativity; to communicate authentically, love; and to participate fully, play. The links to Freud's Pleasure Principle and to Marcuse's vision of a non-repressive culture should be obvious.

In consumer culture, these basic needs are distorted. Our will to self-realization becomes a will to power; our will to communicate becomes dishonesty; and our will to participation is converted into our membership in anonymous, lonely crowds (ibid., ch. 23). Yet all is not lost. Vaneigem argues (far too optimistically as it turned out) that our constantly stimulated creative energy cannot be absorbed fast enough by consumer society. The

Table 4.2 Vaneigem's Triads of Repressive and Free Everyday Life

Repressive Forms of Power Found in Consumer Society	Goals for a Non-Repressive Everyday Life	Methods to Achieve a Non-Repressive Everyday Life
Coercion	Self-realization	Creativity
Seduction	Communication	Love
Mediation	Participation	Play

key to revolutionizing everyday life was to turn loose this creative energy upon the world.

An important weapon in the Situationist arsenal is sensual speech, the sort of silent communication that lovers know all too well (ibid., ch. 11). Vaneigem argues that the revolution to come will emphasize erotic communication, the passion for play found in love, ideas, and the construction of situations. The surest way to the revolution of everyday life involves the 'unchaining of pleasure' by drawing on the passions of everyday life (ibid., ch. 13). Vaneigem lauds the power of an impassioned daydream, of love, of desire, of even a rush of sympathy for another. Spontaneity is the stuff of these impassioned daydreams, leading to play, which will transform roles from straitjackets to roads to freedom (ibid., ch. 15). To take these roads, Vaneigem argues that we must turn from alienated to immediate experience, from analysis to life itself (including away from his own book). More concretely, we must follow the path suggested in different ways by Freud, Marcuse, and the surrealists and reconstruct the unconscious, which he hoped would simultaneously reconstruct society (ibid., ch. 20). This reconstruction is surely an ambitious project—one that our culture has done little since 1967 to accomplish.

Yet Vaneigem remains the optimist to the end. He argues that human beings have a creative core full of unsatisfied desires and dreams in operation 24 hours a day (ibid., ch. 20). In fact, our consciousness of our creative energy increases as consumer society tries harder and harder to co-opt it. Vaneigem's revolution will be a poetic one, for poetry is the fulfillment of radical theory, 'the revolutionary act par excellence'. The precondition for poetry is spontaneity, with its impulse to change the world along the lines of a radical sub-

jectivity, for subjectivity is the only truth (ibid.). This is a far cry from Marx's vision of the dialectical march of the class struggle. In the following passage Vaneigem echoes uncannily the Romantic poet Percy Bysshe Shelley's essay, *The Defence of Poetry* (1821):

> The laboratory of individual creativity transmutes the basest metals of daily life into gold through a revolutionary alchemy. The prime objective is to dissolve slave consciousness, consciousness of impotence, by releasing creativity's magnetic power; impotence is magically dispelled as creative energy surges forth, genius serene in its self-assurance. . . . The creative spark, which is the spark of true life, shines all the more brightly in the night of nihilism which at present envelops us. (Ibid.)

Vaneigem concludes with the notion that nothing is more difficult than one's own self-regeneration. Yet within each of us is a hidden room where passions' flowers bloom, where, like a fantastic tyrannical God, we create our own universes (ibid., ch. 23). Vaneigem's solution to the alienation, isolation, and boredom of consumer society is to embrace our radical subjectivity, to communicate erotically, to unleash the three horsemen of a non-repressive everyday life: creativity, love, and play. Whether the proletariat will come along for the ride is a much more dubious proposition.

CULTURE JAMMING

The Basics of Culture Jamming

An important echo of Situationism is the culture jamming movement spearheaded by the Estonian-born Canadian Kalle Lasn in the 1990s and later. He founded *Adbusters* magazine, which promotes Buy Nothing Day and other anti-consumerist events. The general goal of culture jamming is to make consumerism uncool, to mock the slick ads of corporations like Nike and Calvin Klein with equally slick anti-ads and anti-commercials, and thus to help us reclaim our uncommodified selves by reclaiming the waking reality of everyday life from corporate branding. *Adbusters*, published in Vancouver, is very much in the Situationist and punk spirit. It uses DIY cut-and-paste text and pictures alongside very professional-looking photo layouts. Lasn is Internet savvy, including e-mails in the magazine. *Adbusters* has also created a series of mock ads and 'uncommercials' available on its website (www.adbusters.org).

Lasn lays out the goal of culture jamming in his 1999 book, *Culture Jam: The Uncooling of America*. Lasn situates culture jamming as the logical heir to such activist movements of the 1960s and 1970s as the civil rights movement, feminism, and environmentalism. Culture jammers are media activists who want to change the world by changing the way we interact with media. He lays down six theses as a foundational manifesto (Lasn, 1999: xii–xvi).

(1) *America is no longer a country, but a multitrillion dollar brand.* This is true both of the obvious brands like McDonald's, Marlboro, GM, and Nike, but also of political concepts like 'democracy' and 'freedom', not to mention youthful rebellion. Political leaders bow to corporate power, yet say that America is the most democratic and freest country in the world.

(2) *American culture is no longer created by the people.* As the Situationists said, we buy our entertainments and regard them like spectacles, whether these are brand-name clothes, celebrities, TV, film, or whatever. We listen, watch, then buy—we make almost nothing ourselves.

(3) *A free, authentic life is no longer possible in America.* Our emotions and values have been manipulated by the media. We have been branded, leading designer lives—sleeping, eating, driving, working, shopping, watching TV,

sleeping again. Our free, spontaneous minutes have been swallowed up by the inauthentic images of cool and happy people dispensed by the media. As the Situationists said, this leads to alienation and isolation.

(4) *The mass media dispense a kind of Huxleyan 'soma'.* Here Lasn refers to the dystopia Aldous Huxley described in *Brave New World* (1932), where the citizens are drugged into submission with a pleasure-inducing drug called 'soma' that was free of side effects (other than passivity). In our less-than-utopian culture, the media hand out the narcotic of belonging, of being cool. This soma is highly addictive—and you can never get enough of it!

(5) *American cool is a global pandemic.* On a global scale, local communities, cultures, traditions, and histories are being wiped out by a barren American monoculture—for instance, Japanese kids buy Calvin Klein jeans, eat at McDonald's, and dream about becoming baseball players. Although Lasn does not mention it, this is even more of a problem in Canada, where American cool dominates pretty well all forms of mass media and entertainment.

(6) *The Earth can no longer support the lifestyle of the cool-hunting American-style consumer.* This orgy of consumption has led to a depletion of the planet's resources, pollution, global warming, and species extinctions. Lasn apocalyptically hints at the possibility of ecocide, or the death of the planet, as a possible outcome of this orgy.

Lasn describes his moment of truth when he first became a jammer—he was shopping in a supermarket and jammed a bent coin into the coin slot on a shopping cart. This led him to discover one of the 'great secrets' of modern urban life: 'Honor your instincts. Let your anger out. . . . Don't be unthinkingly civil all the time' (Lasn, 1999: xv). Cynicism is the dark side of the drug of consumerism—it's why we don't vote, we watch TV too much, accept our meaningless jobs, become bored, and shop compulsively. He hopes that our cynicism will dissolve once we realize that consumer capitalism is unethical and that we're not merely consumer drones.

Our Media-Induced Trance

Lasn takes a lot of his ideas from the Situationists. They knew how hard it is to hold onto our core self in a world of manufactured desires, goals, and values. He agrees that the desire for liberty is hard-wired and that the goal of a revolution today is helping people to live authentic, free lives. The Situationists were right that our lives have become spectacles, that most of our intimate gestures are clichés and stereotypes borrowed from film, TV, and other media. As a result, we become 'emulators', buying products that make us feel like someone else (ibid., 102). The power of the mental slavery Lasn sees in modern media lies in the fact that we can resist it, but it never (or almost never) occurs to us to do so. The spectacle is the illusion of freedom, a freedom to choose items from a set menu of experiences—movies, celebrity stories, sports, or Net surfing. To escape this mind control, we should follow the path taken by generations of poets, prophets, and drug-takers, and pursue a mystical oneness with the world. To do so we have to escape our market-structured consciousness by means of authentic gestures. In the 'postmodern world of mirrors' created by the mass media, we have to uncool the Corporate Cool Machine to feel alive again.

But for now, the society of the spectacle has won. We live in an age of Walmartian 'have a nice day' sort of happiness. We're distracted and pharmacologized by entertainments (ibid., 109). We're like the Buddha before he became enlightened to the reality of suffering and how to deal with it. We need a paradigm shift, a new way of seeing, a surge of Enlightenment under our own bo tree to wake up.

How to Jam Consumer Culture

Lasn borrows the idea of a meme from biology as part of his anti-mass media strategy. The idea of the meme was pioneered by the British biologist Richard Dawkins. He defined memes as coded, non-physical organisms that nest in physical organisms. They adapt to their environment just

A typical mock advertisement from *Adbusters*.

like physical bodies; values and concepts are examples. The culture-jamming 'meme warrior' fights to produce anti-consumerist memes. He or she will jam pop cultural marketing and uncool billion-dollar brands with anti-ads and uncommercials. Lasn celebrates the spontaneous, radical gesture that fights the powers of consumerism—when you leap into the unknown you're like 'a cat on the prowl, alive, alert, still a little wild' (ibid., 129). In short, it's fun to take down the titans.

One culture jamming strategy is to find your enemy's leverage point, the Achilles heel (ibid., 130–6). Lasn's favourite form of *détournement* is to subtervise—to produce magazine ads like those in *Adbusters* that look like real ads, but on closer scrutiny are seen to ridicule them. By mimicking these ads, you can uncool them. Buy Nothing Day is exactly what it sounds like: a day when we are asked to stop buying all commodities. He also mentions cyberpetitions, virtual protests on corporate websites, virtual sit-ins that flood these sites, or anti-websites that uncool specific brands. TV jamming is yet another form of culture jamming—the broadcasting, via TV directly or on the Internet, of uncommercials. These parallel real commercials, but have an anti-brand or anti-consumerist message. Of course, many TV stations and networks might be nervous about airing these uncommercials, even if paid. But if they are reluctant, TV jammers can publicize their refusal, which wins points in itself. In the end, Lasn suggests the classic strategy of a pincer movement consisting of both media thrusts like these uncommercials and of grassroots movements. He thinks that this pincer strategy can get people thinking about their lives—eating better, driving less, feeling guilty about eating a Big Mac or wearing Nike caps and Calvin Klein jeans. He hopes that this could lead to a sputtering of the corporate cool machine and a great planetary transformation in the next few decades.

Culture jammers don't simply want to downshift into a more leisurely lifestyle where they work and consume less. They are more radical, rejecting the American dream of the endless buying of consumer goods. Lasn suggests a threefold campaign to 'demarket' key elements of the consumer economy.

(1) His first gambit is to uncool fast-food franchises like McDonald's (ibid., 172–5). Even eating food can be a political act—every meal is a vote for the kind of world we want to live in. Much of what transnational food corporations do is invisible—they 'distance' us from the sources of our food, connecting to the consumer only at the supermarket. Where are those apples we're buying from? Down the road, or a thousand miles away? The average pound of food in America travels 1,300 miles before being eaten (ibid., 174), which certainly says something about our inefficient, energy-driven market economy. Other problems with mass-marketed food include the hawking of unhealthy junk food to kids of all ages and the genetic alteration of food, which has only recently become a political hot potato in North America. Lasn suggests we 'strike the gong of freedom' by demarketing junk and fast food

through uncommercials and by shopping at local farmers' markets. By ridiculing the fat content of McDonald's food we can uncool the brand and create an anti-fast-food meme that will spread throughout the populace. In short, up with flavour and nutrition and local control of food.

(2) His second attack is on the fashion industry (ibid., 175–9). Calvin Klein and his ilk dehumanize us and turn us into commodities, making young women feel insecure about their sexuality with their glossy magazine ads featuring semi-anorexic teens in provocative poses. These ads commodify sex, using beautiful young models to promote insecurity among women. Lasn pictures Klein as propositioning the daughters of North America, then turning them into prostitutes and finally dumping them on the streets. Women's magazines join in this campaign of fetishizing the female body, seeking to turn women into sexual machines with '10 Tips to the Best Sex Ever' and other such articles. He suggests a campaign of demarketing the fashion industry, which is more vulnerable to culture jamming since it depends on fads and trends. One way is through uncommercials like the 'Obsession Fetish' one featured on the *Adbusters* website.

(3) Finally, Lasn suggests uncooling the car (ibid., 179–81). He wants to cut the intimate connection of people to their vehicles. Optimistically, he mentions cases where resistance to cars seems to be building, e.g., cyclists who jam the roadways, demands for more bike lanes, research by companies such as British Petroleum into more ecologically friendly fuel sources, and the development of electric cars. Lasn argues that the car stands as the best example of the failure of consumers to pay for the 'true cost' of the product they consume. Sure, car owners pay for the costs of manufacturing the car and for gas and insurance. But they don't pay directly for roads (these are paid for by all taxpayers), pollution, accidents, noise, traffic policing, and the military protection of oil supplies. There are also the costs to future generations in terms of global warming, ozone depletion, and oil running out. In effect, the future generations are subsidizing our bad habits. In fact, if drivers paid the true cost of their cars, they

would cost $100,000 (ibid., 150). Lasn suggests a slow switch over to this true cost. This would increase public demand for subways, streetcars, and monorails. He also hopes for the development of human/fuel-powered and solar cars which reduce or eliminate the need for gasoline. Maybe in the future a new urban psychogeography will develop where we would be scornful of drivers and their vehicles for 'belching carbon' into the atmosphere.

Jamming the Jammers

In general, Lasn wants to uncool the society of the spectacle—a tall order indeed. He wants us to demarket our bodies and minds, to restore our social and cultural rituals to their original authenticity. While these are noble goals to be sure, some criticisms of the culture jamming movement can't be avoided:

- *Economic:* The sort of structural economic changes Lasn calls for might lead to massive job losses and a sharp upward spike in unemployment. They could even lead to a second Great Depression.
- *Political:* Governments and corporations have far too much at stake to allow the entire consumer economy to be 'uncooled', so culture jamming is politically unrealistic. By its very nature it is too avant-garde to attract mass appeal.
- *Moral:* Culture jammers are hypocrites since they manufacture and sell commodities themselves, including *Adbusters*, Buy Nothing Day T-shirts, and Blackspot sneakers. So culture jammers have become part of the spectacle themselves.

- *Hedonistic:* The ordinary working person actually *likes* consumer goods and media spectacles: people enjoy the diversions provided by Hollywood blockbusters, the convenience of fast food, the fun of playing with gadgets like CD players and computer game systems. Why should they give these up for a lifetime of either political activism or anti-consumer pranks? In short, consumerism is fun.

Despite these criticisms, the culture jammers' attempts to defend the ordinary citizen against the blandishments of advertisers and corporate culture are an important element of social theory and practice today, and their critique of the consumer economy points to the possibility that the business-as-usual practice of endless consumption cannot be sustained much longer.

We end our tour through critical theory with a question: Is consumer capitalism the final and highest stage of economic development for our species? The answer all the critical theorists we've looked at in this chapter would no doubt give is, 'We sure hope not!' Even granting the abundance it has created, consumerism clearly has brought in its train a host of serious social problems that critical theory is quite right to point out—not to mention the destruction of the natural environment caused by unchecked industrial growth, an issue that has grown in importance in the last few decades. Taken in a broad sense, then, critical theory is and should be at the core of modern social theory. It is absolutely indispensable to understanding society.

In the next two chapters we switch gears, looking at micro-sociological ways of understanding society that focus on individual meaning, symbols, and constructs.

STUDY QUESTIONS

1. Why is Hegel important to critical theory? How did he influence Marx specifically?
2. How did Nietzsche distinguish master and slave morality? Evaluate his distinction.
3. In outline, what is Freud's model of the mind? What are our basic drives? What are the weaknesses of this model for social theory?

4. What did Freud think were the sources of human suffering? What solutions has civilization come up with to deal with suffering? Which of these solutions is most effective today?

5. What, for Freud, was the meaning of civilization? How did this idea influence the Frankfurt School?

6. What were Adorno and Horkheimer's chief criticisms of popular culture in general? Were these valid, or was Adorno too much of a sourpuss?

7. Why did Adorno object to popular music? Does his critique still apply to contemporary pop music? Give a few examples of currently popular artists or genres to make your case.

8. Does popular culture encourage social conformity, as Adorno claims?

9. How does Marcuse distinguish true from false needs? Is his distinction valid? Why or why not?

10. What does Marcuse mean by 'surplus repression' and 'repressive desublimation'? How does he think modern industrial society uses sexuality? Does he improve on Freud's picture of modern civilization?

11. For Marcuse, why do we work as hard in modern industrial society today as a century ago if technology has reduced our need to labour? Is he right?

12. Outline four or five criticisms of the Frankfurt School in some detail.

13. Outline the basic psychological characteristics of narcissism described by Lasch. In what ways are these characteristics manifested in our culture?

14. According to Lasch, what effect does the propaganda of commodities have on our everyday life? Illustrate this with several examples.

15. What are the main causes of the sex war today? Does Lasch exaggerate the level of the antagonism between the sexes today?

16. Outline Habermas's picture of the stages of history. Does he follow Marx's picture exactly? How does he differ? Which picture is the most compelling? Why?

17. What does Habermas mean by an 'ideal speech situation'? Does his theory of communicative action qualify him as a critical theorist? Why or why not?

18. What are the Situationists' main criticisms of consumer culture? How did Marxism, existentialism, and Dada influence these criticisms?

19. Outline the main Situationist concepts, then evaluate them as ways of combatting the boredom and alienation of consumerism.

20. What did Debord mean by the 'spectacle'? What, in his terms, is the role of commodities in the society of the spectacle?

21. What does Vaneigem have to say about the power of roles in our lives? How does he see roles as connecting us to consumer society? Is he right?

22. What does Vaneigem see as the three forms of repressive power? What are the three equivalent methods to escape these forms of repression? Could we ever have the sort of revolution of everyday life envisaged by Vaneigem?

23. Compare and contrast the Frankfurt School's and the Situationists' critiques of consumer society. Do either of them offer us realistic ways out of our current cultural dilemma?

24. Evaluate Lasn's six theses on modern America.

25. What are some of the techniques suggested by culture jammers? Can culture jamming ever put a significant dent into the armour of consumer culture? Do we want it to?

SHORT BIBLIOGRAPHY

Adorno, Theodor. 1996 [1975]. 'Culture Industry Reconsidered', in J.M. Bernstein, ed., *The Culture Industries Revisited: Theodor W. Adorno on Mass Culture*. Lanham, Md: Rowman & Littlefield.

———— and Max Horkheimer. 1993 [1944]. 'The Culture Industry as Mass Deception', in Adorno and Horkheimer, *The Dialectic of Enlightenment*. New York: Continuum. Available at: <www.societyofcontrol. com/library/htm_pdf/adorno_horkheimer_dialecticoenlightenment_e.htm>.

Ball, Edward. 1987. 'The Great Sideshow of the Situationist International', *Yale French Studies* 73: 21–37.

Beiser, Frederick C. 1993. 'Hegel's Historicism', in Beiser, ed., *The Cambridge Companion to Hegel*. Cambridge: Cambridge University Press.

———. 2005. *Hegel*. New York: Routledge.

Benjamin, Walter. 1968. 'The Work of Art in the Age of Mechanical Reproduction', in Benjamin, *Illuminations*, trans. Harry Zohn. New York: Harcourt, Brace & World.

Chtcheglov, Ivan. 1953. 'Formulary for a New Urbanism', reprinted in *Internationale Situationniste* 1 (1958). Available at: <library.nothingness.org/articles/SI/en/display/1>.

Debord, Guy. 1958. 'Theory of the Dérive', *Internationale Situationniste* 2. Trans. Ken Knabb. Available at: <library.nothingness.org/articles/SI/en/display/314>.

———. 1967. *The Society of the Spectacle*. Originally published by Black & Red. Trans. Black and Red. Available at: <library.nothingness.org/articles/SI/en/pub_contents/4>.

Forster, Michael. 1993. 'Hegel's Dialectical Method', in Frederick C. Beiser, ed., *The Cambridge Companion to Hegel*. Cambridge: Cambridge University Press.

Freud, Sigmund. 1961 [1930]. *Civilization and Its Discontents*, trans. James Strachey. New York: Norton.

———. 1962 [1927]. *The Ego and the Id*, trans. Joan Riviere. London: Hogarth Press.

———. 1969 [1940]. *An Outline of Psychoanalysis*, trans. James Strachey. New York: Norton.

Gardiner, Michael E. 2000. *Critiques of Everyday Life*. London: Routledge.

Giddens, Anthony. 1985. 'Jürgen Habermas', in Quentin Skinner, ed., *The Return of Grand Theory in the Human Sciences*. Cambridge: Cambridge University Press.

Gray, Christopher. 1996 [1974]. 'Essays from Leaving the 20th Century', in Stewart Home, ed., *What Is Situationism? A Reader*. Edinburgh: AK Press.

Habermas, Jürgen. 1972. *Knowledge and Human Interests*, trans. Jeremy J. Shapiro. London: Heinemann.

———. 1975. *Legitimation Crisis*, trans. Thomas McCarthy. Boston: Beacon Press.

———. 1979. *Communication and the Evolution of Society*, trans. Thomas McCarthy. Boston: Beacon Press.

———. 1984, 1988. *The Theory of Communicative Action*, 2 vols. Cambridge: Polity Press.

———. 1987. *The Philosophical Discourse of Modernity*, trans. Frederick Lawrence. Cambridge, Mass.: MIT Press.

———. 1989. 'The Tasks of a Critical Theory of Society', in Alex Honneth and Douglas Kellner, eds, *Critical Theory and Society*. New York: Routledge.

Hegel, G.W.F. 1956 [1822–30]). *Philosophy of History*, trans. J. Sibree. New York: Dover.

———. 1977 [1807]. *The Phenomenology of Spirit*, trans. A.V. Miller. Oxford: Oxford University Press.

———. 1991 [1821]. *Elements of the Philosophy of Right*, trans. A. Wood and H. Nisbet. Cambridge: Cambridge University Press.

Klein, Naomi. 2000. *No Logo: Taking Aim at the Brand Bullies*. Toronto: Knopf.

Lasn, Kalle. 1999. *Culture Jam: The Uncooling of America*. New York: Eagle Brook.

Mann, Douglas, and G. Elijah Dann, eds. 2005. *Philosophy: A New Introduction*. Belmont, Calif.: Wadsworth.

Marcuse, Herbert. 1955. *Eros and Civilization*. Boston: Beacon Press.

———. 1960 [1941]. *Reason and Revolution: Hegel and the Rise of Social Theory*. Boston: Beacon Press.

———.1964. *One-Dimensional Man*. Boston: Beacon Press.

Marx, Karl, and Friedrich Engels. 1978. *The Marx-Engels Reader*, 2nd edn, ed. Robert C. Tucker. New York: Norton.

Nietzsche, Friedrich. 1967. *The Portable Nietzsche*, ed. and trans. Walter Kaufmann. New York: Viking Books. Contains *The Twilight of the Idols*, *The Antichrist*, *Thus Spake Zarathrustra*.

———. 1967. *The Basic Writings of Nietzsche*, ed. and trans. Walter Kaufmann. New York: Basic Books. Contains *The Birth of Tragedy*, *Beyond Good and Evil*, *On the Genealogy of Morals*.

Redding, Paul. 2006. 'Georg Wilhelm Friedrich Hegel', *Stanford Encyclopedia of Philosophy*. At: <plato.stanford.edu/entries/hegel/>.

Strinati, Dominic. 1995. *An Introduction to Theories of Popular Culture*. London: Routledge.

Vaneigem, Raoul. 1963. 'Basic Banalities', *Internationale Situationniste* 7. Available at: <library.nothingness.org/articles/SI/en/display/10>.

————. 1967. *The Revolution of Everyday Life*. Originally published by Black & Red. Available at: <library.nothingness.org/articles/SI/en/pub_contents/5>.

Wallace, Ruth A., and Alison Wolf. 1999. *Contemporary Sociological Theory*, 5th edn. Upper Saddle River, NJ: Prentice-Hall.

Wartenberg, Thomas E. 1993. 'Hegel's Idealism: The Logic of Conceptuality', in Frederick C. Beiser, ed., *The Cambridge Companion to Hegel*. Cambridge: Cambridge University Press.

Wicks, Robert. 2006. 'Friedrich Nietzsche', *Stanford Encyclopedia of Philosophy*. Available at: <plato.stanford.edu/entries/nietzsche>.

CHAPTER 5 | **MEANING IN SOCIETY: HUMAN AGENCY AND SOCIAL EXPLANATION**

STRUCTURE VS AGENCY: THE BASICS

Athena's Tale

Athena Parthenos is a bundle of contradictions. She is 25 years old, the offspring of a family of Greek immigrants who are Orthodox Church-goers and deeply committed to traditional family values. Athena's father Apollo wanted desperately for her to attend law school, graduate into a good job, marry a nice Greek boy, and settle down to raise a couple of grandchildren. Her mother Aphrodite wanted her to marry, too, but to a doctor or some other professional man who would support her so she could follow in her mother's footsteps by raising a big family.

Yet things don't always work out the way we want them. Athena did go to a good school, but to an art college, not a law school. She will soon marry, but to Rolf Wolfenstein, a handsome German exchange student she met in college. They're not so sure they'll have children right away, preferring to spend a few years working and travelling.

Athena attends church on special occasions, but is nowhere near as pious as her parents. Yet she won't give up her Christian faith, unlike many of her school chums, who are agnostics or atheists. She does follow her school friends when it comes to consumerism and popular culture: she spends many an afternoon shopping for clothes, jewellery, and other accessories at the local mall with these friends, and likes the same bands and musical styles that the majority of her pals do. She gabs to them constantly on her cell-phone (which annoys Rolf to no end), and loves to show off the same fashion items that are popular with other young women in her generation. She makes fun of the traditional types of films and music her parents enjoy, even mocking the musical tastes of her older brother Hermes for being a decade behind the times.

This is a story about two key sociological concepts: agency and structure, which parallel a very old debate in philosophy between advocates of free will and determinism. I'll spell out this debate in greater detail in the next section, but suffice it to say for now that agency refers to our ability to make free decisions as separate individuals, while structure refers to the power of society to shape us in its own image. In the story above, Athena's decisions give us evidence of both agency and structure. Her decisions to study art and marry a German lad against her parents' preferences show Athena exercising human agency; yet her love of consumerism, of technology, and her commitment to the pop cultural tastes of her narrowly defined generation show the controlling influence of social structure. Her commitment to Christianity is more ambiguous; if it is a result of following in the traditions of her family, then it's the product of structure; but if she chooses to remain religious as a personal choice, perhaps a way of rejecting the secular culture she finds all around her, then her practice is a matter of human agency.

Human Agency vs Social Structure

We all face the sorts of decisions that Athena has made. Most of us fancy ourselves to be free human agents who can fully explain why we do what we do. Yet when push comes to shove, most of us are also all too willing to justify at least some of our less pleasant decisions as forced on us by social structures beyond our control. 'Society made me do it' goes the refrain when we have to fire a favourite employee, keep up the pretense of a political or religious belief we don't really accept, or dress in a way that imitates how everyone else in our class and generation dress. All the same, few are willing to admit that we're *entirely* controlled by social structures: most of our actions certainly don't feel that way.

The tension one experiences between human agency and social structure is paralleled by a similar debate in philosophy between the advocates of free will and of determinism. Defenders of human freedom, like Jean-Paul Sartre and the existentialists, argue that human beings are more than just dead physical matter: human consciousness is 'for itself', free to make choices. Indeed, the ideas of legal and moral responsibility are based on the principle of free will; for example, if the criminal wasn't in control of his actions when he did the crime, we tend to see him as less guilty, and perhaps hand him a less severe sentence.

On the other side are the determinists, who argue that the universe is structured according to set physical laws that we can't change at will. This includes the molecules that make up the human body, which is entirely physical, and therefore is just as subject to physical law as rocks and trees. If simple physical systems, such as a ball falling from the Tower of Pisa, obey the laws of gravity and acceleration, then more complex physical systems, such as the human organism, must also obey a fixed set of scientifically determinable laws— even if our science is too simple at present to know all of them.

This distinction also gets played out in the arena of social scientific method as the debate between holist and methodological individualist approaches to research. The holist believes that we understand the human animal best in groups, and that social institutions and structures have a reality distinct from the actions of individuals. The individualist argues that only human individuals are real and that social institutions and structures have no reality independent of these individuals; thus, for example, 'the state' is merely a collection of individuals acting in a particular political way in a given place and time. Of the first two members of the holy trinity of major classical social theorists, two—Karl Marx and Émile Durkheim—basically are holists. Marx believed that large-scale economic forces control human destiny; Durkheim spoke of the collective conscience and organic and mechanical solidarities as similarly large-scale phenomena at the core of what drives human actors to act socially.

The defenders of a social structure approach, who tend also to be philosophical determinists and methodological holists, may use parallel terms like social 'forces' or 'systems' or 'institutions' to describe social structures. The most important of these specific structures are family, class, sex, race, culture, and religion, though individual thinkers vary greatly in how they rate the respective power of each of these structures. We can follow Durkheim's model of social facts in laying out the three basic qualities of social structure: (1) they exist prior to action; (2) they are independent of the actor; and (3) they constrain that actor in some way. In Athena's case, consumerism fits the bill: it existed before she was born, she didn't create it, and it encourages her to act in ways not entirely of her own choosing. Structuralists have been criticized for underestimating human freedom, for overgeneralizing the power of one structure above all others (as when Marxists overemphasize the influence of class structure on history), and for giving human beings too little credit for being creative actors who change their social world according to new values and ideas.

A human agency approach emphasizes how one can escape the constraints of family, class, sex, and the other basic types of social structure by making free decisions as an individual, not just as a preconditioned member of a group, mass, or herd. The human agency approach also says that even if we *do* admit to being influenced by social structures, we are still obliged, as a question of method, to try to understand *how* the individual actor is influenced by these structures. We have to understand an actor's *motives* or *reasons* for acting as he or she did. These motives and reasons give the action *meaning*, both to the actor and to an external observer trying to understand that actor. In Athena's case above, it's not good enough to argue that she has adopted the Greek Orthodox faith *because* it's the faith of her parents. If family were such a powerful influence, she would honour her parents' wishes in all things, which, as we all know, is a rarity with children. So we may ask *why* Athena obeyed her parents in the field of religion, but not in those of education and marriage. The best way to figure out *why* an actor did what she did is simply by asking her. Yes, she may attempt to deceive either us or herself with her answer. If the supporters of the human agency approach argue that the individual actor knows his or her motives and reasons for acting better than anyone else, however, that's where we must start our inquiry.

We will look at several theorists, some of them sociologists, some of them philosophers with an interest in social life, who have taken human agency and individual meaning to be a key element in social explanation. We start with the founding father of this approach, the third member of the holy trinity of classical social theorists, Max Weber.

WEBER ON UNDERSTANDING SOCIETY

Weber's Background and the Iron Cage of Rationality

Max Weber (1864–1920) was an academic German sociologist who studied law and economics, and who taught at several universities, including Heidelberg and Munich. For parts of his life, especially in the period after the German defeat in 1918 and the end of the Austro-Hungarian Empire, he and his wife were active in the political life of their country. He was a liberal who championed democracy in Germany against conservative and socialist forces. We'll deal with

his thinking in some detail here since his *Verstehen* sociology influenced all social theorists who see human agency as the foundation of sociological understanding (indeed, *Verstehen* means 'understanding' in German). Weber's wife Marianne Weber (1870–1954) was an important sociologist and feminist theorist in her own right. She also helped to get his works published after he died in 1920, publishing in 1926 the biography, *Max Weber: A Picture of His Life*.

As Marx was the father of materialist and social structuralist approaches to social theory, so Weber was the parent of micro-sociological accounts of social life that emphasize individual choice and human rationality. Indeed, much of his social theory was a sort of debate with the ghost of Marx. Weber disagreed with Marx that economics was the sole cause of social stability and change—political, religious, and military factors play independent roles in Weber's analysis. In place of a monocausal view of society, he wanted to substitute a plurality of causes. He said at the very end of *The Protestant Ethic and the Spirit of Capitalism*, his most famous work of historical sociology, that he didn't want to substitute a one-sided spiritualistic interpretation of history for what he saw as Marx's one-sided materialistic interpretation.

Weber did want to pay attention to how material interests and the ideologies or rationalizations associated with them influenced social relationships. Yet he also believed in the independent role of ideas like the Protestant ethic in creating or changing social bonds. History is the product of a collection of both ideal and material factors. Ideas are not just reflections of material interests (though in some cases they could be). What Marx called the 'superstructure' of society has a life of its own, though there are interests associated even with ideas (say, in religion, art, or philosophy), and not just economic positions. Interests and ideas are related not causally, but in terms of affinities.

Weber came from a school of thought in late nineteenth-century Germany that emphasized the historical underpinnings of society, hence its name historicism. The historicists were reacting to the positivist view that since human beings are not significantly different from physical objects, our behaviour could be studied in the same way that geologists study minerals or biologists study germ cells. German historicism argued that there was a sharp division between the historical/cultural sciences and the natural sciences. The latter—the *Naturwissenschaften*—dealt with physical things and processes without any rational consciousness; the former, the *Geisteswissenschaften*, dealt with human beings who could think, reason, and create politics, art, and culture. Historicists argued that we can't use the same standards in sciences, which deal with non-thinking things, that we used with human beings, who can attribute some subjective meaning to their actions. In other words, social facts, if they exist at all, are nothing like natural facts. The historicists concluded that the individual was ineffable: we cannot reduce human actions to general types, as we do in physical science. Wilhelm Dilthey, a nineteenth-century German thinker in the historicist tradition, had already outlined the importance of 'understanding' in the human or social sciences before Weber picked up the idea.

Weber tried to steer a course between the extremes of positivism and historicism: he definitely agreed that human subjectivity and rationality made sociology a human science, ruling out positivist methods; but he countered the historicist view that only individual actions could be scientifically described with the claim that sociology needs to generalize by using ideal types of action to explain social life in the mass. Weber distinguishes sociology, which uses 'type' concepts and general uniformities of social action, from history, which deals with individual people, actions, and structures, and how they're connected causally. Sociology is more abstract than history, though its concepts are more precise. It formulates ideal types of people, actions, and events, even though these can rarely if ever be found in reality.

Weber did agree with the natural scientific view that sociology has to be value-free, although it can of course talk about values. To be scientific, it has to be neutral as to the basic ethical or political values it espouses. Of course, the researcher must make a value-based decision right at the start of his or her research, asking 'what topic should I study?' Yet, once this decision is made, Weber believed it was clear sailing for the researcher into the calm waters of scientific objectivity.

Weber's general view of modern history is that society is becoming more and more rational, suffering from 'the disenchantment of the world'. Gods and demons and spirits have disappeared from our world, having been replaced with cogs and gears and punch cards. He thought we're caught more and more in an iron cage of rationality thanks to the domination of the ideas of bureaucratic efficiency and technological productivity in modern life. He called such a state a 'polar night of icy darkness' (Weber, 1946: 128), but saw this dark night as inevitable.

Modern capitalism for Weber, with its championing of the bureaucratic mode of administration, is very rational and efficient. He criticizes the Marxists for thinking that socialism would be able to get rid of bureaucracy—quite the opposite, in fact. Socialism would require that we be trapped even more in the iron cage of bureaucratic rationality, as the history of the Soviet Union later showed. But he imagined interrupting this process, almost like the antithesis in a Hegelian dialectic, the coming to the fore of the charismatic leadership of a hero, prophet, or some other revolutionary figure (remember, this was before Hitler, Stalin, and Mao, though they each embodied what Weber meant by charisma). He got the idea in part from the Romantic notion of the 'genius' who transcends rational or traditional rules to create great art. Freedom and democracy aren't the product of capitalism, and require the defence of resolute men and women. Freedom is defended by charisma, for its opponents are capitalism and bureaucracy, which tend to rationalize and formalize social relations, creating the rule of the technical expert instead of that of the democratic citizen.

Subjective Understanding

At the beginning of his great unfinished study of social theory, *Economy and Society* (1978

[1922]: 4), Max Weber lays his cards on the table—sociology is a science:

> ...concerning itself with the interpretive understanding of social action and thereby a causal explanation of its course and consequences. We shall speak of 'action' insofar as the acting individual attaches a subjective meaning to his behavior—be it overt or covert, omission or acquiescence. Action is 'social' insofar as its subjective meaning takes account of the behavior of others and is thereby orientated in its course.

Weber's sociology takes a *Verstehen* approach—it attempts to *understand* social action as meaningful on the individual level by interpreting the subjective meaning given an act by the actor. He is ultimately a microscopic theorist, though he often talks about large-scale institutions and movements such as capitalism or religion. A major criticism of Weber lies here: if all sociologically meaningful action is individual, how can we even talk about social structures? Weber got around this in a number of ways.

Weber defines social action as an act with a subjective meaning for the actor that takes the behaviour of others into account. He distinguishes physical behaviour from social action. Only the latter has a subjective meaning associated with it: for example, it's the difference between unconsciously blinking my eyes and winking at a cute woman at a party. Yet there's no clear line between meaningful action and merely reactive behaviour. Sociology is about the study of meaningful social action. This mostly involves actions with intentions behind them, things done on purpose and directed to other people.

We can understand a given act two ways: *rationally*, when we understand intellectually the place of the act within a context of meaning; or *empathetically*, in terms of sympathetic appreciation. We can understand a person's action rationally when it reflects the best choice of means connected to a certain goal, though the goal itself might be difficult to appreciate, e.g., if cult members kill themselves to achieve salvation, we can see the connection but think the goal is crazy. If we are subject to strong emotions like love, jealousy, pride, or anger, we'll be more able to empathize with the irrational actions of others. In addition, we can construct purely rational ideal types of action to compare real actions with. Only in these senses can Weber's sociology be seen as rationalistic. Weber makes it clear he's *not* saying that the rational element dominates all human decision-making.

Sociology must also take into account processes and phenomena that have no subjective meaning, i.e., things that have no intention behind them. This includes natural disasters like floods and earthquakes and human diseases. These have social effects, but have no direct social meaning: they are mere data in themselves.

Weber (ibid., 8) argues that there are two ways we can understand a social action, methodologically speaking:

- In *direct observational understanding*, we have a direct understanding of an action, e.g., the meaning of the expression 2 + 2 = 4, or the anger of our friend because of the strained look on his face. We understand the action by simply observing it.
- In *explanatory understanding*, we understand the motive behind an action by placing the act in a general context of meaning and understandable sequence of motivation. This is explaining the act, figuring out its intended meaning; e.g., we explain the anger in our friend by connecting it to his being jealous of his girlfriend or due to an insult he's suffered.

Explanatory understanding can happen on one of three levels: (1) historically, we can understand the actual intention or meaning behind a specific action, e.g., Brutus went to the Senate to kill Caesar; (2) in mass social phenomena, as an average of intended meanings; or (3) the meaning connected to an ideal type, e.g., a capitalist seeks to make a profit.

Weber admits that not all motives are conscious; some are repressed. Also, our motivations are usually mixed; we are subject to conflicting ideas and desires. In most cases, people are only half-conscious of the subjective meaning of their actions. Most actions are governed by impulse and habit; most people are only dimly aware of their motivations. The ideal type of meaningful action, where people are fully aware of their intentions and thus of the subjective meaning of their actions, is rare.

Weber distinguishes the 'adequacy' of our understanding on the levels of cause and meaning. On the level of *meaning*, we just want to figure out if our account of the situation makes sense. A motive is a complex of subjective meanings that the actor takes as adequate ground for the action in question. Our interpretation of the action is adequate if we can identify typical ways of thinking and feeling that connect the actor's subjective meaning to the action he or she took. For example, if a friend seems to have committed suicide because her parents broke up, we would ask whether marriage breakups of parents are typically connected to children's suicides.

On the level of *cause*, we look for situations similar to the one we're trying to understand to see if the same causes are linked to the same effects. In the previous example, we would look at other broken families to see what happened to the kids. We can say that event X caused event Y if there's a probability that given X, Y will happen. A correct causal interpretation of an action comes when both the action and the actor's motives have been understood and meaningfully connected. As part of this process, the sociologist must take into account collective concepts like the state, the family, and the nation, since they obviously have a meaning in the minds of social actors, even though they have no reality outside of individual minds.

Not all actions are social: actions with regard to inanimate objects are not. Our subjective attitudes are not social if they have nothing to do with others. Further, not all contacts with human beings are social. Weber gives the example of running into a cyclist by accident: since neither person intended the encounter, and they just happened to wind up in the same place at the same time, their meeting isn't social. Lastly, not all actions similar to those of others are social—getting caught up in the emotion of a crowd may

not be a meaningful act, but just a psychological or physical reaction. But the line between a fully self-conscious act oriented towards others and an unconscious reaction is not always clear. For example, we might strike up a conversation with the clumsy cyclist and become friends.

Ideal Types and Social Action

For Weber, ideal or pure types like 'charismatic leadership' are concepts invented for practical research purposes to clarify the nature of social life. They are logically precise analytical tools, not attempts to grasp the pure substance or nature of a given type of phenomena, or to create an 'ideal' for human actors to aspire to. In fact, he says that in the real world we might never find the ideal type of a charismatic leader, legal order, bureaucracy, or rational self-conscious decision-making.

Ideal types are abstractions whose purpose is to escape from the narrow methodological individualism of the German historicists. Weber seems to have wanted to take all real-world actions of a rough type and force them through a strainer to distil out the pure essence of that type of action. Ideal types are abstractions that help us to make causal connections between types of people and action. They're what make his *Verstehen* sociology scientific. Yet, Weber argues that ultimately the individual is the sole carrier of meaningful social action. Classes, institutions, or nations are only collections of the meaningful actions of individuals. Only individuals have ontological reality.

Weber argues (ibid., 24–5) that there are four basic ideal types of social action, only two of which are meaningful in the sense that they involve some thought-out purpose or reason. In concrete cases, actions usually are mixtures of two or more of the following ideal types.

- *Traditional action* occurs when when an actor says, 'This is the way we've always done things, so this is the way I'll do it now.' This is the most common form of action in everyday life. It is only barely meaningful, since it usually involves little thinking. An example is an old-fashioned marriage ceremony.

- *Affectual action*, based on an actor's emotions. This type of action also could be barely meaningful, since it doesn't involve a lot of thinking. A bar fight and road rage fit the bill (my examples, not Weber's).
- *Value-rational action*, which is connected to a conscious belief in some ethical, religious, or aesthetic value for its own sake. This could be action aimed at some political cause, defending one's nation, or pursuing a religious calling. The actor feels that the value in question 'commands' him or her to do the action in question, perhaps as part of an existential commitment. Joining the priesthood is an example.
- *Instrumentally rational action*, which seeks to use objects and people to achieve rationally calculated ends. Here the end, the means, and the secondary results all are rationally considered, and various means to a given end weighed. Even the goals of action themselves are evaluated. To this sort of actor, value-rational action seems irrational, since it ignores the consequences of action. For example, from an instrumentally rational point of view, joining the priesthood might seem highly irrational, since it doesn't 'pay off' like a good job in a corporation would. Most of modern economic life is instrumentally rational: it seeks to make money in the most efficient way possible.

Legitimacy and Domination

Weber is probably most famous for laying out a set of concepts and distinctions to do with political legitimacy, forms of authority, social classes, and status groups. Most of this theorizing is found in his great work, *Economy and Society*. His typologies of the types of social action and forms of legit-

imacy and domination roughly parallel each other, as can be seen in Table 5.1.

One of Weber's major concerns was where the legitimacy of social order comes from. Social actions are often guided by a sense of a legitimate order over and above concerns for self-interest. Such a sense resides in the belief that a given social order is valid, and therefore we must follow its rules or commands. Weber gives the example of a civil servant showing up for work at a certain time not due to custom or considerations of self-interest, but due to such a belief in the legitimacy of the order he or she serves.

Weber argues that a person can ascribe legitimacy to an order in four basic ways (1978: 36–7):

- *Tradition:* the order is valid because things have always been that way. Orders based on the sacredness of tradition are common throughout history—the fear of magical evils or the vengeance of the gods reinforces the fear of change typical in such societies. Such orders only change due to a prophetic oracle seen as sacred, or to a leader announcing that the people have lost their way from the sacred truth and have to be put right (i.e., the truth has been obscured for some reason).
- *Affective legitimacy*, perhaps based on faith: the order is backed by god or is seen as special in some way.
- *Value-rational faith:* the order embodies some absolute value. The most common type of value-rational order is one based on natural law, which is absolutely valid, independent of its human consequences.
- By positive enactment, since the order is seen as *legal*. A legal order can come about either by mutual agreement or by the imposition by some authority. This is the most common

Table 5.1 Weber's Typologies of Social Action and Power

Type of Social Action	Form of Legitimacy	Form of Domination
Traditional (habit)	Traditional	Traditional
Affective (emotions)	Affective (based on faith)	[Charismatic]
Value-Rational	Value-Rational Faith	[Charismatic]
Instrumentally Rational	Legal (positive enactment)	Legal

form of order today. It is the belief in the *formal* validity of the enactments of the ruling bodies, whether or not they represent a majority of the population.

In reality, most modern regimes are a mixture of legal and traditional orders.

Weber defines the state as having four elements. First, it's an association we're compelled to be a member of because of the territory we live in. Second, and most important, it's the only body within that territory that can legitimately use force. Third, the modern state has a legal and administrative order regulated by legislation; and fourth, it has an administrative staff to implement those laws.

Weber (ibid., 215ff.) identifies three basic ideal types of authority or domination, all of which justify themselves:

- *Traditional authority* is based on the sanctity of age-old traditions and parallels traditional legitimacy. In such a system, loyalty is to the chief, whose power is sanctioned by tradition.
- *Legal authority* is the belief in the legality of enacted rules and in the authority of those making them. This form of authority is impersonal. Leaders rule only within limited spheres—the Prime Minister can't tell you what to eat for breakfast, nor can a police officer force you to listen to country music.
- *Charismatic authority* comes from the devotion by the people to the sanctity, heroism, or special character of the leader. It's usually connected to some sense that the leader has revealed the moral order of things. Charisma means 'gift of grace' and its recognition is a form of faith, so the acceptance of a charismatic authority could employ either affective or value-rational forms of legitimacy.

Traditional Authority

To start with the simplest first, traditional authority exists where people believe in the sanctity of age-old rules and powers. The leader is a personal master with a number of personal followers, with the rest of the people being comrades or subjects. The traditional master's commands are limited by tradition itself—if he ignores these limits, he risks losing his status. But the obligation of personal obedience owed him is essentially unlimited outside these boundaries—how he leads is at his discretion.

The master does favours for his most loyal followers in order to retain power. Opposition to such authority isn't to the system itself, but just to the power of the individual leader. Changes to the system can occur only if phrased in terms of truths from 'the old days' that current leaders are ignoring. In the pure type of traditional rule, the staff: (a) does not operate within a clearly defined sphere of competence, (b) does not have a rationally established hierarchy, (c) does not have a regular system of appointment and promotion, (d) might not be technically trained, and (e) might not have a fixed salary paid in money. Legal bureaucracies have all of these characteristics.

The patriarchal family is, historically, the original form of traditional authority. Later, the traditional master surrounds himself with relatives, slaves, and freed slaves in what Weber calls 'patrimonial recruitment'. In extra-patrimonial recruitment, the master employs favourites, vassals who owe him personal loyalty, and a few free officials who volunteer to serve him. Although Weber claims that his types of authority do not represent three historical stages (in the order traditional to charismatic to legal, as one would suppose), it's pretty clear that most traditional forms of authority historically predate legal ones.

Legal Authority

Weber argues (ibid., 217–18) that the following interlocking set of general ideas is associated with the pure type of a legal authority. These are the moral and political foundations of modern capitalist and socialist societies, except for those few ruled by charismatic leaders:

1. Legal norms are based on agreement or are imposed from above on the grounds of expediency or rationality.

2. Bodies of law, made up of consistent systems of abstract rules, are created.
3. The chief or superior is subject to impersonal rules.
4. People obey the law as members of an organization, not the chief or superior person.
5. Members obey their superiors within a limited sphere; their real loyalty is to the impersonal order, not to the actual superior.

Next comes what Weber calls the 'fundamental categories' of rational-legal authority (ibid., 218–19). These flesh out the details of the foundational elements listed above:

- Official business is conducted according to general rules. For example, government offices are open during regular hours, not whenever the employees feel like showing up.
- Each organ or agency has a specified sphere of competence, e.g., bus drivers can't do social work, bank tellers can't be doctors. Each office has a limited jurisdictional area.
- There is a hierarchy in each office—lower offices work under higher ones.
- Offices are run by technical rules or norms that require technical training to be mastered. Only officials who pass tests or have certificates are hired.
- The office staff does not own the means of production or administration. Also, their office is not their home. The official's private domicile is separate from his or her public workplace. That's why it's wrong to steal office supplies.
- The official doesn't have a 'right' to his office: it's not his or her property.
- Administrative rules and acts are written down and kept as documents in the bureau or office. Thus, the core of bureaucratic administration is the 'files', which are kept by a series of minor officials or scribes. These files plus an organization of functions equal 'the office'.

The main form of organization for the legal form of authority is bureaucracy, which is largely responsible for the 'iron cage of rationality' we all find ourselves in today. Weber lists (ibid., 220–1), somewhat repetitively, the 10 major characteristics of modern bureaucracies:

1. The officials are personally free and subject to authority only at their jobs.
2. There is a hierarchy of offices. The higher offices supervise the lower ones; a member of a bureaucratic organization can appeal the decision of a lower office to a higher one.
3. Each office has a clearly defined sphere of operations.
4. Offices are filled by a free selection on a contractual basis (e.g., office-holders are not slaves or the relatives of the chief). If this isn't true, and the officials are in some sense forced to work for their chief, then the bureaucracy is in part a traditional form of authority.
5. Officials are chosen by means of technical qualifications—exams or diplomas. This technical side of bureaucracy is becoming more and more prevalent. Only at the top of modern organizations do we find leaders not chosen according to their technical qualifications and thus not purely bureaucratic, e.g., a president and a capitalist entrepreneur, who are more like traditional monarchs.
6. Bureaucrats are paid a fixed salary based on their rank, usually in money.
7. Their job is their main or only occupation. Their job demands their full working capacity.
8. Their job is part of a career, with the possibility of promotion by their superior.
9. The officials do not own the means of administration.
10. The official is subject to strict discipline and control at work.

Bureaucracy can be applied to a wide variety of forms of organization: government, private enterprises, churches, clinics, political parties, trade unions, universities, or the army. In fact, one could say that bureaucracy is the essence of modern social life: more and more all these and other forms of organization are becoming bureaucratized.

Weber thinks that a pure bureaucracy is the most rational and efficient method of exercising control over human beings. It operates stably and precisely in a disciplined way, with very predictable results. In fact, due to modern technology and business methods, bureaucracy has become absolutely essential to modern life: it's the only effective way we can manage government, the production of goods, or any other large form of organization. Whether an economy is capitalist or socialist is irrelevant: both need bureaucracies. Bureaucratic administration is only fully developed in the modern state and in modern capitalism.

As to the social position of the bureaucrat, he does not 'own' his office, nor is his loyalty to an individual, as in traditional societies. His loyalty is of an impersonal and functional character: he is an official in Widgets Incorporated or in the Department of the Environment. Naturally, he strives for as much social esteem as he can get. This esteem is highest in civilized societies with a strong demand for expert administration, and where there is a degree of social differentiation, with the bureaucrats coming from the upper strata of society. The opposite is true in societies with little call for technical administration.

Officials are assumed to have tenure for life, though they can be dismissed if they really screw up. Tenure isn't seen as a right of the official, but as connected to competence in the official's position. Bureaucrats aim at a career and expect to be able to move up the administrative ladder if they perform adequately. In fact, the bureaucrat usually prefers a mechanical fixing of the conditions of promotion.

Charismatic Authority

Charismatic authority derives from the special qualities of the leader, who is seen as having some extraordinary, superhuman, or supernatural powers or extraordinary qualities. These could be of divine origin, as in the magical powers thought to reside in ancient prophets, or it could be some sort of legal, military, or psychological wisdom, as found in leaders of the hunt or great warriors. We

can't see charismatic authority as solely a primitive phenomenon, nor should we imagine the move from tradition or charisma to rational authority as a straight-up evolutionary line. All cases of transcending the routines of everyday life release charismatic forces.

In primitive societies in normal times, the hero or magician is usually not very busy. But when an extraordinary event or troubles happen, like a big hunt, a crop failure, or a military threat, they are called out of semi-retirement. When the leader's manipulation of gods and demons becomes a regular affair, the magician or prophet turns into a priest. When wars become chronic and a systematically trained army becomes necessary, the charismatic war leader becomes a king.

Weber mentions berserker warriors, shamans in tribal societies, the Irish hero Cuchullain, and Joseph Smith, the founder of Mormonism, as examples of charismatic authority figures. We could add many of the powerful dictators of the twentieth century—Hitler, Mussolini, Mao Zedong, Fidel Castro, Juan Peron, and many lesser lights—along with cult leaders such as David Koresh, Reverend Moon, and Jim Jones. These leaders all ruled in large part through their personal charisma, and not through the legal validity of their rule or by their being the traditional leaders of their nation or religion.

Weber (ibid., 242–5) makes a number of points about the nature of charismatic authority:

1. The key to the power of the charismatic leader is the recognition by his followers of the validity of the leader's special powers. This recognition is given freely, but is usually connected to some pretended miracle or revelation made by the leader.
2. If the leader appears to lose his magical or heroic powers and meets with failure, his charismatic authority will wither away.
3. A charismatic community is a group following a charismatic leader and bound together by emotional allegiances. The community has no regular officials: the prophet has his disciples, the war leader his bodyguards or agents.

The leader and his agents have no regular bailiwick and aren't paid a regular salary. The charismatic aristocracy is made up of followers chosen for their loyalty or degree of discipleship. There is no system of formal rules or legal principles. The leader says 'it is written . . . but I say this!'

4. Pure charisma also ignores economic considerations; the leader is more concerned with his mission or spiritual duty. He rejects the economic exploitation of his charismatic power by traditional or rational everyday business practices. Charisma rejects everyday routine buying and selling—think of the disdain Jesus felt for the moneylenders in the temple.

5. Charisma is a great revolutionary force in traditional periods, breaking through the walls built by traditional rules and precedents. It depends on the highly personal experience of the master, which is said to be based on divine grace or heroic strength.

Charismatic authority is opposed both to rational and to traditional forms of authority. Bureaucratic authority is opposed to charisma by virtue of its rational, analytical rules, while charisma is irrational, based on the whims or revelations of the leader. Traditional authority is similarly hostile to charisma; it's based on precedents and rules handed down from the distant past, while charismatic authority rejects the past in a revolutionary way. Charisma also rejects the social power of property ownership.

Bureaucratic rationality can be a revolutionary force with respect to tradition, too. But it revolutionizes from without, by technical means, by changing the material and social order of things and making people adapt to these changes. Charisma revolutionizes from within, changing people by revelation, heroism, or magic. The leaders then bend the material and social order to their wills. Bureaucracy merely replaces the belief in traditional norms with rational rules. Charisma disrupts both traditional and bureaucratic rules, enforcing an inner obedience to the 'divine will', as manifested by the charismatic leader's 'divine will'. It rejects most if not all laws and customs already in place. It is the truly revolutionary force in history.

Bureaucracy and traditional authority share the quality of continuity: the traditional patriarch is the ancient equivalent of the modern administrator. Charisma, on the other hand, upsets this continuity. All extraordinary needs that transcend everyday life have to be satisfied on a charismatic basis. Charismatic authority has no formal bureaucracy, no regular way of appointing or dismissing officials, offers no formal career with the possibility of promotion or a regular salary, and has no permanent institutions. It ignores abstract rules and regulations. Charismatic leaders write their own rules and set their own limits—they are highly individual.

Charismatic communities tend to be anti-economic and communistic. Bureaucracy requires a steady inflow of cash; but charismatics live in, but not of, this world (St Francis is a case in point). Yet they might still pursue booty, as have pirates and warlords. What they reject is orderly, rational economic conduct. They might live off this booty, or from gifts, dues, or other voluntary contributions (e.g., the gifts given to Buddhist monks).

Charismatic communities require the preservation of the heroism or saintliness of their members. To be effective disciples, the followers of the Master must be free of family and job worries and other worldly concerns. This makes charismatic authority unstable. Eventually the leader's mission comes to an end, he loses his powers, and his followers abandon him as a false prophet. As long as he can work miracles, or perform heroic deeds, he will be followed; but as soon as he can no longer guarantee the well-being of his followers, they leave him. Also, the followers give in eventually to the temptations to have a family, own property, or engage in ordinary economic activities. Weber talks about how the turbulent emotional life of the charismatic community eventually burns out, being slowly suffocated by material interests. Biology and material life eventually wear down such communities.

Charisma comes from extraordinary political or economic situations or from psychic and religious states. When the collective excitement that comes from these special events calms down, the tide of charismatic domination flows back into everyday routines and becomes institutionalized. Charismatic leadership is then traditionalized or bureaucratized and worn down by economic necessities, and it becomes routine. Everyday life can't be managed by the direct intervention of a charismatic leader—passports need to be stamped, forms filled out, people hired and fired. This is the work not of prophets but of officials. In addition, as we've seen, people begin to look to their family lives and to their everyday economic interests. When this routinization of charisma sets in, the war leader forms a state, or the community surrounding a prophet, artist, or philosopher becomes a church, sect, or school. The charismatically dominated masses become tax-paying, law-abiding citizens, or dues-paying members of a church, club, or political party. Even though the 'routinized' disciples admonish the followers to maintain a pure spirit, the message becomes a dogma, doctrine, or law. Then charisma and tradition merge—indeed, they both surround loyalty and obligation with a religious aura. In its setting up of a sacred source of authority, charisma establishes the basis of more traditional regimes.

Of course, charismatic authority tends to be very unstable because so much depends on the person of the leader. What happens when the leader dies? The problem of succession rears its ugly head. Weber sees six ways that this problem can be dealt with: by finding a leader with similar charismatic qualities; by using oracles or lots or some other form of divine judgement; by having the old leader nominate a successor; by delegating the new leader's selection to a qualified charismatic staff; by heredity; or by transmission through a religious or magical ritual.

Class, Status, and Party

In a section in *Economy and Society*, Weber takes on Marxism's attempt to reduce all social con-flict to class struggle. He says instead that we have to distinguish three types of social groups: classes, status groups, and parties. In general, classes belong to the economic order, status groups to the social order, while parties are associations struggling for power by aiming at specific objectives. Classes are stratified according to the production and acquisition of goods; status groups are stratified according to the way that these goods are consumed in certain special styles of life associated with each status group. The status order of society is the way that social honour is distributed in a society. It may or may not map onto the structure of economic power in a given society.

Power means the ability of a person or a group to realize its will in a social action even against the resistance of others. Weber thinks that people seek power for its own sake, and not just to get rich by it. All power is not economic at its base, as Marx thought. Even the naked power of money may be disdained by certain status groups.

A class is a group of people with similar economic interests who relate to the economy in the same way. Property relations determine our life chances. Specifically, a class is a group of people with similar power to get a supply of goods and to sell those goods or a skill in the marketplace. Only the propertied minority can take a part of their wealth and use it as capital, i.e., invest it to gain more property. Over against the propertied classes, the workers have only their labour and so are relatively powerless. Weber sees many more class situations than does Marx: owners of workshops, stores, land, mines, cattle, etc. are viewed by Weber as distinct class situations. Even those without property who offer services can be differentiated according to the services they offer. In other words, there are many bourgeoisies, just as there are many proletariats. For Weber the class struggle isn't so obviously a political struggle as it is for Marx. Yet, he admits that for capitalism to work, it requires a legal order to protect capitalist forms of property. In earlier times, the class struggle tended to take the form of struggles over debt bondage, the price of bread or other essential commodities, or slavery. In modern times the class struggle is about wages.

Classes act according to their interests in the marketplace. The degree to which a class can act socially in a common way is linked to the cultural situation in place, especially the ideas afloat at a given time. For example, in Canada modern industrial workers no longer tend to vote en masse for a workers' party—though some might vote NDP, others might be Liberals, and some even support the Conservatives.

Status groups are formed around the allocation of social honour, not economics. Status groups can parallel class divisions, but don't have to: the pretensions of a status group might stand opposed to the power of property or of money. People without property can belong to the same status group as propertied people. A status group is defined by its style of life, i.e., by its pattern of consumption, not according to its power to buy and sell property. This might involve restrictions on social intercourse. Weber talks about how living on a certain street helped to qualify an American as a 'gentleman', along with a number of other things. Gentlemen had greater employment opportunities in certain types of swank establishments and certain privileges in social intercourse, and could marry into established families. Ironically, American status honour was based on usurpation and pure convention—the 'old' New England families descended from the Pilgrims who landed in Massachusetts were originally low-status refugees from England. But if such usurping status groups obtain economic power, they can create legal privileges for themselves, even in democratic societies.

Sometimes status groups can evolve into closed castes supported by religious or other strong sanctions. Contact with members of lower castes is seen as a ritualistic impurity and carries a great stigma. Intermarriage and social intercourse between castes are strictly prohibited. This is especially the case in extreme situations where the status group's superior social honour is backed by supposed ethnic divisions. This could result in the creation of pariah peoples within a given society who are tolerated solely due to the economic functions they perform. History offers a number of examples of pariah peoples: the untouchables in the Indian caste system, the Jews in most of Europe, and blacks in the American South from the end of slavery after the Civil War (1865) until about the 1970s.

Status-based social differentiation goes hand in hand with the monopolizing of ideal and material goods and opportunities. High-status groups claim certain political, religious, and economic honours for themselves: restrictions on intermarriage, a monopoly of certain political offices or landownership, the right to own slaves or to engage in certain trades. High-status groups disdain physical labour, artistic or literary activities performed for money, or even rational economic pursuits in general, e.g., the nineteenth-century gentleman didn't have a job but got an income from his family or the family estate. The market, on the other hand, knows no personal distinctions—such functional interests as money, job skills, and managerial effectiveness rule the marketplace. It has no time for honour. That's why status groups often oppose themselves to purely economic acquisition as low-status money-grubbing—having a big bank account doesn't get you into the country club. That's why Canadian press baron Conrad Black got himself knighted in 2001—to win the social honour his money couldn't buy.

Class situations are most influential in times of technological and economic transformation, while status groups tend to be more important in stable societies. This is so because, when the bases of the production and buying of goods become unstable, class interests tend to dominate. This was the case in the early days of capitalism.

Weber's third type of group is the political party, which tries to influence social action to gain social power. It always involves some type of association with a plan, unlike classes and status groups, which usually have no formal association at all. Parties always have some sort of rational order and a staff of officials to develop and implement their plans. There are all sorts of parties, some with a class basis, like a working-class social-ist party, and some affiliated with a status group. They use various means to achieve power: naked violence, canvassing for votes, speeches, advertis-ing, bribes, and so on. Weber makes a basic dis-tinction between *patronage parties*, which aim at gaining power and divvying up the spoils, and *parties of principle*, which fight for values, yet tend to become patronage parties as they become bureaucratized. Internally, parties have various structures of domination. But since parties are out for conquest or political control, quite often they are organized in an authoritarian manner.

The Protestant Ethic

Marx explained the origins of capitalism in terms of a class struggle between the bourgeoisie and the feudal aristocracy, aided in part by technological developments, like the steam engine that made industrialization possible. He said that the old feu-dal mode of social organization was a fetter on the new mode of production offered by industrial cap-italism, so the former was slowly destroyed by the social and political power of the bourgeoisie. It was an economic change with social repercus-sions. In *The Protestant Ethic and the Spirit of Cap-italism* (1958 [1905]), Weber argues that a major cause of modern industrial and bureaucratic cap-italism was the religious ethic of certain Protestant sects in Western Europe, notably the Calvinists and Puritans. They considered work fundamental to their salvation, but embraced a modest lifestyle. The result was ever-growing profits that might be ploughed back into their businesses. So capitalism cannot be explained in purely economic terms, but also requires an understanding of moral and religious ideas.

Weber begins *The Protestant Ethic* by noting that a number of important cultural phenomena have appeared in their most important forms only in the West: a rational and systematic science, cer-tain types of music, art, and architecture (e.g., per-spective in art and the dome in architecture), and, very importantly, the trained government or eco-nomic official. Even the state itself, with a written constitution, rational laws, and a regular adminis-tration of trained officials, is a uniquely Western product. Most importantly, to Weber, modern cap-italism is a uniquely Western development. Unlimited greed isn't the same as capitalism: artists, prostitutes, gamblers, and crusaders of all periods and places have pursued money. What Weber means by capitalism isn't the simple act of making money, but of making a profit that is for-ever renewed by means of a continuous, rational enterprise of some sort. It is the peaceful pursuit of profit by means of exchange. The capitalist compares his expenses with his income in a rational way. Capitalism in this sense existed in fits and starts in the ancient world, but only in iso-lated cases such as moneylenders and among booty capitalists, such as colonialists and pirates. Modern capitalism requires a rational organization of free labour, the separation of business from the household, and a rational system of bookkeeping.

Also, modern capitalism needed a rational legal system and form of administration, both peculiar to the West. People had to have a sense that their investments would be rewarded and not arbitrarily taken away from them. But why didn't economic interests in China or India create such systems? Weber thinks the key is the peculiar rationalism of the West. We see this in science, economic life, techniques, military training, and law and administration. A rational economic life is based partly on rational techniques and law, but even more on the ideal of practical rational con-duct. This conduct is based on an ethical ideal of duty, supported by magical and religious forces.

Weber starts the main part of his book with an interesting fact: the huge majority of capitalist business leaders, owners, skilled labourers, and technically trained commercial officials in modern Europe and America are Protestant. The Protestant Reformation of Christianity started in the early 1500s with Martin Luther's reform movement in Germany, taken up later in the sixteenth century by John Calvin in Geneva and by John Knox and the Presbyterian Church in Scotland. Protes-tantism spread throughout Germany, England, and other parts of Northern Europe, and was exported to North America by the Puritans and other sects in the seventeenth century.

Weber contends that in places like England, Scotland, and Holland, Puritanism wasn't resisted, but embraced as heroic. Its greater control over people's behaviour gave birth to an ethic that favoured capitalism. The old Protestantism of Luther, Calvin, and Knox wasn't materialistic, but ascetic, hostile to bodily pleasure. The point of working hard to make money was not to spend it, but to fulfill a calling, to do God's work on Earth. The early capitalist spirit, to earn more and more money, yet not enjoy life too much, is not hedonistic. The accumulation of capital may not be to make the capitalist happy, but rather can be an end in itself. This accumulation is the purpose of life, not just a way of satisfying our material needs. It's a religious calling.

Weber argues against Marx's historical materialism that the spirit of capitalism existed before capitalist economic structures did, for example, in the Protestant colonies of New England in the early seventeenth century. It's not a question of modern capitalism coming out of large sums of capital, but out of a unique spirit—indeed, it was usually started by men with limited capital. Capitalism required men with strong character, clarity of vision, and moral qualities that would inspire confidence in workers and customers. These new entrepreneurs were bourgeois who had grown up in the hard school of life, being calculating and daring, moderate and reliable all at the same time. They weren't adventurers. Weber makes clear that the ideal type of the early capitalist entrepreneur is not a show-off or social climber, but a man who prefers to avoid ostentation, unnecessary expenditures, or enjoyment of his power or social status. He is an ascetic, modest person. He doesn't use his wealth for personal happiness. It seemed so irrational and mysterious to the pre-capitalist mind for a person to go to his grave loaded with a great mass of money and goods, yet this is precisely what happened in many such cases.

In his chapter on asceticism and the spirit of capitalism, Weber looks in detail at the work of the seventeenth-century English Presbyterian minister Richard Baxter. Baxter defends worldly asceticism, i.e., the idea that we should avoid temptations of the flesh yet still take a full part in the life of this world. His work was typical of the Puritan spirit. The Puritans, even more than medieval Catholics, condemned wealth and money. But their real moral objection to the enjoyment of wealth was the security and relaxation of effort it leads to. It creates idleness and temptations of the flesh. It's not leisure but activity that glorifies God and gets the sinner into heaven. Baxter sees wasting time as the greatest sin, e.g., in socializing, idle chatter, luxurious pursuits, even too much sleep. He argued that hard work (whether physical or mental) was the key to salvation. Labour is a classic ascetic technique, good as a defence against such 'unclean' pleasures as sex, which should only take place in marriage, and then only to create children. Work was seen as an end in itself, and unwillingness to work as a sign of a lack of grace. This Protestant work ethic was connected to the Calvinist and Puritan doctrine of predestination: as God's children, our souls are already saved or damned; yet since we can't be sure which, we feel anxious about our status and work hard to offer (at least to ourselves) a 'proof of election'.

The Puritan view differs from the medieval view of work as necessary to maintain the individual and community. Baxter says that even the rich have to work if they want to eat, for this is God's command. Martin Luther saw the division of labour as it stood as a direct result of the Divine will—it was a religious duty to persevere in one's allotted place in life. But the Puritans argued that we could see God's hand at work only in the division of labour and by its fruits. Not knowing in advance what God has planned for us, everyone has to pursue a calling in a methodical, rational way. The Puritan's worldly asceticism saw God as demanding the use of rational work in the pursuit of this calling, not just blindly accepting one's lot in life. God wants us to pursue a profit. Wealth is only bad if it leads to laziness or sinful enjoyment, to living merrily without any purpose or goal.

The Puritans opposed all spontaneous enjoyment of life. They were sober ascetics and hated idle talk and vain ostentation, even in dress: they wore simple black clothes, establishing a custom that persists to this day among modern people of business. When they did tolerate cultural goods, they had to be free, not expensive commodities. They rejected the idea of spontaneously and frivolously spending money on luxuries. But their ethic had the positive effect of freeing up traditional ethical limitations on making money—not only was this now legal, it was directly willed by God. The limit on ethically permissible spending was comfort: it was acceptable to spend money for necessary and practical things, but not for the glitter and showiness of the aristocrat's estate. The clean and solid comfort of a middle-class home became the Puritan ideal. The pursuit of wealth became an end in itself, a sign of following a calling given one by God. The religious support for restless, continuous, systematic work in a worldly calling became a powerful element of the spirit of capitalism. The combination of the release of money-making activity from traditional moral bonds and a strict limitation on consumption led to an ascetic compulsion both to save and to reinvest profits as productive capital. This investment fed on itself in ever-increasing cycles.

As the eighteenth century wore on, the Puritan search for the Kingdom of God through work turned into the economic virtues of utilitarian worldliness. The seventeenth century gave the modern world 'a good conscience' about the legal acquisition of money, along with a sense that the poor were poor because God wanted them that way, and that they should remain obedient to God, i.e., to the social system in place.

Next to the Divine blessing of capitalist profiteering was the parallel idea that faithful work, even for low wages in joyless employment devoid of intrinsic meaning, was pleasing to God. That, too, was a calling. With capitalism firmly in the saddle, no further transcendental sanctions were required for demanding joyless work from its workers. Baxter had seen material goods as a light cloak that could be easily thrown off, but did not foresee that cloak would become an iron cage: material goods now have an almost inexorable power over our lives. Capitalism no longer needs religious supports: the idea of a duty to our economic calling is rarely questioned. No one knows whether this cage will last forever, or whether there will be a rebirth of old ideals. Weber concludes that we live in an age of specialists without spirit, and sensualists without heart.

The Protestant Ethic is a paean to the power of moral and religious ideas over social structures. We now turn from Weber to a group of twentieth-century thinkers who also emphasized the notion of the centrality of subjective meaning to understanding human thought and action: Ludwig Wittgenstein, Peter Winch, R.G. Collingwood, and H.G. Gadamer.

LUDWIG WITTGENSTEIN AND LANGUAGE GAMES

The Early Wittgenstein: Logical Atomism

Ludwig Wittgenstein (1889–1951) was an Austrian philosopher who first studied engineering, then went to Cambridge University to study mathematics and philosophy, working with Bertrand Russell (1872–1970) and G.E. Moore (1873–1958). This trio of thinkers, along with A.J. Ayer (1910–89), created the foundation of analytic philosophy, which still dominates the Anglo-American academic scene. This school of thought holds that a close analysis of language and the use of formal logic will resolve centuries-old philosophical problems. They largely failed in this regard, but some of their ideas were important for a social theory that tries to understand social life as the product of human agency.

In his short 1921 book, *Tractatus Logico-Philosophicus*, which he wrote mostly during World War I while fighting with the Austrian army, Wittgenstein held the position that philosophers should help to build a language that was logical and clear. His central theory here is logical atomism. He saw the world as made up of simple facts, or atoms, which are pictured in thought. The proper function of language was either to lay out these thought-pictures in propositions, or to make mathematical and logical statements that, although true, are ultimately tautologies, such as 'all red apples are red.' These tautologies add nothing to our knowledge, unlike descriptions of facts, such as 'the apples on that tree are red.' Any statement that failed either to picture a fact or to express a logical truth was literally 'without sense', nonsense. Therefore, he said, metaphysical, ethical, and aesthetic statements are nonsense. Nonsense would include the following everyday claims, along with many others like them:

- God exists.
- It's wrong to commit murder.
- Beethoven's Ninth Symphony is beautiful.

Wittgenstein argued cryptically that the limits of language are the limits of our world, and ended the *Tractatus* with the famous statement: 'Whereof one cannot speak, thereof one must remain silent.' In other words, if it's not empirically provable, or not a logical truth, we can't speak about it. Needless to say, this approach lay by the wayside many of the traditional concerns of social theory, not to mention philosophy, and he later abandoned it. Regardless, his early work gave solace to an influential movement in twentieth-century thought: logical positivism—Ayer was a main player in it—which rejected the idea that philosophy could meaningfully discuss moral, political, or artistic life. This is one of the principal reasons why so much of Anglo-American philosophy in the twentieth century had so little to say to social and political theory. Wittgenstein himself soon tried to end this silence.

The Late Wittgenstein: Rules and Language Games

Starting in the early 1930s, Wittgenstein began to reconsider his earlier ideas. He turned from his vision of a logically clear and transparent language to the analysis of ordinary language, which is considerably messier and more contradictory than logic and mathematics. Over the last 20 years of his life he wrote down his ideas as a series of numbered paragraphs and aphorisms that were published after his death as *Philosophical Investigations* (1953). The late Wittgenstein sees language as a series of games whose rules vary according to the use to which the game is being put: there is one game for praising people, another for cursing them, one for academic discussion, another for baseball umpiring, and so on. There are countless types of language games. Wittgenstein lists a variety of these games in section 23 of the *Philosophical Investigations*:

> Giving orders, and obeying them.
> Describing the appearance of an object, or giving its measurements.
> Constructing an object from a description (a drawing).
> Reporting an event.
> Speculating about an event.
> Forming or testing a hypothesis.
> Presenting the results of an experiment in tables and diagrams.
> Making up a story; and reading it.
> Singing catches.
> Guessing riddles.
> Making riddles.
> Making a joke; telling it.
> Solving a problem in practical arithmetic.
> Translating from one language into another.
> Asking, thanking, cursing, greeting, praying.

For the late Wittgenstein the meaning of a word depended on its use. We use words like we move pieces in a game of chess. There are specific rules for *how* to move the pieces—for example, the bishop must be moved along diagonals only—but there are still many different *ways* they can be moved. Language is a diverse phenomenon, with many different uses. It cannot be seen as having one common pattern or structure. The meaning of words isn't carved in stone, but varies with the language game being used. We use a given word in a variety of ways, yet these ways are governed by rules; these different ways of using a word can be said to have only a 'family resemblance'. You may look something like your sister, but you aren't identical to her—unless she's your twin, of course. Similarly, the way we use the same word varies from situation to situation. For example, the simple expression 'I'm happy' could express joy in a love affair, resignation about not getting a promotion, sarcasm about getting a bad mark in a class, or a blasé attitude to life in general. The rules governing the use of words form complicated networks of overlapping and criss-crossing similarities that cannot be expressed in simple logical relationships or mathematical formulae (ibid., section 66).

Another metaphor Wittgenstein used to illustrate his view of language was to see words as like tools in a toolbox (ibid., section 11). In the toolbox we find a hammer, nails, pliers, a screwdriver, and so on. Each tool can be used 'correctly' in a variety of ways. The hammer always looks like a hammer, but there are many different uses to which we can put it: pounding a nail into the wall, breaking a piece of wood in two, smashing beer cans, and so on. Words are like this: they may look the same in each sentence we find them in, but they have many distinct uses. Every language game has a set of rules. Wittgenstein describes a primitive language game used by two builders that consists of only four words: block, beam, pillar, and slab (ibid., section 2). Each of these four words refers to an object used by the builders and is understood by them as such. Of course, real language games have many rules. Yet, we mustn't imagine that these rules are hard and fast; they are loose and vague. Wittgenstein compares a rule to a signpost at a crossroads: it points towards one or more destinations, but does not compel us to go to any of them, to stay on the road, or to even continue our journey (ibid., section 85).

Wittgenstein also makes the argument that there are no private languages, no languages in the mind of one person alone. Even 'pain' is a public concept: I can call the twinge in my arm as I type these words 'pain' only because I am a participant in language games that have already defined this feeling for me. Languages are based on what Wittgenstein called a 'form of life', a way of living

for a given community of people. The only way that we can decide on right and wrong ways of using a given word is by its social context. We cannot invent a private language without connecting it to a language we already know. For the Wittgenstein of the *Philosophical Investigations*, language is governed by a series of rules that can only be understood through social interaction. In a word, language is not logical or mathematical, but social at its very core.

R.G. COLLINGWOOD'S HISTORICAL IDEALISM

Collingwood on Metaphysics and History

The social sciences—sociology, psychology, economics, and political science—had their origins in the philosophical and historical research of the eighteenth century. Sociology came out of the philosophical and historical work of Montesquieu, Adam Ferguson, John Millar, and the Marquis de Condorcet; psychology from the philosophical empiricism of John Locke and David Hume and from such French thinkers as Condillac and La Mettrie; economics primarily from Adam Smith; and political science from Thomas Hobbes, Montesquieu, and Locke. All of these thinkers were either philosophers, historians, or both. The twentieth-century English thinker R.G. Collingwood (1889–1943) was both a philosopher and a historian, not to mention a practising archaeologist interested in Roman Britain. Collingwood's ideas about the nature of philosophy and history, and how the two are related, place him firmly in the camp of those who see social relationships as the product of human agency. His idealism links him to the social theory of Max Weber, Peter Winch, and Anthony Giddens. An 'idealist' in epistemology is someone who sees all of reality as a series of ideas. If we see a dog crossing the street, the dog is real to us only because we have an idea of it. In the related though separate sense the term is being used here, a 'historical idealist' is someone who sees history as either driven by ideas (as did Hegel) or as understandable only *through* ideas (Collingwood). It would be more proper to call

Collingwood a 'methodological idealist' because he thinks we can understand the past only through ideas, although he doesn't especially believe that ideas in themselves drive history—his histories of ancient Britain discuss geography, climate, and economics as much as philosophy, religion, and science. And in case you're wondering what a philosopher of history is doing in a book on social theory, remember that history is the story of past events, which includes everything that has happened in society other than that small slice of time we call 'the present'. So history is the foundation of all good social science.

In *An Essay on Metaphysics* (1940), Collingwood describes metaphysics not as abstract speculations about the nature of the cosmos, but as the historical study of the foundational beliefs of natural science in each period of the past. His theory of absolute presuppositions grounds metaphysics in history and, thus, in social relationships. Collingwood starts by assuming that all statements we make are answers to questions: so if I say, 'The wall is three feet high', I'm answering the question, 'How high is this ruin of a Roman wall?' Next, he argues that all statements involve some sort of presupposition: they suppose something to be true that the speaker and his or her audience will agree on. In the statement above, I am assuming that the pile of stones in front of me was in fact a wall and that we can agree on what a 'foot' as a unit of measurement represents. Then, Collingwood follows (ibid., 29, 31) with three claims that need a bit of untangling:

- A presupposition is either relative or absolute.
- A relative presupposition stands relatively to one question as a presupposition and to another as its answer.
- An absolute presupposition is related to all relevant questions as a presupposition, never as an answer.

Collingwood is making a basic distinction here between relative and absolute presuppositions. The latter are foundational beliefs that cannot be verified; they are neither true nor false. They are merely presupposed. This includes beliefs like 'God exists' and 'all things have a cause.' A relative presupposition is presupposed by one question, yet is the answer to another. Let's return to the ruined wall. If I measure it with a tape measure, I am presupposing that my tape measure is accurate. The statement 'My tape measure is accurate' is presupposed by the question, 'How high is the wall?', while at the same time it's an answer to the question, 'Is your tape measure accurate?' So the presupposition that my tape measure is accurate is not absolute, but is relative to another presupposition, perhaps 'The company that made it is reputable.' However, if we asked what the presupposition 'God exists' is relative to, we cannot answer the question: it's an absolute assumption (at least according to Collingwood). The believer takes it as a given.

Collingwood concludes that the proper job of the metaphysician is seeking out the absolute presuppositions of science at each stage of history. All metaphysical questions are thus historical questions (ibid., 49). It's a mistake to try to figure out whether a given metaphysical belief is true or false. Saying that 'God exists' is an absolute belief that no amount of evidence will shake. Collingwood's theory of absolute presuppositions is interesting because it so closely parallels Thomas Kuhn's theory of scientific paradigms (see Chapter 1) and Wittgenstein's notion of a form of life as the foundation for language use. All argue that each age and culture share a set of foundational beliefs that are not based on empirical evidence or logical deductions. Collingwood's metaphysics thus parallels Kuhn's scientific principles and Wittgenstein's language games: they're all grounded in historically shifting social relations.

Collingwood argued in *The Idea of History* (1946: 318) against seeing history, thus by implication sociology, as a natural science. Just as rational activity is free from the domination of nature, historical thought is free from the domination of natural science. Rational beings are free to choose what to do and to avoid doing. Further, history is the story of the human mind, and the mind is historical (ibid., 209). There can be no science of human nature, because human nature changes, unlike the basic physical structure of animals, plants, and minerals. Giraffes always have long necks and spots; the chemical formula for water is always H_2O. Yet the very ideals of human societies change—feudalism is dead, having been replaced by capitalism, at least in the modern West (ibid., 211). Human societies change their absolute presuppositions and social forms from age to age because they are shaped by ideas.

History is knowledge of the human mind (ibid., 219). What else would it be? Coins and pottery shards and tattered parchments written in long-dead tongues mean nothing by themselves without our interpreting them, as we attempt to rethink the thoughts of those who made them. If we find a Roman coin in a village in northern England, we might ask questions like, 'Whose picture is on the coin? When was it minted? Does this prove that there was a Roman town in the area at the time? What could this coin buy in basic staples?' and so on. Collingwood believed that there's no point generalizing too much about historical events: we can't understand Napoleon's military strategies better by comparing them with Hannibal's or Julius Caesar's (ibid., 223). In this Collingwood seems to be rejecting Weber's ideal types, except insofar as these ideals influence the actions of individual actors. Yet he admitted that individual acts are connected to other individual acts through thoughts that potentially can be shared by everyone. Further, Collingwood admitted that historical actors always find themselves in a given situation: 'For a man about to act, the situation is his master, his oracle, his god', a god he can neglect only at his peril (ibid., 316). In summary, Collingwood sees history as grounded in individual actions within given situations, which we can understand only by interpreting the thought that went into them. In this he echoes Weber's emphasis on subjective meaning as the centre of sociological understanding.

The Idea of History

What is history? In his most influential work, the posthumously published *The Idea of History*, Collingwood provides a precise answer (ibid., 10–11). History is:

1. a science that asks questions,
2. whose object is past human actions,
3. which proceeds by interpreting evidence, and
4. whose goal is human self-knowledge.[1]

History is knowledge of the past that the historian revives in the present. It is thus a form of self-knowledge of the historian's own mind (ibid., 175). This is where Collingwood's idealism is clearest: we have no direct access to a past event, say, Napoleon's defeat at the Battle of Waterloo, whether or not we have lots of evidence for it. We can't replay the event; even if we did (say, as part of a lavish film production), it still wouldn't be *the* Battle of Waterloo but a theatrical restaging of the battle. All we have is our ability to relive or revive that event in our own mind. Every man who fought in the battle is long dead, along with all witnesses of the event. Furthermore, even if Napoleon came back to life so we could interrogate him, all he'd have would be his own personal memories of the battle, which the historian would still have to weigh against other accounts and evidence. So, Waterloo as a real event is dead for us. It lives in the present only as a set of ideas in our mind.

This is important for understanding Collingwood's attack on natural science as being on foreign territory in analyzing social and historical events, along with his defence of human agency. He uses the example of his own British homeland to make his case against a materialist or determinist view of history. The fact that Great Britain is an island is not what shaped British history, but the way the British regarded their insularity (ibid., 200):

> The fact that certain people live, for example, on an island has in itself no effect on their history; what has an effect is the way that they regard the seas as a barrier or as a highway to traffic. Had it been otherwise, their insular position, being a constant fact, would have produced a constant effect on their historical life.

. . . In itself, it is merely a raw material for historical activity, and the character of historical life depends on how this raw material is used.

In other words, the 'hard facts' of the situation are the hard facts of the way we *see* the situation (ibid., 317). Here Collingwood comes down clearly on the human agency side of the agency/structure debate: social, geographical, and other structures only influence human actions by giving us different menus of choices. But we still *choose* in the above case either to stay on our island or to sail the briny seas to distant lands.

Based on his notion that the past is accessible to use only through ideas, Collingwood lays out three principles of history (ibid., 215):

1. All history is the history of thought.
2. The history of thought, and therefore of all history, is the re-enactment of past thought in the historian's own mind.
3. This re-enactment is not the passive surrender to the spell of another mind, but an active and critical thinking: the historian re-enacts in the light of his own knowledge, criticizes it, and corrects errors.

Collingwood argues that as historians, and by implication social theorists, we are obliged to re-enact past thought in its widest sense (ibid., 282). In fact, we do this in our everyday life: to understand other people's actions, we re-enact their thought processes in our own minds. If we see a man chasing someone down the street, we run over several motivations in our mind—the man is angry at the person he's chasing, he's a police officer chasing a thief, or he is trying to catch up to a friend to speak with him. We don't usually think of his running as a random burst of activity. Further, re-enactment assumes that each form of life

has its own problems, and the historian/theorist must come to that form of life with some sympathy and insight to understand it (ibid., 329). The historian's thought must spring from the 'organic unity' of his or her total experience, which may or may not allow for an understanding of a past epoch (ibid., 305).

Collingwood made a basic distinction between human historical *acts*, which have a thought-side to them, and natural *events*, which happen according to natural laws. This was a distinction between the inside and the outside of a historical happening. Flowers sprout out of the ground every spring without pondering the question, 'Should we grow this year?' But German voters in 1933 *did* ponder the question, 'Should we vote for the Nazi Party?', or something like it. People think, plan, reason, and establish goals, even if these goals are in part irrational. They act. Rocks, trees, and mountain streams don't think or plan or reason; their changes are governed by physical laws. Human actions are the combination of inner thoughts and outer physical actions; natural events have an outer physical side, but no inner-thought side. This is summarized in Table 5.2.

History is concerned with human acts, not natural events, unless they impact human acts, thus giving past actors reasons for choosing one path of action over another, e.g., a volcanic eruption leads people to leave town before being covered with lava (this, of course, would be a quite rational course of action). We can re-enact only past actions in our minds, not past natural events: I can reconstruct why I went to a given movie or avoided talking to a colleague at work, but I cannot reconstruct a cloud's 'decision' to rain or a volcano's 'choice' to explode, since neither even has an inner-thought side.

Collingwood makes a second basic distinction, echoed by most theorists of human agency,

Table 5.2 Collingwood's Theory of Acts and Events

Type of Phenomena	Basis of Phenomena	Content
Events	Natural (non-thinking parts of nature)	Outer bodies and their movements
Acts	Historical (humans as rational beings with goals, plans, purposes)	Inner thoughts *and* outer bodies and their movements

between natural and human or historical causes. Returning to *An Essay on Metaphysics* (1940: 285), we find that Collingwood describes three ways in which the word 'cause' is used. The first way is in its historical sense:

> Here that which is 'caused' is the free and deliberate act of a conscious and responsible agent, and 'causing' him to do it means affording him a motive for doing it.

His other two senses of 'cause' are those found in the natural sciences, where a 'cause' is an event or state of things that produces or prevents the thing being caused (this is the practical sense of a natural cause), and where the cause is prior to the effect, necessary for the effect to happen, and always leads to the effect (this is the theoretical sense of a natural cause) (ibid., 285–6). So, a historical cause is simply the motive or reason in the actor's mind that led to his or her act. It is a thought inside the mind of the historical or social actor. This analysis of 'cause' is a more radically idealist version of Weber's notion that the sociologist understands a social act by understanding the subjective meaning behind it. Weber admitted that we could use the term 'cause' to describe how collective events could lead an individual to act in a certain way, but Collingwood reduces all historical causality to subjective meaning. What he calls a historical cause is simply a reason or motive for an action: in this sense physical or structural factors never *directly* cause human action, but merely provide actors with reasons to do one thing or another.

Collingwood argues in *The Idea of History* that since historical actions are the product of rational choices, the historian (and by extension the sociologist) isn't interested in people's animal appetites. The fact that social actors eat, sleep, and have sex is not of interest to Collingwood's historian, only the social customs that sanction some appetites and prohibit others (Collingwood, 1946: 216). This leads him to brand psychology as the science of sensations, feelings, and appetites, not rational thought, which is the province of history

and philosophy (ibid., 231). Psychology has no role to play in re-enacting the past. Individual emotions are not properly historical—we can't re-enact feelings of the wind blowing through Nietzsche's hair on the mountaintop, but we can read *Beyond Good and Evil* and try to figure out what he was saying in it. The subject matter of history is reflective thought, of things done on purpose for a reason. This is where one of the major criticisms of Collingwood's view of history comes to light. He is *too* rationalistic, too quick to throw out human passions and subjective feelings. Yet, when we look at his list of the things history can talk meaningfully about, we find it quite extensive: politics, war, economic life, morality, science, philosophy, and art. In all of these fields actors face problems, set goals for themselves, and act for reasons or purposes.

Historical Method: Evidence and Imagination

The basic problem with historical research is that the events being studied have already happened, in some cases a long time ago. If we are studying modern history, a few survivors of important events might still be alive who we can interview. But even in this case we must supplement this sort of direct research with other types of evidence to arrive at a complete understanding of a historical period: diaries, newspaper accounts, maps, government and church documents, works of literature, archaeological fragments (pottery, coins, jewellery, grave remains, statues, buildings), and earlier histories. A diary, shard of pottery, or statue of a goddess cannot give us a complete account of a historical event, much less of a whole historical period. We need some sort of historical method to transform the evidence at our disposal into a narrative of the past.

Remember that Collingwood thought all history was the history of thought. Even with good historical accounts and a bundle of evidence before us, we don't know every relevant thought from the past, but have to connect together the facts and actions we are sure of in a meaningful way. Collingwood argues we do so through the a priori imagination, which produces a 'web' of imaginative construction that links together the various actions and facts for which we have strong evidence (ibid., 241–3). Studying history is like writing a novel, except that history takes place in real space and real time, must be internally consistent, and must cohere to the evidence we have available. So if we ask, 'Why did Hitler invade Poland in 1939?', a sensible answer—given his rantings in *Mein Kampf* and speeches at mass Nazi Party rallies that the German people needed *Lebensraum* (living space) in Eastern Europe— would be 'To obtain new land for Germany.' Other possible answers also cohere to the evidence we have, but many others do not, such as 'Because Hitler was afraid of Polish expansionism, and decided to strike first.'

To figure these things out, Collingwood argued we have to act a bit like a detective who must use his imagination to take the series of physical facts and statements from witnesses he has available to him to reconstruct the crime he is investigating. In this both the detective and the historian use Francis Bacon's (1561–1626) method of scientific investigation. Bacon argued you must 'put nature to the question', that is, torture it for answers to our questions. The historian is like the detective whose criminal investigations are driven by questions. If a bloody glove is found at the scene, the detective asks, 'Whose blood is on the glove? Who owns this glove? Why was it left behind?' Like Sherlock Holmes, the detective keeps asking himself and others questions until he gets enough answers to put together a complete picture of the crime. Collingwood concludes that the criterion of historical truth is this idea of history, where the past is imaginatively reconstructed from available evidence by historians rethinking past thoughts.

Collingwood is important for social theory because his principles of history, especially the notion that all history is the history of thought, state the case for human agency in stark terms. In a sense, he says that Weber's basic principle of *Verstehen* sociology is even truer than Weber himself thought: we can understand a historical or social action only by interpreting the actor's subjective meaning, or in Collingwood's formulation, their thoughts. Generalizations, comparisons, statistics, and ideal types only muddy the waters. Only by re-enacting the thoughts of individual human beings can we understand how and why they acted the way they did. Without this re-enactment, their actions are mere dead events, like a rock rolling down a hill or a dandelion casting its seeds into the wind. To understand *any* human action, past or present, we have to understand that actor's conscious, purposive thoughts. Their sensations and feelings can't be re-enacted, and are thus of secondary interest to the historian or social scientist.

We now turn to Peter Winch, who explicitly applied the insights of Wittgenstein and Collingwood to the social sciences.

PETER WINCH ON THE IDEA OF A SOCIAL SCIENCE

Philosophy and Social Science

Peter Winch (1926–97) picked up Wittgenstein's theory of language games to show how social science must deal with concepts and, therefore, is deeply philosophical at its core. Winch was an English thinker who worked in the same intellectual borderland between philosophy and sociology as the other thinkers in this chapter. His convincing short book, *The Idea of a Social Science and Its Relation to Philosophy* (1958), picks up a number of insights in Wittgenstein and Collingwood and applies these to social science in general. He warns us that we have to beware of the extra-scientific pretensions of natural science. Social science, since it deals with human agents, must operate according to a different set of principles from natural science. It must deal with an understanding of the concepts we apply to social life, so at base it is a philosophical inquiry. Both our social relations and our very sense of reality are based on concepts, which we express through language. And as Wittgenstein made clear, the meaning of words in a given language depends on how they are used. Here's how Winch sees the relation of language, concepts, and society:

Words used according to certain Rules → Meaningful Language → Concepts of Reality → Social Relations → Form of Life

Winch starts by noting that the philosopher is concerned with the nature of reality as a whole, unlike the scientist who is concerned with particular causes and effects (Winch, 1958: 8). This is a conceptual issue, not an empirical one. He does agree that philosophy should attempt to correct linguistic confusions, especially confusions surrounding the question of how language is connected to reality and whether reality is intelligible (ibid., 12). But he rejects the idea of separating our language from our social world, for our concepts and language define this world for us. The world is presented to us through our concepts. In talking about language philosophically, we are discussing 'what counts as belonging to the world' (ibid., 15).

Echoing Collingwood, Winch argues that people make decisions based on their understandings of the situations in which they find themselves. Someone's social relations are permeated with ideas about reality; indeed, social relations are expressions of ideas about reality (ibid., 23). This conflicts with the structuralist and materialist social theories, which look for the causes at play in social action independent of the consciousness of social actors. Winch follows Wittgenstein in seeing the meaning of a word as the way it is used, which must follow some sort of rule for us to be able understand one another. If every time I say 'dog' I mean what you call 'cat', our conversations about pets will be very confusing. Winch goes on to investigate Wittgenstein's notion of what it means to follow a rule. Language follows rules insofar as words are used in the 'same way' from one occasion to another. That is what following a rule means—to do the same sort of thing in different times and places. It would be very strange if I described my pet feline Fluffy as

a 'cat', a 'dog', and a 'fish' to three distinct groups of people yet insisted that I was following some sort of linguistic rule.

Winch argues that reasons and actions can be connected only if the actor is following a rule, whether or not the actor can explain what this rule is. This might seem a bit abstract, but think about the following scenario: Janet buys a lottery ticket for five dollars. Her husband Bill asks her, 'Why did you buy the ticket?' and Janet replies, 'To win the million-dollar jackpot!' The rule here is something like 'if you don't buy a ticket, you can't win!' But if Janet had said that she bought the ticket without also understanding that it was somehow connected to a lottery jackpot, say on a lark, there seems to be no comprehensible rule in effect, hence, no way to rationally explain her actions. The moral of the story is that it must be possible for someone else to discover the rule the actor is following in order to say that she is following a rule at all (ibid., 30). Meaningful behaviour is behaviour others can understand as connected to some prior motive that makes sense both to the actor and to her observers—a point on which Weber and Collingwood would agree heartily. Connected to this point of logic, says Winch, is the fact that meaningful actions can be understood only in a social context where mistakes are possible (ibid., 39). There must be right *and* wrong ways of using words and of interacting socially. If Janet enthusiastically asserted that 'this lottery ticket is my ticket into heaven!', whether or not we're atheists or fervent religious believers, we can certainly correct her—there's nothing in our form of life to connect lottery tickets with celestial paradises.

When a sociologist decides that the same thing has happened in two diverse situations, he or she believes that the same rule can be applied to those two situations (ibid., 88). However, this similarity is 'internal' to the actors' minds, in terms of concepts, not physical characteristics. For example, what makes a Japanese kamikaze pilot's attack on an American aircraft carrier in 1945 and a Palestinian suicide bomber's self-destruction inside a Tel Aviv restaurant in 2005 both cases of

Durkheim's altruistic suicide'? What makes these two acts 'the same'? It's the fact that each actor sees him or herself as sacrificing his or her life for 'a greater cause'—whatever we may think of their respective 'causes'. Winch thus builds Wittgenstein's rather thin notion of a 'form of life' into the connecting bridge between the latter's philosophy and social science. Underlying the sameness of the linguistic and social rules we all follow is the form of life we live in—our social, cultural, and ethnic community. To understand another's actions, we must understand the place of this action within our form of life, within the sum total of our social relations. This opens Winch to the charge of relativism. We may ask, does this mean we cannot understand words and actions in *other* forms of life, say, those of an eleventh-century monk or a contemporary New Guinea tribesman? Is true knowledge of the past impossible? We'll return to this problem when we look at Gadamer, but suffice it to say that it's not so easily resolved.

In sum, for Winch the central problem of sociology—giving a general account of the nature of social phenomena—belongs to philosophy (ibid., 43). Social life should be understood as a web of concepts and rules, some of which we do not always follow. These concepts and rules are tied to the form of life that the actors practise. As Weber said, meaningful social behaviour has a subjective sense. This leads Weber and Winch to the idea that, first and foremost, we have to understand people's reasons for acting before explaining these actions, and not base our explanations on causes or laws of which actors aren't conscious.

Maximizing Max

As we've seen, Weber argued that the sociologist must look to the subjective meaning behind an act to understand it. This is the actor's motive or reason for the act. At the same time, Weber suggested that some behaviour is without such a subjective meaning—for example, the instinctive swatting of a fly—while other types have a large degree of habit associated with them, thus depriving the actor of a meaningful reason for acting. The bone

of contention for Winch is Weber's notion of traditional behaviour, which the latter often describes in terms of blind impulse. Suppose Susie marries her handsome beau Bart. When asked, 'Why did you marry Bart? Why not just live together?', Susie replies, 'That's just the way we do things around here!' Weber might wonder whether Susie actually has a *reason* for marrying Bart, since she frames her action in terms of community traditions. Yet Winch argues that this action *does* have a sense to it: it represents commitment to a form of life. Susie is applying a rule: 'Women in my community marry their mates instead of living common law.' Also, Susie understands to some degree what 'getting married' means, including the moral, legal, and religious differences between being a married couple and being girlfriend and boyfriend. For all these reasons, her action is meaningful.

Whether or not Susie can formulate the rule she's following in getting married is beside the point for Winch, as long as she can tell the difference between a right way and a wrong way of doing things (ibid., 58). Another way of saying this is that principles underlie meaningful actions, while meaningless actions have no such principles governing them. In the above example, Susie's principle might be that 'marriage is a sacred state' or that 'the children of unmarried couples are bastards.'

Winch argues that Weber should have stuck to his guns and not seen subjective meaning as the cause of an action, but as a reason or motive for it (except in Collingwood's historical sense of the term 'cause'). Further, sometimes Weber speaks of collective concepts as causes and of sociological laws as statistical regularities among a mass of individual intentions. Statistics and laws are *sometimes* of use to Weber. Yet Winch retorts that Weber should have maximized the ground principle of his *Verstehen* sociology: that everything depends on the individual actor's subjective meaning. Statistics don't help us to *understand* a person's action. For example, noting that the word '*Katze*' appears in 7 per cent of all German paragraphs tells us nothing about what the word means. Indeed, a language teacher who merely listed the frequency of various words in the language being taught would be seen as an idiot by her students. Understanding a person's action involves grasping the meaning or point of that action—statistics or causal laws can't help us here (ibid., 115). If we explained a teenager's suicide by noting that the suicide rate in Canada has risen by 10 per cent over the last decade, we're not really saying *anything* about that particular suicide. This leads Winch to conclude that we cannot make historical or sociological predictions, because whether or not a trend continues depends on human decisions, which aren't determined in advance (ibid., 93). In other words, human beings are, at least in part, free.

Society as a Conversation

Following in the spirit of Wittgenstein's later philosophy, Winch says that 'social interaction can more profitably be compared to the exchange of ideas in a conversation than to the interaction of forces in a physical system' (ibid., 128). One might add that seeing society as a set of material or functional structures would also be out of the question. Social change is based on language changes: new ways of talking imply new social relationships. This is true since understanding the meaning of a word involves understanding the way it is used; and to describe how it's used involves understanding the social relations underlying it (ibid., 122–3). Social change comes about when language games change. The entire process of social interaction, excepting feral children and mental vegetables, is internal to one or more languages. Think of how the civil rights and feminist movements of the 1960s and 1970s changed the way our society talked about and, hence, treated racial minority groups and women. It is impossible to separate words and actions. Our very concepts of 'equality' and 'justice' changed thanks to these movements, with widespread social changes being the result.

Not surprisingly, Winch agrees with Collingwood that all history is the history of thought, though he doubts that we can re-enact extinct ways of thinking exactly as they were originally experienced because being a contemporary historian gets in the way of being a full member of the past community that we're trying to revive in our minds (ibid., 131). We can't think of our lady exactly as would a medieval knight, although we have some inkling of what chivalry and courtly love involved. Nevertheless, Collingwood was right in rejecting the idea that historical explanation is not the application of theories and generalizations to specific historical events. Instead, both history and sociology trace *internal* relations between sets of ideas or elements of a language game (ibid., 133). Winch discusses the classic Western film *Shane*, where a look by the hero becomes meaningful only within the context of the events of the film. A good film is a form of life. It creates characters with motivations and actions that we can understand as meaningful; as a result we may either sympathize with them or reject them as villainous. This is a metaphor for all of social life: looks, gestures, and words are meaningful only within the context of a form of life, a set of social relations. Both in films and in social interactions, context is everything: we excuse the film action hero for killing if he's getting revenge for the murder of his family; we know the difference between a hockey fight and a physical assault in a dark alley; we can tell whether a wave from a friend is a greeting or a farewell.

In the end, Winch is perhaps *more* of an idealist than Collingwood in that he chooses to define both our past *and* present social relations in terms of ideas and concepts. For Collingwood, we can only know the past by re-enacting past thoughts in the present. This method was for him a basic principle of historical analysis, although he probably would have applied it to social science as a whole. For Winch, on the other hand, the very fabric of social relations is based on concepts and ideas that we can understand only by focusing on the subjective meanings of social actors. And these meanings always are embedded in a given form of life. This leads us to Gadamer's hermeneutics, which takes this notion of historical embeddedness very seriously.

HANS-GEORGE GADAMER'S HERMENEUTICS

The life of Hans-George Gadamer (1900–2002) spanned the twentieth century. After finishing the first of his two doctorates in 1923, Gadamer worked for five years under the great phenomenologist Martin Heidegger (1889–1976). He taught at the universities of Marburg, Kiel, and Leipzig in the 1930s and 1940s before finally settling down in Frankfurt in 1947, where he taught until his retirement in 1968. For the rest of his life he was a travelling scholar, visiting a number of North American campuses, including McMaster University in Hamilton, Ontario. His most famous work is *Truth and Method* (2000 [1975]).

Gadamer's thought is a form of hermeneutics. Originally, hermeneutics was the systematic attempt to interpret the Bible in order to recover the original meaning of these ancient, sacred writings. In the nineteenth century, Friedrich Schleiermacher (1768–1834) and Wilhelm Dilthey (1833–1911) moved hermeneutics away from strictly Biblical interpretation to an attempt to understand the meaning of texts in general in terms of their authors' intentions and how these intentions were shaped by the cultures in which they were written. By Dilthey's time, hermeneutists had begun to move from the interpretation of texts to that of historical events and social relations. Their hope was to ground the human sciences (*Geisteswissenschaften*) in a scientific method as sound as that used by their cousins in the natural sciences (*Naturwissenschaften*), leading to the possibility of the 'objective' interpretation of a text or event. Gadamer's hermeneutics went one step further, arguing that we can never reconstruct the ideas and way of life of a past community in its entirety because we're inevitably mired in the values and presuppositions of our own age. All views of a text (or, by extension, of a society) take place within a given historical horizon: there is no horizon-less view of the past or present.

For Gadamer (1976: 3), language isn't an instrument or tool we pick up to communicate with others, but is the basis of all social life. 'Language is the fundamental mode of operation of our being-in-the-world and the all-embracing form of the constitution of the world.' He follows Winch in arguing that language is the ground of all thought and social relations. We don't relate to the world outside of language: reality happens *within* language (ibid., 35). And to learn a language, we have to learn its rules within a given form of life.

Gadamer's key concepts are 'interpretation' and 'understanding'. In this he echoes Weber's *Verstehen* social theory, though Gadamer is referring more to historical texts than to social acts. The point of hermeneutics is to *interpret* texts (and, by extension, human actions) and thus to *understand* them. This interpretation isn't simply a matter of understanding the subjective meaning of the author of the text (Weber), or of re-enacting the thought contained in it (Collingwood). Gadamer's goal is not to reconstruct an author's intentions—indeed, such a reconstruction is impossible because we're all historical beings immersed in the ebb and flow of shifting values and presuppositions. We're immersed in a horizon of tradition made up of a series of 'prejudices'. In both German and French, the word 'prejudice' means a 'pre-judgement', and that is the sense of the term Gadamer has in mind. When we encounter a thing or idea, we come to it with prejudgements. We can never escape the prejudices of the time and place we live in. Indeed, our prejudices constitute our being (ibid., 9). All interpretations of texts and events are tied to the interests and concerns of the present. Gadamer's hermeneutics argues that textual and social interpretation is less like a scientific experiment and more like a dialogue, paralleling Winch's view of society as one big conversation. When we interpret the past, it's like a dialogue between the known—our minds—and the unknown—the text or event we're trying to understand. Dialogue is a process of negotiation where two parties with distinct interests arrive at an agreement through a figurative meeting of minds. Of course, the only one of these minds to be active is that of the contemporary interpreter. Gadamer, like Collingwood, recognizes that both texts and human actions are the products of past thoughts, so the metaphor of a 'meeting of minds' seems appropriate.

Understanding involves reconstructing the past by fusing our horizon with that of the past epoch under study. Metaphorically speaking, it's like a merging of minds where each shares some of the contents of the other. Gadamer called this merging of minds a fusion of horizons. He agreed with Collingwood that historical investigations are driven by questions, but disagreed that we could recover past thinking in its entirety; we always filter it through the prejudices of our own age. Yet this isn't especially a bad thing, for tradition and prejudice situate us in our world and allow us to understand that world. And this fusion of horizons is always shifting—obviously, history is always in flux. For example, the basic social and political values of 2007 differ from those of 1957 on a number of fronts, hence our interpretation of a text or of an event today could be quite different from that of someone of 50 years ago. In this sense, the meanings of texts and of events are also always changing, since our interpretations of them are linked to current interests that change over time. This relativism moves the process of interpreting texts and events far away from natural science, which aims at a single true interpretation of its objects of study throughout time. Naturally, the notion that an interpretation of an event can legitimately change from time to time—and not just because the earlier interpretation was 'wrong' and the later interpretation was 'right'—would be seen as horribly relativistic by the more scientifically minded.

As an example of how this fusion of horizons works, say the hermeneutist is trying to understand a medieval romantic poem like *Le Roman de la Rose*. He or she must try to understand the prejudices of the medieval poet, some of which are radically different from our own. The poet would tend to see nature and social relations in allegorical and spiritual terms, unlike most moderns. And he probably saw love in courtly terms, as full of high-mindedness, subtle seductions, and self-denials, which are again alien to most modern people. The interpreter must attempt to fuse the poet's values and social horizons with his or her own. The following diagram (Figure 5.1) shows how the hermeneutical process works.

The interpretive process is the same in social relations as with texts. Suppose Kate, a liberal pro-abortion atheist, encounters Brigitte, a conservative Christian pro-life protestor, on a city street. Their horizons are quite different. But as they talk, they discover that they share many values. They

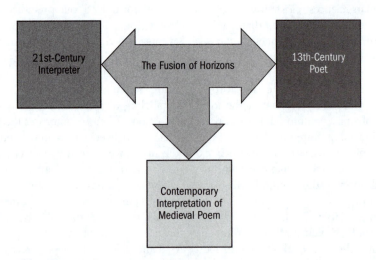

Figure 5.1 The Hermeneutical Process

both value life, but in different ways; they agree that happiness, health, and financial well-being are good things; and they both enjoy good literature and classical music. But they find out these common traits only by engaging in dialogue, by fusing their horizons a bit. Only then do they come to understand each other a little more.

Our 'dialectic of experience' involves the confrontation with elements of experience that contradict our prejudices. That's how we expand our horizons and evolve as theorists and as human beings. In a sense, travelling to foreign countries is a hermeneutical adventure: we encounter foreign languages, cultures, and geography on such trips, expanding our awareness of the human experience. Gadamer argues that when we become aware of the historically conditioned nature of our experience of the world we have 'historically effective consciousness'. Then, we can use our own personal experiences and cultural prejudgements to effectively interpret the past.

This led Gadamer to uphold the role of authority and tradition against Enlightenment skepticism and modern critical theory, both of which attacked traditional values. Habermas, in an extended intellectual debate, called Gadamer a conservative for his defence of tradition. Gadamer replied that since prejudices, hence tradition, are always changing and thus our social horizons are always changing, he is not a defender of a static status quo. In any case, Gadamer's idea of interpreting texts and events through a fusion of horizons between present interpreter and past author based on the cultural prejudices of each gives him a place in the current of social theory that emphasizes human agency.

RATIONAL CHOICE THEORY

Rational choice theory has been developed in a series of distinct disciplines—anthropology, sociology, political science, and economics—to explain why people make the sorts of choices they do. Its subsidiary branch in social theory is called social exchange theory, which is micro-sociological in its focus, looking at individuals as rational actors seeking rewards in a self-interested fashion. Rational choice theory is a bit of an oddball in this chapter—it is largely unrelated to the stream of thought moving from Weber and Wittgenstein through Winch, Collingwood, and Giddens. Yet insofar as it places human agency and individual choice at its core, it fits here as well as anywhere else. As interesting as some of its ideas are, we'll spend considerably less time reviewing rational choice theory than in most other standard texts on social theory since its assumptions are so riddled with problems that its defenders have yet to meaningfully solve. Because of this, I'll treat it much more critically than the other schools of thought dealt with so far.[2] Tim Delaney (2005) calls it 'the most underrated theory in sociology'. Yet Delaney's judgement is a very provincial one. The model of human nature that rational choice theory posits—of the rational utility-maximizing individual—is one of the basic underlying mythologies of mainstream American culture, notably its capitalist element, and American theorists, therefore, also take it much more seriously than do outsiders, who are legitimately more skeptical about this ideal 'rational chooser'.

The Foundation of Rational Choice Theory in Economics and Psychology

The basic assumption of rational choice theory—and social exchange theory, its sociological counterpart—is that people make rational choices to maximize their rewards and minimize their punishments. In this it follows the classic utilitarian philosophy of Jeremy Bentham (1748–1832) and of John Stuart Mill (1806–73), which claims that all people seek to get as much pleasure (Bentham's version) or happiness (Mill's version) as they can and to avoid pain or unhappiness. Further, it assumes that people try to use the most effective or efficient means to achieve these rewards. These rewards could be any of a number of things: survival, shelter, money, physical objects, social approval, sympathy, fame, love, sex, or any other thing desired by people in general. It also assumes, quite realistically, that we live in a world of scarcity—there aren't enough of these things to satisfy everyone. Lastly, it is a universalistic theory in the sense that it argues that people of all cultures engage in this utility-maximizing behaviour in some way that is not peculiar to the modern Western world.

Social exchange theory is grounded in three fields of study—two major ones, classical capitalist economic theory and psychological behaviourism, and one less influential one, cultural anthropology. First, a word about anthropology. Bronislaw Malinowski (1884–1942) concluded from his study of the Trobriand Islanders of the southwest Pacific (today the Trobriands are part of Papua New Guinea) that gift-giving is a key factor in cementing social bonds in all societies. Clan-based relationships in tribal societies are rein-

forced by formal gift-giving ceremonies. In times past, kings and queens exchanged gifts and married into each others' families to solidify alliances. Families offer visitors drinks to welcome them to their houses. At times of celebration, such as Christmas, birthdays, and anniversaries, friends and families exchange gifts, sometimes in a competitive manner. So, the mutual exchange of gifts helps to create social cohesion.

The premises of classical economic theory, which was pioneered by Adam Smith in his *The Wealth of Nations* (1776), are the theoretical touchstone of all rational choice theory. Classical economics assumes that society is a free marketplace where rational individuals interact. Its basic principles are shown in Table 5.3.

Table 5.3 The Principles of Classical Economics

Basic Principle of Economics	Critiques
1. *Law of rational utility maximization:* People, as rational beings, seek to get as much as they can of the things they want (whether physical objects, pleasure, or psychological well-being). What they want is a matter of personal preference.	People *sometimes* rationally maximize their preferences, but not always; they might work long hours to make more money, but decide to skip a chance to work on a weekend in order to go to the beach. 'Well, then, what they *really* wanted was to go to the beach, so the principle is still true!' Then the statement becomes a tautology: we know what people want by the choices they make, and whatever they choose to pursue must be the preference they're maximizing! Since the principle can't be proven false, it is close to meaningless. It also seems to ignore lazy people (unless relaxation is their supreme good, in which case it once again becomes a tautology).
2. *Law of diminishing returns:* The more I get of what I want, the less I want more of it.	This is true of some things but not of others. I may not want any more chocolate ice cream after eating a litre of it. Yet billionaires often seek to add endlessly to their fortunes, working as hard as when they were young entrepreneurs; smokers buy new cigarettes every day—the nicotine addiction is never-ending; having sex might actually make you want more, awakening repressed desires.
3. *Law of supply and demand:* In a free market, if the demand for a product increases and its supply is limited, its price goes up; if the supply of a product increases with demand holding stable or decreasing, its price goes down.	This law says that when things are in short supply and desired by many people, they become more valuable. This assumes a number of things: • That even in a strictly economic sense, a free market exists in Western societies. It does not; government regulation and intervention ended the free market long ago. • That people will actively seek out the best price for a product. In reality, people can be lazy, and favour convenience over price (and if you factor in convenience as part of the 'price' of a product, the whole thing becomes a tautology). • And most importantly, that advertising does not create people's desires for consumer goods. In fact, advertising often manufactures demand where none existed a short time before—think of the technological gadgets that have appeared on the market in the last two decades that were mere dreams a half-century ago.
4. *Law of competition:* The price of goods decreases if firms compete with each other and the market is not controlled by monopolies.	The reality of the modern market in most fields is that it's controlled by a small number of giant firms, which in theory compete with each other, but often tacitly fix the prices of goods at minimum levels. In addition, these giant semi-monopolistic firms may be able to mass-produce goods more efficiently than many small competitors and thus sell their products at lower prices. In social life the law of competition is even less true: if people compete for a desired object, say a beautiful member of the opposite sex, the price of that 'object' may actually increase thanks to the competition.

Source: Adapted from Wallace and Wolfe (1999: 299–300).

Overall, the assumptions of economic theory are based on that famous mythological beast, *homo economicus*, economic man, that rational profit-seeking animal we so rarely see in the real world. In truth, much of economic theory is based on the simple capitalist world view of Adam Smith whereby free competitors try to sell their goods at the highest price they can get and buy at the lowest price. It holds in some cases: unions always bargain for higher, not lower, wages (utility maximization); rich men are more likely to have beautiful wives (supply and demand); while unregulated monopolies can arbitrarily increase prices for the products they sell (competition). Yet the fact that the laws above hold true in some cases doesn't remove the fact that they are plainly false in so many others.

The second major influence on rational choice theory is the behaviourist psychology of B.F. Skinner (1904–90) and his followers. Skinner's behaviourism asks us to see the human mind as a black box into which stimuli flow, out of which come various behaviours. We don't need to know too much about what's inside the black box, just the fact that certain stimuli evoke certain responses. Skinner believed psychology should study people's behaviour, not the subjective conceptions of their minds, their consciousness—hence the term 'behaviourism' for his school of inquiry. Skinner argued that the human organism is shaped by 'operant conditioning', by the positive and negative stimuli it encounters in the world. If a particular behaviour is positively rewarded, the organism is likely to repeat it; if the behaviour is punished, the organism will tend to avoid it. This way of thinking goes back to Pavlov's classical experiments on conditioning—he was able to condition dogs to salivate by ringing a bell associated with food whether the food was there or not. Skinner wrote a novel called *Walden II* that describes a utopian society run by benevolent behaviourists who used operant conditioning to create healthy, happy human beings. He believed that freedom and dignity were largely illusions created by schedules of positive reinforcement.

In the cases both of economic theory and of behaviourism, human beings are seen as reward- or pleasure-seekers who alter their future actions based on the consequences of their past choices. The major difference between the two is that economic theory does put forward a theory of human agency—that people seek to maximize their utilities—whereas behaviourism doesn't care what subjective meaning the social actor assigns to his or her act.

George Homans and Social Exchange Theory

George Caspar Homans (1910–89) spent his entire academic life at Harvard, where he started out studying English, not sociology, though he never did a doctorate in either subject. His most important work is *Social Behavior: Its Elementary Forms* (1974 [1961]). He believed that certain basic psychological principles govern all human behaviour and that classical economics was right to see human interaction as based on the exchange of rewarding goods (Homans, 1974 [1961]: 68). Following common sense and a long line of philosophical speculation, Homans believed that human beings seek to maximize their preferences and respond in more positive ways to rewards than punishments. Since his social exchange theory focuses on the choices and actions of individual actors, it's deeply micro-sociological. Homans grounds his entire theory of social behaviour in a set of five principles (ibid., 16–25), which we'll review into two groups.

1. *Success proposition:* 'For all actions taken by persons, the more often a particular action of a person is rewarded, the more likely the person is to perform that action.'
2. *Stimulus proposition:* 'If in the past the occurrence of a particular stimulus, or set of stimuli, has been the occasion on which a person's action has been rewarded, then the more similar the present stimuli are to the past ones, the more likely the person is to perform the action, or some similar action, now.'
3. *Value proposition:* 'The more valuable to a person is the result of his action, the more likely he is to perform the action.'

In general, Homans is basing his propositions about the elementary forms of social behaviour on Skinner's experiments with pigeons pecking grain as a reward for various behaviours. One need hardly note that most people have more complex motivations than the average pigeon. Yet leaving this aside, the notion that people tend to repeat actions they get rewards for—whether money, social approval, or pleasure—seems intuitively true. Homans adds that the shorter the interval of time between action and reward, the more obvious the connection between the two and the greater the likelihood the action will be repeated. Similarly, if a present situation looks like one in the past where the actor was rewarded for an action, he or she probably will repeat the action. This is even more certain if the reward from such a past action was substantial rather than marginal. Homans rushes to add that the value one gets out of an action need not be hedonistic—he mentions an altruistic friend of his family who took great pleasure in helping others.

These first three principles work best in simple economic situations, which isn't surprising given their origins in classical economic theory. For example, factory workers usually demand 'time and a half' pay to work overtime and 'double time' to work on holidays. Most value their evenings and weekends enough to refuse to work for regular pay. From a buyer's point of view, the value proposition works in reverse: once Jennifer the rational consumer has decided to buy a new car, she will shop around and try to get the best price for the model she has in mind. She will make the most valuable decision, which means spending the least money for the product she wishes to buy.

Homans (ibid., 43) summarizes his first three principles with the following proposition:

The rationality proposition: 'In choosing between alternative actions, a person will choose that one for which, as perceived by him at the time, the value, V, of the result, multiplied by the probability, p, of getting the result, is the greater.'

In terms of an abstract formula, Homans symbolized the above proposition as $A = pV$, or in plain English, people choose actions (A) they think will probably (p) give them the most valued rewards (V). Homans is rather reasonable about how to interpret his propositions: he admits that people aren't always right about what the most rational decision is in a given situation. As the interactionists said in a different context, people's actions are governed by their definition of the situation, not by a God's-eye view of reality. Yet the problem with Homans's general analysis of rationality, rewards, and values is that much of it seems like after-the-fact reasoning. Human beings are emotionally complex and value many things other than birdseed (unlike Skinner's pigeons). Suppose slick Sammy takes out lovely Lucy for a night on the town. Sammy spends hundreds of dollars on a limousine, an expensive restaurant, and a pricey bottle of wine to impress Lucy. At the end of the night Sammy gets lucky, winding up in bed with his lovely date. Homans would say that Sammy's heavy spending was beside the point—what he really wanted was sex. Yet we know this only after the fact. Would Sammy have taken Lucy to a fast-food joint if he knew he would spend the night alone? Is everything an actor does linked to a rational pursuit of some value formulated in advance? And what if Sammy has never wined and dined a desirable woman before? Where's the history of rewards that would make his behaviour explicable in terms of the success proposition? These are tough questions.

Next Homans's version of the law of diminishing returns (ibid., 29):

4. *Deprivation-satiation proposition:* 'The more often in the recent past a person has received a particular reward, the less valuable any further unit of that reward becomes for him.'

This is usually true in economic life for buyers: the value of a first car, computer, or squash racquet is considerably more than the second, and a lot more than the third to the hundredth. Only madmen and millionaires own a hundred cars. It does explain the passion felt by long-separated star-crossed lovers when they finally get together and satiate their desires. Homans even qualifies the proposition by saying that if someone plays too hard to get—manipulating an admirer's feeling of deprivation—the admirer may just give up and look for another source of pleasure.

We can be quickly satiated by food, drink, and sex, and we feel some pain when totally deprived of these physical necessities. But our desires for these things always return—their being satisfied is a fleeting state of affairs. And the desire for fame, power, and money is not so easily satiated. Movie stars continue to work in film even after $10 million paydays, while political leaders hold on to power until forced out or killed—think of the fate of Charles I, Louis XVI, Hitler, Mussolini, Richard Nixon, and other leaders defeated in wars and revolutions. So this proposition applies to only a limited field of social life.

Homans's last proposition, the *aggression-approval proposition*, is divided into two parts (ibid., 37, 39). It presents a social exchange version of Aristotle's ancient definition of distributive justice:

5. *Frustration-aggression proposition:* 'a. When a person's action does not receive the reward he expected, or receives punishment he did not expect, he will be angry; he becomes more likely to perform aggressive behavior, and the results of such behavior become more valuable to him.'
Approval proposition: 'b: When a person's action receives the reward he expected, especially a greater reward than he expected, or does not receive punishment he expected, he will be pleased; he becomes more likely to perform approving behavior, and the results of such behavior become more valuable to him.'

In his *Nicomachean Ethics* Aristotle proposed that justice is when two people of equal merit (however we define this) get equal rewards, while those of superior merit get more than others in an equal proportion to their superiority. For example, if Judy works 10 hours and Heather works five

hours in the same job, Judy should be paid twice as much as Heather. If they were paid the same, Judy would justifiably feel angry. Yet, according to Homans, if Judy's boss gives her an extra week's pay as a bonus for her labours, she will be very pleased and probably feel better about her job.

Homans seems on stronger ground with his fifth proposition—everyday life is full of cases where people make arguments phrased in terms of distributive justice. Think of the student who is bitter at getting too low a mark for what she thinks is a brilliant essay, or an experienced worker's frustration at being passed over for a promotion in favour of a bright young thing fresh out of college. The idea that equal efforts should pay off in equal rewards is almost universal. Of course, just what 'equal efforts' means in concrete situations is all too often a matter of subjective interpretation.

Lastly, a few words on how Homans envisaged power and conformity. Not surprisingly for a social exchange theorist, Homans saw power was based on one's ability to give out valued rewards. He adds the caveat that for one person to have power over another there must be an imbalance between them. The company president can hire and fire his underlings, so he has power over potential employees. The beautiful woman in a crowded bar has power over her suitors, yet less power over a handsome young man who can walk away and court another women than she has over less attractive and older men. Homans adds that non-coercive power is more effective in the long run, since if you use coercion, you have to be constantly on watch for rebellion, having created resentment in those you coerced. Threats of violence work best where the victim's escape route is blocked, for example, with prisoners or members of a racially oppressed minority.

Homans sees conformity as being created by social approval, a valued commodity for most people. When a group of people live near each other or interact on a daily basis, they tend to conform to others' values and expectations in order to get their approval. And once people have established bonds of friendship, a feedback loop is set up between social approval and conformity, as the friends develop a greater stake in the relationship and become reluctant to reject each others' basic values and lifestyles.

Peter Blau and Some Institutional Applications of Social Exchange Theory

Peter Blau (1918–) was born in Vienna, Austria, and emigrated to the US in 1939. He taught at several American universities, most recently the University of North Carolina. His only substantial contribution to rational choice theory is *Exchange and Power in Social Life* (1964), which moves social exchange theory from an analysis of individual psychology to one of larger social groups. As the title of his book hints, his two main concerns are how exchanges lead to social integration and differentiations of power.

Blau attempted to use social exchange theory to explain how social institutions and large-scale practices come into existence. In this sense, he moves exchange theory from Homans's micro-sociological focus to a macro-sociological one (though he agrees for the most part with Homans's basic propositions). Blau thinks that social exchange is an important element in human action, but not its only determinant. The main thing he adds to the mix is norms and values, and how these can put a brake on certain types of social exchanges. An example of a Blauian analysis of social exchange could be the film *Indecent Proposal* (1993), in which Robert Redford's character offers Demi Moore's a million dollars to sleep with him despite the fact that she's happily married to her husband, played by Woody Harrelson. She does so, performing the social exchange that will allow the happy couple to build their dream house. Yet the norm of monogamy gets in the way of their happiness, as they agonize and quarrel over her infidelity. The moral of the Blauian story is that social exchanges have a moral component that the buying and selling of commodities does not (or, at least, not in the same way).

Blau sees social exchange as increasing social integration by creating greater trust, conformity, collective values, and differentiation (Wallace and Wolf, 1999: 329). He spends some time analyzing friendship and love relationships in terms of social exchange. Friendships are more stable where the friends have roughly equal status; a friendship between a company president and a mailroom clerk is unlikely to flower. As for love, couples tend to trade off valued rewards in choosing a mate, whether these are physical beauty, athleticism, or financial success. Successful people have attractive mates, and vice versa; beautiful people can pick and choose between more potential suitors than can the plain. The case of love is especially interesting, since Blau sees it as having a power component: the lover who has the least stake in continuing the relationship has the greatest power within it (Willard Waller's 'principle of least interest') (Blau, 1964: 78). In general, people stay in relationships as long as they're profiting from them, and leave when they're not. Here and elsewhere Blau brings in Erving Goffman's idea of impression management. Part of our value to other people is the impressions we make on them: if they're positive, others will value our company and seek it out. Our 'market price' in the process of social exchange will go up. The opposite is true for botched impression management.

A series of social exchanges can lead to greater trust between those doing the exchanging. This trust is based on, and helps to further, the basic norm of reciprocity. If a group of individuals is to become a functioning community, it must assume that when each of the members gives out something, he or she will get back something in return. Indeed, social and economic exchanges differ for Blau in that social exchange implies a series of unspecified obligations not found in the simple 'X amount of money for product Y' exchange typical of economic life (ibid., 92–4). Once trust is established, people seek out the social approval of others, which leads them to conform to collective values. If friends or colleagues find themselves interacting regularly but disagreeing about important values, the tendency for those in the minority is to overcome their 'cognitive dissonance' with the majority view by altering their values to conform to it or rationalizing away any differences.

Lastly, Blau draws on both Weber and Homans to define power as 'the ability of persons or groups to impose their will on others despite resistance through deterrence either in the form of withholding regularly supplied rewards or in the form of punishment' (ibid., 117). Power can be the result of an uneven exchange situation or of certain social norms. A power structure or form of leadership becomes legitimate when the rewards it offers those who accept it outweigh its costs. Over time, a legitimate power structure is seen as a political authority, and people follow its commands as much from the norm of obedience it generates as from a calculation of the costs and benefits of doing so.

Others have made a mark on social exchange theory, including Richard Emerson and Karen Cook. However, the entire project is flawed by its questionable assumptions about human nature.

Game Theory

An allied form of rational choice theory, which is popular in political science, is game theory. Political scientists have long analyzed political conflict, especially international relations, in terms of a series of games played by rational players in order to understand and predict events. The classic game played by game theorists is the Prisoner's Dilemma. Suppose two jewel thieves, Jake and Rocko, are arrested by the police. The pair have hidden their loot cleverly and the cops don't have very good descriptions of the culprits from witnesses of their most recent robbery. The law's only solid chance of convicting Jake and Rocko is on a charge of possession of an illegal firearm, which we'll say carries a penalty of two years in jail. The police offer each of the suspects a deal: if either one of them confesses and implicates his partner in crime, the partner will get an eight-year jail sentence, while they'll waive the illegal firearm charge and let the confessor go free. But if both suspects confess, each will get five years. Jake and Rocko are held in separate cells and can't communicate. Table 5.4 outlines their dilemma.

Experiments done on various versions of this dilemma have proven that in situations where the prisoners can't talk to each other, they usually both confess and each gets five years in the clink. The test subjects reason like this: the most rational outcome is for both to stay silent and serve two years each. Yet, if I confess and the other prisoner doesn't, I get off with no jail time at all, an attractive option. And since I can't trust my fellow prisoner to remain silent, I had better confess anyway and reduce my jail time from eight to five years. As a result, the most irrational outcome usually happens, with an overall score for the game of minus 10. Game theorists claim that this dilemma explains many of the irrational outcomes of supposedly rational but selfish decision-making we find all around us.

This dilemma has been applied to international conflict, specifically to the nuclear balance of terror between the US and the USSR during the Cold War. The Americans and Russians were like two scorpions in a bottle: each could literally wipe out in one day most of the other's military forces and major cities with the thousands of nuclear-armed rockets and atomic bombs in their arsenals, with the potential side effect of destroying the planet in the process. The best outcome is what really happened: the rockets stayed in their silos and both powers survived. Nevertheless, some

Table 5.4 The Prisoner's Dilemma

What should they do?	Rocko Confesses	Rocko Stays Silent
Jake Confesses	*Both Defect* They each get 5 years in jail. Total penalty = 10 years.	*Jake's Free Ride* Jake gets 0 years, Rocko gets 8. Total penalty = 8 years.
Jake Stays Silent	*Rocko's Free Ride* Rocko gets 0 years, Jake gets 8. Total penalty = 8 years.	*Rational Outcome* 2 years for illegal weapon charge. Total penalty = 4 years.

generals felt tempted to massively attack the enemy power before it could retaliate in force, hoping for a 'free ride' (this almost happened during the Cuban Missile Crisis of 1962). Yet, if both sides think this way, war seems inevitable. So, how do we assure peace? By playing a modified, more rational version of the Prisoner's Dilemma, where each side clearly communicates to the other its intentions to *not* use the nuclear option unless the other side does so first.

Rational choice theory highlights one element of human decision-making—the purposive pursuit of rewards and avoidance of punishments. Whether all of human action can be seen in this light is a difficult question. What the theory calls a 'reward' is so vague that it's tempting to think that its propositions can be boiled down to a series of tautologies. We now turn to Anthony Giddens, who attempts to synthesize human agency and social structural approaches.

ANTHONY GIDDENS ON AGENCY AND STRUCTURE

The English sociologist Anthony Giddens (1938–) is arguably the most important living social theorist, certainly the most influential in the English-speaking world. He was a professor at the University of Cambridge from 1969 to 1997, when he took the post of Director of the London School of Economics, where he stayed until 2003. In 2004 Queen Elizabeth knighted him Baron Giddens, and he sits in the House of Lords for Labour. Giddens has an impressive resumé of publications, listing 35 books on his website, including textbooks, works of social theory, and more recent books on contemporary political issues such as globalization and social democracy. He is an adviser to British Prime Minister Tony Blair, his 'Third Way' policies an attempt to adapt and renew Labour Party policies for a globalized world. Our main concern here is with his social theory at its most general level, which he calls structuration theory. He sets this out in *Central Problems in Social Theory* (1979), *Profiles and Critiques in Social Theory* (1983), and *The Constitution of Society* (1984). We'll return to Giddens's ideas on the nature of modern social, cultural, and economic life in Chapter 12 on globalization.

Giddens is the grand synthesizer of human agency and social structural approaches. For him, these are two ways of looking at social action. He argues against the theoretical imperialism on the one side of structuralist and functionalist approaches, which overemphasizes the power of social forces unknown to human actors, and on the other, phenomenology and symbolic interactionism, which lend too much credence to the freedom of human agents to act as they please. Giddens argues that social life is constructed and reconstructed based on the meaning people attach to their actions, although this meaning may not be in the actor's conscious mind or contained in a set of reasons which the actor can formulate in advance. Sociology is about both the reproduction of social relations and their transformations, which is brought about both intentionally and through the unintended consequences of people's actions (Giddens, 2003). In other words, it's about both social stability and social change, about the things we want to do and the things that happen even though no one planned them. His use of terms such as 'system' and 'structure' makes him sound a little like Parsons. But Giddens insists on the importance of social change and sees systems and structures as having reality only in social practices carried out by knowledgeable agents. He stands with Collingwood, Winch, and Gadamer in refusing to see sociology as allied to the natural sciences, since human action is distinct from events in the world of nature. Unlike the functionalists, he sees the study of sociology as tied to social critique and to practical social reforms, a connection he has acted on as a public intellectual.

Structure, System, and the Duality of Structure

Giddens is a sort of Buddha of modern social theory, in most things advocating a 'middle way' between extremes. Social science is not about isolated rational decision-makers or about abstract functions and structures. 'The basic domain of study of the social sciences, according to the theory of structuration, is neither the experience of the individual actor, nor the existence of any form of social totality, but social practices ordered across space and time' (Giddens, 1984: 2). He sees most of the phenomena of social life as a series of feedback loops linking past, present, and future thought and actions. The most basic feedback loop links the individual agent and social structure, where each influences the other on a regular basis.

Giddens's basic concepts are agency, system, structure, and the duality of structure. When human beings act, they create social practices having certain rules (as Wittgenstein and Winch said) and allocate certain resources, leading to social and economic inequality. Social structure is not a mysterious force acting on individuals, but is reproduced every time social actors follow the rules of the social game. In other words, structure is a set of properties of the various types of social practices we engage in, and would cease to exist if we stopped doing these things. Yet social structure is what allows social practices to happen in the first place: practices can no more happen without structure than fish can live without water. Structure is the medium in which practices live. Giddens (1979: 69) calls this the 'duality of structure':

> The concept of structuration involves that of the duality of structure which relates to the fundamentally recursive character of social life, and expresses the mutual dependence of structure and agency. By the duality of structure I mean that the structural properties of social systems are both the medium and the outcome of the practices that constitute these systems.

For example, the relation of domination of a manager or a foreman over assembly-line workers in a factory exists only insofar as the factory is still in business and these people all go to work. If a worker quits, or if the factory goes out of business, the structure of domination ends. In this case, the worker can ignore his or her old boss's orders. Yet while at work, this structure of domination allows the factory to operate, as managers order raw materials and parts and set production goals, and

foremen ensure factory floor discipline and quality control and make sure enough workers are available to run each shift. The structure is, thus, the medium in which the factory operates in the first place, whatever alienating effects it might have on the average worker.

Giddens distinguishes, somewhat precariously, system from structure. A system is pattern of conduct that is repeated over time in some sort of group, whether small like a family or large like a nation. This pattern of conduct is reproduced by people as a social practice within the nexus of a given span of time and continuum of space. In our factory example, the workers showing up at 7 a.m. for the day shift is a regular pattern of conduct reproduced at the start of each day. Similarly, these workers walking to their stations on the line and taking up their tools is another practice they repeat each day. Both of these sets of actions are part of the factory system.

Structures are sets of rules and resources, or sets of transformation relations, that are organized as properties of systems and thus embedded in social practices. Structure isn't something outside of the actor's actions, but is 'both the medium and outcome of the human activities which it recursively organizes' (Giddens, 1986: 531). What Giddens means by a 'rule' is very close to what Wittgenstein meant: a right way of doing something socially, whether speaking or acting. Actors understand what they're doing insofar as they understand the rules of social life as embodied primarily in their 'practical' consciousness. Social structure is not just a barrier to action, but plays the positive role of structuring the day-to-day practices of the human agents. It has no reality separate from the knowledge agents have about what they're doing—in other words, social structure is virtual, a set of structural properties of systems of actions that survive only as memory traces in actors' minds (Giddens, 1984, 2003). In this Giddens rejects the metaphors for structure of rigid girders in a building or a skeleton in a body; structure is a property of repeated actions, not a concrete thing outside of and prior to all actors' minds. Yet structures aren't located in space and time and don't have a subject 'doing' them, unlike systems, which Giddens sees as the patterned conduct of spatially and temporally situated subjects (ibid., 25). Figure 5.2 gives an idea of what his theory looks like.

Power is a type of structure. Power is not a resource like money or food. Resources are the media that power uses to produce and reproduce structures of domination. Power is a regular relation of freedom and dependence between actors or groups in a series of social interactions (ibid., 16). Inherently, power is neither good nor bad. For one thing, Giddens thinks that societies require systems of domination to operate in the first place (ibid., 32). Back in the factory, money is the principal medium by which management exercises power over the workers—if they don't show up to work on time and follow orders, they won't get paid. The relation of domination between managers and workers is a structural property of the factory system, reproduced every time the workers show up for their shift and do their job. Yet if the factory goes out of business, this structure disappears, since the patterns of conduct that make up the factory system cease to exist.

The Social Actor and Three Levels of Consciousness

Giddens's social actor or agent is knowledgeable about his or her actions. We're all social theorists since we all know a lot about the 'conditions of reproduction' of the society we're a member of (Giddens, 1979: 5). We know what it's like to go to school, to work in a factory, or to vote, even if we don't always know the consequences of these acts. And whenever we act in a repetitive way, doing the same thing over and over, our knowledge of our actions becomes reflexive: we monitor our actions in a self-conscious way. The student thinks about what it's like to 'go to school', the worker about factory wage labour, the voter about what effect his or her vote will have on the election. This monitoring of action takes place within a given physical setting, as Erving Goffman, one of Giddens's major influences, points out (Giddens, 1984: 3–4).

Giddens argues that we can't break down a set of social practices into a set of distinct acts, each brought about by a distinct intention or set of intentions. Instead, a 'context of intentionality' saturates our actions (Giddens, 1986: 543). Everyday life is not a set of discrete acts X, Y, and Z, each with its own separate conscious motivations, but a *durée* or flow of actions that we can separate and understand rationally only after the fact. Think about the act of 'going to a movie'; is it one act, or a series of acts? We drive or walk to the cinema, pay for our ticket, walk through the entrance, buy some popcorn, chat with a friend, then sit down to watch the film. It's really a flow of acts each connected to the other. If we 'intended' to go to the movie, did we also consciously intend paying for the ticket? Buying the

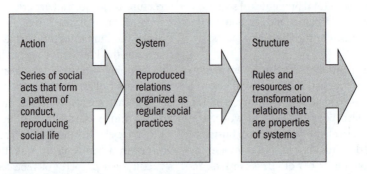

Figure 5.2 Giddens's Theory of Structuration
Source: Adapted from Giddens (1984: 25).

popcorn? The truth is that we usually act first, and only rationalize the act by explaining it to others if they find it puzzling. There is no need for me to explain going to work at my regular time in the morning; yet, if I suddenly burst into the song 'I Am a Pirate King' from Gilbert and Sullivan's *The Pirates of Penzance* during a lecture on Weber, *this* action would require some sort of explanation. Giddens means by 'rationalization' a theoretical understanding of our action, which, he argues, we usually have as knowledgeable actors, but can't always express in discourse until after we've acted.

Second, our unconscious motivations impel us to act in ways we can't especially understand (at least, without a session on the psychoanalyst's couch). Our motive for an act isn't our intention; a man on a date may *intend* to wine, dine, and sweet-talk his special lady, but his *motivation* is sexual desire or affection. Third, we reflexively monitor our actions to see how successful they are and how much social approval we get from them. If our sweet talker finds that a red rose impresses his date, he may buy her a whole batch of roses on the second date. Fourth, our actions often produce consequences we neither intend nor desire that influence our future actions as the 'unacknowledged conditions' of our acts. Here's what his theory of agency looks like in diagrammatic form (Figure 5.3).

Giddens's theory of agency emphasizes the unintended consequences of human action in our lives, which in some cases he includes as an element of human agency. To quote the poet Robert Burns, 'The best laid schemes o' mice an' men gang aft agley [go often astray]'. If I flick on my light switch and startle my pet cat Fluffy, who leaps off a table and knocks down and shatters my precious Ming dynasty vase, Giddens argues that I caused the destruction of the vase, though I certainly didn't intend to do so. If something further away in space and time happens, say, the now skittish Fluffy gets into a fight with a neighbourhood cat, which causes a marital spat between my neighbours that leads to their divorce, it's not reasonable to say that I was responsible for their breakup. So agency isn't about just intentions, but about what events we have the power to bring about within some limited span of space and time. We are the agent of an event within the immediate context of our action if by acting differently the event would not have happened (e.g., if I come home later and don't startle Fluffy, thus saving my vase).

Giddens argues that the social actor is knowledgeable about the situation he or she finds himself or herself in, yet is not always consciously aware of the reasons for his or her actions. He expands Weber's notion of subjective meaning into three categories of knowledge or consciousness:

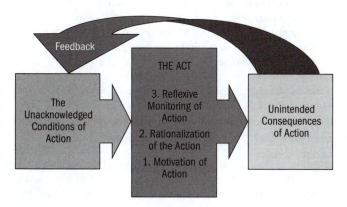

Figure 5.3 Giddens's Theory of Agency
Source: Adapted from Giddens (1984: 5).

- *Discursive consciousness:* The actor is consciously aware of what he is doing, and formulates this knowledge as an account of or reason for his action, e.g., 'I go to work each day in order to earn a paycheque and pay for my rent, food, and clothes.' It comes out only from time to time, usually when an actor has to explain why he did something out of the ordinary.
- *Practical consciousness:* This is 'the tacit knowledge that is skillfully employed in the enactment of courses of conduct, but which the actor is not able to formulate discursively' (Giddens, 1982: 31). In other words, it's knowing how to do things without being able to explain how you know. Giddens argues that much of everyday life, contrary to the claims of the other theorists studied in this chapter, is based on custom and habit, and thus lies in the domain of practical consciousness.
- *Unconscious motivation:* Thinkers like Wittgenstein and Winch have failed to acknowledge the degree to which our unconscious impulses motivate our actions. Giddens argues that we have to return to Freud's model of the mind (in part) and take into account our unconscious drives. He also argues that the body, with all its irrational needs and drives, is the centre of the self, a fact that reason-centred theorists such as Winch tend to forget.

So social actors operate in everyday life on all three levels continuously. Their actions are motivated by a combination of conscious and unconscious motives. Their lives are full of activities that they have known how to do for a long time, but have never formulated in a series of conscious rules; and yet they can provide reasons for most of their actions when called on to do so.

The main criticisms of Giddens's theory of structuration are: (1) his language is so convoluted and pitched at such a high level of abstraction that the theory is difficult to prove or disprove; and (2) in combining agency and structure in a convenient series of feedback loops, he produces tautologies, i.e., he is attempting to have his theoretical cake and eat it too. Yet the notion that human agency and social structure are mutually dependent and impossible to separate in day-to-day life is rather difficult to deny. His grand synthesis of agency and structure, or freedom and determinism, is a good way to end this chapter.[3]

STUDY QUESTIONS

1. What are the main differences between structuralist and human agency approaches to social theory? How does Athena's tale illustrate these differences?
2. How does Weber's emphasis on subjective meaning affect his view of the proper methodology for social science? What sort of methods would his approach rule out?
3. What does Weber mean by 'ideal types'? What are the ideal types of action? What's the point of establishing such ideal types?
4. What are the main characteristics of traditional and charismatic authority? How do they differ? Give examples of each type of authority in modern life.
5. What are the main elements of rational authority for Weber, and how do these elements apply to bureaucracies? In what sense are we trapped in an 'iron cage' of rationality? Is he right? Why or why not?
6. How does Weber distinguish class, status groups, and parties? Give examples of each.
7. What elements of the Protestant ethic does Weber connect to the development of capitalism?
8. What do Wittgenstein's notions of language games, rules, and forms of life have to do with social theory?
9. What is Collingwood's theory of absolute presuppositions and how does it apply to history? Is he correct in thinking that there are such presuppositions? Explain why or why not.

10. What are Collingwood's three principles of history? Why does he think history (and by implication, social science) is very different in its purpose and methods from natural science?

11. What is Collingwood's historical method? How does it connect with the other human-agency-centred approaches in this chapter?

12. Why does Winch see social science as an inherently philosophical endeavour? How was he influenced by Wittgenstein in this regard?

13. What is Winch's criticism of Weber? Is it justified?

14. How does Gadamer suggest that hermeneutics comes to understand a past text or event? What does he mean by a 'fusion of horizons'?

15. Discuss how the principles of classical economics and psychological behaviourism have influenced social exchange theory.

16. Outline Homans's five basic propositions. Evaluate each of them as universal descriptions of human behaviour. Are human beings rational-utility maximizers?

17. How does Blau use social exchange theory to explain conformity and the creation of social institutions? Are there weaknesses in this explanation?

18. How does Giddens define structure, system, and the duality of structure? Is his view of structure an improvement on functionalism and/or on Marxism?

19. Outline the main elements of Giddens's theory of human agency. Is his theory too abstract to explain actual human actions?

20. What are the three levels of consciousness Giddens describes? Give examples of each from your everyday life.

21. Do the human agency approaches outlined in this chapter represent an improvement on functionalism, materialism, and critical theory? What can they explain that more structurally oriented approaches cannot? What are their weaknesses as compared to them?

SHORT BIBLIOGRAPHY

Blau, Peter M. 1964. *Exchange and Power in Social Life*. New York: John Wiley.

Collingwood, R.G. 1924. *Speculum Mentis*. Oxford: Clarendon Press.

———. 1939. *An Autobiography*. Oxford: Oxford University Press.

———. 1940. *An Essay on Metaphysics*. Oxford: Clarendon Press.

———. 1946. *The Idea of History*, ed. T.M. Knox. Oxford: Oxford University Press.

Craib, Ian. 1997. *Classical Social Theory*. Oxford: Oxford University Press.

Delaney, Tim. 2005. *Contemporary Social Theory: Investigation and Application*. Upper Saddle River, NJ: Pearson Prentice-Hall.

Dray, William. 1980. 'R.G. Collingwood and the Understanding of Actions in History', in Dray, *Perspectives on History*. London: Routledge.

———. 1989. 'Collingwood's Historical Individualism', in Dray, *On History and Philosophers of History*. Leiden: E.J. Brill.

Gadamer, Hans-Georg. 1976. *Philosophical Hermeneutics*, trans. and intro. David E. Linge. Berkeley: University of California Press.

———. 2000 [1975]. *Truth and Method*, 2nd edn rev., trans. Joel Weinsheimer and Donald G. Marshall. New York: Continuum.

Giddens, Anthony. 1979. *Central Problems in Social Theory*. London: Macmillan.

———. 1982. *Profiles and Critiques in Social Theory*. London: Macmillan.

———. 1984. *The Constitution of Society: Outline of the Theory of Structuration*. London: Polity Press.

———. 1986. 'Action, Subjectivity, and the Constitution of Meaning', *Social Research* 53: 529–45.

———. 2003. Web page at the London School of Economics: <www.lse.ac.uk/Giddens>.

Harrington, Austin. 2005. *Modern Social Theory: An Introduction*. Oxford: Oxford University Press.

Homans, George. 1974 [1961]. *Social Behavior: Its Elementary Forms*. New York: Harcourt, Brace and World. Rev. edn 1974.

Kenny, Anthony. 1973. *Wittgenstein*. Harmondsworth, UK: Penguin.

Malpas, Jeff. 2003. 'Hans-Georg Gadamer', *Stanford Encyclopedia of Philosophy*, at: <plato.stanford. edu/entries/gadamer/>.

Ritzer, George, and Douglas J. Goodman. 2004. *Classical Sociological Theory*, 4th edn. New York: McGraw-Hill.

Wallace, Ruth A., and Alison Wolf. 1999. *Contemporary Sociological Theory: Expanding the Classical Tradition*, 5th edn. Upper Saddle River, NJ: Prentice-Hall.

Weber, Max. 1946. *From Max Weber: Essays in Sociology*, ed. H.H. Gerth and C. Wright Mills. New York: Oxford University Press.

———. 1978 [1922]. *Economy and Society*, vol. 1, ed. G. Roth and C. Wittlich. Berkeley: University of California Press.

———. 1958 [1904]. *The Protestant Ethic and the Spirit of Capitalism*, trans. Talcott Parsons. Foreword by R.H. Tawney. New York: Charles Scribner's Sons.

Wittgenstein, Ludwig. 1922. *Tractatus Logico-Philosophicus*, trans. C.K. Ogden. London: Routledge & Kegan Paul.

———. 1974 [1953]. *Philosophical Investigations*, trans. G.E.M. Anscombe. Oxford: Blackwell.

Winch, Peter. 1958. *The Idea of a Social Science and Its Relation to Philosophy*. London: Routledge & Kegan Paul.

CHAPTER 6 SOCIETY AS SYMBOLS OR CONSTRUCTS: SYMBOLIC INTERACTIONISM AND PHENOMENOLOGY

COOLEY, MEAD, AND THE BIRTH OF SYMBOLIC INTERACTIONISM

In this chapter we'll continue on from the micro-sociological analyses of social life in terms of human agency discussed in the previous chapter to three related, though distinct, schools of social theory—symbolic interactionism, ethnomethod-ology, and phenomenology. All three are micro-sociological, taking the motivations of the individual actor and the events of everyday life as their foundation. These three schools of thought see society as made up of symbols or constructs whose principal residence is the human mind act-ing socially, not the external structures or abstract functions of the larger society. In the first half of the chapter we'll look at the major symbolic interactionist theorists, first, its founders Charles Cooley and G.H. Mead, then, two of its later lumi-naries, Herbert Blumer and Erving Goffman.

The General Approach and Intellectual Roots of Symbolic Interactionism

The school of social theory now called symbolic interactionism came out of the Chicago School of sociology in the early twentieth century. Interac-tionism focused on how individual human inter-actions create a universe of symbols that human minds share, thereby creating a society. The Chicago School, so named because it was most strongly associated with the University of Chicago's sociology department, was from the start a branch of social psychology. It de-emphasized social rules, social structure, and institutions,

focusing instead on how small-scale social inter-actions create a society.

Symbolic interactionism, a term coined by Blumer long after the school had already estab-lished itself, was opposed to a number of other approaches. It argued against the stimulus-response psychology of the behaviourists, who saw human beings as the passive product of externally imposed stimuli. The interactionists choose to see human beings as at least in part active shapers of their destinies, not Pavlovian dogs yelping at the commands of social forces. They also opposed functionalism for similar rea-sons—it made human beings the passive prod-ucts of socialization, of the norms and rules of the social system.

Interactionism has a number of roots. First, we can look back to Weber, who wanted to arrive at an interpretive understanding of people's social actions by trying to figure out the subjective meaning an act had for the individual. Weber's action theory, insofar as it focused on the active decision-making and ideas that the individual social action brought to the table, has a similar methodological starting point as interactionism. Second, but more directly, the early Chicago the-orists were influenced by the German sociologist Georg Simmel (1858–1918), who was interested in how the comings and goings of everyday life between the 'atoms of society' create a series of forms and symbols that give shape to society.

Third, they were influenced by American pragmatist philosophy, notably the work of William James (1842–1910). The pragmatists argued that truth was not an eternal entity in some sort of Platonic heaven, but a practical outcome of social life. Something was 'true' if it worked, 'false' if it didn't. Also, James proposed the idea of a social self, where our thoughts and feelings flow into each other and in and out of their social environment. This flow coagulates around concepts like 'I' and 'me'.

A fourth important source was the urban sociology of the early twentieth-century Chicago School, notably of Robert Park (1864–1944) and of William I. Thomas (1863–1947), who were themselves loosely interactionist. This school produced many studies of city life, including ones on Polish immigrants, gangs, and Jewish ghetto life. Park and his students used a 'moving camera' approach to their studies of urban life, trying to catch city dwellers in their natural modes of life. Thomas introduced the important idea of the 'definition of the situation'. Thomas believed that if 'men define things as real, they are real in their consequences' (Thomas, 1923). If we see a situation as real, it affects what we do and thus has social effects. For example, if Trevor is convinced that Tim hates him, he'll act towards Tim in a way that will sour their relationship, whether or not Tim's hatred was real or an illusion. This obviously is connected to Weber's idea that we have to focus on the subjective meanings of people's acts, not their 'objective' purpose. The value a given symbol has for one person or group might be quite different from the value it has for someone else—a Christian cross has tremendous meaning to a devout Catholic, yet very little for a skeptical atheist. What counts is the way the actor defines the meaning of that symbol, not what the symbol may mean to the sociologist investigating the actor's actions.

Charles Horton Cooley and the Looking-Glass Self

An early major interactionist figure of importance was Charles Horton Cooley (1864–1929). He taught for his entire career at the University of Michigan at Ann Arbor. He was an introspective scholar, somewhat sickly, who quite sensibly avoided petty academic politics in favour of a life of quiet reflection (Delaney, 2004: 154). His observations on the development of the self were based to a large degree on his experiences with his own children, whose early life he describes in his books. Cooley's works are peppered with literary references, quite often from Shakespeare's plays, which helped him to understand the way we use pronouns like 'I' and 'me' in the English language as much as any field research did. He also read and imbibed the wisdom of the German poet Goethe and the nineteenth-century American transcendentalists Thoreau and Emerson, giving his social theory a literary flair.

Scientifically, Cooley was influenced by Charles Darwin's theory of evolution, especially as it was laid out by Herbert Spencer (1820–1902), though he rejected the vicious struggle for existence proposed by social Darwinists like Spencer, preferring a kinder, gentler, more progressive politics. Cooley did see society as an organic whole where everyone was linked to everyone else: the individual and society depend on each other to constitute themselves. Yet he didn't see it as an organism that swallows up the motives and intentions of the individual in abstract functions. In this sense he anticipates Parsons's functionalism only in part. His organicism also enters into his view of the self. He saw the 'I' as like a nucleus in a living cell: it was formed from the surrounding organic matter, though more active and organized than the remainder of the cell (Cooley, 1964 [1902]: 182).

Cooley followed the Scottish Enlightenment thinkers David Hume and Adam Smith in arguing that sympathy was the ground of social life. By 'sympathy' he meant not an emotional sense of pity for others, but simply the sharing of any mental state. We share these mental states through symbols, the most important of which are words. Indeed, Cooley says that the range of sympathy a person has is a measure of his or her 'social power': a capacity for sympathetic insight into other minds is required by all great leaders (ibid., 140–1). When we're part of a social group, we have sympathy with it; and conversely, our minds are microcosms of the groups we belong to.

If a person plays a vital part in the life of a time or country it's because that life is 'imaged' in the sympathies of the person in question (ibid., 145). Cooley writes almost poetically of the need for a spirit of freedom in the greatest of people, and that a healthy self 'must be both vigorous and plastic, a nucleus of solid, well-knit private purpose and feeling, guided and nourished by sympathy' (ibid., 189).

Not only does he see sympathy as important in establishing social connections between people, but he uses sympathetic introspection as his basic methodology. To understand people's actions, we should put ourselves in their shoes, sympathetically enter into their lives. Cooley's optimistic nature is shown in the fact that he largely ignores our dark and dangerous unconscious drives as motivational factors.

Cooley distinguished between primary and secondary groups. A primary group involves people who have feelings for one another and interact in a face-to-face way, for example, a family, a group of children playing together, or a neighbourhood. A secondary group is one where the relationships between people are more professional, distant, cool, and contractual. Bureaucracies, workplaces, and professional associations fit the bill here. Cooley argues that healthy children are socialized by primary groups, which are tremendously important in creating healthy adult selves.

Cooley contended that the 'imaginations' we have of each other are the 'solid facts of society, and to observe and interpret these must be the chief aim of sociology' (ibid., 121). Society cannot be understood without understanding the imagination of individual actors, the way we see each other. This leads us to Cooley's most important idea, the looking-glass self, a concept that returns with a vengeance in the work of Blumer and Goffman. Cooley quite sensibly argues that the self is formed and developed by looking in the mirror of society at the judgements of others. Cooley thought this self had three elements (ibid., 184):

- You imagine how you appear to the other person.

- You imagine the judgement of the other person.
- You feel some sense of pride, happiness, guilt, or shame.

In other words, in taking into account the judgements of others, we regulate our own actions (including our appearance) according to how we *think* other people will judge us or seem to judge us according to their facial expressions and gestures. That's why most people tend to conform to common standards of dress, hair style, and manners: they implicitly or explicitly fear the negative judgements of others if they are seen as too nonconformist. Try wearing an item of clothing that is clearly out of fashion and see the looks you'll get from those around you.

George Herbert Mead on the Self

George Herbert Mead (1863–1931) had a long and varied career. He was a railway surveyor for a while and studied philosophy at Harvard and in Germany. He was also an active social reformer. He eventually wound up at the University of Chicago in 1893, where he taught until his death. He was a highly respected teacher despite the fact that he had no graduate degrees himself, and among the many students he influenced was Herbert Blumer. He didn't publish any books in his lifetime, and is known today mainly by the efforts of his students to make his ideas known through posthumously published lecture notes, the most important of which is *Mind, Self, and Society* (1934). He called his philosophy of society 'social behaviourism', but it was also the foundation of symbolic interactionism. Like Cooley, Mead was influenced by the pragmatism of William James and John Dewey. Yet it was the stimulus-response language of behaviourism that Mead used to describe many of the main phenomena of human social life, including mind, self, symbols, gestures, and meaning. His major divergence from behaviourist psychology is that he didn't see the mind as a black box that we should ignore, but a series of functions that comes into existence through acting socially. The mind is a social phenomenon, a view contrary to much of the Western philosophical tradition from Descartes to Kant. Consciousness is real, but comes into being only through society. We can study the mind because we can see how it 'behaves' in the social world, not because we have special powers of introspection into other people's thoughts. When studying social psychology, we don't start with isolated consciousnesses but with a social whole, for 'the whole (society) is prior to the part (the individual), not the part to the whole; and the part is explained in terms of the whole, not the whole in terms of the part or parts' (Mead, 1934: 7). The social act is part of a complex 'organic' process, 'no part of which can be considered by itself'. As the title of his principal work indicates, mind, self, and society are closely linked.

Mead saw the self as at least in part active and creative, the result of a social process in which the actor in a situation takes on the roles of others in making decisions. People create their own environment, their own social universe, peopling it with symbols that are important to them. This leads to the first important distinction that Mead made: between 'things' and 'objects'. A thing merely is what it is: a stimulus that exists prior to the responses of any individual. It becomes an object once someone acts in relation to it in some way. A pen can be a number of things: an object you write with, a tool to poke holes in a can or bag, or a makeshift pointer to help with a presentation. Just sitting there in front of you, it's not inherently any particular one of these objects, just a thing. Similarly, a tomato can be an object of nutrition, part of a still life, or a way of commenting on a particularly bad theatrical performance (Wallace and Wolf, 1999: 198). Parallel to this distinction between things and objects is Mead's distinction between a stimulus and an object. The former is something we react to instinctively, like a mosquito bite; the latter is something to which we give symbolic meaning, like a book we pick up and read.

The self has to be distinguished from one's body. There are parts of our body that we can't directly perceive; further, we can't experience the body as a whole. But we can always experience our self. So the physical part of us is essential to the self, but we can imagine the self without it. Mead talks about ghosts and the idea of the self leaving one's body at death. He calls this the idea of a 'double', which all primitive tribes imagine exists. The self is both subject and object. We only experience the self insofar as we can objectify our selves, a social phenomenon that involves taking the attitudes of other people towards us into our minds. We put ourself in their shoes and see ourself as an external object. We do this when we communicate—we share significant symbols, and thus create a self in a world of other selves. We can't imagine the self arising outside of social experiences—even the prisoner in solitary confinement talks to himself as if he's talking to other people. The self always involves the experience of another person. The response of the other is essential to our experience of our self. Also, we find out what we are going to say and do only by saying and doing things and seeing what happens. Once again, the mind is a social thing.

Mead's most famous distinction is that between the 'I' and the 'me'. The 'I' is the acting subject, the freely choosing and unpredictable disposition to act, as when someone asserts 'I wrote that book.' It's the response to the community the self makes that in turn changes the community. It's when we try to create a situation that is novel and unpredictable, when we assert ourselves against others, when we reject the traditional way of doing things. It's firmly based in the present. On the other hand, the 'me' is the acted-upon object, as when a student says, 'The professor gave me an A+ in this course!' The 'me' is the attitudes of others that have been socialized into us, what we have learned from those others. The 'me' is the part of our selves that maintains itself in the community by recognizing others, and thus that socialized part of us that follows the dictates of convention and habit. The 'me' is our connection to the organized social world within each of us. So the 'I' is the creative, active part of us, the 'me' the passive, socially controlled part of us—the 'self' of the functionalists. Mead saw these as two phases of the self that are required by society to function as a dialectic of creativity and conformity. They interact in our daily lives: the active 'I' may take over for a while, but will likely slip back into the passive 'me' when encountering the strongly held judgements of others.

Mead thought that before we act, we tend to have an internal conversation with ourselves that helps us to take others and the symbols important for us into account. We talk over the consequences and values associated with our decisions internally before we act, and make indications to ourselves—'self-indications'—that assign meanings to social objects. Mead said that this putting oneself in the shoes of others is the core of social communication. This is what he meant by 'role-taking': we mentally put ourselves in the role of others before making a decision. This goes back to Cooley's looking-glass self: our social behaviour is modified by looking back at ourselves after we have taken on the role of the other. Indeed, Mead says that our social intelligence is measured by our ability to put ourselves in the place of other people. In our internal conversations we try to see how other people understand the social objects in front of them and the meanings of symbols and gestures, and then adjust our actions according to this understanding of the attitudes of others. This is like rehearsing for an action you are contemplating: you play over in your mind the results of your intended action, e.g., 'Should I go to the movies tonight instead of reading my sociology text?', trying to judge its consequences.

Mead also notes the phenomenon of people who do and say things they don't mean. We might say that such a person is not 'himself' or 'herself'. In addition, we are different selves to different people (an idea that Goffman would pick up from Mead). Since the process of social interaction brings forward the self, each social situation brings forward a different self, at least potentially. Mead also notes that we experience parts of our selves only in relation to our selves, in our internal conversations. Within any given community the person experiences a sort of unified self, which can be broken up by varying social situations. The var-ious simple selves of which an individual is made up are reflections of various aspects of the structure of the social process as a whole. Each component self reflects our interactions with a specific social group. We can imagine the self in a psychologically healthy person as like a jigsaw puzzle made up of many different pieces that all fit together. As Mead explained, an extreme example of the breakdown of the complete self can be seen in schizophrenia or multiple personality syndrome. Here the complete, united self breaks down into its component selves: the jigsaw puzzle falls apart into individual pieces. The individual relates to all social groups at the same time—thus appearing to be crazy.

Mead on the Development of the Self

Mead saw the self as developing through stages associated with infants' ability to use symbolic interpretations of their actions to make these actions and, thus, social life meaningful to them. Meaning for Mead comes from our taking the attitudes of other people into account in the way we react towards an object, hence, we don't steal other people's pens because we know they see them as their 'property', though we might feel free to pick up a newspaper left on a bus or a cafeteria table and read it, even though it was bought previously by someone else.

Mead saw three stages in the development of the self:

- *The pre-play stage* begins around age two, when the child engages in imitative acts like mimicking sounds or grabbing toys that have no social meaning.
- *The play stage* occurs when the child can put him or herself into the position of one other person, filling a series of separate and discrete roles. The child as player has only one alternative player in mind. This is when the child scolds her toys for being bad, or pretends to be a doctor, parent, or superhero.
- *The game stage* becomes active when a player is able to play as a member of a team, taking

into account the attitudes of other players. There are now many others to relate to, and the child at this stage sees how their roles are related to each other. The game stage is the jumping-off point from being an egocentric child to becoming a socially oriented adult. Any team sport can serve as an example: the baseball player must co-operate with other team members to win—it does no good to throw the ball to first base to get a batter out if your teammate isn't in position to catch it.

As the child matures into adulthood, she or he develops a sense of a generalized other, the imaginary person who embodies the organized attitudes of a whole community. This generalized other is akin to Freud's notion of the super-ego, the internalized judge that regulates conduct without the need for fresh punishments. As the generalized other is internalized, the social actor is 'good' and follows social rules without having to be scolded by parents or parent substitutes. This is how structure and social roles enter interactionist analyses: the player identifies with what he or she imagines to be the attitudes of the generalized other with regard to his or her position in society, and applies these attitudes in behavioural choices. For example, a man may go to a job interview wearing a suit, even though no one has ever actually told him to wear one; people line up for a movie or sports event without any threat of coercion; a person holds a door open for a stranger without the expectation of reward. We meet the generalized other every time we walk down a street full of strangers. A community is in essence one big, generalized other. In fact, we are nationalists— Canadian or American or Russian—because we see our nation as the grandest expression of our generalized self.

Mead on Symbolic Meaning and Gestures

Symbolic interactionism developed its definition of a 'symbol' from Mead's notion of a gesture. A gesture is an act that calls for some response from others and thus has some symbolic content, without the gesturer especially knowing what the content or response will be. Mead's example of dogs fighting, barking, snarling, and biting at each other shows us a conversation of gestures where the gesturers' actions are modified by the stimuli provided by others without their consciously plotting out how they respond to these stimuli. Dogs don't pause in mid-battle to muse, Hamlet-like, 'To woof or not to woof, that is the question!' Their communication is neither introspective nor conscious. Mead defined a symbol as 'the stimulus whose response is given in advance' or, in other words, an act (including linguistic acts) that the actor and the audience both understand will bring about a finite series of consequences (ibid., 181). For example, if you insult someone, this could lead to a fight, to yelling back and forth or at least to a counter-insult or sarcastic comment, depending how serious the insult was. An insult is unlikely to lead to a warm embrace, or to an offer of free beer, unless the insult was meant ironically. A gesture becomes a significant symbol when it has the same meaning for an entire social group, arousing in others the same response as it evokes in the person making it (ibid., 47). Language provides the best example of gesture: when we use words in the same way, we are exchanging significant symbols. Significant symbols are gestures that possess wide social meaning that we can consciously understand. Mead argues that social interaction can be seen as a conversation of gestures, both within us and with others. It can be an unconscious form of communication, as in the dogfight, or a conscious communication of significant symbols, as in a conversation. Indeed, Mead saw thinking itself as an internal conversation using significant symbols.

Mead, like all the interactionists, is quite good at micro-sociological analysis and not so good at explaining social structure and large-scale inequalities. Furthermore, he spends little time with unconscious processes, seeing the exchange of symbols that creates society as largely a conscious process (for humans at least, if not dogs).

HERBERT BLUMER AND MATURE SYMBOLIC INTERACTIONISM

Background on Blumer

Herbert Blumer (1900–87) was a follower of Mead who taught at the University of Chicago from 1927 to 1952. He studied under Mead, who at the end of his career bequeathed his course in social psychology to Blumer. Blumer led a varied life; he played pro football, was a mediator in labour disputes, and interviewed the Al Capone gang. After his long stay in Chicago, he moved to the sunnier climes of Berkeley in California for the last 25 years of his teaching career. He became the leading symbolic interactionist. His book *Symbolic Interactionism* (1969) is the clearest theoretical statement of the school of thought's main ideas.

Blumer, like Mead, was arguing against the mechanical behaviourism of John B. Watson and B.F. Skinner, which saw human behaviour as part of a simple stimulus-response relation. Instead, he wanted to include individuals' sense of subjective meaning in the equation. Thus, the social act became:

Stimulus → Interpretation → Response

Although he vehemently claimed to be a follower of Mead to the bitter end, Blumer moved even further away from behaviourism than had Mead, dispensing with behaviourist language in favour of talk about subjective consciousness and symbolic meaning.

Blumer did take up Mead's idea that to understand the meaning of a social interaction, we have to put ourselves in other people's shoes to understand the social symbols they take to be important. We do this through the internal conversations we have before acting by means of what Blumer calls 'self-indication'.

Blumer's Three Premises of Symbolic Interactionism

In *Symbolic Interactionism* (1969: 2), Blumer lays out the school's three central premises:

1. Human beings act towards things on the basis of the meanings they have for them.

Here Blumer is emphasizing the consciousness of actors in interpreting their actions, against macro theorists like Marx and Parsons, who reduce consciousness to something less autonomous. Our intentions are always linked to the meaning of the social objects that make up our world, which includes physical objects, people and their actions, institutions, and ideals. We don't always agree about these objects. Some people might value friendship more than others, so would do anything for a friend. Others might value money more than friendship, so would invest more meaning in a nice car than in being loyal to a friend. Blumer criticizes the contemporary social science of his day for falsifying the behaviour it studied by reducing human decisions to social positions and roles, norms, values, and cultural rules. He worries that the subjective meanings of our actions are swallowed up in these norms and roles, distorting the nature of social life.

2. The meaning of things arises out of the social interactions one has with one's fellows.

Blumer is saying that meaning is a social product and is not inherent in things. No thing has meaning in and of itself—it requires social actors to give it meaning. For example, a curling rock might be meaningless to most Peruvians, even though most Canadians would instantly recognize its purpose. There are two traditional ways of understanding the meaning of things. Realists say that meaning is inherent in the thing itself—a chair is a chair and a cat a cat by their very nature—and when we perceive this nature, we understand the meaning of the thing in question. The opposite extreme is the subjective theory that attributes meaning to the psychological makeup of the person doing the perceiving. Symbolic interactionism rejects both of these theories, seeing the meaning of a thing as arising from a process of interaction between people. If a person offers you a chair and you sit in it, the social meaning of the chair becomes clear to both of you.

3. These meanings are handled in, and modified through, an interpretive process a person uses in dealing with the things he or she encounters.

Blumer sees meaning as the product of a series of acts of interpretation by the social actor. In this process we give objects meaning, we act based on these meanings, then we revise these meanings to guide future action. Like Mead, Blumer thought that we have internal conversations to sort out the meaning of things. We especially do this when we have to deal with an out-of-the-ordinary situation. For example, a customer in a store tries to talk the price of a product down (to which the clerk might respond, 'The prices are marked clearly!'), or a stranger of the opposite sex makes what seems like a sexually suggestive remark (you think, 'Is he (she) hitting on me? I'm not sure!'). We go through an internal conversation to try to sort out what this new situation means and how to respond to it—although we go through it with conventional situations too, it doesn't take as long to sort them out, since the cues are all there.

Social Actors, Roles, Structures, and Objects

Sociology is the study of human groups existing in action. Too often sociologists attribute behaviour to static things like social structure, social roles, cultural norms, or pre-set psychological motivations. These sociologists forget that all social life consists of groups of individuals interacting—social interaction is where these things come from in the first place. Social interaction is between actors, not between social roles, social structures, or cultural values. Blumer often calls social structure a 'straitjacket', even though he talks about how social roles, hierarchies, and institutions shape and guide action. Structure doesn't determine action. Obviously, our actions are guided by our perceptions of the roles we play— a sales clerk in a clothes store probably won't make a habit of insulting her customers since this is clearly outside her job description (and bad for

business besides!). But it's still us acting, not the roles. As Blumer notes, 'social interaction is obviously an interaction between *people* and not between roles': people confront problems or engage in conversation; they don't encounter or talk to 'roles' in a literal sense (ibid., 75). And as Goffman points out, even by our teenage years we learn to engage in a considerable amount of 'role distance' in our daily lives. You might work at The Gap, but you may have other career goals; you are not *really* a Gap sales clerk. The same applies to being a student; students realize that one day they will graduate and take on new roles: corporate executives, scientific researchers, fathers and mothers. In fact, in some cases we disdain our roles, especially if they're low-paying jobs in the service industry.

Blumer isn't denying that social structures influence our actions — he's only saying that they don't *determine* them. Social interaction is more than structured responses to others. We usually sketch out our plans in our minds before putting them into effect. In doing so, we might totally disregard the effects of social structures on our thinking. This is especially the case in situations involving conflicts or unique events such as economic crises, deaths in one's family, fires, wars, riots, terrorist attacks, or serious sicknesses. In such crises we have no firm social roles to guide us, the events being unprecedented. He mocks Parsons's pattern variables for dealing with this sort of situation: if people really went through each of these variables before acting, they'd be paralyzed from acting—no one would ever do anything. We have to invent new meanings for dealing with such situations, and can't fall back on our traditional social roles and functions. In short, the less structured and habitual a situation, the more effective a symbolic interactionist is in understanding it.

When we act, we have to take the actions of others into account. We have to fit our actions into theirs somehow. Blumer repeats in his own language a distinction made by Mead. Symbolic interaction is an interaction based on an interpretation of the actions of others; non-symbolic interaction, like a boxer defending himself against a blow, is a direct response to the actions of others without this interpretive element.

One way we communicate meaning is through gestures. Gestures form part of an act in a way that indicates the act's larger context or meaning, e.g., saluting an officer indicating obedience, or giving an apple to the teacher indicating that you're a good student. When the gesture has the same meaning for both parties, they've understood each other. He also follows Mead regarding the importance of role-taking in interaction—i.e., when we take each other's roles to understand each other's actions we see ourselves as others see us. Human social interaction is a dual process of indicating to others how they should act and then interpreting others' indications of how to act when deciding what to do oneself. This is a symbolic interchange of meanings. Social life is a process of exchanging such meanings.

Our worlds consist of objects created by symbolic interactions. Blumer divides these objects into three classes (ibid., 10–11):

- Physical objects like books, trees, and cats (except talking cats of course).
- Social objects like teachers, students, mothers, and friends.
- Abstract objects like ideas of justice and morality, philosophies, or religious views.

Different objects might have different meanings for different people: a diary might be precious to its writer but mere scrap paper to her roommate. The meaning of objects arises usually through social interaction, so when we agree about the meaning of an object we can say it has become a common object for us.

Blumer makes a couple of points here. First, people's social worlds consist of objects that they recognize and know, not mystical entities like social functions. Second, objects are social creations—human group life is one vast process where people form, sustain, transform, and cast aside their objects in giving and taking away their meanings. A social world is a world populated by meaningful objects.

The Self and Group Action

Blumer agreed with Mead that to interact symbolically with others, we have to possess a self that is an object to our self. This self guides our actions reflexively, based on how we see ourselves and by role-taking with other people. We interact with our self through self-indication, we make indications to our self such as 'it's time to go to school!' or when we become angry with ourselves for making a foolish mistake, or talk to ourselves about whether we want to pursue one course of action over an alternative.

This self is distinct from that imagined from most schools of thought in the social sciences, where the self is seen as a responding organism, the product of factors that determine its nature. Here it's social only in the sense that it's a member of a social species. Blumer's self, with its use of self-interaction, is an acting organism that isn't programmed by its environment or psychological makeup, but one that makes choices. Blumer thinks human action involves taking into account the things around us and then interpreting their meaning before acting. One has to get inside this interpretive or defining process to understand an actor's choices.

Blumer notes that group action also has to be understood in this way—we still have to understand the ways that actors interpret their social objects to understand the group's actions. We might be tempted to see joint actions as of a different nature from individual actions if we forget that the participants have to guide their actions by forming and using meanings. Yet most social action seems to take place within terms of standard patterns. In most situations, people share common and pre-established meanings that guide their behaviour. For example, when you walk into a variety store and give the clerk a $20 bill to pay for a bag of chips, you don't expect her to keep the change as a 'tip' and order you out of the store. And you assume that when you go to the washroom in a restaurant, other customers won't rush over and steal your food, even if it's particularly tasty.

Most social science assumes that we live according to some established order of rules. Blumer makes three observations on this notion (ibid., 18–20):

- The full expanse of human action isn't just following pre-established rules and patterns. New situations are arising constantly.
- Repetitive and standard actions are just as much the product of an interpretive process as are ones based on creative thinking. When we follow a set of rules, we on some level interpret the situation we're in, know the relevant rules for that situation, and then apply them. Just because most people follow the rules doesn't mean that these rules are not the product of social interaction. It's social action that upholds the rules, not the rules which uphold social action. The mistake of seeing networks and institutions as self-operating entities led Parsons and the functionalists to see society as a social system. They failed to see the meanings located at various points in the social network that actors use in their processes of social interaction.
- New joint actions always arise out of a background of others' previous actions. We can't slice off a given action from its historical linkages. Our having dinner at a restaurant is linked to all the other people who ever have eaten out. These other 'eating-outs' help to shape the actions we engage in when we eat out—wearing shoes, ordering food politely, giving a tip, maintaining certain standards of personal hygiene, and so on. Joint action involves not only a horizontal linkage to other actors' actions in the present situation, but also a vertical linkage to past actions.

Blumer's View of Methodology

As we've already seen, symbolic interactionism is definitely a micro-sociological approach to understanding social life. The theory promotes a methodology that deals with individual social interactions. Since it is a form of social psychology, it seeks to understand the private and inner experience of the individual through an examination of life history, diaries, letters, and interviews. It seeks to understand the values and meanings different objects had for the individual in question and to see the social world from that point of view. It requires that the sociologist constantly observe the empirical social world. It seeks to understand 'from the inside' the way an individual or group of people define their social worlds. To do so, it has to be inductive, relying on reasonable inferences instead of on logical reasoning or physical scientific experimentation. As Blumer says at the end of his methodological chapter in *Symbolic Interactionism*, it has to respect 'the nature of the empirical world and organize a stance to reflect that respect' (ibid., 60).

Blumer sees himself as an idealist, somewhat at odds with Mead, who considered himself a 'social' behaviourist. An idealist is someone who thinks that we know the world only through our pictures and ideas of it. We perceive the world through our senses and then develop ideas about it—we have no direct experience of, for example, 'being a tree'. So our world consists of the ideas we and others have of it. Yet that doesn't mean we can see the empirical world in any way we like, for that world can 'talk back' to us (ibid., 22). The reality of the outside world is based on the fact that it's usually pretty tough to change it—it's stubborn and resistant to our wills. You may want everyone to love you, and to get A's in all your classes, but it probably won't happen.

Interactionist methods parallel the methods that lawyers use to defend an accused criminal when they try to get the jury to put themselves in the mind of their client to create sympathy for him or her. For example, they might try to explain how a murderer was in fact a victim of child abuse and how the act of killing was an emotional response to this abuse. In general, Blumer advocated a direct 'naturalistic' examination of the empirical social world. This would involve a qualitative understanding of that world, not a piling up of statistics. Interactionists tend to be quite suspicious of number-based sociology, since this tends to distort the subjective meanings actors have of their social worlds.

Blumer thinks that sociologists should go directly to the social world. Spending all one's time collecting hard data like census numbers, polls, questionnaires, and so on violates the basic principle of interactionism—that we have to get close to the people we're studying to understand the meanings they assign to their most important social objects. Hard data usually fail to catch these meanings. For example, he attacks the IQ test for trying to assign a number to intelligence, which is really diverse—it could involve university mathematics, the sales techniques of a businessman, the creative skills of a poet, or the practical intelligence of a slum dweller dealing with the problems of everyday life. One would assume that he would have been similarly suspicious of number-based student ratings of teachers.

Blumer saw symbolic interactionists as going through two methodological stages in their work. First, they had to explore the part of the social world they were interested in. This had two purposes:

• to arrive at a close and comprehensive acquaintance with a sphere of social life they probably did not know much about before;
• to sharpen and focus the researcher's investigation so that the problem is rooted in the empirical world.

Blumer wanted social research to be flexible and open-ended, becoming better and better defined as the research progressed. This is in sharp contrast to how much graduate and funded research is done. Researchers usually have to define their problem, research methods, methodology, and hypothesis well in advance of their research, especially if they are requesting funding from a government or other grant-giving agency. They must, in Blumer's terms, already know the results of their research before it's even started, which makes no sense. The irony is that Blumer saw his own open-ended style of research as truer to the social world, and thus, one would have to conclude, more 'scientific'.

Blumer (ibid., 41) saw a number of techniques as connected to the interactionist approach:

• the direct observation of social life;
• interviewing people and listening to their conversations;
• listening to radio and watching television;
• reading newspapers;
• reading letters and diaries, going over actors' life histories;
• reading public records and histories;
• finding expert participants who are especially well informed.

Thus, if an interactionist wanted to investigate the drug subculture, he or she might observe drug addicts in action, interview addicts and cops involved in enforcing drug laws, read newspaper accounts of drug use, or convene a panel of experts (both users and enforcers) to comment on drug use.

In the second stage of interactionist research the researcher engages in a close inspection of whatever analytical elements can be found in the empirical information that has been gathered. Blumer distinguishes 'sensitizing concepts', which are loose ideas that merely suggest directions for research, from 'definitive concepts', which tell us what to look for in the data, including some things, excluding others. Sensitizing concepts act as a bridge between the theoretical concepts of sociologists and the practical ideas of social actors.

When we combine these two stages of inquiry, exploration and inspection, we can call interactionist analysis a naturalistic inquiry—it echoes the 'nature' of what it's studying. One part of the naturalism of sociological inquiry is the fact that for the interactionist, all stages of research are going on at the same time. The researcher explores the relevant social fields, does interviews and checks the mass media, develops sensitizing concepts, goes back to the social field with these concepts in hand, does more research, develops more concepts and perhaps a preliminary model, and so on. In other words, theory and practice are always flowing into each other: they are simultaneous.

Interactionist Models

The interactionists come out of their naturalistic inquiry with one of several possible models, depending on the nature of what they are studying (based on Wiseman, 1973):

- The idea of a 'career model' with a beginning, a middle, and an end, as with Howard Becker's description of the marijuana smoker in his book *Outsiders* (1973).
- The idea of a cyclical model where a phenomenon starts, builds up, is reacted to by the forces of social order, declines, then starts all over again in some other form. Stan Cohen applied this sort of model to the moral panic caused by the mods and rockers subcultures of 1960s England in his book *Folk Devils and Moral Panics* (1980 [1972]). An interactionist might apply a cyclic model to modern moral panics such as the recent disease scares (e.g., the SARS epidemic) and the fear of terrorism in the US after the 11 September 2001 attacks, despite the fact that no one in the US died at the hands of terrorists from that time to the present (April 2007).
- The 'social types' model, where a number of people in a given social field are categorized according to types, e.g., an interactionist might divide university students into hard workers, socializers, marginal hangers-on, 'jocks', and artsy types.
- A model that focuses on the different types of settings and scenes where social actions take place. An interactionist might analyze university student life according to sub-scenes in the lecture hall, the library, the campus centre, the gym, and the campus bar.

Some Methodological Implications

Symbolic interactionism seeks a direct examination of the empirical social world. It doesn't try to fit that world into the straitjacket of a pre-established research protocol, or a fixed logical or mathematical model. It wants us to dig out this world's nature through a careful probing and examination of that world. Is this unscientific? Blumer says that even his three premises have to be tested scientifically, though he says we can do so by observing what's going on under our very noses. He sees four basic methodological implications of symbolic interactionism:

1. People act on the basis of the meanings of the objects in their social world.

This means we have to try to understand the meanings actors bring to the situation, not meanings we *impose* on their actions. Blumer sarcastically observes that when a scholar tells us to be 'objective', often what he *really* means is that we should see things from his own point of view. This implies three things for researchers: they must (1) see the world and its objects as the social actor being studied sees them; (2) have a body of relevant observations to understand the actor's central objects of concern; (3) guard against bringing their own pre-established images and ideas into their research (Blumer, 1969: 51–2).

2. Joint action takes place in terms of a process where people make indications to each other and interpret each other's indications.

Two conclusions flow from this implication. First, approaches such as functionalism, which see social interaction as a mere medium through which determining factors come into play, are wrong in that they ignore the fact that interaction is the very process whereby these determining factors are *formed*. People shape, form, and alter their actions based on the indications they get from others, not according to overarching structures and functions. Second, this also means that we shouldn't compress the process of social interaction into a specific form, such as Parsons's pattern variables or AGIL paradigm. This is a particular vice of social science. It's easy to see that social actors respond to each other's actions in a variety of ways; they are not constrained to a single form. We cannot fix the form of social interaction in advance, as Parsons's variables and systems attempt to do (ibid., 54).

3. Social acts are constructed through a process where actors note, interpret, and assess their present situation.

We have to observe social action before remembering categories that give conceptual order to that action. Social action is constructed by the actor; he or she is no mere responding organism, but actively copes with a situation and forges a line of action. To understand circumstances, we have to try to see things from the actor's point of view. For example, if studying heroin addiction, a researcher first should ask the addict how and why he or she uses the drug, before consulting social workers and doctors about its effects. Blumer is astonished that social scientists fail to pay attention to the formation of a social action by the acting unit (ibid., 57).

4. Interlinked actions, such as organizations, institutions, and the division of labour, are fluid, not static, affairs.

Here Blumer attacks functionalism specifically for seeing social actors as mere media for the play and expression of systemic forces, mere cogs in the functional machine. Symbolic interactionism doesn't see people's actions as the result of systemic principles, but as the way they define and interpret their situation. This applies even to institutional action where actors have to define their own meanings and take others' meanings into account. In addition, group action is always tied to past group actions, the ways things are done to the ways they've been done in the past. Most social science ignores these historical linkages. For example, we queue up at movies, bus stops, and supermarkets because that's the way we and others have dealt with the situation in the past, not because we've been socialized into these rules by some omnipresent queuing system.

The strength of interactionist analysis is also its main problem; it can deal quite well with micro analysis but has a harder time with macro analysis. Blumer makes an attempt to deal with social institutions, yet without much success. He can also be criticized for not seeing the historical underpinnings of social life in the broad sense, and thus too facilely regards social actors as free in their choices. Micro-sociology is the 'home base' for symbolic interactionism. Its greatest contribution to social theory lies in its questioning of the idea that we can understand social life by imposing abstract theoretical concepts on it or quantify it in statistics and surveys. It also gives us a powerful methodology for researching everyday life.

ERVING GOFFMAN'S DRAMATURGY

Background on Goffman

Erving Goffman (1922–82) was born in Manville, Alberta. He received his BA from the University of Toronto in 1945, then studied sociology and social anthropology at the University of Chicago, receiving his MA in 1949 and his Ph.D in 1953. As part of his doctoral studies he spent a year in the Shetland Islands off the northern coast of Scotland doing research for his thesis and for his first and most famous book, *The Presentation of Self in Everyday Life* (1959), a true sociological classic that we'll look at in detail below. He taught at Berkeley from 1958 to 1968, then at the University of Pennsylvania from 1968 until his death. Goffman's general project was the micro-sociological or small-scale analysis of the forms of talk, rituals, and habits found in everyday life and how these help to create our personal identities. His other works include *Asylums: Essays on the Social Situation of Mental Patients and Other Inmates* (1961), *Stigma: Notes on the Management of Spoiled Identity* (1963), *Interaction Ritual* (1967), and *Forms of Talk* (1981). In *Stigma*, Goffman looks at how stigmatized individuals must try to manage the impressions that others have of their stigma in order to be accepted by mainstream society. In *Interaction Ritual*, he looks at such mundane experiences as how people interact when boarding a crowded elevator or bus.

Goffman is considered to be a symbolic interactionist, though he is also linked to phenomenology and ethnomethodology. He took seriously Blumer's idea of the 'definition of the situation' as a determinant of human behaviour, along with Mead's 'I' versus 'me' distinction. For Goffman, life is a stage where we perform for an audience, where the 'I' is always concerned with how it looks to others, and thus always is slipping into 'me-ness'.

The Interaction Order

Shortly before he died of cancer, Goffman was made president of the American Sociological Association. He wrote an address for its 1982 meeting, though it was never delivered due to his failing health. This essay, 'The Interaction Order' (1983: 2), presents a general rationale for his micro-sociological approach to social life. He defines the interaction order as an environment where two or more people are in each other's physical presence—telephone conversations and letters (and one would presume e-mails) are watered-down versions of the real thing. Most of daily life is spent in such orders, where we're engrossed in personal encounters with fairly clear spatial and temporal limits, e.g., driving to work, attending a concert, or ordering a plate of Chinese food. Goffman finds five types of 'animals' in the 'interactional zoo' (ibid., 6–7):

- People seen as *vehicular units*, as physical beings moving in space.
- *Contacts* between people who can respond to each other, e.g., a conversation.
- *Encounters* between people who share some undertaking, which includes at least three subtypes: a small informal circle of actors discussing some issue, hearings and trials managed by a chairperson, and situations where talk is superfluous, e.g., card games and sex.
- *Platform performances* like plays, movies, and lectures, where the performers occupy some special elevated place.

- *Celebrations* like weddings and birthday parties that have a common mood and are seen as unitary events though they can break down into a series of mini-encounters without ceasing to exist.

Interaction orders are usually orderly things governed by strong norms, though this does not mean that most actors would resent their being changed. Obviously, such normative orders can lead to social inequality. Yet, to get on with any sort of business, we need some sort of conventions and norms to guide our interactions (ibid., 5–6). As for the critique of interactionist analyses as ignoring structural factors, Goffman replies that face-to-face contacts can both reinforce and disrupt social structures (ibid., 8). The interaction order is only loosely coupled to broader structures: such structures are flaunted in a myriad of ways in everyday life.

All the World's a Stage

Goffman's masterpiece of social theory is *The Presentation of Self in Everyday Life*. In it he compares everyday life to a theatre where we engage in dramatic performances and thereby construct our 'self'. The self is the product of an effectively staged and performed scene, not the thing that performs that scene: the actor exists only in acting. In Latin the self is a 'persona', which also means 'mask'. This is the root of our word 'personality'. When we go out into the social world, we assume various personae: we wear various masks. These masks will highlight certain parts of our selves while hiding other parts. The very structure of the self can be seen 'in terms of how we arrange such performances in our Anglo-American society' (Goffman, 1959: 252). Goffman sees the individual as playing two basic parts: as a performer, a 'harried fabricator of impressions', and as a character, hopefully with various sterling qualities. After a correct performance, the audience assigns a self to the perfected character, but this is a *product* of the scene, not its *cause*. This character is housed in the body of the performer in some way. The self is not an organic thing with a specific location, but a dramatic effect of the presented scene. The possessor and his or her body are merely the peg on which something of 'collaborative manufacture' will be hung for a certain time (ibid., 253).

Although explicitly denying it at one point, Goffman follows Shakespeare in arguing that 'all the world's a stage' where various players are constantly making their entrances and exits. He also echoes to a degree the gloomy view of life that Macbeth pronounces:

> Life's but a walking shadow, a poor player
> That struts and frets his hour upon the stage
> And then is heard no more: it is a tale
> Told by an idiot, full of sound and fury,
> Signifying nothing. (*Macbeth*, Act V, Scene V)

Goffman calls his view the dramaturgical theory of the self. His theory focuses on indoor settings in our Anglo-American world, so it is not a universal theory, though it certainly covers much of everyday life. At its core is the idea that the way we present ourselves in this theatre—whether a school, a workplace, a shopping mall, or a social event—is by means of impression management. We want to 'look good', to be an effective worker, a good student, the life of the party, attractive to potential romantic partners, and so on. To do so, we have to manage the impressions that we give off to others. The major way we do this is by means of the creation of a series of 'fronts' associated with our various social roles that we show our audiences. It's a bit like putting on a mask to fit each situation we're in: our front helps to define the situation for those observing our social performance.

Goffman divides the stage of everyday life into three regions. Two key qualities of a region are (1) that it's physically bounded in some way, usually by a wall, and (2) that the impression fostered by the performance in a given region tends to saturate that region for a limited span of time (ibid., 106). The front region or stage is that part of a public performance that an actor *wants* the audi-

ence to see—it's when an actor is seriously trying to manage the impressions of his or her audience. It's where the performance takes place: where a university professor gives a lecture, a pop band plays to adoring fans, or an office manager sits at his big oak desk surrounded by paperwork. We see the actor or team's formal or official position being played out on the front stage. This usually involves invoking conventions that have meaning to the audience, for example, a lawyer wears a suit and carries a briefcase into court, a judge wears robes and is very serious while on the bench, while a prime minister doesn't hang around with working-class gents in a pub wearing a T-shirt and jeans unless it's a campaign photo-op.

This is exactly like an effective play or film. The actors play the roles of their characters successfully enough that we suspend our disbelief in the fiction being promoted by the drama and 'play along' with the story. We believe that Arnold the Hollywood star is really a hero fighting terrorists. Of course, on one level we know that Arnold isn't really a hero but just an actor, but we ignore this for a couple of hours. Similarly, we know that Dan the lawyer might have all sorts of personal habits that shed a bad light on his personal hygiene (he might be a slob at home), his morals (he might cheat on his wife), or his honesty (he might withhold evidence from the police). But as long as he keeps these items off the front stage and represents his clients effectively, we take his performance seriously.

The back stage is the part of the theatre of our everyday lives where we get ready for our front-stage performances, and where we hide anything that's inconsistent or which contradicts our public persona. Here the public performer can 'let his or her hair down', so to speak. It's where the props are stored and one's personal front is prepared. Examples include a kitchen in a restaurant, where the waiters and waitresses can gossip about their customers or the boss; or a bathroom in a dance club, where women can fix their hair and makeup and chat about the cute boys in the bar. The audience is barred from the back stage: it's strictly off-limits, even to paying customers.

When we are on the back stage, we might do things that contradict our front-stage performances. Goffman mentions how 'loose language', such as swearing, sexual remarks, and kidding, are more likely to take place there (ibid., 128). The lawyer might make a rude noise in the courthouse's bathroom, or make jokes about his or her clients behind their backs. Similarly, Richard Nixon's vulgarity-laced Watergate tapes revealed a nasty, small-minded back-stage persona that became a significant factor in the front-stage president's forced resignation, just as the inadvertent open mikes of broadcasters and politicians have sometimes led to embarrassment and in some cases career changes. We also see contradictions in team performances: conflicts within a team might be played out in the locker room or at a practice, but are almost never shown to the public during a game. Yet we do see these conflicts emerging from time to time in the media, e.g., the members of a government cabinet or party hierarchy break solidarity and criticize each other or the prime minister or party leader; or when members of a sports team criticize their teammates for bad play, or their coach for incompetent leadership. This sort of thing can cause a severe disruption in the unity of the team.

The third region of a performance is outside or off-stage, where outsiders live. This is a residual region, defined as everywhere other than the front and back stages. In an actual theatre, it would be the world outside its walls. Here actors are neither performing nor getting ready for a performance.

One of the major issues raised by Goffman's analysis of the self is the question of whether there is an authentic, inner self underneath all those fronts or masks. Once we eliminate all the social roles we play—boyfriend, wife, mother, student, father, teacher, sister, lawyer, brother, doctor, coach, clerk—is there anything left over? This question revisits David Hume's view of the self as just a bundle of perceptions that holds together only thanks to our memory of how past events connect to present ones. For Goffman the self seems to be a bundle of fronts. As you read this section, ask yourself a question: can you think of any part of what you call your 'self' that isn't in some way connected to a social role you're performing in the theatre of everyday life? Once all the masks have been removed, is there a face beneath them, or just empty space?

Merchants of Information and Morality

For Goffman, social life is about impression management. When we encounter people in everyday life, we look for clues or 'sign-vehicles' that will enable us to gain information about the person—status, trustworthiness, competence, and so on. He distinguishes the expressions that a person gives in verbal symbols from the expression that an actor gives off through less direct communication. His book is about this second form of expression, the non-verbal type.

Regardless of the object an actor has in mind, it's in the individual's interests to control the conduct of others by controlling the definition of the situation so they will act voluntarily according to his or her plans. If going on a date, for example, a male of the species might be careful to promote the image of being a successful or potentially successful person in the economic sense by dressing in an expensive leather jacket and picking up his date in a nice car. A performer's audience can use the expression a performer gives off to check the validity of his or her verbal expressions. For example, if a person claims to be a professional of some type, we might look at that person's clothes or shoes to see if they match what we expect of such a status. Of course, a con artist can manipulate such cues, dressing in an expensive suit and carrying a laptop computer, for example, to convince an unwitting dupe that he is a successful corporate type.

Goffman compares social encounters to an information game—'I will give you some information that helps to define the role I am claiming to play, in exchange for which you give me some information about your intended role.' In this game, each person can establish the tentative official ruling on things vital to him or her, in exchange for non-commitment on things vital to others in the encounter, which Goffman calls an interactional modus vivendi (ibid., 9). We create a working consensus about our overall definition of the situation each time we interact. Sometimes events occur that contradict or discredit the definition of the situation being fostered by the main actor or actors. When this happens, the interaction can come to an embarrassing halt, for example, when someone claiming a special skill botches the simplest of actions.

Goffman says that interactions usually have a moral character. Performers want to engineer a convincing impression that they really *are* the role they're playing, and thus they're making at least an *implicit* moral claim on the respect of others. When a person projects a definition of a situation and makes an implicit or explicit claim to a person of a specific kind, 'he automatically exerts a moral demand upon others, obliging them to value and treat him in the manner that persons of his kind have a right to expect' (ibid., 13). He also forgoes claims to be things he does not appear to be. In this sense we are 'merchants of morality' displaying a variety of goods (ibid., 251). Communicative acts become moral ones.

Goffman's book is about how people manage the impressions they give off to others. 'Interaction' or 'encounter' for Goffman means the influence of people on each other in face-to-face situations. A performance is everything an actor does in a given situation to influence other participants in any way. A 'part' or 'routine' is a preestablished pattern of action we see being played out during a performance that can be repeated in other similar situations (ibid., 15–6).

Fronts and Roles

When a performer plays a part, he or she implicitly asks people to take seriously the impression being fostered, so that the audience will believe that matters are as they appear to be. The performer can either be totally taken in by his own act, or not at all. A cynical performer is someone who doesn't really believe in his or her own act or

care about his or her audience, while a sincere performer believes in the reality of the role he or she is playing. Goffman talks about how people in service occupations, even if sincere, must from time to time act cynically towards their public. An example might be a sales clerk who pretends to be nice to a despised customer. Really, though, the difference between cynical and sincere performers lies on a continuum—sincerity is a matter of degree. We start by wearing social masks, personae, but eventually take our roles so seriously that they become an integral part of our personalities. Cynical performers can become sincere ones over time. Goffman gives the example of an army recruit who follows the rules to avoid punishment, but later follows the rules out of a sense of esprit de corps. Goffman also notes the opposite phenomenon—of a sincere performer becoming more and more cynical over time. An example is the law student who enters law to defend human rights and ecological organizations like Greenpeace, but succumbs to the lure of riches and becomes a corporate lawyer defending oil interests.

A person's front is the part of the expressive equipment used in performances. Our fronts are the major ways we present our selves in public performances. Such fronts are associated with our various social roles that we show our audiences. We put on a mask to fit each situation we are in: our front helps to define the situation for those observing our social performance. Goffman defines a front as 'that part of the individual's performance which regularly functions in a general and fixed fashion to define the situation for those who observe the performance' (ibid., 22). We use fronts to communicate to others the essential elements of the social role we presently are playing, just as actors use physical movements and different ways of delivering their lines to communicate the inner feelings and motivations of the characters they play. Of course, we do not want things to appear too contrived, too phony, so once in a while we inject an element of spontaneity into our performances.

Goffman defines the personal front as the expressive equipment most closely identified with a performer, dividing it into appearance and manner, which should match each other in a well-played show. Our personal front includes:

- insignia of office or rank, e.g., an officer's cap in the military, or a judge's robe;
- proofs of high status, e.g., a diploma on the wall of a dentist or doctor;
- our clothing, e.g., the cap and uniform of a nurse, the team uniform and peaked cap of a ball player;
- indicators of our sex, age, and racial characteristics;
- our size and looks: for example, children are taken less seriously in most roles than adults;
- our posture, speech patterns, facial expressions, and bodily gestures: if you're being interviewed for a job you wouldn't sit slouched in the chair, or greet the interviewer with a 'How's it going, man?'

Also, more and more pieces of technology are becoming parts of the personal fronts of at least members of the professional classes. We've all seen the business person, or even academic, with a laptop in hand—evidence that they're so serious about their work that they take it with them.

The setting of a performance is also important. It includes the physical layout of the space, the furniture, decor, and other items that act as scenery or stage props for the human action played out there (ibid., 22). A setting tends to stay put, geographically speaking. People using a particular setting as part of their performance cannot begin to perform until they've got to the appropriate setting, and usually have to end the performance when they leave that setting. For example, to be a waiter, one needs to be in a restaurant; if you tried serving people food in a library, they would think you were crazy (even if you *really* are a waiter). In other cases, the setting of our performances is more flexible—you can be a student in any number of places. But most settings connected to work and professional careers are less flexible, whether an office, a hospital, a factory floor, a boardroom, or a café.

Our appearance includes those stimuli we use to tell others our social status (ibid., 24). They also tell the audience about our 'temporary ritual state', i.e., whether we are engaging in some formal social activity, in work, or in informal recreation. Expectations about appearance often are standardized within a given culture: police officers wear blue or black uniforms; business people wear suits and are neatly groomed; hospital personnel wear uniforms of white or pastel colours. Most of the characteristics related to personal front are important parts of our appearance—a uniform or insignia, certain clothes, body language, ways of speaking, gestures, props, and so on. These serve to communicate social status, occupation, age, gender, and personal values and commitments to others.

As opposed to our appearance, our manner is made up of those stimuli that warn us of the role the performer expects to play in the situation at hand (ibid., 24). So, if you're sitting in a doctor's office and a man with a white lab coat enters and asks you in an authoritative manner for your urine sample, you assume that he is a doctor, and not a janitor come to empty the trash cans. A performer's manner may indicate how central a role he/she expects to be taking in the coming interaction. A haughty, aggressive manner may give the impression that the performer expects to control the interaction, while a meek and humble manner gives the impression that the performer will let others take command of it. Each role has a different manner associated with it. You expect your doctor to tell *you* what's wrong with you. It would be strange to be offered a diagnosis and then asked nervously and hesitatingly, 'What do you think?'

We often expect some consistency between appearance and manner that confirms that the persons performing really are who they claim to be. You wouldn't expect an on-duty cop to slap you on the back and ask you to go for a beer if you stopped to ask him for directions. Appearance dictates a certain manner, in this case, to serve and protect the public. We also expect some consistency between appearance, manner, and setting; we expect a billionaire like Bill Gates will have an opulent mansion and servants, not to mention an expensive car and a chauffeur. If we saw him by himself driving an old jalopy we would be taken aback.

When we encounter a performer playing a certain type of role indicated by appearance and manner, we can slot his or her performance into a manageable vocabulary of fronts that we know how to respond to. We do not have to know all the details about the performer's individual character to appreciate the performance. In fact, if the individual's character comes out too much, this could be an annoyance, for example, if, when we go to a bank teller to withdraw some money, she tells us how sad she is because her boyfriend left her. Goffman says this creation of a small number of fronts to encompass a large number of social acts is probably a natural development. When an actor takes on a social role, there's usually an established front waiting for them. One may be able to select from a variety of fronts, but will have trouble trying to create an entirely new one.

Performers usually have to add signs to their performances to dramatize their conception of the role they're playing. For example, a baseball umpire makes a dramatic sweep of his arms to indicate that a runner is 'safe', while a hockey referee points authoritatively to a penalized player, indicating the player's infraction with a dramatic motion of the hands. In some cases, dramatic gestures and acts are built into a player's performance, for example, a rock star cavorting on stage. In other cases, the dramatization is harder to define, as when a car mechanic proffers a bill for services unseen, but which took a lot of time and effort on the mechanic's part.

Idealization, Control, Misrepresentation, and Mystification

Performances make abstract claims upon their audiences because they present an idealized view of the situation. Professions project an idealized picture of themselves onto the world supposedly to make individual performances more effective. When a performer presents himself before others, his or her performance tends to incorporate officially accredited social values. Performances often are rejuvenations of the moral values of the community, even a celebration of these values. In this sense 'the world is a wedding'.

Societies tend to idealize the powerful and moneyed upper classes. The most important way in which this is done is through status symbols that express wealth: an expensive car, designer clothes, a Rolex watch, or glittering jewellery. Goffman is fascinated, however, by the phenomenon of people who underplay wealth, intellect, spiritual strength, or self-respect in a way that seems to undermine their position but contributes to some long-term goal. He gives the example of the Shetlanders refusing to improve the appearance of their cottages because they feared having their rents increased. He also mentions beggars, who used to engage in staged dramatizations of their poverty where the beggar's family appeared in tattered but clean clothes, or the beggar implored his 'mark' with his sad eyes. A few years ago a similar story was heard in Toronto of a street beggar who writhed about on the pavements, apparently in great pain, yet earned a comfortable living from her performance.

Actors have to avoid or hide actions that discredit their performances. Once the falseness of the Toronto beggar's performance was exposed, the police, public, and media turned against her. The most basic things that actors must hide are 'inappropriate pleasures and economies' (ibid., 43). For example, an alcoholic might hide a flask of whisky in his jacket; an impoverished family might buy cheap versions of goods to give the image of having more status than they actually do. There are more ways things are concealed in performances: (1) shady but profitable activities like bribe-taking are hidden; (2) previous mistakes are covered up; (3) the performer shows only the final product, not rehearsals and rough sketches; (4) dirty business and illegal acts are covered up; (5) less important standards are sacrificed to more important ones (e.g., in a greasy-spoon café cleanliness is sacrificed for speed); and (6) the actors try to give the impression they have ideal qualifications for their roles, even if it took years of pain and humiliation to get those qualifications.

Performers tend to conceal or underplay those activities, facts, and motives that are not compatible with an idealized version of themselves and their products (ibid., 48). Performers also often cause their audiences to believe they are related to them in a more ideal way than is really the case. Goffman makes a couple of points here. First, performers try to make sure that the performance they're doing *right now* seems like their most essential one, in other words, that the present audience is special. A stand-up comedian might open her act by saying, 'It's great to be here in Saskatoon this time of year', even though outside the temperature is −25° and the snow piled up to her knees. Goffman calls this 'audience segregation', without which urban life would collapse. Second, effective performers like to create the illusion that their performances are special and unique and full of spontaneity, hiding their routine aspect. This is a problem for stage actors, singers, and comedians who have to 'get up' for performances, plays, songs, and routines they've already done dozens of times, and for professions like sales or teaching where one's emotional state directly affects one's job performance.

We shouldn't analyze performances in terms of mechanical standards, where a big gain can outweigh several small losses, but use artistic imagery, in that a single off-key note can disrupt an entire performance. Goffman identifies three ways in which this type of performance disruption can occur:

1. The performer shows incapacity or disrespect through a loss of muscle control, e.g., by tripping or belching.
2. A performer may do something to indicate that he or she is either too much or too little concerned with the show being put on, e.g., by appearing very nervous, by showing a lack of interest, or by laughing at his or her audience.
3. The performer might use bad dramaturgical direction, e.g., come prepared for the wrong performance, show bad timing, or allow embarrassing lulls.

Goffman concludes that we must be prepared to see that 'the impression of reality fostered by a performance is a delicate, fragile thing that can be shattered by very minor mishaps' (ibid., 56). Like an inadvertent trumpet blast in a symphony's performance of a classical piece of music, one goof up can throw off an entire public performance.

The expressive coherence required in performances points out a crucial discrepancy between our all-too-human and socialized selves. As human beings we are creatures of emotional ups and downs, yet our performances must not be subject to these. 'A certain bureaucratization of the spirit is expected so that we can be relied upon to give a perfectly homogeneous performance at every appointed time' (ibid., 56). We have to hide our animal habits and our moods when we put on our social masks.

Most of the signs that performers use to foster impressions can also be used to dupe or mislead their audience. We tend to see it as more of a crime for an impostor to impersonate someone with a sacred status, like a priest or a doctor. This probably has something also to do with the trust we place in these professions. However, the social legitimacy of misrepresenting one's age and sexual status varies with the situation. It's considered very wrong for a 15-year-old to drive a car and order drinks in a bar; but it's not considered terribly wrong for an adult woman on the prowl to claim she's younger than she really is to attract a man. Another example is dying one's hair to cover grey—for women it's totally acceptable, but for men it's frowned upon. If an actor tells a barefaced lie and is caught, it will throw a dark shadow over her future performances—she won't be trusted. But it's fine to tell a white lie to save the audience's feelings, e.g., a clerk in a clothes store telling a customer 'you look fabulous, dahling!' as she tries on a new dress.

Points of secrecy are found in complicated relationships such as a marriage. A married couple may hide all sorts of things from each other: flirtations with work friends, the wasting of money on frivolous things, or a dim view of their spouse's relatives. Yet sometimes one sour note in a performance of such a relationship can spoil the whole thing: a minor secret withheld by one spouse is discovered by the other, who then becomes paranoid about whether he or she has been lied to about more important matters, thinking, 'How can I trust you anymore?' But in the end, Goffman notes, we can't say that the cynical view of a performance gets to its 'reality' more accurately than a more naive view. There are truly false performances. But it's one thing to say that a given performance has been discredited; it's another to say that it's false.

Performers must try to regulate information to keep their definition of the situation going strong. But they must also regulate contact with the audience to prevent their ritual contamination—if the performer gets too close to his or her audience, the performer's front might quickly collapse. One way that an actor can create a state of mystification in an audience is by maintaining a certain social distance and thereby creating awe. Kings, the ultra-rich, and military leaders often stand aloof from the crowd to help maintain this sense of mystery and awe. After all, the people don't want leaders with too many human failings—witness the debate over the various scandals that Bill Clinton was involved in. The awe, which this mystification of the audience is intended to create, may also hide things that the performer is ashamed of. The audience senses secret mysteries and powers behind the wizard's curtain, even though there is only a little old man there.

The performances of everyday life aren't acted or 'put on' in the sense that actors know in advance what they will be doing and aim at some specific effect. Large elements of everyday performances are improvised. Honest and sincere performances are less rooted in the real world than slightly off-kilter ones. The details of a given role don't come from a script, but from the command of an idiom—in general, we learn how to act while playing out a role. To be a particular kind of person is to sustain certain ways of acting, often unconsciously. A status, position, or social place isn't a material thing we possess and display, but a pattern of appropriate conduct, 'coherent, embellished, and well articulated. Performed with ease or clumsiness, awareness or not, guile or

good faith, it is none the less something that must be enacted and portrayed' (ibid., 75).

Teamwork and Impression Management

Obviously, many of our public performances are as part of a team. A team is a group of people who co-operate to stage a specific routine (ibid., 79). As we've seen, teams also co-operate to conceal unpleasant and embarrassing facts, knowing all along that any team member can give away the show. That's why whistle-blowers are despised in some circles, like the legendary Deep Throat who told reporters about the Watergate cover-up connected to Richard Nixon's early 1970s presidency and was hated for years afterward by members of Nixon's inner circle. Open disagreement between team members is very bad for a performance. As a result, team members must swallow their anger at each other's mistakes, at least until the audience has retired (ibid., 89). Have you ever seen actors stop in mid-play and yell at each other for botching lines? Not likely. Some performance teams have stars who act as a centre of attention; most have directors who discipline performers when they step out of line. In general, teams are secret societies who carry with themselves the 'sweet guilt of conspirators' (ibid., 105).

Much of the second half of Goffman's book has to do with the various techniques performers use to keep their show alive. The past life and current actions of a given performer always contain a few facts that could discredit claims about the self the performer was attempting to make and thus weaken the performance. Also, a performer can make a faux pas, gaffe, or boner during a performance (ibid., 209). When an actor deliberately threatens the polite appearance of consensus found in a given scene, she or he has 'created a scene'. A new drama is introduced with new scenes, and everyone has to take sides, joining either the old conservative team or the new disruptive team. Examples include when a team member blurts out criticisms of another member publicly, when an audience gives up on the game of polite interaction and confronts the performers, or when two or more people are showing off or loudly arguing and force onlookers to take sides in their debate, e.g., a pair of drunken men on a crowded bus.

When a performance is disrupted and ugly incidents occur, the reality sponsored by the performers is threatened. People become nervous, flustered, ill at ease. To avoid this, performers use three sets of defensive practices to save the show. First, they encourage dramaturgical loyalty (ibid., 212–16). Performers mustn't betray the secrets of the team between performances. They must show a united front in public. One way to do this is to create high group solidarity and to mock and belittle the audience while backstage to justify the team's use of deceptive techniques while performing. Another way to promote dramaturgical loyalty is to change audiences from time to time. That way the performers do not get too close to any given audience.

Second, dramaturgical discipline is employed. Performers must show intellectual and emotional involvement in their activities, while not letting themselves get carried away by their own shows. They must show self-control, not letting themselves be bothered by their personal problems, teammates' goof-ups, or audience adoration or hostility. They must learn to suppress their spontaneous feelings to stick to the expressive status quo established by the team's performance (ibid., 217). A large part of this self-control involves the control of one's face and voice. Goffman mentions how Becker found that marijuana smokers learn how to hide being high from family and co-workers.

Third, dramaturgical circumspection is important. The interests of the team require that performers exercise prudence and care in staging a show, preparing in advance for any problems or opportunities that might arise (ibid., 218). Several techniques can aid this circumspection: picking loyal and disciplined team members, picking an audience unlikely to cause trouble, and reducing the size of the performing team to the smallest number necessary to carry out the performance. If a performance is short and relatively anonymous, it's easier to maintain a false front than it is

during a long, involved performance, e.g., the smooth telephone voice used by telemarketers soliciting strangers by telephone can be kept up only for awhile. Great care must be taken where a performance has important consequences, such as job interviews. In such a situation, every little detail of the person's appearance and actions is seen as highly symbolic. Radio and TV performers are another example—massive audiences impel them to take great care with the details of their performance, such as the plastic perfection of the TV news anchor's hairdo.

Goffman says that these defensive techniques of impression management have a counterpart in the tactful tendency of the audience and outsiders to protect performers and thus save their show. For one thing, audiences voluntarily stay away from the backstage region: hamburger eaters don't visit slaughterhouses, while theatrical audiences don't demand entrance to the actors' dressing rooms. In Anglo-American societies like ours, people are supposed to mind their own business and to keep their noses out of other people's lives. This is part of the tact and respect for privacy we exercise as audiences in our everyday lives—we let people get on with their jobs as long as they are not totally incompetent. Audience members are usually willing to pay attention to performances, not interrupt them, avoid scenes, and not try to make the performers slip up. When performers make a mistake, showing a discrepancy between the impression they are aiming at and the reality disclosed, the audience may tactfully choose not to see it. In moments of crisis, the audience may come out in tacit collusion with them to help them out. This is especially true of beginners, who are encouraged to 'go on' with their performance after a mistake, e.g., 10-year-old Jenny playing at her first piano recital.

The performer must also show his or her audience tact regarding tact, and not push this first tact beyond limits. For example, if a group of people are having a private conversation that others can overhear, they should avoid discussing blatantly personal things that the pseudo-audience can't ignore. Also, performers must be sensitive to hints from the audience, and only tell limited untruths. And if people maintain a show before others they don't believe themselves, they can experience a special kind of alienation from themselves and a special kind of wariness of others. Goffman talks about college girls playing dumb on dates: they feel contempt towards their boyfriends, who are so easily taken in by their tricks. They felt like they were 'slumming'. Yet sometimes their boys see through their tricks, and the young ladies feel embarrassed (ibid., 237).

In summary, Goffman's book is concerned with the structure of face-to-face social encounters in everyday life, within the interaction order. Yet this is only one of the several alternative approaches to the study of social establishments as fixed systems that Goffman envisages. One can also look at them technically, in terms of efficiency; politically, in terms of power relationships; structurally, in terms of status divisions; or culturally, in terms of moral values, customs, and fashions (ibid., 240). Yet one must assume that Goffman saw dramaturgy as the first among these equals in social theories.

We now switch gears to the second set of 'interpretive' approaches in this chapter—phenomenology. We'll spend less time on each individual author since the central ideas of phenomenology tend to be repeated in the three theorists considered here.

THE PHENOMENOLOGY OF EVERYDAY LIFE

Phenomenology as a social theory asks us to look on the world of everyday life as a foreign country with strange customs that the sociologist visits to describe and map, like the early European explorers during the age of discovery. Yet unlike the European explorer, the phenomenologist is asked to 'bracket' his or her own assumptions about the reality and value of these customs, however familiar they might seem to be. Phenomenology seeks to make the everyday world all around us seem less mundane, as full of ordered practices and rituals, and then try to understand how these orders

and rituals operate. It aims to reduce the phenomena of social life to their essential qualities in order to understand society.

Husserl and the Phenomenology of Consciousness

Derived from two ancient Greek words, phenomenology is the *logos* (study or logic) of *phenomena* (appearances). What phenomena? Edmund Husserl (1859–1939), the founder of modern phenomenology—the term had been used before him by the philosophers Kant and Hegel—wanted to study the phenomena of our consciousness, the thoughts in our heads. He saw phenomenology as a purely descriptive discipline that did not pretend to prescribe any values or offer any solutions to practical problems. Later, Alfred Schutz shifted phenomenology from the purely mental world to social life, wanting to study the stocks of knowledge and common-sense assumptions about everyday life that make that life possible. This project is quite similar to Goffman's, though the phenomenologists tend to use more philosophical language than the interactionists. Schutz and his followers saw social reality as constructed by human thinking and action. We require phenomenological inspection of that thinking and action in order to understand society.

Husserl aimed to make philosophy a rigorous science in pursuit of what he called eidetic (essential) ideas and the transcendental ego. He saw his project as akin to that of the seventeenth-century French philosopher René Descartes, who used a system of methodical doubt to arrive at the one thing he was sure was true: 'I think therefore I am.' In other words, Descartes was sure he existed as a thinking thing, whatever the status of his physical body and other people and objects in the world might be. He called this thinking thing, in Latin, the *ego cogitans*. Husserl aimed higher than Descartes: he wanted to discover the transcendental ego, the pure form of thought independent of its relation to objects in the world, social relations, and ethical, political, and aesthetic values. He called his project 'transcendental phenomenology' since he aimed to transcend both the subjective world view of everyday life and the objective world view of natural science.

Husserl believed that all thoughts were thoughts *of* something: they were intentional. They point towards something. This isn't just a matter of thinking of physical objects like trees and pens and bottles of whisky; it also includes future or past courses of action and abstract ideas. Yet consciousness is also a process continually in flux, governed by a sense of inner time. Husserl saw the purpose of phenomenology as the close inspection of the phenomena of consciousness, free from assuming that the objects they refer to exist and free from any ethical, political, or cultural interests or values. Traditionally, philosophy has assumed that our ideas correspond to something in the world, even if it's abstract—my idea of a dog corresponds to some real dog, of freedom to a real relationship between people. Husserl calls this set of correspondences of ideas to reality the 'natural attitude', which most people are trapped in most of their lives. They assume the reality of the things their thoughts picture, including the reality of social relations they're part of. Even science does this—scientists believe in the reality of concepts like force, mass, and acceleration, even though these are only theoretical constructs. To counter this natural attitude, Husserl proposed a 'phenomenological attitude' that would sever the connection between consciousness and the 'natural' world of objects.

Husserl's key method is what he called the *epoché* or phenomenological reduction, or in humbler terms, 'bracketing'. He argued that we could take the contents of our consciousness and 'reduce' them to pure thoughts by bracketing out their connection to real-world objects and values. Husserl wanted to strip away from our ideas their connection to the objective world and any values we associate with them to get at their purest form, which he thought would lead us to discover a 'transcendental ego' common to all human beings akin to the thinking being Descartes discovered in his *Meditations*. He wanted us to abstain from assuming that the objects of our consciousness are

real, though by no means was he a naive skeptic who doubted that the real world is really out there.

The thing that natural science misses is the fact that everything actually happens in the life-world, our everyday experiences. We do not experience the force of gravity in that lifeworld but apples falling from trees and tired muscles after a long walk. Husserl's phenomenological reduction aimed to bracket out both natural science and the lifeworld to discover the essential structures of consciousness. But here's the rub: once we strip away assumptions about the connection of our ideas to objects in the world and get rid of any subjective values connected to them, is there anything left? His transcendental phenomenology may in the end be like the proverbial cat chasing its own tail. It was left to Alfred Schutz to turn Husserl's philosophical ideas into a workable social theory.

Schutz and the Phenomenology of the Social World

Alfred Schutz (1899–1959) was born in Vienna, Austria, and studied both law and the work of Weber and Husserl, his two main influences. He worked much of his life as both a bank executive and a part-time social theorist, escaping from the Nazis to America in 1939. He wound up at the New School for Social Research in New York City in 1943 and taught part-time there until 1956, when he took a full-time position. His basic goal in his work was to translate Husserl's phenomenology of pure consciousness into a phenomenology of the social world, which he did in his major work, *The Phenomenology of the Social World* (1967 [1932]), and in later works. He was also influenced by Weber, especially by his notion of the ideal type and his demand that social science be value-free. Schutz wanted the social scientist to bracket out their personal lives and interests to reach this value-free state.

Like all the social phenomenologists, he argued that social actors construct their social worlds, yet they wind up seeing these worlds as objective facts. Instead of bracketing the lifeworld as Husserl did, Schutz examined it in depth. He wanted to *study* the lifeworld of everyday life rather than seeing it as a troublesome cloud blocking the sunny horizon of the transcendental ego. Just as Husserl believed that people adopt a natural attitude towards the connection between their ideas and objects in the world, Schutz argued that people take social reality as objectively given to them, adopting a natural attitude to the social world. Schutz wanted to reduce the naturalness of the social world, trying to understand the assumptions and processes that underlie everyday life.

Our intersubjective world is created and maintained by the common-sense knowledge that underlies our actions. Schutz discovered that people draw on common stocks of knowledge in navigating their way through the various situations in their lives: we know how to speak a language, greet people, use technological objects, be polite to bureaucrats, and order a pizza (and a lot of other things, too). Schutz argued that human beings love to classify or typify things. We use typifications to aid us in our voyage through everyday life. We typify objects, people, situations, even ourselves. We also typify ways of doing things. A Parisian might see a rude tourist speaking English as 'a typical American'; a critic might classify a formulaic Hollywood movie as a 'typical action film'; a young man out for a drink might see a pub as a 'typical pickup bar'. Typifications also happen on an even more fundamental level, in the reports our senses give us of the objects in the external world. We associate a loud wailing sound with a police or ambulance siren, a red octagon with a stop sign, the smell of burnt cheese with a local pizza parlour. We understand the social world through an endless series of typifications, some of them peculiar to us as individuals, some of them more generally valid. The collection of typifications within our mind makes up our lifeworld. They provide us with myriad linguistic and practical tools that allow us to interpret, label, and understand our social worlds.

When we have to act, we rely on stocks of knowledge Schutz calls 'recipes'. Just as a recipe for pasta sauce tells us that we have to add so much tomato paste, so many onions and olives, and so much oregano to the mix, a recipe for a job interview tells us to show up on time, be polite to the interviewer, dress formally, and play up our qualifications for the position. Recipes are ways of doing things socially. Anthony Giddens would later pick up Schutz's ideas of stocks of knowledge and recipes, including them within what he calls 'practical consciousness'.

The typifications people create in their lives are first-order constructs. When the sociologist arrives on the scene, he or she can only produce second-order constructs based on the original first-order ones. The sociologist produces ideal types of actors and action, as Weber did: these are not real human beings but puppets to be manipulated for scientific purposes (Schutz, 1973: 255). We can play with the ideal type of charismatic leadership as much as we like, but not real charismatic leaders like Lenin or Mussolini. Also, we're constantly changing our typifications and recipes based on experience. For example, we discover easier and better ways of performing routine tasks like cooking, while preconceptions about a racial group melt away as we get to know a few members of the group.

For Schutz, an action is some activity oriented towards the future. Whatever one is projecting in the act is the goal of the action. A motive is the reason why a social actor performs a given action. We can look at a social act from two directions: (1) its 'in-order-to' motive, the subjective meaning of the action as projected into the future by the actor; and (2) its 'because' motive, which is when we look back on the action after it has happened and interpret it in terms of the actor's biographical and historical circumstances. Alexandra says that she takes the bus to school *in order to* attend her sociology lectures and get a degree; yet she wants the degree *because* her parents encouraged her to be educated from an early age and convinced her that she'll get a better job with a degree than without one. The in-order-to motive looks into the future, and because of its subjective quality it cannot be scientifically investigated with any rigour. But our 'because' motives, being grounded in past circumstances, *can* be systematically examined. In-order-to motives exist within a realm of free choice, the action not having yet happened; but because motives are determined by past factors and involve social types, not individual choices. Thus Schutz seemingly solves the age-old philosophical debate between free will and determinism by saying, in effect, 'it all depends on how you look at it.' This is not surprising, as he saw individual actors living in a dialectical relationship with social structure (and thus as both free and determined at the same time). We change the world by our actions, which then change us in return (ibid., 209).

Further, Schutz more or less agreed with Weber's definition of social action. He defines social behaviour as 'conscious experiences intentionally related to another self which emerge in the form of spontaneous activity' (Schutz, 1967: 144). If we previously projected or planned this behaviour, it's a social action. This embraces acts directed towards a 'thou' (in German *Du*) as a self with consciousness and duration, a thinking person, as opposed to a mere physical thing. Echoing Weber, Schutz argues that a doctor working on an anaesthetized patient or a soldier marching in time with the man in front of him is not engaging in social action since each of them is ignoring the conscious experience of the other person. In each case they see the other person as a mere body. For both Schutz and Weber, social action involves including another person's subjective meaning as part of one's projected act, in Schutz's language treating the other as a 'thou'.

Provinces, Realms, and the Lifeworld

Schutz quite rightly pointed out that we live in various realities, that we have a number of provinces of meaning in our lives. Not only do we have the waking world of everyday life, of civil society, but we also spend part of our lives in the worlds of fantasy, dreams, the theatre, the cinema, religion, and science (to name some of the more common ones). Each of these worlds has its own logic, its own spatio-temporal relations, its own

type of physicality, its own rules and forms of knowledge. In everyday life we have to walk to work; but in a fantasy world we can fly. In our dreams we meet people we have not seen for years, not to mention fictional beasts and movie stars. To get to each of them, we have to bracket out other worlds—we have to fall asleep to dream, to sit in a darkened theatre to enjoy a film, to suspend logic to understand the Holy Trinity. The borders between these worlds are poorly guarded by the watchdogs of the mind: we can daydream at work or see the Big Bang as a divine act. Yet in the end, Schutz admits that the world of everyday life is the paramount reality.

The lifeworld has a variety of realms, a variety of ways we relate to our fellow human beings:

- The *Vorwelt* (past world): This world is full of 'predecessors', people who lived before our time. Napoleon is one of my many predecessors. I will never share the same time or space with him, though I know a bit about his life, including the facts that he lost the Battle of Waterloo and was a Leo.
- The *Folgewelt* (future world): This world is full of 'successors', future people we'll never meet. We can only guess about this world.
- The *Umwelt* (surrounding world): This is the world of everyday interactions, populated by people existing in the same time and space as us. We can talk to them, shake their hands, or smell their perfume. Schutz calls these people 'consociates'. This is the realm of individual human action and first-order constructs (e.g., recipes).
- The *Mitwelt* (shared world): This is full of 'contemporaries', people who share the same time in history with us, but not the same space. Bill Clinton is my contemporary and is still alive, but I have never been in the same place as him. In this realm we find types of people and social structures.

We have a 'We-relationship' with our consociates, with whom we have sympathy and intimate connections. Yet we encounter people in the *Mitwelt* as types, as part of a series of 'they' relations, as when someone says of a large impersonal organization, 'they cheated me!' When we think of people living in a country we have never visited, it's hard to think of them as real individuals; instead, they are generic 'Albanians' or 'Mongolians', each with some vague set of typified customs learned from travel books or television documentaries. Yet Sandy your hairstylist cannot be typified in the same way, since you chatted with her just last week about her vacation in Costa Rica and can remember quite clearly her orange mohawk, pierced nose, and high-pitched laugh. Sandy is in our well-lit *Umwelt*; the Albanians are in a darker cognitive region, our *Mitwelt*. Naturally, these four categories of people are ideal types and can change—an unknown contemporary becomes a consociate when we meet and befriend her. But if she moves far away and we lose contact, she becomes a mere contemporary.

We can imagine our social world as a solar system[1] with our personal self and its *Umwelt* at its fiery centre illuminating a *Mitwelt* made up of eight orbiting planets (what Schutz called 'levels') that fade off into dark oblivion as we move further and further away from the sun of 'me':

1. People we have met before and could meet again.
2. People who have been encountered by someone we know, but not by us directly.
3. Those who we are about to meet (and thus who will enter our *Umwelt*).
4. Strangers we know only as filling a position or role, e.g., the person who checks my tax return in Winnipeg, or the mayor of some distant town.
5. A group of people whose general identity and function we know without knowing any of them individually, e.g., the Boston city police force or the Jamaican bobsled team.
6. Collective entities that are anonymous and by their very nature we can't meet, such as the French state.
7. Objective structures of meaning we and our consociates had no hand in creating, e.g.,

pretty well anything to do with language except local slang.
8. Physical artifacts our *Umwelt* had no hand in creating, e.g., Rodin's *The Thinker* or the doomed cruise ship *Titanic* (ibid., 280–1).

Naturally, the boundaries between these eight levels are permeable as we move through life: by sheer chance I might actually meet a Boston cop or a Jamaican bobsledder. Yet, for the time being, our social planets tend to spin in their set orbits.

Schutz fleshes out a bit what he means by the 'lifeworld', the world of everyday life and common sense. He sees it as having six characteristics. While in it, we: (1) are wide awake and paying attention to our lives; (2) believe in its reality; (3) are working on something, setting projects for ourselves that we try to complete; (4) experience our working self as a 'total' self; (5) live in an intersubjective world of communication and action; and (6) feel our inner flow of time matching the flow of time in society at large (Ritzer and Goodman, 2004: 416). It's you right now reading this book, plus the flux of experiences surrounding you.

THE SOCIAL CONSTRUCTION OF REALITY

Peter Berger (1929–) and Thomas Luckmann (1927–) were both directly connected to Schutz. Berger was one of his students at the New School in New York, while Luckmann co-wrote one of Schutz's later works, which appeared after his death. Their short book *The Social Construction of Reality* (1966) presents its basic thesis in its title: human beings construct a shared social reality. This reality includes everything from ordinary language to large-scale institutions. In general, they see reality as a quality of things where they cannot be affected by our will. 'The reality of everyday life is organized around the "here" of my body and the "now" of my present' (Berger and Luckmann, 1966: 22). In other words, we're once again in Goffman's interaction order. They focus on the 'sociology of knowledge' in that common-sense bodies of knowledge come to be seen as part of this social reality and thus as constitutive of society (ibid., 3).

Berger and Luckmann echo many of Schutz's principal ideas. Consciousness is intentional—it is directed towards objects. Most of the time we live within the world of common-sense knowledge, in the natural attitude. This commonsensical world, the world of face-to-face interactions, is the paramount reality. Yet within all our streams of consciousness flow inner streams of time; and we only have so much of this time to complete our life projects. This temporal structure is coercive; we can't reverse it and replay the past or avoid death (ibid., 27).

Everyday life is governed by stocks of knowledge, including recipes, that give us 'pragmatic competence in routine performances' (ibid., 42). As you go through everyday life, you project a metaphorical cone of light in front of, around, and behind you that creates a 'zone of lucidity' or familiarity surrounded by a much greater zone of darkness (ibid., 44–5). This region lit up by our personal stock of knowledge depends largely on what we find to be relevant in our surrounding world, which is usually a practical question. For example, we ignore a steady stream of traffic yet pay attention to the bus we intend to catch as it approaches our stop. The darkness represents that which we don't know or don't care about. Like Schutz, Berger and Luckmann see typificatory schemes as governing our everyday lives. We 'negotiate' the validity of these schemes as we encounter others; the further we are from a face-to-face situation, the more abstract such typifications become (e.g., the 'typical Englishman' as opposed to Henry Jones from Birmingham) (ibid., 31). Social life is a continuum of such typifications, from the most abstract and distant to the most immediate and concrete. Social structure is the sum total of these typifications and the recurring patterns of interaction based on them (ibid., 33).

Berger and Luckmann also see the world as divided into consociates, contemporaries, predecessors, and successors. They argue that language is central to understanding the reality of everyday life. Language objectifies and typifies experience,

and can transcend the 'here and now' of immediate experience temporally, spatially, and socially (ibid., 39). We can read Isaac Asimov's *Foundation* series of science fiction novels and be transported to distant planets 10,000 years in the future, or more prosaically, tell our friends about our recent summer vacation. Language builds great edifices of symbols that 'appear to tower over the reality of everyday life like gigantic presences from another world' (as in religion, philosophy, and science), yet later brings these edifices back to earth as objective parts of social reality (ibid., 40). Our social world is built of shared symbols and stocks of knowledge; our common participation in these is what 'being a society' means.

Social reality exists on two levels for Berger and Luckmann. Subjectively, it's something we find personally meaningful, such as a friendship; objectively, it exists in social institutions and structures like government bureaucracies and large corporations. These two levels roughly parallel Schutz's 'we' relations and 'they' relations: we are part of our friendship but deal with the government bureaucrat as part of the 'they', even though the state supposedly represents the people. So the actor experiences social reality as both created by human beings (as in the friendship) and objectively 'out there' (as in the bureaucracy).

One of the main questions in the book is how an actor's subjective meaning can become an objective fact (ibid., 18). We experience each other daily in an intersubjective world of face-to-face interaction, Goffman's interaction order. We create our own meanings within that order, yet these meanings often escape us, giving birth to or sustaining larger structures. Berger and Luckmann set up a dialectic between the individual actor and larger structures based on the three moments of externalization, objectivation, and internalization. These three moments happen simultaneously for the adult social actor, as shown in Figure 6.1.

Externalization occurs when social actors knowingly create their social worlds. It's the productive element in the social construction of reality, where the actors both build something *and* know that they're building it. When two partners

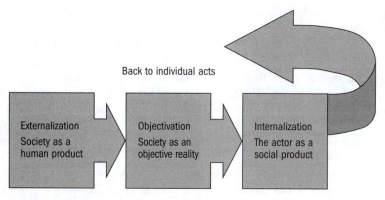

Figure 6.1 The Social Construction of Reality
Source: Berger and Luckmann (1966: 61).

start up a business, or a couple gets married, we see this moment in action. 'Objectivation' is when we look at some social practice or institution and see it as an objective reality that for the most part can't be changed. The reality of everyday life appears objectified, as 'constituted by an order of objects that have been designated as objects before my appearance on the scene' (ibid., 21–2). Corporations, bureaucracies, the army, and the police all fit the bill here. Yet perhaps the most powerful objective social reality is language, both because we usually can't choose which language to speak and because, once speaking it, we have to use words in more or less the same way as others to be understood (i.e., we cannot call dogs 'cats', say we're happy when we're actually sad, or interpret '200 dollars' to mean '50 dollars').

Finally, internalization comes close to what the functionalists mean by socialization, where the social actor internalizes norms and values and accepts them as givens, as valid both for the 'they' and the 'we'. This moment ensures that the social order is seen as legitimate by the vast majority of the populace (and breaks down during times of revolutionary change). We internalize what we saw as an external objective reality and make it *our* reality. We know who we are thanks to internalization; we have our own place in the world. For example, in North America today the great majority of people have internalized consumer capital-

ism as the most legitimate way of organizing economic activity *and* as providing the happiest lifestyle. This internalization could one day change if consumerism led to environmental collapse and its de-objectivation for the majority of former consumers.

Indeed, one of the dangers of this third moment, internalization, is that it leads to reification, a concept derived from Marxist thought. It's when we see human phenomena as physical things. Reification is the process where we see the things human beings make, such as the state, churches, or economic institutions, as if they were part of the natural order or the results of some cosmic or divine will. 'Reification implies that man is capable of forgetting his own authorship of the human world, and further that the dialectic between man, the producer, and his products is lost to consciousness' (ibid., 89). Such a world is a dehumanized one to Berger and Luckmann, who see it in a way reminiscent of Sartre's practico-inert. Roles, which are typifications of conduct for a given social position, can become reified to the point where a person totally identifies with the typifications attached to one of them and says, 'I have no choice. I have to do this because of my position' (ibid., 91). This sort of logic is common with soldiers and bureaucrats. In this sense phenomenology presents the social and political reformer with an understanding of why reform is often so hard to accomplish—the corrupt or unjust systems in place have become reified and turned into rock-hard social objects by the masses that participate in their ongoing renewal.

Berger and Luckmann argue that we go through two levels of socialization. The first—primary socialization—takes place in childhood through significant others such as family and school chums. It ends when we internalize the generalized other (borrowing from Mead a bit). Secondary socialization happens during adult life, when we find ourselves slotted into various positions in the economy, and thus into the objective lifeworld. These specific positions in the lifeworld socialize us for specific roles, such as bank clerks, librarians, corporate CEOs, and garage mechanics. It's the internalization of a variety of institutional subworlds. Berger and Luckmann see socialization as so powerful that it even channels our sexual and nutritional choices. Out of the many objects our body, in theory, could have sex with or eat, social reality determines that we choose only a few of these things to satisfy our biological needs (ibid., 181–2).[2] Our objective social world trumps our subjective choices to such a degree here that tabooed objects of desire arouse only disgust in most of us. The utility of phenomenology comes from the way it connects our subjective choices to social reality without making that reality a hard-and-fast structure independent of all human decisions.

ETHNOMETHODOLOGY

Harold Garfinkel (1917–) is the founder of ethnomethodology, an approach to research that has drawn many adherents to its cause over the last two generations. Garfinkel finished his Ph.D. at Harvard in 1952. After a few years at Ohio State and in Chicago, he wound up at UCLA, where he established a training centre for budding ethnomethodologists such as Aaron Cicourel. Garfinkel was influenced by both Husserl and Schutz, and many of his main ideas are attempts to adapt phenomenology to empirical research. Yet he was also influenced by Talcott Parsons's

theory of action, whereby an actor aims at a goal within a social field in which certain situational conditions and norms and values guide or restrain what they can do. Garfinkel wanted to add a strong dose of the actor's own understanding of his or her situation and choices to Parsons's mix. In this sense, we can call ethnomethodology a 'phenomenological theory of action'.

Ethnomethodology (or as Anthony Giddens calls it, 'ethmeth') came out of Garfinkel's attempt to analyze audio tapes of a Chicago jury discussing a case in 1945. He wanted to try to understand how the jurors knew how to act as jurors, how they learned the rules of the 'jury game'. After seeing a list of other sciences such as ethnobotany and ethnophysics, he decide to invent the term 'ethnomethodology' to describe the study of how a people or folk uses various methods to make sense of their social world. Garfinkel is convinced that there is 'endless orderliness' in the methods people use in 'immortal, ordinary society' (Garfinkel, 2002: 139). Since these methods are so much embedded in our natural attitude to everyday life, like almost invisible veins of gold in a mass of meaner ore, the ethnomethodologist has to treat this life as problematic. The ethmeth practitioner has to figure out ways of shaking us a bit so we (i.e. students of social life) can see that everyday life isn't as objectively valid as we often think. This is Garfinkel's equivalent of the phenomenological reduction.

He would often give his students bizarre assignments composed of impossible-to-answer questions to shake them out of their natural attitudes towards academic work. But more importantly, Garfinkel and his followers performed breaching experiments to expose the nature of the rules and order keeping a given social situation working. These sought to disrupt the taken-for-granted nature of the social world through experiments that would show its subjective character. Basically, they make trouble within a given interaction order (to use Goffman's term) to try to make sense of that order. Suppose a professor came into her class at the regular time, sat down, and started reading a copy of *The Lord of the Rings*, ignoring her students and not doing the expected lecture. Presumably the students would soon get restless and either leave or question the professor. Ethnomethodologists have done similar experiments and found that an audience like this one tries to make sense of, or account for, the professor's strange behaviour—'Are we supposed to be working an assignment during class? Is the professor angry at us for some reason?' They try to give an *account* of the professor's odd actions.[3] Indeed, Garfinkel thought that social actors in general produce and manage their settings using procedures that make those settings 'accountable' to themselves and others (Garfinkel, 1967: 240). We try to give a plausible, meaningful account of all situations, even those that are inherently meaningless.

Garfinkel saw such breaching experiments as disruptions of the subject's background expectations. To be successful, such an experiment had to do three things: (1) make sure the subject couldn't see the experiment as a game, play, or elaborate joke; (2) force the subject to re-evaluate the 'natural facts' of the breached reality, yet not give him or her enough time to reconstruct the breached situation into a new reality that can be mastered; (3) make sure that subjects reconstruct the facts of the new situation by themselves (ibid., 54). In short, Garfinkel wanted his experiments to be taken seriously and to be forceful enough so that their subjects had to react quickly.

An experiment that Garfinkel and crew actually did was having students go into shops to try to barter for goods instead of paying the marked prices. The normal method of consumption here is based on a 'one-price rule': one enters a shop, chooses what one wants, and then pays the marked price. Garfinkel's students found that some shop assistants were confused or angry at such violations of the social code of shopping, though in other cases the bartering actually worked and the successful students became quite good at it. That this is just a subjective code is clear. In the summer of 2004 I visited Mexico, where street vendors can be seen at all major corners, city squares, and tourist destinations. On the main avenue between the ancient pyramids at

Tenochtitlan, vendors sell carved statuettes of Aztec gods, masks, jewellery, and other trinkets to tourists. Yet their prices are quite flexible and they seem to expect some bargaining. An opening price of 'cincuenta pesos' might be met with a reply of 'treinta' and so forth until either a mutually acceptable price or an impasse is reached. The normal method of buying things in North American shops is not normal at all in Mexican markets and streets.

Social order is created by individuals in part through the accounts they can give of their everyday practices. Garfinkel says that ethmeth analyzes everyday actions as people's 'methods for making those same activities visibly-rational-and-reportable-for-all-practical-purposes, this is, "accountable" as organizations of commonplace everyday activities' (ibid., vii). A Mexican street vendor might account for bartering by noting that it's more important to sell the goods and make *some* profit rather than not to sell them at all. Yet most of the time we don't enunciate these accounts: they're buried deep in the rocks of our everyday actions like that gold ore just mentioned. The ethnomethodologist must disrupt the continuity of everyday life and its taken-for-granted nature to get at the precious ore of the accounts that keep this life going.

An account of a situation contains the meaning the actor assigns to it. Some of our accounts are fully verbal, as when a player makes a mistake in a sport and tries to justify it to his teammates. Others involve shortcuts and abbreviations, while still others aren't put into language at all. When we encounter a term that all of the people in a situation understand but that is not explained verbally, Garfinkel calls this an 'indexical expression'. We leave a lot out of our verbal accounts of typical situations that we fill in with indexical expressions based on common stocks of knowledge of the situation or activity at hand and specific knowledge of the people involved in it. If your friend asks you if you want to go to a movie, she assumes that you will show up on time, pay for a ticket, perhaps buy some popcorn or treats, and sit relatively quietly in the theatre and watch the movie (as opposed to listening to music on a portable CD player and singing along). Most of this need not be stated verbally—most people would provide this account for what 'going to a movie' means. Of course, all of this is contextual and thus is indexed to a specific type of situation. If we were attending a baseball game instead of the film, drinking beer and cheering loudly would be acceptable; likewise, if our movie-going friend is habitually late, our showing up a bit late might not be out of order. Where and when social actions take place are important to ethnomethodologists: place and time help to define a social encounter. In this sense, they feel a greater need to be part of what they're investigating than most other social theorists.

Ethnomethodology is micro-sociological: in-depth interviews, audio and videotaping, breaching experiments, the study of personal documents, and participant observation. They all share the desire to 'get close' to social life in order to understand how and why people do the things they do. These methods are thus closer to everyday discourse, and very far from the more scientific quality of statistical research. Ethmeth sometimes uses a documentary method, where appearances are seen as documents of underlying patterns (ibid., 78). Institutions often have unwritten codes of conduct that emerge from time to time in verbal descriptions of action. For example, even though college students might be obsessed with getting good grades, they often want to avoid 'sucking up' to the teacher, being seen as a 'teacher's pet'. Only a certain amount of interviewing and observation of students would bring this part of the student code out. Yet a student coming to a teacher's office to discuss class material in greater detail, away from other students, might document this fear.

Ethnomethodology is not a system that explains or predicts social action. Like phenomenology in general, it is a descriptive discipline. Garfinkel criticized most of traditional sociology for trying to impose its own sense of social reality and reason on social actors, borrowing some form of rationality from science (he was probably thinking of rational choice theory here). This limited definition of rationality is then used by researchers to evaluate 'pathological, prejudiced, delusional, mythical, magical, ritual, and similar features of everyday conduct, thinking and beliefs' (ibid., 262). Naturally, such a procedure will reflect social reality like one of those funhouse mirrors that distorts the gazer's body in a comical way. Garfinkel's ideal mirror is much flatter and well-polished, as free from distortion as possible.

We end with some criticisms of ethnomethodology specifically and of phenomenology more generally. First, its focus on small-scale qualitative analysis might leave out the 'big picture' view of things, including how social structure and historical changes affect individual actions. Second, power and economic interests seem to be left out of the equation. Why are some stocks of knowledge more powerful than others? How does economic inequality affect the accounts people give of their behaviour? Third, like most of the theorists covered in the last two chapters, phenomenology can be seen as politically inert, hiding behind its claim to be 'value-free' when the question as to whether we need to critique society arises. Yet having said this, phenomenology's commitment to studying the details of everyday life should be given its due as an important hue in the great kaleidoscope of modern social theory.

STUDY QUESTIONS

1. What was the symbolic interactionists' criticism of behaviourist psychology? Were they right?
2. What role does sympathy play in Cooley's social theory? How is it connected to his theory of the looking-glass self? Are we all looking-glass selves?
3. How did Mead differentiate the 'I' from the 'me'? Do we need both of these elements to operate in daily life? Why?
4. Describe Mead's theory of the development of the self, offering any relevant criticisms.
5. How do the following Meadian concepts fit together: self-indication, role-taking, symbols and gestures? Can we do macro-level sociology based on these concepts?
6. What are Blumer's three principles of symbolic interactionism? Give examples of each from your everyday life.
7. How would Blumer respond to the idea that social structure regulates our behaviour?
8. What are the two stages in interactionist method that Blumer outlines? What are some of the specific investigative techniques he approves of? Which ones is he suspicious of?
9. What are the methodological implications of symbolic interactionism Blumer lays out? Are any of these a problem for seeing sociology as a science?
10. What are the five basic types of interactions Goffman outlines? Is he right to focus on face-to-face interactions as the prime focus for sociology?
11. In what sense is Goffman's self a 'persona'? Is he right that the self is a product of a performance, not something that exists *before* the performance? Explain.
12. What are the three basic regions Goffman outlines as part of all performance settings? Use his division to analyze your favourite bar or restaurant.
13. What does Goffman mean by 'front', 'setting', 'appearance', and 'manner'? What are some of the main elements of your personal front? How do these four things interact in a given performance, e.g., a student's attendance at a lecture?
14. What are some ways performers idealize, control, and misrepresent their performances in everyday life? Is Goffman saying that these processes make social life 'phony'?
15. What three general practices do team members use to avoid performance disruptions? Give examples of each.
16. What is Husserl's general approach to phenomenology? What did he mean by the 'phenomenological reduction'? What was the major fault of his approach?
17. What types of knowledge did Schutz see as holding together everyday life? Give examples of each form.
18. How did Schutz distinguish 'in-order-to' motives from 'because' motives? Why?
19. How did Schutz define behaviour and social action? Did he agree with Weber's definition?
20. What are the four realms of the lifeworld delineated by Schutz? How is each related to space and time? What sort of people do we find in each?
21. Outline the eight regions of the *Mitwelt* according to Schutz, giving an example of each other than the one listed in the text above.
22. Outline the social process whereby Berger and Luckmann argue that our subjective meaning becomes an objective fact. Give an example from your own life of each of their three stages.
23. Describe what Berger and Luckmann mean by 'reification'. Is it a serious social problem?
24. What is ethnomethodology? Why are breaching experiments important to ethnomethodologists? Design your own breaching experiment to show what sorts of rules apply to either the classroom or your place of work.
25. What are 'accounts' and 'indexical expressions'? Why are accounts important to everyday life?
26. What are the strengths and weaknesses of the research methods of ethmeth practitioners?
27. Compare the basic ideas of symbolic interactionism and phenomenology. Where do they agree? Where do they disagree?

SHORT BIBLIOGRAPHY

Becker, Howard S. 1973 [1963]. *Outsiders: Studies in the Sociology of Deviance*, rev. edn. New York: Free Press.

Berger, Peter L., and Thomas Luckmann. 1966. *The Social Construction of Reality: A Treatise in the Sociology of Knowledge*. Garden City, NY: Doubleday.

Blumer, Harold. 1969. *Symbolic Interactionism: Perspective and Method*. Berkeley: University of California Press.

Cohen, Stan. 1990 [1972]. *Folk Devils and Moral Panics: The Creation of the Mods and Rockers*. Oxford: Blackwell.

Collins, Randall, and Michael Makowsky. 2005. *The Discovery of Society*, 7th edn. New York: McGraw-Hill.

Cooley, Charles. 1964 [1902]. *Human Nature and the Social Order*. New York: Schocken Books.

Delaney, Tim. 2004. *Classical Social Theory: Investigation and Application*. Upper Saddle River, NJ: Pearson/Prentice-Hall.

Garfinkel, Harold. 1967. *Studies in Ethnomethodology*. Englewood Cliffs, NJ: Prentice-Hall.

———. 2002. *Ethnomethodology's Program: Working out Durkheim's Aphorism*, ed. Anne Warfield Rawls. New York: Rowman & Littlefield.

Goffman, Erving. 1959. *The Presentation of Self in Everyday Life*. Garden City, NY: Doubleday.

———. 1963. *Stigma: Notes on the Management of Spoiled Identity*. Englewood Cliffs, NJ: Prentice-Hall.

———. 1967. *Interaction Ritual: Essays on Face-to-Face Behavior*. Chicago: Aldine.

———. 1981. *Forms of Talk*. Philadelphia: University of Pennsylvania Press.

———. 1983. 'The Interaction Order', *American Sociological Review* 48, 1: 1–17.

Husserl, Edmund. 1931. *Ideas: General Introduction to Pure Phenomenology*, trans. W.R. Boyce Gibson. New York: Macmillan.

———. 1970. *The Crisis of the European Sciences and Transcendental Phenomenology*, trans. David Carr. Evanston, Ill.: Northwestern University Press.

Mead, George Herbert. 1934. *Mind, Self, and Society from the Standpoint of a Social Behaviorist*, ed. Charles W. Morris. Chicago: University of Chicago Press.

Ritzer, George, and Douglas J. Goodman. 2004. *Classical Sociological Theory*, 4th edn. New York: McGraw-Hill.

Schutz, Alfred. 1967. *The Phenomenology of the Social World*, trans. George Walsh and Frederick Lehnert. Evanston, Ill.: Northwestern University Press.

———. 1973. *Collected Papers I: The Problem of Social Reality*. The Hague: Martinus Nijhoff.

Thomas, William I. 1923. *The Unadjusted Girl*. Boston: Little, Brown.

Wallace, Ruth A., and Alison Wolf. 1999. *Contemporary Sociological Theory: Expanding the Classical Tradition*, 5th edn. Upper Saddle River, NJ: Prentice-Hall.

Wiseman, Jacqueline P. 1974. 'The Research Web', *Journal of Contemporary Ethnography* 3: 317-328.

CHAPTER 7

STRUCTURALISM, SEMIOTICS, AND POST-STRUCTURALISM

THE BASICS OF STRUCTURALISM AND SEMIOTICS

Structuralism and Semiotics Defined

Structuralism and semiotics are related theoretical approaches developed for the most part by twentieth-century French theorists. Both of them focused at first on the nature of language but were later applied to culture and society. They are popular in anthropology and literary and cultural studies, and have important repercussions for social theory.

Structuralism is simply the idea that we can explain a given 'surface' phenomenon in terms of some structure that lies beneath our conscious or perceptual awareness of the phenomenon in question. This structure causes the surface phenomenon to exist or operate, or conditions it strongly in some way. Think of an iceberg where we can see the upper 10 per cent or so of its mass. But hidden beneath it is a deeper structure, the majority of its mass (Figure 7.1). This is the iceberg's deep structure, that which keeps it afloat, even though we can't see it from the surface.

The surface phenomena are largely determined by its deeper structures.

Surface Phenomena

Saussure: *parole* (specific words and sentences)

Lévi-Strauss: myths in various cultures

Freud: dreams, jokes, slips of the tongue

Campbell: various mythical hero stories

Pop Culture: films, TV shows, novels

Deep Structures

Saussure: *langue* (deep structures of language)

Lévi-Strauss: universal structure of myths, binary oppositions

Freud: the unconscious mind (id, superego)

Campbell: the monomyth

Pop Culture: structures of each genre (e.g., Umberto Eco has analyzed Ian Fleming's James Bond novels as having a recurring structure)

Figure 7.1 The Structuralist Iceberg. (Ralph A. Clevenger/CORBIS)

Structuralists tend to see their favourite structures—e.g., the unconscious mind for Freud,[1] the universal structure of myths for Lévi-Strauss, cultural myths for Barthes—as universal in their power, affecting all peoples and cultures in some way. For Freud, *everyone* has an unconscious mind that develops through certain psychosexual stages and the Oedipus or Electra complex in childhood. Surface phenomena like dreams, jokes, and slips of the tongue give evidence of a deeper structure we're only dimly aware of. This deeper phenomenon, the unconscious mind, is where our basic drives work themselves out—the Love and Death instincts. Culture and social structures can be seen as akin to Freud's model of the mind, each with its own surface phenomena and deeper structures. Structuralism is especially useful in the study of culture because it can understand books, movies, songs, and other cultural artifacts in terms of the recurring underlying structures they exhibit.

Semiotics sees languages, cultures, and other phenomena as systems of signs, as codes. A system of signs is a way of communicating meaning to other human beings—but only to others who understand the code on some level. These signs aren't universally the same for everyone at all times—they depend in most cases on historical events. For example, the fact that a red traffic light means 'stop' is a historical accident: it could just as easily have been green or yellow. The job of the semiotician is to understand and decode these systems. Sometimes, as in structuralism, the users of a system of signs don't understand fully what their own signs mean, for example, when you speak a sentence in English—'I saw a black cat lurking in the moonlight'—you might not understand the grammatical function of each sentence unit. What grammatical role does 'moonlight' play here? Or 'in'? Yet you can understand it all the same because you share the same system of signs with other English speakers, even if this system isn't entirely conscious. We can apply semiotics to culture and social relationships, as Baudrillard did with consumer goods, if we see the objects within a culture as making up a system of signs, a sort of language.

Saussure and the Foundations of Structural Linguistics and Semiotics

The founder of both structuralism and semiotics in linguistics was Ferdinand de Saussure (1857–1913), who, in his lectures on linguistics (student notes published as *Course in General Linguistics* in 1916), proposed a view of language as a formal structure defined by differences between its systemic elements. He saw language as a structure where the relationship between its elements was arbitrary. Language does not reflect 'the real world', as philosophers like Plato have claimed. Instead, the meaning of words has come about by a series of historical accidents (even if a small handful of them are onomatopoeic, like 'bang' and 'sizzle'). As all semioticians believe, language is made up of a series of signs that come together in a code that allows us to transmit meaning, just as in a much more limited way traffic signs or referees' signals in a hockey game transmit meaning to drivers and players. The fact that such a code is fixed within the community using it (e.g., the rules of English grammar are fairly rigid) doesn't detract from the fact that the meaning of words is in no sense 'natural'.

Human languages are made up of signs, each of which has two elements. A given linguistic term—a sign—is the union of a written mark or a sound—the signifier—and the idea or concept it represents—the signified. Saussure also called the signifier a 'sound image'. Figure 7.2 shows Saussure's model of the sign in pictorial form, using the standard comic-book code for thought and speech.

Words in a language are signs that combine marks or sounds with ideas or concepts: in Figure 7.2, the woman's idea of a cat plus the spoken word 'cat' produces the sign for a cat. Signification is the process whereby a given signifier and a given signified come together to produce a meaningful sign.

Signifiers obviously differ from language to language—'cat' refers to a furry little beast in English, but not in other languages. As we can see in the diagram, various languages have various sig-

Figure 7.2 Saussure's Model of the Sign

nifiers for the same signified. The relation between signifier and signified is arbitrary. 'Dog' in English is nothing like 'chien' in French, yet they both mean the same thing and neither has anything to do with actual canines, except by historical accident. Real dogs do not have the word 'dog' stamped on them at birth in English-speaking countries. There is no natural connection between signifier and signified, between mark or sound and concept—if there were, we'd all speak the same language. What maintains the independence of signifiers is their difference from each other—a 'dog' is not a cat, or a tree, or any of a thousand other things. And so on through all the other nouns in the English language.

Saussure maintains that signifiers and signifieds alike have meaning only by virtue of the formal structure they share. And he proposed that we look to the rules and conventions of language, to grammar, for data. This sort of investigation could result in our understanding of the deep structure of language that influences all speakers at an unconscious level. Within the system of language

Saussure distinguished its *langue*—the overall structure and rules of a language (like the rules of a chess game) from its *parole*—the way words are used in specific circumstances (like the moves in a game of chess). You can't play chess without knowing its rules or *langue*, but spending all afternoon discussing chess rules without moving any pieces would not constitute a game of chess. You have to make some moves, to engage in *parole*. Structural linguistics studies *langue* as an abstract system or structure. Hence it tends to ignore the historical context of the signs it studies.

Saussure called the linear relation of elements in a sentence its 'syntagmatic' structure or sequence, which is related to *parole*. A sentence makes sense because the units that make it up follow a certain order. Consider the following line from a poem:

'My love's like a red red rose.'

Here the basic elements of the sentence are 'my', 'love', 'is like', and 'red rose'. Imagine that the elements of this sentence are like those refrigerator magnets with words on them that we can put in any order we like to write a poem. If we rearrange the order a bit we get:

'My red red rose is like love.'

This makes sense, yet a very different sense from the first sentence. The point is that the syntagmatic structure of a sentence helps to determine its meaning.

Aside from this syntagmatic order, Saussure talked about the paradigmatic dimension of language, which is related to *langue*. Here elements of a sentence are associated with other elements outside the sentence, to a sort of 'inner storehouse' of signifiers in our minds. If we can't make a proper paradigmatic substitution, the meaning of what we're trying to say can change drastically. Consider a couple of paradigmatic substitutions for 'red red rose':

'My love's like a warm spring day.'
'My love's like a squealing hog.'

Obviously, the poet's love will be less impressed with the second substitution than the first—'warm spring day' is paradigmatically similar to 'red red rose', but 'squealing hog' most certainly is not.

Saussure wanted to focus on the *synchronic* structure of language, how it exists at a given point in time (like a snapshot), over its *diachronic* nature, how it changes over time. To understand the structure of a language we must, in effect, freeze it in time. Saussure thought that we could study language as an abstract system of signs frozen temporarily in time. The science of these signs he called semiology. Later, semiology got applied to other sorts of cultural phenomena that could be seen as systems of signs. But unlike language, the relation between signifiers and signifieds in culture isn't arbitrary, but constructed by their makers or their audience. For example, we all know what such signs as a police uniform, a laugh track on a TV show, or a painting of a muscular hero and winsome damsel in distress on the cover of a romance novel signify—we don't have to take a wild guess, as we might with words in a foreign language. In other words, there are economic, political, and aesthetic dimensions to the construction of cultural signs: their makers want their audiences to associate a given concept with a given signifier (e.g., social order with a policeman's badge, or a sexy woman on a TV ad with a new make of car).

Saussure's structuralism was also important in that it looked at language as a total system that must already exist in order for human beings to create meaning within it. Saussure called *langue* an 'absent totality' that exists outside of language yet is instantiated in all meaningful acts of speaking and writing (Ashenden, 2005: 200). Language allows us to plug into reality; it makes us instead of us making it. Language isn't a set of tools we can pick up and use as we see fit, as Wittgenstein thought, but a system that structures our very thinking. This concept later led to the 'anti-humanism' and the idea of the death of author found in post-structuralist theory, where human beings are seen as the playthings of linguistic structures. Both structuralism and post-structuralism are thus at odds with the active, creative view of the human agent found in hermeneutics, symbolic interactionism, and phenomenology.

Lévi-Strauss and Structural Anthropology

Claude Lévi-Strauss (1908–) applied structuralism to anthropology, especially the study of myths. His main works are *The Elementary Structures of Kinship* (1949), *Structural Anthropology* (1958), *The Raw and the Cooked* (1964), and *The Savage Mind* (1966). He saw certain common, universal cultural and mythological principles underlying all specific historical manifestations of culture and myth. These are lodged in the unconscious mind. Lévi-Strauss saw the myths of the Polynesian, Australian, and African tribal cultures he investigated in person, along with those of the ancient West, as sharing common structures, though they varied in details. Myth is like a structural language that gets replayed over and over again in different cultures: the hero fighting a great monster, the intrepid voyage to strange lands, myths about incest taboos, tempting female demon-goddesses, and so on. The specific examples of these myths Lévi-Strauss sees as the *parole* of the myth system, while its recurrent structures are its *langue*. So the structure of myth is both unconscious and an organized system, a language. Its purpose is to express our unconscious hopes and fears, to resolve psychic contradictions that cannot be resolved on the conscious level (think of how the myth of King Oedipus expresses the cultural fear of incest, and of how the Christian picture of heaven expresses the hope for a beautiful afterlife).

One way that these mythological principles are structured is in terms of pairs of binary oppositions like the raw and the cooked, humans and gods, good and evil, man and woman, life and death, nature and culture. These binary pairs structure mythological thinking. For example, in Greek mythology Zeus appears from time to time as an ordinary human or animal to have sex with a young maiden he's taken a fancy to. This myth explores the binary opposition between 'human beings' and 'gods' and how it's important not to forget this distinction. The notion of binary oppositions reappears in other structuralist and post-structuralist thinkers: indeed, one could say that the debate between these two camps is to a large degree over whether or not such oppositions are natural to the human mind (the structuralists) or constructed by culture (the post-structuralists). They were important to Lévi-Strauss because they helped to give shape to individual myths. In *The Elementary Structure of Kinship*, Lévi-Strauss discusses how cultures implement the incest taboo by setting up a variety of binary oppositions in their myths between two groups of people: 'those I can mate with' and 'those I cannot mate with'. Marriage is possible with the former but not with the latter. Even more fundamentally, the nature/culture pair helps to define, through myth, who or what is inside a given culture and who is outside it, e.g., normal human beings versus demons, witches, or the insane.

In totemism Lévi-Strauss saw evidence of these binary oppositions. In totemism, each social group was represented by a given animal or natural phenomenon—by a lion, a bear, an eagle, a sun god, a river spirit. Societies manifest the distinction between nature and culture by using these totems, not to mention differentiating themselves from each other. The totem acts as a symbol for the group that has chosen it. A modern version of totemism is how sports teams use the names of animals, e.g., the Boston Bruins and Miami Dolphins, and how families and universities use images of animals on their crests, e.g., a stag and a lynx on a Canadian university crest. So we're still totemists. The abstract structure of this totemism is a property of the logical structure of the mind, though the actual totems chosen—the stag and lynx in one case—are obviously a reference to our Canadian environment.

This idea of myths having abstract structures based on binary oppositions is of obvious usefulness in the study of popular culture. We love stories with heroes and villains representing good and evil, thrillers that play with the boundaries between life and death, and comedies based on differences between the sexes, national groups, or classes. Popular culture is littered with myths that primitive human beings would have understood all too well. Also, we can see things like fashionable clothes, cars, jewellery, magazines, and so on as modern totems. They connect us to more universal principles such as good taste, the upper class, rebellion, or being a member of a certain generation or subcultural tribe.

JOSEPH CAMPBELL AND THE HERO WITH A THOUSAND FACES

The American theorist of myths, Joseph Campbell (1904–87), argues in *The Hero with a Thousand Faces* that behind all religion and myth is a common, unconscious structure. Myth is:

> the secret opening through which the inexhaustible energies of the cosmos pour into human cultural manifestation. Religions, philosophies, arts, the social forms of primitive and historical man, prime discoveries in science

and technology, the very dreams that blister sleep, boil up from the basic, magic ring of myth. (Campbell, 1968 [1949]: 3)

Just as dreams play out in fantastic landscapes the unconscious problems of the dreamer, myths play out on a much vaster field the collective problems of humanity (ibid., 19).

Campbell convincingly argues that all the great mythical sagas are basically one story, the monomyth. This monomyth is the hero's journey, which has a rough-and-ready common structure of stages in myths taken from a wide variety of cultures. It is the quest saga, the same story told in Jason and the Golden Fleece and Odysseus's journey, in the legends of King Arthur and the Round Table, in the ancient Sumerian epic of Gilgamesh, in the Irish legends of Finn McCool, even in the story of the Buddha (not to mention hundreds of tribal myths from all over the world). Campbell got this idea of an unconscious myth from Carl Jung's notion of cultural archetypes and of the collective unconscious, which he felt provided the foundation of mythological thinking in a great diversity of cultures. He mixed in a hefty dose of both Freudian and Jungian psychoanalysis in his work, seeing the hero's journey as a simultaneous journey of the ego to achieve oneness with the world, to overcome its fears of both id and super-ego and of the seductive Mother and the ogre-like Father.[2] Campbell doesn't talk much about being influenced by French structuralist theory, though the monomyth is a clear attempt to find an underlying structure beneath the many surface manifestations of the story of the great quest found throughout the world.

The journey has three major parts to it—Departure, Initiation, and Return, each with a number of subsections. In its shortest form, the hero ventures out from his common world into a supernatural one, encounters and defeats strange and magical forces arrayed against him, and returns to his ordinary world with a marvellous boon for his comrades at home (ibid., 30). The hero cycle also contains a number of familiar repeated characters—the hero, a mentor, a villain (which Campbell sometimes calls the 'dragon'), a

goddess (sometimes also a mother figure), magic potions or forces, helpers, sometimes a rogue, and jesters or tricksters. They also feature the struggle of good versus evil, light versus darkness. Campbell's model of the hero's journey can be applied to the original *Star Wars* movie, and to an extent to the entire original trilogy. Indeed, *Star Wars* creator George Lucas was an admirer of Joseph Campbell and consciously patterned the *Star Wars* saga on the hero's journey. This use of a universal archetype of myth explains why *Star Wars* was so popular, since it appealed to our unconscious patterns of thought. Table 7.1 applies the archetypal characters and stages in the hero's journey to three films that fit Campbell's model rather well: *Star Wars*, *The Matrix*, and *Oh Brother, Where Art Thou?*[3] It no doubt fits many others, including *The Lord of the Rings*. Campbell would argue that these films are successful in part because they draw on mythic archetypes of the monomyth lodged deep in our unconscious minds. As it turns out, structuralism is big box office. Given the power of mass media over our lives, this is a fact that social theory cannot afford to ignore.

So the monomyth lives on in contemporary cinema. George Lucas, the director and writer of *Star Wars* (1977) and co-writer of the second and third instalments in the saga, *The Empire Strikes Back* (1980) and *Return of the Jedi* (1983), has on several occasions admitted to being influenced by Campbell's work; before his death, Campbell returned the favour in interviews by commenting on how Lucas's films embody the monomyth.

I Departure

1. *The Call to Adventure* The call to adventure is the point in the future hero's life when he is told that things are about to change radically. He is called to leave his home by some herald or message.[4] Sometimes it's mere chance or a blunder that starts his journey. The call leads him to a dark forest, an underground kingdom, a secret island, or some other hidden place where the adventure takes place (ibid., 58). In *Star Wars*, the call comes when the young hero of the movie, Luke Sky-

Table 7.1 The Hero's Journey

Character	Star Wars (1977)	The Matrix (1999)	Oh Brother, Where Art Thou? (2000)
Hero	Luke Skywalker	Neo	Ulysses Everett McGill
Mentor (Magician)	Obi-Wan (later Yoda)	Morpheus	Blind Railwayman
Goddess	Princess Leia	Trinity	Penelope McGill
Villain (the Dragon)	Darth Vader	Agent Smith	Sheriff Cooley
Rogue	Han Solo	Tank or Cypher	Pete Hogwaller
Jesters and Tricksters	Chewbacca, droids	Mouse	Delmar O'Donnell
Magical Power	The Force (dark and light)	Control of the Matrix	Music

Stages in the Hero's Journey

1. Call to Adventure	Luke watches holo-recording from Princess Leia asking for help	Trinity hacks into Neo's computer with warning: 'Wake up Neo'	Everett, Pete, and Delmar escape from the chain gang
2. Refusal of Call	Luke feels he has to help with the harvest	Neo reluctant to go with his friends to the club	
3. Supernatural Aid	Obi-Wan rescues Luke from the sand people, gives him a light sabre	Morpheus's magic phone call, later tells Neo that his world is an illusion	Blind railwayman offers them a prophecy (= Tiresias in Homer)
4. Crossing of the First Threshold	Luke's aunt and uncle killed, Luke leaves Tatooine via Mos Eisley spaceport	Neo takes the red pill, leaves the Matrix	Trio visits cousin Washington's farm
5. The Belly of the Whale	Trio trapped in garbage compactor	Neo captured by agents or Neo ejected into underground wet cavern	Trio trapped in burning barn by Sheriff
6. Road of Trials	Light-sabre practice, rescue of Leia	Neo undergoes training, meets Oracle, battles three agents	Encounters with Big Dan (= Cyclops in Homer) and Baby Face Nelson
7. Meeting with the Goddess	Luke meets Princess Leia	Neo meets Trinity in dance club	The meeting with Penny (Penelope), Everett's wife, later in the film
8. Woman as Temptress	Not literal: Luke is tempted by the dark side in *Empire Strikes Back*	[Cypher tempted by the promise of oblivious pleasure in the Matrix]	The sirens tempt our heroes, turn Pete into a frog? (= Circe in Homer)
9. Atonement with the Father	'Luke, I am your father' in *Empire Strikes Back*	Neo returns to the Matrix to save Morpheus from the agents	
10. Apotheosis	Luke becomes a Jedi in *Return of the Jedi*	Neo killed by agents, resurrected by Trinity's love, now invincible	Trio records song 'Man of Constant Sorrow' as Soggy Bottom Boys
11. The Ultimate Boon	The Death Star is destroyed (out of order)	Vaguely, the destruction of the Matrix (not resolved in first film)	Supposedly bank heist money, but really Penny and 7 Wharvey gals
12. The Refusal of the Return	Luke wants to stay to avenge Obi-Wan during shoot-out in docking bay	Neo stays in the virtual subway station to battle Agent Smith	
13. The Magic Flight	The *Millennium Falcon* escapes from Death Star, pursued by fighters	Vaguely, Neo's running battle with the agents in last third of film	The rescue of Tommy from the Klan, escape from angry Klansmen
14. Rescue from Without	The *Millennium Falcon* shows up during the battle, saves Luke	Perhaps Neo's being resurrected by Trinity's kiss	Governor Menelaus 'Pappy' O'Daniel pardons trio after song
15. Crossing the Final Threshold	The *Millennium Falcon* fights a running battle with TIE fighters	Neo 'kills' the three agents after his apotheosis	Caught by Sheriff, about to be hung, saved by the Great Flood (cow on roof)
16. Master of Both Worlds	Luke destroys the Death Star; the force is with him	Trinity's love has saved the physical Neo, and he has become the 'One'	'Ulysses' freed from prison and gets his family back
17. Freedom to Live	Victory ceremony at end of *Star Wars* (or the defeat of the empire in *Return*)	Neo back in Matrix at end, his phone call prophesies revolution	'Ulysses' is free to live a normal life

walker, discovers Princess Leia's holographic call for help in the memory banks of a discarded droid (R2-D2). Luke lives on Tatooine, a desert planet where he, his aunt, and uncle eke out a meagre living. He's bored and looks forward to leaving.

2. *Refusal of the Call.* Sometimes after the call to adventure is given, the hero is reluctant or refuses to heed it. This may be from a sense of duty or some obligation, a fear of the new world that looms before him, or some other reason that holds him in place. In *Star Wars*, Luke tells Obi-Wan that he can't leave his aunt and uncle, who need help with the harvest. But once Imperial storm troopers murder them, he is suddenly free to leave.

3. *Supernatural Aid.* Once the hero has decided to go on the quest, a mentor or guide with special powers appears to aid him. The helper gives the hero magical aids, amulets, talismans, or weapons. The helper is usually a wise old man, like Merlin in the Arthur sagas, Gandalf in *The Lord of the Rings*, or Obi-Wan in *Star Wars*. In the latter, Obi-Wan Kenobi, a former Jedi (a knight with supernatural powers based on the Force), rescues Luke from the sand people raiders and gives him his father's light-sabre (the equivalent of Excalibur in the King Arthur legends). He also starts to teach Luke about the Force, the 'magical' power of the *Star Wars* universe. After Obi-Wan's death, Yoda becomes Luke's new mentor, training him to become a Jedi on the swamp planet of Dagobah.

4. *The Crossing of the First Threshold.* The hero now ventures forth into the unknown, leaving his old world behind. Beyond the threshold are darkness and danger—Columbus's men believed there to be mermaids and sea monsters in the Atlantic Ocean beyond the limits of European navigational knowledge. 'Beyond here there be dragons!' as the ancient mariners used to say. The hero has to cross some sort of barrier, having to defeat a threshold guardian to do so. In *Star Wars*, Luke leaves his home and travels to the Mos Eisley spaceport, where he visits a cantina full of odd-looking aliens. Campbell sees this as the traditional seaport scene where our hero is about to cross over into a new world. The bar patrons are threshold guardians who threaten our young hero with their strange customs and sudden outbursts of violence. Yet at the same time Luke meets the mercenary trader Han Solo and his sidekick Chewbacca: they seem untrustworthy at first, but turn out later to be solid allies. Luke has given up on his old life at this point and crossed over from being a farm boy to the hero with a thousand faces.

5. *The Belly of the Whale.* Early in his adventure the hero is often trapped in the belly of the whale—in a sea monster like Jonah, in a cave, underwater, or in some other enclosed space. The hero appears to die, but is resurrected, perhaps in a new form. The hero's old self has died, a new one born. Although the belly is dark and scary, it represents the final split between the known and unknown worlds and thus the start of enlightenment. Here the hero shows his willingness to undergo a metamorphosis and get on with his adventure. Campbell (1988) suggests that in *Star Wars* the scene where Luke, Princess Leia, and Han are trapped in the trash compactor represents the belly of the whale—especially when Luke is pulled underwater by the slimy beast and appears dead, though he reappears a minute or two later. He sees the water in the scene as representing the unconscious. Yet it could also be argued that the scene where Han's ship the *Millennium Falcon* is pulled inside the Death Star by a tractor beam also represents the belly of the whale.

II Initiation

6. *The Road of Trials.* The road of trials is a series of tests and tasks that the hero must complete to achieve his goal. This road of trials usually takes place in a tricky setting—there could be a labyrinth, an enchanted forest, or dangerous waters along the way. There is usually some sort of dragon or dragon-substitute to slay. The hero may fail one of these tests, yet doesn't give up, for he's aided by a magic amulet, secret agents of a greater power, and a rogue or trickster. This stage is often the core of the quest saga. In *Star Wars*, Luke's tests include light-sabre practice, rescuing the princess from her cell, and escaping from the Death Star. The labyrinth is the Death Star itself.

Luke Skywalker (Mark Hamill), Princess Leia (Carrie Fisher), and Han Solo (Harrison Ford) in *Star Wars*. (*Star Wars: Episode IV—A New Hope* © 1977 and 1997 Lucasfilm Ltd. & ™. All rights reserved. Used under authorization. Unauthorized duplication is a violation of applicable law.)

One sees the enchanted forest in The Return of the Jedi, inhabited by the cuddly Ewoks, the hero's hidden helpers, while another labyrinth appears in the form of the Cloud City ruled by Lando Calrissian in The Empire Strikes Back.

7. *The Meeting with the Goddess*. The hero meets a woman who represents an all-encompassing love. Campbell sees the goddess figure as mixed up with the earth Mother. This stage represents a mystical marriage with the 'Queen Goddess of the World' who is simultaneously mother, sister, mistress, and bride (ibid., 109–11). In the *Odyssey*, this occurs when Odysseus tarries for seven years with the beautiful nymph-goddess Calypso. In *Star Wars*, this stage is loosely symbolized by Luke's meeting and infatuation with Princess Leia, who later turns out to be his sister.

8. *Woman as the Temptress*. Here the hero is tempted to fall off his chosen path by either a seductive woman or, more metaphorically, by the temptations of a material life he chose to abandon as part of his quest. At this stage the hero feels the temptations of the flesh, temptations he can't give into if he is to win the boon. Campbell talks of how the hero, a pure soul, becomes tainted with the odour of the flesh and feels revulsion for the goddess (ibid., 121–2). This is when Oedipus realizes he has slept with his mother, and when Hamlet becomes disgusted with his mother's marrying his uncle. In the *Star Wars* trilogy, it's not a literal woman, but Darth Vader's attempt to seduce Luke with the Dark Side of the Force to make him a servant of the Empire.

9. *Atonement with the Father*. Here the hero must confront his father, or a father figure, who represents great power and the balance between life and death. This is the centre of the journey, when the hero undergoes a transformation of some sort, perhaps resulting from his apparent death and transfiguration. Campbell says that this stage is where the hero abandons the 'double monster' of a dragon thought to be God (in Freudian terms, the superego) and the dragon seen as sin (the repressed id), coming to see the father as merciful (ibid., 130). This stage is represented by Darth Vader's revelation in *The Empire Strikes Back* that he is Luke's father and his attempt to win Luke over to his side. It's also represented by the ultimate reconciliation of Vader to the light side of the Force at the end of the trilogy as he dies in Luke's arms.

10. *Apotheosis*. Here the hero gains some godlike or spiritual power or becomes enlightened. Like the Bodhisattva, our hero throws away the terrors born of ignorance and sees the world as illuminated and free from pain. Campbell hints that in some cases the hero takes on an androgynous quality at this point, like the Hindu god Shiva. In the *Star Wars* saga, this is obviously when Luke becomes a full Jedi and is able to defeat enemies like Jabba the Hutt with his magical powers. The Force is Luke's divine power. Note that after Leia is revealed to be his sister, Luke no longer shows any interest in women: he has become Campbell's bisexual god (or more strictly speaking in this case, an asexual god).

11. *The Ultimate Boon*. The goal of the hero's quest could be the milk of paradise, the elixir of life, a holy object, a magical talisman, or simply a great feat. In the Arthur legends, it was the Holy Grail; for Jason of Argos, it was the Golden Fleece; for Gilgamesh, immortality; for the Buddha, enlightenment. Although the hero may win the prize with ease, he may also, like Prometheus, have to trick the gods of their treasure and beat a hasty retreat afterwards. In *Star Wars*, the first great boon is the destruction of the Death Star. In

the bigger picture of the original trilogy, the death of the Emperor is the ultimate boon.

III Return

12. *Refusal of the Return*. Once the prize has been won, the hero must return it to the kingdom of humanity from the magical realm. Yet the hero is often reluctant to return to ordinary reality after having lain with the goddess and drunk her sweet nectar. Thus, he stays awhile in the blessed isles. This stage is vague in *Star Wars*. It could be during the shootout in the docking bay when Obi-Wan is apparently killed by Darth Vader in a light-sabre battle and Luke wants to go back to avenge his death, but Han yells, 'Luke, come on!'

13. *The Magic Flight*. Where the boon has been stolen from the gods, or they have been tricked to give it up, the hero must flee from the scene with the villain and his or her minions in hot pursuit. The road home is a dangerous one in such cases, the adventure by no means over. The hero uses magical evasions or throws behind him delaying obstacles. The magic flight in *Star Wars* is the escape of the *Millennium Falcon* from the Death Star and its fighting off of pursuing Imperial fighters.

14. *Rescue from Without*. Just as the hero uses helpers and guides during his adventure, he may need some help on the return journey to get the boon back to humanity. This is especially so if the hero has fallen under the spell of the magical realm and needs society to come knocking at his door to remind him of his ordinary duties. Yet that society might feel resentment at the prize of life-redeeming elixir and be at a loss to comprehend its value (ibid., 216). In *Star Wars*, this stage is the *Millennium Falcon*'s sudden appearance during the battle over the Death Star, which saves Luke's fighter from destruction (though there are several cases of characters being rescued by others throughout the trilogy).

15. *The Crossing of the Return Threshold*. The hero must cross over from the land of darkness to the land of light and bring his newly won wisdom to the people living there. How can he pass his soul-satisfying experience on to those consumed by banalities and low passions? Why even come back to such a world? (ibid., 218). Yet return he must to complete the journey. In *Star Wars* the parallel could be the destruction of the pursuing Imperial fighters by the *Millennium Falcon*, though this happens before the rescue scene mentioned above.

16. *Master of the Two Worlds*. For the Buddha, this was the moment of enlightenment: he became a master of both the material and spiritual worlds. In general, when the hero loses attachment to limitations, ambitions, hopes, and fears, winning victories on both physical and spiritual planes, he has achieved this mastery. He is now the cosmic dancer, able to move from the sunlit to dark worlds and come back again as he sees fit. In *Star Wars*, it's when Luke uses the Force to destroy the Death Star. Later in the trilogy, it's when Luke balances the light and dark sides of the Force.

17. *Freedom to Live*. Finally, the hero is victorious and has overcome his fear of death. He lives in the now, and sees a connection of individual minds with the universal will. We see this stage in the final scene in *Star Wars*, the victory ceremony in a great hall in the rebel base. It comes again in *The Return of the Jedi* with the death of the Emperor and the victory of the rebellion.

In the monomyth we see a powerful recurring mythical structure that appears not only in a multitude of ancient tales, but also in some of the better examples of modern popular culture. Yet this and other structuralisms are open to a few fairly biting criticisms (Strinati, 1995: 123–7). First, the structuralist idea of myth is too abstract and lacking in empirical evidence. Yes, there are similarities between the myths of different cultures, but that doesn't mean that there are identical underlying logical structures in all these cases. Indeed, this essentially psychoanalytic view of myth fails to account for the proven role of oral transmission and diffusion of specific types of myth from one culture to another. Still, one must admit that Lévi-Strauss and Campbell have made a good case for recurring structures in widely divergent myths.

Next, structuralism is too synchronic and ignores how myth and culture depend on their historical and social contexts. Third, structuralism tends also to be too deterministic, making us robots controlled by linguistic or mental structures. It ignores the role played by human agency in the production of culture. Finally, perhaps the binary oppositions the structuralists emphasize are overstated. Is there really such a sharp difference between nature and culture, as they think? Between male and female? Or between any of the other binary pairs they mention? This last point is one of Derrida's major critiques of structuralism.

SEMIOTICS AND POPULAR CULTURE

Barthes on Cultural Myths

As we have seen, semiotics is the idea that language and culture are systems of signs or codes. Roland Barthes (1915–80) pioneered the application of semiotics to popular culture, seeing films, novels, clothes, music, and images in magazines as such systems. Semiotics has the advantage over structuralism of being able to deal with signs as historically and culturally located—it doesn't believe in abstract structures that apply to all cultures at all times, except the general structure of the science of signs itself. Barthes's *Mythologies* (1957) contains 54 short newspaper articles analyzing various aspects of French consumerism and popular culture in the 1950s, including wrestling, toys, cars, striptease, soap detergents, and jet pilots. The most important part of the book for our purposes is the extended theoretical essay 'Myth Today', which concludes the book.

Barthes wanted to expose how the ruling bourgeoisie tried to make its values into universal ones, to turn history into nature, thus mystifying their power. This is what Barthes calls 'myths' do: they transform history into nature, make people see current social relationships and power structures as part of the natural order of things. According to Barthes, this is accomplished through mass media and popular culture, the world of everyday life. He says that he 'resented seeing Nature and History confused at every turn' and wanted to track down '*what-goes-without-saying*, the ideological abuse' he found hidden in myths (Barthes, 1957: 11). Thus, what Barthes calls myth is close to what the Marxists call 'ideology'. Although Barthes denies in *Mythologies* that his criticism is ideological, the similarities between his semiotics and the Marxist critique of ideology are clear enough. He argues that reality is always constructed by cultural codes of meaning. These codes are always related to the material interests of their creators. There's no such thing as an objective, unbiased, uncoded experience of the cultural world (Strinati, 1995: 110). No one is innocent of these ideological constructions.

Myths in popular culture express a message through a variety of signs. We can see texts, photos, films, magazines, news reports, sporting events, and pop songs as a series of semiotic systems each containing their own myths. Barthes sees myth as a second-order semiotic system. The first-order system is Saussure's triad of signifier (marks or sounds), signified (concept), and sign (meaningful word). So the sound 'rose' added to the concept of a rose produces the linguistic sign 'rose' to designate a flower traditionally given to women by men to symbolize love or passion (or to smooth over marital spats). Barthes argues that cultural myths start from the first-order sign (its 'form'), in this case a rose, using it as a signifier in a new semiotic triad, linking it with a cultural concept—a signified—'passion' or 'love'. The combination of form and concept, the signifier (a rose) and the signified (romanticism), produces a cultural sign or myth: the notion that love is like a rose, or that the gift of a rose represents the passion of the giver for its recipient. This two-stage process is outlined in Figure 7.3.

In this sense, what Barthes calls 'myth' is like a meta-language that uses other languages to express meaning. Yet Barthes had a more explicitly political purpose in his semiology: exposing

Figure 7.3 Barthes's Semiology of Culture

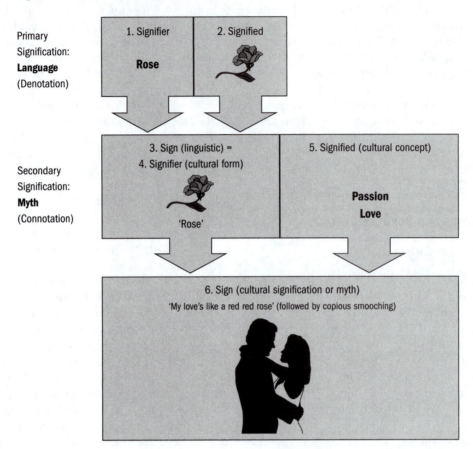

Primary
Signification:
Language
(Denotation)

Secondary
Signification:
Myth
(Connotation)

1. Signifier

Rose

2. Signified

3. Sign (linguistic) =
4. Signifier (cultural form)

'Rose'

5. Signified (cultural concept)

Passion

Love

6. Sign (cultural signification or myth)

'My love's like a red red rose' (followed by copious smooching)

the cultural myths of bourgeois society. He argues that just as myths are a language, they are also depoliticized speech, speech where the politics is hidden. His most famous example comes when he picks up a copy of *Paris Match* magazine in a barbershop and sees a picture of a black colonial soldier on its cover.

The signifier or form of the myth is the picture of the black soldier reverently saluting what we take to be the French flag; the signified or concept, military glory or Frenchness. The sign as a whole means that France's empire transcends race and has the enthusiastic support of its subjects, despite the recent defeat in Vietnam and coming defeat in the Algerian war of independence, in full swing at the time Barthes's book was written. The cover photo is thus a myth that tries to naturalize a historically transient situation: France's colonial empire, which is now little more than handful of sandy islands scattered around the world.

Barthes argues that the power of a myth like that of the *Paris Match* cover lies in the fact that its reader sees the ideologically motivated connection between the image and French imperialism as an inductive or causal one (Barthes, 1957: 131). In fact, it's a *semiotic* system, yet the naive reader takes it to be a *factual* one. Myth performs a conjuring trick, depoliticizing speech, purifying it of contradictions so that people can wallow in a world where everything is self-evident

On the cover, a young Negro in a French uniform is saluting, with his eyes uplifted, probably fixed on a fold of the tricolour. All this is the *meaning* of the picture. But, whether naively or not, I see very well what it signifies to me: that France is a great Empire, that all her sons, without any colour discrimination, faithfully serve under her flag, and that there is no better answer to the detractors of an alleged colonialism than the zeal shown by this Negro in serving his so-called oppressors. I am therefore again faced with a greater semiological system: there is a signifier, itself already formed with a previous system (*a black soldier is giving the French salute*); there is a signified (it is here a purposeful mixture of Frenchness and militariness); finally, there is a presence of the signified through the signifier. (Barthes, 1957: 116) (*Paris Match*)

and natural (ibid., 143). People really believe in the naturalness of the politically motivated links between the form and concept of cultural signs like the one above. In other words, Barthes's semiotics assumes that many of us (to borrow a phrase from Stuart Hall) are cultural dopes and take at face value the ideologically loaded messages we get from mass culture.

A more contemporary example, from the world of advertising, is a magazine ad for Kool cigarettes that centres on an attractive woman sitting in a car while a man pumps some gas in the background. We see a large male hand in the foreground holding a package of Kool cigarettes. The hand, cigarettes, car, and woman are the main signifiers of the ad. The ad is intended to sell the cigarettes by the creation of a myth that connects these elements in a chain of signification with three main concepts: coolness, success, and sexiness. The meaning of the ad is that it's 'cool' to smoke Kool, that people who smoke Kool drive nice cars and are carefree (it's a convertible after all), and most importantly, Kool smokers get beau-

tiful women. Such an ad is probably aimed at a man who is concerned with his self-image and who takes economic and sexual success seriously. Such semiological systems are everywhere in advertising—in magazines and newspapers, on billboards, television, and the Internet. Indeed, ads are the best examples today of cultural signs with clear semiotic structures.

Yet there are a few problems with semiotic interpretations of culture. First, how do we know that the meaning we assign to a myth is really valid and not just the product of our subjective imagination or political biases? Semioticians of pop culture are notoriously ideological in their attributions of meaning, often imposing an ideology onto the artifact being studied. For example, radical feminist theorists tend to read almost all of popular culture as a series of attempts to impose patriarchy on the unwary masses.

Another problem is that the meaning of a cultural sign is fairly obvious to most observers because we see it as existing in a certain context, which practitioners of semiotics tend to ignore.

Barthes divorces the meaning of a sign from the social context where it occurs, ignoring the intention of the sender and the reaction of the receiver of the sign. It may not be all that difficult to decode cultural signs. A gift of roses usually means 'romance'. Yet the meaning of a sign depends on the social relationships of the two people exchanging it—the roses *could* mean 'romance', but they could also be a joke or insult or even be seen by their receiver as a case of sexual harassment (say if Joe sends Josephine a bunch every day for a month after she's warned him to leave her alone) (Strinati, 1995: 126). In other words, we're back to intentionality and subjective meaning, not culture-spanning semiotic structures.

Lastly, the meaning of a cultural sign doesn't remain hidden until the semiotician comes along and decodes it—the audience interprets it in various ways, often quite critically. In the case of the Kool ad discussed above, while some people might actually buy into the equation of smoking = success + sex, many others reject it as a puerile fantasy. People aren't robots, and are known to occasionally think for themselves. Certainly, most students in a class of undergraduates will figure out that the ad creators are trying to set up a dubious mythical connection between smoking, sex, and being 'cool'. To paraphrase Horatio in *Hamlet*, there must needs come no semiological ghost from the grave to tell us this!

The Birmingham School and the Semiotics of Style

We now turn to a school of thought that is a heady hybrid of Gramsci's Marxism and Barthes's semiotics, the neo-Marxist subcultural theory of the University of Birmingham's Centre for Contemporary Cultural Studies (CCCS). Its members published their ideas from the early 1970s on in a series of working papers and longer studies, notably their seminal collection *Resistance through Rituals* (1976). The main theorists associated with the Birmingham School in its glory days were Phil Cohen, Stuart Hall, Dick Hebdige, John Clarke,

Tony Jefferson, and Angela McRobbie. Their theory of subcultural deviance was specifically applied to the British experience in the four decades after World War II, though it can be adapted to other contexts. The Birmingham School members were neo-Marxists with a semiotic twist. Marx thought that the ruling ideas of each epoch were the main ideas of the ruling class. They picked up on this notion, defining culture as forms of material and social organization for a given class that provide it with 'maps of meaning' that help to structure its social life (Clarke et al., 1976: 10). Subcultures are smaller, more local, and more differentiated structures within a larger cultural network (ibid., 13). The CCCS saw postwar British subcultures as attempts by working-class youth to resist the power of the bourgeoisie through arcane ensembles of rituals, dress, language, and music.

The CCCS was reacting against the transactionalist or labelling theory approach to deviance, which was grounded in symbolic interactionism. The transactionalist sees deviance as the outcome of a process of social interaction wherein a group of people is labelled 'deviant' by those with the power to make rules. This theoretical school focuses on the *process* of becoming a deviant, not on some set of inherent characteristics shared by deviants, such as coming from broken homes or underprivileged backgrounds. Howard Becker's *Outsiders* (1963) stands as a landmark in this tradition. Becker's central thesis is that certain social groups he calls 'rule creators' create deviance by making rules whose breaking constitutes deviance, after which the breakers are labelled 'deviant'. Thus, deviance is the outcome of a transaction between rule creators and rule breakers. A deviant is someone to whom the label 'deviant' has been successfully applied. Later, rule enforcers, such as the police and the court system, are brought in to institutionalize these newly created rules. These enforcers are not concerned with the *content* of the rules they enforce; they are just 'doing their job'. This labelling of the rule breaker as an 'outsider' does not come out of nowhere; it is the result of moral enterprise. The rule creators are moral entrepreneurs: they try to start moral crusades against social groups or practices they feel are active threats to the social order. These crusades add to their power. Examples of such crusades include the temperance movement that led to Prohibition in the 1920s, the House Un-American Activities Committee and McCarthy hearings in the US of the late 1940s and early 1950s, President Ronald Reagan's war on drugs in the 1980s, and the Bush administration's war on terror from 2001 on. In each case a group of people were successfully labelled as 'outsiders', at least for a while: drinkers, Communists and 'fellow travellers', drug takers, and Islamic fundamentalists.

The Centre for Contemporary Cultural Studies criticized labelling theory for failing to show the structural and historical underpinnings of deviance and how subcultures can be read as semiotic systems. The Birmingham theorists found the focus on public labelling as the chief origin of deviance naive. They believed the class struggle was alive and well in Britain in the 1960s and 1970s, but that it was being played out largely in the realm of culture. They centred their picture of the meaning of deviance on Gramsci's notion of hegemony: in capitalist societies class struggle takes place not only at the economic and political levels, but also at the ideological level, within the realm of culture. The ideological struggle between classes is a struggle over cultural power (ibid., 12). The ruling class seeks to dominate other classes not only through direct economic and political power, but by seducing the oppressed classes into accepting the cultural values of the ruling class through its domination of such cultural industries as radio, film, television, the arts, and the press. Their hegemony makes their social and economic power seem natural, yet this hegemonic power is not automatic or permanent—the consent of the lower classes has to be continually won. The working class is never totally absorbed culturally by the bourgeoisie. Hegemony is part subjugation, part negotiation. Subcultural groups are a reaction to such ideological struggles within a given

oppressed class, winning space for the group in question. They are working-class responses to bourgeois hegemony.

The Birmingham School refused to see the music, styles, and leisure activities of British youth culture as classless—they had deep social and economic roots. The CCCS took up the problem of the origins of deviance by questioning the basic assumption of labelling theory, metaphorically asking the labelling theorists, 'why do moral entrepreneurs label only *certain* subcultural groups as deviant?' Their answer was that British subcultures like the Teddy boys of the 1950s, the mods, rockers, and skinheads of the 1960s, and the punks of the 1970s were oblique expressions by working-class youth of class resistance to the social and cultural hegemony of the bourgeois ruling class. British moral entrepreneurs were thus defending bourgeois values—the family, religion, and most importantly capitalism—in condemning these folk devils to a cultural hell. Only rarely did the transactionalists look at the relation between the poor and the powerful in *structural* rather than interactional terms. The Birmingham School's search for structural explanations of deviance and skepticism with regard to middle-class values made them critical of both traditional (largely American) subcultural theory *and* interactionist approaches because of their attempts to frame their analyses in terms of an assumption of the need for some sort of bourgeois social consensus. The fact that these earlier schools of thought largely *wanted* to preserve this consensus distorted their understanding of deviance.

The Birmingham School saw subcultural resistance as taking place within the realms of popular culture, consumption, and leisure. Working-class youth resisted bourgeois values through subcultural rituals, dress, slang, and music, offering magical solutions to real class contradictions. These magical solutions centred on subcultural styles, such as the mods' smart jackets and Vespa motor scooters and the punks' green mohawks and ripped T-shirts held together by safety pins. They won cultural space for these youth groups.

They are 'coded' expressions of a working-class consciousness held in check by the ideology of increasing affluence in post-war Britain, where some argued that everyone was becoming middle class. Small rebellions of this sort were part of a post-war generational consciousness that saw limited upward mobility for working-class kids set against a background of rapid and widespread social changes in Britain.

To decode these stylistic ensembles, the theorists of the CCCS turned to the semiotics of Roland Barthes. As we've seen, Barthes thought that modern cultures are held together by mythologies embodied in a variety of cultural signs. So the CCCS saw subcultural groups like the skinheads and punks as forming alternative mythologies, alternative semiotic systems that rejected bourgeois hegemony. The way they dressed, talked, and acted, along with their music of choice, formed an ensemble that could be decoded as a rejection of mainstream bourgeois cultural signs. The CCCS borrowed from Lévi-Strauss and Barthes the idea of *bricolage* (Clarke, 1976a: 177). A *bricoleur* is a handyman, someone who uses whatever is at hand to fix something that doesn't work. He is an improviser, like the eponymous hero of the TV series *MacGyver* (1985–92). *Bricolage* in this context is the notion that deviant groups mix and match elements of their ensembles with commodities taken from other contexts and give new meanings, such as the punks' use of the swastika or Union Jack on their 'uniforms' (they were neither Nazis nor old-fashioned patriots, though they did mock such beliefs, as in the Sex Pistols' 'God Save the Queen'). These cultural signs were given new meanings in a sort of 'semiotic guerrilla warfare'. The result of subcultural *bricolage* is a stylistic ensemble that is homologous—it hangs together in a coherent way (including clothes, hairstyles, music, and leisure activities) and expresses their social plight, giving it some new meaning. This involved distinct forms of dress, music, and ritual, along with an argot (a special way of talking).[5] It also involved subverting and transforming the raw materials provided by mainstream culture to express some opposition to the social status quo, as when the skinheads appropriated Doc Martens boots and suspenders to express their aggressive proletarian outlook, or when the punks turned pop music against its flower-power, California-dreaming world view in the late 1970s and 1980s. As Barthes showed, cultural artifacts have no natural meaning, but only become meaningful within a cultural code. The swastika was a holy symbol to Tibetan Buddhism; to the Nazis it was a sign pointing to the domination of the master race over Europe; to the punks it was a slap in the face to middle-class British society in the 1970s. It has no meaning in and of itself.

The CCCS theorists produced studies on a number of specific subcultures. The mods of the mid-1960s were largely clerks and petty functionaries who worked in offices in London and other large cities. They expressed their alienation from their jobs by dressing in smart Italian suits, riding Vespa scooters, taking speed, and listening to mod rock bands like the Who and the Kinks in their spare time. The imagined glamour of their leisure world was at odds with their humdrum work life. On the other hand, the skinheads of the late 1960s were a magical attempt to reclaim a vanishing working-class community based on the exaggerated adherence to the values of territoriality, collective solidarity, and masculinity (Clarke, 1976b: 102). These values were expressed in their black boots and short hair, their loutish behaviour at football matches, and their violence towards immigrants and anyone they saw as 'queer'. Yet the CCCS researchers argued that the hippie counterculture of the 1960s and early 1970s, although its pro-drug stance and sexual permissiveness challenged traditional bourgeois values, was really a sort of middle-class adaptation to the shift in capitalism from an economy of production to one of consumption. The hippies' search for immediate gratification, narcissism, and 'doing your own thing' individualism fitted the needs of consumer society rather well (Clarke et al., 1976: 64–7). One could argue that a buttoned-down version of the hippie philosophy has become the new hegemony a generation after they flourished as social dropouts in Haight-Ashbury, Carnaby Street, and Yorkville.

However, the 'magical' solutions to class contradictions created by these subcultures do not address the real material causes of their class subordination. They were not mounted on the real terrain of economic and political struggles, and thus failed to pose a challenge to the hegemony of their parent culture (Clarke, 1976a: 189). Their importance lies in their winning of space for working-class youth through the distinctive leisure styles that embodied their way of life, even if this winning of space, for most of the participants in these subcultures, lasted for only a few years. Unfortunately, subcultural styles usually wind up as little more than novel consumption styles once the capitalist marketplace gets a hold of them and redefines them as the fleeting fad of a generation instead of part of the class struggle.

Hebdige on Subcultures

Dick Hebdige reflected the general orientation of the CCCS on subcultures in his 1979 book *Subculture: The Meaning of Style*. He argues that everyday commodities can be symbolically repossessed by groups resisting the hegemony of the dominant culture, magically appropriating them as a coded opposition to the ruling class. Thus the job of the cultural theorist is to 'discern the hidden messages inscribed in code on the glossy surfaces of style', in other words, to be a semiologist (Hebdige, 1979: 18). Hebdige adds two new elements to the analyses of subcultures provided in the earlier work of his CCCS colleagues. First, his book leans heavily on the punks—a subculture that did not exist when *Resistance through Rituals* was written—to make his point that British subcultures can be decoded as oblique forms of resistance to the cultural hegemony of the ruling class in a capitalist society. Second, Hebdige sees most of the British subcultures as responses to or incorporations of the black immigrant experience in Britain from the

1950s on (for example, through the influence of reggae music on punk bands like The Clash).

Hebdige's *Subculture* shows how subcultural styles make sense to their bearers insofar as they communicate a significant difference between the subculture and mainstream culture. He discusses in some detail the punk stylistic ensemble. The cheap trashy fabric of their clothes, their orange and green hair, their ripped and graffiti-covered T-shirts held together by safety pins, their borrowing of sexual bondage gear to wear as everyday clothing, and the 'blank robotics' of their favourite dance, the pogo, all added up in Hebdige's mind to subcultural guerrilla warfare waged in the clubs and council estates of Britain in the 1970s by predominantly working-class youth. The punks constructed a homologous ensemble of symbolic objects out of 'the trashy cut-up clothes and spiky hair, the pogo and amphetamines, the spitting, the vomiting, the format of the fanzines, the insurrectionary poses and the "soulless", frantically driven music' (ibid., 114). Underneath their clownish makeup Hebdige discerned the 'unaccepted and disfigured face of capitalism', which the punks thought had led Britain down a dead-end alley with no future (ibid., 115).

He sees the punks as showing off a perceived condition of exile from their parent society (ibid., 66) and compares their styles to Dada, an anti-art movement from the early twentieth-century that spawned nonsense poetry generated by random bits of newspaper clippings, and Marcel Duchamp's sculpture *The Fountain*, an ordinary urinal that he signed and displayed in a gallery. Even the names of punk bands express a sense of 'wilful desecration' and their perceived outcast status: The Sex Pistols, The Clash, The Damned, The Slits, The Vibrators, and Canada's DOA. He also mentions the cheaply cut-and-pasted fanzines, full of spelling and grammar mistakes, and the use of spray-paint graffiti or ransom note typography on record covers and posters.

Hebdige is clearly interested in the social meanings of subcultural styles. Like the rest of the CCCS researchers, he reads these meanings through structurally tinted sunglasses. From Hebdige's point of view, subcultural style acts as a coded response to community changes. Indeed, coding (and the need for decoding) is one of the key contributions of the Birmingham School to the analysis of subcultural styles. They linked these codes back to their structural roots, usually class. As did the other members of the CCCS, Hebdige took from Barthes the idea that the dominant class tries to make its rule appear natural through a series of cultural signs that appear to be depoliticized common sense, though in fact these are part of an attempt to maintain hegemony.

Sadly, as one can imagine from Hebdige's general tone, these symbolic acts of resistance to hegemony are destined to self-destruct, as the original innovations of the style become frozen commodities for sale at the local mega-mart (e.g., when contemporary youth buy gangster rap and too-baggy-pants at a suburban mall). Hebdige concludes that youth 'cultural styles may begin by issuing symbolic challenges, but they must inevitably end by establishing new sets of conventions' (ibid., 96). The engine of consumer capitalism consumes these styles and spits them back out as mass-produced objects no longer tied to the counter-hegemonic meanings they originally signified.

So, in the CCCS sense of the term, are there subcultures today? A few goths and punks still roam the netherworlds of downtown streets and high school classrooms a generation after these subcultures were born, though by no means are these lively expressions of a working-class rejection of the bourgeois status quo (even though a few punk bands such as Green Day manage to create best-selling albums). The main candidate for an authentic subculture today would seem to be rap or hip-hop culture. It certainly has the main components of a subculture: distinctive clothes, rituals, slang, and music. Yet despite its lower-class origins in American black ghettos, hip-hop has long since emigrated to white middle-class neighbourhoods, its current message being about sexual conquest, gang violence, and the blind pursuit of wealth. And when hip-hop

millionaires are interviewed on nationally broadcast TV talk shows, you know the jig is up. Hip-hop culture does form a semiological system, but one without any firm class foundation. In other words, it has become yet another consumer good, though perhaps one with a bit more edge than the minivans and Fleetwood Mac CDs owned by its practitioners' parents.

In conclusion, the Birmingham School saw the meaning of subcultural style as expressing in code class contradictions, exhibiting from the 1950s to the 1970s an increasing alienation by working-class youth from the bourgeois hegemony in Britain. The form of these subcultural styles can be seen in a multitude of cultural signs, from the mods' smart suits to the punks' ripped T-shirts held together by safety pins. Their meaning lies in the fragmented social structures that gave them birth. This brand of subcultural theory is open to one major criticism—the theorists merely imposed meanings on subcultural styles, which the bearers of those styles neither understood nor intended. This critique is easier to make with some subcultures than others. In the case of the largely self-aware punks, for example, it is far from outrageous to claim that they were very much aware of subverting the normal meanings of the cultural objects they appropriated. Yet in some other cases, the semiotic decodings offered by theorists may well have been massaged a bit, and quite unconnected to the subjective meaning of the actual members of these subcultures. Yet most of the CCCS's mappings of the various subcultures they turned their semiotic telescopes towards still ring true today, whether or not the members of these subcultures were really aware of what they were doing.[6]

POST-STRUCTURALISM: THE THEORETICAL LOGIC OF POSTMODERNISM

A New Country

In talking about post-structuralism, we inevitably enter the territory of postmodernism, the subject of the next two chapters. We must chart our trip through this territory in general terms if we're to make sense of post-structuralist theory, which is the theoretical logic of postmodernism. To do so I'll use a geographical metaphor. Imagine a large and complex country called Postmodernism that is divided into two provinces called Postmodern Culture and Postmodern Theory. Each of these provinces contains a number of substantial cities, themselves divided into a number of diverse neighbourhoods. To be precise, Postmodern Culture contains seven such metropolises, while Postmodern Theory contains five. Most of the people in the province of Postmodern Theory speak a language called Post-Structuralism and are very loyal to their country. The province of Postmodern Culture, on the other hand, contains a number of distinct ethnic groups and languages. Some of its inhabitants are indeed loyal Post-Structuralists; but others are Marxists, Feminists, Phenomenologists, Hermeneuticists, or even Liberal Humanists (who are hated by the Post-Structuralists). These minority ethnic groups aren't always enthusiastic Postmodernists—indeed, some of them are in active revolt against their country. Yet they all spend a lot of time talking about what it means to be a Postmodernist.

Of course, this is just a metaphor. To make its meaning clearer, thinkers who discuss postmodernism as a cultural phenomenon are not especially in favour of either postmodern culture or post-structuralist theory: in fact, many, like Frederic Jameson, are rather hostile to both. They may be post-structuralist; but they may also be Marxist, feminist, or liberal. These theorists of postmodern culture are describing and criticizing a form of culture that most agree came into place in the 1960s with the triumph of consumer capitalism and the post-industrial society (and later the computer age and the information economy).

On the other hand are the theorists who put forward a positive philosophical program along 'postmodern' lines, though most such thinkers (e.g., Jacques Derrida) don't like being called postmodernist. They are broadly post-structuralist since they come after structuralism, having

absorbed its lessons. It's not that they're hostile to structuralist theory, but simply thought that it didn't go far enough. The post-structuralists agreed with some of the tenets of structuralism: that language is fundamental to human self-understanding, being a system of signs whose meanings are arbitrary; that these signs are made up of signifiers and signifieds; and that binary oppositions are important in the structuring of human societies. Yet they deny the notion that we can look for deeper structures to explain the meaning of texts, the mind, or human social interactions. In effect, they sever the connection between signifier and signified, between surface words or events and their deeper structures.

So we can divide 'postmodernism' into two broad territories: cultural theorists and post-structuralists. Naturally, there is considerable emigration from one territory to another, and some theorists have lived comfortably in both. The 12 basic principles of postmodernism are outlined in Table 7.2. Note that our 12 'cities' contain a series of connected though separate 'neighbourhoods' or sub-principles, most of which we shall visit in this chapter and the next two.

In the remainder of this chapter we'll visit the territory of postmodern theory, whose citizens are almost entirely post-structuralist. We'll leave our exploration of the larger province of postmodern culture for the following two chapters. The ontology of post-structuralism parallels a major issue in postmodern culture. The post-structuralists argue that we can no longer take the Enlightenment idea of rational progress very seriously. Enlightenment reason has been bankrupted not only by Nietzsche's philosophical critique and Freud's psychology, but also by such real-world developments as two world wars, the Holocaust, the atomic bomb, and any number of genocides, from Armenia in 1915 to Pol Pot's Cambodia. How can we take human rationality and progress seriously now? Modernism celebrated a number of meta-narratives or big stories: the use of reason and science to enlighten the species; the praiseworthy forward march of technology; the liberal progress towards equal rights for all; the innate human

Table 7.2 Mapping Postmodernism

Postmodern Culture	Key Theorists
1. The Postmodern Condition: The critique of Enlightenment reason and the incredulity towards meta-narratives.	Lyotard, Derrida, Foucault
2. Political Economy: The post-industrial society, where services dominate industrial production. Knowledge now the primary good. Consumerism and the commodification of culture. A flexible workforce, contractual obligations, globalization. The decline of the nation-state and the end of ideology.	Bell, Lyotard, Jameson, Giddens, Ritzer, Baumann, Saul (among many others)
3. Communications: The network society, with a domination of mass media and computers. The global village and the age of the Internet. Cyberspace, data smog, hyperreality, and the death of the real.	Castells, McLuhan, Baudrillard, Shenk, Kroker
4. Pop Culture: Irony, pastiche, self-referencing and recycling in film, TV, music, and popular literature. Surface over depth, style over substance. Fusions of genres and of high and pop culture.	Jameson, Hutcheon
5. Dimensions: Space-time compression. Loss of local public space. History as a simulation of the past. The 'no time' society—everyone always on the move. The narcissism of the eternal now.	Harvey, Jameson, Baudrillard, Menzies
6. Architecture: Double-coding and the use of such classical motifs as columns, statues, and colour in buildings. A rejection of modernist functional/machine aesthetic. Humour and eclectic borrowing from the past.	Jencks, Venturi
7. Art: A return to the human figure and a parodic appreciation of classicism. A rejection of modernist abstraction, minimalism. Play, humour.	Jencks

Postmodern Theory (mostly Post-Structuralist)	Key Theorists
8. Ontology: The critique of Enlightenment reason and logocentrism, the incredulity towards meta-narratives. No unified field for science, politics, art.	Derrida, Foucault
9. Agency: The fragmentation of the subject and the death of the author. There is nothing outside the text. Texts open to many readings, meanings.	Nietzsche, Freud, Barthes, Lacan, Derrida, Foucault
10. Epistemology: The critique of truth as correspondence with reality, of representation, and of objectivism. Power/knowledge. Radical constructivism and contextualism. Intertextuality.	Derrida, de Man, Feyerabend, Kristeva
11. Method: Skepticism and deconstruction. Différance. Playfulness over scientific rigour. No interpretation is final.	Derrida, de Man (many minor deconstructionists)
12. Strategy: A more positive attitude towards intuition, myth, fantasy, and mysticism. Acceptance of fringe religions, political ideas, world views. Micro-narratives. Postmodern ethics.	New Age movement, Irigary (feminism), Bauman

drive to freedom, or the end of the class struggle in a communist paradise. Postmodern theory rejects all of these as at best only partially true, at worst illusions. As J.F. Lyotard announced at the beginning of his *The Postmodern Condition*, postmodern society is defined by its incredulity towards meta-narratives. We just can't believe in these big stories anymore.

So we can characterize the 'ontology' of postmodern theory as the notion that there is no unified field for art, science, or politics (Ermath, 1998). Modern art (up to the twentieth century) tried to picture 'reality'; modern science tried to interpret 'nature'; modern democratic politics tried to represent the 'people' or the 'nation'. These and other unified fields, along with the realism, empiricism, and humanism that support them, are all disrupted by postmodern theory. 'Reality', 'nature', 'people', and 'truth' become unstable signifiers for postmodern theory, never quite connecting to the concepts they supposedly stand for. In other words, there are many realities, many natures, many truths, but there is no absolute centre of things. Yeats's poem 'The Second Coming' (1922) says it best:

Things fall apart; the centre cannot hold;
Mere anarchy is loosed upon the world.

If we add Nietzsche's pronouncement that 'God is dead', we get a sense of the intellectual climate in which postmodernism was born, one where all certainties were undermined.

Agency: The Fragmentation of the Self and the Death of the Author

The fragmentation of the self in Western thought can be traced back at least to the late nineteenth century in the work of Friedrich Nietzsche, a relentless critic of almost all the major theoretical systems of his day. Nietzsche talks in *The Twilight of the Idols* (Part 6, Section 3) about the 'error of false causality', which is our faith in 'inner facts', phantoms like the will, spirit, or ego as the causes of our thoughts and actions. Motives are just surface phenomena that cover up deeds. 'It was out of himself that man projected his three "inner facts"—that in which he believed most firmly, the will, the spirit, the ego. . . . Small wonder that later he always found in things only that *which he had put into them*.' Time and time again Nietzsche criticized the primacy of conscious rational thought and of a unified self in our lives. One of his main ideas was that all living things seek to manifest a *will to power*. Yet this will is a complicated thing, being in fact a plurality of sensations (*Beyond Good and Evil,* section 19). It's really made up of many competing tiny wills. We deceive ourselves that the synthetic concept 'I' connects a unitary will to the decisions we make, but the feeling of exercising one's will is like the feeling of delight felt by a commander ruling a group of under-souls, for the self is a social structure of many such souls. We see our actions as the effects of our unified will:

> *L'effet c'est moi*: what happens here is what happens in every well-constructed and happy commonwealth; namely, the governing class identifies itself with the successes of the commonwealth. In all willing it is absolutely a question of commanding and obeying, on the basis, as already said, of a social structure composed of many 'souls'. (Ibid., section 20)

This is where our sense of moral responsibility comes in, from the illusion that we are all autonomous, sovereign individuals able to exercise freedom of will. In fact, we're driven as much by instincts like fear, lust, cruelty, and revenge as by rationality. Freud aided Nietzsche in the deconstruction of the self by splitting it into three psychic processes, the id, ego, and superego. Not only had the self become a trinity, but part of this trinity is directly unknowable—the unconscious part (mainly the id), which we repress. Of course, Freud was no postmodernist, being a firm believer in scientific truth and objectivity. Yet his psychology furthered Nietzsche's project of showing the unified self to be a fiction.

If we move forward to the late twentieth century, we find postmodern theorists picking up this fragmented self from Nietzsche and Freud. Structuralism saw the self as submerged in linguistic structures, with Lévi-Strauss seeing the human subject as a plaything in the binary logic of myths. The psychologist Jacques Lacan (1901–80) argued that the mind is structured like a language, even the unconscious. He agreed with Freud that the mind is trinary in structure, but he called the three elements the Real, the Imaginary, and the Symbolic. The infant starts out as 'really' a part of its mother's body. In the 'mirror stage' of development, from about 6 to 18 months old, the baby lives in an imaginary world where it creates a false idea of its self by looking in a mirror, where it sees a signified for its signifier (e.g., a picture of Pierre to go with its name 'Pierre'). The imaginary stage is reflexive: the child becomes conscious of itself as reflected in the eyes of others (its social mirrors). Later it enters the symbolic order thanks to the learning of language, and thus enters the world of social relations. This symbolic world is centred on the father/phallus, and is a world of loss for the infant, which is no longer part of the mother. Unfortunately, says Lacan, women cannot identify with the patriarchal nature of the symbolic order, which is centred on the phallus and which the male child enters upon resolving the Oedipus complex by identifying with the symbolic power of the phallus. The Bulgarian-born post-feminist Julia Kristeva (1941–) ridicules Lacan's connection of symbolic and phallic power, seeing the unconscious mind and the body as prior to linguistic meaning. She also criticizes the idea of female sexual identity as a metaphysical illusion. The category 'woman' doesn't exist as some essence, but is always in the process of being created. In other words, sexuality is individual, not a property of a collective group.

Postmodern theorists in general argue for less emphasis on the subject as the preconstituted centre of the experience of society and history, questioning the value of a unified, coherent self— they see the self as the source of the outmoded subject/object dichotomy, a fossil relic of liberal humanism, a locus of power, or an oppressor creating world views that exclude some to favour others (Rosenau, 1992: 42).[7] Not surprisingly, Michel Foucault (1926–84) and Jacques Derrida (1930–2004), the two best-known post-structuralist theorists, tend to see the self as a side effect of discourse (talking and writing), not as the active centre of decision-making. In fact, at the end of The Order of Things, Foucault proclaimed the 'death of man'. Like Nietzsche speaking of the death of God, he did not mean that 'man' once existed but has since expired, but that the humanist notion that we are the authors of our own existences is false. Of course, the fragmentation of the self tends to put into question the idea that human beings are purposeful agents, as Weber, the interactionists, and ethnomethodologists all believed. It thus throws into question our notion of moral agency: if we cannot say 'Rocko robbed the bank' but instead blame it on his id, some fugitive aspect of his will to power, or a vague 'subject position' that we may or may not name 'Rocko', then it becomes pretty hard to prosecute him for his crime. And more importantly for the purposes of social theory, if there is no coherent subject, then we have no one to attach a subjective meaning or intentions to. If skeptical post-structuralists such as Derrida and Foucault are right that there is no concrete subject, then human agency and causality disappear and the whole hermeneutical and phenomenological proj-

ect we've looked at in the last two chapters is a huge waste of time.

The fragmentation of the self in Western thought led directly to the post-structuralist notion of the death of the author. In his later period Roland Barthes (1977: 148) announced that 'the birth of the reader must be at the cost of the death of the author.' What he meant was that readers contribute as much if not more to the meaning of a text as its author. Establishing the meaning of a text is a collaborative effort involving both writer and reader, though ultimately it's up to the reader since the author is a sort of absent presence (especially if he or she is dead). The postmodern novelist and critic Umberto Eco put it another way: a text is 'a machine for generating interpretations' (Eco, 1983: 2). Barthes and Eco are making points about the nature of reading in itself. Michel Foucault makes the socio-historical case for the death of the author in his essay 'What Is an Author?' (Foucault, 1979b), in which he claims that the author is a function of writing and a product of a text, not the other way around. The idea of an author being responsible for creating a given text had to do with bourgeois notions of property, copyright, and controlling the distribution of ideas that only came into being in the seventeenth and eighteenth centuries.[8] In the Middle Ages texts were produced collectively by holy orders of monks, while in primitive societies mythic texts were created by the tribe. In other words, post-structuralists argue that the 'author function' is a historical concept that will fade as bourgeois humanism gives way to postmodernity.

The reason this is important to social theory is that the post-structuralists see every organized system or set of practices human beings involve themselves with as like a language. This includes not only speech, books, and other actual texts, but films, television shows, moral codes, forms of dress, habits, social relations, political hierarchies, and economic interchanges. 'There is nothing outside the text', as Derrida says in Of Grammatology (1982: 158).[9] Given the so-called death of the author, there's no sense in looking at an author's social and economic background to understand his or her motivations, as is done in many schools of modern criticism. Nor is there any point in examining in detail the author's intentions. Derrida says that reading a text 'has nothing to do with the author as a real person' (ibid., 158). So for the post-structuralists the self as author of texts or events becomes a ghost-like wraith, a shadow of intentionality.

On the positive side, since the author is dead, the reader becomes much more powerful. Postmodern theory allows many different readings of the same text: to deny the validity of a person's reading is to marginalize and oppress that person (which makes marking essays difficult). In fact, postmodern theory pretty well demands that the reader construct the text. Still, the reader's power is handicapped by the post-structuralist denial of the capacity of language to give us true or objective descriptions of reality. The post-structuralist program goes through three stages that subvert traditional social science: (1) first, it transforms cultural objects and social practices into text-like things; then (2) it argues that we can't take the intentions of the authors of these things too seriously in interpreting them; then (3) it deconstructs the notion of a 'final' and 'true' interpretation of any text. Of course, we've already seen how the fragmentation of the subject removes moral responsibility for actions. Similarly, if there are no authors of texts or text/events (remember, the post-structuralists see everything humans do as texts), then we cannot associate intentions, reasons, or moral judgements with anyone. This is difficult for most social scientists to swallow, unless they stop talking about people entirely and focus purely on social structures (even this is tricky business for postmodernists, given the 'post' in post-structuralism). And on the level of common sense, it makes little sense to say that a reader 'creates' a text in reading it. For example, if one reads a good science fiction novel, one is transported to 'a galaxy far far away', full of characters and events that the reader in no way invented. Reading is as much a matter of being absorbed into another's mind as it is an active re-authoring. Having said this, the post-structuralist

criticism of active authorship does warn us not to be too hasty in assigning the meaning of social events to rational, conscious, unified subjects. Yet this isn't the same thing as saying that there are no subjects there at all.

Epistemology: The End of Truth, Power/Knowledge, and Intertextuality

Epistemology is the study of how we know things, and thus of the nature of truth. Postmodern theorists distrust the modern ideas of abstract truth and objective knowledge. They reject truth as a goal because it is linked to the Enlightenment, to reason, order, rules, and logic, and thus to all the usual modernist suspects (Rosenau, 1992: 77). The more skeptical among the post-structuralists object to truth claims as arbitrary propaganda or rhetoric, whether these occur in university literature classes or scientific laboratories. Followers of Foucault assert that truth is always part of a power game, of power/knowledge, so it depends more on economic and political hierarchies than fair-minded scientific research. If Foucault is right that truth is tied to a power/knowledge equation, then epistemology becomes a political question (we will return to this issue at the end of this chapter). Lyotard and Baudrillard argue in roughly the same way that truth is terroristic, for it seeks to silence or eliminate those who do not agree with it. Of course, many times in Western history the ideas of unpopular individuals and minorities *have* been silenced for political reasons, from Socrates' trial in ancient Athens to Galileo's astronomical problems with the Catholic Church to the Nazi burning of 'Jewish' literature. Yet to claim that all 'truth' tries to do this is quite another matter.

Part of the post-structuralist argument against truth goes back to the Saussure's claim that the relation of signifier to signified is an arbitrary one, and thus that a given language is a huge net of arbitrary meanings cast over reality. The post-structuralists agree with this, adding that since our notion of reality is constructed both linguistically and socially, the arbitrariness of language is double: both the words we use and the supposed reality they refer to are mental constructions. Since language is so deeply constructed, we never really match up our linguistic utterances to reality. Truth cannot be a mirror of the essence of the world, for the world has no essence. To believe it does would be to engage in what Derrida calls 'the metaphysics of presence', the notion that we can capture in philosophical language the essence of things as though our words made them present (for example, by saying 'God is good' because we think he has blessed us with a new job or our favourite football team with victory). What truth does exist for postmodern theorists is in traces and fragments. Truth is rhetorical in the sense that it tries to convince an audience of something on the emotional level. And it's always in flux. In a way postmodern theory sees truth as having more of an aesthetic than an epistemological character since it's the fleeting creation of an individual artist/actor, like a painting or a statue.

Just as truth is suspect, so is representation. To represent something is to make it present again, as when politicians 'represent' their constituents—they (figuratively speaking) make their voices 'present' in Parliament. One of the key issues in postmodern theory is the debate over the cultural status of representation—the capacity of science and philosophy to represent reality, art to represent beauty, literature to represent human values, or history to represent the past. Postmodern theory is anti-representation, since representation is central to the politics, social structure, and philosophy of modernity. We see this modern idea of representation in democracy's political delegation of powers, in painting's resemblance to the world, in the photograph's replication of a scene, in the writer's repetition of life events, in the lawyer's substitution for her client, in the photocopier's duplication of a document (ibid., 92). Representation is everywhere. Postmodern theorists claim that it's wrong to assume that representation is carried out without any loss of content. Representation is like taping a record on a low-quality cassette tape, then copying that tape onto a second tape, and then onto a third, and so

on. Each time we lose a bit of the original music's clarity and depth.

Postmodern theorists herald the end of the 'Order of Representation'. They see representational democracy as alienating, representational art as boring, representational literature as desecrating, and representational history as deceptive (ibid., 94). The whole idea of representation in language, and thus in social science, assumes that there is a reality out there to be represented and that we can capture that reality in a meaningful way in language. Our words can 'stand for' that reality, which exists outside of our representations of it. Yet as the American postmodernist and pragmatist thinker Richard Rorty (1931–) says, while the world is out there, truth is not. When we try to represent the world in language, we assume that the words we use are meaningful both to us and to others. Yet post-structuralists tell us that there are many meanings for a given word or symbol and that language can have no direct relationship to reality. We can't represent external reality, since representation assumes an objective observer independent of the thing or person being represented (ibid., 97). Who is to judge the accuracy of a given representation? Who can escape from the vicious circle of language, which is symbolic in its very nature?

So, postmodern theorists question our ability to authentically represent anything. Not surprisingly, they are also skeptical about theory, which depends on truth. Skeptics see most modern theory as totalizing, 'logocentric' meta-narratives. People, events, and objects are unique, yet theory tries to reduce this uniqueness to systems and categories. Since language is our only link to reality and language contains no firmly grounded meanings, all theory is distortion—it is ideological in nature. The more skeptical postmodernists see theory as a weapon of power, a form of rhetoric. The Yale critic Paul de Man (1919–83) talked about modern theory closing off the multiplicity of interpretations, hinting that only postmodernism really reflects the perspectival nature of the world. Thus, postmodernists claim that they will not construct rational systems of theory grounded in observation and experience—although sweeping claims like the 'author is dead' and that modernism is bankrupt certainly have the smell of theory about them (ibid., 81–2).

Since everything is a text, what smaller truths we can create are the products of intertextuality, Kristeva's idea that we live in a world of interrelated texts unconnected to a non-textual reality. To arrive at a truth we have to plunge into the ocean of texts all around us, for there is no beach where this ocean of texts ends and we can rest and dry off, epistemologically speaking. We can only prove that our interpretation of one text is valid by connecting it to other texts. Think about doing research for an essay: you go to the library to photocopy articles and borrow books, or sit down at your computer and look up information on the Internet. At no point do you encounter real theorists or real social events. In fact, the Internet is a good model for what the post-structuralists mean by intertextuality: web pages link to other web pages and to search engines, which themselves have links to still more pages, in an endless swirl. To coin a phrase, there is nothing outside the web.

Intertextuality leads post-structuralists to embrace some radical form of constructivism or contextualism (or both). The former argues that the meaning of all things is constructed by the human mind, which is not all-knowing or the same everywhere, and therefore its products are quite fallible. For example, 'power' and 'justice' are cultural constructions sensitive to the ebbs and flows of history. A contextualist is someone who says that our interpretation of an idea or event depends entirely on the context we make it in. To the seventeenth-century gentleman, it may have made sense to own slaves; yet to do so today in the West would be both illegal and looked on in horror by all sensible people. Was the slave owner wrong in the absolute sense? It is difficult for a true postmodernist to say he was, for our seventeenth-century gent was a child of his times as much as we are of ours. To say he was is to assume an absolute moral centre from which to judge all those outside this centre to be inferior. But postmodern theory rejects all such centres.

Method: Genealogy, Deconstruction, and Play

Post-structuralist method combines extreme skepticism with a certain playfulness. In general, postmodern theory follows the advice of the philosopher of science, Paul Feyeraband, that 'anything goes'. If it works, we'll use it. Yet this oversimplifies things, since it leaves open the question of just what 'works'. Postmodern theory is playful in that it's less tightly tied to rationality and objectivity than modern theory, and thus, often feels free to experiment with ideas in a free-form manner (indeed, some of Derrida's texts are so loose and experimental that they are painful to read). Such an approach is more likely to highlight creativity, feelings, and empathy than calm reason. Yet having said this, there are three specific methodological routes the post-structuralists have taken, which we'll deal with in the rough order of their chronological appearance.

First, Michel Foucault has proposed genealogy as a key method, borrowing the idea from Nietzsche's work *On the Genealogy of Morals*. In the intellectual sense, genealogy is the search for connections between ideas, practices, and institutions. Of course, all good history and much of sociology does this anyway. The difference that Foucault introduces is that his genealogy doesn't look for the deep structures, origins, or causes behind a given phenomenon, but for ruptures, local and illegitimate knowledge, discontinuities, and other traces of forgotten meaning ignored by 'scientific' analyses (Foucault, 1980: 83). He says that genealogy must 'record the singularity of events outside of any monotonous finality', looking for them in the most unpromising places: in sentiments, love, conscience, and our instincts (Foucault, 1977: 139–40). It aims to analyze the descent of things, especially the way that history imprints itself on the human body, a central concern in all of Foucault's works (ibid., 148). This genealogy isn't looking for a higher truth or a deeper structure to explain the phenomenon, but for a wider picture of it, a picture not under the control of the dominant form of power/

knowledge. In this sense, Foucault's genealogy is close to Derrida's deconstruction.

The main method of post-structuralism is deconstruction, Jacques Derrida's brainchild. In the most basic terms, deconstruction is a way of systematically critiquing texts. The word itself doesn't mean to 'destroy' but to 'take apart'. The deconstructionist aims to tease out the 'warring forces of signification' in a text, to uncover its hidden hierarchies and the traces of opposed meanings in its main concepts. In short, deconstruction tries to discover the latent meanings in a text ignored by traditional readings of it. Like the structuralists, deconstructionists believe that modern discourse is structured around a series of binary opposites—culture/nature, man/woman, speech/writing, reason/emotion, good/evil. These binary opposites are hierarchies where the first term in the pair is seen as superior to the second, with this hierarchy helping to structure the discourse. A deconstructionist does a careful reading of a text to show how traces of the second term undergird or leak into the first. For example, Derrida might reread a dialogue by Plato that praises reason to tease out how the Greek applauds play or passion in a quiet way—yet without claiming that play or passion is the 'real' subject of the dialogue. These binary opposites support a variety of metaphysical or moral centres that have (according to Derrida) haunted Western thought: God, reason, truth, essence, the Forms, Christianity, or the Good (Powell and Lee, 1998: 100). Derrida feels that Western thought has frozen the play of opposites in binary pairs like reason/emotion and culture/nature to keep these metaphysical centres in power. Deconstruction aims to decentre these centres, to show how each centre contains some part of its margins, yet without putting a new metaphysical structure in its place.

Third, Gilles Deleuze (1925–95) and Félix Guattari (1930–92) developed a 'rhizomatic' view of knowledge that parallels the epistemological stances of both genealogy and deconstruction. They argued that Western thought has constructed 'trees' of knowledge with a central trunk of essential beliefs and branches and roots of less essential information growing from that trunk. We see these trees of knowledge in chemistry, linguistics, and philosophy, among other disciplines (ibid., 108–10). A rhizome is a plant's underground stem made up of a series of nodes, each of which sends out a group of separate roots. An intellectual rhizome does the same: it has a number of distinct nodes, each with its own tangle of epistemological roots. In the view of Deleuze and Guattari, the first three principles are connection, heterogeneity, and multiplicity: all the nodes of knowledge connect to each other (unlike in a tree, where they connect to the branch); they are distinct; and they have multiple roots. You can pull out a rhizomatic root, but a similar one will sprout up somewhere else. The key to a rhizomatic system is that it is non-hierarchical and non-centred. An example of such a system is the Internet, which has no overall 'controller': anyone with access to a computer and a server can use and contribute to it. Deleuze and Guattari hold out rhizomatic knowledge as an alternative to the more centralized and structured paradigms of modernism.

Strategy: Intuition, Micro-Narratives, and Counter-Canons

Finally, we should say a few words about postmodern theory's general strategy in the moral, political, and religious arenas. Here we leave some of the rigours of post-structuralist analysis behind to discover the more populist side of postmodern theory. First of all, since postmodernism rejects reason and objectivity, postmodernists are more open to intuition, fantasy, humour, personal desires, and gratification (Rosenau, 1992: 53). Part of this openness to the non-rational elements of life is a focus on micro-narratives, myths, folk wisdom, and local stories as opposed to the universal meta-narratives of science, truth, and freedom. Everyday life, personal stories (like those on Internet blogs), and communal experience gain a new credibility for the postmodern strategist.

Part of the postmodern strategy is to decentre things, to highlight what's going on at the margins. Thus some postmodern theorists seek out the fringes of intellectual life in such areas as post-colonial and queer studies (though one should point out that these fringes are not entirely dominated by postmodern theory). According to post-colonial theorists, if one deconstructs the Western canon of literature, one discovers on its margins a collection of under-appreciated non-Western authors. This leads to the creation of a counter-canon of little-studied non-white authors who post-colonialists argue should be read more often and more seriously. Queer studies seeks to deconstruct the traditionally hostile view of heterosexual society to gays, bringing the history and literature of gay men and lesbians into the intellectual mainstream. Postmodern feminists also seek to make marginalized female voices heard, although these feminist theorists aren't especially postmodernist.

Some examples of postmodern life strategies include New Age religiosity, fusions between Western and Eastern art forms (e.g., the marriage of Indian traditional and Western rock music), the sampling of cultural goods from distant lands (e.g., sushi restaurants, recordings of Tibetan chants, snippets of Buddhist wisdom), and alternative politics (e.g., the Green Party). Some of this is a result of globalization; but it's just as much the result of the decline of meta-narratives and the hunger for something of a spiritual or deeply political nature to fill the void left by decline of Western rationality, science, and liberal progress. Of course, the problem with all of this is that it opens the door to endless egoism and narcissism, as postmodernists claim a freedom to think and do whatever their heart's desire suggests given their abandonment of modernist notions of rationality, objectivity, and universal truth. Yet there's no doubt that this decentering of Western culture has made things interesting.

JACQUES DERRIDA AND DECONSTRUCTION

Derrida's Post-Structuralist Pharmacy

Jacques Derrida was born in El-Biar in Algeria in 1930 to a middle-class Jewish family. He went to France in 1949, where he studied philosophy under Michel Foucault, Louis Althusser, and others in the early 1950s at the École Normale Supérieure. He taught at the Sorbonne from 1960 to 1964, and then from 1964 to 1984 at the École Normale Supérieure. From the 1970s on he also travelled extensively and taught at a series of universities in America. Derrida was part of a generation of French intellectuals who, giving up on existentialism and Marxism, turned away from political revolution—especially after the failure of the May 1968 revolt of students, radicals, and workers in Paris—to a linguistic one, looking not so much at *what* language says, as *how* it says what it says (Powell and Lee, 1998: 99). Derrida and his intellectual allies became increasingly distrustful of the idea that language conveys a single, authoritarian message, focusing on its ambiguity and complexity. Derrida takes several ideas from the structuralists, including the importance of binary thinking in the modern world (although he seeks to deconstruct such thinking) and the omnipresence of language. As Derrida argues, 'there is nothing outside the text': as thinking beings we're always caught in a web of linguistic signs. Yet he rejects Saussure's firm distinction between signifier and signified as a metaphysical distinction between a transcendental world, that of the signifier, and the world of the physical senses, where we find the signified. Because of this Saussure wrongly thought that the sole purpose of writing was to represent spoken language (Derrida, 1976: 30).

At the root of the Western philosophical tradition is a basic distinction between speech (in Greek *logos,* which also means reason or logic) and writing. Derrida claims that the Western philosophical tradition has privileged speech over writing. Speech is given precedence as the expression of what is immediate and present, and is thus seen as more real, more true. Writing is a poor imitation of speech, what's left over when speech is no longer present. It offers us appearances, what Plato called 'doxa' or opinion. 'Phonocentrism' is the idea that speech presents the speaker's immediate meaning, which Derrida thinks is an illusion. For the Greeks, only a living discourse, the *logos*, could be fertile and have children, while written texts are 'disseminated' into a void, parentless and wandering.

Derrida lays out this view of the relation of speech and writing in his deconstruction of Plato's dialogue, *Phaedrus*, in his extended essay 'Plato's Pharmacy' (1981). In *Phaedrus* Socrates introduces the myth of the god Theuth, who offers King Thamus the gift of writing, which he calls a 'recipe' or 'remedy' (in Greek *pharmakon*) for memory and wisdom. The king rejects this gift, fearing it will induce both forgetfulness and arrogance in students who think that now they have books, they will no longer need wise teachers. For Plato only speech has a living father, its speaker. Texts are like wasted seeds thrown onto barren fields. Derrida traces the origins of the god Socrates calls 'Theuth' to the Egyptian god Thoth, also a god of writing, along with being the god of medicine and the mighty Osiris's scribe, recording the names of the dead in his book as they pass into the underworld (Derrida, 1981: 91). Thoth's medicine is both a science and an occult practice; he is both god and magician, a wild card in the pack, a joker, a floating signifier (ibid., 93). In a similar way, the *pharmakon* offered to King Thamus is a floating signifier: it can be a beneficial remedy or drug, but it's also a poison, both in terms of its Greek meaning and as a metaphor for writing, which remedies our weak memories temporarily while debilitating them in the long term. The translation of *pharmakon* as 'remedy' removes its magical and hard-to-master qualities, preferring to equate it with a safe, scientific word (ibid., 97). Derrida wants to open up the duality of meaning of this drug in Plato's pharmacy, this *pharmakon*, and thus the duality of writing as both a medicine refreshing weak memories and a poison that kills the living *logos*, the directness of speech. Derrida therefore tries to show how Plato's assumed intent in the dialogue—to praise speech over writing—is not as clear as one might think. In the end we get a much more ambiguous picture of Plato's use of the myth of Theuth and a deconstruction of the binary pair, speech (*logos*)/writing (the *pharmakon*). Derrida shows that such key philosophical concepts are always in play, their meaning always deferred, and that maybe writing is not such a bad thing after all, despite King Thamus's cavils.

Logocentrism and the Metaphysics of Presence

Logocentrism, the centring of a discourse on the *logos*—reason, speech, or the word that presents thought—is what Derrida calls this focus on speech over writing. Derrida sees all Western thought as based on the idea of a centre, on Truth, the Forms, Reason, Essence, God, or some other metaphysical certainty. The problem is that every centre—e.g., Christianity—excludes or marginalizes the 'Other'—i.e., Judaism, Islam, Buddhism, and so on. It tries to make the privileged term the only one that counts, tries to make the centre hold against all comers, thus refuting Yeats. Further, he sees the entire Western tradition (except maybe Nietzsche and Martin Heidegger) as dominated by Reason, by an attempt to *re*-present the world in a perfectly rational language. Such a language would make the world 'present' to the philosopher, to speak the Truth, to make the Word flesh. This philosophical attempt to make the truth 'present' Derrida calls 'the metaphysics of presence'. The classic case of the metaphysics of presence is Plato's theory of forms, in which he saw all real objects as pale reflections of purer, divine archetypes of them (e.g., all dogs participate in the Form of Dogginess). Yet there's no Trojan Horse that Reason can't conquer. This is why Derrida cannot use 'rational' discourse to attack reason, but can only indicate the traces of what he's pointing at in his writings. His attacks on logocentrism and the metaphysics of presence are more like guerrilla ambushes than frontal assaults.

Philosophy and science assume the presence of a real world of truth, causes, and origins that can be captured in ordinary discourse: the metaphysics of presence. Derrida argues that the need to place a reassuring end to the reference of one sign to another inclines us to logocentrism, to the idea that language is subservient to non-linguistic objects, intuitions, or ideas. But nothing is ever directly present to us: signs always mediate everything. We can't escape the intertextual world. So the seduction of logocentric reason is that it can offer a pure communion with the world. Derrida finds this idea arrogant and totalitarian, for reason exercises a tyranny over the uncertain, the different, and the marginalized. It is indifferent to the 'Other'. In the worst cases, rationality has been used to justify and organize genocide, mass destruction, and death, from the well-oiled Nazi bureaucracy that implemented the Holocaust to the massive iron cage of co-ordination involved in keeping the American military machine, with its arsenal of potentially world-destroying nuclear weapons, merrily rolling along.

In his essay 'Freud and the Scene of Writing', Derrida (1978: 198) speaks of the whole history of Western thought as tied to the idea that the self is present in consciousness, even in the opposition of consciousness to the unconscious. Freud is no post-structuralist to Derrida, though he admits that his unconscious text is a 'weave of pure traces', not a copy of a prior text. In this essay Derrida is fascinated with Freud's idea of a 'mystic writing pad', a block of wax or resin over which sheets of wax paper and plastic are placed. One writes on the plastic with a stylus, and can erase the words by lifting the sheets off the wax. Yet a trace of one's writing remains on the wax block. This wax block is a metaphor for the unconscious, which one writes on consciously then erases, leaving traces behind. Derrida wants to radicalize this idea of the trace and remove it from Freud's metaphysics of presence based on the duality of conscious/unconscious, to see writing as connected to traces of meaning, as part of the play of the world.

Structure, Sign, and Play in the Human Sciences

Another essay from *Writing and Difference* is Derrida's important 1966 address at Johns Hopkins University, 'Structure, Sign, and Play in the Discourse of the Human Sciences'. On the surface this essay is a critique of Lévi-Strauss's structuralist anthropology, but underneath it broadly critiques logocentrism and the metaphysics of presence. Derrida says that the very idea of a structure goes back to the start of Western science and philosophy, to what Plato called *epistēmē*, knowledge. The sorts of structures Lévi-Strauss talks about have centres to orient themselves, but also to make sure that the organizing principle of the structure would limit its play (ibid., 278). Anthropology tries to conceive of a structure that is fully present and beyond play. In this sense, his structures freeze the very myths he seeks to understand, caging them like circus lions.

The history of metaphysics in the West is that of substituting one centre for another: *eidos* (Idea or Form), *archē* (origin), *telos* (goal or final cause), transcendentality, consciousness, God or Man. In the end these are all different versions of being as presence, different ways of giving the human race a firm centre as a ground for its existence (ibid., 279–80). Yet when 'language invaded the universal problematic', everything became discourse, everything became part of a system of signs. Without an extra-linguistic foundation in the Forms, God, human nature, or something else of a transcendental nature as an anchor, we are cast adrift once again upon the sea of signification with nothing more to hold on to than floating signifiers. 'The absence of the transcendentally signified extends the domain and the play of signification infinitely' (ibid., 280). It's no accident that what the French call 'ethnology' (i.e., anthropology) was born at the moment when European culture was feeling dislocated and was forced to stop considering itself as the culture of reference.[10] The Europeans' criticism of the ethnocentrism of their early colonial days and the decentring of European culture went hand in hand with the deconstruction of the history of metaphysics in the work of Nietzsche and Heidegger (ibid., 282). In other words, the shift away from Europe as the cultural and political centre of the world paralleled the Europeans' loss of faith in their former metaphysical certainties.

In the end Derrida sees history and anthropology as caught up in the metaphysics of presence, to which he opposes play as the disruption of presence. What sort of play? Nietzsche's type, 'a joyous affirmation of the play of the world and the innocence of becoming, the affirmation of a world of signs without fault, without truth, without origin', where the non-centre is seen as something other than a loss of centre (ibid., 292). There are thus two interpretations of the relation of structure, sign, and play in the social sciences: one seeks to decipher a truth or origin that escapes play and the arbitrary nature of the sign, as with Lévi-Strauss and the structuralists; the other, turned away from questions of origin, tries 'to pass beyond man and humanism, the name of man being the name of that being who, throughout the history of metaphysics or of ontotheology—in other words, throughout his entire history—has dreamed of full presence, the reassuring foundation, the origin and end of play' (ibid.). Derrida opts for this latter strategy, which affirms the play of the world. That he can be a social scientist while engaging in such linguistic play is a dubious possibility at best.

Binary Oppositions and *Différance*

As we've already seen, human thought is pervaded by binary oppositions like culture/nature, reality/appearance, truth/falsity, knowledge/opinion, man/woman, and good/evil, the first element in each case being privileged. This freezes the play of the system and marginalizes the other member of the pair. Derrida wants to show how these distinctions, which some thinkers take to be true and absolute, can be shown to be fuzzy and will shade into each other when deconstructed. He wants to decentre the centre, to allow these binary pairs to freely play.

One of Derrida's key concepts is *différance*. This word is a combination of two meanings of the French verb *différer*: to make different, and to defer or put off. The meaning of words is in part defined by what they're not, by how they're different from other words, occupying their own unique linguistic space. At the same time, the full meaning of a text is always put off or deferred to the future, which never comes. With this concept Derrida wants to emphasize two things: first, the difference between systematic theoretical struc-

tures and the objects (for example, experiences, events, or texts) they try to explain, and, second, the way in which the attempt to make an absolute distinction is always deferred by the involvement of one polar opposite in the other. This latter phenomenon Derrida also discusses in terms of how the 'trace' of its opposite always lingers at the heart of any polar term. For example, within each man there is a little bit of woman, within culture a bit of nature, and so on. He also employs the term 'dissemination' to refer to the way that objects of analysis slip through the conceptual net spread by any given system of knowledge we devise: when writing, we disseminate texts into the world, without knowing how they will be read or used. As he says in his essay 'Différance' (1982, 1968 in French), the circulation of linguistic signs puts off the moment when we can encounter the thing itself. Following Saussure's idea of the arbitrary character of the sign, languages and codes are constituted historically as a weave of differences. *Différance* is older than the concept of Being: there is no depth to the bottomless chessboard on which Being is put into play. In other words, linguistic signs, like pieces on the bottomless chessboard, have nothing beneath them to stop them from floating away (Derrida, 1982: 22). We have no metaphysical guarantee that they mean what we think they mean.

Deconstruction

Derrida proposed the French word *deconstruction* as a translation of Heidegger's *Destruktion*, which first appears in Heidegger's 1927 phenomenological magnum opus, *Being and Time*. According to Heidegger, to see time as a fundamental element of human Being, we need a *Destruktion*, or loosening of the structure of the history of Western metaphysics. For Derrida, too, the term means, 'destructuring', not 'destruction'. Derrida starts with the structuralist assumption that the meaning of a signifier doesn't come from what it refers to, but from the way it interacts with all other signifiers. For Derrida all words are 'floating signifiers' cast adrift on the ocean of texts. His post-structuralist point is that *we* give meaning to all signifiers in speaking or writing, and thus we are implicated in the production of meaning: there can be no detached, rational, scientific observer, and there is nothing outside the text. Everything is a type of discourse. Texts are never simple unitary things— they are full of suppressed or hidden meanings. We can't be satisfied with figuring out the author's intentions. We have to peel away the constructed meanings of a text, to deconstruct it, to move beyond the merely 'present' meanings, as Derrida sought to do in his essay, 'Plato's Pharmacy'. This is what Derrida has done in his many essays on literature, philosophy, and anthropology.

Deconstruction is a 'careful teasing out of the warring forces of signification *within the text itself*' (Johnson in Derrida, 1981: xiv). It sees meaning not as produced by the static closure of binary oppositions, but through the free play of the signifier (the sound image). Signifier and signified lose their status as fixed points in the stable order of discourse. 'A text is not a text unless it hides from the first comer, from the first glance, the laws of its composition and the rules of its game' (Derrida, 1981: 63). But these laws are never entirely clear: they are not a secret waiting to be discovered, like the origins of the Nile River for nineteenth-century explorers. One has to deconstruct the text to get a sense of one or more ways they operate. One way to do this is by taking apart the binary pairs, to show how binary pairs like 'nature/culture', 'man/woman', and 'Christian/Islam' aren't as solid as some like to think. These binary pairs help to exclude the 'Other' from our culture, and thus deconstruction can be seen to have a peripheral role in fighting the oppression of minorities.

Deconstruction, Literary Criticism, and Social Theory

Traditional literary analysis has understood the meaning of a text as the expression of its author's mind, that is, as thoughts the author intended to convey in writing the text. The first stage of deconstructive criticism is the structuralist one of detaching meaning from authorial intention, locating it instead in the text itself as a linguistic structure. But the post-structuralists take the further step of denying a fixed meaning to even the autonomous text itself. It's not that a text lacks all meaning but that, on the contrary, the text is the source of an endless proliferation of conflicting meanings. As deconstructionists delight in showing, any proposed privileged meaning of a text can be undermined by careful attention to the role in it of apparently marginal features.

The moral of the story for social theory is that since human agents, social events, and structures are all text-like things, they, too, can be deconstructed. As a social theorist, Derrida would look at classical analyses like those of Marx, Durkheim, and Weber and try to show how traces of non-dominant readings lay buried within their texts. In addition, he would show how on the one side the notion of a unified, purposeful human agent and on the other that of deterministic social structures both close off the free play of signifiers, creating too-rigid interpretations of social life. So he would distrust all attempts to fix the understanding of social life on some firm centre, whether anthropological structures, the class struggle, subjective meaning, or the collective conscience.

Some Critiques of Deconstruction

Deconstruction has roused the ire of theorists around the world, who have accused Derrida of everything from closet fascism to a hatred of modern science. Four substantial accusations can be made against Derridean deconstruction that his defenders have yet to answer successfully:

1. It abandons the idea of a true interpretation of a text, always looking for traces of opposing meanings. But how can one tell a good interpretation from a bad one? Doesn't evidence count? If it does, then truth re-enters the picture. If not, then in Derridean play clever rhetoric or temper tantrums could easily trump reasoned debate. We thus arrive at a very rel-

ativistic picture of things—which, of course, might be what Derrida wanted all along.

2. It encourages obfuscation in language and endless talk about nothing. This could lead to total irrationalism, where only one's personal feelings count in academic and scientific debates. Without some notion of rationality, even if it's only pragmatic, the human sciences *will* become forms of rhetoric, as some post-modernists said they were all along.

3. It falsifies the world, including real problems, by treating everything as a text. Hunger, poverty, disease, an⌐ ⌐ re not texts—they're rea¹ . Only those tr⌐ towers would

[handwritten note: Links to Goffman?]

We can just ⌐ct all that ⌐ swirling ⌐on-logo- ⌐ng.

Yet so ⌐ Derrida behind on too sour a note, ⌐ must acknowledge that his critique of Western metaphysics and deconstructive method have certainly shaken things up in modern theory, making people much less willing than they once were to construct grand explanatory structures out of the floating signifiers of social life.

We finish the chapter with a look at Derrida's former teacher and contemporary, Michel Foucault, who combines elements of structuralism and post-structuralism in his archaeologies and genealogies of madness, forms of knowledge, prisons, and sexuality.

MICHEL FOUCAULT ON POWER AND THE DOCILE BODY

Michel Foucault (1926–84) is a postmodern (though he disliked this term) philosopher, historian, sociologist, and theorist who has had a wide influence in social theory, literary studies, feminism, criminology, and other academic fields. He was born in Poitiers, France, and his early education was in both philosophy and psychology. He

is difficult to categorize. His work starts out with some strongly structuralist assumptions in its early and middle periods, and then slides into post-structuralism in his mature works. Foucault was, generally speaking, interested in how systems of knowledge and definitions of the self become concretized in such institutions as asylums, hospitals, schools, prisons, the military, and sexual practices. In this general sense he can be seen as a distant theoretical relative of Goffman, who studied the ways that social institutions strongly encourage specific types of performances. Foucault was interested in how society defines the mad, the sick, the criminal, and the sexual 'deviant' as different from so-called 'normal' people, and then used its mechanisms of power to make the general populace internalize these arbitrary definitions as valid, resulting in the ostracism and oppression. In a way, then, his life's project was a massive historical-sociological deconstruction of the binary pair 'normal/abnormal'. We can trace this project back to Foucault's awareness as a young man that he was gay, which led to depression, a suicide attempt, and a visit to a psychiatrist where he first encountered an institutional definition of normality (heterosexuality in this case, which excluded Foucault).

Further, he was very suspicious of the Enlightenment idea of progress, being more sympathetic to the historicist notion that the basic truths about human nature change over time. The ideas of one age are very different from those of another, which affects the way human nature is defined. Foucault's work can be roughly divided into three periods, even though there is lots of intellectual leakage between them. In his early period (1950–9), during which he worked on his doctoral thesis on Western views of insanity, Foucault was very much under the influence of Marxism and phenomenology, as was common among French intellectuals of the day. He taught at the universities of Lille, Uppsala (in Sweden), Warsaw, and Hamburg during this period. In 1954 he published his first book, *Mental Illness and Personality*. While in Sweden in the mid-1950s he came upon a huge library of medical literature dating back to the sixteenth century. His perusals of this library led him to write his first two major works, *Madness and Civilization* and *The Birth of the Clinic*.

Archaeological Period (1960–9)

Foucault taught at the University of Clermont-Ferrand from 1960 to 1966, then at the University of Tunis from 1966 to 1968. In 1968 he became Chair of the Philosophy Department at the University of Paris at Vincennes; in 1969 he was elected to the College de France. In this middle period in his career, he abandoned his earlier influences and became interested in tracing out the archaeology or origins of the various *epistemes*, or systems of thought (roughly parallel to Thomas Kuhn's paradigms of science), that have dominated the human sciences in Western history.[11] This is the structuralist element in Foucault's work: these *epistemes* determine the sort of valid knowledge claims one can make with the historical period they govern, like Kuhn's paradigms. They are structures of discourse (written and spoken language), meta-systems of signs. In seventeenth-century Massachusetts I could validly claim that my next-door neighbour is a witch in league with the devil; today such a claim would be laughed at. *Epistemes* don't evolve from one to the next gradually, but take epistemological leaps that wipe out the authority of the previous *episteme* in one fell swoop (Ashenden, 2005: 208). The problem with the notion of an *episteme* is that Foucault saw them as the totality of rules governing discourse in a given period, yet was reluctant to connect them with social, political, economic, or other extra-discursive factors, as a Marxist or critical theorist would. Consequently, he winds up with the argument that discourse *causes* discourse, without explaining how this happens. So seventeenth-century people believed in witches because of their *episteme*, but why did they accept this *episteme*? Why not some other one? We're back in the realm of causes and origins, a realm that neither Foucault nor Derrida feel comfortable in. In short, too much description, not enough explanation.

In any case, this period starts with the publication of his first important work *Madness and Civilization: A History of Insanity in the Age of Reason* (1961), which examined how the Western view of madness changed from the Middle Ages to the modern period. In this book he wants to write an 'archaeology of silence' (Foucault, 1973 [1961]: xi), since the unreason of the mad cannot speak in rational discourse. He saw three *epistemes* or paradigms of madness from the Middle Ages to today:

- *Pre-Modern Episteme:* In the Middle Ages and early Renaissance, the mad were tolerated, even seen as divinely inspired. Their madness was a path to supernatural wisdom. Look at how the mad are pictured in Shakespeare's plays for evidence of this view: madness is seen as a sort of spiritually inspired fall from grace. Here it was possible to speak of 'the wisdom of fools'.
- *Classical Episteme:* Later, in the classical age, from about 1650 to 1800, Foucault argues that madness was seen as a sort of 'unreason', a descent into animality that had to be restrained by or hidden from rational society. This age starts with the 'great confinement' in the mid-seventeenth century of the mad, the unemployed, libertines, and other undesirables. The insane were now left to rot in the dark prisons once occupied by lepers.
- *Modern Episteme:* Later, after the insane were 'liberated' by modern psychological discourse, madness was seen as a treatable illness, a disease to be cured by skilled doctors. This regime was initiated by Phillipe Pinel in France and Samuel Tuke in America at the end of the eighteenth century. They 'freed' the mad from their prisons only to impose bourgeois notions of morality on the insane, whose descent to animal-like behaviour was an affront to these norms.

The essence of the classical view of madness was that it was a form of Unreason, a descent into animality that should be dealt with by discipline and brutality (ibid., 75). But the madman was *not* sick to the classical mind; he was not the victim of a disordered nature, but was swallowed up in a darkness that allowed his brute passions too much liberty (ibid., 83–4). Hence the need to chain him up, to confine him. In the modern age, asylums open to house the mad, who are no longer quartered with ordinary criminals and the poor. They are now medical patients, not chained animals. Tuke, a Quaker, implemented a regime of surveillance and judgement of the mad, treating them like children who had to be taught morality and religion. Under Pinel, the asylum becomes a place where ethical uniformity is imposed, where the mad were denounced socially as failing to live up to bourgeois moral standards (ibid., 259). Madness was put on eternal trial in the moral world of the asylum to get the mad to feel remorse about their crazy ways and allow them to return to the 'normal' world. The doctor was seen as having daemonic secrets that allowed him to effect a magical cure (ibid., 273–5). Freud demystified the asylum, concentrating all its powers in the analyst, using talk therapy to return the mad from the province of unreason to a more reasonable place. Yet all of psychiatry retains the moral tactic of trying to normalize madness that dates back to the late eighteenth century.

In his first explicitly 'archaeological' work, *The Birth of the Clinic: An Archaeology of Medical Perception* (1963), Foucault talks about how, starting in the eighteenth century, doctors began to use their medical gaze to impose order on the chaos of disease. This clinical gaze could penetrate the surface of the patient's body and reveal hidden truths. Later, in *The Order of Things: An Archaeology of the Human Sciences* (1966), a difficult book that amazingly became a best-seller in France, he painstakingly showed how the *epistemes* operating in early modern European versions of biology, linguistics, and political economy (in those days called natural history, general grammar, and the analysis of wealth) were strikingly different from those operating in these same fields today. Codes of culture establish what sort of scientific research people of a given period can engage in (Foucault, 1994 [1966]: xx). Here's

how Foucault describes his general strategy for investigating these codes:

> I am not concerned, therefore, to describe the progress of knowledge towards an objectivity in which today's science can finally be recognized; what I am attempting to bring to light is the epistemological, the *episteme* in which knowledge, envisaged apart from all criteria having reference to its rational value or its objective forms, grounds its positivity and thereby manifests a history which is not that of its growing perfection, but rather that of its conditions of possibility. . . . Such an enterprise is not so much a history, in the traditional meaning of that word, as an 'archaeology'. (Ibid., xxii)

The book is about how forms of knowledge classify their objects of study and create 'orders' of things. As *Madness and Civilization* was about how some people were 'others', this book is about how things are the 'same'. Once again he discovers three distinct *epistemes* operating in the human sciences from the Renaissance to today:

- *Pre-Modern Age:* In the Renaissance (until the mid-seventeenth century), things were ordered in terms of their *resemblance* with related things and other orders of things. Foucault sees resemblance operating in four ways in this age: in terms of convenience (being physically adjacent), emulation, analogy, and sympathy, with the latter being the strongest type of resemblance.
- *Classical Age:* In the late seventeenth and eighteenth centuries, the main technique of classification became one of *representation*, where things were ordered in terms of what they stood for. Knowledge is collected in tables.
- *Modern Age:* From the nineteenth century to today we see history as shaping nature, language, and society, with time ordering things.

It is indeed strange to look back to the sixteenth century to see how the natural historians of the Renaissance thought that certain plants liked and disliked each other, that the stars determined our destinies, or that nature contained signs of divine will. To the Renaissance mind 'the face of the world is covered with blazons, with characters, with ciphers and obscure words' (ibid., 27). Language itself was seen as resembling the world, as a series of God-given signs of things (ibid., 36). The profound kinship between language and the world seen in the Renaissance disappeared in the classical age, when language was seen as a way of representing the world, as an instrument of analysis and combination whose meaning wasn't guaranteed by the order of things (ibid., 43, 63). The thinkers of the classical period, according to Foucault, saw the main task of discourse as *naming* things, and thus their primary goal was to create a type of language that was perfectly transparent with the things it names. In other words, they wanted science to represent the world clearly.

The classical age loved to arrange knowledge in tables, for example, economic data and taxonomies of plant and animal species. This created a static view of the order of things. Under the modern *episteme*, economics was seen in historical terms (as in Marxism), human existence becomes finite, and even the natural world is seen as developing over time (ibid., 262). Instead of dreaming of past golden ages, thinkers now dream of the end of history and thus of time. The stream of time has washed away the static grid of the table—the modern mind sees in the world a 'profoundly historical mode of being of things and men' (ibid., 276). Nature is no longer a peaceful garden, but wild, even bloody and murderous. A language expresses the fundamental will of the people who speaks it, being a reservoir of tradition and folk memory. The modern age discovers a finitude, a shortness of time, where the mode of being of my life is delineated by the space occupied by my body, the mode of being of economic production by the things I desire, and the mode of being of language by the slender chains of my speaking thoughts (ibid., 314–15). Just as the classical age imagined knowledge contained in timeless grids, the modern mind sees knowledge floating like little boats along the river of time.

Foucault argues in *The Order of Things* that the concept 'man' is a recent invention dating back about two centuries (ibid., xxiii). At the end of this book he predicts the death of man when the *episteme* of the modern age comes to an end. Foucault saw human beings as chained by linguistic and knowledge structures not entirely of their own making, only one of which—the modern—saw humanity as an object of study. Prior to the Age of Reason, the concept of 'man' didn't exist (ibid., 308). Eighteenth-century thinkers like Immanuel Kant developed the notion that human beings are both knowing subjects and known objects, thus allowing social institutions to be objectified and the human sciences to be employed to discipline the human beings living and working in them. 'Man' became an object of intensive study. We should point out that Foucault's idea relies on a somewhat odd interpretation of the 'science of human nature' found in many eighteenth-century thinkers, e.g., David Hume, which talked about human beings collectively before the concept of 'man' supposedly—at least according to Foucault—came into existence.

This period can be said to close with his theoretical treatise *The Archaeology of Knowledge* (1969), his theoretical summary of the archaeological method, which defines archaeology as the study of forms of knowledge in a given historical period. In it he repeats the notion found in his previous three works that the *episteme* of the classical Age of Reason was quite distinct from that of the modern age.

Genealogical Period (1970–84)

From the early 1970s and on, Foucault shifted his focus to a 'genealogical' approach, an investigation of the family trees of various social and intellectual phenomena. He had become skeptical about finding the 'true' origins of the various things he was interested in investigating. Instead, he looked for dead ends, traces of knowledge, and unconnected facts as ways of explaining the various phenomena he was investigating. This was largely the result of the influence of Friedrich Nietzsche's search for a genealogy of moral codes, as laid out in his *On the Genealogy of Morals.* Nietzsche focused on the 'little truths' of politically motivated language shifts, climate, diet, sexual repression, and other such unphilosophical events to explain how modern moral codes came to be. Foucault didn't entirely abandon his archaeological method, but he submerged it under his search for the family trees of the sciences of criminology, social psychology, and sexuality. He announced the start of this period in his important essay 'Nietzsche, Genealogy, History'. In his genealogies he looked at the apparatuses by which modern subjectivity is constituted by discourse and by disciplinary practices that inscribe regimes of control upon the body. In other words, he examined how we become the types of selves we are.

In this period Foucault became more relativistic, seeing Power and Knowledge as intertwined twins. Simplifying somewhat, for the mature Foucault to *know* something in a systematic way meant having *power* over people. Foucault argues that power/knowledge defines such categories of people as the mad, the criminal, and the sexual deviant to keep in power a certain type of social order. On a broader scale, modern societies control the bodies of their citizens through human sciences, such as psychiatry, criminology, and medicine, which define what it means to be 'normal' and punish those who aren't. Mind you, he saw power as also a positive thing, as essential to social and economic order; for example, the operation of power/knowledge in factories made possible worker discipline and thus the Industrial Revolution. Despite the moral relativism that seemed to mark his work in this period, Foucault didn't hesitate to campaign for prisoners' rights in the early 1970s, later also championing gay rights.

His most famous work of this period is *Discipline and Punish* (1979a [1975]), a history of forms of punishment. Here he gives his clearest statement of how power/knowledge works. He says his book is about the 'political economy of the body' and how one could read in the 'micro-physics' of the power to punish a genealogy of the modern soul (ibid., 29). And since no power relation is unconnected to the constitution of some field of knowledge, his book also connects penal institutions to broader fields of study in the human sciences (ibid., 27). Yet one can't see power in a purely negative sense, since it produces reality, domains of objects, and rituals of truth (ibid., 194). In other words, power creates settled social relationships. Part of this power/knowledge equation is *biopower*, the power over life, and *biopolitics*, the ways the body is disciplined by regimes of power/knowledge. Both of these are connected to the way that modern authorities punish criminals and sexual 'deviants' and to the psychological and medical sciences that legitimate that punishment.

Foucault finds several apparatuses of punishment in history. In the days of the absolute monarchs, a crime was seen as an attack on the person of the king, a declaration of war on his sovereignty, so it was punished in public in a gory and spectacular way. Up until the mid-eighteenth century (at least in France), punishment was a spectacle that inflicted pain on the body. It was preceded by torture, a game of truth between prisoner and torturer. Yet legal reformers in the latter days of the French Old Regime and during the French Revolution helped put an end to punishment as a public spectacle since it was seen as 'inhumane': even the guillotine was seen as a step in the right direction since it was a quick and relatively painless death. In the nineteenth century punishment was moved indoors, its target no longer the body and its sensitivity to pain but the mind and its capacity for 'normalization'. Its goal was not the vengeance of the king but the restoration of an obedient subject.

Foucault sees Jeremy Bentham's model of the ideal prison, the Panopticon, as a model for the 'disciplinary society'. The Panopticon has a central observation tower containing guards surrounded by circular banks of prison cells facing it, each with a window facing outside to let light in. They were like well-lit little theatres of punishment. Since the cells all face the central tower, the prisoners never know when the guards are observing them, so they in theory regulate their own conduct. Foucault saw the Panopticon as a metaphor for the disciplinary powers of contemporary institutions like the military, schools, prisons, and the clinic, all of which localize observation and graduate punishment within their claimed local bits of space and time through timetables, the correction of gestures, the enclosing and partitioning of space (think of a modern factory or office), the control of talk and sexuality, promotions and demotions, grades, rankings, and isolation. All this discipline led to normalization, one of the 'great instruments of power' at the end of the classical age (ibid., 190). It was also a part of a military dream where people would be turned into docile cogs in the machine by exhaustive training (ibid., 169). This dream was good for the development of capitalism, for it produced workers willing to work for long hours in grimy factories for a mere pittance.

Further, by making the 'field of visibility' infinite, Panopticism caused people to police themselves: you never know if you're being watched, so you had better be good just in case. Foucault argues that the model of the Panopticon slowly spread throughout all of society, having the great advantage of being a disciplinary machine that anyone can operate. This all led to a society of 'docile bodies'—the disciplinary society. In such a society physical punishment is almost entirely abandoned, being replaced by psychological discipline, which is at least in part self-discipline and is backed by the sciences of medicine, education, psychology, and criminology. So the great accomplishment of the nineteenth century in the field of punishment was to deprive criminals of their liberty and technically transform them at the same time by throwing them all in panoptic-style prisons (ibid., 233). Yet for the last century it has been clear that prisons don't reduce the crime rate and produce reoffending inmates and delinquency. They're a colossal failure as reformatories. Whenever this is pointed out, however, the proposed solution is only more penitentiary techniques (ibid., 265–8). Why the reluctance to try other methods of punishment? Because the carceral network is deeply rooted in our disciplinary society, and because small-time criminality like prostitu-

tion is actually useful to the dominant classes. After reading the book one gets the impression that Foucault harbours some nostalgia for the good old days of blood-and-guts public punishments, where the prisoner was mentally free even if his body was in chains, where Captain MacHeath in John Gay's *The Beggar's Opera* (1728) could make a gallows speech to a throng of admiring pickpockets, prostitutes, and other petty criminals at Tyburn Tree and die a hero.

Foucault concludes that:

> The judges of normality are everywhere. We are in the society of the teacher-judge, the doctor-judge, the educator-judge, the 'social worker'-judge; and it is on them that the universal reign of the normative is based; and each individual, wherever he may find himself, subjects to it his body, his gestures, his behaviour, his aptitudes, his achievements. The carceral network . . . has been the greatest support, in modern society, of the normalizing power. (Ibid., 304)

Yet his model of the Panopticon as a vast conspiracy engine imposing power relations on everyone has brought Foucault a lot of criticism: just who is oppressing whom, if power is 'everywhere'? And why are they doing this? A Marxist would say that all this discipline is about controlling the working class; Foucault dances around this issue, only flirting with the notion that the disciplinary society is a class-based one. This element of Foucault's theory has been tremendously popular in postmodern feminism, queer studies, and post-colonial studies, all of which revel in the notion of unseen oppressors subtly punishing sexual and racial outsiders without using overt physical force. It supports the ideology of victimhood that would have made Nietzsche, with his scorn for slave morality, roll in his grave. Ironically, however, in many ways Foucault is a dedicated Nietzschean. He has nothing but kind words for the great German thinker.

Foucault's last efforts involved the application of his genealogical method to sexual practices in his three-volume *History of Sexuality* (*Volume I: An Introduction*, 1976; *Volume II: The Use of Pleasure*, 1984;

Volume III: The Care of the Self, 1984). This unfinished *History*[12] is about how the sexual self has been constructed in different historical phases in the West. Foucault describes how discourses on sex, like those on punishment, are connected to forms of power legitimated by the human sciences—medicine, psychiatry, psychoanalysis, and the philosophy of education. These disciplines create a 'sexual science' that defines sexual normalcy for the period in question. In Volume I, Foucault attacks the 'repressive hypothesis', the idea that in Western culture from the seventeenth century to the mid-twentieth century talk of sexuality was almost silenced and the sexual act restricted to the marriage bed. The Victorian period was seen as especially guilty of repressing sexuality. In reality, people talked endlessly about sex in this era: in the Victorian age it became the subject of numerous serious scientific studies from the likes of Kraft-Ebbing and Havelock Ellis. The nineteenth and early twentieth centuries witnessed an explosion of 'unorthodox' forms of sexuality with strange scientific names like 'onanism', 'auto-monosexualism', 'presbyphilia', and 'zoophilia' (Foucault, 1990a [1976]: 43, 49). This explosion of discourses about sexuality led to Freud's development of psychoanalysis, a *scientia sexualis* (sexual science) where someone is paid to sit and listen to others talk about their sex lives. In contrast, societies like China, Japan, India, and ancient Rome developed an *ars erotica* (erotic art) where the goal wasn't to tie sex to power/knowledge and the confessing of forbidden fruits, but to derive as much pleasure from it as possible without endangering one's body or soul. Foucault concludes that modern industrial-

capitalist societies did not refuse to recognize sex, but sought to produce true discourses about it (ibid., 69). Today we feel like proud rebels to speak out against sexual repression in order to attack the powers that be, 'to utter truths and promise bliss, to link together enlightenment, liberation, and manifold pleasures; to pronounce a discourse that combines the fervor for knowledge, the determination to change the laws, and the longing for a garden of earthly delights' (ibid., 7). In other words, we in the West feel just a little bit subversive and dangerous when we attack sexual repression even though it was never more than a muted reality in the first place.

In Volume II, Foucault claimed that the ancient Greeks (e.g., Plato and Xenophon) put forward an 'aesthetics of the self' that aimed at a pleasurable and happy life in which sexual practices of different types should play a full role, as long as they weren't engaged in excessively. Later, the early Christians turned to a 'hermeneutics of the self', to the notion that there is a true, inner self that religion and philosophy must attempt to discover, a self that should be purified of sexual drives. Foucault tried to show how there is a difference between individual sexual practices, such as the habitual practice of ancient Greek male aristocrats of having sex with young boys, and the modern tendency in psychological and moral discourse to define and categorize the participants in such practices in some way, in this case as 'homosexuals'. This is a political act of definition, the operation of power/knowledge on the body of an oppressed minority—gays. Ironically perhaps, Michel Foucault died of AIDS in 1984, the unfortunate victim of his gay lifestyle.

STUDY QUESTIONS

1. How did Saussure apply structuralism to the analysis of language? How did he define a 'sign'?
2. How was Saussure's view of language different from Wittgenstein's? Why do words mean what they do according to Saussure?
3. How did Lévi-Strauss apply structuralism to myth? How do totems fit into his theory?
4. What does Campbell mean by the 'monomyth'? How is this a case of structuralism?
5. Outline the stages in the hero's journey, then apply Campbell's model to a contemporary film.

6. What does Barthes's semiology aim to analyze? In what sense is it a 'second-order' system of significa-tion? Apply his semiology to a magazine ad or television commercial.

7. Where does the Birmingham School think that British subcultures come from? How was their posi-tion a critique of labelling theory?

8. How did the Birmingham School use semiotics to analyze subcultural styles? Pick a subculture and do a Birmingham-style semiotic analysis.

9. Do we have any subcultures in modern North America in the sense of the term used by the Birm-ingham School? Explain why or why not.

10. What is the difference between the analysis of postmodern culture and postmodern theory? How does post-structuralism fit in this distinction?

11. What do the post-structuralists mean when they say that 'the author is dead'? How does this affect their view of agency? Is their position too extreme?

12. How did Nietzsche and Freud influence the post-structuralist view of the self?

13. Why do the post-structuralists attack truth and representation? Given their views on this issue, can we have a meaningful 'postmodern' social science?

14. Outline genealogy and deconstruction as general methods. Can you see any weaknesses in each of them? Can deconstruction be applied to sociology?

15. How do post-structuralist ideas get translated into postmodern life strategies? Are these strategies becoming dominant in our society?

16. Why does Derrida think that Western thought has privileged speech over writing?

17. What does Derrida mean by 'logocentrism' and 'the metaphysics of presence'? What is he attacking when using these concepts?

18. What do binary oppositions and *différance* have to do with Derrida's notion of deconstruction? Choose a text containing binary oppositions and deconstruct it.

19. Outline the main principles and weaknesses of deconstruction.

20. What does Foucault mean by *epistemes*? What *epistemes* did he discern in the history of madness in the West?

21. What does Foucault say are the three distinct *epistemes* of classification found in the human sciences since the Renaissance? Give examples from biology, linguistics, and economics to illustrate these stages.

22. What does Foucault mean by 'power/knowledge'? How does he apply power/knowledge to ideas about punishment in the modern world?

23. What was the Panopticon? Why did Foucault discuss it? Is he right that we live in a 'disciplinary society'? Apply Foucault's notion of panopticism to a specific institution that affects your life.

24. What is the 'repressive hypothesis' and why does Foucault attack it? Was he right to do so? Do we live in a repressive society today?

Short Bibliography

Ashenden, Samantha. 2005. 'Structuralism and Post-structuralism', in Austin Harrington, ed., *Modern Social Theory: An Introduction*. Oxford: Oxford University Press.

Barthes, Roland. 1972 [1957]. *Mythologies*. New York: Hill and Wang.

———. 1977. 'The Death of the Author', in Barthes, ed., *Images, Music, Text*. New York: Hill and Wang.

Becker, Howard. 1963. *Outsiders: Studies in the Sociology of Deviance*. New York: Free Press.

Campbell, Joseph. 1968 [1949]. *The Hero with a Thousand Faces*, 2nd edn. Princeton, NJ: Princeton University Press.

———, with Bill Moyers. 1988. *The Power of Myth: The Hero's Adventure*. New York: Mystic Fire Video (PBS television show).

Clarke, John. 1976a. 'Style', in Hall and Jefferson (1976).

————. 1976b. 'The Skinheads and the Magical Recovery of Community', in Hall and Jefferson (1976).

————, Stuart Hall, Tony Jefferson, and Brian Roberts. 1976. 'Subcultures, Cultures and Class', in Hall and Jefferson (1976).

Cohen, Phil. 1972. *Sub-cultural Conflict and Working-Class Community*. Working Papers in Cultural Studies. No.2. Birmingham: University of Birmingham.

Derrida, Jacques. 1976 [1967]. *Of Grammatology*, trans. Gayatri Chakravorty Spivak. Baltimore: Johns Hopkins University Press.

————. 1978 [1967]. *Writing and Difference*, trans. Alan Bass. Chicago: University of Chicago Press.

————. 1981 [1972]. *Dissemination*, trans. Barbara Johnson. Chicago: University of Chicago Press.

————. 1982 [1972]. 'Différance', in Jacques Derrida, *Margins of Philosophy*, trans. Alan Bass. Chicago: University of Chicago Press.

————. 1994. *Spectres of Marx*, trans. Peggy Kamuf. New York: Routledge.

Eco, Umberto. 1983. *Travels in Hyper Reality*. San Diego: Harcourt Brace Jovanovich.

Ermath, Elizabeth Deeds. 1998. 'Postmodernism', in *Routledge Encyclopedia of Philosophy*, vol. 7. London: Routledge.

Foucault, Michel. 1972 [1969]. *The Archaeology of Knowledge*, trans. A.M. Sheridan Smith. New York: Pantheon.

————. 1973 [1961]. *Madness and Civilization: A History of Insanity in the Age of Reason*, trans. Richard Howard. New York: Vintage Books.

————. 1973 [1963]. *The Birth of the Clinic: An Archaeology of Medical Perception*, trans. A.M. Sheridan Smith. New York: Pantheon.

————. 1977. 'Nietzsche, Genealogy, History', in Foucault, *Language, Counter-Memory, Practice: Selected Essays and Interviews*, ed. Donald F. Bouchard, trans. Donald F. Bouchard and Sherry Simon. Ithaca, NY: Cornell University Press.

————. 1979 [1975]. *Discipline and Punish*, trans. Alan Sheridan. New York: Vintage Books.

————. 1979b. 'What Is an Author?', in Josue Harari, ed., *Textual Strategies: Perspectives in Post-Structuralist Criticisms*. Ithaca, NY: Cornell University Press.

————. 1980. *Power/Knowledge*, ed. C. Gordon, trans. C. Gordon, L. Marshall, J. Mepham, R. Soper. New York: Pantheon Books.

————. 1987. 'Questions of Method: An Interview with Michel Foucault', in Kenneth Baynes, James Bohman, and Thomas McCarthy, eds, *After Philosophy: End or Transformation?* Cambridge, Mass.: MIT Press.

————. 1990a [1976]. *The History of Sexuality, Volume I: An Introduction*, trans. Robert Hurley. New York: Vintage Books.

————. 1990b [1984]. *The History of Sexuality, Volume II: The Use of Pleasure*, trans. Robert Hurley. New York: Vintage Books.

Hall, Stuart, and Tony Jefferson, eds. 1976. *Resistance through Rituals: Youth Subcultures in Post-War Britain*. London: Harper Collins Academic.

Hebdige, Dick. 1976. 'The Meaning of Mod', in Hall and Jefferson (1976).

————. 1979. *Subcultures: The Meaning of Style*. London: Methuen.

Lévi-Strauss, Claude. 1963 [1958]. *Structural Anthropology*. New York: Basic Books.

————. 1966 [1962]. *The Savage Mind*. Chicago: University of Chicago Press.

————. 1969 [1949]. *The Elementary Structures of Kinship*. Boston: Beacon Press.

————. 1970 [1964]. *The Raw and the Cooked: Introduction to a Science of Mythology*. London: Jonathan Cape.

————. 1973 [1955]. *Tristes Tropiques*. London: Jonathan Cape.

Martin Ryder's Contemporary Philosophy, Critical Theory and Postmodern Thought links (these are very comprehensive, with a set of links for each major postmodern/post-structuralist theorist). At: <carbon. cudenver.edu/~mryder/itc/postmodern.html>.

Martin Ryder's Semiotics links. At: <carbon.cudenver.edu/~mryder/itc/semiotics.html>.

Miniature Library of Philosophy (Marxists Internet Archive contains selections from the works of Saussure, Lévi-Strauss, Barthes, Derrida, Lyotard, and Jameson). At: <www.marxists.org/reference/subject/philosophy/index.htm>.

Nietzsche, Friedrich. 1967. *The Portable Nietzsche*, ed. and trans. Walter Kaufmann. New York: Viking Books. Contains *The Twilight of the Idols, The Antichrist, Thus Spake Zarathrustra*.

———. 1967. *The Basic Writings of Nietzsche*, ed. and trans. Walter Kaufmann. New York: Basic Books. Contains *The Birth of Tragedy, Beyond Good and Evil, On the Genealogy of Morals*.

Powell, Jim, and Joel Lee. 1998. *Postmodernism for Beginners*. New York: Writers and Readers.

Rosenau, Pauline Vaillancourt. 1992. *Post-Modernism and the Social Sciences*. Princeton, NJ: Princeton University Press.

Saussure, Ferdinand de. 1960 [1916]. *Course in General Linguistics*. London: Peter Owen.

Storey, John. 1998. *An Introduction to Cultural Theory and Popular Culture*, 2nd edn. Athens: University of Georgia Press.

Strinati, Dominic. 1995. *An Introduction to Theories of Popular Culture*. London: Routledge.

Filmography

Star Wars. 1977. Written and directed by George Lucas.

The Empire Strikes Back. 1980. Directed by Irvin Kershner. Written by George Lucas, Leigh Brackett, and Lawrence Kasdan.

The Return of the Jedi. 1983. Directed by Richard Marquand. Written by George Lucas and Lawrence Kasdan.

The Matrix. 1999. Written and directed by Andy and Larry Wachowski.

Oh Brother, Where Art Thou? 2000. Directed by Joel Coen. Written by Ethan and Joel Coen, with help from Homer.

CHAPTER 8 | POSTMODERNISM: POLITICAL ECONOMY AND COMMUNICATIONS

The Postmodern Guy

Allow me to introduce for your consideration one Bart MacLean, a typical citizen of postmodernity. Bart rises at 8:30 to the buzzing of his electronic alarm clock, rubs his eyes, and then switches on his computer to check his e-mail. He lives in a tiny bachelor apartment in a large modern city, and is three years out of a university degree in sociology and mass media. Every morning he rubs gel into his blond-streaked hair, grabs his cellphone, and rushes off to the neighbourhood Starbucks for a quick cappuccino and a few moments with a manga novel before rushing off to his waiting 'job', as he ironically refers to it, at El Jaguar restaurant. The restaurant is exotically decorated with Aztec and Mayan motifs, including a mural of a snarling jaguar on the front wall and a five-foot-tall mock pyramid at its centre that doubles as a fountain. Of course, El Jaguar is nowhere near the jungles of the Yucatan, but in a strip mall with chain hardware and computer stores as next-door neighbours. After he knocks off around six, Bart rushes to the subway station and home to work on his real passion, web page design, which doesn't pay as well as waiting tables, but gives him a technological kick he can't get from any of the many service industry jobs he's had over the last eight years. As he moves from place to place in his home megalopolis his cellphone is almost constantly at his ear as he talks to his friends or listens to messages received during his work hours. He's a busy guy, acknowledging callers with his trademark phrase 'you've got 30 seconds!' to indicate the severe time pressures he sees affecting his life.

Bart has fairly eclectic tastes: he loves hip-hop (though he's never been to an inner-city ghetto), Indian traditional music (though he's never travelled in Asia), Thai food, and Japanese anime videos. His favourite television show is, of course, *The Simpsons*, with its dark irony and endless parodies of politics, religion, and elements of the mass media. Bart doesn't believe in big stories about politics, religion, or the meaning of life. He has never voted (though reasonably well informed politically), has never been associated with any church (though he read *The Celestine Prophecy* a couple of years ago and found it interesting), and lives from day to day. On the weekends he goes clubbing, and he knows what music is hot not only in North America but in Europe and the Far East as well. He travels whenever he can, both in person and much more often by surfing the Net. Bart is the postmodern guy. He is tied to all major elements of postmodern culture: its incredulity towards meta-narratives, its political economy, its communications, its pop culture, its space/time compression, its art and architecture. This chapter is about what it's like to be Bart, and quite probably what it's like to be you.

Revisiting Postmodern Culture

In the last chapter postmodernism was divided into two territories: postmodern theory, which we've already dealt with, and reflections on postmodern culture, the subject of this chapter. Postmodern theory spoke mostly in the language of post-structuralism, inheriting and critiquing the main principles of Saussure and the structuralists. Now we move on to discuss a wide variety of thinkers who have written on the nature of culture and society in the last half-century. Many of these thinkers are neither structuralists nor post-structuralists—in fact, some of them want nothing to do with Barthes, Derrida, or Foucault, theoretically speaking. Yet they all are interested in the idea that the culture we live in is something unique, a break with the past.

The core element shared by the thinkers dealt with in this chapter and the next is a basic question—do we live in an era we can conveniently call 'postmodern' that is culturally, socially, economically, and politically distinct from all previous eras? There are a variety of answers to this question. In his survey of postmodernism, Barry Smart (2005: 259) argues vehemently that any notion of a radical rupture between modernity and postmodernity has to be rejected. Frederic Jameson agrees, seeing postmodern culture as a form of late capitalism. Yet Daniel Bell argued in the 1970s that in the postwar period in America a post-industrial economy replaced the industrial form of production still in place in much of the rest of the world; while a decade later Jean Baudrillard spoke of an era where the hyperreal dominates society to the extent that we are living through the death of the real. Without especially using the term 'postmodern', a number of the commentators on our present culture certainly believe we are witnessing something quite new.

After several false starts earlier in the twentieth century, the term 'postmodern' finally entered our intellectual vocabulary in a permanent way thanks to Charles Jencks's use of it to describe the new architecture of the 1970s that rejected the sterile steel, glass, and concrete boxes of utopian modernist architects such as Le Corbusier and Ludwig Mies van der Rohe. Since then it has entered the language, coming to mean dozens of distinct and semi-distinct things. Yet amid all this terminological confusion all is not lost, for as we saw in our first journey into the territory of postmodernism in the Chapter 7, we have a map of the region (see Table 7.2).

In this chapter we begin by looking at J.F. Lyotard's argument that the postmodern condition is one where we no longer believe in meta-narratives, the big stories that once powered the metaphysical and moral engines of Western culture. We then consider political economy and the nature of communications in postmodern society. Daniel Bell argues that the 1960s saw the birth of a post-industrial society where services and information-processing replaced heavy industry as the backbone of Western economies. Finally, we'll move on to Manuel Castells's recent work on the nature of the information society, which his massive study *The Age of Information* explores in depth.

In the following chapter we'll look at some critical responses to postmodernity and venture into the other realms of postmodernism—art, architecture, pop culture, and the compression of time and space into an eternal present. In our journey through the territory of postmodern culture in this chapter and the next we'll visit all of the seven 'regions' listed in Table 7.2, thus providing the reader with a grand tour of this recently settled country.

THE POSTMODERN CONDITION

Lyotard on the Postmodern Condition

Jean-François Lyotard (1924–98) was born in Versailles, France, and taught in Algeria, Brazil, California, and, from 1968, at the University of Paris. He was a prolific writer, and addressed many philosophical issues over his long career. In the 1950s and 1960s Lyotard was a member of 'Socialism or Barbarism', a Marxist group that rejected the authoritarianism of Soviet communism. The May 1968 Paris revolt of workers and students against the government of Charles de Gaulle disillusioned Lyotard with leftist politics (the revolt was a great show, but accomplished little), and in the early 1970s Lyotard rejected Marxism, in part because of the 'systematization of desires' that Marxists tried to impose with their emphasis on industrial production as the ground of culture. He became more and more associated with the French post-structuralist school of thought, rejecting what he saw as the rigid structuralist approach of Marxism.

Lyotard's short book *La condition postmoderne* (1979) was commissioned by the Council of Québec Universities as a report on the status of science and technology. In it Lyotard defines postmodernism as an *incredulity towards meta-narratives*, a lack of belief in the master stories that formerly powered Western culture. These meta-narratives include those of Christian salvation, liberal progress, Communist revolution, and Darwinian evolution. But the two master narratives Lyotard sees as truly powering Western culture as far as education and science go are:

- *The March of Liberty:* the French Enlightenment narrative of Reason, Progress, and revolutionary emancipation, culminating in the French Revolution. Here science fights side by side with political liberalism against the priests and tyrants holding back enlightenment and thus human freedom. The hero of this meta-narrative fights for liberty.
- *The Unity of Knowledge:* the German Idealist narrative from the early nineteenth century of the speculative Unity of all Knowledge and the self-conscious march of the World Spirit. Hegel was its main defender in philosophy, Wilhelm von Humboldt in education. Under this meta-narrative the purpose of education is not utility or liberty, but the advancement of the speculative spirit in itself. The hero here fights for knowledge.

Within the last generation or two, according to Lyotard, we've lost faith in these meta-narratives. Lyotard sees this crisis as afflicting science, art, and literature, though his book focuses on how modern science deals with this crisis. As a result of this fading of meta-narratives, science suffers a loss of faith in its search for truth and must thrash about in search of other ways of legitimating its efforts.

Connected to this crisis in scientific legitimacy is the growing dominance of information machines and information-processing in post-industrial society. Knowledge has become *the* post-industrial force of production. Lyotard argues that, very soon, all knowledge will have to be convertible into computer data for it to be considered valid or useful. If it cannot be, it will quickly become irrelevant. In fact, Lyotard sees the self as a node in a complex web of circuits of communication, a conduit through which flow endless quantities of knowledge or data. With the growing use of e-mail, cellphones with Internet connections, and computers in general, this is even truer today than it was in 1979. Data banks will be the encyclopedias of tomorrow, 'nature' for the postmodern individual (Lyotard, 1979: 85). Lyotard was dead on in his prediction of the computerization of society: more and more research today is done directly through computers, and it is not unusual for university students to never open an actual book when doing research on an essay. Lyotard fears that the dominance of these data banks will sound the death knell of the era of the professor, as he or she is no more competent to hand down information to students than computers and has thus become obsolete (ibid., 87). This has not happened yet, though it certainly looms large as a technical possibility. On a broader scale, there is the very real danger that the state has become a form of 'noise', an unnecessary filter, serving to block too much communication in a global village where knowledge has become a valuable form of international commerce (ibid., 15–16). Lyotard mentions the problem of nations trying to regulate the data flowing through orbital satellites owned by large multinational corporations such as IBM. Who will watch these watchers?

Further, the central criterion for scientific research is now 'performativity', roughly economic utility or efficiency. Knowledge is produced to be sold. An equation of wealth, efficiency, and truth has thus established itself in our age. Research that doesn't pay off isn't performative and will slowly fall through the cracks (with destructive effects on university life). A 'move' or strategy in the game of education or science is good if it works better than other moves and costs the same or less than the others. Science is part of the capitalist system, part of a system whose goal is to maximize profits. Business enterprises and governments do not 'buy' the scientists, technicians, and the machines they need to discover the truth, but to augment their power (ibid., 76). Truth and justice will be more and more linked to performativity, an uncanny prediction on Lyotard's part given the obsession with fiscal responsibility and deficit slashing in conservative and centrist Western governments from the 1980s on. Performativity also affects higher education, as universities and colleges over the last generation have concentrated their efforts on offering programs that 'pay off' in jobs for their students, along with putting education institutions at the service of larger political and economic powers. The question put to educators and researchers today concerning their work is no longer, 'Is it true?', but 'What use is it?' or 'Can we sell it?' (ibid., 84).

Lyotard is concerned that the computerization of society could have nightmarish political effects, as computers represent a dream system of control, one that could act in a terrorist fashion. Yet if the public has free access to data banks, then this computerization could open up discussion on important societal issues (ibid., 107). Once again Lyotard's book seems to prophesy the dualistic nature of the Internet today: it hooks us into a global information network that allows for greater intrusions into our private lives, but at the same time opens up a whole world of useful information (not to mention sizable amounts of data trash).

Philosophically, Lyotard sees forms of discourse as governed by language games with varying sets of rules, echoing Wittgenstein. Remember how Wittgenstein speculated that the meaning of a word is determined by the way that it is used, which in turn depends on what language game is being played by those who use the word. For example, players in a rough football or hockey game might use very foul language they would never dream of using with their families or in a television interview. For Lyotard, to speak is to fight or play, the aim being to win the game. Language games have three qualities: (1) their rules

are determined by a sort of contract between their players; (2) moves that violate the rules of the game push the player outside the game or modify its nature; and (3) all statements made by players are 'moves' in the game (ibid., 22–3). Social bonds are made up of these language games. The game one plays is determined by one's social position. Of course, the language game Lyotard is especially concerned with in the postmodern condition is that of science.

For Lyotard, what counts as a valid statement (a 'good move') in a given form of discourse depends on what language game one is playing. Lyotard sees two basic types of discourse in the West: *traditional narrative discourse* (e.g., storytelling around the tribal campfire) and *scientific discourse* (e.g., the language physicists, biologists, and computer programmers use). Each has its own rules. Yet the narrative form is the dominant form of knowledge. Traditional storytelling implies a triple competence: of knowing how to speak, how to hear, and how to do things properly. These stories transmit a set of pragmatic rules about what holds society together (ibid., 40). They define who has the right to speak and act in it. For example, traditional myths help to define who is and isn't a member of a community, its place in the world, and the social practices the gods approve of or reject. Science, however, can't accept traditional fables and myths as serious discourse: talk of Zeus hurling lightning bolts or of the Tuatha de Danaan hiding beneath the bogs of Ireland with hordes of gold does not go very far with nuclear physicists. These are stories for children.

Lyotard argues that scientific knowledge is no more 'true' or necessary than traditional narratives: both are merely collections of statements within language games that are judged as good or bad by the internal rules of each game (ibid., 47). What makes a 'move' in science a good one? If the experts agree that it follows the rules of the game of science. In other words, there are no 'meta-rules' that justify all language games, all forms of discourse. This is just like board games: the rules of chess are irrelevant to checkers or Monopoly. One does not roll a pair of dice to determine how far a knight can move or use imaginary money to buy one's opponent's pawns. Similarly, the rules of tribal storytelling, at least *on the surface*, are irrelevant to nuclear physics or geology. We can't judge the relative values of traditional storytelling and modern scientific forms of discourse, even though the traditional form is more tolerant of science than science is of the traditional. Thus Lyotard is a relativist on this issue—we can only 'gaze in wonderment' at the variety of species in the zoo of discourse (ibid., 47). We cannot turn the zebras into horses or the hippos into elephants. We just have to accept their differences.

Part of the crisis of modern science is its loss of legitimacy. Once upon a time it could appeal to either the meta-narrative of the liberation of the human subject or that of the unity of knowledge. Now these have become quaint anachronisms in postmodern culture. Given the decline and fall of meta-narratives in the postmodern condition, the sciences are left to drift on the seas of culture without any metaphysical or moral anchor. They can't legitimate themselves purely by performativity (though this is their real goal), since this leaves open the question as to what or who all this performativity is for. Yet scientific discourse still has to legitimize itself. It does this by turning to the very narrative discourse it had previously discredited, describing its research as an epic tale to conquer ignorance and disease, to unlock the secrets of nature, or to eliminate poverty through better genetics or chemistry. Lyotard's *La condition postmoderne* is largely the story of how contemporary science has attempted and failed to find a new source of legitimacy that does not depend on tribal chanting around a campfire. Oddly enough, we find out at the end of Lyotard's book that the science he has been talking about throughout is *modern*, not postmodern. Yet he briefly opens up the Pandora's box of postmodern science towards the end, describing it as 'immanent to itself' (ibid., 89) and no longer interested in the drive for greater and greater performance. Postmodern science embraces quanta, fractals, chaos theory, paradoxes, discontinuity, and catastrophes, which Lyotard connects to the central principle of paralogy—

a playful and competitive conversation that stimulates the talkers to new ideas without their especially arriving at firm conclusions. He opposes this to modern science's drive to efficiency and desire to shut down traditional tale-telling. Little tales, not meta-narratives, are what drive the inventive spirit of postmodern science. Yet he leaves open the question whether it can legitimate itself by paralogy alone, for the innovations that sometimes come out of paralogical battles can be turned into useful aids in the drive towards performativity.

Lyotard on Aesthetic Postmodernism

In a later essay, 'Answering the Question: What Is Postmodernism?', included in the English translation of *The Postmodern Condition* (1984), Lyotard sees postmodernism as an extension of the avant-gardist theme in modernist art and literature. The essence of modernity is a shattering of traditional beliefs and a sense of the lack of reality of what's around us, along with the invention of other realities. This notion echoes Marx's famous claim that under capitalism 'all that's solid melts into air', that we come face to face with the economic nature of our relations with each other and the material power of the ruling class. Lyotard agrees with Marx's argument that capitalism has a corrosive effect on the metaphysical, religious, and political certainties of old, an effect that modern science helps to accentuate. The result is an open market where everything has exchange value, where everything can be bought and sold. When capital rules art and culture:

> Eclecticism is the degree zero of contemporary general culture: one listens to reggae, watches a western, eats McDonald's food for lunch and local cuisine for dinner, wears Paris perfume in Tokyo and 'retro' clothes in Hong Kong; knowledge is a matter for TV games. . . . Artists, gallery owners, critics, and public wallow together in the 'anything goes', and the epoch is one of slackening. But this realism of the 'anything goes' is in fact that of money; in the absence of aesthetic criteria, it remains possible and useful

to assess the value of works of art according to the profits they yield. Such realism accommodates all tendencies, just as capital accommodates all 'needs', providing that the tendencies and needs have purchasing power. (Lyotard, 1984: 76)

Lyotard's postmodern culture is a cosmopolitan one where money talks so loudly that it drowns out any discussion of aesthetic criteria for works of art. But what is postmodernism in this aesthetic sense? In the early twentieth century, artists and artistic movements attacked each other in quick succession: Cezanne attacked the Impressionists, Picasso attacked Cezanne, Duchamp and the Dadaists attacked Picasso, and so on. In the modernist framework, a work is 'modern' only if it's first 'post'-modern, attacking the modern. So aesthetic postmodernism is modernism 'in the nascent state', being born (ibid., 79). Lyotard thus sees artistic postmodernism as directly tied to artistic modernism, a somewhat different take on postmodernity than seen in *The Postmodern Condition*.

THE POST-INDUSTRIAL INFORMATION SOCIETY

Daniel Bell on the Coming of the Post-Industrial Society

One of the key props holding up the idea that we live in a distinctly postmodern culture is the notion that our political economy today is quite different from what it was 50 or 100 years ago. The Harvard-based sociologist Daniel Bell (1919–) argued in *The Coming of the Post-Industrial Society* (1973) that we have entered the beginnings of a new era economically and politically, at least in North America. This is the era of post-industrialism, where services taken in the broadest possible sense are replacing industrial production as the engine that drives our economy. Although some of his political predictions were overly optimistic, his economic forecast for the decades that followed the publication of his book turned out to be accurate.

So what is a post-industrial society? We can make sense of it best by comparing it with pre-industrial and industrial societies. Table 8.1 outlines the main differences among each of the three ideal types of societies Bell sees in history. Bell sees his idea of a post-industrial society as a logical construction of what 'might be' if the social trends current in the early 1970s continued (ibid., 14). His three ideal types do not exist in their pure form—even post-industrial societies still have plenty of factories, while industrial societies have computers and shopping malls. Yet we can distinguish these types of society in terms of what dominates their economies, even if fragments of earlier social types remain in some strength.

Bell divides society into three elements: its social structure (which includes its economic structure), its polity, and its culture (ibid., 12). These three elements, in Bell's view, are semi-independent and can conflict with each other. We can imagine them as the three points of a triangle, with the relations between them differing from society to society. For example, the culture of modern society is centred on the enhancement of the self, while its social structure is based on *economizing* the allocation of resources according to the principle of least cost and maximum output. These traits don't need to be causally connected. In studying post-industrial society, Bell is primarily interested in the social structure of that society and its consequences for political life.

Pre-industrial societies are organized around land as their principal resource, exploited through agriculture, mining, fishing, and logging. They focus on the extraction of raw materials and foodstuffs. The 'game' being played in such societies is against nature, as its inhabitants try to eke out a living from farms, forests, lakes, and seas. Its technology is human and animal muscle power, and being tied to nature, it's dependent on the elements much more than industrial society and its artificial environments. Pre-industrial societies are ruled by kings and nobles, who own most of the land and control its military forces. Their axial (basic) principle is tradition. Pre-industrial societies have large service classes, but these are made

Table 8.1 Bell's Typology of Types of Society

	Pre-Industrial Society	Industrial Society	Post-Industrial Society
Main Economic Activity	Agriculture, mining, fishing, timber	Manufacturing	Services
Resource	Land	Machines	Knowledge
Technology	Raw materials and muscle power	Energy (steam, coal, oil, gas, electricity)	Information
Game Played	Against nature	Against fabricated nature	Between people
Methodology	Common sense and experience	Empiricism and experimentation	Abstract theory, models, simulations
Leading Social Figures	Nobility (own land, control military)	Businessmen	Scientists, researchers, technical innovators
Common Occupations	Farmer, fisher, miner, unskilled worker	Semi-skilled worker	Technical work, retail, finance, entertainment
Basis of Power	Property in land (military force)	Property and political organization	Technical skill and political organization
Axial Principle	Preservation of tradition	Economic growth	Codifying and applying theoretical knowledge
Time Frame	Up to late 1700s	Late 1700s to 1950s	Late 1950s to present
Regions where each type exists (1973)	Asia, Africa, Latin America	Western Europe, Soviet Union, Japan	North America
Update on regions (2007)	Africa, parts of Asia	Russia, Eastern Europe, China, Pacific Rim	North America, Japan, Western Europe

Source: Adapted from Bell (1973: Tables 1-1 and 6-1).

up of personal servants like cooks, cleaners, gardeners, and tenant farmers. We can still see examples of pre-industrial societies in Africa and parts of Asia and Latin America.

Industrial society moves from agriculture to manufacturing as the backbone of its economy. It uses machines driven by various forms of energy—steam, coal, oil, electricity—to mass-produce products for the marketplace. Because of these new forms of energy and new forms of organization, it is far more productive than pre-industrial society. Yet the dark side of these new forms of organization, from Taylorism[1] in industry to bureaucracy in government, is the fact that human beings are treated as things (ibid., 127). Its leaders are businessmen (and in rare cases businesswomen), its most common occupation the semi-skilled worker. Power can be found in the class with the greatest property and ability to organize itself politically. Its axial principle is economic growth. Contemporary Russia, Eastern Europe, China, and parts of the Pacific Rim

today are industrial societies overlaid with post-industrial veneers.

Bell (ibid., 14) notes five distinctive characteristics of post-industrial society that involve some basic economic, social, and technological changes:

- a change from a goods manufacturing to a service-based economy;
- the dominance of a professional and technical class;
- the centrality of theoretical knowledge in innovation and political goal-setting;
- a future orientation based on the control of technology;
- the creation of new intellectual technologies to aid in decision-making.

The most important characteristic of the post-industrial society is that most people no longer work in agriculture or in factories, but in services. By services Bell means various economic activities:

transportation, recreation, entertainment, trade, finance, real estate, health, education, research, and government. Even as early as 1960, 53 per cent of the labour force in North America worked in services, as opposed to 39 per cent in industry and only 8 per cent in agriculture. The figures for Europe at the same time were 34 per cent in services, 38 per cent in industry, and 28 per cent in agriculture; in Asia, 71 per cent of the labour force still worked in agriculture (ibid., 16). By 1969, the percentage of American workers in services had risen to 61 per cent. In June 2005, service workers took up 78.7 per cent of the US economy, with manufacturing and construction the occupation of only 15.6 per cent of the workforce (www.bls.gov/news.release/empsit.nr0.htm). As one can see, Bell's prediction of a rising percentage of service workers in post-industrial societies like the US has certainly been proven true, with a crossing of the 80 per cent barrier in sight. Canadian statistics follow the US closely: in June 2005, 75 per cent of the labour force worked in services, with 25 per cent in all forms of 'goods production', including agriculture (www.statcan.ca/english/Subjects/Labour/LFS/lfs-en.htm). For the majority of North Americans, the factory and the farm are places visited only on sightseeing tours or jaunts through the country to buy a bushel of apples or to sample the newest vintage from a local winery.

Part of the rise in services is in the growing numbers of workers in the professional and technical class. But their influence is felt beyond their numbers, as their control of technological innovation and theoretical knowledge gives them both economic power and significant input into political decision-making. Home base for this class is universities and research institutes. Bell argues that the very nature of the knowledge sought in post-industrial society has changed. Increasingly, theoretical, not empirical, knowledge that can be codified in symbols is emphasized (ibid., 20). It's easy to see what he means in the field of current technology: computers work thanks to a symbolic digital code made up of a multitude of ones and zeroes, and computers are *the* way knowledge is stored and communicated in post-industrial soci-

eties. According to *Forbes* magazine, the richest person in America over the last 10 years has been Bill Gates, head of Microsoft Corporation, which has a virtual stranglehold on computer operating system software, along with producing a wide array of other computer programs. So if we see computer software as theoretical knowledge, then once again Bell's book is prophetic. Of course, he also means by 'theoretical knowledge' basic scientific research in physics, chemistry, and biology not especially related to empirical experiments and business payoffs, as it would have been in an industrial society. Yet theoretical knowledge does pay off in more public policy control of the economy thanks to computer-aided economics. Overall, the centres of post-industrial society will be the university and privately funded research institutions, where human capital developed through education will supplant physical capital, such as land and machines, as the economy's most valuable asset.

Bell thinks that post-industrial societies can plan and control their technological growth, unlike industrial societies, where technological leaps were sporadic, at the whim of clever inventors like Thomas Edison and Alexander Graham Bell. Lastly, post-industrial societies create new intellectual technologies that substitute problem-solving rules for intuitive judgements (ibid., 29). Modern economics and game theory both rely on the notion of rationality to predict the decisions of large, complex groups of people. They hope to order mass society through such predictions, though Bell admits that human irrationality has caused them to stumble and falter as intellectual technologies (ibid., 33). In any case, the game in post-industrial societies is between people, not against nature (whether in its raw or fabricated versions). This is to be expected of a social structure dominated by the provision of services, not raw materials or manufactured goods. We buy CDs for the music or computer software on them, not to own the plastic; we pay good money for mere sounds (e.g., live concerts), images (e.g., films), electrical impulses (e.g., cable TV), experiences (e.g., travel), well-being (e.g., health), and theoretical knowledge (e.g., education), none of which in themselves leave us with any material goods.

The ideal post-industrial society is more concerned with the quality of life than the quantity of goods produced. This quality is guaranteed with growing access across all social classes to health, education, entertainment, and the arts (ibid., 127). As a result, more and more people travel, buy real estate and luxury goods, go to restaurants, stay at hotels, and attend sporting events, along with using a bevy of other services. As people use these services they need to employ more people, thus pushing society towards a service economy. This is exactly the way things have gone in North America, Western Europe, and Japan over the last three decades.

We can see the differences between the three types of society as based on differences in cosmologies or world views. Pre-industrial societies are caught up in an endless struggle to wring a living from nature, not always succeeding. Along came industrial society, which tried to substitute a technical order for a natural one, relying on the rational control of production to overcome the vagaries of nature. Finally, in post-industrial society reality is no longer either nature or techniques for reworking nature but the social world itself. Society becomes a social construction based on the 'reciprocal consciousness of self and other' (ibid., 488). Nature and physical objects will fade away as people take control of their social life. This is the utopian side of Bell's thought, one that pictures a world still far in the future.

As for the political side of post-industrialism, Bell argues that technical skill gained through education will become the basis of power. Now we have a mixture of three factors that act as the basis for power: property, technical skill, and political organization (ibid., 361). Yet as knowledge and planning become more important to the economy, military, and political institutions, the power of the professional and technical class will increase. Bell divides this class into four 'estates': the scientific, technological, administrative, and cultural. Their ethos is not economic self-interest so much as a sense of professionalism, an ethic of

service. Despite their high status, however, there's no intrinsic reason that this class will work together to gain political power or will develop a collective economic self-interest. In fact, given the great concern with the self in modern culture, it's more than likely that distinct groups within the technocratic and professional class will pursue separate interests, e.g., teachers will squabble with government bureaucrats, while entertainment stars see themselves as having nothing in common with university researchers. In fact, Bell argues that specific 'situses' (locations), such as government bureaucracies, universities, hospitals, and the military, will have greater cohesiveness than the whole professional/technocratic class in post-industrial society.

Writing shortly after the turbulent late sixties, with its wave of student protests against the Vietnam War and the more general flowering of the counterculture (including the beginnings of women's liberation), Bell sees an 'adversary culture' in place which is partially at odds with the rise of post-industrialism. Tied to the adversary culture is a resistance to bureaucratization. Bureaucracy, with its impersonal rules, was once an ally of freedom; yet in a world caught in its iron cage, its mechanical rules start to look stultifying (ibid., 119). Bureaucracies are the home turf of much of the professional classes. Given this fact, the central conflict of post-industrial societies is no longer the battle of capital versus labour but that between professionals and the less skilled masses (ibid., 129).

This leads Bell into a critique of corporate culture. Industrial societies have three important distinguishing features: the power of large corporations, the imprint of machines on work, and class conflict between workers and capitalists (ibid., 160). In industrial societies corporations are basically economizing machines whose goal is to produce goods as efficiently as possible in order to maximize their profits. The rhythm of work is mechanical in such societies, even in offices, where the same economizing principles apply. The man in the grey suit working in his generic cubicle from nine to five according to a set, rigid corporate policy is the standard for industrial society. The economizing mode of thinking emphasizes the optimal use of resources and the minimization of wasted time and effort. It seeks to connect means to ends in a rational manner and to convince people to work according to a methodology aimed at increasing productivity as much as possible.

Bell talks about the 'new criticism' of corporate culture, which argues that corporations have made industrial countries dirtier, uglier, and more polluted because they fail to take into account the social costs of their actions (ibid., 272–4). The costs of these 'externalities'—roads, sewage systems, pollution cleanup, and health care—are borne principally by either the state or individual citizens. Yet corporations in industrial society don't assign a value to things such as clean air, beautiful scenery, or peace and quiet—these are 'free goods' beyond the pale of the economizing frame of mind (ibid., 279). Added to this is the fact that most North Americans resent paying taxes—they are seen as pure costs, with the schools, hospitals, libraries, and parks they buy just magically appearing out of the ether. This is also part of the mindset of corporate culture. In a post-industrial society Bell hopes the corporation will become a sociological institution where people are no longer treated as things and that takes its social obligations seriously. He hoped that the corporation would take more seriously employees' job satisfaction, the employment of minorities, the great gap in pay between average workers and corporate chiefs, the environment, the community, and moral issues. Against the idea that corporations are only responsible to their shareholders, Bell argues that corporations today are not really private property institutions since those truly concerned with their fate are their employees, not their largely absentee stockholders (ibid., 294). Unfortunately, most corporations today have not become the sociological institutions Bell hoped for, even if many of them have hired more minorities and pay some attention to the environment. The corporation of the early third millennium is still profit-oriented and must be compelled by the state to pay attention to such things as pollution and the exploitation of workers.

Bell's rather sunny prognosis of the nature of post-industrial society is open to a number of criticisms. First of all, it's crystal clear that even with the growing importance of the professional and technical class in post-industrial societies, we're still talking about capitalism, where a small minority of people control most of the economy, where capitalists make a profit by exploiting workers (at least in Marx's technical sense of extracting surplus value from their labour). A shift from an industrial to a service economy doesn't especially change the fundamental economic and political power of property owners: information may be a valuable commodity, but it's still money that buys it. However, we can perhaps get around this criticism by using Manuel Castells's distinction between modes of production, which have to do with how economic surpluses are allocated, and modes of development, which centre on the resources worked on by a given society and the technology it uses to develop those resources (Castells, 2000a: 14). So capitalism and socialism (or what Castells calls 'statism', i.e., domination by the state) are modes of production, while agrarian, industrial, and post-industrial societies (which Castells calls 'informational') are modes of development. Castells argues that the modes of production and development in a society are different kettles of fish. An industrial society can be either capitalist or socialist—America in the early 1940s was a capitalist society, the Soviet Union was statist and socialist, and Japan was statist and mildly fascist. Similarly, post-industrial societies can be either capitalist or statist, though the great majority of them are the former. Thus, there may be no contradiction in saying that a post-industrial society can be capitalist, as most industrial societies have been. Yet as we've seen, Bell thinks that education and technical skill are the basis for power in post-industrial societies. But money still talks and corporate property is an important source of political power. Bell doesn't clearly separate means of production from means of development in his analysis of post-industrialism.

Second, even a generation after Bell's *The Coming of the Post-Industrial Society*, most Western societies have stalled in improving their provision of affordable health care and education to all social classes, and thus have failed to develop this important aspect of post-industrialism. Societies like Britain and Canada have questioned their own deeply entrenched state-managed health-care systems, while America has yet to develop one. Conservative governments in the 1980s and 1990s withdrew from active support of health, education, and scientific research (except, one might note, military-related research), as more and more of these essential services have become privately funded. However, there's no denying that they remain important social needs for Western societies.

Third, how can the culture of a post-industrial society remain aloof from its social structure, as Bell claims? Aren't the two inextricably linked? Doesn't a post-industrial economy produce a postmodern culture? Conversely, can we imagine an information-dominated economy that *does not* produce forms of culture centred on computers, digital information, and audiovisual electronics? In the world today there are no such cultures. We'll take up these criticisms when we consider the thought of Frederic Jameson. First, however, we turn to Manuel Castells's vision of the network society.

MANUEL CASTELLS: THE NETWORK SOCIETY AND THE INFORMATION AGE

Manuel Castells (1942–) is a sociology professor at the University of California at Berkeley. Born in Madrid, Spain, he is best known for his mammoth three-volume study of the general state of things today, *The Information Age: Economy, Society, and Culture* (1996–8). We'll be concentrating on the revised edition of the first volume of this work, *The Rise of Network Society* (2000). Castells isn't, strictly speaking, a 'postmodernist'. In fact, he claims he has no desire to add to the mountain of already existing postmodern theory. Nonetheless, he clearly argues for an updated version of Daniel Bell's thesis that we live in a new age, one that Bell called post-industrial and Castells calls informational. Castells describes

the political economy of postmodern culture, acting more as its champion than its critic. In his tendency to use arcane language, his occasional slippage into functionalist terminology, and his desire to build a vast theoretical system covering all aspects of society, he is the Talcott Parsons of the digital age.

His overall position is that since the 1970s we've entered a qualitatively different type of society and a new epoch, the Information Age. He agrees with Bell that there are three ages of man (to borrow a line from Shakespeare): the Agricultural Age, in which nature dominated culture for thousands of years; the Industrial Age, where mass production allowed culture to dominate nature; and our own Information Age, where human culture is so free from its natural constraints that we feel compelled to recreate nature artificially in the environmental movement, national parks, zoos, and so on (Castells, 2000a: 508). In the first age, increased surpluses came from working harder or finding more natural resources. In the second, productivity was improved with new energy sources. In the Information Age economic improvement comes from the application of new information technologies and the generation of new (and a bit of old) knowledge by means of them.

For Castells, as we have seen, a mode of production is the structural principle whereby economic surpluses are controlled, appropriated, and used (Castells, 2000b: 8). Over the last century the two most common modes of production have been capitalism, which presently dominates the world, and statism, a catch-all category that includes Nazi Germany, imperial Japan, and Soviet Russia. In the former, private capitalists reap the rewards of economic surpluses; in the latter, the state does. Modes of development are 'the technological arrangements through which humans act upon matter (nature), upon themselves, and upon other humans' (ibid., 9). The mode of development is how workers and managers use technologies to produce things of economic value. As just mentioned, there are three modes of development in history: the agricultural, the industrial, and the informational. Unlike Marx, Castells analytically separates the development of modern technology from the development of capitalism, though he recognizes that the two are intimately linked. Yet he points out that there have been a few examples of statist industrial societies, e.g., the USSR and Japan in the 1930s and early 1940s.

Social structure for Castells is a combination of relations of production and consumption, human experience, power relations, and how these are expressed in culture. Production is how human beings appropriate and transform nature to produce a product, which is then consumed, generating a cash surplus for various people. This leads, as Marx thought, to various social relations of production, until recently, expressed in terms of social classes. Experience is the action of human beings upon themselves, and is expressed in our biological and cultural identities, especially in family life and the unequal relations between the sexes. Power is the attempt to impose one's will on others through the actual or potential use of violence, whether real or symbolic. The state has tended to monopolize power, though Castells also mentions Foucault's idea of the 'micro-physics' of power found in smaller institutions such as schools, hospitals, and prisons. Culture is about the symbolic interaction of human actors based on their place in the hierarchies of production, consumption, and power and on their experience. This interaction leads to the formation of ethnic, national, sexual, and other identities, usually crystallizing in specific territories (Castells, 2000a: 14–15).

Despite his insistence that the modes of production and development are distinct ideal types, as we can see from Table 8.2 they tend to pair up. Feudal social structures were paired to an agri-

cultural mode of development; industrial societies were usually capitalist but sometimes statist; all the informational-mode societies today are capitalist or semi-capitalist. In fact, Castells sees as one of the great political events of recent history the failure of the Soviet Union to become an informational society, which he implies, among other factors, led to its collapse.

For Castells the greatest event in modern history was the informational revolution that started in the 1970s and accelerated in the 1980s and 1990s. The centre of this revolution is the development of new information-processing technologies—basically, the personal computer—along with the Internet, new technologies in communications, optics, and genetics. The Information Age is defined by a technological paradigm powered by microelectronics-based information and communications technologies and genetic engineering. This paradigm speaks a universal digital language. As a result there is a conflict between our local, particular identities—as English, French, Canadian, Indian—and the abstract, universal identities promoted by modern technology. This creates a situation where our societies are increasingly structured around a bipolar dialectic of the Net and the self (ibid., 3). In other words, although our bodies live in specific places and cultures, our minds—thanks to computers and television—exist in a global space of instant information.

What is technology? It's 'the use of scientific knowledge to specify ways of doing things in a reproducible manner' (Castells, 2000b: 8). Thus, technological systems use tools, rules, and procedures to apply scientific knowledge to a task in a

Table 8.2 Castells's Modes of Production and Development

	Mode of Development		
Mode of Production	Agricultural	Industrial	Informational
Feudal	Europe in the Middle Ages	None	None
Statist (Fascist, Communist, etc.)	[Ancient societies; not discussed by Castells]	Nazi Germany, Imperial Japan, Soviet Union	None really (though China today to a degree)
Capitalist	[Third World in early twentieth century; not discussed by Castells]	Most of Western world from nineteenth century to late 1970s	All advanced societies from late 1970s on (US, UK, Canada, Japan)

way that can be repeated over and over. Modes of development are defined by their central technological paradigms and by their principles of performance. Castells argues against technological determinism, despite the fact that it seems so obvious to us today that technology constantly moves our society forward. He argues that we can't give free-thinking 1970s Silicon Valley entrepreneurs like Bill Gates and Steve Jobs all the credit for the personal computer revolution: the state also had a large hand in its development (e.g., the Internet's direct ancestor was ARAPNET, a US military communication network designed to survive a nuclear attack). In general, the state plays a key role in stalling, unleashing, or leading technological change (Castells, 2000a: 12). Castells notes how China was a leading innovator in technology until about 1400 and then stalled when various emperors decided to hold off disseminating new technologies out of fear of the social changes that would result. The opposite extreme is that of Japan in the late nineteenth and early twentieth centuries, where a dynamic series of governments actively promoted technological changes, even hiring foreign teachers and firms to modernize the country's schools and infrastructure. Thus, nothing is inevitable in the advance of technology: it all depends on how it's used by those in power.

Castells calls this new mode of development an 'informational' instead of 'information' society because all societies depend on information and knowledge to develop: think of the invention of the railway, the steamship, and the telegraph in the middle of the nineteenth century. What's new about the informational or network society—Castells is quite fuzzy on the distinction, though he implies that the network society is a *type* of informational society—is the fact that 'information generation, processing and transmission become the fundamental sources of productivity and power because of new technological conditions emerging in this historical period' (ibid., 21). In it we see a positive feedback effect between technical knowledge and the creation of new machines to store and process that knowledge. In simple terms, technical knowledge is not used just

to improve the manufacture of goods, as in the industrial age, but to improve the machines and techniques through which knowledge and information flow—computers, televisions, music players, optical and medical devices. Of course, this means we live in a digital world. As Lyotard predicted, more and more information must be either computer-coded, or fail to be even recognized as usable or genuine. This leads to a close relation between the creation and manipulation of symbols and the production and distribution of goods—what large manufacturer or retail chain doesn't use computers to manage its buying and selling? Castells concludes rather optimistically that for the first time in history 'the human mind is a direct productive force, not just a decisive element in the production system' (ibid., 31). We'll have more to say about his cheerleading for globalized capitalism later.

This new society is shaped by the interests and logic of advanced capitalism without being reducible to it in any simple fashion (ibid., 13). All major societies today are both informational and capitalist, yet they retain a large degree of cultural diversity. Compare China and Brazil, or Scotland and Japan: these are all informational societies, but they are hardly carbon copies of each other. The interface between the capitalist mode of production and the informational mode of development is the fact that financial capital—banks, stock traders, currency speculators, and other large-scale investors—relies on information-processing machines and the data they provide to generate profits. In this sense financial capital, big industries, and high technology are interdependent, the three corners of the triangle of the postmodern political economy (ibid., 504). In short, then, the overhaul of capitalism over the last generation has proceeded hand in hand with the development of computer networks and modern telecommunications.

Castells argues that the restructuring of capitalism from the 1970s to today is distinct from the rise of the informational or network society, though they tightly parallel each other. This *informational capitalism* has been the most powerful force channelling and shaping the new informational paradigm. It has four general aims (ibid., 19):

1. a deepened desire to seek profits, often at the expense of organized labour;
2. enhanced productivity thanks to the new information-processing machines;
3. globalized production and markets;
4. state support for its efforts to increase productivity and global trade.

Specifically, this restructuring involved such things as more flexible management systems, a decentralization of corporate structures, an attack on the power of unions, the deregulation of markets in goods and services, the gradual undoing of the welfare state, the globalization of trade, and a tighter integration of the world financial system (ibid., 1–2). Capitalism rules the planet today, even if a few countries like China still adhere to ideologies that seem to be at odds with it. This new brand of capitalism is both global and structured around networks, notably financial networks such as banks, stock exchanges, currency traders, and the futures market. The global financial market does not exist in specific spaces and operates at the speed of light (the speed of electronic impulses). As a result, this mode of production is capitalism in its purest sense, an 'endless search for money by money and the production of commodities by commodities' (ibid., 505).

Money today is almost entirely independent from production, escaping into vast electronic networks that even corporate managers do not entirely understand. These financial networks work only in part according to a market logic. Castells theorizes that instant telecommunications in themselves produce 'information turbulences', just as in chaos theory the flapping of a butterfly's wings in China produces a hurricane in the Caribbean. A good example of the way this new financial system works is currency exchange rates. On 1 January 2000, one Canadian dollar could buy 69 US cents; on 14 February 2007 it could buy 86 US cents. This shift has almost nothing to do with changes in production or productivity lev-

els in the Canadian and US economies, but was the product of speculation and variations in political perception by currency traders.

The new form of society that dominates the Information Age is the network society. Whether all informational societies are also network societies is difficult to judge from Castells's work—in *The Network Society* he says that the latter is a subcategory of the former, while in a summary article from 2000 he wants to abandon the expression 'Information Society' (Castells, 2000b: 10). In any case, the network society is clearly the social form typical of the Information Age. In fact, Castells argues that networks, being flexible, adaptable, and able to evolve, are a 'superior morphology for human action' (ibid., 15). What is a network? A set of interconnected nodes; a node is point where a curve (of interaction or communication) intersects itself. The distance between two or more nodes is shorter than that between levels in a vertically integrated hierarchy like an old-fashioned business before the Information Age. Network-based social structures are dynamic and open, and are thus good instruments for capitalist innovation, globalization, and a decentralized processing of people's values and moods (Castells, 2000a: 501–2). Yet they have a dark side: their binary logic switches some people and places on, others off. If a node ceases to perform its function (note the echo of Parsons), it is phased out, just like dead cells in a biological organism. For Castells, networks are neutral as to values: 'They can equally kiss or kill: nothing personal' (ibid., 16). Castells is not terribly critical of this amorality in his work.

The network society has a number of material foundations:

1. Information is its raw material, with technologies acting on it just as nineteenth-century factory machines worked on iron, cotton, or wood.
2. The new technologies are pervasive, affecting all human efforts.
3. These information technologies use a networking logic that strongly penalizes those outside the networks.

4. The new information technology paradigm is based on flexibility.
5. There is a growing convergence of specific technologies into a highly integrated system, e.g., digital satellite television relies on the integration of digital processors and actual television receivers (ibid., 70–1).

The nodes of information networks are equivalent to the nodes of the industrial paradigm, the factories that mass-produced goods. The information nodes, however, produce more information. Of course, industrial production still takes place. Yet for Castells it no longer defines the societies we live in, and to succeed must be managed by computers.

Network society has created a new global economy with three central features: it is *informational*—productivity and competitiveness come from a firm's ability to generate knowledge and process information; it is *global*—finances, trade, production, consumption, skilled labour, and science are all de-nationalized and globalized; and it is *networked*, i.e., based on competition between business networks (Castells, 2000b: 10). The new unit of production is not the individual company but the business project itself. The capitalist enterprise becomes a node in a global network of financial flows. The new economy as a whole is an intricate weave of global networks of money, management, and technical know-how.

The process of globalization did not just happen by itself: it was pushed by elites in both wealthy and poor nations for a variety of both noble and selfish reasons, in the case of the Third World often by leaders who expected to profit personally by the deregulation, privatization, and free trade that was part of the globalizing process. Yet Castells is certain these changes can't be easily undone: if you disconnect your country from the global network, it's simply bypassed as a dysfunctional node. This decoupling from the global economy would come at a staggering cost— short-term economic devastation; long-term closing of access to sources of growth (Castells, 2000a: 147). Once a country has anted up to the global economy, it's in the game for good. To use an everyday example, imagine a major retail chain refusing to accept bank or credit cards: this would cripple their sales, if not ruin the entire business.

Not surprisingly, the new global economy is run by *network enterprises*. These have a number of features: they have abandoned the mechanical assembly-line style of mass production in favour of flexible production; they have moved away from the traditional corporate model of rigid vertical hierarchies, in some cases emphasizing the creative potential of smaller units within a corporate network; and they have embraced 'Toyotism'—Japanese management methods such as 'just-in-time' delivery, workers' involvement in production decisions, teamwork on the shop floor connected to rewards for effectiveness, 'total quality control' aimed at reducing product defects to zero, and a flatter management hierarchy (ibid., 166–9). Added to these are a greater emphasis on customer satisfaction, increased contacts with suppliers, and a continual retraining of employees. These organizational changes are possible thanks largely to the computer-based information networks within and between companies. There was a quantum leap in information technology in the early 1990s involving the digitization of communications, the development of broadband transmission, and a rapid increase in computer performance. All this new technology helped to make the network enterprise a sociological reality.

So what exactly *is* a network enterprise? It is 'that specific form of enterprise whose system of means is constituted by the intersection of segments of autonomous systems and goals' (ibid., 187). In other words, it's a firm that is willing to systematically co-operate both within and outside its hierarchy to increase productivity. Castells says that the network enterprise's job is to transform signals into commodities by processing knowledge (ibid., 188). But is our economy essentially or simply about the transformation of signals into goods? Can we describe a gold mine or a pizza parlour or a car dealership as doing this? Even if he's only giving us a Weberian ideal type here, Castells may be once again exaggerating to score some theoretical points. Which brings us back to Daniel Bell's question: are we living in a post-industrial economy with fundamentally new features?

Castells looks at the nature of work and employment structures to answer this question. The information revolution has *not* resulted in a massive spike in the unemployment rate, as many feared. Instead, it has led to new types of jobs and a more diversified employment structure, along with the growing phenomenon of the flex-timer. Part-time and contract work form an ever-increasing part of the economy, with women filling many of these new temporary positions. Castells makes two basic distinctions between types of labour in the network society: first, between networked and switched-off workers; second, between self-programmable workers committed to the goals of their network and generic workers who are disposable and mainly interested in their own survival. These distinctions have served to increase social inequality over the last few decades, the networked self-programmable types forming an elite, the switched-off generic workers falling into the reserve army of the semi-employed or semi-employable.

Castells argues that Bell had things only partly right. The new type of society that emerged in the last few decades of the twentieth century isn't post-industrial but informational, with a different mix of agricultural, industrial, and service jobs in each country. From 1920 to 1970, the G-7 countries—the US, UK, France, Germany, Italy, Japan, and Canada—became post-agricultural economies, with England leading the way early in the century. But the real shift in employment was from agriculture to services and construction, not away from industry. Later, in the 1970–90 period, these countries became post-industrial in their employment structures, but at quite different rates. This led to two different models of the informational society: the *service economy model* of the US, UK, and Canada, which have largely deindustrialized; and the *industrial production model*, as found in Japan and Germany, where a high level of industrial employment remains.

Castells believes that post-industrial theorists such as Daniel Bell and Alain Touraine overlook the diversity of things that count as 'services', the revolutionary nature of the new information technologies, and the cultural and historical diversity of advanced societies. Yet having said this, Castells admits that Bell's post-industrial theory was basically correct, though he could not have predicted the personal computer revolution and the Internet. Castells offers a detailed list of the common features of informational societies that echoes Bell's own predictions (ibid., 244):

- the phasing out of agricultural employment;
- a decline in the number of manufacturing jobs;
- the rise in and diversification of services;
- an increase in the number of managerial, professional, and technical jobs (these now make up about 17 per cent of the workforce in Japan);
- the stability of the retail trade and the solidification of a white-collar proletariat of clerks and sales workers;
- an increase in the number of workers in the upper and lower pay levels;
- an upgrading of the skills needed for a given type of employment, with more and more jobs requiring an advanced education (i.e., the undergraduate university degree becomes the equivalent of the high school diploma of 50 years ago).

As a result of these changes the social relations between capital and labour have changed, mostly to capital's benefit. Capital is global and networked, while labour is largely local. Capital exists in a hyperspace of pure circulation (ibid., 505–6), in what Castells calls the space of flows and in timeless time. Labour still works in specific places, still punches the clock, counting off the minutes until quitting time.

Castells on Media, Space, Time, and Politics

A key issue in the Information Age is how new technologies affect culture and everyday life. Thanks to the minimum of effort taken to use it, television became the most popular medium of the late twentieth century, ending the typographic mind. It is the cultural epicentre of our societies, being so seductive and easy to use. Castells quotes a study showing that the average American used 6.43 hours of media per day, over half of it television, while spending only a meagre 14 minutes in interpersonal interaction (ibid., 361). Only work takes up more of our time. Yet the effects of mass media are very modest, making one wonder about the value of the billions of dollars spent on advertising each year. Castells argues that there is no true mass culture, as such critical theorists as Adorno and Marcuse have claimed. Yet television and the media in general still frame the language we use to communicate, with messages sent outside the media disappearing from the collective public mind rather quickly.

The real change in media of late is the segmenting of messages and the diversification of audiences. Walkmans and MP3 players allow people to wander about the town lost in their private audio environments; cable television has exploded to 100 or more channels, catering to specialized tastes from gays to history buffs, from science fiction fans to gardeners; VCRs allow for flexible viewing and ad zapping; and radio stations have become more and more specialized, focusing on limited demographics. The share of the US television audience controlled by the major networks has dropped from 90 per cent in 1980 to 55 per cent at the end of the century. Yet all this diversification and customization hasn't stopped the growth of larger and larger multimedia oligopolies such as AOL/Time Warner/CNN, Viacom/CBS/MTV, and Disney/ABC, to mention the main ones in America. So television has become both more diverse and segmented and more commercialized and centrally controlled at the same time.

The hot new medium is the Internet, with its ephemeral symbolic environment and interactive audiences. Hypertext allows this interactivity, providing Net surfers with a flexible, inclusive universe in which to while away the hours. Given the diversification of radio and TV programming and the arrival of the Internet, Castells concludes that McLuhan's global village, with its one-way communication, has faded away, and we live instead in

'customized cottages globally produced and locally distributed' (ibid., 370). The medium is no longer the message; instead, the message is the medium, by which Castells seems to mean that media programs are tailored to suit specific groups of people with specific cultures, values, or tastes. But to deny the obvious effects of technologies like TV, cellphones, and computers on our perceptions and sense ratios—which is what McLuhan meant when he said 'the medium is the message'—seems a tad silly, even given the obvious flowering of diversity in the media in the Information Age. An increase in the number of messages doesn't especially alter the nature of the medium transmitting them.

Castells *does* defend an important thesis in postmodern theory: the idea that our reality is essentially virtual. Cultures are constituted by communication processes, which involve the production and consumption of signs (as the structuralists said). Thus, all communication—whether computer code or a simple 'hello'—is symbolic. Reality has always been virtual since it has always been perceived through symbols. When critics of electronic media 'argue that the new symbolic environment does not represent "reality"', they implicitly refer to an absurdly primitive notion of "uncoded" real experience that never existed. All realities are communicated through symbols' (ibid., 404). This leads Castells to conclude that we live in a culture of real virtuality, not virtual reality. Real virtuality is a system where reality itself—our material and symbolic existences—is entirely captured and immersed in virtual images, in a world of make-believe. As a result, these screen images *are* experience, not just a communication of experience. And from our society's point of view, electronically based communication *is* communication. Castells's position is remarkably similar to that of Jean Baudrillard, who we'll visit in the next chapter. But it suffers from one remarkable fault: it doesn't follow from the fact that linguistic communication involves symbols that *all* reality is symbolic and thus virtual. Direct experience of non-human nature—howling cats, leafy trees, and babbling brooks—isn't in itself symbolic, and is certainly distinguishable from watching a television show about cats or trees or watercourses. Also, we can have direct experience of other people that doesn't involve symbolic communication, as in the act of falling in love. In other words, all of reality is *not* virtual, despite Castells's view of the symbolic nature of all communication. Whether it's becoming *more* virtual is another question.

Space is an expression of society. It's not a photocopy of society—it *is* society, as well as being crystallized time (ibid., 441). Social practices always take place within one or more spaces. The culture of real virtuality shortens the time it takes to communicate to the speed of light and disembodies local places from their geo-historical meanings. We might have pictures of the Grand Canyon, the Eiffel Tower, and the Great Wall of China on our computer, using them as electronic wallpaper without knowing exactly where they are or their geological or historical significance. In the Information Age, we live in a space of flows and a timeless time. Money and information flow through global networks constantly, ignoring real places. They travel in this space of flows, a virtual space. In this space social relations happen without the actors being in the same place, geographically speaking. Yet it still requires three material supports:

- the actual circuits on which these flows take place—computer, telecommunication, and transportation systems;
- the nodes and hubs where real things happen, e.g., the Mayo Clinic in Rochester, Minnesota, or the New York Stock Exchange;
- the places where the managerial elite actually live.

The space of flows is further anchored in real physical places. The privileged spatial form of the new global economy is the *mega-city*. Castells counts 13 such cities with 10 million or more population in 1992: Buenos Aires, Rio de Janeiro, São Paulo, Mexico City, New York, Los Angeles, Bombay (Mumbai), Calcutta, Seoul, Beijing, Shanghai, Tokyo, and Osaka.[2] To this list we can add such important economic and cultural centres as London, Paris, Chicago, Frankfurt, Milan, Singapore, and Moscow (and, in the Canadian context, Toronto), even though they don't make the cut population-wise. These mega-cities are major nodes of trade and finance, media, information flows, politics, and the symbolic capacity to create images (ibid., 434). Yet just as they are connected to global networks both physically (through transportation and communication links) and socially, they are often disconnected from their own hinterlands. The Chinese peasant would find the glittering shops of downtown Shanghai more foreign than would the visiting Japanese or American corporate chieftain. The mega-city acts like a tornado, sucking into its environs the best and the worst: innovators and agitators, the rich and the destitute. Yet despite the social problems that agglomerate in their midst, mega-cities are the key nodal points in the space of flows that dominates the Information Age, the centres of economic and technological dynamism and of cultural and political innovation. They are the future.

In the Information Age, time is sped up and de-sequenced. Past, present, and future mix together in the culture of real virtuality, where all events seem to be simultaneous. Modern computers and telecommunications allow for light-speed financial transactions, flexible work schedules, a denial of death through its over-representation in film and TV, instant wars, and virtual simulations of historical events. The control of reproduction and the increase in the average duration of life have disrupted traditional biological and social rhythms. Busy women put off having children until middle age, while men retire in their fifties with a third of their lives still ahead of them. Wars are fought using machines that look remarkably like video-game consoles and are beamed directly to our living rooms via satellite TV in real time. It's easy enough to understand what Castells is driving at—within a generation we have gone in formal communication from writing letters where we expect a reply in several weeks to writing e-mails where we expect the reply within hours, if not less.[3] The bottleneck for information flow is no longer technological but human: how quickly does one get around to answering e-mail or looking over the results of an Internet search? The dominant functions in network society take place in a global space of flows and in timeless time (where information travels at the speed of light), while the less important functions—from garbage collection to pottery—take place in real places according to biological and clock time.

As a result of modern communication technologies, primarily the Internet, traditional 'senders' of information such as religions and moral authorities have become secularized and lost their super-human status. When everything is on line, the world loses some of its enchantment, and when television reporters speak to the whole world from caves in Afghanistan and planes fly across the Atlantic in hours, one's native soil doesn't seem so special any more. This leads to a crisis over personal and collective identity. This crisis causes a clustering of many around traditional or primal identities such as tribe, race, territory, or religion. 'In a world of global flows of wealth, power, and images, the search for identity, collective or individual, ascribed or constructed, becomes the fundamental source of social meaning' (ibid., 3). In such a world religious fundamentalism gains momentum, as seen in the spectacular rise of Islamic terrorism in the years after Castells's trilogy was published. When the Net switches off the self, 'the self, individual or collective, constructs its meaning without global, instrumental reference' (ibid., 24). People cling to whatever solid ground they can find as they're swept along by the rivers of timeless time and the ever-shifting space of flows. Rejecting universalism, they exclude the excluders.

On top of the return of identity politics is the fact that *official* politics has become all about image, thus personalizing leadership. Although Castells doesn't mention this, the story of US presidential politics in the television age makes this clear, from Richard Nixon's dripping brow and shifty eyes in his 1960 television debate with John

F. Kennedy to George W. Bush's staged photo-ops aboard aircraft carriers and in front of cheering soldiers. The same, of course, has been true in Canada, where Pierre Trudeau epitomized the charismatic leader who maintained a symbiotic love-hate relationship with the media over his long career as Prime Minister. From the late 1960s to the early 1980s, Trudeau used television effectively, upstaging clumsier and less media-savvy Conservatives such as Robert Stanfield and Joe Clark.

People get almost all their information about political leaders and parties from the media, thus bringing to the fore trivial stories about sex and corruption instead of policy differences. The state has its sovereignty questioned by global flows of wealth and information, its legitimacy questioned by scandals and broken promises. According to Castells (who was no doubt thinking more about Europe than the US at the time), the state adapts by sharing sovereignty with other governments and international organizations like the UN and the WTO, and by devolving powers to provinces, states, or national regions within federal unions such as Quebec, Scotland, and Catalonia. It becomes a 'network state', sharing power with other network states through international treaties like the Kyoto Accord and with local and regional governments (Castells, 2000b: 14). If you can't beat them, join them.

Castells's picture of the Information Age is certainly comprehensive. Yet it's not without its faults. First, it returns in part to the difficult terminology and abstract system-building of the functionalists, squeezing out the individual human actor in favour of sweeping descriptions of social structure and processes. Second, he exaggerates the degree to which the informational paradigm dominates our entire world—there are simply too many exceptions to trends such as the networking of labour, real virtuality, the space of flows, and timeless time to see them as anything more than interesting ideal types with some application to the real world. Third, and most troubling, is the creeping conservatism in his view of the network society. We've already seen that he is quite certain that the new global economy cannot be opted out of without severe penalties. He says baldly that there is 'little chance of social change' within network society. This can only be accomplished by either rejecting entirely the logic of networks (he calls this the formation of 'cultural communes'), or by creating alternate networks based on alternative values such as human rights and ecology (ibid., 21–2).

Yet anti-globalization groups have won major support all across the Western world, staging major protests in Seattle in 1999 at the World Trade Organization meeting, in Quebec City in 2001 at the Summit of the Americas, and at numerous other summits of political and economic leaders in Europe and elsewhere. These groups would beg to differ with Castells that social change is a dead issue in our society. Reversing Marx, Castells argues that there's no such thing as a global capitalist class but instead a wide collection of human-flesh capitalists, capital-owning groups like pension funds, and the faceless capitalist of global financial flows (Castells, 2000a: 505). He suggests in sunny tones that more and more workers own stocks today, hinting at a world historical merger between capital and labour. Admittedly, Castells does mention in passing the growing inequalities in network societies, and tells us early on that his theory is meant to be exploratory and value-free. But the ideological sympathy for informational capitalism lurking just below the surface of much of his work makes Castells's impressive survey of the state of the world today something of a sociological Trojan Horse for those with money and power—though a big and shiny one all the same.

STUDY QUESTIONS

1. Explain how Bart MacLean's life typifies the aspects of postmodern culture discussed in this chapter and the next. Which theorists can you find hints of in his story?
2. How does Lyotard define postmodernity? What are the two major meta-narratives he sees in modern history? Do we still believe in either one?
3. What does Lyotard predict will happen to the postmodern university? Is he right?
4. According to Bell, what are the three main types of societies in human history? Discuss the economy, technology, and social structure of each.
5. What are the main elements of post-industrial society? What evidence did Bell offer that we are living in one now? Have his predictions concerning post-industrialism turned out to be true?
6. What is Bell's critique of corporate culture? Can we find a similar critique in Castells's work?
7. What does Castells mean by 'mode of production' and 'mode of development'? How does his typology of societies differ from Bell's?
8. How does Castells define the Information Age and the network society? Is the network society still capitalist? If so, how so?
9. What does Castells mean by the 'culture of real virtuality'? Give some examples.
10. What sort of space and time dominate Castells's Information Age? Provide illustrations of each.

SHORT BIBLIOGRAPHY

Baudrillard, Jean. 1984. *Simulacra and Simulation*, trans. Sheila Faria Glaser. Ann Arbor: University of Michigan Press.

———. 2001. 'Symbolic Exchange and Death', trans. Charles Levin, in Mark Poster, ed., *Jean Baudrillard: Selected Writings*. Stanford, Calif.: Stanford University Press.

Bell, Daniel. 1973. *The Coming of Post-Industrial Society: A Venture in Social Forecasting*. New York: Basic Books.

Castells, Manuel. 2000a. *The Rise of the Network Society*, 2nd edn. Oxford: Blackwell. (Vol. 1 of *The Information Age: Economy, Society and Culture*.)

————. 2000b. 'Materials for an Exploratory Theory of the Network Society', *British Journal of Sociology* 51, 1: 5–24.

Giddens, Anthony. 1991. *Modernity and Self-Identity: Self and Society in the Late Modern Age*. Stanford, Calif.: Stanford University Press.

Harvey, David. 1989. *The Condition of Postmodernity: An Enquiry into the Origins of Cultural Change*. Oxford: Blackwell.

Jameson, Frederic. 1984. 'Foreword' to Jean-François Lyotard, *The Postmodern Condition*, trans. Geoff Bennington and Brian Massumi. Minneapolis: University of Minnesota Press.

Lyotard, Jean-François. 1979. *La condition postmoderne*. Paris: Minuit.

————. 1984. 'Answering the Question: What Is Postmodernism?', trans. Régis Durand, in Lyotard, *The Postmodern Condition*, trans. Geoff Bennington and Brian Massumi. Minneapolis: University of Minnesota Press.

Powell, Jim, and Joel Lee. 1998. *Postmodernism for Beginners*. New York: Writers and Readers.

Rosenau, Pauline Marie. 1992. *Post-Modernism and the Social Sciences*. Princeton, NJ: Princeton University Press.

Smart, Barry. 2005. 'Postmodernism', in Austin Harrington, ed., *Modern Social Theory*. Oxford: Oxford University Press.

Strinati, Dominic. 1995. *An Introduction to Theories of Popular Culture*. London: Routledge.

CHAPTER 9 POSTMODERNISM: TIME, SPACE, AND CULTURE

In the previous chapter we explored that part of the territory of postmodern theory having to do with politics, economics, and communications. Now we forge on into new lands, the provinces of postmodernism to do with changes in the structure of space and time and in the nature of the popular culture. Frederic Jameson takes a Marxist perspective, arguing that postmodernism is nothing more than the cultural logic of late capitalism. He explores not only postmodern theory, but also art, architecture, and pop culture. We will also have a brief look at Terry Eagleton's similar critique of postmodern culture. Jean Baudrillard, perhaps the best-known theorist of postmodernity, believed that with the density of modern communication and the omnipresence of electronically mediated entertainment, we now inhabit a desert of the real. Following up on the previous two sections, we will consider the basic elements of postmodern popular culture, then examine Baudrillard's short work, *The Evil Demon of Images*, and finally see how postmodern culture is reflected in a number of films. In the final section on postmodernism we will look at a number of postmodern attitudes to space and time: David Harvey's argument that postmodernity is afflicted with a rather severe case of time/space compression; Charles Jencks's description of the main elements of postmodern architecture; Jameson's analysis of the 'hyperspace' of postmodern architecture; and finally, Albert Borgmann's picture of the celebrative postmodern city. We start with a prominent critic of postmodern culture, Frederic Jameson.

THE CULTURAL LOGIC OF LATE CAPITALISM

Postmodernism, the Highest Stage of Capitalism

Frederic Jameson (1934–) is one of the main critics of postmodern culture and the social and economic structures that support it. Jameson is an enthusiastic Marxist who has tried to understand the nature of contemporary culture through an updated version of Marx's historical materialism. In *Postmodernism, or, The Cultural Logic of Late Capitalism* (1991), Jameson views postmodernism as the first specifically North American style. This style proclaims that it's looking for the moment in time when everything changed, when the modernization process is complete and nature has receded to the margins (Jameson, 1991: ix). Its place has been taken by culture, the new nature for the postmodern person. Television and computers have replaced horses and ploughs as means of production and communication; a trip to the shopping mall has replaced a walk in the woods as an amusement for our idle hours. Jameson is sarcastic about the whole process of cultural change. The success of postmodernism deserves to be written in best-seller format: it's a mystery why a truly motley crew of strange bedfellows ran to embrace postmodernism until we look at the philosophical-social function of the concept (ibid., xii). He concedes that postmodernism gives intellectuals new and exciting tasks, and creates a sense of a revolutionary era. Yet its coming is at best 'a very modest or mild apocalypse, the merest sea breeze'. What do these postmodern intellectuals and artists *really* do? Their ideological job is to co-ordinate new forms of practice and new social habits with new forms of economic production and organization created by global capitalism. (ibid., xiv). In other words, their job is to make sure that the culture we live in suits its new economic base, to create postmodern people to suit the late capitalist socio-economic structures all around us.

So postmodernism is nothing more than a reflex or modification of a new stage in the history of capitalism. We don't live in a 'post-industrial society', but in a late capitalist industrial society that still contains the avatars of its earlier incarnations (ibid., xii). There are still factories, wage labour, and a social divide between capitalists and workers. But now the division of labour has been internationalized, and the system is pushed forward by automation and computerization into a state where it looks like something 'post'-industrial, if not post-capitalist. Yet it is neither. Jameson borrows from Ernest Mandel (1975) the idea that capitalism has gone through three stages, each of which is powered by a distinctive form of energy:

Table 9.1 Mandel's Stages of Capitalism

Form of Capitalism	Time Period	Principal Technology
Market	1780s–1880s	Steam
Monopoly/ Imperialistic	1890s–1940s	Electricity, petroleum
Multinational (Late)	Late 1940s– present	Electronics, nuclear power

Market capitalism was driven by steam engines and trade between industrial nations. This changed under monopoly capitalism, as the imperial powers exploited their colonies in Africa, Asia, and Latin America, their machines now being driven by electricity and gasoline. Finally, under late or multinational capitalism, electronics and nuclear energy drive technological change, helping to create a Third Machine Age. In the previous age, F.T. Marinetti and the Futurists got excited over the appearance of automobiles, airplanes, and machine guns, while the architect Le Corbusier built utopian buildings he called 'machines for living in'. The utopian energies of the Second Age of machines have subsided. Our favourite machines are now the television and the computer, which, as Jameson points out, are machines of reproduction, not production. Yet we shouldn't get too hung up on the newness of contemporary technology, which is mesmerizing and fascinating not in itself but insofar as it offers a sort of 'representational shorthand' for coming to understand the nature of the decentred global network of power and control that exists within Mandel's third stage of capital (ibid., 37–8). When did this third age start? Its preparation can be traced back to the post-war shortage of consumer goods and the conversion of war factories to their production in the 1950s. Its true beginnings, however, can be found in the psychic break with the past in the 1960s, with the flowering of the counterculture, rock 'n' roll music, the generation gap, and mature consumer society.

So what does Jameson think of late capitalism? Well, capitalism as a whole is at the same time the best and worst thing that has ever happened to the human race (ibid., 47). Like Marx, he seems to think that the development of capitalism is something we all have to suffer through until something better comes along. Yet the main point of postmodernism, politically speaking, is:

> that this whole global, yet American, postmodern culture is the internal and superstructural expression of a whole new wave of American military and economic domination throughout the world: in this sense, as throughout class history, the underside of culture is blood, torture, death, and terror. (Ibid., 5)

From the napalmed jungles of Vietnam to the bloody sands of Iraq, American imperialism and multinational capitalism have worked hand in hand. Jameson is suspicious of theories of the coming of a distinct post-industrial or postmodern society as theoretical Trojan Horses justifying late capitalism as a kinder, gentler system than its predecessors. But late capitalism is still driven by industrial production and class struggle, despite ideological smog created by pro-postmodern theorists. Jameson sees no possibility of neutrality on the issue of the value of postmodern culture: every position on its value is 'also at one and the same time, and *necessarily*, an implicitly or explicitly political stance on the nature of multinational capitalism today' (ibid., 3). Late capitalism says, in effect, 'you're either with us or against us.'

One of the core events in late capitalism is the commodification of the world, notably of culture. As the Frankfurt School first realized, the culture industries try to commodify all of 'aesthetic production', churning out books, films, and pieces of art like cans of soup to be sold to the masses. A commodified thing is something we can assign an exchange value to. Jameson takes the position that unlike under the modernist movement in the arts in the early twentieth century, in postmodern culture art objects have become commodities through and through. Late capitalism feels a particular urgency in producing fresh waves of new and improved goods, a process that assigns a structural role to 'aesthetic innovation and experimentation' (ibid., 5). To do so it tries to colonize what had previously been left uncommodified— nature and the unconscious. National parks are full to the hilt on summer weekends; consumers buy New Age CDs with whale chants and the soothing sounds of flowing water; and sex is used to sell everything from toothpaste to vodka. These pre-capitalist enclaves of nature and the unconscious were once 'extraterritorial and Archimedean footholds for critical effectivity', as in Romantic poetry and critical theory (ibid., 49). Now they're used to sell soap.

Because Jameson sees Marxism as an activist philosophy, he is concerned that the semi-autonomy of culture under modernism has been destroyed by late capitalism. Culture is now just another form of capitalist production. Capitalism today has become a vast bog of quicksand, swallowing up all critical impulses: even if a critic is a

partial success, he or she only creates one or more critical commodities for sale in the marketplace. Yet, thankfully for Jameson, not all of cultural production today is postmodern, even if it's the force field in which it all operates.

Modern vs Postmodern Culture

Postmodernism proclaims the end of ideology, history, art, man, or whatever to express its sense of a radical break with the past. This started when the impulse of high modernism was coming to an end in the arts, as a series of modernist movements ran out of steam in the 1950s and 1960s: abstract expressionism in the art, existentialism in philosophy, representation in literature, and auteurs like Hitchcock and Fellini in film (ibid., 1). A new generation saw the work of Picasso, Joyce, and Stravinsky as dead classics, not living rebellions. Modernism came to an end about the same time that multinational capitalism was approaching its heyday. When a new global consumer capitalism came to dominate the Western world, a new type of culture was needed to reflect this system: postmodernism. Jameson outlines five features of postmodern culture:

- a new depthlessness in the art, film, and other aesthetic products of the era;
- a weakening of the sense of history;
- a new emotional ground tone based on the waning of affect;
- a new technology connected to a new economic world system;
- a new political mission for art in the world space of multinational capital (ibid., 6).

Jameson uses several specific examples to illustrate these five points. As for the depthlessness of postmodern art, he mentions two pieces of modern art that make his point in a contrastive way. Van Gogh's painting of a pair of peasant shoes can be understood via some quick hermeneutics as pointing to a world of stark rural poverty and backbreaking work: it's a symptom of a greater reality (ibid., 7–8). And that trumpet blast opening up modernism in painting, Edvard Munch's *The Scream* (1893), is a classic expression of the modernist themes of alienation, fragmentation, and anxiety (ibid., 11). The screamer, surrounded by undulating waves of colour and indifferent bystanders, expresses his inner torment to the outside world. Yet postmodern culture repudiates a variety of 'depth models' in art, film, and popular culture. Where there was once surface and depth, there is now only an outside, a shiny surface.

Jameson outlines five depth models abandoned by postmodern culture:

1. The hermeneutical model of the outside and inside of a text, with the latter reached by good interpretation.
2. The dialectical model of essence and appearance found in Hegel and Marx.
3. The Freudian model of the manifest and latent meaning of dreams, jokes, and other manifestations of the unconscious mind.
4. The existential model of authentic and inauthentic action, connected to the theory of alienation, as found in Heidegger and Sartre.
5. The semiotic opposition between signifier and signified found in the structuralist linguistics of Saussure and his followers (ibid., 12).

The subject is now killed off or decentred, and with it the modernist idea of individual artistic style. The anxiety and alienation we see in a modernist painting like *The Scream* are foreign to the world of postmodern culture: the alienation of the self has been replaced by its fragmentation. Jameson worries that postmodern culture's liberation from the older *anomie* of the centred but alienated subject may be not just a liberation from anxiety but a freedom from every other kind of feeling as well, as the self becomes a patchwork of free-floating, impersonal feelings without a clear focus (ibid., 16). What Jameson seems to be pointing to here is the idea that the greatness of modernist culture was its obsession with the possible meaninglessness of the individual's life, something we get a strong sense of in existentialist works like

Sartre's play *No Exit* and Albert Camus's novel, *The Outsider*. Its works explored the depths of this threatening emptiness. Yet postmodernism, the ally of a globalized consumer capitalism, replaces the dualities found in these five depth models with shifting practices, discourses, complex surfaces of intertextuality, and literary play (ibid., 12). Successful postmodern theorists such as Foucault have their critical capacity paralyzed by this refusal to plumb the depths of social life, leading to a situation where the impulses of revolt found in Marxism and critical theory are now seen as 'trivial and vain' (ibid., 6).

For Jameson a key feature of postmodern art and architecture is its flatness and lack of depth, and thus its superficiality. What Jameson calls 'postmodern art' celebrates the mass-produced commodities it emulates. He compares Andy Warhol's painting *Diamond Dust Shoes* (1980) to Van Gogh's painting *A Pair of Shoes*. Warhol's work shows us a random collection of dead objects, mere commodity fetishes. Indeed, Warhol's entire opus centres on commodity fetishism: his paintings of Coke bottles and Campbell soup cans, his coloured photos of celebrities like Marilyn Monroe and Elvis Presley and of political figures like Che Guevara and Mao Zedong all celebrate the surfaces of mass production without any real criticism of the art object as a commodity. The revolutionary Che becomes just another pretty face on a canvas or T-shirt. Jameson doesn't see any critical depth in Warhol's work, which makes him the artist par excellence of postmodern culture.

So what replaces the search for depth meaning characteristic of modernist art? The fragmentation of the subject in postmodern culture leads to the dominance of pastiche, the gluing and cobbling together of elements of several things into some sort of artistic object, whether a painting, piece of music, film, or novel. It's the imitation of another style, but without the critical energy of parody, which presents a skewed version of what it's attacking to ridicule it. In other words, pastiche for Jameson is a sort of 'blank parody', a parody without laughter, a parody without any sense of a healthy form of culture we long to return to. Now, with the collapse of the modernist ideology of style, 'the producers of culture have nowhere to turn, but to the past: the imitation of dead styles, speech through all the masks and voices stored up in the imaginary museum of a now global culture' (ibid., 17–18). Postmodern culture cannibalizes all styles to feed the consumer's appetite for an endless series of new images and pseudo-events.

Yet Jameson overstates his case here for the decline and fall of parody, as the last two decades have seen many old-fashioned parodies at least in film and television, from the TV cartoon show *The Simpsons*, most of its episodes ridiculing other aspects of popular culture, to mockumentaries such as *This is Spinal Tap* (1984) and darker political satires like *Wag the Dog* (1997). Pastiche and the recycling associated with it, however, are powerful forces in postmodern art and pop culture, for example, in the dozens of remakes of older films by Hollywood from the early 1990s to today.[1] A more solidly grounded argument made by Jameson is his repetition of Guy Debord's claim that we live in a society of the spectacle, where the image itself has become the ultimate commodity. This reinforces the logic of late capitalism, which, after all, is about selling false images of things on a global scale through advertising. We are surrounded by what Baudrillard calls 'simulacra', copies of things that don't exist. Our addiction to film, television, and computer images transforms the past into a series of visual images and computer texts, which Jameson thinks effectively abolishes any sense that we can make social and political changes in the future (ibid., 46).

Jameson discusses historical nostalgia films to make his point about the waning of our sense of history, mentioning George Lucas's *American Graffiti* (1973) and Lawrence Kasdan's *Body Heat* (1981). He argues that such films try to appropriate a missing past by recreating it as a simulacrum of what it actually was. Yet we've lost the ability to actively experience history thanks to the concentration on images and the time compression of late capitalism: every act of consumption is simultaneously the death of one desire and the birth of another. Instead, we're 'condemned to seek His-

tory by way of our own pop images and simulacra of that history, which itself remains forever out of reach' (ibid., 25). Of course, film and television drive this forgetting of the real past and its reconstruction as simulations, the classic case being American war films such as *The Deer Hunter* (1978), *Platoon* (1986), *Glory* (1989), *Black Hawk Down* (2001), and *We Were Soldiers* (2002). These simulacra of the past, while aspiring to realism, inevitably promote the notion of the glory of the American soldier and the greatness of *Pax Americana*.[2]

Jameson's postmodern culture is one where depthless but technologically sophisticated commodities are embraced by consumers who lack any depth of feeling, sense of authenticity, or awareness of history except by means of the images fed them by mass media. The *culture* of postmodernism is a reflection of social changes and ideological needs of a new *economic* structure, late or multinational capitalism, with Marxism its privileged mode of analysis (Jameson, 1984: xiii). If we are skeptical towards meta-narratives, it's because such skepticism serves the needs of consumer society.

Eagleton on Postmodernity

In his essay 'Capitalism, Modernism and Postmodernism', which appeared in *New Left Review* (1985), the British Marxist critic Terry Eagleton (1943–) echoes Jameson's critique of postmodernism, adding a few unique flourishes of his own. For Eagleton, postmodern culture is once again the product of late capitalism. It turns all artistic creation into commodity production while parodying the avant-garde art of the modernists. Art and society are integrated into each other as the modernists hoped, but this time as depthless, styleless, dehistoricized surfaces divorced from any sense of artistic authenticity (Eagleton, 1985: 60). In other words, art objects become consumer products. Just as art is commodified, commodities become art objects— think of Warhol's paintings of soup cans. Eagleton sees art and commodities in postmodern society as swirling in a feedback loop where they lend one another legitimacy and allure. For example, think of the power of the corporate icon today, two decades after Eagleton's essay: students of the new millennium proudly wear the logos of major corporations on their caps and shirts as expressions of a fashionable hipness, a habit that students of the previous generation would have looked upon with horror.

Modernism in the arts was born in the early stages of commodity culture, yet it resisted that culture, holding out 'by the skin of its teeth against those social forces which would degrade it to an exchangeable commodity' (ibid., 67). Modernist art objects like Marcel Duchamp's dressed-up urinal may have been fetishes, but at least they resisted becoming exchangeable commodities. The modernist artist or writer didn't sell out to capitalism. Yet modernism eventually failed because just as it bracketed off the social world to remain critical of bourgeois culture, it cut itself off from the social forces at work in late capitalism. It stayed free from the bourgeois order, protesting against it aesthetically. Yet postmodern artists, theorists, and *literati* are more than willing to play ball with late capitalism. Rather than getting stuck in some limbo between art or ideas and material reality, postmodernists admit that their productions are commodities for sale in the late capitalist marketplace. They sell out with gusto.

So far Eagleton is speaking the same language as Jameson. Yet he makes some interesting epistemological and psychological observations that expand on Jameson's work. Postmodern art echoes modernism in that it doesn't reflect reality—it is anti-representational—but this time because there's no reality or truth to reflect except that which is *already* an image, a spectacle, a simulacrum (ibid., 62). The truest art in postmodern culture is that which reflects commodities (we are back to Warhol's soup cans). The same goes for theoretical speculation: post-structuralist criticisms of reason and truth go hand in hand with corporate power, which is all about manipulating desires, not seeking deep meanings. Not surpris-

ingly, classical models of truth 'are increasingly out of favour in a society where what matters is whether you deliver the commercial or rhetorical goods', for the goal of both post-structuralist theorists and boards of directors is not truth but performativity, not reason but power (ibid., 63). Eagleton, however, is scornful of Lyotard's hopes that paralogical scientific experiments will somehow save the day: these noodlings don't threaten the massive power of modern capitalism.

Modernism stands outside postmodern commodity culture. It refuses to turn away from the angst of the screamer, from the dream of authenticity found in existentialist literature. It's stubborn, for it:

> obstinately refuses to abandon the struggle for meaning. It is still agonizingly caught up in metaphysical depth and wretchedness, still able to experience psychic fragmentation and social alienation as spiritually wounding, and so embarrassingly enmortgaged to the very bourgeois humanism it seeks to subvert. Postmodernism, confidently post-metaphysical, has outlived all fantasy of interiority, that pathological itch to scratch surfaces for concealed depths. (Ibid., 69–70)

As with Jameson, Eagleton sees postmodernism as abandoning the depth models so important to the great modernists from Nietzsche and Freud to Picasso and Sartre. Postmodernism is all about surfaces, being a sort of strip-mall philosophy.

As for the self under postmodernism, it's dispersed and slightly schizophrenic, as suits a consumerism with nothing left to struggle against other than illusions like objective ethics, the class struggle, or Freud's Oedipus complex. The irony is that the post-structuralists saw the unified self or subject as a core concept of contemporary bourgeois ideology and thus in urgent need of deconstruction, whereas in truth late capitalism had already done a pretty good job of tearing it apart. Eagleton thinks that the originality of postmodern theory on the self is vastly overrated, for the contemporary subject is already:

less the strenuous monadic agent of an earlier phase of capitalist ideology than a dispersed, decentred network of libidinal attachments, emptied of ethical substance and psychical interiority, the ephemeral function of this or that act of consumption, media experience, sexual relationship, trend or fashion. The 'unified subject' looms up in this light as more and more of a shibboleth or straw target, a hangover from an older liberal epoch of capitalism, before technology and consumerism scattered our bodies to the winds as so many bits and pieces of reified technique, appetite, mechanical operations or reflex of desire. (Ibid., 71)

Late capitalism has turned us into bundles of desires and appetites to be fulfilled by consumption. Our consumer selves don't need to be deconstructed by postmodern theorists: Nietzsche and Freud have already done the job on the psychological level, while consumerism finished the job on the level of practical everyday action. For Eagleton, like Jameson, postmodern culture is the ideological expression of late or consumer capitalism. Given the power of the latter on our lives, it is no wonder that postmodernism is such a cultural force today.

We now turn from Marxist criticisms of postmodern culture to the ex-Marxist Jean Baudrillard's theory of the simulacrum and hyperreality, which seems to both critique and celebrate postmodernism at the same time.

POSTMODERN SOCIETY AS THE DESERT OF THE REAL

As we saw in Chapter 3, Jean Baudrillard (1929–2007) was a French theorist and cultural analyst who started his academic life as a Marxist sociologist interested in consumer society. He described how what was formerly a society of production became, after World War II, one of consumption. Becoming slowly dissatisfied with Marxism, he went on to incorporate structuralism and semiology into his work, seeing the objects we consume as a system of signs or code embedded in structures of consumption and leisure. From the late 1970s on, Baudrillard turned away in a large degree from Marxism and structuralism to post-structuralism. He became the high priest of postmodern culture, being inspired at first by the Canadian thinker Marshall McLuhan's communications theory. He was fascinated by how media affect our perception of reality and the world. He agreed with McLuhan that in late industrial societies the medium is the message. McLuhan argued that it is not *what* the media tell us and show us that is important, but their physical and psychological effects on us. Baudrillard argued that today medium and message are in the process of merging to the point where our lives are becoming media-created simulations of reality. He concludes that in the postmodern media-laden condition, we experience something called 'the death of the real': we live our lives in the realm of hyperreality, connecting more and more deeply to television sitcoms, music videos, virtual reality games, or Disneyland, things that simulate a reality that doesn't exist. This notion connects with his earlier work. In his critique of Marx's dialectical materialism Baudrillard argues that our culture is witnessing the death of production and of the reality of labour, as consumerism and the welfare state have turned work from a vital necessity for survival into a general system of social control tied to the need to consume.

The Precession of Simulacra and the Desert of the Real

The central notions in Baudrillard's mature social theory are the 'simulacrum' and 'hyperreality'. To understand these, we turn first to his important essay 'The Precession of Simulacra' (1978)—from *Simulacra and Simulation* (1984 [1981]). He starts by recounting the feat of imperial map-makers in a story by Jorge Luis Borges who make a map so large and detailed that it covers the whole empire, existing in a one-to-one relationship with the territory underlying it. It is a perfect replica of the empire, so perfect that it precedes the territory it maps. After a while the map begins to fray and tatter, the citizens of the empire mourning its loss, having long taken the map—the simulacrum of the empire—for the real empire. Under the map the real territory has turned into a desert, a 'desert of the real'. In its place, a *simulacrum* of reality—the frayed mega-map—is all that's left.

The term 'simulacrum' goes all the way back to Plato, who used it to describe a false copy of something. In general, a simulacrum is an image or copy of something that closely resembles its original yet seems unreal. Baudrillard built his whole post-1970s theory of media effects and culture around his own notion of the simulacrum. He argues that in a postmodern culture dominated by TV, films, news media, and the Internet, the whole idea of a true or false copy of something has been destroyed: all we have now are *simulations* of reality.

Indeed, in some cases these simulations *precede* the reality they are supposedly simulating: the TV family becomes a model for 'real' families, or news reporters create the news they are supposedly just reporting on by playing up a minor political or sexual scandal. In our culture we take 'maps' of reality—television, film, the Internet—as more real than our actual lives; these 'simulacra' or hyperreal copies precede our lives. Our television 'friends' seem more alive to us than their flesh-and-blood equivalents. We communicate by e-mail and relate to video-game characters like Lara Croft better than to our own friends and family. We drive on freeways to shopping malls full of identical chain stores and products, watch television shows about film directors and actors, go to films about television production, vote for ex-Hollywood actors for president or governor. Is he really an actor? Or a politician? It doesn't matter in postmodern culture: they are both just simulations. We get nervous and edgy if we're away too long from our computers, our e-mail accounts, our cellphones. Now the *real* empire lies in tatters, while the hyperreal map of it is clear and bright. We have entered an era where third-order simulacra dominate our lives, where the image has lost any connection to real things.

Baudrillard talks about the murderous power of images and how they were once linked to an absolute belief in God. Religion and language both made wagers on the reality of representation, in the first case that images of the divine referred to a real deity, in the second that words referred to an objective reality outside language. They believed that a sign 'could refer to the depth of meaning, that a sign could be exchanged for meaning and that something could guarantee this exchange—God, of course' (Baudrillard, 1984 [1981]: 5). But what if God was only a simulation of human hopes and fears? If so, then the whole system becomes without foundation and weightless, a giant simulacrum, no longer guaranteeing the truth of representation.

Representation starts with the utopian idea that the sign and the real are equivalent, while simulation negates the reality of an image or sign. When language or art tries to represent the world, it rejects simulations or fakes as cases of false representation. A fake Picasso isn't real—what's more, the artist producing it is a criminal if he or she tries to pass it off as real. Yet simulation absorbs all so-called 'fakes' into its order of things, since something can't be fake where there's no reality to compare it to: think of reality TV shows that create highly artificial situations to supposedly get in touch with 'real' social life. To understand the historical progression of representation from the attempt to capture reality to simulations of things that don't exist, Baudrillard lays out four phases of the image. Our culture has seen images:

- as the *reflection* of a basic reality (a good appearance of the image, like a landscape painting from the early modern period);
- as a *mask* and *perversion* of a basic reality (an evil appearance of the image, like a masked highway robber or a fake *Mona Lisa*);
- as a mask of the *absence* of a basic reality (a form of trickery or sorcery, as in *The Wizard of Oz*);
- as bearing no relation to any reality at all: a pure simulacrum (like a computer game about space battles or a television reality show) (ibid., 6).

The key move here is from cultures that contain fakes and counterfeits of reality to ones that try to disguise the fact that there's no reality there at all. It's the move from stage 2 to 3, from 'a theology of truth and secrecy' to one of simulacra and simulation, to one where God is dead and there's no divine guarantee of the difference between the true and the false. Baudrillard gives several examples of how modern culture produces simulacra that try to keep alive a sense of reality after it's long gone. In 1971 the Philippines government returned the recently discovered primitive Tasaday people back to their original state despite the fact that their contact with modern culture had turned them into mere 'mummies' of a primitive culture. They now exist in a 'glass coffin' as a simulation of a hunter-gatherer forest tribe (ibid., 8). Baudrillard also mentions the effort to exhume the actual mummy of the Egyptian pharaoh Ramses II to prevent it from rotting in a museum. And in France the Lascaux caves, covered with 17,000-year-old paintings of animals, were closed to the public and reconstructed 500 metres away as a simulation of the original. Baudrillard predicts that like Borges's map of the empire, the public will over time forget the original caves and take their simulation as the 'real' ones.

Disneyland, Capital, and Hyperreality

Baudrillard sees Disneyland as the perfect model of the nature of cultural simulation today. By an extraordinary coincidence, this deep-frozen infantile world was created by a man who is himself now in cryogenic sleep: Walt Disney (ibid., 12).[3] Disney himself has only a simulated life, to match the simulated social life found in his California creation Disneyland, a third-order simulation (see below) of all of America. Disneyland conceals the fact that all of 'real' America is Disneyland. In a typically outrageous attempt to provoke us, Baudrillard claims that Disneyland is presented to us as an imaginary place to make us believe that the rest is real, when in fact all of Los Angeles and the America surrounding it are no longer real, but hyperreal simulations. 'It is no longer a question of a false representation of reality (ideology), but of concealing the fact that the real is no longer real, and thus of saving the reality principle' (ibid.,

12–13). The imaginary world of Disneyland is neither true nor false. Its elements—the Enchanted Village, the Magic Mountain, and Marine World—encircle LA as imaginary stations that feed it reality energy. Los Angeles is as a city of endless, unreal circulation, a 'town of incredible proportions but without space, without dimensions', and so it needs this imaginary place made up of childhood signals and faked phantasms to supply power to its sympathetic nervous system (ibid., 13). LA is one big pan shot, a huge power plant energized by cinema studios. Of course, Disneyland is only one of the many hyperreal simulations feeding us reality energy. What do you do when you go home at night: watch the TV news? rent a DVD of a Hollywood film at the local video store? surf the web? play a computer game? These are all simulations that hide the fact that what they represent is little more than a desert of the real. Every day of our lives we go to Disneyland.

Why all these attempts to feed us reality energy? Postmodern capitalism (my term, not Baudrillard's) fears the contagious hyperreality it finds all around us, so it tries to confuse the reality and desire principles, to make us think that our artificially created desires are real human needs. The only weapon of power, of capital, is to re-inject realness everywhere using the talk of crisis and desire: 'Take your desires for reality!' is its ultimate slogan (ibid., 22). Capitalism, as Marx observed, turned all that's solid into air. Baudrillard picks this up, arguing that it destroys every human goal and the distinctions between truth and falsity and good and evil while it makes everything equivalent to and exchangeable for everything else (Baudrillard elsewhere calls this the 'law of equivalence', the idea that commodities are 'equivalent' to a given amount of money). Capitalism destroyed a sense of the use value of things by turning everything into commodities with exchange values. Baudrillard makes the metaphysical argument that the hysteria of mass production today is aimed at a return to a representation of the real because capitalism knows it is threatened by simulation and needs to remanufacture artificial social, political, and economic stakes (ibid.). But it's too late: the hyperreal cat is already out of the bag. The production of goods and commodities today no longer makes any sense on its own. 'What every society looks for in continuing to produce, and to overproduce, is to restore the real that escapes it. That is why today this "material" production is that of the hyperreal itself' (ibid., 23). In simple language, our society no longer produces only what we need to survive or to make our lives moderately comfortable. It produces things no one needs and then stimulates our non-existent desires for these things. At the same time capitalist society convinces us that all this production proves that our desires for consumer products must be real, and thus the economic system that makes them is needed and morally justified.

Baudrillard also talks about a 1971 PBS reality-show experiment with the Loud family, which consisted of 300 hours of non-stop broadcasting of this family's daily life, later parodied in the films The Truman Show (1998) and Ed TV (1999). Baudrillard finds a perverse joy in the microscopic simulation of this middle-class California family's life that transformed the real into the hyperreal. Baudrillard says that Mrs Loud, the ideal heroine of the American way of life, acted like a martyr of old when she was chosen to be glorified and die under the fiery glare of the studio lights as the Loud family self-destructed on air (ibid., 28). The television lens cut through ordinary reality like a laser, killing it. The result was a sort of sacrificial process, a religious drama of a mass society. One would imagine that he would say the same thing about more recent reality shows such as Survivor (several versions from 2000) and Joe Millionaire (2003). On them real people—well, usually attractive want-to-be actors, models, and singers— sacrifice their time and dignity to become media celebrities, to become simulations of the rich and famous. Most watch these shows because they present us with simulacra of real personal conflicts, emotional traumas, and sexual transgressions. Yet they are controlled, managed, and channelled by casting agents, producers, and marketing executives. They are hyperreal.

Baudrillard argues that Foucault's image of the Panopticon, with its universal surveillance by prison guards and their surrogates in schools, hospitals, and asylums, no longer applies. We should forget Foucault because the eye of TV is not an absolute gaze of malevolent control, for this assumes we live in an objective space (like a prison) and that the gaze is all-powerful and despotic. It isn't. We can turn the TV eye off, unlike the prisoners in Foucault's Panopticon, even if we don't bother. We have moved from a society dominated by Foucault's sense of panoptic surveillance to one of deterrence. There is no longer an implied command to submit to a universal gaze. Now the media tell us 'YOU are the model! . . . YOU are information, you are the social, you are the event . . .' (ibid., 29). We're no longer being watched by malevolent keepers; rather, we have become part of the show. We're witnessing the end of panoptic space and the end of Guy Debord's idea of the spectacular. We are no longer in the society of spectacle, with its alienation of the audience from power and authentic needs. Baudrillard credits McLuhan as having uttered the first great formula of our age: 'the medium is the message.' But now there is no longer any concrete medium we can put our finger on: everything is intangible, diffuse, and diffracted throughout the real, and it cannot be said that the message is distorted by it. Restaurants and bars are festooned with TV screens; news reporters stop men and women on the street for their 10-second opinions; movies are made about video-game characters, while video games based on movies are released at the same time as the films themselves. Media have become more like a genetic code that 'directs the mutation of the real into the hyperreal' (ibid., 30). In short, television and life have dissolved into each other. We are our own TVs; we are all Louds, ecstatically doomed to infiltration by the media.

The Orders of the Simulacrum

Elsewhere Baudrillard has discussed the relation between images and reality throughout Western history, finding four distinct 'orders' of simulacra. In Symbolic Exchange and Death (1976) he talks about how the relationship between reality and simulations of it has changed throughout history.

In the Middle Ages there was a *symbolic order* where knights in shining armour symbolized the feudal morality through their noble deeds and heraldic devices and damsels in distress like Guinevere symbolized the Virgin Mary (Powell and Lee, 1998: 48–9). Codes of behaviour, dress, courtly love, and religious devotion all pointed to a fixed system of signs, a fixed social space based on a rigid hierarchy. This system of signs pointed to a world modelled on an image of God. The signs of the medieval world 'stood for' real things: they were symbols, not simulations. Given this rigid hierarchy, symbolic orders were cruel societies, offering little hope for the lower classes.

From the Renaissance to the Enlightenment, the rigid symbolic order broke down, and signs and symbols began to move about more freely. The mark of this new order, what Baudrillard calls the *first order of simulacra*, was the era's fascination with the counterfeit or fake, from stucco angels to automatons (mechanical men). These counterfeits had a theatrical quality to them, as did baroque art with fantastic statues of God and Jesus found in seventeenth-century churches. They stood in opposition to the idea of natural law, the moral foundation of the classical era. Baudrillard gives the example of the French cook Camille Renault, who used concrete to make chairs, trees, a sewing machine, an orchestra, and sheep with real wool attached (Baudrillard, 1976: 81). Even though these were counterfeit forms, they were made of a deathless, indestructible material. They were meant to last, even though they were fakes. Concrete and stucco were 'the democratic triumph of all artificial signs, the apotheosis of the theatre and of fashion . . . the Promethean aim of the bourgeoisie being first achieved in the *imitation of nature*, before throwing it into *production*' (ibid., 79–80, my translation). These counterfeits symbolized the first order of simulacra. Their goal was to use individual creations to imitate nature before nature itself was eclipsed by industrialism, urbanization, and mass production.

The *second order of simulacra* coincides with the Industrial Revolution. This is an era of production, its basic value being the law of the marketplace. Now, unlike Renault's concrete simulacra, objects could be mass-produced by modern industry. While Camille Renault made his concrete sheep as a unique object, a Renault factory turned out endless replicas of a given model of car. Photography and cinema later allowed the mass production of images. The essence of the mass-produced good is that the first one made should be the same as the last one made: a hundred copies of a given photo or car should all be identical. Yet the hundredth copy is no more or less real than the first one. They are not simulations of nature, but simulations of each other or of some original blueprint. In contrast to the stucco angel, Baudrillard mentions the robot as the ideal symbol of the second order. A robot isn't a theatrical device that tricks us into believing it's human, but an instrument of work whose value lies in its mechanical capacity (ibid., 83).

The second order is one where production is taken as real and where labour power is seen as something we can assign a value to and thus see as exploited by capital, which takes 'surplus value' from the sum total produced by the worker. Here the law of equivalence rules: all products produced by industry are equivalent to some money value. The same goes for language: all words are equivalent to some meaning in the overall structure of language, as Saussure asserted. This era believed that production, meaning, and consciousness were all realities, foundations for the sciences of economics, linguistics, and psychology. It had a rage to 'civilize' everything, not letting any parcel of land or natural resource remain undeveloped. In the industrial era the rule is simple—'produce!'

The *third order of simulacra* comes when we no longer have a single simulacrum of nature, or a large number of mass-produced copies, but models, pure simulacra that are copies of nothing at all, that exist only as code. This is the age of hyperreality, where simulacra of things precede their real-world cases (e.g., as when a movie like

The China Syndrome 'predicted' the real nuclear accident at Three Mile Island in 1979). This is the era of consumer icons, virtual reality, genetic engineering, and electronic communication, all controlled by a code. Baudrillard emphasizes DNA, the code of life, as the mother of all codes, which replaces industrial production as our dominant cultural symbol. Yet this is also the digital age, as on/off switches rule computers, communications, consumerism, and politics. Computer software is made up of a massive number of ones and zeros; our consumer choices are often reduced to a pair of major products (e.g., Coke or Pepsi); in America politics is polarized between the Democratic and Republican parties; while referenda ask us to vote 'Yes' or 'No' to new taxes, Quebec sovereignty, or membership in the European Union. He also pointed to the digitality of the rule of the two superpowers, the US and the USSR, though this digital code was decompiled by the events of 1989.

In the third order, which for our purposes we can see as almost identical with postmodern culture (though Baudrillard rarely uses the expression), such concrete reference points as levels of production, linguistic meaning, deep emotions, philosophical substances, and history itself melt away, replaced by a 'total relativity' of signs (remember structuralism) and the rule of simulation in all fields. 'This means simulation in the sense that from now on signs will exchange among themselves exclusively, without interacting with the real' (Baudrillard, 2001a: 128). The theatre of representation has been closed. Of course, we have capitalism to thank at least in part for this liberation of signs to roam freely, for capital freed things from their use values by turning them into exchangeable commodities.

He sees this third age as the end of labour and of production in the sense that neither is strictly necessary: our society is engaged in a hysteria of overproduction, while its general level of well-being allows the welfare state to support the unemployed. The ritual of labour is still important, however, at least as a simulacrum:

Work (in the form of leisure as well) invades all areas of life as a fundamental repression, as control, and as a permanent job in specified times and places, according to an omnipresent code. People must be *positioned* at all times: in school, in the plant, at the beach or in front of the TV, or in job retraining—a permanent, general mobilization. But this form of labor is no longer productive in the original sense: it is now merely a mirror of society, its imaginary, its fantastic principle of reality. (Ibid., 137)

It's true that the long hours and dangerous work of the early factories is a thing of the past. Yet now we're all tiny terminals in the consumer system. Baudrillard wonders whether we're still in capitalism if we no longer believe that commodities have 'real' values, but concludes that we're in an age where capitalism has become a general mode of domination where capital has 'finally attained its purest form of discourse' free from talk about markets, finance, and class (ibid., 133). In other words, capitalism has become like computer code that programs our entire lives, both our work and our leisure.

What does Baudrillard mean by the 'real'? One 'possible definition' he gives is that the real is something for which we can provide an equivalent representation (ibid., 148). So if we can meaningfully represent God in a holy text or in a painting, then God is 'real' to us. Of course, in the third order, hyperreality takes over. This is beyond representation because it only *simulates* the real (ibid., 149). A Hollywood action film about a terrorist attack is not meant to represent a *real* attack, but to simulate one that hasn't happened. Our political, social, historical, and economic lives are now all caught up in this hyperreality. This is neither reality nor fiction, but simulations of things that don't exist, at least so far. We can see all of this summarized in Table 9.2, which also refers to the four phases of the image discussed by Baudrillard in 'The Precession of Simulacra', along with how the orders apply to science fiction.

Table 9.2 Baudrillard on the Orders of Simulacra

Orders of Simulacra	Phases of the Image	Utopias and Science Fiction
1. *Symbolic order:* Society is organized as a fixed system of signs distributed according to rank and obligation (e.g., in the feudal era a peasant could not become the King). The question of reality does not arise: the meaning of signs is already established in advance (by God or power structures).	Art reflects a basic reality (see 'Precession of the Simulacra' for an extended discussion). Example: Gothic paintings depict the birth of Jesus as the true son of God, replete with signs of his divinity (the Three Wise Men, a halo over the Madonna's head, etc.).	No need for utopian or science fiction writing: the utopian order already exists in the here and now.
2. *First order of simulacra:* The early modern period, from the Renaissance to the Industrial Revolution. Natural law the basic value. A competition for the meaning of signs starts. Simulacra aim to restore an ideal image of nature. Fakes and counterfeits enter the scene: stucco angels, concrete chairs, theatre, fashion, masks. But true originals underlie the fakes.	Art masks and perverts a basic reality. Example: baroque paintings of an impossibly beautiful Jesus ascending to the heavens like Superman, with the Madonna watching with a blissful look on her face.	Utopias: Transcendental or romantic dreams, counterfeit copies of the real world. 'If only we got everything right, life would be beautiful!' Thomas More's *Utopia*; Francis Bacon's *New Atlantis*.
3. *Second order of simulacra:* From the Industrial Revolution until the middle of the twentieth century. The law of the market the basic value. Mass production of copies or replicas of a single prototype: cars, planes, fridges, clothes, books. Liberation of energy through the machine (Marx's world). Copies more or less indistinguishable. Reproduced things aren't counterfeits: they're just as 'real' as their prototype (though we can still recognize the prototype).	Art masks the absence of a basic reality. Example: photography and the mechanical reproduction of paintings (see Walter Benjamin's important essay 'The Work of Art in the Age of Mechanical Reproduction'). A framed reproduction of a Renaissance painting of the Madonna hung over one's bed, right beside a velvet image of Elvis.	The classic science fiction of the age of mass production: robots, rocket ships to Mars, space exploration, alien invasion, intergalactic wars. Present technology projected into the future and outer space. Robert Heinlein's *Starship Troopers*; Isaac Asimov's *I, Robot* and the *Foundation* series. Fifties Hollywood sci-fi films: *Them*; *It Came from Outer Space*; *War of the Worlds*. The original *Star Trek* television series. Borges's imperial map.
4. *Third order of simulacra:* The present age—dominated by simulations, things that have no original or prototype (though they may parallel something). Era of the model or code: computers, virtual reality, opinion polls, DNA, genetic engineering, cloning, news media make the news, Nike sneakers as status symbols, Disneyland. The death of the real: no more counterfeits or prototypes, just simulations of reality—hyperreality. Information replaces the machine as the basic mode of production.	Art bears no relation to reality at all. Example: a virtual reality female talking head reads news headlines to us over the Internet. Is she real? A fake? The question has lost its meaning—there is no original to compare her to. Or Madonna (the singer, not the mother of Christ) made up like Marilyn Monroe vamping it up with a troupe of lithe male dancers in a music video on MTV.	The end of science fiction: the real absorbed into a hyperreal, cybernetic world. Not about an alternative universe, but about a simulation of the present one. Philip K. Dick's *Simulacra*; J.G. Ballard's *Crash*; William Gibson's *Neuromancer*; Ridley Scott's *Blade Runner*; Paul Verhoeven's *Total Recall*; David Cronenberg's *Crash* and *eXistenZ*; the Wachowski brothers' *The Matrix*. The Borg, the holodeck, and virtual reality characters (*Voyager's* doctor) in the later *Star Trek* television series.

Note: Many of the examples used in this table and in the following section are my own, not Baudrillard's.
Source: Adapted from Mann and Dann (2005).

The essence of the third order of simulacra is the death of the real, which once acted as a concrete reference point for linguistic meaning, economics, politics, religious belief, psychology, and sexuality. Words are no longer seen as referring to objectively real things; mass production has long since escaped from any sense of fulfilling real needs; political leaders and revolutionary movements have become media images; God is dead, at least in the West; psychoanalysis is seen as based on a series of fictions; while the idea of a 'natural' form of sexuality is laughed at by most. Baudrillard has hit upon a central element of postmodern culture with his notion of the death of the real. Much of what our culture once fervently believed in is now seen as a form of fiction, as something people in the past just 'made up' or, to use the current jargon, socially constructed. The desert of the real is empty of metaphysical exit signs—we're stuck in it.

Simulacra and Science Fiction

In the essay 'Simulacra and Science Fiction', from *Simulacra and Simulation*, Baudrillard applies his theory of orders of simulacra to one specific field: science fiction literature, taken in the broadest possible sense. He argues that the three types of utopian and science fiction writing parallel the three orders of the simulacrum that have ruled our culture since the Renaissance, with the cutting-edge utopian writing of today no longer being, strictly speaking, 'sci-fi' but merely an extension of our own technological and cultural landscape (e.g., J.G. Ballard's novel *Crash*, or William Gibson's cyberpunk stories such as *Neuromancer* and *Count Light*). In other words, Baudrillard is saying that our imagination itself is tied into the development of the orders of simulacra.

When society has yet to experience the death of the real and sees copies of real things as suspect counterfeits, its imaginary products are seen as extensions of the real, as in Thomas More's *Utopia*. Later, we arrive at the classic science fiction of Isaac Asimov, Arthur C. Clarke, and Robert Heinlein, the sci-fi of robots, spaceships, the conquest of the galaxy, and wars with giant alien bugs. Asimov's

seven-novel *Foundation* series stands as a landmark in this tradition: religion, spaceships, robots, and cultural differences are all present, but in a galaxy where the only intelligent beings are humans and their creations. The technology and conflicts of the present were extended into outer space and the future in this phase of sci-fi. This is why the original *Star Trek* series so often dealt with the moral and political themes of the 1960s—the Cold War (see the episode 'Balance of Terror'), racism, sexual equality, and the counterculture.

Later, sci-fi turned from moral issues to simulations of reality, as in the works of William Gibson and David Cronenberg, not to mention *Blade Runner* and the Borg and holographic characters of the later *Star Trek* series. Although this division cannot always be sharply made, we see in these later efforts a creeping awareness of how virtual realities and genetic manipulations are more interesting themes than rocket ships to Mars and interstellar empires. The science fiction (if we can even use the term) of this era of third-order simulacra is about fractured identities and inner dangers, and has a much more pessimistic view of the utility of technology. A good case in point is David Cronenberg's *Dead Ringers* (1988), where the director uses cinematic tricks to allow Jeremy Irons to play identical twins in their long slow slide into drug addiction and death. They are simulacra of each other and find it impossible to work out their separate identities before it's too late. Similarly, Gibson's *Neuromancer* (1984) is about a society where characters can jack mentally into cyberspace, one where corporate power and street violence drive the story, not laser blasters or alien invasions. The moral of the story for Baudrillard is that each of these forms of science fiction writing—utopianism, classic technology-based science fiction, and hyperreal simulations—symbolizes the type of society that produced it.

Further Explorations of the Desert of the Real

In *The Ecstasy of Communication*, Baudrillard argues that our bodies and the universe around them have become monitoring screens, with television the perfect symbol of this process (Baudrillard, 1998 [1983]: 12). Formerly non-commercialized public space disappears thanks to the mass media, and advertising invades everything: streets, monuments, later the cinema (think of the giant TV commercials one is now forced to watch before movies) and the World Wide Web (pop-ups and spam). This invasion of our former privacy by TV and computer screens is both ecstatic and obscene. By 'obscene' Baudrillard means that there's no more spectacle, theatre, or illusion in mass entertainment or life; instead, everything has become 'transparent, visible, exposed in the raw and inexorable light of information and communication' (ibid., 21–2). He compares our lives to the forced and exaggerated sex in porn films: like the porn star, we act out a blown-up simulation of a life. Our lives have become obscene like these sex scenes:

> We no longer partake of the drama of alienation, but are in the ecstasy of communication. And this ecstasy is obscene. Obscene is that which eliminates the gaze, the image of every representation. Obscenity is not confined to sexuality, because today there is a pornography of information and communication, a pornography of circuits and networks . . . . (Ibid., 22).

This obscene ecstasy is cool and seductive: it feeds us excessive images, penetrating our private spaces along with our public ones. Our intimate moments have become media fodder, from deconstruction of the Loud family in the 1970s to the many reality TV shows that now dominate the airwaves.[4] Yet we feel an ecstasy at this penetration of media as every night we see the whole world played out on our TV screens. Hysteria was the great mental disease of an age that took theatre and the staging of the subject seriously (i.e., the end of the nineteenth century), and paranoia of an age where organization was too rigid and dominating (i.e., the first half of the twentieth century). Schizophrenia is our prime pathology, a disease caused by the promiscuity and close interconnection of information and communication networks (ibid., 26–7). Things have become too close, too

confused, overexposed. As pure screens ourselves, we are *too* plugged into things and thus ecstatically schizoid.

In the early 1980s Baudrillard hit the road. He travelled across the United States and recorded his enigmatic though stimulating reflections on the country in *America* (1986). For Baudrillard, America is the last primitive society, one that had achieved a radical sense of modernity that Europe had only dabbled in. In fact, America *is* a hyperreality, a place where real culture is found in the streets, in wide open spaces, speed, movies, and technology, not in museums, galleries, or churches (Baudrillard, 1988 [1986]: 100). The authentic America isn't contained by these old repositories of culture, as it is in Europe; it's found in Disneyland, Hollywood, TV, Safeways, the sandy deserts of the Southwest and the urban deserts of Santa Barbara and Los Angeles (ibid., 104). America is a culture centred on technology and images, on orgies of goods and services, on expulsing excesses of energy both in a wasteful consumerism and on war against much weaker nations like Vietnam and Iraq.

Early in the book Baudrillard describes visiting New York, which he proclaims is one of the two great centres of the world, along with Los Angeles. European snobs shouldn't be too quick to dismiss the power or authenticity of American culture because:

> the latest fast-food outlet, the most banal suburb, the blandest of giant American cars or the most insignificant cartoon-strip majorette is more at the centre of the world than any of the cultural manifestations of old Europe. This is the country which gives you the opportunity to be brutally naïve: things, faces, skies, and deserts are expected to be simply what they are. This is the land of the 'just as it is'. (Ibid., 28)

He describes New York as a place with wall-to-wall prostitution where only tribes, gangs, the Mafia, and secret societies can feel at home and people refuse to look at one another. Yet he also lauds the beauty of the black and Puerto Rican women of the city, whose looks he finds animalistic and sublime (ibid., 15–19). He especially sees the emptiness and simulated nature of what he calls 'astral' America most clearly in California, with its freeways and urban deserts. Baudrillard found there ample proof of his ideas of the death of the real and of the social, especially as he drove through Death Valley, where the 'desert of the real' is no mere metaphor. The realities of earlier orders of simulacra vanished like mirages in his rear-view mirror. In California he sees evidence that America is a *utopia achieved*, with its soft resort-style civilization and sexual freedom.[5] Yet it also has an ascetic side: its inhabitants cryogenize their emotions and punish their weak flesh with diets, jogging, and the semi-medieval instruments of torture found in gyms. It is an anorexic culture of disgust and fear of death suffocated by its own plenty (ibid., 40).

In California he found a 'stunning fusion' of the pure simulacrum and natural beauty, from the desert's geological marvels to Los Angeles's fantastic lack of depth or charm (ibid., 124–5). Cinema and life mix in America. Deserts, cities, and freeways are all like giant sets of the latest Hollywood epic. One should look at films to understand American urban life, not the other way around. In fact, the American utopia has been so successfully promoted in the movies that its culture fascinates even those it harms the most, to the point that they believe in the American dream and risk their lives to emigrate there. In the end, Baudrillard finds in natural deserts a vision of the desertification of signs in America. America, as the original place of radical modernity, is the model for the rest of the world, which is also becoming hyperreal, full of simulations. America is a desert, especially in its large cities, where real life has disappeared from their inner core and retreated to the suburb. In his odyssey Baudrillard surrendered to what he sees as America's primitive, animalistic, vital, potent, hyperreal energy. He sees it as the model of things to come throughout the rest of the world, which will become considerably sandier, hotter, and more barren of cultural vegetation—except for the odd televisual cactus.

Baudrillard's short work, 'The Gulf War Will Not Take Place' (1991), is based on an article he wrote for *Libération* in which he claimed that the 1991 war wouldn't take place because in our hyperreal age virtual war has replaced actual hostilities. The hostage and the media have replaced the warrior, and war has become like safe sex, never too risky or dangerous. The atomic apocalypse is not a real possibility. Yet once the Gulf War had started, Baudrillard stuck to his guns and asked whether it was really taking place. The Western audience was aware of it only as a series of hyperreal images on our TV screens presided over by expert talking heads on CNN, 'raiders of the lost image' spewing endless streams of stupidity (Baudrillard, 2001b: 248). These experts, to Baudrillard, were as much concerned with their looks and sophistication as with the horrors of the war itself. The media promote the war, the Western military promotes the media, and advertising pays for the whole televisual circus (ibid., 236). Even Saddam Hussein gets in on the act by using the media in a cynical and purely instrumental way, kissing children and waving to adoring crowds on TV. The West might see him as immorally perverting the media, but Baudrillard argues that he understood better 'the structural unreality of images and their proud indifference to the truth' (ibid., 245). In other words, Saddam knew that TV is only a simulacrum, not a mirror of reality.

The war was also about the shedding of huge stocks of weapons by the Western powers, by over-equipped societies committed to the production and elimination of waste (ibid., 237). Yet it was a 'clean' war fought by men glued to computer screens launching missiles, planes, and bombs against a distant enemy.[6] Thus the war was virtual, like a computer game, as witnessed in that famous video of the American smart bomb being guided down the chimney of an Iraqi bunker. Added to the virtuality of technology was the virtuality of the politics of the war. Saddam was a fake enemy, a Western ally against Islamic Iran during the 1980s, then suddenly a champion of Islam against the West in the 1990s, yet always a deceiver of the Arab masses (ibid., 240). The bloodiness and pointlessness of the 1980–8 Iran-Iraq War was the hidden sin, the heinous crime, that both sides avoided discussing. So despite the horrible loss of life (mostly on the Iraqi side), the war was a hyperreal war, a simulation.

Baudrillard's work in the 1990s continued to focus on this theme of the hyperreality of postmodern culture, his writing becoming more disjointed and aphoristic (perhaps echoing Nietzsche's style). His work since the mid-seventies gives us an impressionistic big picture of the media-dominated, information-driven, virtual culture of the age. He may exaggerate the degree to which we have moved away from the reality of linguistic meaning, art, social life, and war, but this movement is undeniably part of the postmodern condition. We now turn to some general reflections on postmodern popular culture based on the theorists considered so far.

POSTMODERN POP CULTURE

Let's take a breath and review some of the main ideas found in the last three chapters to refresh our memories. When we speak of postmodernism, we really mean two different things that are in part related. First, we have postmodern theory, a broad set of ideas that finds its origins in the nineteenth-century philosopher Friedrich Nietzsche and the early twentieth-century theorist Ferdinand de Saussure. Perhaps the most famous postmodern theorist is Jacques Derrida, who developed the method of deconstruction. In general, deconstruction means to take apart a text and discover its conflicting meanings. Derrida saw everything as a potential text—books, films, TV shows, even pieces of pictorial art. Everything could be read as a text. And everything contains conflicting meanings that cannot be determined in a final way. Derrida is a post-structuralist. That means he comes after and critiques structuralism while preserving some of its concepts. The post-structuralists believe that languages, texts, and social orders lack the rigid structures that the structuralists found in them. Other important thinkers influenced by post-structuralism include Roland Barthes and Michel Foucault.

The second sense of postmodernism is the idea that we have lived in a 'postmodern culture'

since roughly the middle of the 1960s, which, as shown in Table 7.2, has seven distinct aspects. Three of these aspects have had a key impact on popular culture.

(1) As we've seen, Lyotard said in *The Postmodern Condition* that the main characteristic of postmodern culture is an 'incredulity toward meta-narratives', that is, a skepticism about big stories. These stories include those about Christian salvation, the Marxist dream of a perfect communist society, the march of scientific progress, the liberal idea of increasing human freedom, and the ability of art to represent the world in a true fashion. This is a central claim about postmodern culture. What it implies is that in the postmodern era many people are becoming relativists: they no longer rely on capital 'T' truths to define their lives. They borrow bits of knowledge from different traditions, e.g., New Age books like James Redfield's *The Celestine Prophecy*, which is a mish-mash of modern science, Buddhism, Taoism, and ancient Hindu mysticism. They're what Levi-Strauss called *bricoleurs*: scavengers who take bits and pieces of ideas from various traditions to make up their world view. This is connected to post-structuralism in the sense that such thinkers question the idea that a text can have a single, unequivocal meaning. It also relates to the use of collage and pastiche in postmodern culture and to the decline of the linear narrative in postmodern novels, films, and TV stories. The truths postmodern writers try to describe are more fragmented and less coherent than those sought by modernists.

(2) We have witnessed, too, the triumph of an economy of consumption over that of production. Now our economy's main problem isn't the ability to churn out products like steel, ships, trains, and machinery, which it can do effectively, but finding consumers to buy the products it produces. As a result, the Protestant ethic of the need to work hard and save money for the future is replaced by a consumer ethic of immediate gratification, hedonism, and buying on credit, and this rampant consumerism is open to the latest trends promoted by advertising. As a result, a number of occupations become more important. Advertising and marketing

companies, TV production firms, web designers, computer programmers, journalists, and all sorts of technicians who support these occupations are important parts of the postmodern economy. These groups encourage consumers to be conversant with the media. Indeed, it can be argued that this new media-based class seeks to promote a hierarchy of taste that relies on media awareness, and thus it helps to bring about the third aspect of postmodern culture, media saturation.

(3) We live in a media-saturated and information-driven society. Radio, film, TV, and computers dominate our lives. As Marshall McLuhan pointed out, we now live in an electronic age dominated not by print-based media but by electronic media that have turned the world into a global village. This has led to the mixing of the economy and popular culture as the 'realities' created by the media get mixed up with the realities of everyday life. We think and live more and more in terms of the stories and images and information given to us by the mass media. We're surrounded by media screens and transmitters: TVs, computers, radios, palm pilots, and cellphones with LCD screens. This has led postmodernists like Baudrillard to conclude that we live in a hyperreal image-obsessed culture.

The Elements of Postmodern Pop Culture

Postmodern popular culture can be seen as a loose constellation of trends that includes five main elements.[7]

1. The Coming of a Hyperreal Media Culture

In postmodern culture our social relationships are governed more and more by images and stories from the mass media. These media no longer hold up a critical mirror to society, as the liberal theory of media suggests, but to a large degree *make* our society. Our consumption of goods is increasingly tied to advertising and promotion in the media. Indeed, media *are* much of what we consume: cable TV, movies, video tapes, DVDs, CDs, and so on. As Baudrillard suggests, in our media-dominated society we encounter reality as a desert of the real. Old-fashioned physical and emotional reality has been replaced by media simulations.

Much of what we experience is not real, but more than real, or hyperreal: think of TV show families, computer games, film special effects, and of late, reality TV. These models of reality *precede* their real equivalents—they give us models of how to think and act. They give us hyperreal models of our lives. Because of the 2003 reality TV show, Joe Millionaire (real name Evan Marriott) became a household name in North America, appearing on TV talk shows, magazine covers, and websites. Joe only *seemed* to be a millionaire—he was really a construction worker. Or was he? Who was the real Joe? The phony millionaire? The construction worker dating a collection of attractive women while living in a French chateau provided by the Fox network? Or the media celebrity?

Baudrillard would argue that phenomena like reality TV show that we live in a hyperreal culture where it's hard to distinguish between the reality of everyday life and the hyperreality of mass media. This idea is echoed in a number of recent films and TV shows. The film *The Truman Show* (1998) is about a man named Truman Burbank (Jim Carrey) who lives in an artificial environment populated by actors and televised 24 hours a day without his knowing it. Even his wife is an actor whose main job is to keep Truman in line and to surreptitiously promote products by holding them up to hidden cameras and singing their praises. The point of the film might be that we are all Trumans, satisfied to live our lives in entirely mediated worlds. Yet we should pause before fully accepting this idea: whether media have taken over our sense of reality entirely is an open question. Most people can still distinguish reality from media stories, and have other sources of meaning in their lives—their families, their careers, or forms of art and culture that aren't just commodities.

2. The Breakdown of High Art

In postmodern culture high art becomes part of popular culture. Its special aura is destroyed, as everything is turned into a consumer commodity. Art becomes a collection of products for sale in the marketplace. For one thing, as Walter Benjamin pointed out, modern printing techniques allow us to mass-produce copies of high art: the poorest student can afford a copy of Renoir's *Boating Party*. Part of this process of breakdown is the entry of jokes, parodies, and self-references into art. Andy Warhol (1928–87) was famous for this: he painted pictures of Campbell Soup cans and Coke bottles, and made prints of coloured photos of Marilyn Monroe, Elvis Presley, Beethoven, and Mao Zedong. As Jameson observes, Warhol's art is a form of commodification. He was the son of Czech immigrants and started out in his hometown of Pittsburgh as a commercial illustrator for magazines, newspapers, and catalogues. He moved from this to the world of pop art in the 1960s and 1970s, ruling it from his New York castle/studio called (appropriately) The Factory. It turned out not only his own pop art, but amateur semi-pornographic films, photography, journalism, and music produced by hangers-on such as The Velvet Underground, all under Andy's direction. Warhol's main technique was to transfer a series of often identical photos onto a silkscreen, which he used to make a print onto a canvas, applying synthetic paints onto the images. He could make endless reproductions from these silkscreens. Both his artwork and his image were cool, distant; he was narcissistic and self-involved, showing how both art and artist under postmodernity become commodities. The only aura left to art and the artist is fame—for precisely 15 minutes, as Warhol once observed.

Postmodern culture does not respect high art as the distinct prerogative of the upper classes. Most people now see TV, video, popular music, and film as art just as much as the works of the old masters. Yet Strinati (1995: 240) argues that this isn't all that new. For one thing, the Frankfurt School made this sort of observation a generation before postmodernism became the rage. Also, postmodern artists make distinctions between good and bad art, so aesthetic criteria still exist. Those who celebrate postmodern culture are not always stupid populists who celebrate ignorance: they are often clever people who like books, films, and TV that are 'in the know', full of parody and ironic references. Think of the Fox network's cartoon show *The Simpsons*: most episodes are replete with references to pop culture that are much funnier if you know the connections. In short, one could argue that instead of getting rid of all aesthetic hierarchies, postmodernists want to create a new one, albeit one based not on class but on insider knowledge.

3. The Emphasis on Surface over Depth and Style over Substance

Jameson and others argue that in postmodern culture surface meanings are more important that deep ones, and style is more important than substance. We live in an 'image culture'. The French Situationist Guy Debord called this a 'society of the spectacle', because we become slaves to the spectacles offered by the media, leading us to live banal, inauthentic lives. Playfulness and jokes take the place of artistic integrity, content, and meaning. Looking good on a media screen is more important than being good at your craft. For example, music videos often highlight the look of the performer—the singer wears fashionable or sexy clothes and gold chains, is surrounded by hot-looking male or female dancers or extras, with the whole thing set in some exotic locale. They may cost a million dollars apiece to make, and act as a 3–4 minute commercial for the artist. It's more and more important that pop stars *look* good, rather than actually be good singers, musicians, or songwriters. Think of N'Sync, Britney Spears, Christina Aguilera, and Shakira. Their fans don't think too much about the music, but consume it as an amalgam of image and sound.

A second example of style over substance can be found in the virtual reality of computer graphics and games. Recent movies often use spectacular special effects to simulate reality—think of

Independence Day (1996) or *Spiderman* (2002). Computer games create rich imaginary worlds where we can lose ourselves for hours. Hollywood film is turning away in part from literature as its source for stories to comic book heroes and computer games—Batman, Spiderman, the X-Men, Daredevil, and Lara Croft, the heroine of the video game *Tomb Raider*, being cases in point. A counter-argument to the importance of special effects in movies today is that cinema from its earliest days was concerned with showing spectacular events using lavish sets and props if producers could afford them. For example, as early as 1916 D.W. Griffith rebuilt the ancient city of Babylon on a Hollywood backlot for his film *Intolerance*. We could argue that if a silent film director like Griffith had access to modern spectacular special effects, he would have used them. Yet it is certainly true that big-budget films today are often more concerned with spectacular special effects than a good story or good acting.

The dominance of style and surface over substance and depth can be seen on television, too. This goes back at least to the 1980s and the crime drama *Miami Vice*, where the main characters' clothes and the visuals they were surrounded by were more important than the stories themselves. Plenty of evidence suggests that television today, at least on the major networks, emphasizes style over substance. Most actors on American TV are aesthetically appealing (it's a bit different in Britain). Many shows seem to focus on the look of their stars, their locations, and a rock or pop music soundtrack rather than substantial storytelling. These shows appeal directly to the pure surface of things: *Sex and the City, Fashion TV, Are You Hot?*, the various *Survivor* series, *Electric Circus, Entertainment Tonight, Blind Date, Melrose Place*, and *The O.C.* are some obvious examples. Of course, one can still watch serious TV with interesting stories or social and political messages, e.g., science fiction shows like *Star Trek*, dramas on such cable stations as A&E, and cutting comedies like *The Simpsons*. It's a question of which type of show dominates the airwaves.

4. The Dissolving of Time and Space and the Eclipse of History

Due to the speed of modern means of transportation and communications, time and space tend to dissolve. We can cross a continent in a few hours, while it may have taken a week in the railway age and several months on top of a horse. We can communicate around the world via a telephone or on the Internet at the speed of light. TV stations report news from Iraq or Afghanistan a few minutes after it happens. As time and space become less stable, we begin to see an eclipse of history. People learn their history by watching films like *Saving Private Ryan* (1998) or *Schindler's List* (1993). The past becomes a movie or TV spectacle. High school students may know who played Oskar Schindler, but not who won World War II. Everything becomes a big NOW, flashed to an inert public on electronic tickers on CNN.

The linear narrative found in most modern literature and films begins to collapse. Instead, we have fragmented narratives with fragmented senses of time and space. Quentin Tarantino's 1994 film, *Pulp Fiction*, for example, is made up of five fragments placed out of chronological order. We see John Travolta's character die in one scene, then alive and well in a later (really an earlier) scene. The non-linear narrative has become a common device in film over the last decade or so. Christopher Nolan's *Memento* (2000) tells the story of one Leonard Shelby (Guy Pearce), who suffers from a mental condition where his short-term memory lasts for only 15 minutes, after which he can only remember events that occurred before the attack that led to his condition. The film sets its scenes in reverse order to duplicate Leonard's strange, schizophrenic awareness of the world: the beginning of the film is actually the last thing that happens in the story. This film echoes Jameson's concern that when we can't unify the past, present, and future into a coherent sequence, we can't experience our biography as that of a unique self (Jameson, 1991: 27). As the temporal order of things breaks down in our schizophrenic postmodern condition, the present engulfs the subject and our awareness of history is narrowed to Warhol's (and Leonard Shelby's) 15 minutes.

5. The Eclipse of the New: Parody, Pastiche, Self-Referencing, and Recycling

Connected to the other elements above is the idea that postmodern culture suffers from an eclipse of the new. Ezra Pound, the noted modernist poet, said to artists to 'make it new'. Modernist artists and writers followed his lead, trying to create new and unique forms of art and literature. But postmodern culture is less interested in creating new cultural forms. Instead it engages in a number of artistic strategies.

Parody. Postmodern TV, film, and art often include parodies of a specific cultural object or of a genre at their core. The essence of the popular cartoon show *The Simpsons* is parody of just about everything—the family, politics, religion, TV, movies, and popular music. Each episode is rich in this sort of omniparody: many explode with pop cultural references (e.g., silly re-enactments of films or TV shows), celebrity guests, and the occasional biting commentary on social or political ills. For example, a 1996 episode shows the aliens Kang and Kodos taking the roles of Bill Clinton and Bob Dole in the US presidential race. When they are exposed as aliens, one of them quips, 'It's true, we *are* aliens. But what are you going to do about it? It's a two-party system; you have to vote for one of us.' Many of these parodies are directly related to old TV shows or films—they endlessly recycle the history of pop culture. Each episode is a pastiche of parodies, a comic simulacrum of the original—which is especially the case if the viewer is not aware of the original. For example, the 1993 episode 'Treehouse of Horror IV' features three shorts entitled 'The Devil and Homer Simpson', 'Terror at 5½ Feet', and 'Bart Simpson's Dracula', which are direct parodies of Stephen Vincent Benét's *The Devil and Daniel Webster*, the *Twilight Zone* episode 'Terror at 20,000 Feet', and Francis Ford Coppola's film, *Bram Stoker's Dracula* (1992). The episode is framed by a meta-parody featuring Bart Simpson

playing Rod Serling on *Night G[...]* we see parodies of classic mo[...] such as David's *Death of Marat[...]* Dali's *Persistence of Memory*, alo[...] Van Gogh, Picasso, and Esch[...] episode, 'Rosebud', casts Home[...] Mr. Burns, in the role of Charl[...] *Citizen Kane*, complete with C[...] flashbacks to his youth.

Pastiche/double-coding. Pastiche is the combining of elements from several cultural objects or genres or cultures into one whole. Double-coding, an idea developed by Charles Jencks in his studies of postmodern architecture, is the combination of modern techniques with more traditional art forms to appeal to a broad public. It reads the past in the present and the present in the past. Numerous examples of pastiche and double-coding can be found in recent popular culture. For example, Ridley Scott's *Blade Runner* (1982) glues together a film noir crime drama from the 1940s to a science fiction film to a romantic drama to produce a pastiche. Many contemporary musicians engage in pastiche-like or double-coded mixtures of musical styles and genres, notably those that appeal to the early days of rock 'n' roll. The late 1990s British band Kula Shaker, led by Crispian Mills, recorded albums that were a pastiche of musical forms, notably the psychedelic rock of the sixties and traditional Indian music. In fact, their songs 'Tattva' (a British hit) and 'Radhe Rahde' are centred on Indian chants sung in Sanskrit.

Self-referencing. This is when a story or art object refers to another cultural object in the same field, e.g., when an ad refers to other ads for similar products. Self-referencing works best with an audience literate in pop cultural references: *The Simpsons* fits here once again. Another example is the American singer Beck (1970–), an expert musician keenly aware of the history of popular music. His albums *Mellow Gold* (1994), *Odeley* (1996), *Mutations* (1998), and *Guero* (2005) cut and paste the past of blues, rock, folk, funk, and rap into self-aware snippets of the history of pop music. He uses samples from old tunes, mocking riffs and vocal stylings, and a general cacophony of double-coding to create what is no doubt a postmodern pop. On *Mellow Gold* we hear him parody Robert Plant's wail from 'The Immigrant Song' in his song 'Truckdrivin' Neighbors Downstairs', transplanting Led Zeppelin's music into a world of trailer parks, velvet paintings, kitsch, and white trash. On the same album we hear Beck's deconstruction of New Age narcissistic hippiedom on 'Nightmare Hippy Girl'. Yet his real self-referencing tour de force is *Odeley*, which is full of oddball tape tricks, electronic noises, and references to different musical genres, including funk, rap, hip-hop, blues, folk, industrial, classical, and even flamenco. Samples are sprinkled throughout the songs on the album. There's even a reference to Dadaism and Marcel Duchamp in the song 'Readymade'. Here are double-coding, an ironic replaying of the past, and parody, postmodern aesthetic forms par excellence.

Recycling. Postmodern culture recycles the past, reusing old forms or stories in the current context. This includes historical nostalgia films such as *Titanic* (1996) and *Pearl Harbor* (2000), which recycle the recent historical past, dealing with events already filmed with some success. It also includes such films as *Blade Runner*, which recycles Humphrey Bogart-type crime dramas, and the original *Star Wars* cycle, which recycles to a degree the Buck Rogers and Flash Gordon-type serials of the 1930s. Of course, the line between recycling, double-coding, and self-referencing is a thin one at best, distinguishable mainly by the intentions of the creator: double-coders and self-referencers may be driven by a genuine postmodern aesthetic, while recyclers may just be suffering from a lack of imagination combined with greed (though this is not a fair assessment of the creators of *Blade Runner* and the original *Star Wars* trilogy).

Four More Examples of Postmodern Strategies at Work in Popular Culture

There are many other examples of how these five strategies play out in postmodern culture and how they interact. We could complain about how Hollywood more and more focuses on sequels to

make money: *Superman*, *Batman*, *Star Wars*, *Halloween*, *A Nightmare on Elm Street*, *The Matrix*, and Harry Potter, to mention a few. These obviously recycle many of the same characters and themes, make references to earlier parts of their own series, and in some cases paste together earlier scenes or plot points and even parody themselves, as with 1994's *New Nightmare*, where the fictional character Freddy Krueger returns to murder his creator, Wes Craven, and the actors in his previous movies. The very notion of a sequel rejects the idea of 'making it new'. Yet to be fair, sequels have been made as far back as the 1920s, for example, the *Sherlock Holmes*, *Tarzan*, and *Thin Man* series (Strinati, 1995: 244). Genres have blurred together throughout the history of cinema, so it's a question of degree. Yet one can't help but feel that recycling in various forms now *dominates* the American film industry.

We can also find these postmodern strategies at work in popular music. Beck is a good example, since he not only uses a pastiche of psychedelic rock, folk, hip-hop, blues, and funk in his music, but literally recycles earlier popular music through the inclusion of samples in his songs. In fact, rap and hip-hop artists have turned sampling into a fine art, leading to many legal battles with the owners of the songs they borrow from. Many other pop artists recycle: the 1980s Anglo-Irish band The Pogues combined traditional Celtic music and punk, for one. The more self-conscious recycling and parodying of techno and dance artists doing covers of old tunes is seen, for example, when Moby does an album of movie songs like the James Bond theme music, or when Shaggy takes an old pop song, *Angel of the Morning*, and gives it a hip-hop/reggae beat. Lastly, the Canadian band Sloan, originally from Halifax, uses a mixture of affectionate double-coding of various older rock forms, notably the Beatles. On their album *One Chord to Another* (1996) they use infectious harmonies, hand-claps, and jangly guitars characteristic of early Beatles songs on tracks such as 'The Good in Everyone' and 'Everything You've Done Wrong' (the latter even starts with a 'Penny Lane'-type trumpet introduction). As with Kula

Shaker, Sloan's referencing of older pop forms could be either parodic double-coding or nostalgic pastiche—it's hard to say.

This is different from the 'modernist' rock 'n' roll of the 1950s to the 1970s, which saw itself as creating something brand new, so new that religious conservatives actually burned the records of its first stars in huge bonfires. The early rock 'n' roll of Buddy Holly, Chuck Berry, and Jerry Lee Lewis was radically different from the swing and jazz music that dominated radio in the 1950s, as was the drug-inspired 1960s rock of the Beatles and The Doors, along with the virtuosity of guitar gods like Jimi Hendrix, Eric Clapton, and Jimi Page (although blues was the basis of their styles). As late as Pink Floyd's *The Wall* and The Clash's *London Calling* (both late 1979), rock could still claim to be 'making it new', as could 1980s electronic bands like New Order and OMD. The fact that rap/hip-hop has lasted *so long* as a popular musical genre, from Afrika Bambaattaa in the late 1970s to 50 Cent and Eminem in 2007 (and no doubt beyond), seems to indicate an exhaustion of the creative shifting of genres that is so clearly evident in popular music from 1950 to 1985 (i.e., jazz, swing, blues, early rock, surf, psychedelic rock, folk rock, punk, reggae, New Wave, and electronic dance music). In short, we live in an age of musical recycling.

Third, advertising uses all of these strategies. For one thing, it uses self-referencing and parodies of other ads—beer commercials often go in for this sort of thing. Other ads parody the practice of advertising. They point to the nature of advertising as a media construction—the narrator might actually talk to the audience about how the product in question won't change your life, as promised by other ads. In addition, advertising recycles culture, especially pop songs—think of all those car ads with Moby songs, of Volkswagen's use of the largely forgotten folksinger Nike Drake's song 'Pink Moon' in its 2000 TV commercial, and of The Gap's trendy commercials from 1998 featuring teenaged models dancing in their khakis to swing music and 1960s pop tunes like Donovan's 'Mellow Yellow'. The old is new for advertisers bitten by the postmodern bug.

Most convincingly, postmodern architecture recycles or double-codes the past. Modernist architecture was cold, functional, and efficient, using glass and steel to create towering boxes like the bank buildings in downtown Toronto and the former World Trade Center in New York. It is rational and scientific, disdaining the past and the context where it exists with its utopian pretensions. But postmodern architecture is more colourful and playful. It uses statues, columns, and elements of classical traditions, such as Egyptian and Greek architecture, to produce more livable public spaces. Instead of black and grey we might see bright red or green or blue walls and playful references to the past or to the purpose of the building. The AT&T building in New York looks like a Chippendale clock on the top. The Portland Public Services Building in Portland, Oregon, has false Egyptian-looking columns on the front and a huge bronze statue of the imaginary goddess Portlandia brandishing a trident mounted above its entrance. Las Vegas is full of what might be seen as postmodern architecture: phony pyramids and sphinxes, baroque palaces, a replica of the Statue of Liberty, a Venetian villa. We also see some of this influence in the film *Blade Runner*. The Los Angeles of the future pictured in the film includes many architectural styles—the run-down Bradbury building is in the art deco style of the 1930s, while the headquarters of Tyrell Corporation looks like a giant Mayan temple. We'll return to architecture when we discuss Charles Jencks in the final section of this chapter.

Baudrillard's Evil Demon of Images

The 'diabolical seduction of images' is the central theme of Baudrillard's lecture on film, *The Evil Demon of Images*, presented in Australia in 1987. Images no longer represent a 'real' world, but are now simulacra that logically and chronologically precede that which they supposedly reproduce— in some sense they 'cause' real-world events to come into being. They're especially diabolical when they are realistic: this is when the resemblance of the image to the real world is most immoral and perverse (Baudrillard, 1987: 13–14). Most of photography, cinema, and TV today gives us images of reality that strike us as real, but actually only *seem* to resemble the things, events, and faces they picture. For example, Woody Allen's 1984 film *Zelig* is about a man who can simulate the looks and skills of whoever is near him—he's the 'Chameleon Man'. Zelig is on an 'adventure of total seduction' where he begins to resemble everyone who approaches him (ibid., 15). For Baudrillard he is symbolic of the way that third-order simulacra work: he seduces us by his resemblance to his surroundings, like a savage seducing his god by wearing a mask resembling his deity. Yet the savage is only a simulacrum of his deity.

Media images start to contaminate all of our reality to the point where we model ourselves on them. Film, television, and life mix together, even in wartime. Punning on von Clausewitz, Baudrillard says that media images are the continuation of war by other means, a point that became even more telling during the Gulf Wars of 1991 and 2003. He is fascinated by the interplay between the images created by the mass media and how modern wars are fought. Take the epic film *Apocalypse Now* (1979):

> Coppola made his film the same way the Americans conducted the war . . . with the same exaggeration, the same excessive means, the same monstrous candour—and the same success. War as a trip, a technological and psychedelic fantasy; war as a succession of special effects, the war become film well before it was shot; war replaced by technological testing. . . . The Vietnam War and the film are cut from the same cloth. . . . If the Americans (apparently) lost the other, they have certainly won this one. *Apocalypse Now* is a global victory. It has a cinematographic power equal and superior to that of the military and industrial complexes, of the Pentagon and governments. (Ibid., 16–18)

The director, Francis Ford Coppola, prolonged the Vietnam War in the jungles of the Philippines, pouring napalm on them like the best American field commander. This was a type of cinematic war, where war becomes film, and film becomes war, the two united by their excessive use of technology. Coppola saw his film as a world historical event, with the actual Vietnam War as a mere pretext, 'a psychotropic dream', not of victory, but of the creation of war as a mass cinematic spectacle (ibid., 17–18).

Baudrillard's central claim in this essay is that cinematic and television images anticipate reality, causing a scrambling of cause and effect. This goes back to his idea of the precession of simulacra: simulations precede the events they are supposedly simulating. This happened when the Three Mile Island nuclear accident near Harrisburg, Pennsylvania, in March 1979 was preceded by the film *The China Syndrome* (starring Jane Fonda), which deals with an accident at a nuclear plant in California. In the case of Harrisburg, the real event arranged itself to produce a simulation of catastrophe. Baudrillard muses that maybe *The China Syndrome* was the real event and the Three Mile Island nuclear accident its simulacrum. In any case, he sees the image (especially the TV image) as having a deterrent effect on real catastrophes, just as nuclear weapons have deterred wars between major powers for over 50 years.

Baudrillard worries that events no longer have any meaning because models precede them. Images now impose their own immoral logic, without depth or reality. The message disappears and the medium is everything. We're foolishly naive to argue that media should only be used for 'good things': the image revolts against this when it implodes meaning. In other words, don't expect to be morally uplifted or meaningfully educated by television: it's not in the nature of the beast. The secret of the image mustn't be looked for in its capacity to represent reality, but in its capacity to short-circuit reality. The blurring of image and reality no longer leaves room for the image to represent something outside itself: e.g., television news doesn't 'represent' the important events of the day, but the nature of the TV medium itself.

Baudrillard is more scornful of TV than film: he calls it an artificial memory that replays the extermination of meaning. Television is the 'veritable final solution to the historicity of every event' (ibid., 23). It kills memory and history. Shows like *Holocaust* (a 1978 miniseries) don't raise collective consciousness; they attempt to reheat a cold historical event. The cool light of television doesn't help to create a sense of the 'imaginary', unlike cinema, which still carries an intense sense of imagination, a sense of myth, a capacity to dream. The TV image, however, is only a screen, a miniaturized terminal in your head that goes through you like a magnetic tape (ibid., 25).

All of America is cinematographic—life there is one long tracking shot. Cinema invests all of American life with a mythical ambience. That's why the cult of Hollywood idols is perhaps the last great myth of modernity, the stars of the day our Apollos and Athenas. Baudrillard was an unrestrained film buff, finding a primal pleasure in images, in their brute fascination unencumbered by moral, aesthetic, or political judgements (ibid., 28). Modern media images mesmerize us not as sites for the production of meaning, but as sites for the disappearance of meaning and representation, sites of the degeneration of the real (ibid., 29). We can see this happening today especially in the spate of reality TV shows, which collectively give 'reality' a bad name. In these, reality has degenerated into plastic surgery and drunken frolics in hot tubs.

Even in cinema, images have become hyperreal, more real than reality, especially in its production of 'dazzling simulacra' of past ages. Baudrillard cites as cases in point the films *Chinatown*, *1900*, *Barry Lyndon*, *All the President's Men*, and *The Last Picture Show*; we might add *Saving Private Ryan*, *Titanic*, and *Pearl Harbor*, among many others. He argues that these 'dazzling simulacra' of the past lack the hallucinatory quality of true imagination. There used to be a living, dialectical relationship between cinema and the imaginary; now that relation is a negative one (ibid., 33). Cinema today plagiarizes and copies itself, remakes classics and silent films, and is fascinated by itself as a lost object. Yet he sees in this only cold collage and a cool, asexual promiscuity (ibid., 34). The third-order simulacrum of the past is to real history as porn is to real sex: both are pale simulations of the original passions they depict.

Some Postmodern Films

It's a widely accepted in social theory that postmodern culture is defined in part by the heavy interplay between media and everyday life. Thus, it is apropos to conclude here by looking at several films that embody the postmodern condition.

Stardust Memories (1980) and *Zelig* (1984). Woody Allen is a master parodist and postmodern individual. If his screen persona is at all an accurate reflection of his 'real' self, he's narcissistic, self-absorbed, and egotistic, but uses self-deprecatory humour to deflect criticism—in *Stardust Memories* he even has a critic ask him about his narcissism. His characters go through series of empty relationships, then spend the rest of their films engaging in endless self-analysis. Indeed, intense self-analysis and self-parody are Woody's trademarks, including lots of psychiatry jokes. His later films brilliantly reflect the psychological space of the postmodern intellectual bourgeois.

Allen's *Stardust Memories* is a postmodern homage to Federico Fellini's modernist classic *8½*. Like Fellini's film, it was shot in a sombre black and white, and deals with a film director, Sandy Bates, played by Allen. In Fellini's film the main character is Guido Anselmi, a middle-aged film director trying to recover his creative impulses at a health spa while dealing with a failing marriage, a flighty mistress, and a film crew and producer who keep pressing him to make decisions about a science fiction epic he's supposedly working on. Allen's film opens with a scene where Sandy Bates is trapped on a train full of morose passengers, while a passing train is full of partying people: this is a direct parody of the opening scene of *8½*, making clear his intention to recycle or parody Fellini. As with Fellini's film, we see characters questioning the director's waning talents: right after the opening scene, the Lorraine Newman character opines, 'his insights are shallow and morbid. . . . I've seen it all before when they try to document their private suffering and fob it off as art.' The public longs for his early, funny films, not his more pretentious, serious efforts. Allen wanders through the film, like Fellini's Guido, trying to figure out if the life of the artist is worth it at all.

Allen's character goes to a film festival in his honour in a country town, paralleling Guido's visit to the spa. There are endless streams of admirers, cameos, and flashbacks to his childhood: in one we see that the young Sandy is able to fly and do magic tricks. The enchanting Dorrie (Charlotte Rampling) is his lost love, and throughout the film Sandy flashes back to scenes with her. Several fantasy sequences appear, as in Fellini's movie, and several women slide into and out of Sandy's life—Dorrie, a French woman named Isabel, the girlfriend of a college film professor (Jessica Harper), and a nameless woman whose husband has given her permission to sleep with Sandy. Allen parodies Fellini's harem sequence with one of a mad scientist who wants to switch one woman's brain into another's body to make the perfect woman. The film is rife with double-coding—it even has a night scene in an elegant café, like one in $8^1/_2$, where Allen has a tête-à-tête with Tony Roberts. As Sandy muses about death and looks for meaning, he has a memory of a wonderful Sunday morning breakfast with Dorrie while listening to Louis Armstrong, paralleling Guido's final realization in Fellini's movie that the pleasures of life are simple. The whole film is nostalgic—filmed in black and white, with Allen's beloved old jazz constantly playing in the background. In short, *Stardust Memories* is a postmodern homage to the great modernist film auteurs—Fellini and Bergman, Godard and Antonioni. It is, as well, a serious case of recycling: Fellini's film is possible without Allen's, but not vice versa.

As we've seen in the discussion of Baudrillard, *Zelig* is about a man who adapts perfectly to his surroundings—a 'Chameleon Man'. Set in the Jazz Age, Zelig turns into a simulacrum of those around him, e.g., when jamming with black jazz musicians, he becomes a black jazz man himself. In the film we see his progress through newsreels and other documentary footage. Like one of Warhol's prints, he is a simulacrum of the celebrities around him. He has no existence in and of himself, no deep 'self' to return to—he is the postmodern individual, depthless, empty, all surface appearance.

Blade Runner (1982). Ridley Scott's seminal film *Blade Runner*, based on Philip K. Dick's short novel 'Do Androids Dream of Electric Sheep?', is a dystopian story of how the flexible accumulation of world capital will pan out in the immediate future, specifically, the decaying post-industrial, multicultural morass of Los Angeles in 2019. Rick Deckard, the Blade Runner (played by Harrison Ford), hunts down renegade 'replicants', androids built to do hazardous off-world work. They are the hyperstrong, intelligent, skilled slaves of late capitalism (Powell and Lee, 1998: 123–4). The replicants have human emotions, but only live for four years. They are the ideal short-contract workers. They are simulacra of human beings, complete with emotions—and, in the case of Rachel (Sean Young), with human-like memories that convince her that she's not an android. The replicant Roy (Rutger Hauer) goes to visit Tyrell, the head of the gigantic Tyrell Corporation (and his maker), to force him to prolong his life. Tyrell tells him that he should enjoy his short life, because it's like a flame that burns twice as bright. Roy kills him when he discovers that he can't prolong his life—he murders his god, thus fulfilling Nietzsche's prophecy that God is dead.

The streets of Scott's Los Angeles are crowded with ads for mega-corporations—Sony, Coke, Budweiser, and so on. The city itself is a postmodern hodgepodge of architectural styles: Greek, Roman, Chinese, art deco, pyramids, and even a Mayan temple. The film offers us a pastiche and double-coding of modern techniques with past styles. Even the style is double-coded: set in the future, but reminiscent of 1940s film noir, such as *The Maltese Falcon*, with Ford's Deckard as a postmodern Sam Spade. Deckard falls for Rachel, making her aware that she is indeed an android and that her memories of the past are only the simulacrum of a life. They even sleep together,

Deckard blocking out the difference between human and android. But remember—the simulacrum is hyperreal, more real than reality. And maybe in the postmodern age, we are all to a degree cyborgs, human computers, due to our reliance on technology. In fact, film critics have debated whether or not Deckard himself is a replicant. *Blade Runner* helped to give birth to the literary genre of cyberpunk, announced two years later in 1984 with the publication of William Gibson's novel *Neuromancer.*

32 Short Films about Glenn Gould (1993). This Canadian film, starring Colm Feore and directed by François Girard, is a postmodern biography of Glenn Gould, the famous Canadian pianist, told as the story of a decentred and fragmented subject, of a postmodern man. Girard and co-writer Don McKellar (who also briefly appears in the film) have written and compiled 32 vignettes, including interviews with real friends and co-workers of Gould, that loosely fit together to tell the story of Gould's life from his childhood to his death. Here we have true postmodern filmmaking: no linear narrative but a series of fragmented episodes, some of them significant, some not so much so. Music and life interweave. There's a lot of jumping around in Gould's life, e.g., from Short 9, his last concert, to 11, when violinist Yehudi Menuhin disagrees with his decision to quit the concert stage; and from Short 18, which raises the question of his sexuality, to 19, where we hear his letter to a mysterious love interest, to 23, where Gould composes a personal ad.

It's not without irony that Gould saw himself as a media figure, prepared CBC radio documentaries, and was obviously familiar with McLuhan's theories of media (discussed in Chapter 11). After his retirement from live performance, Gould became a media or electronic personality: indeed, in Short 5, 'Gould on Gould', spoken in Gould's own words, he says that he gave up concerts because his involvement with recording and the media represents the future, while the concert hall is the past. Further, he says that he doesn't like the hierarchy of artist and audience, and wants to operate unaware of the presumed demands of the

marketplace, to have the artist abandon a false sense of responsibility. In short, the film is about a sort of death of the pianist as the author of the musical performance.

The Matrix (1999). The Wachowksi brother's popular science fiction fantasy is about an entirely virtual world. Two hundred years in the future artificial intelligence machines have taken over a darkened earth and have imprisoned millions of human beings in vast fields of cocoons, using their bodies for power. While their bodies are imprisoned, the humans' minds unknowingly participate in a virtual reality computer simulation of the Earth at the end of the twentieth century, which keeps most of them contented enough to not question the reality of their non-lives. A small group of rebels led by Morpheus (Laurence Fishburne) and Trinity (Carrie-Anne Moss) recruit Neo (Keanu Reeves) to their cause, removing him from his virtual world to the grim reality of the devastated planet. Morpheus is convinced that Neo is a saviour with the power to control the virtual world created by the artificial intelligence machines, which turns out to be true at the end of the film. Although the film has clear Christian themes—the Holy Trinity, the coming of a saviour, the power of faith over technology—it also makes both explicit and implicit references to Baudrillard's ideas. We see a copy of *Simulacra and Simulation* early in the film; later, after Neo is shown the true nature of things, Morpheus proclaims 'welcome . . . to the desert of the real!' And of course the matrix itself is one big hyperreal simulacrum, a 'prison for your mind' as Morpheus puts it.

The film seems to suggest that the hyperreality of the matrix is a distorted exaggeration of where our culture is headed today: towards a greater and greater reliance on virtual realities and artificial intelligences. The moral message of the film is that we have the power to wake up from our matrix dreams, to fight the power of virtual reality and avoid living in the desert of the real surrounded by computers, televisions, cellphones, Blackberries, and other electronic gadgets common to this environment.

POSTMODERN SPACE/TIME

Harvey on Space/Time Compression in Postmodernity

In *The Condition of Postmodernity* (1989), David Harvey (1935–) presents a view of postmodern culture and society that parallels that of Frederic Jameson and, to a lesser degree, Jean Baudrillard. Like Jameson, he is a historical materialist who believes that although we have an endless capacity to create things, we always do so within historically situated conditions, mainly of an economic nature. Added to this historical materialism is a second powerful theoretical element: his argument that postmodern culture, which he defines as starting roughly in the 1960s, has undergone a 'fierce round' of space-time compression. This is hardly surprising to Harvey, for the annihilation of space and time has always been at the heart of capitalism's dynamic (Harvey, 1989: 293). Yet the advances in the production and distribution of goods and in computers, communications, and transportation sped the whole process up so much in recent times that a qualitatively new state of affairs has arisen. His position on capitalism is clearly similar to that expounded by Marx and Engels in *The Communist Manifesto*:

> Capital is a process and not a thing. It is a process of reproduction of social life through commodity production, in which all of us in the advanced capitalist world are heavily implicated. Its internalized rules of operation are such as to ensure that it is a dynamic and revolutionary mode of social organization, restlessly and ceaselessly transforming the society within which it is embedded. The process masks and fetishizes, achieves growth through creative destruction, creates new wants and needs, exploits the capacity for human labour and desire, transforms spaces, and speeds up the pace of life. (Ibid., 343)

Culture, to Harvey, is becoming increasingly commodified, bound up with the circulation of money. He echoes Jameson in saying that in postmodernity both high and popular culture are rooted in the daily circulation of capital (ibid., 299). Yet the economy and our experience of space and time are only the *necessary* conditions for political and cultural change. A semi-autonomous dialectic of ideas and knowledge drives such change on its own as its *sufficient* condition. In other words, Harvey is no simple economic determinist.

To understand how space-time compression came to dominate our lives, we have to go back in time to the Middle Ages. Under feudalism people lived in definite places with legal, political, and social meaning. Outside the territorial boundaries of their communities, space was ruled by a mysterious cosmology, populating it with heavenly hosts or sinister demons, witches, and monsters. The European voyages of discovery, linked to advances in map-making and increases in international trade, ended all that. The globe became finite and knowable. The use of perspective in the art of the Italian Renaissance bled over into other techniques—maps were made with abstract, fixed grids (borrowed from the ancient cartographer Ptolemy) to portray realistically the surface of the Earth, while commerce and banking were conducted with greater rigour and mathematical precision. The new maps of the Renaissance applied mathematics to a flat surface: space went from the medieval conception of islands of known friendly territory surrounded by *terra incognita* to that of a vast but chartable area open to conquest and habitation. The domination of nature, the conquest of new territories, and the ordering of space according to a mathematical grid went hand in hand in the project of modernity (ibid., 249).

Medieval maps might have a picture of a barn that was as big as a whole city down the road—the question of relative scale wasn't too important. Such quaintly subjective notions of the nature of space, however, didn't survive the end of feudalism. This whole idea of objectivity in spatial representation was valued in the Renaissance and Enlightenment as an aid to navigation, to clearly define property rights and political boundaries, and to determine rights of passage (ibid., 245). As space compressed, its political and economic value was accentuated. Land became private property—a commodity—and as such had to have an owner. Accurate maps were the means whereby this valuable resource was divided between the contending powers.

Time also had to be measured more accurately. In the Enlightenment, chronometers of various types moved the human race from biological or seasonal time to clock time. The Enlightenment operated within Isaac Newton's vision of the cosmos, with absolutes of homogeneous time and space forming limiting containers for thought and action. An hour in Inverness, Scotland, is exactly the same as an hour in Perth, Australia; ten feet of wood in the wilds of Canada is the same as ten feet of wood in the Palace of Versailles. Yet the breakdown in these absolute views of space and time under the stress of time-space compression 'was the central story of the birth of nineteenth- and early twentieth-century forms of modernism' (ibid., 252). Picasso's cubism, Einstein's theory of relativity, T.S. Eliot's disjointed narrative in 'The Waste Land', and many other aspects of modernist culture followed suit from the space-time compression caused by modern technology and economic changes by picturing a world of fragmented spaces and disjointed temporal structures.

Moving back a bit, Harvey argues that the key year when it all changed was 1848. From then on, capitalism made a huge investment in the conquest of space: witness the development of the railway, steam-powered ships, the telegraph, the building of the Suez Canal, then later radio and the automobile. These technological changes, added to the expansion of world trade from the mid-nineteenth century on, put capitalism firmly on the road to globalism (ibid., 264), and led to imperial rivalries between Britain, France, Germany, Japan, Russia, and the US, winding up in the Great War. Picasso called it a 'cubist war', no doubt because the suppression of spatial barriers had made the world one big political canvas full of distorted objects. In the end the power of money and 'aesthetic' politics like fascism tri-umphed over the modernist movement, the only artistic movement that tried rationally to control time-space compression. This brings us to postmodernism.

For Harvey, postmodern culture represents a crisis in Enlightenment thought. Abstract reason is denounced, while universal projects of human emancipation are instinctively distrusted. Postmodern culture willingly embraces ephemerality, fragmentation, discontinuity, and chaos (ibid., 44). The modernists may have resisted having their art and literature commercialized, yet the postmodernist embraces the market with gusto. This goes hand in hand with the fact that today large corporations are the main patrons of the arts. From the 1960s on, high culture lost its authority over culture as a whole, as pop art, shifting fashions, and mass taste were promoted by capitalist consumerism addicted to a mindless hedonism (ibid., 60). Telecommunications aided in the process of eroding high culture and compressing space and time: the average American family (at least around 1990) watches seven hours of TV each day, yet spends only a fraction of that time in meaningful interaction with other people. As a result, people see history and the world as a collection of simultaneous and equal events. Surfaces dominate depths and people's local roots are pulled out by jetliners and news reports from around the globe.

Over the last few decades a particularly intense phase of space-time compression 'has had a disorientating and disruptive impact upon political-economic practices, the balance of class power, as well as upon cultural and social life' (ibid., 286). Economic life has seen a number of important changes: a bevy of new technologies, led by computers; the subcontracting and outsourcing of production, which has overturned the old-fashioned corporation with its Fordist (after Henry Ford, a pioneer in assembly-line mass production) methods and vertical integration; the Japanese-inspired just-in-time delivery system for raw materials and parts; and the electronic control of production, to mention just the most important changes (ibid., 285). This has led to quicker turnover times in production. Improved communication and distribution chains quicken the circulation of commodities through the world market. And buying all these new commodities is easier, too, with electronic banking and plastic money in the form of bank and credit cards. Lastly, there has been a partial shift from the consumption of goods to that of services, as one would predict from the post-industrial economy Daniel Bell saw the beginnings of in the 1960s.

Yet two economic developments have had an especially striking impact on postmodern culture. First, fads and fashions have been mobilized in mass markets for clothes, ornamentation, personal technologies, pop music, video, and other such things. This lends a volatility and transient nature to products, labour processes, ideas, and tastes: today's fad melts into air tomorrow; pop stars rise and fall like waves hitting a shoreline. Second, everything has to be instantaneous and disposable, from fast food and packaging to values, relationships, and commitments to physical locales. Our throwaway society discourages attachments to products, people, and places, bombarding us with images that offer newer and better versions of what we already have. Advertising manipulates our desires through the unholy trinity of money, sex, and power to keep us buying, to keep us changing, to keep us on the move. All of this compresses the time we feel attached to things—to our new car, to our hometown, to our mate.

Harvey offers a few specific examples of the effects of time-space compression and the culture of the media image. Both corporations and political leaders rely increasingly on the media to provide them with positive images. Such images are more important than production levels or good policies. In fact, politics has become in part 'aestheticized': charisma and look are more important than political wisdom, as witnessed in Ronald Reagan's bellicose presidency and Margaret Thatcher's fight over the Falklands, and more recently in George W. Bush's manipulation of the media, Congress, and the American public to justify the bombardment and invasion of Iraq in 2003. The power of the media has created a world of simulated images, Baudrillard's simulacra. Yet

Harvey notes that it's not just TV and advertising images that dominate our culture—it also builds material simulacra such as environments copied from other times and places, spectacles, even obsolete means of transportation and labour (e.g., the copy of Columbus's ship, the *Santa Maria*, in the West Edmonton Mall).

Art is now churned out like sausages to appease a mass market. In the late 1980s New York could boast 150,000 artists and 680 galleries in its greater area; a generation before it had only a handful of galleries and a few full-time artists (ibid., 290). Ironically perhaps, postmodern culture has seen a series of religious revivals (e.g., Islamic and Christian fundamentalism) along with regional outbreaks of extreme nationalism (e.g., the nations of the former Yugoslavia and Soviet Union) as responses to the compression of space and the speeding up of global communications. The idea of being everywhere at once thanks to the mass media leaves one rootless, without a clear identity. To reject this unhappy condition, local loyalties and archaic religious values are embraced by some with fervour, leading to the many simmering regional conflicts of our age.

Harvey, being a historical materialist, sees money as the root of all the simulated evils of our times. We are going through a crisis of representation fuelled in part by a crisis in the way money represents value. Once upon a time—in the postwar period up until the early 1970s—the world's currencies were tied to the US dollar, itself convertible into gold. The collapse of the Bretton Woods agreements (signed in 1944) and the end of the gold standard led to floating exchange rates, which quickly became unstable. The 1970s saw rampant inflation, making money itself worth less and less every day. At the same time the world financial system was separated from actual production, becoming a huge casino where speculators meet in a global poker game. Money is now a sign without any material foundation, what Derrida would call a 'floating signifier'. The collapse of energy giant Enron in a massive stock manipulation swindle in 2001 illustrates Harvey's point well. The company's managers made no pretense of producing any real 'value' by their actions other than the manufacture of a dynamic corporate image, which they used to increase stock prices and thus enrich themselves.

Finally, postmodern culture raises a number of spatial issues. Modernity aimed to make space uniform and homogeneous, and capitalism succeeded to some degree—think of how suburbs, strip malls, chain stores, and expressways look pretty well the same everywhere in North America. As a result, capitalist firms seek out local spaces that are at least a bit unique to please their employees. A few 'world cities' may act as centres of finance and communications, but local differences in the availability of materials and in taste become important under conditions of global economic competition. Corporatist local governments flourish as cities compete to forge distinctive images and interesting traditional atmospheres to lure investment and the 'right' people. Yet, too often, the result is what Harvey calls 'serial monotony': the same quaint markets and fishermen's wharves in New York, Boston, and Baltimore (ibid., 295). This isn't too surprising, for the annihilation of space has ramped up the mix of commodities available to the consumer in most parts of the world. North Americans buy French cheese and German beer, while Europeans sample genuine American pizza and hamburgers. The world's cuisine can be assembled in one place, sometimes as confined as that of a shopping mall food court. The same goes for other forms of recreation: simulacral samples of local culture buzz around the world in the wink of an eye without leaving traces of their origins in the history or labour processes of where they came from. 'The general implication is that through the experience of everything from food, to culinary habits, music, television, entertainment, and cinema, it is now possible to experience the world's geography vicariously, as a simulacrum' (ibid., 300). Global space shrinks to a 20-inch television screen or a take-out paper box from the local Thai restaurant.

For Harvey, two attitudes to this intense phase of space-time compression result (ibid., 301–2). The first is that expressed by Charles Jencks and, one would imagine, the majority of Westerners: let's just enjoy the multicultural ride, with a sushi roll in one hand and an Aztec mask in the other. What's so bad about escape and fantasy? The world is our oyster; eclecticism is the 'natural evolution' of a culture of choice. The second reaction is to reject globalization and to search for personal and collective cultural identity. We saw the dark side of this search for collective identity in New York City on 11 September 2001 and in the events in the Middle East that flowed from these attacks. Neither option seems to offer a satisfactory way out of the cultural condition of postmodernity.

Charles Jencks and Postmodern Architecture

Charles Jencks (1939–) is important to social theory for two reasons: first, he revived the use of the term 'postmodern' in the mid-1970s after a long hiatus (it had been used previously by the historian Arnold Toynbee in the 1940s, along with several others); second, he attacks modernist architecture as a failed experiment, defending what he called 'postmodern architecture' as offering more livable public spaces. By the early 1970s, people were growing tired of the concrete, steel, and glass boxes produced by modernist architecture, which dates to around 1900 but really picked up steam in the 1920s and 1930s. Modernist architects like Le Corbusier (1887–1965) and Ludwig Mies van der Rohe (1886–1969) pioneered the International Style, which emphasized simple geometric forms made of concrete, steel, and glass, designed to be as free from ornamentation as possible as part of a utopian break with the past. Le Corbusier's 'machines for living in' and van der Rohe's black-and-grey monoliths dominate the skylines of most North American and not a few European cities. One example is van der Rohe's TD Centre in Toronto, a typical soulless modernist black box, though we can see similar structures in the downtowns of all larger North American cities. This building is a close cousin of his more famous Seagram Building in New York (finished in 1958), a flagship of modernism.

In a public lecture Jencks proclaimed the death of high modernist architecture as taking place on 15 July 1972, when the huge Pruitt-Igoe modernist housing project in St Louis was blown up. Jencks agreed with the literary critic Umberto Eco that the past cannot be destroyed, as in modernism, but instead should be revisited with irony. Jencks calls this quoting of the past 'double-coding': postmodernist architecture uses modern techniques but quotes traditional elements. That way it can appeal both to other architects and to the public, for whom modernist minimalism offers little inspiration. Postmodernist buildings use eclectic mixes of two or more different periods to create ambiguity, contradiction, and paradox, for example, when they reintroduce colour, columns, ornamental facades, and statues. For Jencks, we can read buildings like post-structuralist theorists read books: they can mean two things at once and participate simultaneously in two distinct codes. There is no need to impose on lived space a single all-encompassing logic.

Postmodern architecture, according to Jencks, has a number of general characteristics. First of all, it rejects the modernist view that the classical style is out of bounds for political reasons. Greek and Roman classicism had left a bad taste in many modernist mouths due to the fascist taste for classical architecture, as witnessed in Hitler and Albert Speer's monumental building projects in Berlin and elsewhere. Also, postmodernist architects want to have a *dialogue with history*. They do this through the use of the column, statues, ornamentation, and colour, as did the ancient Egyptians, Minoans, Greeks, and Romans, along with Renaissance and Enlightenment European architects. Jencks lists 10 specific characteristics of postmodern architecture (1987: 330–46):

1. *Pluralism:* A celebration of difference, otherness, and radical eclecticism. Things don't have to be rigidly symmetrical and uniform, as with modernism. This could include the use of ambiguous signs about the function or aesthetics of the building.

2. *Dissonant beauty:* Elements of the building may clash, but the overall effect is pleasing.

3. *Urbane urbanism (contextualism):* New buildings fit into and extend the urban context, e.g., renovating a downtown warehouse instead of dynamiting it and building a modern apartment building.

4. *Anthropomorphism:* The use of ornaments, mouldings, and statues that suggest the human body.

5. *The relation between past and present:* The parody, nostalgic replaying, and making of a pastiche of past styles.

6. *Yearning for content:* Making a building *about* something, e.g., using elements of a Greek temple for a 'temple of commerce'—that is, a bank. Buildings can tell a story.

7. *Double-coding:* As we have seen, this is reading the present in the past and the past in the present, a drawing on tradition while using modern building techniques. In other words, a use of both traditional and modern codes of architecture.

8. *Multivalence:* The use of several codes simultaneously and coherently.

9. *Tradition reinterpreted:* When architecture returns to the past, it must be to a degree inventive, not just copy what came before.

10. *The return to the absent centre:* The desire for a communal space combined with the admission that there's nothing adequate to fill it.

Jencks feels that postmodernism is of two minds about the past: it wants to retain and preserve aspects of the past while also wanting to escape its dead formulas. Contemporary communications, scholarship, and fabrication methods make all styles equally possible. There's no reason we can't choose our own codes and conventions: this is much more interesting than adhering to the rigid rules of modernism.

Postmodernist architecture tries to create a dissonance between the past and present by means of irony, play, humour, and paradox. Its double-coding makes it accessible not only to the average person, but also to the most discerning professional architect. An example is Michael Graves's Portland Public Services Building, which has coloured ornamental garlands/ribbons on its sides, hints of an Egyptian motif with false monumental columns on the front, along with a 36-foot-tall bronze sculpture of the imaginary classical goddess Portlandia poised over the front door, who creates a playful mood with her Greek toga and trident. Critics had harsh words for Graves's design. Yet when Portlandia was transported to her permanent place by barge and then truck in 1985, crowds lined up to watch, touching her before she was out of reach forever. Such could not be said of the steel beams and panes of glass in one of van der Rohe's corporate towers.

Postmodernist architecture seeks to regenerate what's already there with the new. It refers to its environment, unlike modernist buildings, whose simple geometric forms soar above their surroundings with their mission to rationally transform society. In their 1972 book *Learning from Las Vegas*, Robert Venturi, Denise Scott Brown, and Charles Izenour attacked the universalistic, utopian, hyper-planned elements of modernism, which tries to enclose space in glass and steel geometric forms without ornamentation, sculpture, or graphics to relieve the harsh mechanical feeling that results. Venturi and his colleagues prefer street architecture that grows up organically and unplanned, a common language of space that the people really like, as in Disneyland or Las Vegas. The chaotic mixture of styles on the Las Vegas strip is more popular than uniform, rigid, and abstract monuments erected by modernist architects. Venturi et al. called for an architecture that combines mass-cultural elements with pop art, comedy, sorrow, and paradox, defending the mix-and-unmatched oriental bazaars and exotic Etruscan, Roman, and Moorish architecture of Las Vegas, which plays with multiple elements of the past. This is the type of architecture suitable to a pluralistic society—non-authoritarian. Architecture should be plural and fun rather than cater to an abstract, utopian concept of Man (Powell and Lee, 1998: 86).

Philip Johnson's AT&T Building (now called the Sony Building) in New York illustrates these principles, showing some postmodernist features—it's in the shape of a grandfather clock with a Chippendale broken pediment at the top. It plays with the past, and parodies the modernist skyscrapers that surround it. Its broken pediment, shape, and monumental entrance suggest a double-coding of the modern office tower with a grandfather clock and a classical temple. Like all postmodernist architecture, it means more than one thing (multivalence), is pluralistic, double-coded, and playfully mocks the past. Postmodern architecture is about reclaiming a livable public space; it rejects Lyotard's performativity, choosing instead a combination of playfulness and history.

In general, modernist art was scientific, experimental, intellectual, and often abstract. It disdained mass appeal, even though it eventually found it. Picasso's cubism broke down everyday reality into flat geometric shapes; the abstract expressionists gave up on the human figure and plant life as subjects, producing paintings with coloured rectangles, lines, circles, even blobs of paint. As Kim Levin notes (1988: 2–3), modern art was austere, puritanical, and elitist, demanding clarity and order. Yet people finally got bored of all that 'arctic purity': one can only look at three geometrical coloured stripes for so long and still expect to see anything meaningful in it.[8] In contrast, postmodern art involves a return to nature that 'quotes, scavenges, ransacks, recycles the past. Its method is synthesis rather than analysis. It is style-free and free-style. Playful and full of doubt, it denies nothing. Tolerant of ambiguity, contradiction, complexity, incoherence, it is eccentrically inclusive' (ibid., 4). If the typical emblem of modernism is the grid—look at the map of a typical modern city, or the blueprint of a modern apartment building—the emblem of postmodern art is the map, with its arbitrary and flexible boundaries based on such natural barriers as rivers, mountains, and seas (ibid., 7). Both Levin and Jencks hold out the hope that postmodern art and architecture will stage a partial return to nature and the human figure, and thus to elements of classicism, romanticism, and other traditional styles.

Jameson on the Glossy Surfaces of Late Capitalism

Frederic Jameson agrees that architecture is 'the privileged aesthetic language of postmodernism', but what he considers to be 'postmodern' architecture or 'postmodern' space is rather different from Jencks (Jameson, 1991: 37). Just as he connects postmodern culture to late capitalism, he sees the architecture of postmodernism as the sort of building that commodifies space in the service of modern capital. These buildings usually have enormous glass surfaces that reflect each other like the hostile glare of two bikers wearing mirrored sunglasses, whatever minor cannibalizations of past styles they might incorporate to soften their appearance. Jameson notes how the 'exhilaration' produced by these bank towers and corporate headquarters can be a delight to our eyes, yet produce a quantum leap in urban alienation as they repel urban squalor and poverty with their reflective surfaces (ibid., 33). They are *not* Jencks's lived spaces, but glossy skins, images without depth, an *architectural hyperspace*. Their goal is to express 'the great global multinational and decentered communicational network in which we find ourselves caught as individual subjects' (ibid., 44). They are like giant nodes of commerce linked to a global network of ever-accumulating capital.

What Jameson calls 'postmodern' buildings— the Eaton Centre in Toronto, the Beaubourg (Museum of Modern Art) in Paris, and the Westin Bonaventure Hotel in Los Angeles—aspire to be miniature cities, hyperspaces in which individuals move and congregate, creating a 'hypercrowd'. They are artificial spaces with artificial communities, all in the service of capital. This new architecture tries to expand our senses to new and yet unimagined dimensions (ibid., 39–40). A case in point is John Portman's Westin Bonaventure Hotel. Its mighty glass skin repels the city outside it. Its escalators and elevators are transportation machines. Its busy nature gives one the feeling that its emptiness is absolutely packed. Jameson sees it as a hyperspace where all depth is suppressed. In general, Jameson sees postmodern architecture as a refinement of modernism, with more space, more glass, and a few naturalistic touches added, yet still giving us artificial, alienating, and hyperreal spaces.

Borgmann's Postmodern Festive City

We end this chapter with a look at the work of Albert Borgmann, a philosophy professor at the University of Montana. Borgmann's *Crossing the Postmodern Divide* (1992) synthesizes a general analysis of the social and philosophical nature of modernism and postmodernism with a defence of the postmodern city as a space for communal celebration. Borgmann is a Roman Catholic, so he tends to see things in trinities. Table 9.3 lists his main ones.

He starts with the traditional trinity of pre-modern, modern, and postmodern societies, roughly the same classification used by Bell, Castells, Lyotard, and many other social theorists. In the pre-modern Middle Ages people had a sense of local boundedness (to their village or castle or town), cosmic centredness (the human race and its world were at the centre of the cosmos), and divine constitution (God ruled the world in a benevolent and just fashion). Columbus, Copernicus, and Luther shattered this medieval trinity. Columbus's voyage to the Americas shattered the European sense of being locally bound to the centre of the world; Copernicus's discovery that the Earth revolved around the Sun, and not vice versa, made people realize that their little orb was *not* the centre of a divinely ordered universe; Martin Luther's Protestant Reformation, with its reliance on the authority of the Bible, fatally weakened (in Borgmann's eyes) the communal power of divinity (Borgmann, 1992: 22).

The end of the pre-modern world opened up nature to conquest by technology and the planet as a whole to conquest by European culture. Borgmann argues that due to technological innovation and economic changes, the project of modernity was characterized by three things: *aggressive realism*, *methodological universalism*, and *ambiguous individualism*. The theorists and artists

Table 9.3 Borgmann's Trinities

Type of Society/World View	Main Characteristics	City Life
Pre-modern (Middle Ages)	Local boundedness Cosmic centredness Divine constitution	The traditional village or town: unplanned; life adjusted to the seasons.
Modern	Aggressive realism Methodological universalism Ambiguous individualism	Cities rationally planned according to a rigid geometric grid/framework.
[Hypermodern, a variation of modernism]	Hyperreality Hyperactivity Hyperintelligence	The car rules: expressways, high-rises, suburbs, and shopping malls result.
Postmodern	Focal realism Patient vigour Communal celebration	Let urban life grow spontaneously; decommodify celebration.

of modernity wanted to picture the real world in terms of universal philosophical and mathematical principles, supported by an ethic that championed the individual over the state and the church. This leads Borgmann to analyze our own recent past in terms of another trinity of ideal types of society and to view postmodern culture in a somewhat different light from other theorists we have looked at. This trinity is *modernism*, *hypermodernism*, and *postmodernism*. He assigns most of the negative aspects of what others call 'postmodernism' to the distorted form of culture he calls 'hypermodernism'.

The aggressive realism of modernism led it on a campaign to conquer nature, as seen most clearly in the conquest of the American West in the nineteenth century by farmers, railways, and the US cavalry. Yet the more recent conquest of nature and modernization of cities came thanks to the automobile. Architects and planners couldn't resist its logic. The car conquered time and space, acting as a symbol of individual freedom. It was the vehicle of modernism, 'the force that empowered builders to reorder the untidy and irrational structures of the late nineteenth and early twentieth centuries' (ibid., 58). Cars forced cities to give up their old complexity and with it the traditional urban fabric in exchange for high-rises, suburbs, and expressways. Modernism ate its own urban children, the cities that failed to measure up to the standards of a rational and enlightened order. The results were a rigid geometrical

purity akin to three-dimensional Cartesian co-ordinates. At the same time, all this traffic-based rationality left the public square naked, a faint image in our rear-view mirrors.

Hypermodernism is connected to a number of things. First, it's linked to what Borgmann calls 'commodious individualism', which replaced the rugged individualism of nineteenth-century America. The commodious individual is a consumer who travels from place to place and through his or her social sphere with ease, a person who consumes products and space in as little time as possible. As a result, advanced industrial countries face a situation unprecedented in human history—goods saturation. One can only buy so much furniture, so many laptops, computer games, DVDs, or brand-name sneakers, and still discover any meaningful use value in them. So with hypermodernism comes the possibility that our emotional hunger for consumable things will run dry (ibid., 63).

Connected to this is Borgmann's fear that we are in danger of losing our sense of reality. In the present age we are faced with two social tendencies related to technology: the *hypermodern* tendency to endlessly refine technology at all costs, and *postmodern realism*, the sense that we should outgrow our obsessive reliance on technology and to put it at the service of reality, of things that command our respect.[9] Borgmann breaks both of these down into further trinities of social trends. Hypermodernism is devoted to the 'design of a technologically sophisticated and glamorously unreal universe, distinguished by its hyperreality, hyperactivity, and hyperintelligence'. Postmodern realism aims instead to recover 'the world of eloquent things', and has the characteristics of *focal realism*, *patient vigour*, and *communal celebration* (ibid., 6). Postmodernism is a check on hyperreality, a 'thickening network' that obscures our connection to natural and traditional realities, choking them off by populating our world with machines and computer fantasies (ibid., 119). Thus, for Borgmann, postmodernism is a partial revival of traditional ways of life, leaving the blame for the death of the real at the doorstep of a supercharged modernity.

We live in hyperreal worlds, work and take our leisure like hyperactive rabbits, and rely on hyperintelligent machines to do our thinking. This hypermodernism can only be met by a genuine alternative, postmodern realism, which takes into account the criticisms of postmodern theorists and tries to deal with the hypermodern condition with a patient vigour centred on communal celebration (ibid., 12). What are these 'eloquent things' that Borgmann thinks we should return to? Primarily they are a combination of wild nature and traditional ways of life, which exist today only in the narrow openings left behind by hyperreality—for example, in parts of the wilderness that are too expensive to develop or in community practices that can't be commodified. The focal reality aspect of postmodernism involves things that engage our mind and body and centre our lives—they have a commanding presence. Borgmann argues that in North America the wilderness has the clearest voice among eloquent things, for it's the closest connection we have to the primeval world. The voice of the wilderness 'has a powerfully commanding resonance . . . because it shows no traces of human intonation. It speaks to us naturally' (ibid., 120). If the focal charms of a horse or forest or stream lack hyperreal thrills, so what: at least they are grounded in an underlying reality, unlike computer games, television, or pop concerts.

This finally leads Borgmann to consider architecture and the postmodern city. Architecture is the most dramatic manifestation of postmodernism, and we should be thankful for the kinder, gentler climate it has brought with it, even if it's ambiguous towards creating truly festive and well-grounded buildings (ibid., 60). To promote postmodern realism, we need to emphasize a sense of community and the space it occupies, to rediscover the connection between focal things, people, and practices. Modernism and the automobile are the real enemies of a healthy urban atmosphere: the car drove out the untidy fabric of traditional cities in favour of a 'pseudopastoral landscape of towers in a park' (ibid., 128). Borgmann wants an urban reality that is ferial (focused on ordinary life) and festal, an urban life where a diversity of human concerns can converge and cohere in an intricate pattern of streets. Echoing Robert Venturi, he says that city life cannot be designed and controlled but only allowed to happen, allowing its utilitarian and extravagant aspects to coexist (ibid., 131). Daily life in the city is sturdy, full of real spaces, real people, real activities. Yet it must be defended against hypermodern activity and hyperreality. If real urban life is restricted to mere islands of daily energy and diversity, the tides of hypermodernism will erode its foundation, and our everyday lives will collapse or float off into hyperreality. In short, daily reality 'needs to be linked to the natural, raised to the festal, and extended to the poor' (ibid., 133). This can be accomplished through means as simple as creating parks connected to rural and wild nature by trails. Although Borgmann doesn't mention this, the alternative is to see suburban shopping malls as the new public squares, complete with plastic trees and purely commercial motivations for existing in the first place. The shopping mall and corporate office tower are the public spaces of hypermodernism, disconnected from nature, with a commodified sense of community where consumers gather only to celebrate their latest purchases.

Borgmann ends by calling for a 'festive city' based on the principles of what he calls postmodern realism. Sadly, our public spaces have been sacrificed to expressways, high-rises, parking garages, and other transportational wastelands. The festive city needs streets, courts, and gardens where people can sit, eat, meet, and read. These need more vigorous support from local merchants, who are all too reluctant to invest in the streets more than a few feet from their front doors. Hypermodern technology has allowed us to mechanize and commodify all celebration, transferring the job of entertaining to hidden machinery that produces a commodity 'guaranteed to excite and entertain' (ibid., 134). With the increasing use of technology, the elements of genuine celebration—reality, community, and divinity—slowly slip away. Borgmann gives the example of pop concerts where reality is transformed by gigantic intricate machinery such as stacks of loudspeakers, huge television screens, lasers, and inflated flying pigs into an alluring hypercharged commodity, a really *big* show (here he echoes Guy Debord, knowingly or not). We've become too used to the idea of having celebration served up to us like a McDonald's burger or Starbucks coffee. Borgmann wants a richer sense of reality connected to a deeper sense of community. He gives as a counter-example to the pop concert a ballpark (minor league, one would guess) where banter and laughter flow naturally between strangers and unite them into a community, hoping that when reality and community conspire, divinity can descend upon the game (ibid., 135). What we need in general is not radical changes, but a move away from the machinery and commodities of hypermodernism to the support of places 'where reality, community, and divinity are joined in celebration' (ibid., 139). Of course, this leaves open the question whether the average citizen of postmodernity really *wants* to escape his or her hypermodern lifestyle; after all, that Starbucks coffee is awfully tasty, and the pop star of the moment does put on a frightfully good show. Yet the fact that travel to less bustling places such as the islands and countries of the Caribbean and Mediterranean is as popular as ever, with its implied need to escape the hyperreal rat race of post-industrial Western societies, leaves one the hope that the festive city is something more than just a mirage in Borgmann's mind. People want to escape hypermodernity—it's just a matter of where they can escape *to.*

STUDY QUESTIONS

1. What does Jameson mean by 'late capitalism'? In what ways is postmodern culture a stage of late capitalism? Give some examples from popular culture.
2. What are the five depth models Jameson feels postmodern culture eliminates? What are some examples from postmodern art, film, and music that illustrate these changes?
3. How does Eagleton defend modernist art and literature against post-structuralism? Is his critique of post-structuralism justified?
4. What does Baudrillard mean by 'simulacrum' and 'the desert of the real'? What is the gist of this argument that we live in such a desert? Is he right?
5. How does reality TV illustrate Baudrillard's ideas about hyperreality? Give some examples from shows currently on the air to make your case.
6. What are Baudrillard's orders of simulacra? What relation to reality characterizes each? Give examples of how the economy and technology worked in each of them.
7. What does Baudrillard think of contemporary America? Does he exaggerate?
8. Outline the five key aspects of postmodern popular culture, giving several examples of each from film, TV, music, or literature. Is most of pop culture today 'postmodern'?
9. Discuss how music or television today embodies postmodernism, using examples both from the text and from your own experience.
10. How does Baudrillard think that film today offers a 'precession of simulacra'? Can you think of any recent examples of this phenomenon?

11. Critically discuss how three of the films reviewed in the text embody postmodern culture. Compare each of them to a recent film of a similar genre.

12. What view of time and space came into existence in the Renaissance and Enlightenment? What did maps and clocks have to do with these new views?

13. How does Harvey connect modern capitalism to the time-space compression we experience in post-modern culture? Is this compression as serious as he thinks?

14. What, according to Venturi et al. and Jencks, is wrong with modernist architecture? Using an example of a modernist building in your own city or town, evaluate their critical attitude.

15. Outline Jencks's 10 elements of postmodern architecture. Apply them to the Portland Public Services Building and the AT&T Building in New York.

16. What does Jameson mean by 'postmodern' architecture? Is it different from or the same as Jencks's version? Explain.

17. What, for Borgmann, are the main characteristics of pre-modern, modern, and postmodern societies? What sort of cities do we find in each?

18. What does Borgmann mean by 'hypermodernism'? What are its three subsidiary elements? Why is he critical of it?

19. Describe Borgmann's festive city. Is this just a pipe dream, or could it become a reality? Explain.

20. Match up each of the seven aspects of postmodern culture to the theorists discussed in Chapters 8 and 9. Which aspect do you think is the most important one? Why?

SHORT BIBLIOGRAPHY

Baudrillard, Jean. 1976. *L'échange symbolique et la mort*. Paris: Gallimard.

———. 1984. *Simulacra and Simulation*, trans. Sheila Faria Glaser. Ann Arbor: University of Michigan Press.

———. 1987. *The Evil Demon of Images*. Sydney: Power Institute of Fine Arts.

———. 1988 [1986]. *America*, trans. Chris Turner. London: Verso.

———. 1998 [1983]. *The Ecstasy of Communication*, trans. Bernard and Caroline Schutze. New York: Semiotexte.

———. 2001a. 'Symbolic Exchange and Death', trans. Charles Levin, in Mark Poster, ed., *Jean Baudrillard: Selected Writings*. Stanford, Calif.: Stanford University Press.

———. 2001b. 'The Gulf War Did Not Take Place', trans. Paul Patton, in Mark Poster, ed., *Jean Baudrillard: Selected Writings*. Stanford, Calif.: Stanford University Press.

Borgmann, Albert. 1992. *Crossing the Postmodern Divide*. Chicago: University of Chicago Press.

Eagleton, Terry. 1985. 'Capitalism, Modernism, and Postmodernism', *New Left Review* 152: 60–73.

Harvey, David. 1989. *The Condition of Postmodernity: An Enquiry into the Origins of Cultural Change*. Oxford: Blackwell.

Hutcheon, Linda. 1989. *The Politics of Postmodernism*. London: Routledge.

Giddens, Anthony. 1991. *Modernity and Self-Identity: Self and Society in the Late Modern Age*. Stanford, Calif.: Stanford University Press.

Jameson, Frederic. 1984. 'Foreword' to Jean-Francois Lyotard, *The Postmodern Condition*, trans. Geoff Bennington and Brian Massumi. Minneapolis: University of Minnesota Press.

———. 1991. *Postmodernism, or, The Cultural Logic of Late Capitalism*. Durham, NC: Duke University Press.

Jencks, Charles. 1977. *The Language of Post-Modern Architecture*. London: Academy Editions.

———. 1987. *Post-Modernism: The New Classicism in Art and Architecture*. New York: Rizzoli.

Levin, Kim. 1988. 'Farewell to Modernism', in Levin, *Beyond Modernism: Essays on Art from the 70's and 80's*. New York: Harper and Row.

Mandel, Ernest. 1975. *Late Capitalism*, trans. Joris de Bres. London: NLB.

Mann, Douglas, and G. Elijah Dann. 2005. *Philosophy: A New Introduction*. Belmont, Calif.: Wadsworth.

Powell, Jim, and Joel Lee. 1998. *Postmodernism for Beginners*. New York: Writers and Readers.

Rosenau, Pauline Marie. 1992. *Post-Modernism and the Social Sciences*. Princeton, NJ: Princeton University Press.

Smart, Barry. 2005. 'Postmodernism', in Austin Harrington, ed., *Modern Social Theory*. Oxford: Oxford University Press.

Strinati, Dominic. 1995. *An Introduction to Theories of Popular Culture*. London: Routledge.

Venturi, Robert, Denise Scott Brown, and Steven Izenour. 1972. *Learning from Las Vegas*. Cambridge, Mass.: MIT Press.

Filmography

8¹/₂. 1963. Directed by Federico Fellini; written by Fedrico Fellini, Ennio Flaiano, Tullio Pinelli, and Brunello Rondi.

Stardust Memories. 1980. Written and directed by Woody Allen.

Zelig. 1983. Written and directed by Woody Allen.

Blade Runner. 1982. Directed by Ridley Scott; written by Philip K. Dick, Hampton Fancher, and David Webb Peoples.

Thirty-Two Short Films about Glenn Gould. 1993. Directed by François Girard; written by François Girard and Don McKellar.

The Matrix. 1999. Written and directed by Andy and Larry Wachowksi.

Memento. 2000. Directed by Christopher Nolan; written by Christopher Nolan and Jonathan Nolan.

The Simpsons. 1989–. Fox TV show. Various writers and directors.

CHAPTER 10 FEMINISM

THE THREE WAVES OF FEMINIST THEORY AND PRACTICE

Feminist theory is a vast field that would require several thick volumes to cover. In this chapter we'll look at a number of feminist theorists who are the most relevant for modern social theory, leaving out many more than we include. There are a variety of schools of feminist theory that disagree with each other on some basic issues. Yet there's one issue they all agree on. According to Marilyn Frye, a feminist is someone who thinks that women are oppressed. Naturally, at some level this implies that men (either individually or as part of some greater social structure) are doing the oppressing. This is a good working definition of feminism.

First-Wave Feminism

We can trace the beginnings of feminist theory back to the 1790s, a turbulent period in Western history. Ordinary women took part in some of the demonstrations and mob attacks on symbols and people of privilege during the French Revolution. They also worked behind the scenes, hosting salons, writing, and agitating for change. The last few decades of the Enlightenment were a time when people like Thomas Paine, Thomas Jefferson, the Marquis de Condorcet, and William Godwin advocated for the rights of man. 'We hold these truths to be self-evident, that all men are created equal, that they are endowed by their Creator with certain inalienable Rights', asserted the 1776 Declaration of Independence of the American rebels against the British Crown penned by Jefferson. Some women of the day took this talk of rights seri-

ously and went a step further. Olympe de Gouges (1748–93) wrote a pamphlet in 1791 called 'Declaration of the Rights of Woman and Citizen' in which she argued for equal legal and political rights for women. The Declaration included a provision for marriage as a social contract between two equal parties that could end with a fair division of property. She was rewarded by the revolutionary government with a trip to the guillotine.

Yet the opening trumpet blast of feminist theory that summoned a regiment of women to its cause was Mary Wollstonecraft's 1792 book, *A Vindication of the Rights of Women*. Wollstonecraft (1759–97), who had a troubled personal life before finally marrying the anarchist William Godwin, argued that women could be just as rational as men if properly educated. Instead, they were encouraged to study the frivolous arts such as dancing, singing, chit-chatting, and looking pretty in order to attract a husband. The fact that men are stronger physically than women was to Wollstonecraft morally meaningless in this Age of Reason. If men wanted good partners and mothers for their children, they should treat women as rational human beings, as friends, not servants.

First-wave feminism started in the nineteenth century and gathered strength in the early twentieth century as the final battles for women's suffrage were fought. Its goal was basic legal rights for women, which didn't exist in most countries until the early or mid-twentieth century. Its specific aims were the rights to vote, to hold property independently of one's husband, to a fair divorce with child custody, to run for and hold public office, and to an education in colleges and universities. In America in the mid-nineteenth cen-

Mary Wollstonecraft. (National Portrait Gallery, London)

tury feminism was tied to the abolition of slavery, which succeeded in 1862 with President Lincoln's Emancipation Proclamation. The American first wave was led by Elizabeth Cady Stanton (1815–1902) and Lucretia Mott (1793–1880), a Quaker like many of the early feminists. Both were abolitionists. When they were restricted from active participation in anti-slavery meetings, Stanton and Mott organized the Seneca Falls Convention in 1848, a meeting of about 300 delegates interested in women's rights who gathered in this small New York town. They drafted a Declaration of Sentiments that declared, among other things, that 'We hold these truths to be self-evident: that all men and women are created equal', paralleling Jefferson's 1776 Declaration. Stanton, Mott, and later Susan B. Anthony (1820–1906) led the struggle for women's rights in America in the nineteenth century, with Anthony voting 'illegally' in the 1872 presidential election, for which she was arrested but later pardoned.

The 'suffragettes' in England, led by Emmeline Pankhurst (1858–1928), used more radical methods to win the vote than their American cousins, including hunger strikes, the harassing of anti-suffrage politicians, civil disobedience, the smashing of windows, and other destruction of property. After a half-century of agitation, the dike of male political privilege broke open. The countries of the British Commonwealth led the way, with New Zealand giving women the right to vote in 1893, Australia following suit in 1909, and Britain and Canada in 1918, though Britain restricted the vote to propertied and educated women over 30 for another decade. The US Congress ratified the Nineteenth Amendment in 1920 giving women the right to vote—a few individual states had beaten Congress to the punch, starting with Colorado in 1893. Most other Western nations passed female suffrage into law between 1918 and 1930, with the bastion of revolutionary liberty, France, waiting until 1945.[1] The rights to own property, divorce, and higher education were won slowly but surely in this same period. After the first wave won its victories, it faded away in the 1920s, leading to a long lull in the gender wars.

One last gasp of first-wave feminism came from its Christian wing. It gave birth to the 'social purity' movement that aimed for the elimination of such social evils as prostitution and alcohol. The temperance feminists, who had been active since the mid-nineteenth century, believed that alcohol was a great evil that led to violence, adultery, and the abuse of women, and so was a feminist issue. They succeeded briefly at slowing down the flow of demon rum in the 1920s after the US Congress passed the Eighteenth Amendment prohibiting the sale of alcohol, but with the failure of prohibition the temperance movement became little more than a historical oddity. Ironically, their arguments were eerily similar to those used by modern feminists to ban pornography.

Second-Wave Feminism

Liberal Feminism

Second-wave feminism started in the early 1960s with Betty Friedan's critique of the closeted lives of suburban housewives in *The Feminine Mystique* (1963).[2] Friedan focused on 'the problem that has no name', the emptiness and anxiety that 1950s

American women felt as housewives surrounded by shiny new gadgets in their suburban homes, a new Chevrolet or Ford in the garage, and husbands working at nine-to-five jobs to pay for it all. Their roles as cooks, cleaners, and baby makers weren't enough: they wanted something more out of life, despite the mystique that psychologists, priests, and journalists built up around the 'sacred' institutions of family and motherhood. Poverty wasn't the problem; rather, social inequality was at the heart of women's malaise. These mothers of the baby boom were what Marilyn Frye later called 'birds in a gilded cage', free to flutter about in their post-war economic prosperity without the freedom to enter higher education, careers, or politics.

Liberal feminism accepted the reality of the legal and political rights won by the first wave, but argued that social and economic inequalities in Western societies prevented women from achieving full equality and freedom. They agreed with the first wave that all men *and* women are created equal, but thought that sexism was alive and well in Western society. Thus, the battle for equality was far from over. Specifically, they argued that Western societies in the mid-twentieth century had reduced women to playing the roles of girlfriends, wives, mothers, and cooks, and little else. Women should be given the option of pursuing careers and gaining social equality in both the home and the workplace. They were 'liberal' in the sense that they thought the real problem with Western societies was that they had failed to extend to women the same rights that the founding documents of democracies such as the American Declaration of Independence and the French Declaration of the Rights of Man and Citizen had promised to 'all men'. If only these rights could be realized in the home and the workplace, women could gain the same status as men. In other words, they did not seek radical social change; they merely wanted their share of the liberal capitalist pie: a progressive enactment of legal and economic reforms that would make women full citizens. Examples include the creation of daycare facilities, the legalization of abortion, greater female involvement in politics, and the removal of barriers to women entering the workforce. The most famous attempt at such a reform was the Equal Rights Amendment in the US, passed by Congress in 1972 but ratified by only 35 of the 38 states required by the Constitution for it to pass, thus leaving it dead in the water by 1982. It would have banned all discrimination based on sex. Yet equal rights for the sexes were institutionalized in several other countries, including in Canada's 1982 Charter of Rights and Freedoms.

Liberal feminists also objected to the media portrayal of women in such traditional roles as wife and mother. Their solution was to promote more and more women into prominent roles in the mass media, which would hopefully solve the problem of negative stereotypes. In addition, women were encouraged to become active consumers of these media, to reject those forms that showed these negative stereotypes. Certainly, liberal feminism did a lot to advance the cause of sexual equality. Abortion is legal in most Western countries, daycare facilities are common, divorce is no longer seen as a disgrace, and 60 per cent of university students in Canada in 2007 are women. But some feminists argued that these slow but steady changes weren't good enough—more was needed.

Radical Feminism

Radical feminism got started in the late 1960s. It argued that the basic problem with Western society wasn't just insufficient rights for women, but the fact that it is a patriarchy, a society with a male-dominated social structure. Patriarchy displayed its power in all facets of our society—in politics, in the economy, in the media, in the home, in romantic relationships. It promoted the domination of men over women everywhere and has produced widespread and deep suffering. The founding text of radical feminist thought is Kate Millett's *Sexual Politics* (1970), which argued for the destruction of monogamous marriage and the nuclear family as outmoded patriarchal institutions. Other radicals, such as Andrea Dworkin (1946–2005), suggested that a woman couldn't really consent to heterosexual sex in such a male-dominated society. Susan Brownmiller (1935–) went one up on Dworkin, suggesting that all men were potential rapists due to their inner bestiality. Others argued that patriarchy was so powerful that dedicated feminists had to give up on heterosexuality as sleeping with the enemy and embrace a lesbian sisterhood. Adrienne Rich (1929–) claimed there is nothing 'natural' about heterosexuality: without the oppressive economic and political relations between men and women characteristic of patriarchy, more women would be drawn towards lesbianism. She proposed that all intimate relationships between women exist on a 'lesbian continuum', whether or not these are explicitly sexual. In short, the radicals argued that a revolution against the patriarchal system was needed, both in the public realm and in the bedroom.

We see a more recent example of the harsh dualism of radical feminist thought in Marilyn French's *The War Against Women*:

> As long as some men use physical force to subjugate females, *all* men need not. The knowledge that some men do suffices to threaten all women. Beyond that, it is not necessary to beat up a woman to beat her down. A man can simply refuse to hire women in well-paid jobs, extract as much or more work from women than men but pay them less, or treat women disrespectfully at work or home. He can fail to support a child he has engendered, demand the women he lives with wait on him like a servant. He can beat or kill the women he claims to love; he can rape women, whether mate, acquaintance, or stranger; he can rape or sexually molest his daughters, nieces, stepchildren, or children of a woman he claims to love. *The vast majority of men in the world do one or more of the above.* (French, 1992: 182)

Radicals hit hard against what they took to be questionable expressions of male heterosexuality. Andrea Dworkin and Catharine MacKinnon (1946–) fought to ban all pornography in several US cities, winning briefly in Minneapolis in 1983.

They argued that explicit sexual images, including the nudes in *Playboy*, were a violation of women's civil rights. MacKinnon's position was similar to that of her friend Dworkin: men use their sexual power through rape, assault, incest, harassment, and the threat of all these things to keep women in place. She pioneered laws against sexual harassment in the workplace in North America. Radicals also marched to take back the night from male crime and staffed rape crisis centres to save women from abusive partners.

At least at first, the radicals saw a sharp biological division between the sexes. They believed there were innate sexual characteristics. Women were seen to be nurturing and non-violent and to have greater emotional depth than men. At the same time, men were inherently analytical, cold-blooded, violent and aggressive, and, with a few exceptions, could not be trusted. This is called *sexual essentialism*, a position radicals had started to abandon by the early 1980s in favour of *social constructionism*, the notion that all psychological gender traits are constructed by culture. Constructionism is now the dominant position in feminist theory.

Radical feminists pushed programs of affirmative action more energetically than the liberals, and attacked vigorously mass media that painted women in traditional roles. Radicals started the feminist tradition of finding patriarchy oozing out of the cracks of pretty well all male-created films, magazines, TV shows, rock videos, and other manifestations of modern culture. It's still very powerful in academe today, with entire courses outlining the patriarchal qualities of films, novels, poetry, and so on. Women's Studies programs in universities are for the most part the product of second-wave radical feminist agitation. Part of the academic side of the radical feminist movement is the attempt to de-patriarchalize the English language, replacing 'history' with 'herstory', 'seminar' with 'ovular', avoiding sex-specific pronouns like 'man' and 'he', and making job descriptions gender-neutral, e.g., 'newsperson' or 'sanitary engineer'. Needless to say, some of this linguistic revisionism came across as farcical to non-radicals, as when first-year university students at some American universities ceased being 'freshmen' and became 'freshpersons'.

The feminist critique of the image of women in the media also came largely from second-wave radical feminists. They argued that media, especially advertising, picture women as sexual objects for men. The media tend to favour young and beautiful women who are not very smart—in a word, bimbos. It objectifies them, propagating what Naomi Wolf (1962–) called 'the beauty myth'. Wolf says that the mass media tend to focus on beautiful women only and create anxiety in the huge majority of women who don't measure up to these impossible standards and who therefore diet and buy expensive clothes, cosmetics, hair-care products, and other instruments of aesthetic improvement. Wolf claims that after women gained social and economic power in the 1970s and 1980s, entering the workforce en masse, patriarchy had to find another way of keeping women in their place, and this was accomplished through the myth that women have to measure up to a media-propagated standard of beauty. Patriarchy struck back by subtly compelling women to spend time, money, and emotional energy on selecting and buying clothes, cosmetics, dieting, plastic surgery, and other aesthetic enhancements.

More generally, radical feminists argue that the use of attractive women in films, TV shows, magazines, and ads plays up to the male gaze, which observes the female body as an object of desire. Laura Mulvey sees Hollywood films as reproducing the structure of male power and female powerlessness in our society by exalting the male gaze, which objectifies the woman as a beautiful mindless body. Feminist analyses of film delight in pointing to the many scenes in Hollywood and other films where the camera lingers over the face or body of a beautiful actress. They argue that this lingering promotes male power by encouraging a controlling male sexual gaze, much like the guards in the central tower of Foucault's Panopticon.[3]

There are a number of important criticisms of the radical feminist argument that the media objectify women, and that this objectification is always bad. First, perhaps film and magazine ads do objectify beautiful female bodies. But the same is done with male bodies, especially in the last couple of decades. Think of those underwear ads with almost naked male models and all those hunky Hollywood actors. Also, isn't sexual attraction inherently objectifying? Do people lust after a fine character or a beautiful mind in *any* society, or is attraction mostly about bodies, even if we assume that culture constructs to some degree what body types are considered beautiful? Given the fact that it's been celebrated in both Western and Eastern art for at least 4,000 years, can't we see the pursuit of beauty as valid? Maybe the beauty myth is not a myth at all, but human nature. Maybe our love of beauty is hard-wired, not just a construct.

Third, aren't women able to use sexuality to gain power, whether in the home or the workplace? Does women's sexuality have to be seen as inherently evil? Third-wave feminists like Camille Paglia see sexuality as a good thing, as the fuel that has energized Western art and culture. She lauds the pop singer Madonna for using her sexuality to become a media icon. Fourth, capitalism has long known that sex sells. Maybe feminists who attack sexism in the media are missing their target—it's not patriarchy they should blame, but consumer capitalism.

Radicals offered several extreme solutions to patriarchal oppression. Some sought to counter-productively wallow in their own victimhood, hating all men and ignoring any evidence that questioned the basic radical view of male bestiality. A second solution was to embrace female separatism, to retreat to purely female enclaves, in some cases becoming politically motivated lesbians or accepting androgyny. They actively promoted the formation of women's groups that formed a separate society from mainstream patriarchal culture. These two solutions aren't mutually exclusive. Allied to these solutions were attacks on art forms that they saw as sexist. Unable to defeat patriarchy, radicals often sought instead to create islands of feminist culture in a sea of patriarchy—Women's Studies departments, study groups, communal households, rape-crisis centres, filmmaking collectives, and so on. Yet their fiery rhetoric did push forward some of the projects already kicked off by liberal feminists: the crusade to legalize abortion, affirmative action hiring, and laws against sexual harassment. We'll have a look at a classic radical feminist text, Shulamith Firestone's *The Dialectic of Sex,* in the next section.

Socialist Feminism

Socialist feminism is linked to radical feminism. It's mainly a shift of emphasis. Socialist feminists follow Marx and Engels in seeing the cause of women's oppression as economic. They argue that uniquely capitalist society creates patriarchal oppression by promoting male domination in the family and in the economy through a division of labour where women are confined in the home to being mothers and housewives, and in the workforce to low-paying and low-status jobs. Women are the sexual proletariat in patriarchal capitalist societies. In a socialist economy, men and women would be freed from their traditional roles of oppressor and oppressed, their economic equality promoting greater social equality. Some socialist feminists even suggest paying housewives a regular wage for their labour, though others argue that a sharing of domestic chores is the smarter approach. Iris Marion Young and Nancy Fraser are two important socialist feminists.

Postmodern Feminism

Postmodern feminists can also be liberal, radical, or socialist, with a twist. Unlike most earlier feminists, the postmodernists argue that gender is entirely a construction. Other than the obvious biological differences, any psychological traits that vary between men and women are purely the product of culture. As a result, they see sexual inequality as socially and culturally constructed, something that could be changed by changing our social values and culture.

Postmodern feminists get most of their ideas from French post-structuralist thinkers, who argue that everything can be seen as a text. Most are influenced by Jacques Derrida's idea of deconstruction, with its critique of binary parts (notably the 'male/female' pair) and logocentrism, which the postmodern feminists translate as 'phallocentrism'. They argue that much of Western literature and popular culture is phallocentric and needs to be deconstructed. Postmodern feminists are quite conscious of the effects of culture on our ideas about gender. They see films, TV shows, magazines, advertising, and books as constructions of various ideas of gender difference. Since there are no real 'natural' differences between men and women, the ideas we get from pop cultural texts are tremendously important in constructing those artificial differences.

Examples of postmodern feminists include Hélène Cixous, Julia Kristeva, Donna Haraway, and Judith Butler. Butler (1956–) is especially interesting since she argues that gender is 'performative': it's a role we perform, just as a Shakespearian actor plays the role of Hamlet or Richard III. Yet unlike the actors, gender performers are largely forced to repeat their act, creating a fiction of a core or stable gender for each of us. This removes any sense that gender is 'natural'. Instead, Butler thinks we should deconstruct the rigid binary of male/female, a binary that second-wave radicals tended to smuggle in by the back door after rejecting the notion that human biology has given women their inferior social and political status. She was influenced by the post-structuralist thinkers Derrida, Foucault, and Kristeva, and in turn influenced queer studies, with its notion that sex, gender, and desire are free-floating variables that are not causally connected (so someone who is sexually 'male' might have 'female' gender traits and desire other 'men').

The big problem with postmodern feminism is relativism. If everything is a construction, then how can feminists argue for practical political changes? Why should we accept one group's view of gender relations over another's if everything is relative? If an ad shows a woman playing the role of a housewife, why is this worse than one showing a female CEO? If there are no universal values but only a variety of subjective feelings, why is your construction of gender any better than mine? Ultimately, postmodern feminists have to appeal to either brute force (which one imagines they would reject) or a general sense of fairness to push their project to completion beyond their own narrow circle. They have to embrace a non-relativistic notion of reason or morality.

Third-Wave Feminism

Since the early 1990s, a small group of feminists, including Camille Paglia (1947–), have argued that women must give up the claim to be victims of patriarchy and seize the day, taking the political and economic power now legally open to them. For this reason it is sometimes called 'power feminism'. They argue that women have to learn to fend for themselves, to play fair and not seek special advantages. Third-wave feminism suggests that the all-powerful patriarchy pictured by radicals is an illusion since the status of women has changed so much over the last 30–40 years. The negative phase of the feminist revolution is over; now it's time to stop complaining and do something with the hard-won rights and equality provided by first-wave and liberal feminism. They also suggest that expressions of heterosexual desire and of female beauty are part of human nature, not moral evils. In fact, Paglia sees all of the history of art as driven by a battle between the Apollonian and the Dionysian, between calm reason and wild passion, with the male desire for the female body (and vice versa) being a big part of this passion. So third-wavers aren't anti-sex (or at least not anti-heterosexual sex) like many second-wave radicals. Quite the opposite.

The third-wavers say that pop culture today can't be seen as saturated with patriarchal oppression. Paglia argues that the two great art forms of the twentieth century were film and rock 'n' roll, both of which are driven by sex. She admires Madonna's explicit sexuality, and points out that gay artists such as the photographer Robert Mapplethorpe can be seen as just as 'pornographic' as heterosexual male artists dealing with erotic sub-jects, so one can't blame explicit sexual imagery on straight white male patriarchs alone. She's pro-sex, unlike the Dworkins and Mackinnons of the second wave. We'll look at Paglia in more detail later.

In *Who Stole Feminism?* (1994), Christina Hoff Sommers launches a withering (and often funny, which is odd for a feminist book) attack on what she calls 'gender feminism', which is basically the radical feminism of Gloria Steinem, the young Naomi Wolf, Dworkin, MacKinnon, and Susan Faludi. She contrasts this with her own 'equity feminism', the feminism of the first wave and of more recent writers such as Betty Friedan and Germaine Greer geared towards equal rights and a level playing field between the sexes.

> American feminism is currently dominated by a group of women who seek to persuade the public that American women are not the free creatures we think we are. The leaders and theorists of the women's movement believe that our society is best described as a patriarchy, a 'male hegemony', a 'sex/gender system' in which the dominant gender works to keep women cowering and submissive. The feminists who hold this divisive view of our social and political reality believe we are in a gender war, and they are eager to disseminate stories of atrocity that are designed to alert women to their plight. The 'gender feminists' (as I shall call them) believe that all our institutions, from the state to the family to the grade schools, perpetuate male dominance. Believing that women are virtually under siege, gender feminists naturally seek recruits to their side of the gender war. They seek support. They seek vindication. They seek ammunition. (Sommers, 1994: 16)

In one chapter Sommers describes the psychodrama of her visit to a feminist conference where radicals competed with each other to express their feelings of personal outrage, victimhood, and resentment against men. Yet her more stinging attack is on the distortion of facts perpetrated by second-wave feminists. She quotes Steinem to the effect that 150,000 women die every year in America from anorexia nervosa and similar eating disorders, a 'fact' that Wolf repeats in *The Beauty Myth*. Well, it turns out that the actual figure varied from about 54 to 101 in the 1980s. The gender feminists offer distortions like this to keep their own troops in order, convinced that a 'war on women' is blazing as strongly in the 1990s as it was a generation or more before. Sommers thinks that this idea of a 'gender war' is a gross misrepresentation of male–female relations that has seeped into all levels of education, from primary school textbooks to university curricula, thanks to the political activism of gender feminists.

More generally, third-wavers have argued that the ideology of victimhood clung to by radical feminists actually helps to perpetuate women's inferior status, as it encourages them to spend their time weeping and holding hands in acts of sisterly solidarity instead of voting, getting a career, running for office, and doing other things that give them economic and political power. Ironically, in *Fire with Fire* (1993), Naomi Wolf gives some theoretical support to the third wave by making a distinction between 'power' and 'victim' feminism. Victim feminism sees women as the passive victims of patriarchy, as naturally non-competitive in the face of male aggressiveness. It is anti-sexual, self-sacrificing, resentful of money and power, self-righteous, judgemental about women's dress and sexuality, and says, in effect, 'women good, men bad!' Power feminism is 'unapologetically sexual', against sexism but *not* men as a whole, and is tolerant of other women's choices about their opinions, body images, and personal lives. Most importantly, power feminism aims to see women as moral adults, as responsible power-seekers in an egalitarian world (Wolf, 1993: xx). Naturally, Wolf urges women to embrace power feminism, and in this sense she has embraced in part the ideas of the third wave.[4]

The third wave is not, however, very popular in universities, since most female faculty came of age under the wing of second-wave feminism. On the other hand, it seems to be the wave of choice for young women today—except for a few Women's Studies students, in my experience

most women university students express bewilderment or hostility towards radical feminism in class discussions.

SHULAMITH FIRESTONE AND THE DIALECTIC OF SEX

Marxism, Radical Feminism, and Sex

Shulamith Firestone's *Dialectic of Sex*, published in 1970, the same year as Kate Millett's *Sexual Politics*, is one of the most important early works in the radical feminist tradition. It also has strong elements of socialist feminism. Firestone (1945–) was born in Ottawa, Ontario. At an early age she launched herself full force into the ferment over civil rights, women's liberation, and the counterculture in the 1960s, editing the journals *Redstockings* and *Notes from the Second Year* and allying herself to feminist groups. Her book gives a detailed critique of the family, love, romance, and modern culture, a critique echoed many times since then in other feminist works. Here is her clarion call for a radical feminist revolution:

> In the radical feminist view, the new feminism is not just a revival of a serious political movement for social equality. It is the second wave of the most important revolution in history. Its aim: overthrow of the oldest, most rigid class/caste system in existence, the class system based on sex—a system consolidated over thousands of years, lending the archetypal male and female roles an undeserved legitimacy and seeming permanence. (Firestone, 1971: 15)

Firestone proposes some radical solutions to the dilemma women face as citizens of patriarchal societies—the death of the nuclear family, economic and sexual freedom for both women and children, and a cybernetic socialism, all designed to overthrow the sexual caste system Firestone sees as dominating our society.

Firestone argues that radical feminists want a revolution based on altering women's fundamental biological condition through a combination of new technology and social changes. Just as Marx suggested that the proletariat seize the means of production from the capitalists, Firestone suggests that women should seize the means of reproduction from male-dominated society. The tyranny of the biological family and the unfair sexual division of labour it's based on have to end in order to create a society where the biological differences between the sexes are of no cultural significance (ibid., 11). Unfortunately, this division of labour has exaggerated psychic differences between the sexes, making men more rationalistic, aggressive, and insensitive, women more emotional and passive. Since sexual difference pervades our entire society, feminists have to question not only the organization of that society as a whole, but the organization of nature itself by controlling the reproductive process.

She suggests that Marx and Engels's dialectical materialism was of some use. Yet Firestone argues that just as there is a dialectic of class in history, as Marx pointed out, there is also a dialectic of sex, a struggle between the sexes for power. Underneath Marx and Engels's class struggle there existed the sexual substratum of this dialectic, a dialectic of sexual difference. She describes how this dialectic has historically affected romance, the family, culture, and economics. Firestone suggests that while recognizing the importance of economics, we develop a new, still materialist, view of history based on sex as its primary category. Not all reality is strictly economic. Underneath economic struggles lies the biological family, based on such natural reproductive differences between the sexes as the uniqueness of menstruation, child-bearing, breast-feeding, and menopause to women. The long period of dependence of a child on its mother made women rely on men for physical protection and economic well-being. Yet these natural conditions can now be overcome with technologies such as the birth control pill, 'test tube' babies, and automation in the workplace.

Love and Oppression

Firestone sees the idea of love as a cornerstone of women's oppression. Male culture depends on the love given by women. While men are thinking, writing, and creating, women pour their energy into loving men. Male culture feeds on women's love like a parasite, sucking emotional support out of it. Firestone sees love as the height of selfishness—but acceptable selfishness if between equals. But both love and marriage suffer many failures. This is largely due to the unequal balance of power between men and women in love relationships. True deep love can only be between equals; in societies where no such equality exists, love is a way men control and oppress women.

Men fall in love with women by a process of romantic idealization. They put women on a pedestal, which seems to wipe out women's class inferiority. This idealization and mystification of love causes women to link their personal identity to finding their ideal prince, their knight in shining armour, thus losing their individuality. This leads to the double standard long decried by feminists. Women are seen as monogamous, loving, possessive, and into 'relationships' instead of mere sex. Men are polygamous, out only for sex, and mistake sexual desire for love, even though they can idealize some women. Firestone is echoing the Marxist idea of 'false consciousness' here: women deceive themselves both about their own nature and about their relationship with men, which is based on a structural position of inferiority. Firestone offers three specific theses on love and family politics.

(1) *Men cannot love*. Men fall in love with their own projected image. They avoid commitment, ogle other women, and sleep around. Even if they marry, they blame their wives for suffocating them, calling them a 'nag' or a 'ball and chain'. She even blames men for using unpredictable behaviour to create a feeling of anxiety in their partners. This is obviously an essentialist position: it seems to be true of *all* men, and is a bit hard to take as a serious pronouncement without some qualifications.

(2) *Women's clinging behaviour is required by the objective social situation*. Women are forced to use clinging behaviour and manipulation to get men to commit. They must use subtle methods of manipulation as part of their Manhunt, for without male approval a woman is doomed. They must

use sex as a weapon and play games to get this commitment. Men do reserve a special pedestal for their wives. But these women are expected to be mothers, housekeepers, cooks, companions, and lovers—all at once. In the society in which Firestone lived, women were an inferior class. Not only do they need male approval, their economic dependence on men makes love between equals impossible. Of course, this raises the interesting question whether the entry en masse of women into the workforce over the last 30 plus years has alleviated this economic dependence, making women less inferior and freer to leave unhappy marriages. Still, as feminists in the 1990s were fond of pointing out, the average working woman only made about 70 per cent of the average man's salary, so this new-found economic power wasn't all it appeared to be.[5]

(3) *This situation has hardly changed today*. Firestone argues that men don't marry liberated women, even if they might admire their intelligence and sleep with them. They want someone they can own and control. Men use the sexual revolution to get women to give up the old games of love. Yet emancipated women are shunned, as their intelligence is not appreciated. She concludes that maybe men are just not worth the emotional upheaval women have to go through to marry or live with them.

The Culture of Romance

Firestone argues that as women become more liberated from their biology through medicine and birth control, patriarchal society brings in romanticism to reinforce the subjugation of women and buttress male power (ibid., 146). Romance is a cultural tool of male power used to delude women into believing they still need a man to run their lives. It uses three techniques:

1. *Eroticism*. Reality is sexualized. All animal needs for love and warmth are channelled into genital sexuality. Women are painted as the only love objects in our society, and men are encouraged to overcome their resist-

ances. In fact, women are so eroticized that they see *themselves* as sex objects instead of rational beings.

2. *Sexual privatization*. A woman's individuality is reduced to an appreciation of her physical attributes, e.g., being a blonde or a brunette. This leads to women adopting a false individuality where men distinguish individual women by means of these superficial attributes. Women are turned into interchangeable 'dolls' for men's appreciation, become clothes horses, and are called names like 'kitten', 'sweetie', or 'honey'. They lose their identity as members of an oppressed sexual class, assuming a purely superficial and private sexual identity.

3. *The beauty ideal*. This forces women to mutilate their bodies with diets and cosmetics and the latest fashions. But the result is that they look more and more alike, as women tend to copy the fashions they see in beauty magazines or the look of movie stars like Marilyn Monroe in the 1950s (or Jennifer Lopez today). The ideals of beauty that women aspire to are defined by men. When women try to match the beauty ideal with diet, exercise, cosmetics, or by dying their hair, this has the political function of keeping them subservient to men. Here Firestone anticipates the argument made by Naomi Wolf 20 years later in *The Beauty Myth*. Both make beauty a political issue for feminists.

Uniquely, Firestone argues that even men get caught up in this drive towards becoming erotic objects. An erotomania develops: breasts, legs, and thighs jump out of every magazine cover, film screen, TV tube, and billboard. Most of these erotic objects are female, so men 'walk about in a state of constant sexual excitement' (ibid., 154). Naturally, this erotomania puts women on the defensive against the marauding male beasts. One can only imagine what Firestone would think of the erotic effects of women's fashions today.

At the end of her chapter on romance Firestone admits that sex objects are beautiful, and says that in attacking them she isn't attacking beauty itself. The same goes for eroticism, which is obviously exciting. The face on the cover of *Vogue* is beautiful, she says. But is it beautiful in a human way? Does it express human emotions? Or is it like an inanimate object? Of course, Firestone's distinction between 'human' and 'objective' beauty is a tricky one, to say the least. What is a cold objective beauty to one person might be quite warm and human to another.

Some Utopian Hopes

Firestone concludes her book with a list of four utopian demands that, if fulfilled, would end the dialectic of sex:

- the freeing of women from the tyranny of their reproductive biology;
- the full self-determination, including economic, of women and children;
- the total integration of women and children into society;
- sexual freedom for women and children to do what they want when they want with whom they want.

Women would be freed from their reproductive biology through daycare (though this, to Firestone, is at best a short-term solution), the birth control pill, and the diffusion of child care throughout the community. Even more fundamentally, child-bearing would be taken over by technology, while child-rearing, which is as much about power relations as about love between parent and child, would cease to be based on the nuclear family.

As for the self-determination of women and children, the present economy fails to reward women fairly for their work. Women are used as a source of cheap and plentiful labour and are asked to sacrifice themselves as mothers to raise their families. Firestone estimates that if mothers were paid for their work, the bill would total one-fifth of the American gross national product (ibid., 208). To replace this system Firestone calls

for a 'cybernetic socialism' where the people would own the means of production and wealth would be distributed based on need, paralleling Marx's famous slogan, 'from each according to his abilities, to each according to his needs'. Firestone hopes that under such a system people could choose their own lifestyles at will, echoing Marx and Engels's utopian hope expressed in *The German Ideology* that under communism one could hunt in the morning, fish in the afternoon, herd cattle in the evening, and write literary criticism at night. This is the *socialist* aspect of her feminism: her revolution depends on a healthy socialist economy to ensure women (and children) the freedom to reject the biological/nuclear family as a source of economic support. She also talks about women adopting traditionally male 'single professions'—sailors, truck drivers, firefighters, detectives, or pilots—as a transitional move towards greater economic equality.

As for the integration of women and children, once again technology will play a key role. Firestone wants to eliminate formal schooling for children and abolish childhood by giving kids full legal, economic, and sexual rights. They would live in communal households of about 10 people (not especially including their biological parents), form friendships with whomever they chose, and 'mingle freely' throughout society (ibid., 239–40). This leads to Firestone's final demand—sexual freedom for all. Since sex would no longer be restricted to making babies and since people would cease to care about the fatherhood of the child for the purposes of handing down an inheritance, we would return to our natural 'polymorphous' sexuality, with all forms allowed and indulged in (ibid., 210). Genital sex would become only one of several forms of erotic satisfaction and monogamy would fade away. The incest taboo would disintegrate since people wouldn't especially know who their own parents were and birth control would prevent the creation of freakish offspring.

As we've seen, Firestone wants to dispense with the traditional biological family of father-mother-children, replacing it with communal households consisting of about 10 people of different ages who would sign a contract to stay together for 7–10 years. About one-third of each household would be made up of children. They would share all domestic chores. The children would be free to leave one household and go to another if they saw fit. As a result of these social changes and the ending of the blood tie between mother and child, pregnancy would only be engaged in as a 'tongue-in-cheek' throwback to an earlier age (ibid., 241). The problem today is that marriage is propped up with sentimental sermons, counsellors, and guidance manuals when it should be allowed to die a natural death. All brides and grooms think they are special: they will be the only ones who escape an unhappy or wrecked marriage. All potential mothers and fathers think they'll be good parents. Yet bad marriages and divorces are increasingly common—not to mention the obvious fact that there are many bad parents, too. Thus, Firestone encourages us to be realistic, to accept the fact that the traditional nuclear family is a recipe for continued failure, producing far too many miserable children. She hopes that the end of the biological family, paired with the end of back-breaking manual labour, could result paradise on earth.

Firestone's *Dialectic of Sex* is radical feminism at its most utopian. Some of her demands have already become social realities: women have entered many occupations formerly reserved for men; more women have their own careers and a degree of economic independence; the nuclear family has been eroded, if not consigned to the rubbish heap of history; and children have more rights than they ever have, to the point were some critics suggest that we are raising a generation of spoiled brats. However, some of her suggestions are still seen as just as radical as they must have in 1970. Children still have to go to school and obey their parents. There are few communal households. The incest taboo is as strong as ever—perhaps stronger—and there's no danger of polymorphous sexuality bursting out any time soon, despite the advances made by gays. And lastly, state socialism is pretty well a dead political issue

in the West, as capitalism won the day (at least for now) somewhere around 1989. Capitalist societies are still structured according to class and still contain extremes of wealth and poverty. So, although there's been some movement on Firestone's first two utopian hopes, the last two are dead in the water.

SUSAN MOLLER OKIN ON THE FAMILY AS A SCHOOL FOR JUSTICE

Susan Moller Okin (1946–2004) was a native of New Zealand. She taught from 1990 on at Stanford University (she was a visiting professor at Harvard at the time of her death). She is the author of *Women in Western Political Thought* (1979) and editor of *Is Multiculturalism Bad for Women?* (1999). We'll focus on her best-known theoretical statement, *Justice, Gender, and the Family* (1989). Okin's book is sort of an update on the feminist critique of the patriarchal family two decades after Firestone's *The Dialectic of Sex*. She describes her work as political theory, though the distinction between political and social theory is a difficult one to maintain, especially in feminist thought since, as the feminist slogan has long proclaimed, 'the personal is political.'

Okin's feminism is grounded in her debate with male theorists of justice, notably with John Rawls. Rawls (1921–2002) was the most important liberal political theorist of the late twentieth century. In his magisterial *A Theory of Justice* (1971), Rawls defends a theory of justice as fairness, which he describes as a combination of the 'social contract' and Kantian views of morality. Social contract theory, which started in the seventeenth century with Thomas Hobbes and was developed by John Locke and Jean-Jacques Rousseau, argues that people in a hypothetical or real 'state of nature' without laws or government cannot guarantee their personal security or property. To escape this nasty and brutish place (as Hobbes called it) they agree to a social contract that limits everyone's capacity to rob and do violence to each other in order to establish social peace and a legal structure that protects property.

So society is the product of a social contract between free and rational beings who seek to promote their mutual welfare. Immanuel Kant was one of the greatest philosophers of the late Enlightenment. His theory of ethics was predicated on his own version of the Christian Golden Rule, which he called the 'Categorical Imperative'. It said: 'act only according to a maxim that you could at the same time will to become a universal law.' In other words, don't do things to people you wouldn't want done to you. If you don't want others to steal things, don't steal things yourself—the maxim here is 'stealing is wrong.' Kant's second version of the imperative is, 'don't treat yourself or others solely as a means, but always at the same time as an end.' In other words, don't use people.

Rawls picks up on these ideas in laying out the two principles of justice by which we should govern modern democratic states:

- *Equality of liberty principle*. Everyone has an equal right to as much liberty as possible up to the point where it conflicts with the liberty of others.
- *Difference principle*. All goods in our society, including wealth, status, and power, should be equally distributed *unless* giving more to one group benefits the least advantaged people in our society *and* the offices and positions that result from this social inequality are equally open to all.

Rawls argues that in his hypothetical state of nature, which he calls 'the original condition', people should be imagined to be blind to all their personal attributes—their race, their sex, their level of wealth and education and intelligence, where they live. They see the world behind a 'veil of ignorance'. We then ask these abstract individuals, 'what principles would you support for *all* people within our society after we sign the social contract?' Rawls argues they would come up with something like his own two principles. After all, if you don't know if you're poor or rich, you won't defend social privileges based on having a lot of money. Similarly, if you don't know whether or not you're

male, you won't defend a social order giving men all the power. So in the original condition, where one is blind to all of one's attributes, you would opt for as much freedom as you can get, along with social equality *unless* a bit of inequality benefits everyone. Rawls's theory is very important for feminist theory for a couple of reasons. On the one hand, it defends equality of liberty and wealth for everyone, men and women. On the other, it also opens up the question of the justice of the sexual division of labour in the traditional nuclear family: can we justify the economic and social inequality between the husband with a career and the wife who stays home to take care of her children and her husband's domestic needs in terms of a 'social contract' that benefits everyone?

Okin endorses Rawls's basic principles that individual liberty should be limited only to make room for the liberty of others, and that economic inequalities are only justified if they benefit the least advantaged and if high positions are open to everyone. But Rawls, says Okin, fails to account for the injustices created by male-dominated family structures, including the general social attitudes that come out of these structures.

Okin begins *Justice, Gender, and the Family* by noting that although American society claims to be just and democratic, deep sexual inequalities still exist. At the time of the book's writing in 1989, women working in full-time jobs made only 71 per cent of what men made. Only two out of 100 US senators were women. Millions of women work in low-paying, dead-end jobs (Okin, 1989: 3). The economy is still based on the assumption that men go to work and women stay home and do the lion's share of housework, even in 'rationally' planned families. This type of thinking is especially harmful after family breakups, when women who have neglected their careers to raise a family are left unprepared to enter the workforce. Okin argues that to have justice between the sexes in society as a whole, we need to establish justice in the family first of all, which would involve changing how families are structured, both economically and politically. To put it plainly, Okin argues that 'marriage and the family, as currently practised in our society, are unjust institutions. They constitute the pivot of a societal system of gender that renders women vulnerable to dependency, exploitation and abuse' (ibid., 135).

Okin says that most feminists see gender differences as socially constructed. 'Biological determinism', or essentialism, is false. Things that used to be seen as based on valid sexual differences, for example, women's 'natural' role as housekeepers and nurturers, are now seen, at least by feminists, as based on artificial gender-based divisions. Family structure is gendered, not natural. Since sexual difference is a social construct that produces sexual inequalities, gender roles should be broken down, thus creating a 'genderless family', one where mom and dad share equally the burdens and benefits of family life. This makes her a postmodern liberal feminist with some radical leanings.

Okin's book contains a three-pronged argument involving theories of justice, family policies, and the family as a 'school' for justice.

(1) *Theories of justice.* Women must be 'counted in' by theories of justice. Too often philosophers thinking about justice have simply assumed that the 'individual' is the male head of a patriarchal household. They also often assume that private, domestic life is outside the realm of justice. Theories of justice have tended to focus on public economic and political life dominated by household heads, which have traditionally been male. They assume public men with wives at home to do the cooking, cleaning, and child care. Okin sees this distinction between public and private spheres as false for four reasons:

1. Power is of central importance in family life, not just public life. Okin gives the example of how physical violence helps to enforce male rule in an unnatural way.
2. The domestic sphere is itself created by political decisions. For one thing, women were deprived of legal personhood in most countries until the early twentieth century, so the family is not a separate 'private' sphere unaffected by the law.

3. We are socialized into our gendered selves within the family. Once again it plays a political role.
4. The division of labour in the gender-structured family raises practical and psychological barriers to women in other spheres. For example, a gender-structured family might discourage young women from pursuing higher education.

Okin also criticizes political theorists for their 'false gender neutrality'. She says that it doesn't do any good for well-meaning theorists to avoid using the pronoun 'he' to describe the abstract citizen of these theories given the fact that society is shot through with sexual difference, with women in an inferior position in family life, the workplace, and politics. A theory of justice has to take into account this inequality, not just paper it over with gender-neutral language.

Finally, Carol Gilligan's 'ethics of care' approach doesn't help here. As we'll see in the next section, Gilligan's psychological work on childhood development convinced her that women tend to embrace an ethics of care and empathy, men an ethics of justice and rights. Okin doesn't want to give up on justice and rights quite yet. For one thing, there's no evidence that women are 'naturally' more inclined towards such an ethics than to one of abstract rights; for another, it's misleading to draw the sort of sharp distinction that Gilligan does, for all good theories of justice are obliged to take care and empathy into account anyway. So feminists still have to debate questions of justice.

(2) *Family policies.* Women's equality of opportunity is seriously jeopardized by current inequalities in the family. For one thing, Okin believes that the power relations in the traditional family tend to be replicated in the workplace, and they wind up reinforcing each other (ibid., 147). If the husband rules his family like a king, then he'll probably want to rule his workplace in a similar way. In addition, many employers assume that 'someone' is at home taking care of the kids when they create policies on the flexibility and length of work hours. The

workplace (at least when Okin wrote her book in the late 1980s) generally doesn't support parents working full-time. Third, when parents divorce, the woman, unprepared for the workplace due to her past role as an unpaid labourer in the traditional family structure, is handicapped economically. As a single mother, she is much less able to support her children as she might not have the education or job skills her ex-husband developed under the traditional sexual division of labour.

As a remedy to these injustices, Okin advocates a 'massive reallocation' of resources away from the military to social services such as daycare, health care, and employment training. In addition, she wants a gender-neutral workplace free from all sexual discrimination. This would involve the provision of leaves for pregnancy and childbirth for several months, along with high-quality on-site daycare in larger companies and institutions supported by direct government subsidies. Further, given problems with the economic dependence of a housewife on her husband, both partners should be legally entitled to all the money coming into the household (ibid., 180–1). Having employers issue two cheques—one to the actual earner, one to his or her domestic partner—would give fair recognition to unpaid work in the home.[6] Most controversially, Okin wants the parent without physical custody of a child to contribute to the child's support *to the point where the standards of living of the two households are the same*' (ibid., 179).[7] The partner who worked outside the home—usually the man—should support the one who stayed home for as long as the traditional division of labour lasted during the marriage, or until their child entered first grade in a marriage that lasted only a short period of time. Lastly, Okin feels that if men participated equally in raising their children, it would be good for not only their wives, but for both of them and their children, too. Nurturing fathers wouldn't ignore their children after marriage breakdowns.

There are some fairly obvious criticisms of Okin's proposals. Isn't the legal mandating of parental leave and daycare discriminatory against people of both sexes who don't want to have children? Why should I have to work all summer while my co-worker Justin gets three months off

to raise his kid? Or why should I pay higher taxes to subsidize Mary's five children in day care when she could have used birth control? As for splitting wages, although Okin denies this is a 'cash nexus', it comes very close to paying housewives (or, in rare cases, househusbands) a wage. Do we really want our spouses to be paid domestic workers? Without wanting a return to the traditional family, such a move might serve only to increase the divorce rate. Third, isn't there a danger that Okin's proposal to equalize post-divorce household incomes would reward laziness and lack of initiative for the spouse being subsidized? What if this spouse decides to stay home all day watching TV instead of pursuing higher education or looking for at least a part-time job? This is a fair proposal only if half of child custody decisions left the fathers with the children, which isn't the case today. Otherwise, it is natural to think that working men would build up some serious resentments at having a large bite of their incomes going to support women they probably no longer want to have anything to do with. This sort of proposal would have to be surrounded by some rather strict limitations on the level and length of time of the child support to make it workable and fair. Lastly, Okin's defence of nurturing dads assumes that all men would make good active fathers, which flies in the face of common sense.

(3) *A school for justice*. Okin demands that the family be transformed into a school for justice. The practices of family life define the possible futures that boys and girls see for themselves. 'Until there is justice within the family, women will not be able to gain equality in politics, at work, or in any other sphere' (ibid., 4). Okin believes that we learn to be just in our childhoods, in our families. The family is a school for injustice if it's structured in the traditional gendered way, with the father as breadwinner and patriarch, the mother as an economically dependent obedient servant. Instead, families should encourage their children to embrace an ethic of equality of opportunity for both sexes. One way they can do this is by setting an example: parents should share such duties and roles associated with family life as careers, housework, and child care.

Okin's basic claims here are (a) that families have a huge influence on the moral development of children, and (b) that unjust families produce unjust adults. It's hard to deny the validity of her first claim. The second, however, is up for grabs, especially since the vast majority of human beings who came of age before the advent of second-wave feminism, by Okin's own admission, were the products of unjust family structures. Were they all unjust adults, too? Although adults are in part the product of their early family experiences, perhaps Okin overestimates the degree to which we are passively programmed by our parents. One could argue that a young girl who sees a clear injustice in her family's life will just as likely rebel against it, seeking greater independence as an adult. Many of the great rebels in history had difficult childhoods. One must also remember that Adolf Hitler grew up in a fairly stable bourgeois Austrian family (though admittedly a patriarchal one—like pretty well all nineteenth-century families). Perhaps a mildly unjust family is at least as good a school for justice as an entirely just one!

In any case, none of this invalidates the moral content of Okin's argument that the traditional family, with its unfair division of labour between father and mother, is unjust. The real question here is whether the traditional male-dominated family structure can be reformed to allow for greater sexual equality, or, as Firestone claims, if it must be done away with altogether for this equality to be achieved. If the state intervened by requiring employers to provide daycare, parental leave, and equal paycheques, along with requiring couples who split to share their combined incomes evenly, would this create a practical family structure ruled by sexual equality, or would it lead to a society of dysfunctional families? These questions only future historians will be able to answer with certainty.

CAROL GILLIGAN AND THE ETHICS OF CARE

Gilligan, Kohlberg, and Development Theory

Carol Gilligan (1936–) did her graduate work in education at Harvard, where she taught for over 30 years in the Graduate School of Education. Her main interest is young women's psychological development, particularly their development as moral beings. Gilligan's *In a Different Voice* (1982) challenges the prevailing dogma on the psychological growth of children established by Freud, Jean Piaget, and Lawrence Kohlberg that only young men are capable of rising to an appreciation of an abstract view of rights and justice, whereas young women are confined to lower levels of moral development centred on their feelings of empathy and the need to nurture. The most notorious case of this view of women's psychological development being by its very nature stunted was Freud's theory of penis envy, the idea that young girls envy the absent penises their brothers have. This leads to emotional insecurity and an unhealthy fixation on the father. Naturally, all feminists reject this idea.

Gilligan argues that what were formerly thought to be sexually neutral theories of moral development, such as those of Freud, Piaget, and Kohlberg, in fact have observational and evaluative biases. They falsely take men's development as the norm. Gilligan found that the qualities deemed by these developmental theorists to be necessary for adulthood—autonomous thinking, clear decision-making, and responsible action—are those associated with masculinity and considered undesirable for women (Gilligan, 1993 [1982]: 17). This stereotype splits love and work, confining work requiring emotions to women and instrumental work to men. She says that, from a different perspective, these stereotypes reflect an unbalanced conception of adulthood, favouring the separateness of the individual self over connection to others, an autonomous life of work over the interdependence of love and care (ibid., 17). Against Freud, Piaget, and Kohlberg, Gilligan sees moral problems for young women coming from conflicting responsibilities, not rights. They resolve them with contextual and narrative thinking. The female ethic of care centres moral development on an understanding of responsibility and relationships, just as the male ethic of justice ties moral development to an understanding of rights and rules.

Her mentor during her graduate studies at Harvard was Kohlberg: she was his research assistant in the early 1970s. Kohlberg studied the moral development of boys, concluding that they go through six stages of moral development. Kohlberg saw these stages as a hierarchy: the higher up you go on the scale, the more morally developed you are. He divided these six stages into three levels.

Pre-conventional level
1. Punishment and obedience orientation: Children obey the commands of others to avoid punishment.
2. Reciprocity and trading orientation: Here they are willing to make deals to satisfy their needs, e.g., trading hockey cards, or giving a girl a candy to get to walk her home from school. Moral principles have nothing to do with behaviour.

Conventional level
3. Conformity/good boy or girl vs bad boy or girl orientation: Children act well to please others, based on a stereotype of goodness and badness. One earns approval by being 'nice'. Intentions start to count. Kohlberg found that girls rarely got beyond this level.
4. Law and order orientation: At this point they obey authority (if they are good) and follow fixed rules to maintain the social order. Here there is a respect for authority for its own sake, without the need for abstract principles.

Post-conventional or principled level
5. Social contract/legalistic orientation: Morality is based on individual rights agreed to democratically by all of society. These rights are protected by law, so this orientation is legalistic. Here people realize the relativism of personal values and opinions, and that the law can be changed for reasons of social utility. So this orientation is also utilitarian, aiming at the greatest happiness of the greatest number of people.
6. Universal ethical principles orientation: Here people act morally because they see themselves as following universal ethical principles such as the Golden Rule or the idea of the equal rights and dignity of all human beings. This is the highest stage for Kohlberg: we act morally not just to avoid punishment, make a deal, or conform to authority, but because we really *believe* in the morality of our actions, and that we can apply this morality to other people in similar situations.

When Kohlberg applied his theory of moral development to young women, he concluded that they rarely made it beyond stage 3, where goodness is seen as helping and pleasing others. They seldom reached the three higher stages, where morality is tied to rules or universal moral principles. Naturally, Gilligan objected to Kohlberg's model as ignoring differences between the moral voices of each sex. He was wrong to think that because girls and women don't get to stages 5 and 6 they are therefore morally handicapped. She points out that the problem with Kohlberg's research was that it excluded female subjects and was thus biased against the 'different voice' that young women use to deal with moral dilemmas.

The Two Voices[8]

In her book *In a Different Voice*, Gilligan uses a number of empirical studies to try to show that young women speak in a different moral voice, one that values care and relationships over abstract rules and moral principles. Gilligan cites Nancy Chodorow's studies that suggested that young girls develop a greater sense of empathy with others than boys. Since masculine identity is shaped by separation, men fear intimacy and closeness; since feminine identity is grounded in attachment, it is threatened by separation and isolation. Janet Lever's studies on how boys and girls played children's games showed that if disputes break out during play, boys usually attempt to resolve them by 'sticking to the rules' to keep the game going, while girls usually stopped the game to keep their relationships intact. Gilligan used these studies and three of her own to show how two distinct 'voices' can be heard in the moral discourse of young men and women. She found that the young women she studied often felt a sense of alienation from mainstream Western culture since they had to stifle their relationship-centred inner voices to avoid a conflict with the ethics of male-dominated culture. Our culture has sought to impose the male moral voice on both sexes, both in the schoolyard and in the academy.

The male voice speaks with an 'ethics of justice', which speaks the language of rules and a respect for individual rights. Tied to this focus on individual rights is a fear of attachment and commitment and a positive view of separation. The male voice sees inequality and oppression as its enemies. Boys learn independence, fair play, and organizational skills in the rough-and-tumble competitive games of their youth, turning these into hierarchies of rules and principles in their adult lives. The male voice views the self individualistically, but sees a 'universal' notion of the self at the centre of moral decision-making: moral rules must apply to everyone, everywhere, regardless of context. The central image here is one hierarchy.

The female voice speaks with an 'ethics of care'. This voice values relationships, connectedness, and intimacy, but fears detachment and abandonment. It wants to maintain peace and care for those in need. The feminine voice sees morality as contextual, as tied to individual stories and not to abstract and inflexible moral principles. Responsibilities to others are what count the most. Moral dilemmas should be solved within relationships, not by tossing them aside. Women's reluctance to judge according to a strict hierarchy of rules is not a simple-minded moral relativism, but an attempt to take into account the intricacies of individuals' lives and experiences in moral decision-making. The web is the central metaphor of the ethics of care.

Gilligan concludes that women care for others by taking a variety of voices into account. While men assume that care in their private lives, they devalue it in their public lives. We wind up with an unbalanced concept of moral adulthood. Yet neither voice is superior: both have to be inte-

grated to produce a full-fledged view of moral life. Rights and responsibilities have to be integrated. We need a greater sense of moral balance.

Gilligan and Essentialism

Gilligan's work raises the important issue in feminist theory of whether the psychological traits traditionally associated with each sex, such as men's greater abstract rationality and aggressiveness or women's greater empathy and need to nurture, are natural or cultural. Those who argue that some sex-specific psychological traits are natural are called 'essentialists' or 'biological determinists', while those who argue that all such traits are culturally determined are 'social constructionists'. An essentialist believes that to a degree there are separate male and female psychologies. Men are logical, mathematically inclined, believe in abstractions and universal rules and rights, and are both more rational and more aggressive, but they are less in touch with their bodies and nature. Women are nurturing, motherly, believe in concrete things and relationships, and are more in touch with their feelings, with the Earth, and with nature. Thus an essentialist might say that to end patriarchal society, we must get men to value female psychological traits more, to accept difference, and thereby end the male need to dominate women.

The other school of thought, which is 'postmodernist' or 'constructivist', believes that all gender traits are constructed by our society, that there are no *natural* male or female traits. Thus the idea that women are more nurturing, emotional, and closer to their bodies is a patriarchal male construction invented to keep women in a position of subservience. Constructivist feminists try to change men and women themselves: they would like men to adopt some of the typically female traits, and vice versa, to overcome male oppressive ways of thinking and submissive female ways of thinking. Part of this could be the pursuit of androgyny in dress and sexual orientation, e.g., bisexuality and lesbianism, as a political statement about the feminist's opposition to patriarchal gender constructions. Thus, unlike the essentialists, who suggest that we should value difference, constructivists seek to deconstruct gender stereotypes both in theory and in practice as a way of ending male domination.

Gilligan waffles on the essentialist versus constructivist debate. She notes that the link between the two moral voices she describes in her book and men and women as distinct sexes is merely 'an empirical observation', and that this association was not meant 'to represent a generalization about either sex' (ibid., 2). For one thing, this distinction between male and female voices may not hold in different cultures at different times. The 'Letter to Readers' that Gilligan added in 1993, 11 years after her book first appeared, doesn't clarify matters much. Here she says that psychological differences between the sexes are the result of body differences, family relationships, and the social and cultural position of the sexes (ibid., xi); in other words, they are both biological *and* cultural. Women have a hard time distinguishing between their own distinct voice and the socially constructed feminine voice, often confusing the two (ibid., xvii). She deliberately refuses to resolve the dilemma because she finds the question of whether gender characteristics are biologically determined or socially constructed 'to be deeply disturbing', since this implies that people are either genetically determined or the products of socialization. This robs women of their distinctive voice, and thus the chance of resistance, creativity, and change (ibid., xix). Gilligan thinks that to make a final decision about whether our gender traits are essentially tied to our biological sex or are socially constructed by our culture would destroy our freedom of thought and action. Whether this is a judicious conclusion or a simple copout I leave to the reader.

The Greedy Druggist

The middle chapters of *In a Different Voice* deal with three case studies done by Gilligan herself. In the key one, Gilligan asked young men and women to imagine a man who is contemplating stealing a drug that he can't afford to buy to cure his ailing wife. They were asked how they would resolve this dilemma originally designed by Kohlberg:

- Heinz's wife needs a rare drug costing $2,000.
- The drug only costs the druggist $200, but Heinz can only afford $100.
- The druggist is stubborn, and won't budge on the drug's price.
- Kohlberg asked boys and girls, should Heinz steal the drug?

Gilligan used this case study in her own research, examining in detail the responses of two 11-year-olds. Jake thought that the situation was like a mathematical equation. He said that it's right to steal the drug since the right to life is more important than property rights. This is a matter of logic, thought Jake. Amy, another 11-year-old, was hesitant. She thought that Heinz and the druggist should talk things out and resolve the conflict through communication. But caring for one's family is also very important. Maybe he could borrow the money? For Jake the problem could be solved by a logic of fairness: it's not fair to withhold a life-saving drug from a dying person just to make an extravagant profit. But with Amy it was a matter of maintaining relationships, which made the problem more complicated. Gilligan argues that Amy's ambiguity and insistence on the need for conflicting parties to communicate is just as sophisticated a solution as Jake's solving the problem by establishing a hierarchy of abstract principles.

Seeing life as a web rather than a succession of relationships, women see autonomy rather than attachment as a dangerous quest (ibid., 48). Therefore women prefer a history of attachment that stresses continuity rather than replacement and separation, whereas men are more willing to replace one relationship with another. So women see themselves as at the centre of a web of relationships, and men see themselves as placed somewhere along a hierarchy. This gives rise to an ethics of care, where no one should be left behind, and an ethics of justice, the idea that we should all strive to be fair to each other:

These disparate visions in their tension reflect the paradoxical truths of human experience—that we know ourselves as separate only insofar as we live in connection with others, and that we experience relationship only insofar as we differentiate other from self. (Ibid., 63)

The Abortion Dilemma

In her third study (the second involved students writing stories about various pictures) Gilligan discusses how her women subjects are concerned with their moral responsibilities in dilemmas, such as whether or not to get an abortion. In this study, 29 women aged 15–33 were interviewed. Their discussions of their decisions to abort or not abort a fetus centred on the issue of avoiding hurting anyone, and thus affected both self and other. In the abortion dilemma she found a distinct moral language evolving. Her subjects tended to go through three stages in their moral reasoning about abortion:

1. The first is a *selfish stage*, when the central concern is the survival of the self. Here the subjects are worried about their lack of power if they keep the baby and see their relationships with men as disappointing. They sometimes choose isolation to save themselves. This stage focuses on social sanctions and it parallels Kohlberg's pre-conventional stage.
2. The next stage focuses on *responsibility and goodness*. Here the woman adopts social values, shared norms, and expectations. The issue of protecting others from hurt and caring for them arises—the woman must accomplish the seemingly impossible task of choosing a victim (her fetus, herself, or the man in her life). This is Kohlberg's conventional stage. Gilligan quotes a woman named Cathy who was pressured into an abortion by her lover but felt a private resentment about it afterwards. She wanted to be good to all parties, but felt pressured into making a choice.
3. In the final *care stage* the subject focuses on the self and other and how they are intercon-

nected. This involves a transition from the goodness of the second stage to truth. The woman now turns inward and acknowledges the need to accept personal responsibility for making a choice. Gilligan uses the example of Ellen, a musician, who gets pregnant as a result of a love affair and fears having to abandon her work life if she opens herself to the vulnerability of love. Yet she also fears turning into a cold, heartless person, of losing her femininity totally.

Gilligan found that at their highest stage of moral reasoning, contrary to Kohlberg's stage of abstract moral principles, women try to include both selfishness and responsibility, the self and others, in their decision (ibid., 98). A desire not to hurt others is no longer just part of a conventional set of social norms, but sustains an ideal of care that understands the psychological complexity of relationships. So here the message is the need to balance self and other in the context of compassion. True development for both sexes would require an integration of rights and responsibilities.

At Gilligan's third, post-conventional level, women renounce moral judgements due to their realization that people's behaviour is psychologically and socially determined, yet they affirm a moral concern with the reality of pain and suffering. This way of thinking raises issues of exploitation and non-violence. Sadly, she says, when Gandhi championed non-violence, he tried to impose it as a truth on others, thereby violating their integrity. In the end, Gilligan sees the abortion study as illustrating the need for an expanded theory of moral development to incorporate the feminine voice, which takes the link between responsibility and care seriously.

Integrating Two Voices

The ideal model for men is distance in relationships. For adult men, Gilligan found that close friendships with other men or women are rare—even with their wives. Men may have had a number of romantic relationships, and a social circle of some sort, but they are unlikely to have a close non-sexual friendship with a woman. As a result, male subjects tended to describe themselves with distancing words like 'intelligent', 'logical', 'honest', 'arrogant', or even 'cocky'. Most moral development texts recognize the need for separation, but not for continuing connection. Gilligan feels that male and female voices typically 'speak of the importance of different truths, the former the role of separation as it defines and empowers the self, the latter the ongoing process of attachment that creates and sustains the human community' (ibid., 156). They represent two different moral ideologies: a separation justified by an ethic of rights and an attachment supported by an ethic of care.

Men are expected to pursue their identity through power and separation, through work, which leaves them distant from others. They then experience intimacy as a transformative experience. Gilligan thinks that this model—separation first and intimacy second— just doesn't fit women. She argues that men should learn to view equality in relative terms and see how truth is multiple. She describes how Alex, a male subject, didn't realize how distant he had been in a relationship that just broke up and how his hierarchy of values acted as a barrier to intimacy. In a typically male way Alex sees equality as fracturing society. On the other hand, women see care and an ongoing attachment as the path that leads to maturity. The danger women share is that relationships in mid-life can break down, if children leave or a marriage breaks up, leaving the woman high and dry, in a childlike dependence on others. The depression and despair she may face in such a situation are caused, says Gilligan, by the negative way society constructs the value of care.

In the end, the moral domain is expanded by including responsibility and care as values. Gilligan concludes that 'the different voice of women lies in the truth of an ethic of care, the tie between relationship and responsibility, and the origins of aggression in the failure of connection' (ibid., 173). We fail to see the value of the different reality of women's lives in part because of the assumption that there is a single mode of social experience. The ethic of justice is based on the premise of equality—everyone should be treated the same. The ethic of care rests on the premise of non-violence—that no one should be hurt. The perspectives come together in the understanding that just as inequality hurts both parties in a relationship, violence is destructive for everyone (ibid., 174). In the end we have to combine the two perspectives for a full view of moral development.

Some Criticisms

A number of fairly strong criticisms have been levelled at Gilligan's work, two of which dominate the secondary literature. First, it would seem likely, despite her protestations to the contrary, that the notion of a distinct female voice plays into an essentialist view of gender: women value care, empathy, and relationships, men abstract rules, rights, and justice. This view might not be embraced too enthusiastically by other feminists since it tends to reinforce traditional sexual stereotypes with a bulwark of psychological research, while also taking away the very valuable weapons of human rights and a sense of justice from the moral arsenal of the women's movement. Second, even if we grant that her research is well grounded and correct, it is based on data that are now about 30 years old and aging rapidly. Isn't this rather like taking a Polaroid of a person and then staring at it every day, assuming that the person's features will remain unaltered as she or he grows older? In other words, perhaps women's very nature has changed as our culture and family structure have become more egalitarian over the last generation, and young women would no longer be as heavily socialized into an ethics of care as they once were. Yet if Gilligan's position were an essentialist one, changes in socialization patterns wouldn't matter. Ultimately this is an empirical question that requires further research—it seems unlikely that childhood behaviour has changed that much within the last few decades.

We now move away from childhood and the family drama to the debate whether there is a distinct female 'way of knowing' the world.

Feminist Standpoint Theory

Women's standpoint theory, feminist epistemology, and feminist philosophy of science all share one basic characteristic: they argue that women experience and know the world in a special way that is ignored by the male-dominated social and physical sciences. In this section we'll explore the ideas of a major standpoint theorist, Dorothy Smith, and a major feminist philosopher of science, Sandra Harding, keeping in mind that other important standpoint theorists such as Nancy Harstock and Patricia Hill Collins share their basic position.

Dorothy Smith and Women's Standpoint Theory

Dorothy E. Smith (1926–) was born in Great Britain. She started her working life as a secretary, but then moved on to study at the London School of Economics, graduating with a BA in 1955. Her next stop was the University of California at Berkeley, where she finished her Ph.D. in 1963. While there she was married to a graduate student and had children, an experience from which she learned that women are seen as mere helpmates to men's intellectual activities: women take care of the kids, of the clothes, of food preparation, and of the house, while men read and think. She notes how few women taught sociology in the 1960s, and thus how little women's perspectives mattered to professional sociologists. After graduating, Smith taught at Berkeley and the University of Essex in the 1960s, then at the University of British Columbia from 1968 to 1976. In 1977 Smith took up the post of professor of sociology at the Ontario Institute for Studies in Education (OISE) in Toronto, and became a central figure in the Canadian sociological scene. Her main works are *The Everyday World as Problematic: A Feminist Sociology* (1987) and *The Conceptual Practices of Power: A Feminist Sociology of Knowledge* (1990).

Smith was influenced by two schools of thought: Marx's materialism, notably his ideas about the relation between work and life as expressed in *The German Ideology* (co-authored with Engels), and the phenomenology of Alfred Schutz coupled with the ethnomethodology of Harold Garfinkel, which, as we've seen, are very much related. Thus she's a materialist/phenomenologist committed to feminist politics. Smith wants to explore the nature of the everyday and everynight world experienced by women from women's own standpoint—hence standpoint theory. She echoes the traditional goal of feminist social science: she wants a sociology *for* women, not just *about* women. It's not good enough just to add a few bricks made up of studies of gender roles, the women's movement, women's sexuality, and so on to the foundation of the sociological edifice. We need to change the very way we see women's lives, to open up the 'discursive fabric' through which a range of repressed, denied, and hidden experiences can break out (Smith, 1990: 12). We can do this by means of a sociology of knowledge.

Smith is a sociologist of knowledge in the sense that she is interested in how knowledge is produced by social systems or structures. Thus, she sees forms of knowledge as the products of given types of society, just as cars and computers and cameras are the products of given types of factories. All forms of knowledge come from a specific location in society, not from some ethereal realm of pure thought.[9] Knowledge is socially organized, not the product of individual minds alone (Smith, 1992: 91). Her starting point is the individual human body—usually the female body—located in a given here and now, a given space and time. Most real, actual bodies do work of various types: they teach university classes, cook, clean, take care of children, drive to the mall, walk to the corner grocery store. Yet the sort of work done by women's bodies is—or at least was a generation ago, when Smith started to sketch out her women's standpoint theory—quite different from that done by men's. Women's bodies occupy a local space concerned with providing for the physical needs of men, themselves, and their children. Smith's feminism is grounded in the belief that women's experience of oppression, 'whatever its form and focus, was grounded in male control, use, domination *of* our bodies. No transcendence for us. We were irremediably (as it seemed) defined by our bodies' relevance for and uses to men' (ibid., 88). Her alternative is an embodied sociology grounded in women's direct experience of the world from within that world. Hence a sociology *for* and *by* women. This would be an insider's sociology, but one that is sensitive to avoiding the construction of sociological fables and then imposing them on unwitting oppressed groups. Smith mentions seeing an Indian family from an Ontario train and recalls musing on how different their experience of the world must be from hers (Smith, 1990: 24–5).

As other feminist theorists such as Susan Bordo have argued, the male epistemological standpoint tends to be that of the 'Cartesian subject', an isolated rational and logical ego cut off from the messy realities of the body's functions, domestic labour, and strong emotions.[10] Smith agrees with this: the reality of women's experience precedes the 'text-mediated discourse' (i.e., books and articles) that dominates academic life. She argues that the typically male Cartesian subject cuts himself off from local times, places, and relationships, from the bodily site of his being (Smith, 1992: 89–90). The male subject sees itself as transcendent, while the female subject sees itself as local. They live in different worlds.

Yet her Marxist side tells her that a simple reflection on this direct experience isn't good enough. We have to connect people's experiences to the larger social and economic order, which for the time being is a capitalist one. This combination of micro and macro approaches leads Smith to conclude that an 'alternative sociology, from the standpoint of women, makes the everyday world its problematic' (Smith, 1990: 27). As Marx and Engels spelled out in *The German Ideology* and elsewhere, the way we work on nature to produce something of economic value creates a material relation between us and the world that is the core of our everyday life. Smith wants to understand the way women work in everyday life, and how that work affects their bodies and their minds.

Smith argues that the established nature of academic life alienates women since sociology is grounded in men's experience. She speaks in the same sort of language as Michel Foucault, though not referring to him: the power of the social sciences is grounded in the knowledge men create and propagate in academic institutions. Sociology is a type of governing practice, one of many ways in which our society is 'ruled, managed, and administered' (ibid., 14). All *relations of ruling* are done through concepts and symbols, through such texts as political constitutions, government and academic regulations, criminal law, and methodological principles expressed in textbooks and articles. So sociology participates in these relations of ruling insofar as it establishes a given methodology as the most valid one, to the exclusion of all others.

Sociology is a man's world. Male sociologists work in the very medium they study, whereas female sociologists must split their consciousness to enter the realm of sociological theory and practice. They must move from the local realm of cooking, shopping, and child care to the 'extralocal' realm of the relations of ruling, which is conceptual in nature. This leads to a 'bifurcation of consciousness' in women:

> Entering the governing mode of our kind of society lifts actors out of the immediate, local, and particular place in which we are in the body. What becomes present to us in the governing mode is a means of passing beyond the local into the conceptual order. This mode of governing creates, at least potentially, a bifurcation of consciousness. It establishes two modes of knowing and experiencing and doing, one located in the body and in the space it occupies and moves in, the other passing beyond it. Sociology is written and aims at the latter mode of action. (Ibid., 17)

Men can be thinkers and theorists *because* their physical needs are taken care of by women. For women to enter into the 'conceptual mode' of life—into academia—they have to cross daily the chasm between the local and the conceptual or extra-local realm, to go from changing diapers to engaging in dialectic. Needless to say, Smith thinks this is a significant chasm for women to leap, especially given the limited number of women teaching in universities in the 1950s and 1960s when she formulated women's standpoint theory. Sociology was an old boys' club, and she wanted in.

Part of this bifurcation of consciousness is the traditional goal of sociology to discard our personal experience and take up an ethic of objectivity that separates the researcher from his or her personal interests and biases (ibid., 15–16). Like many standpoint theorists and feminist epistemologists, Smith suggests that the idea of bias-free objectivity is a peculiarly male assumption, one that shuts women's ways of knowing out of the academy. This is tied to the collusion of traditional social science with the 'relations of ruling', the way our society is governed by leaders through texts and text-mediated discourses.

Smith sees teaching sociology as a political act. Yet real resistance to oppressive political structures doesn't start in theory—it requires more practical politics (Smith, 1992: 96). Even though power is created and maintained by texts—think of all those bureaucratic regulations that govern the institutions you study and work in—writing more texts does not change the nature of that power. Talk in itself is cheap. Smith is no postmodernist who believes that there is nothing outside the text. Actual people exist in real worlds, and our dialogue with them stops us from dreaming up crazy ideas about how those worlds operate (ibid., 93). She compares our map of social reality to a Toronto subway map: its symbols allow us to navigate from one end of the line to the other, but they look nothing like the actual stations we see as we zoom from downtown to the city's northern limits.

A powerful criticism of Smith's standpoint theory is that although this bifurcation of consciousness was once true, today more and more women are having academic careers where they share the burdens of housework and child care with their male spouses, or don't have children at all, or have female partners. So the male/female and extra-local/local dualisms don't align as neatly as they once did. And her criticism of men's dependence on women obviously doesn't apply to most single men, since they have to enter the 'local' realm of cooking and cleaning as much as women were traditionally forced to do. The gender gap between the bifurcated female consciousness and the unitary male consciousness has narrowed considerably of late; whether it still significantly oppresses women in academic life is an open empirical question.

Smith's work is open to several other criticisms. *Having her cake and eating it too.* Smith (1990: 28) argues that women are 'the authoritative speakers of our own experience'. Yet it would seem that enlightened women are also the authoritative speakers of *men's* experience, since Smith argues with some energy that men participate in relations of ruling by means both of sociological method, with its emphasis on objectivity, and of their domination of the extra-local realm in everyday life. Standpoint theorists claim that most men don't understand the unique experience of women, or in many cases even their own experience as patriarchs. It would seem that women not only have a unique experience but a superior understanding of both sexes. Smith suggests that some women are able to transcend their own standpoint, unlike most men. Women's standpoint is epistemologically liberating, men's merely stultifying. In simplest terms, women can understand both sexes, while men only understand their own. This smacks of inconsistency and unfairness.

Subjectivism and relativism. Following up from this first point, Charles Lemert and others have accused Smith of being a subjectivist, of being caught up in chronicling the lives of women in specific social locations and ignoring the larger structures of action and belief that govern their lives. No man *or* woman is an island, an isolated subject. Yet standpoint theory would appear to enjoy building islands of subjective experience in larger oceans of social actors. Smith (1992: 90–1) says explicitly there's 'something distinctive' in the standpoint of women, yet that her notion of standpoint doesn't aim to give any special privilege to women's ways of knowing. In other words, men and women have different ways of seeing the world, thus echoing Gilligan's view of sexual difference. Yet how different are these ways of knowing? Can they understand each other at all? This returns us to the first critique: the epistemological bridge between men's and women's standpoint seems to have one-way traffic only.

Closely related to her possible subjectivism is the danger of standpoint theory sliding down the slippery slope of relativism. If Smith wants to focus on the standpoint of women, why not the standpoint of black women, as Patricia Hill Collins, a black American theorist, has suggested? Or why not the standpoint of poor Latina women? Or Asian immigrants in Vancouver? Or McDonald's employees? Or *Star Wars* fans? Aren't all these standpoints equally valid? The ramifications of this slippery slope for science should be obvious: we wouldn't want uneducated Peruvian immigrants running our nuclear reactors or teaching engineering simply because we want to be sensitive to their 'standpoint'. It's hard to get around the idea that in *some* parts of science and social science, the standpoints of skilled, knowledgeable groups are superior to those of their opposites. How they got to be skilled and knowledgeable is another matter.

Historical change. Third, it goes without saying that the last generation or so has seen tremendous changes in gender relations in the Western world. For example, about half the professors and 80 per cent of the students (both undergraduate and graduate) in the sociology department where I taught while writing this chapter are female. This is a far cry from Smith's Berkeley department in the 1960s, where she was one of two female professors. Women are no longer officially and systematically discriminated against in most North American universities, whatever piecemeal bias might crop up here and there from the old guard. Indeed, almost all Canadian universities have employment equity programs to promote the hiring of women over men with better qualifications. The claims of feminist theorists that women are

oppressed must be constantly updated to take into account the very real social changes of the 1970s, 1980s, and 1990s. Without this updating, standpoint theory is in danger of holding up sepia-tinted snapshots of an all-powerful patriarchal order that is little more than an angry memory in the minds of aging feminist academics.

Sandra Harding and the Feminist Epistemology

Sandra Harding (1935–) is an American academic who came to fame during the two decades she taught in the Philosophy Department at the University of Delaware. From 1996 she has taught social science and comparative education as Director of the Center for the Study of Women at UCLA. Her work is more eclectic than that of Smith. Much of it is taken up with explaining the views of other feminist thinkers, notably standpoint theorists, and it's often difficult to tell the difference between her views and those of the people she summarizes. However, she is clear about the central thesis of feminist epistemology: that both the physical and social sciences are dominated by white, bourgeois, Western men who import into their work 'androcentric' (male-centred) and sexist biases. This is just as true of the study of monkeys in the jungle (primatology) as of the study of human beings in society (sociology). There's no such thing as pure science, since all research is situated in a given social and political location. In other words, science always has a political side. She even goes so far as to muse that:

> theorizing itself is suspiciously patriarchal, for it assumes separations between the knower and the known, subject and object, and the possibility of some powerful transcendental, Archimedian standpoint from which nature and social life fall into what we think is their proper perspective. (Harding, 1986a: 647)

There is no sexless, timeless, culture-free place from which to theorize, no view from nowhere. Indeed, the idea of the dispassionate, value-free, objective pursuit of knowledge according to a rigorous scientific method is itself an androcentric, white, bourgeois male prejudice (ibid., 653). These nasty patriarchs defend a 'logic of discovery' that only tries to answer the sort of questions about nature and social life *they* want answered. When they ask questions about women, their motivation is all too often to 'pacify, control, exploit or manipulate' them, for traditional social research has always been for *men* (Harding, 1987: 8). Harding's view of patriarchy as a powerful force in sexual politics links her to the radicals of the second wave, even though some of what she says about the reality of gender differences comes close to postmodernism.

Harding is perhaps best known for her exploration of the role of women in the sciences. She has championed the cause of several female scientists who have been 'erased' from the history of scientific discovery, notably Rosalind Franklin, a key background figure in Crick and Watson's discovery of DNA. Certainly these forgotten figures should be resurrected from obscurity. Yet it's not good enough just to add a few female scientists to the mix and stir, nor simply to add a few facts about women to traditional research to even things out. The problem is that male researchers take their own presuppositions as the norm for all human beings. Even the ideal of objectivity is androcentric, for among other things, it concentrates on the way we justify our scientific claims—the logic of justification—and ignores the contexts of discovery and justification. The origins of scientific problems don't matter to men. *Why* Einstein explored theoretical physics instead of insect behaviour or geography isn't important; only his results are. And these results are often seen by traditional science as the result of inspired hunches, as coming out of the pure blue skies of male genius. Yet even Einstein had a context of discovery, which no doubt included women doing his laundry and cooking his supper, not to mention a world view that saw science as an entirely male pursuit. Harding believes that science always has a political context and political effects—who funds it, who benefits from it, and which social

order it buttresses. A science for all human beings would have to be directed by politically engaged feminist researchers, whether male or female (Harding, 1989: 706). Just adding women without overcoming the sexist biases of traditional science would leave these prejudices in command, to the detriment of the women's movement.

One proposed solution to the male domination of science is feminist empiricism. This is the idea that if male scientists were compelled to live up to their own standards of objectivity and fairness, and stick to the empirical facts, they would mend their sexist ways. Female researchers could pressure their male counterparts to be better empiricists to eliminate sexist and androcentric biases from their research. Harding argues that feminist empiricism fails because the very way men select their problems is at fault, not just how they justify their research claims. They choose to research problems of value to men, not women. Also, following the logical and sociological norms found in traditional science will produce androcentric results (Harding, 1986a: 652). Sticking to the facts won't make science gender-neutral. In fact, Harding still maintains that the social sciences actively work to support men's control of women (Harding and Norberg, 2005: 2009). Their goal is less truth than power.

Harding has also chronicled the rise of standpoint theory, for the most part sympathizing with it. She obviously agrees with Smith that women have a distinct way of knowing the world. As we've seen, Harding is less concerned with the logic of how scientists justify their beliefs—the central aspect of most academic discussions of epistemology—than with how they choose their problems and the context of their discoveries. She hopes that standpoint theory can provide a less partial and less perverse understanding of the world than traditional male-dominated social science (Harding, 1986a: 655). Standpoint theory is politically engaged in women's liberation and sees aspects of the social world that male-dominated theory cannot. It avoids what Donna Haraway calls the 'God trick' of speaking from on high about all things, yet having no specific social location. It battles against this 'view from nowhere', arguing that its specific location can advance the growth of knowledge. Its other major advantage lies in the fact that it is so good at stirring up debate (Harding, 2004: 26–9). Standpoint theory must have some truth to it, or its enemies wouldn't be so passionate in attacking it.

What she calls the 'successor sciences'—those based on standpoint theory or feminist epistemologies—aim to provide 'more complete, less false, less distorting, less defensive, less perverse, less rationalizing understandings of the natural and social worlds' (Harding, 1986a: 654). This is part of a struggle for power. Like Smith, Harding sees conceptual practices as ways in which groups rule over one another, especially in bureaucracies, which thrive on abstract ideas and mounds of paperwork. So it matters very much in our society *who* controls all that paperwork. Standpoint theory aims to 'study up' from oppressed groups to dominant social institutions, to see behind the curtain of sexist ideologies (Harding, 2004: 30). One part of this 'studying up' is looking at how the consciousness of the age selects certain problems as more interesting than others (ibid., 35). Obviously, these will be the problems that serve the dominant social institutions.

Yet Harding thinks that her partial defence of standpoint theory doesn't open the door to relativism. If a women's epistemology, why not those of other groups? She admits that there might also be Asian, African, and other ethnic epistemologies alongside feminist epistemology—after all, one cannot ignore the 'colonized social experiences' of these groups while trumpeting women's oppression (Harding, 1986a: 659). Perhaps, however, one could concentrate on the shared goals of these various oppressed groups rather than seeing them as a series of isolated solitudes. Harding believes that relativism becomes a problem and a possibility only when the hegemony of ruling powers is challenged by those they rule. Calling feminist epistemology 'relativist' is just a fancy way of trying to preserve the legitimacy of male domination of the sciences (Harding, 1987: 10). Of course women have a different view of the social world

than men. To insist that we must all think the same way is just another way of saying that we should all think like *men*.

Harding has some sympathy for postmodernism, though she doesn't think that standpoint theory can accept it entirely since it leads to political inertia. The claim of postmodernism that truth is a logocentric illusion has been tempting for many recent feminist theorists. Feminist critiques led to the dissolving of the essential 'Man'. Yet there is no essential Woman either, just myriads of women in different races, classes, and cultures (Harding, 1986a: 647). In fact, Harding defends the instability of feminist theory. It should be in part standpoint theory, in part postmodern, and borrow from 'male' theories such as liberalism, Marxism, and psychoanalysis. Feminists should embrace the instability of analytical categories since 'consistent and coherent theories in an unstable and incoherent world are obstacles to both our understanding and our social practices' (ibid., 648–9). There are many feminisms, just as there are women in different races, classes, and cultures. She likens a good feminist theorist to a guitar player playing a riff over the beats provided by patriarchal theory, as opposed to inventing a whole musical form herself. All three of the feminist approaches to science Harding mentions— feminist empiricism, standpoint theory, and postmodernism—have their strengths and weaknesses. They should be freely sampled by feminist epistemologists (though feminist empiricism is the most flawed of the three).

Yet when push comes to shove, Harding argues that women *do* have a better grasp of certain types of problems than men (and, one presumes, unenlightened women). The prior beliefs and actions of researchers are part of the evidence for the validity of their research, and not just the facts they marshal and the quality of their arguments.[11] Despite flirting with a total social constructionist view of knowledge, she's not saying that sexist and anti-sexist claims are equally true. In fact, 'women's and men's experiences are not equally reliable guides to the production of complete and undistorted social research' (Harding,

1987: 10). Women are more likely to produce such research. Men just aren't equipped to do this:

> Dominant groups are especially poorly equipped to identify oppressive features of their own beliefs and practices, as standpoint methodologies have argued. . . . Their activities in daily life do not provide them with the intellectual and political resources necessary to detect such values and interests in their own work. (Harding and Norberg, 2005: 2010)

The sexual determinism here is rather obvious: men can't overcome their social status as an oppressive class. Men are stuck in the quicksand of sexual privilege whether they want to be or not:

> Objectively, no individual men can succeed in renouncing sexist privilege any more than individual whites can succeed in renouncing racist privilege—the benefits of gender and race accrue regardless of the wishes of the individuals who bear them. (Harding, 1986a: 658)

The job of feminist theory is to fight this male power. Harding hopes it will create a 'liberatory, transformative subjectivity' in women what will contribute to a general social progress (Harding and Norberg, 2005: 2011). Its goal isn't truth, but political equality.

On the basis of the above, one would think that Harding sees us as prisoners of our sex. Yet she also criticizes feminist theory for reproducing the dualisms of gender vs sex and society vs biology. She hints that there may be a contradiction between saying that in theory biology is not destiny when in fact women should have their biological differences recognized by government policies (Harding, 1986a: 662). Her solution to the problem of saying that gender is constructed by society, but that women as a sex should be given special recognition, is to accept the nature vs nurture and sex vs gender splits as outmoded figments of our imaginations and at the same time to insist that they're relevant to our lives. In other words, she is suggesting a feminist version of Plato's Noble Lie: it if works politically but is false empirically, let's believe it anyway. Biology and society are actually interwoven influences, but for the sake of the women's movement, so her argument goes, we'll focus on social construction in the realm of theory and biological difference in the field of political action. In the final section we'll hear Camille Paglia's colourful rejection of this Noble Lie.

Harding argues for a 'reasonable constructionism' for the sciences and for the need to resocialize men in the political arena. Knowledge isn't abstract and universal, but is always situated in a given historical and social location. Nature doesn't dictate to us a single solitary truth. Instead, 'many possible hypotheses are consistent with nature's order', and the best ones we put forward are only 'temporarily less false' than all the others (Harding, 2004: 38). The question isn't whether we construct our knowledge, but whether we do it in a reasonable way. Standpoint theory is only a stepping stone to a world where truth and power aren't mixed together, where research is free from all sexist biases. Yet Harding thinks that we have a long way to go before we get to such a world.

Men can contribute to feminist research. Harding mentions John Stuart Mill and Marx and Engels in this regard. We can't blame entire classes of people for designing oppressive social institutions if some of them individually had nothing to do with building these (Harding, 1987: 11). She urges men trained by sexist institutions to courageously 'take advantage of that evil and use their masculine authority to resocialize men', in part by engaging in 'phallic critiques' of the boardroom, locker room, and military. These last remarks are rather condescending if not insulting to men, arguing that male social scientists retreat to research ghettos that are too uncomfortable for female researchers. They are typical of the casual reverse sexism of second-wave feminists. In the end Harding argues that those who don't 'actively struggle against the exploitation of women in everyday life are unlikely to produce social science research about any subject at all that is undistorted by sexism and androcentrism' (ibid., 12).

Unfortunately for her, this would exclude not only most male researchers today, but a good number of women too.

We've already seen some of the problems with Harding's feminist epistemology above and in the section on Dorothy Smith. A number of other serious questions arise. Is a well-grounded empiricism really sexist? Can't men partially overcome gender bias, at least in the context of justifying their research? And would sciences dominated by women be any less biased in the long term—if standpoint theory is right, wouldn't they tend to focus on 'women's' problems, just as male science focuses on men's problems? One way of looking at the problem of sexist bias in the sciences is in terms of a basic dualism: either there's some zone in scientific endeavour that is free from gender bias, however covered in twilight it might be, or such a zone is an illusion. If this zone exists, objectivity isn't a doomed project, and what Harding calls feminist empiricism can at least force male researchers to reduce their gender biases (though it can't force them to choose problems that don't interest them). If there isn't any such zone, it's difficult to see how Harding can escape from relativism—we would need male and female Geography, Physics, and Mathematics as much as male and female Philosophy and Sociology, since all forms of knowledge would be mapped along gender lines. It would be as if men and women were speaking distinct theoretical languages without any Rosetta stone to translate one into the other.[12] Further, it's difficult to see *why* each sex would want to learn the other's language if no zone of objectivity exists. Science would become half politics. Of course, Harding would reply that science was *always* political, and feminist epistemology just forces us to recognize this fact.

Lastly, as one reads Harding's work from the 1980s to 2005, it seems that nothing much has changed in the sciences, despite a considerable influx of female researchers into universities in that period. She does note the large amount of good work done in the fields of standpoint theory and feminist epistemology. Yet the problem these theorists discuss—male sexist bias in the sciences—seems almost frozen in time, whether the background music is seventies disco or post-millennial hip-hop. This might be evidence of Harding having no little cultural capital tied up in the problem of male bias *not* being solved any time soon, and not of the continued almost total male domination of the sciences.

DONNA HARAWAY'S CYBORGS

Donna Haraway (1944–) was born in Denver, Colorado. She studied zoology, philosophy, and English at Colorado College, graduating in 1966. After studying for a year in Paris, she went to Yale, earning her Ph.D. in biology in 1972 through her interdisciplinary research in developmental biology. She has taught at the University of Hawaii and at Johns Hopkins University, and is now a professor in the History of Consciousness Department at the University of California at Santa Cruz, where she has taught feminist theory and its relations to science since 1980. Haraway is the author of *Crystals, Fabrics and Fields: Metaphors of Organicism in Twentieth-Century Developmental Biology* (1976), *Primate Visions: Gender, Race, and Nature in the World of Modern Science* (1989), *Simians, Cyborgs, and Women: The Reinvention of Nature* (1991), and the oddly titled *Modest_Witness@ Second_Millennium: Femaleman Meets Oncomouse: Feminism and Technoscience* (1996).

Haraway's greatest claim to fame is her 'Cyborg Manifesto', which first appeared in *The Socialist Review* in 1985. In it she mixes together socialist feminism, a 'contructivist' idea of gender differences, and an appreciation of a feminist science fiction peopled by post-gendered androids and aliens in a heady postmodern brew.

Haraway argues that our modern high-tech culture breaks down the distinction between the organic and the machine, turning human beings into a hybrid of the two. We've started to become cyborgs, like the Borg in *Star Trek* or Arnold Schwarzenegger's character in the *Terminator* films: 'By the late twentieth century, our time, a mythic time, we are all chimeras, theorized and fabricated hybrids of machine and organism; in short, we are cyborgs. The cyborg is our ontology; it gives us our politics' (Haraway, 1985: 231). This cyborg status isn't just a question of our being reliant on electronic devices in our everyday lives. It's also a question of how we reshape our bodies with exercise machines, of robotic automation in factories, and of genetic research. Her ideas about cyborgs have been especially influential on cyberpunk writers, who start from the assumption that the electronic machines we rely on in the information age fundamentally alter both our physical nature and our consciousness.

Haraway wants to move beyond both traditional socialist feminism, which finds the origins of oppression in class structure and economics, and radical feminism, which ties oppression to the narrow gender roles created and enforced by patriarchy. She feels that science and technology have created the conditions where these economic and sexual dialectics are no longer as powerful as they once were.

Her 'Cyborg Manifesto' aims to create an 'ironic' political myth for socialist feminism, that of the cyborg, a hybrid of machine and organism that's part science fiction, part social reality. In fact, the boundary between the two is collapsing in our high-tech, gadget-laden information economy. This myth is a way of mapping our social and bodily realities that is both socialist, since it reflects the new economic realities of our age, and postmodernist, since it points at a world without gender, where we can take pleasure in confusing boundaries.

Haraway argues that because the electronic age blurs the distinction between nature and culture in our lives, the breakdown of three other crucial boundaries helps to make the image of the cyborg a potent political possibility. These boundaries are those between humans and animals, humans and machines, and the physical and the non-physical. Cyborgs are the monstrous, illegitimate offspring of these boundary blurrings, potent feminist myths for resistance to patriarchy and for the recoupling of diverse groups of women.

Haraway's social constructivist view of gender can be seen most clearly in her statement that nothing about being 'female' naturally binds women. Differences in gender, race, and class are constructed by patriarchy, racism, and capitalism. These differences cause painful fragmentation among feminists, for the concept of 'woman' is elusive, and is sometimes used as an excuse for women's dominations of each other. In fact, Haraway agrees with the black American feminist bell hooks that white women's embarrassing silence about race illustrates their guilt with respect to the racial domination of whites over blacks. All types of feminism try to annex other forms of domination to the one they see as central. Socialist feminists view class and labour as key, extend this to sexual inequality, and only later add in race; radical feminists see gender divisions as the key form of domination, bringing in labour by analogy, and once again adding race almost as an afterthought (ibid., 242). Haraway sees all these categories as historical and unstable, and is dubious about the tendency of most forms of feminist thought to concentrate exclusively on a single dualism (e.g., 'male/female' or 'exploiter/exploited').

Later in her 'Manifesto' Haraway argues that we're moving from an organic industrial society to a 'polymorphous' information or post-industrial society (ibid., 243). This moves us from the old forms of domination produced by the division of labour, the nuclear family, and white capitalist patriarchy to an 'informatics of domination'. Information is now the central commodity, mediated by electronics. This turns labour into robotics and word processing, sex into genetic engineering, and the mind into artificial intelligence (ibid., 248). Here she echoes Baudrillard's postmodernism and Castells's theory of the network society.

This new economy is still exploitive. However, it breaks down the old dichotomies of mind and body, human and animal, organism and machine, civilized and primitive, culture and nature, men and women. These distinctions, which were once used to support various forms of domination, are challenged by high-tech culture. We zone out in front of our computers, symbolically jumping from our bodies to cyberspace; we connect to tribal societies in the Amazonian rain forest with satellite dishes and hand-held video cameras; we change our biological sex with surgery; we decorate ourselves with body piercings and tattoos. Modern technology and culture jumble together mind, body, organism, machine, civilization, tribalism, and male and female into one constantly shifting cultural blob.

Why should our bodies end at our skin? As Marshall McLuhan had already said, modern machines and media are extensions of our minds, bodies, and central nervous systems. Haraway describes the cyborg as the uniquely postmodern self, disassembled and reassembled. Cyborg monsters in feminist science fiction give us different pictures of the political possibilities of a post-gender world. An intense pleasure in machine skill can now become part of our sense of embodiment—we could stop seeing such pleasure as a 'fetish' and finally realize that we *are* our machines and they are us. Haraway argues that we should seek out renewal in the form of the regeneration promised by cyborgs, not that of rebirth promised by the old gender-driven reproductive matrix. Cyborgs open up the possibility of a 'monstrous world without gender' (ibid., 253). She concludes that science and technology are best seen as a source of great satisfaction: she would rather be a cyborg than a goddess.

Since she doesn't favour the rigid prohibitions on sexual self-definition and sexual practices that more repressive modern feminists like Catherine MacKinnon argue for, Haraway can be seen as straddling the second and third waves, although her idea that one's gendered identity is a social construction is hardly news to most second-wavers. Haraway's 'cyberfeminism' argues that one's sexual identity can be constructed as one pleases, since there is no natural state for either men or women (or for human beings as distinct from the machines we create, for that matter). As cyborgs, we are free to choose our sexual identity. If we choose to speak in a different voice, that voice can be whatever we choose it to be.

The uniqueness of Haraway's vision is a product of her study of higher-order primates and of biological theories in general, her conclusion being that *nature itself* is largely a social construction. Her work in primatology led her to conclude that science brings to the study of sexual difference culturally relative ideas about gender differences. These mostly male scientists try to find in the animal world the culturally imposed differences between the sexes that exist in our own society. For Haraway, the constructed nature of the difference between the male and the female of the species penetrates through the upper layer of the socially defined gender roles we find in human cultures right down to the biological sexual differences found in higher-order primates. Her constructionist view of gender difference is thus all-inclusive.

Haraway can be criticized on a number of fronts. First, perhaps she exaggerates the influence of new technologies on the breakdown of distinctions between the organism and the machine and the physical and the non-physical. After all, we still have basic physical needs and drives to fulfill, and these appear to be in no danger of disappearing. Second, many people don't want to live in a post-gendered world, to give up the pleasures of sexual difference in exchange for test-tube babies and computer sex. This could be independent of any desire we have to use sexual difference to dominate others. Third, if Haraway is using the cyborg as a postmodern fictional metaphor to describe our place in the new information and electronic economy, in what sense is this 'materialist' or 'socialist'? Don't socialists usually advocate a fundamental change in the economic arrangements of capitalism in the name of human equality? It's not clear, at least in the 'Cyborg Manifesto', that Haraway wants any such change.

Yet the 'Cyborg Manifesto' is a challenging essay all the same. Its central message is Haraway's proclamation that modern science and technology have started to turn our cherished distinctions between human beings and machines, between men and women, into artifacts of a disappearing industrial, patriarchal culture. For all we know, perhaps her brave new world of genderless cyborgs will arrive in some dimly perceived future.

CAMILLE PAGLIA'S ATTACK ON THE SECOND WAVE

Camille Paglia (1947–) is the most important of a small group of feminist theorists who are actively critical of second-wave radicalism, especially its academic version. They can be characterized as a 'third wave' of feminist social theory. Paglia's early teaching career was a checkered one, but she is now University Professor of Humanities and Media Studies at the University of Arts in Philadelphia, Pennsylvania. Her background is in art, literature, and literary theory; her mentor at Harvard was the great literary critic Harold Bloom. Yet much of what she says overlaps with social theory, notably her ongoing debate with academic feminism.

Paglia is notoriously confrontational in print and in person. She has written extensively in magazines and newspapers and on the web, and has been interviewed frequently in the mass media. Paglia follows Oscar Wilde's motto that the only thing worse than being talked about is *not* being talked about. She is an unabashed fan of modern popular culture, writing essays championing Madonna, the Rolling Stones, and other popular artists. She is also very sympathetic to male gay culture, arguing for the artistic merit of Robert Mapplethorpe's sexually explicit photographs. Paglia's main works of relevance to social theory are *Sexual Personae* (1991 [1990]), *Sex, Art and American Culture* (1992), and *Vamps and Tramps: New Essays* (1994). A self-confessed bisexual, she has challenged the orthodox beliefs of both second-wave feminism and gay activism. Her basic message is that Western culture never entirely defeated ancient paganism, which lives on today in both popular culture and in certain schools of literature and high art. Her work represents the most serious challenge to second-wave academic feminist theory today.

Nature, Culture, Sex, and Art: The Eternal Battle of Apollo and Dionysus

Paglia sets out her 'metaphysics' of art, culture, and sexuality in her first major work, *Sexual Per-*

sonae. This weighty tome sketches a history of how sexual masks or 'personae' have affected Western art and literature. The history of art is a long dream of artists trying on an endless variety of sexual masks that continuously fluctuate between masculine and feminine patterns. Although much of the book is of more interest to critics than social theorists, in the early chapters Paglia lays out in some detail her view of sexual difference and of how modern feminism has distorted Western culture for ideological ends. She sees the history of culture as a great battleground between two metaphorical Greek gods—Apollo, god of sunlight, reason, and prophecy, and Dionysus, god of wine, women, and song.

> The Apollonian and Dionysian, two great western principles, govern sexual personae in life and art. My theory is this: Dionysus is identification, Apollo objectification. Dionysus is the empathic, the sympathetic emotion transporting us into other people, other places, other times. Apollo is the hard, cold separatism of western personality and categorical thought. Dionysus is energy, ecstasy, hysteria, promiscuity, emotionalism—heedless indiscriminateness of idea or practice. Apollo is obsessiveness, voyeurism, idolatry, fascism—frigidity and aggression of the eye, petrifaction of objects. . . . Dionysus is energy unbound, mad, callous, destructive, wasteful. Apollo is law, history, tradition, the dignity and safety of custom and form. Dionysus is the *new*, exhilarating but rude, sweeping all away to begin again. Apollo is a tyrant, Dionysus a vandal. (Paglia, 1991 [1990]: 96–7)

Paglia identifies women with the Dionysian, men with the Apollonian, with a number of qualifications. The Dionysian world is one of caves, wombs, liquids, the changing, the murky—of what Paglia refers to as the *chthonian*, from the Greek word for 'of the earth'. Its religion is the earth cult of the mother goddess, with her pregnant belly and roly-poly undefined body. The Apollonian world is one of clarity, objectivity, sunlight, straight lines, efficiency, rationality—the world of capitalism, modern science, and the 'sky-cults' of the great monotheistic religions with their father-figure gods. It starts with the stern statues of the ancient Egyptian pharaohs; shines brightly in the Greece of the classical age, with its geo-metrical temples and shining god-images of Athena, Apollo, and Hermes; and comes down to our own day in the gigantic economic engine of modern capitalism and the colossal endeavours of modern science. Yet prowling in the shadows of all this Apollonian art is the chthonian cat, hun-kered close to the ground, still in touch with mother earth. This Dionysian impulse has been largely submerged by modern art and literature, though it seeps through in the works of the Romantic poets, of the Marquis de Sade, Friedrich Nietzsche, and Oscar Wilde, to name just the most obvious culprits. Rarely do these two forces com-bine happily in the same person or culture, though they often meet in dialectical conflict.

The Apollonian seeks to *concentrate* and to *project*. Pulling a leaf out of Freud's book, Paglia notes that on the most primitive level—in urina-tion and ejaculation—men have to project their precious bodily fluids outward to express their masculinity. This projection leads to abstraction and conceptualization in art, to physical science, and to technological progress. The Apollonian draws borders between things, setting up struc-tures and hierarchies. The very idea of represent-ing the world through art, of turning reality into an object, is Apollonian. Paglia follows the creed of nineteenth-century 'aestheticism', with its motto of 'art for art's sake'. Civilization *is* art (Paglia, 1992: 22), and art and morality don't mix. Art is Apollonian at least in form, for it freezes the flux of nature in making a thing of beauty. A large part of art is the creation of a series of female-inspired sex objects, contrary to the puritanical view of feminist theorists like Catharine McKin-non and Andrea Dworkin, who see the objectifi-cation of the female body as part of an attempt by 'patriarchy' to oppress women.

On the other hand, the Dionysian is liquid and flowing, refusing to fix nature into an objec-tive form. In the womb-world of nature there are no objects, no art (Paglia, 1991: 93), hence there have been precious few great female artists. Paglia sees the adult woman's body as a prisoner of repro-ductive urges, as 'submerged in a world of fluids', a 'dank primal brew of earth and water' (ibid., 91–2). Dionysus is the god of liquids, of the bow-els of the earth, of swamps full of gators and snakes. Yet the Apollonian and the Dionysian must meet from time to time to perpetuate the species. Since we have to make babies, female beauty acts like a drug that allows the male of the species to break free temporarily of his Apollon-ian shackles and re-enter the realm of the Dionysian. It enchants men into the bedroom.

The Western personality, with all its great achievements, also comes from the 'superhuman purity' of the Apollonian imagination (ibid., 12). Men spend much of their early lives trying to sep-arate themselves from their mothers, hence their obsession with building things, projecting them-selves, and solidifying their selves in isolation from others: think of the cowboy riding the range or the architect designing a palace of commerce. The Apollonian is a 'male line drawn against the dehumanizing magnitude of female nature' (ibid., 28). One of the principal products of the Apollonian is capitalism, going all the way back to Homer's bronze-clad warriors, which Paglia sees as 'the Apollonian soup cans that crowd the sunny temples of our supermarkets' (ibid., 37). This notion that capitalism is an Apollonian conquest of nature dating to ancient Greece is something of an exaggeration on Paglia's part. Although it makes sense on the level of metaphor, it makes lit-tle sense on the economic level, unless we define capitalism as any system that produces things sold for money. Yet her point that capitalism is in its very essence Apollonian is fair enough, even if we follow Weber in seeing modern capitalism as beginning only in the seventeenth century. Nonetheless, Paglia credits capitalism with being an efficient economic machine that has brought a decent standard of life to the greatest number of people (Paglia, 1992: 246). But being a good capitalist or consumer isn't the same thing as being fully human.

Nature is the most powerful force in the universe, yet everything great done by the human race was in defiance of nature (Paglia, 1994: 20–1). To defend ourselves against nature we build civilization. Civilization is a palace of reason and ethics built by the Apollonian to defend us against our primal instincts, namely sex and aggression. It's mind's battle to imagine itself free of matter, Apollo's pulling himself out of the murky Dionysian cave. Paglia (1991: 1) sees sex as the 'natural in man' or as a dynamic interplay between nature and culture (Paglia, 1992: 19). It's still largely hidden and mysterious. To defend ourselves against unbridled sexuality, we build up repression, defence mechanisms, and art. In fact, repression actually *increases* sexual pleasure: as Paglia (1991: 36) notes, there's nothing less erotic than a nudist colony. Sex and nature are the brutal pagan forces within and without us,

leading to real sexual differences that culture can paper over only in part (ibid., xiii). Historically, we witness an eternal battle between sexual repression and debauchery, as seen in the move from the conformity of the 1950s to the relative freedom of the 1960s and 1970s and then the AIDS crisis of the 1980s. Sex and civilization are at two ends of a teeter-totter, swinging up and down in eternal motion.

Paglia has repeatedly stressed the fact that although *some* aspects of sexuality are socially constructed, it's childish and false to claim that our entire sexual lives are just social conventions that could be changed by altering our social institutions or laws. Sex is the point of contact between nature and culture, it's the *daemonic*—the animal within us (ibid., 3). Feminism has cheated a generation of young women of sexual wisdom by trying to convince them that problems like rape,

Zippy the Pinhead cartoons, from Paglia's *Vamps and Tramps* (1994). (Printed with permission of the author. © 1992 Bill Griffith.)

sexual harassment, prostitution, and pornography can be dealt with by re-educating men and passing a few regulations that will reshape an already malleable human nature. Human beings aren't purely the products of social conditioning. Sexual differences are not the result of this or that arbitrary social construction. Women have been identified with nature and fertility going back to prehistory (ibid., 7). The connection of women with nature in ancient mythology is an eternally valid truth, however much we try to revolt against nature's limitations today. 'The female body is a chthonian machine, indifferent to the spirit who inhabits it. Organically, it has one mission, pregnancy, which we may spend a lifetime staving off' (ibid., 10). In short, women aren't in control of their bodies: nature is (Paglia, 1992: 31). Second-wave feminism has distorted this fact in moving from a battle for legal and political equality to a campaign to erase real sexual difference.

Grass Huts and Civilization: The Culture Wars

Paglia argues that a civilization led by women would be still living in grass huts, which hardly endeared her to radical feminists. Men have built pretty well everything of value in modern societies: bridges, highways, skyscrapers, plumbing, computers, modern capitalism, the mass media, antibiotics, and the birth control pill, not to mention liberal democracy. Without these accomplishments, feminism wouldn't exist, and all those second-wave feminist writers wouldn't be sitting at their desks writing:

> What feminists call 'patriarchy' is simply *civilization*, a system designed by men but augmented and now co-owned by women. Like a great temple, civilization is a gender-neutral structure that all should respect. Feminists who prate of patriarchy are self-exiled in grass huts. (Paglia, 1994: 26)

Men bonded together against nature, using science and technology—their 'defensive head-magic'—to create the 'spectacular glory of male civilization' whose language and logic feminists today use to attack patriarchy (Paglia, 1991: 9). The fact that men have traditionally dominated art, science, and politics is explained by the fact that they are natural projectors: their sexual anatomy proves this. Men project in erection and ejaculation, leading them to conceptualize in art and science (ibid., 17, 20). Women are by nature more self-contained: they have no need to project their essence into the world. This point of view has embroiled Paglia in the 'culture wars' of late twentieth- and early twenty-first-century America over such related issues as affirmative action, the 'rape crisis', homosexuality, political correctness, and the degradation of higher education.

Paglia argues that most second-wave feminists—though she rarely uses this term—have given up on the laudatory goal of seeking the legal and political equality of the sexes in exchange for a dubious attempt to socially re-engineer men and dominate academic life for their own selfish purposes. The only way to make the sexes the same is by killing the imagination, lobotomizing the brain, and castrating men. This would be bad not only for men (especially the third part!), but also for culture as a whole, since male aggression and lust 'are the energizing factors in culture . . . tools of survival in the pagan vastness of female nature' (ibid., 23, 26). The fact that men feel incomplete leads them to project outward, to build the citadels of art, science, and politics as defences against a feminine nature. American feminists have gotten caught up in the empty fantasy of male oppressors and female victims turned into pure sex objects by patriarchy. Paglia sees woman as the dominant sex. They've always ruled the emotional and sexual realms, and of late women have started to gain power in the formerly male-dominated public realm. Women's sexual power has bewitched men from the time of Helen of Troy—whose face launched a thousand Apollonian ships—to the modern glamorous Hollywood actress. Paglia's heroines are those women who accomplished great things without taking off their feminine sexual mask and sacrificing their strength, from Amelia Earhart and Hillary Clinton to Elizabeth Taylor and Madonna.

Most of academic feminism today is prudish and puritanical about sex, as seen in Dworkin and McKinnon's attempt to ban all pornography, even *Playboy* and *Penthouse*, from store shelves in the 1980s. It is also naive about the psychology of sex, which they think can be managed in a rational and egalitarian manner. 'Leaving sex to the feminists is like letting your dog vacation at the taxidermist's' (Paglia, 1992: 50), which, one must confess, would be ruff for poor Fido. Sex is a dark and powerful force: we're not, deep down, all kind and wonderful nurturers. Second-wave feminists want to castrate and make eunuchs of men, although they have had no success in working-class, black, and Latino culture (ibid., 63).

At least part of what makes men men and women women are some real hormonal differences between the sexes. As a pagan priestess of nature, Paglia thinks it arrogant to believe we can construct ourselves in any way we wish. The AIDS crisis proved this: the sexual freedom exercised by the gay community in the 1970s came at a grim price. The so-called 'double standard', whereby men seek to spread their seed far and wide while women want to remain pure, has a strong grounding in biology and evolution. Men want to spread their genes; women want to take care of their children. These missions conflict with each other. Women have to be on their guard. They have to be picky, for promiscuity in women is a loss of identity, a contamination (Paglia, 1991: 27). Paglia is a firm supporter of the political and legal equality of women, thus echoing the goals of first-wave feminism. Yet equality of opportunity is not the same thing as erasing sexual difference, which Paglia sees as grounded in part in nature.

Round two of the culture wars takes place in the arena of academe. The modern university is dominated by an army of 'pedestrian, toadying careerists who wave Sixties banners to conceal their record of ruthless, beaverlike tunneling to the top' (ibid., viii–ix). The sixties generation turned on, tuned in, but dropped out of academic life, leaving the fields of the arts, humanities, and social sciences to conformist fifties types who embraced French theorists such as Jacques Derrida and Michel Foucault as badges of their phony rebellions. These French poststructuralist theorists:

are perfect prophets for the weak, anxious academic personality, trapped in verbal formulas and perennially defeated by circumstance. They offer a self-exculpating cosmic explanation for the normal professorial state of resentment, alienation, dithery passivity, and inaction. (Paglia, 1992: 211)

Paglia heaps scorn upon the contemporary professor throughout her essays on academe. American universities are dominated by a genteel code where the bland lead the bland, and promotion requires self-censorship, respectability, restraint, and a lack of a sense of humour (unlike British schools, where a good-natured eccentricity is more acceptable) (ibid., 121). Academic assessment is based on a 'murky mire of words, gossip, connections, stroking, conspiracy, backstabbing', not hard work or excellence in teaching (ibid., 246). Universities have become places where students are coddled by administrators and teachers, where vigorous intellectual debate is the exception, not the rule. Minority opinions are not respected by academics: those who refuse to toe the line are simply passed over when it comes to hiring and promotion, while the academic old guard handpicks conservative conformists to replace itself.[13] Paglia's critique of academe echoes John Stuart Mill's nineteenth-century warning against the 'tyranny of the majority' in liberal democracies, which he feared would promote mediocrity and ignore true genius.

Ironically, given her suspicion of Marxism, Paglia makes a Marx-like argument that the academic job shortages of the 1970s and 1980s led these tunnelling beavers to market themselves more and more at conferences and other academic conclaves as slick prepackaged products, ignoring serious research and scholarship in exchange for 'smarmy whimsy', inert personalities, and narrow politically correct 'wisdom'.

Despite the fact that conferences are a huge waste of money and diversion of energy away from research and teaching, academics are still hired today in part because they have cruised, back-slapped, and glad-handed at conferences. Paglia says we should dump them entirely.

What is Paglia's solution? Return to the basics of history, politics, art, and literature. Make students learn facts and dates. Decommodify education, and merge all our overly specialized university departments into three faculties: the arts and humanities, the sciences, and the social sciences. Return humour and playfulness to teaching and dump conformist clones and scenarios of victimhood. Overall, recruit professors who have a mastery of the great artistic and intellectual traditions and who have a passion for learning and teaching, not specialists who deliver dull pedantic papers at conferences attended by other dull pedants (ibid., 234–8)—all of which sounds like rather a good idea.

Round three of the culture wars has to do with the political meaning of masculinity. Paglia defends male homosexuality as intellectually and artistically stimulating. Many of the great cultures of the past—the Athens of Socrates and Plato, the Renaissance of Michelangelo and Shakespeare, even the American scene in the 1960s and 1970s—had lively gay male underworlds. Homosexuality, decadence, and peaks of artistic creativity have been constant historical bedfellows. Paglia (1994: 72) defends bisexuality as a noble ideal, for she wants to break down the distinction of gay vs straight in favour of a 'fluid continuum of human sexuality'. Somewhat inconsistent with her general view of the power of nature over nurture, she argues that being gay is largely a choice, not something forced upon one. Yet being gay will never be 'normal', a fact that gay activists refuse to acknowledge. Nature exists, whether we like it or not, and in nature 'procreation is the single, relentless rule': the fact that penises fit into vaginas isn't an accident (ibid., 71). Homosexuality will never be entirely accepted by the straight majority, who will always have the making of babies in the back of their minds.

On the other side, lesbianism for Paglia is cozy and regressive, an attempt to return to a blissful state of union with one's mother (Paglia, 1992: 23). Although she supports youthful explorations of bisexuality for women, Paglia warns her female readers not to get stuck in the lesbian lifestyle and its separation from male culture. Gay men are spontaneous and funny, while lesbians are notoriously humourless. Feminists who assert women's moral superiority over men while ignoring the vast achievements of male civilization are living in a world of illusion. The modern world is largely a male accomplishment:

> Male lust . . . is the energizing factor in culture. Men are the reality principle. They created the world we live in and the luxuries we enjoy. When women cut themselves off from men, they sink backward into psychological and spiritual stagnancy. (Ibid., 24)

The problem today isn't too much male rule, but collapsing masculinity, which gay men remedy in part with a glamorous cult of the masculine (ibid., 37). Paglia wants both strong men and strong women, not male eunuchs who work under the twin tyrannies of office work and radical feminist rhetoric. Paglia heaps scorn on academic feminists who see their nerdy bookworm 'partners' as the ideal models of manhood (ibid., 4). They lack the wit and the swagger of both the gay male *artiste* and the straight construction worker, not to mention the intellectual strength of ballsy thinkers such as Nietzsche and Freud.

Rape, Sexual Harassment, Porn, and Prostitution

In *Vamps and Tramps*, and to a lesser degree in *Sex, Art, and American Culture*, Paglia takes aim at radical feminist dogmas with respect to rape, sexual harassment, prostitution, and pornography. For Paglia, sex is a natural urge inextricably related to power and violence. Controlling it is up to culture, to society. She charges academic feminists with taking the sunny view of Jean-Jacques

Rousseau (of 'noble savage' fame) that human beings in a state of nature would live violence-free and happy lives, and for believing that modern culture is to blame for problems related to sex and violence. *Au contraire*: by nature we're all savages, and we have society to thank for controlling our innate beastly urges. Her general position is libertarian: we shouldn't try to control sexual conduct with laws, for all intrusion of authority figures into our sexual lives is totalitarian (ibid., 24). This libertarianism leads her to defend the legalization of drugs and prostitution and the continued legality of abortion and pornography. The state has no place, to quote Pierre Trudeau, in the bedrooms of the nation. Anything goes, as long as it doesn't interfere with public health or cause direct harm to others.

Aggression and eroticism are deeply intertwined, so as each generation of boys hit puberty, they have to be refined and educated to restrain their violent and aggressive drives (ibid., 51). Yet feminists have claimed that rape is an act of violence rather than sex, naively seeing the two as separate things. Sex and power are always linked, and rape is male power fighting female power (Paglia, 1991: 23). Rape is caused by a *failure* of social conditioning, not by the power games of patriarchy. It comes from the brutish realm of pure animal appetite, being a sort of sexual gorging. It is also an act of desperation and envy by men who feel suffocated by the allure of women and by their dependence on them (Paglia, 1994: 32–3). Men are tormented by the hemming and hawing of women, by the humiliating rejections they face at women's hands. In all higher species, the female chooses, while the male makes a fool of himself by prancing about and flapping his wings to attract the female's attention (ibid., 35). Paglia's boldest claim in this debate is that although all people have an absolute right to their own bodies, consent to sex can be *non-verbal*, in terms of either words or actions. For example, going to a stranger's apartment after a night on the town could be seen as a signal that you want to sleep with him.[14] College-aged women have to take responsibility for their mannerisms and mode of

dress, even if they did grow up in the 'artificially pacified zone' of suburbia (ibid., 36).

Rape should be punished as an assault on the person of another, like any other form of assault. But all forms of consensual sex should be left alone, though for reasons of taste and fairness to others we can legitimately ask that shared public places be sex-free. However, on campuses in America the definition of rape was extended to cover all unpleasant and embarrassing sexual encounters, with feminists painting women as victims and men as oppressors. This 'shrill feminist rhetoric' of victims and oppressors comes 'straight out of nickelodeon strips of mustache-twirling villains and squealing maidens tied to train tracks' (ibid., 25). It feeds the emotional hunger felt by the sheltered, coddled, and flattered white middle-class girls found so often at elite American colleges.

One of Paglia's main fears concerning too-stringent sexual harassment guidelines is that they turn campuses into 'hysterical psychodramas of sexual transgression' (Paglia, 1992: 53) where the false accusations of 'grandstanding neurotics' go unpunished and minor beefs become major political issues. Paglia relates several examples. At the University of Nebraska, a graduate student had a picture of his wife in a bikini on his office desk. Female students said they found it offensive and successfully campaigned authorities to have it removed. At Penn State a copy of Goya's painting *The Naked Maja* hung for decades at the back of a classroom. A feminist professor found all that naked flesh obscene, so she demanded it be removed, and it was. Paglia finds this sort of 'Stalinism' reprehensible. Words shouldn't be censored by public institutions. Since pictures are 'pagan speech', they should be free from censorship, too. When hurt feelings trump intellectual freedom, the university has committed suicide (Paglia, 1994: 50–1).

Harassment in the form of stalking and attacking ex-lovers comes from the fact that many men divinize their women as goddesses and can't endure the idea that another man might enjoy her love. Paglia warns women that they have to realize that by making a commitment to a man they are merging unconsciously with that man's mother. If you reject a man, you have to treat him with an icy indifference to terminate this maternal fantasy (ibid., 45–7). A sex-free workplace is neither possible nor desirable, and the attempt to make it so is a slap in the face to proletarian values: a *Playboy* centerfold is for a construction worker what a Manet nude is for the educated bourgeois. Besides, the attempt to desexualize and pacify the workplace actually encourages the glass ceiling that prevents women from moving from the mail room to the boardroom since they are discouraged from developing the 'hard-nosed, thick-skinned tactics' needed to get there. All workplaces are hostile. If you want to be leader of the wolf pack, you need to bare your fangs from time to time (ibid., 51–3).

Paglia confesses that she is a pornographer. Pornography is about lust, not power, though there may be an element of aggression in the sex act. In porn we see a pagan arena of beauty, vitality, and brutality where we can explore our deepest forbidden selves. Porn has the positive role to play of stoking the fires of sex in a world where those fires have been dampened by bureaucracy, mechanization, and bourgeois politeness (ibid., 110–11). The academic feminist view of porn is a narrow one to say the least. Paglia's main critique of academic feminists on this issue is that they never actually look at porn—apart from a few inflammatory examples culled from the vast amount of product put out by the porn industry—and therefore don't know what they're talking about. They're like those Victorian ladies who dressed table legs in fabric to avoid naughty thoughts. Second, academic feminists simply ignore the huge gay male porn industry in trying to make their case that the point of porn is the degradation of women (ibid., 66). Third, the claim that porn causes rape and violence against women is absurd since these things existed for thousands of years before the first modern pornography was printed or filmed.

Paglia feels that the imagination cannot and should not be policed, even as found in the most lurid porn. The idea that the male gaze alone objectifies and renders passive everything it touches is a mistake: *both* sexes objectify things, whether in art or everyday life. There's nothing degrading about displaying *any* part of the human body (ibid., 62). The idea that we can legislate an equality of beauty and talent in either the arts or personal life is a pipe dream. Pornography strips the romantic veneer from sex and makes the female porn actress the 'high priestess of a pagan paradise garden . . . animated by the cruel pre-Christian idolatry of beauty and strength' (ibid., 66–7). It is the revolt of our inner pagans against the harsh repression of our Judeo-Christian superegos. It is art.

Lastly, Paglia defends prostitution as a return of the pagan goddess. Other than the strung-out junkies academic feminists tend to focus on, prostitutes are not victims. They are the ultimate liberated women since they have sex with whomever they wish, usually on their own terms. Needless to say, prostitution carries risks with it, as does any sexual adventurism. Yet academic feminists are stuck in their contradictory bourgeois world view of simultaneously expressing solidarity with 'sex workers' while seeing 'whores' as exploited victims of patriarchy. Paglia suggests that brothels be legalized and licensed and that whores not be harassed as long as they're not a public nuisance (ibid., 56–60).

Epilogue: The Power of Pop

For Paglia (1992: vii) the two great cultural forms of the twentieth century are film and rock music. Popular culture today is an 'eruption of the never-defeated paganism of the West'. It's the third revival of paganism in Western history, the others being the Renaissance of the fifteenth and sixteenth centuries and the Romantic movement in art and literature in the early nineteenth century. In rock music we see a return of the Romantic themes of energy, passion, rebellion, and demonism (ibid., 20). It's a short leap from William Blake and Samuel Taylor Coleridge to Jim Morrison and Mick Jagger. Further, some women in rock and pop aren't just passive sex objects, but positive role models for young women. Paglia enthusiastically defended the pop singer Madonna as a pagan princess of the late twentieth century. She is a true feminist who 'exposes the puritanism and suffocating ideology of American feminism' by showing girls how to be fully female and in control of their lives, how to be 'attractive, sensual, energetic, ambitious, aggressive, funny' at the same time (ibid., 4). Paglia argues that the true genius of modern American culture is found in rock music and Hollywood films. The French, defeated in World War II, turned to deconstruction as a way of explaining their world. Yet the message of post-structuralist French theory—that language is full of conflicting meanings and the self is a myth constructed by culture—doesn't suit the more confident American cultural landscape. Paglia prefers Hendrix to Foucault: the 'thunderous chords of hard rock smash the dreary little world of French theory' (ibid., 229). The self in America is the product not of military defeat and literary deconstruction, but of pop cultural energy.

The cinema is the supreme Apollonian machine, the movie projector 'an Apollonian sharpshooter', a 'blazing lightbeam' that shows clearly the link between aggression and art (Paglia, 1991: 31). Cinema is an eye-intense flaunting of sexuality, a pagan spectacle that restores the exhibitionist cult to the public realm (ibid., 33). It *shows off* our sexual personae. Scholarship's worship of words makes it difficult for the modern university to deal with mass media. There's far more truth about sexuality in a good film than in all of second-wave feminist discourse.

Paglia's overall message with regard to power of pop is that it represents the most vital force in American culture. Her view is a far cry from the Frankfurt School's suspicion of the culture industry, second-wave feminists' condemnation of the sexual objectification of women in film and music videos, and the post-structuralists' reduction of music, film, and TV to a series of language games. Paglia loves art and beauty. Anyone who tries to destroy a young person's blossoming love of the beautiful—whether it's a feminist like Andrea Dworkin or a postmodernist like Jacques Derrida—is perverted (Paglia, 1992: 261). Sex, art, and beauty are eternal bedfellows, and no amount of feminist theory will ever change this fact.

Study Questions

1. What were the main objectives of first-wave feminism, and how did it differ from the second wave? Which theorist in this chapter is closest to being a first-wave feminist? Explain.

2. What are the main beliefs of radical feminists such as Dworkin and MacKinnon? How do these beliefs differ from those of liberal feminists? What are some of the weaknesses of radical feminism?

3. What do postmodern feminists have to say about gender? What is the main problem with their position? Are all gender differences constructed by culture?

4. How have third-wave feminists attacked their predecessors? Do they go too far?

5. Which of the waves and varieties of feminism makes the most sense? Defend your view critically.

6. In what sense is Firestone a 'materialist'? Explain.

7. How does Firestone critique love and the culture of romance? Are her critiques outdated or are they still relevant today?

8. What does Firestone think of the nuclear family? What does she think should replace it? Is her position a reasonable one?

9. What are Rawls's principles of justice? What does Okin think of them?

10. Why does Okin think that the modern American family is *not* a school for justice?

11. What is Kohlberg's theory of moral development? Why did Gilligan criticize it? Do you think that her critique is valid?

12. According to Gilligan, what are the characteristics of the female and male ethical 'voices'? How does she support her claims with the druggist and abortion dilemmas?
13. Is Gilligan a sexual essentialist? Defend your view.
14. What are the basic claims of Smith's standpoint theory? How have Marxism and phenomenology influenced Smith's ideas?
15. What does Smith mean by the 'bifurcation of consciousness'? Do young women feel this bifurcation today as acutely as Smith did in the 1960s and 1970s?
16. Why does Harding criticize 'feminist empiricism'? Can a researcher who sticks to empirical facts also be a good feminist? Explain your view.
17. Outline the main criticisms of Smith's and Harding's feminist standpoint theories. Do men and women have different ways of knowing the world? Why or why not?
18. Why does Haraway want women to embrace the notion of the cyborg as an ironic myth? Would you like to be a cyborg? Explain.
19. In what sense is Haraway a socialist feminist? Or a postmodernist?
20. What does Paglia mean by the 'Apollonian' and the 'Dionysian'? How does she connect these two concepts to sexual difference? Does her distinction make sense?
21. What does Paglia mean by 'sexual personae'? How does she connect sex, art, and civilization?
22. What is Paglia's view of the social constructionist theory of sexual difference? How does she connect this to her critique of academic feminism?
23. Outline Paglia's criticisms of American academic life. Do her criticisms ring true for your university or college?
24. What is Paglia's position on sexual consent? How is this connected to her fears about the 'rape crisis'? Do you agree with her libertarian position on sexual matters?
25. What are the two great art forms of the late twentieth century for Paglia? Compare Paglia's view of pop culture with that of the Frankfurt School or of radical feminism.

SHORT BIBLIOGRAPHY

Beauvoir, Simone de. 1952 [1949]. *The Second Sex*, trans. H.M. Parshley. New York: Vintage.

Bordo, Susan. 1987. *The Flight to Objectivity: Essays on Cartesianism and Culture*. Albany: State University of New York Press.

Brownmiller, Susan. 1975. *Against Our Will: Men, Women and Rape*. New York: Simon & Schuster.

Butler, Judith P. 1990. *Gender Trouble: Feminism and the Subversion of Identity*. New York: Routledge.

Dworkin, Andrea. 1974. *Women Hating*. New York: Dutton.

Faludi, Susan. 1991. *Backlash: The Undeclared War against American Women*. New York: Crown.

Firestone, Shulamith. 1971 [1970]. *The Dialectic of Sex: The Case for Feminist Revolution*. New York: Bantam Books.

French, Marilyn. 1992. *The War Against Women*. New York: Simon & Schuster.

Friedan, Betty. 1963. *The Feminine Mystique*. New York: Norton.

Gilligan, Carol. 1993 [1982]. *In a Different Voice: Psychological Theory and Women's Development*. Cambridge, Mass.: Harvard University Press.

Greer, Germaine. 1970. *The Female Eunuch*. New York: McGraw-Hill.

Haraway, Donna. 1985. 'A Manifesto for Cyborgs: Science, Technology, and Socialist Feminism in the 1980s', *Socialist Review* 80: 65–107.

Harding, Sandra. 1986a. 'The Instability of Analytical Categories of Feminist Theory', *Signs* 11, 4: 645–64.

————. 1986b. *The Science Question in Feminism*. Ithaca, NY: Cornell University Press.

————. 1987. 'Introduction: Is There a Feminist Method?', in Harding, ed., *Feminism and Methodology: Social Science Issues*. Bloomington: Indiana University Press.

————. 1989. 'Women as Creators of Knowledge', *American Behavioral Scientist* 32, 6: 700–7.

———. 1992. 'After the Neutrality Ideal: Science, Politics, and Strong Objectivity', *Social Research* 59: 567–87.

———. 2000. 'After the Common Era', *Signs* 25, 4: 1041–4

———. 2004. 'A Socially Relevant Philosophy of Science? Resources from Standpoint Theory's Controversiality', *Hypatia* 19, 1: 25–47.

——— and Merrill P. Hintikka, eds. 1983. *Discovering Reality: Feminist Perspectives on Epistemology, Metaphysics, and Philosophy of Science.* Dordrecht, Holland: D. Reidel.

——— and Kathryn Norberg. 2005. 'New Feminist Approaches to Social Science Methodologies: An Introduction', *Signs* 30, 4: 2009–15.

MacKinnon, Catharine. 1987. *Feminism Unmodified: Discourses on Life and Law.* Cambridge, Mass.: Harvard University Press.

Millett, Kate. 1970. *Sexual Politics.* Garden City, NY: Doubleday.

Moi, Toril. 1985. *Sexual/Textual Politics: Feminist Literary Theory.* New York: Methuen.

Nicholson, Linda J., ed. 1990. *Feminism/Postmodernism.* London: Routledge.

Okin, Susan Moller. 1990. *Justice, Gender, and the Family.* New York: Basic Books.

Paglia, Camille. 1991 [1990]. *Sexual Personae: Art and Decadence from Nefertiti to Emily Dickinson.* New York: Vintage Books.

———. 1992. *Sex, Art and American Culture: Essays.* New York: Vintage.

———. 1994. *Vamps and Tramps: New Essays.* New York: Vintage Books.

Rawls, John. 1971. *A Theory of Justice.* Cambridge, Mass.: Harvard University Press.

Rich, Adrienne. 1980. 'Compulsory Heterosexuality and Lesbian Existence', *Signs* 5 (Summer): 631–60.

Smith, Dorothy E. 1987. *The Everyday World as Problematic: A Feminist Sociology.* Boston: Northeastern University Press.

———. 1990. 'Women's Experience as a Radical Critique of Sociology', in Smith, *The Conceptual Practices of Power: A Feminist Sociology of Knowledge.* Toronto: University of Toronto Press, 11–28. Reprinted from *Sociological Inquiry* 44 (1974).

———. 1992. 'Sociology from Women's Experience: A Reaffirmation', *Sociological Theory* 10, 1: 88–98.

Solanis, Valerie. 1970. *The SCUM Manifesto.* New York: Olympia Press.

Sommers, Christina Hoff. 1994. *Who Stole Feminism? How Women Have Betrayed Women.* New York: Simon & Schuster.

———. 2000. *The War against Boys: How Misguided Feminism Is Harming Our Young Men.* New York: Simon & Schuster.

Spivak, Gayatri Chakrovorty. 1987. *In Other Worlds: Essays in Cultural Politics.* New York: Methuen.

Thomson, Judith Jarvis. 1971. 'A Defense of Abortion', *Philosophy and Public Affairs*: 47–66.

Wolf, Naomi. 1991. *The Beauty Myth.* Toronto: Vintage Books.

———. 1993. *Fire with Fire: The New Female Power and How It Will Change the 21st Century.* Toronto: Random House.

———. 1997. *Promiscuities: The Secret Struggle for Womanhood.* Toronto: Random House.

Woolf, Virginia. 1977. *A Room of One's Own.* London: Grafton Books.

Young, Iris Marion. 1990. *Justice and the Politics of Difference.* Princeton, NJ: Princeton University Press.

CHAPTER 11 THE GLOBAL VILLAGE

WELCOME TO THE GLOBAL VILLAGE

Jessica McMillan, a Media Studies student at a large Canadian university, sashays into her morning class with a smile on her face and a backpack full of technological goodies on her shoulder. After sitting down, she lays out her gadgets like a tribal shaman might have laid out his charms and talismans in days of yore: her laptop in the centre, plugged into the outlet beneath the desk, instantly connected to the university's wireless network; then her MyPod mpeg music player on the left, her cellphone on the right (set to vibrate instead of ring to avoid the professor's wrath), and finally her Blueberry personal digital assistant behind her cellphone. As the professor boots the class computer and turns on the projector on which to display his lecture slides, Jessica turns off her MyPod and scans her cellphone for any messages received in the 10 minutes it took her to walk across campus. She has three new messages, two from students asking her about an assignment the professor announced last week but they didn't hear about since they had 'no time' to attend the lecture. She promises herself to return their calls right after class: if she herself has time, that is.

After the lecture starts, Jessica revs up her multi-tasking mental engine. As she types additional notes into the outline the professor posted on the class website last night, she plays a game of digital solitaire in the background, carries on four instant message conversations with her friends (two of whom are actually in the same room), and from time to time reads e-mails on her private account, jessicamac@coolmail.com, or checks for new postings on the digital bulletin board attached to her www.PersonaPage.com personal profile. All around her other students are doing the same, immersed in private digital worlds of their own creation. Jessica, like her classmates, looks as though she's trapped in a virtual bubble. Fragments of the professor's lecture penetrate this bubble; other bits bounce off into the vast nothingness of non-attention surrounding it. Yet these bubbles aren't self-enclosed monads unconnected to each other. Instead, they are linked by streams of computer code, fibre optic cables, and microwave transmissions to hundreds of other such monads scattered across the campus, the city, even in some cases the continent. Jessica is both disconnected and plugged in at the same time—disconnected from her immediate physical environment, but plugged in to a global network of communications. She is a global villager whose neighbours could be next door or thousands of miles away. She lives in a virtual space that more and more of us call 'home' today.

In this brief chapter we'll look at pictures of this global village painted by two Canadian theorists.[1] We start by going back to the 1960s for a road map to the village provided by a wily cartographer named Marshall McLuhan.

THE MEDIUM IS THE MESSAGE: MARSHALL McLUHAN

Marshall McLuhan was born in Edmonton, Alberta, in 1911, and went on to become the most widely known philosopher of communications and media in the last century. He later became the 'patron saint' of *Wired* magazine and the informal patron saint of modern communications theory. Although he started out as a scholar of literature— he earned a Ph.D. in English from Cambridge in 1943—he became interested in advertising and mass media in the 1950s after settling down to a teaching career at St Michael's College at the University of Toronto. In 1963 he took up residence in an old coach house there, forming the Centre for Culture and Technology, which he ran until his death in 1980. McLuhan's most famous book is *Understanding Media: The Extensions of Man* (1994 [1964]). McLuhan also published *The Mechanical Bride* (1951), *The Gutenberg Galaxy* (1962), *The Medium Is the Massage* (1967), and *War and Peace in the Global Village* (1968), the last two with the aid of graphic artist Quentin Fiore. McLuhan revelled in the combination of images and texts (the two works with Fiore are full of photos and drawings), the quoting of Shakespeare and modernist poets like T.S. Eliot, puns and jokes, and television interviews. He was and is Canada's greatest thinker, yet sadly is usually ignored outside of communications and media departments.

In his Introduction to *Understanding Media*, McLuhan sees the Western world as imploding. The mechanical age extended our bodies in space: 'Today, after more than a century of electric technology, we have extended our central nervous system itself in a global embrace, abolishing both time and space as far as our planet is concerned' (McLuhan, 1994 [1964]: 3). With our electronic age's extension of our central nervous system, we participate in depth in the actions of the whole world. 'It is no longer possible to adopt the aloof and dissociated role of the literate Westerner' (ibid., 4). Electronic technology urges us to get involved, to plug in. After 3,000 years of specialism, the world has become compressed: today it's no more than a village. We have a heightened awareness of responsibility thanks to electronic speed, which brings social and political functions together with our technological means. The modern aspiration for wholeness, empathy, and depth of awareness is a product of technology. So McLuhan's book is about the shape of how we

extend our beings in our technologies, trying to understand what those shapes look like. It's about the way that we mediate our relation with the world through our tools.

Yet McLuhan wasn't in favour of the new electronic age; he just wanted to understand it. As he said in a 1966 CBC interview on *This Hour Has Seven Days*:

> I am resolutely opposed to all innovation, all change, but I am determined to understand what's happening. Because I don't choose to sit and let the juggernaut roll over me. Many people seem to think that if you talk about something recent, you're in favour of it. The exact opposite is true in my case. Anything I talk about is almost certainly something I'm resolutely against. And it seems to me the best way to oppose it is to understand it. And then you know where to turn off the buttons. (Quoted in Benedetti and DeHart, 1996: 20)

Many saw McLuhan as heralding the end of the book culture in a TV age, but in reality he was urging us to recognize and understand the power of the new televisual medium. In fact, he tried to have his grandchildren deprived of TV. Yet in order to fight something, you must first understand it.

Lewis Lapham, who edited the 1994 reissue of *Understanding Media*, says that we can draw two basic premises from McLuhan's work: (1) we become what we behold,[2] and (2) we shape our tools, then our tools shape us (McLuhan, 1994: ix). He saw media as actually changing us and the world, not just providing us with information. Media aren't just passive tools. They actively reshape our bodies and our minds.

McLuhan didn't define media in the traditional way, as something that brings us information or entertainment—though they obviously do this, too. Media can be technological, but aren't necessarily so. Media are anything that extends our bodies, minds, or complete beings. At the same time they amputate a part of us. So clothing extends and protects our skin, but cuts us off in a tactile sense from our natural environment (think of the joy of wearing sandals on a warm summer's day after a winter of socks and boots). A car extends our legs in its ability to transport us great distances, yet encloses us in a steel box and amputates our leg muscles from the exercise they get in walking. And the Internet—I speculate here, since McLuhan missed the coming of the World Wide Web by about a decade—extends our minds in cyberspace, as seen quite literally in William Gibson's cyberpunk novels such as *Neuromancer* and *Mona Lisa Overdrive*, yet amputates our senses of touch, smell, and taste, not to mention forcing us into immobility in front of a computer screen.

McLuhan says that in a culture like ours that splits and divides things in order to control them, it's a shock to be reminded that the *medium is the message*. His famous mantra means that the content of a medium, e.g., the stories a TV news anchor reads on a given newscast, isn't as important as the psychological and physical effects of that medium, which in this case might be to numb us to dramatic world events by confining them to two-minute video clips and glib commentaries. McLuhan thought that a medium shapes and controls the scale and form of human social action. The 'message' of any given new medium or technology is the changes in scale, pace, or pattern that it introduces (ibid., 7–8). The personal and social consequences of any new medium result from the new scale of things it introduces into social life. Just as the railway created 'railway suburbs' clustered around train stations, the automobile has created modern suburbs serviced by shopping malls, usually combined with the decline of city cores. Both extended living patterns further away from urban centres.

Each medium has a unique set of sense ratios associated with it: in print our visual sense rules; in radio, the aural; in television, we combine via our tactile sense the visual and aural. The 'content' of any medium is always another medium: the content of the telegraph is print; of print, the written word; of writing, speech; while the basic content of speech is thoughts. McLuhan uses the example of electric lights to illustrate this point. Lights aren't a medium until they're used to spell out a brand name on an electric sign: their content is a form of print. As we open up each medium theoretically, we find another medium contained within it, like Russian dolls hidden inside each other.

McLuhan mocks those who separate technologies in general, and media specifically, from their effects. It's like saying that guns aren't inherently good or bad: it just depends on how they're used. He says that people who believe that media are 'neutral' in their effects are hypnotized by the amputation and extension of their own beings in a new technical form. Media are not neutral: they shape and change us. As we modify our technology, it modifies us in return. We become the 'sex organs of the machine world' (ibid., 46), endlessly spewing out our spiritual seed via our favourite forms of media. In this sense McLuhan is something of a *technological determinist*: our machines change our very natures as we use them. A recent example from the field of education can be seen in the fact that video games, music videos, cellphones, and Internet web pages and message services have caused serious attention deficit problems with students of all ages.

Media in general cause changes in the ratios between our sense perceptions. And when these change, our thinking and acting change, and thus we change. So we can see McLuhan as a prophet of things to come when looking at the Internet, which definitely seems to extend our minds in a 'global embrace', as Net gurus such as Kevin Kelley have proclaimed, whatever its downsides. Global villagers today are different types of creatures from the book-loving children of the Enlightenment.

Electricity made things instant. McLuhan makes clear the great importance of our new electric media, of radio, film, TV, and computers: they 'constitute a total and near instantaneous transformation of culture, values and attitudes' (quoted in Benedetti and DeHart, 1996: 22). For example, movies speed up mechanical relationships and move us from a linear world of sequences and connections to a world of more creative configurations.

McLuhan saw the first great media revolution in modern times as Gutenberg's invention of the printing press in the fifteenth century. It introduced the linear thinking of print-based cultures (think of reading line after line of text in a book, always left to right, at least in English). The French Revolution was initiated by literary types and lawyers, and aimed at universal rights for all men. It showed how the 'typographic' principles of uniformity and continuity had overlaid the non-linear, even squiggly complexities of ancient feudal and oral societies. Although he gets carried away with the idea that changes in media can explain social and political shifts, this notion that a print culture has its own unique way of looking at political life is certainly a new way of looking at politics.

Any medium has the power of imposing its own assumptions on those who aren't paying attention. The ultimate confrontation between sight and sound, between written and oral communication, is with us today. McLuhan thinks that we can moderate the fierceness of this conflict by understanding the media we use to extend our bodies and minds, including the conflicts they create within us.

McLuhan says that electric speed mingles prehistory with modern industry, the preliterate with the literate and the post-literate. As we experience endless patterns of information in modern media, we are in danger of experiencing a mental breakdown. Cultures get jumbled up by the new electronic speed of communications media. The electric technology is within the gates. Yet we shouldn't shoot the messenger who carries this news:

> I am in the position of Louis Pasteur telling doctors that their greatest enemy was quite invisible and quite unrecognized by them. Our conventional response to all media—namely, that it is how they are used that counts—is the numb stance of the technological idiot. For the 'content' of a medium is like the juicy piece of meat carried by the burglar to distract the watchdog of the mind. (Ibid., 18)

Further, McLuhan says that the effect of the medium is made strong and intense because it is given another medium as content. The content of a movie is a novel, a play, a short story, or in some cases an opera. Yet the effect of a movie is not just its content; it introduces a new set of sense ratios when it adapts a novel or play. Letters on a page become visual images on the big screen, enveloping us in the darkness of the movie theatre.

When the Europeans colonized Africa, they imposed a literate culture on the natives and thus detribalized them—they tried to turn them into good Europeans. But today, in our electronic world, we're like the Africans when they first experienced print culture—we are as numb in our new electric world as they were to our own literate and mechanical culture. The effects of a new technology can't be found in new opinions and concepts but in changes in our sense ratios, our patterns of perception. Only the serious artist can encounter a new technology with impunity, for only he or she is expertly aware of changes in sense perceptions caused by new media.

Since McLuhan defines media as extensions of the mind or body, he wants to know how these extensions affect our senses and perceptions. He asks, 'to what extent do we depend on one sense relative to another?', and 'what happens when this sense ratio changes?' The senses can be ranked according to how complex the perceptions are we get through them. Sight is the most complex, then hearing, touch, smell, and taste. According to McLuhan, this is why human languages are based on visual and aural symbols, not smells and tastes, which could hardly generate a very sophisticated series of interactions. McLuhan urged us not to separate the psychological and physical effects of changes in media: he seemed to believe that new media *literally* create changes in the powers of our senses and thus in our awareness of the world. For example, he seriously argues that print created individualism and nationalism. So in this case a new medium had profound political effects. Yet, too often, we ignore these effects: 'Subliminal and docile acceptance of media impact has made them prisons without walls for their human users' (ibid., 20). As the Buddha thought of life in general, we have to be awake to the influence of new media if we seek enlightenment.

In the second chapter of *Understanding Media*, McLuhan lays out his famous distinction between hot and cool forms of media. A *hot medium* extends a single sense in high definition, giving us a lot of information and little to fill in. Such a medium doesn't ask us to participate much or engage our other senses. A medium is 'high definition' if its message is well-defined, sharp, and detailed. Think of letters of the alphabet, numbers, photos, and maps. Hot media feed a single sense a lot of data.

In contrast, a low-definition medium gives us only a little information and more work to do. We have to fill in the blanks, to participate. It also tends to engage more than one physical sense. He calls these low-definition media *cool*. Such low-definition shapes, images, and sounds are less distinct. Our eyes or ears must 'scan' our perceptual field and make sense of what we're seeing with *closure*, by filling in gaps between the information bits we do have. Think of the difference between a photo and a comic book. The former—if competently done—is complete in itself, requiring no closure to understand what is being pictured. Yet the latter requires us to leap from panel to panel, closing up the 'gutter' between each 'snapshot' of an action or event to come to an understanding of what's happening overall. In addition, comics use 'shorthand' such as thought and speech bubbles and visual icons for emotions and other mental states—e.g., wavy lines coming from Spider-Man's head indicate that he's using his 'spidey sense' to warn him of danger. The reader must have some

basic understanding of comics to interpret these images (see McCloud, 1994).

A telephone and speech are cool media, because the ear receives only partial information, and you have to fill in the rest by participating. Yet print and radio are hot media. We use our eyes to read a book or newspaper without any need for further sensory participation. And there's simply no point in talking back to your radio: it won't answer (unless it's a two-way shortwave set or walkie-talkie). Our participation with a medium isn't for the most part in terms of intellectual involvement, but in terms of how it engages our senses. Table 11.1 provides a list of the some of the media classified by McLuhan arranged in hot and cool couples.

As Freud noted of the role of the superego in our psychosexual lives, intense experiences must be censored or 'cooled down' before they can be assimilated. Our psychic 'censor' protects our central system of values and our physical nervous system by cooling off intense new experiences. If we didn't do this, and we assimilated all shocks to our awareness, we'd become nervous wrecks. Think of how you instinctively plug your ears when surprised by a loud noise, filter out conversations in a noisy place so you can listen to a friend talk, or ignore reports of horrible deaths in distant countries on the TV news so you can get on with your dinner. For McLuhan each medium affects our psychic censor differently.

The printed word helped end the Middle Ages by encouraging specialization in the pursuit of knowledge and individual enterprise. The hotting-

Table 11.1. McLuhan's Hot and Cool Media

Hot Medium	Cool Medium	Sense Ratio Shift
Print	Speech	From visual reception to aural involvement
Radio	Telephone	From aural passivity to speaking
Film	Television	From aural/visual passivity to tactile closure
Photos	Cartoons and comics	Comics must be 'closed' up, interpreted
Lectures	Seminars	From listening to participating
Maps	[Directions?]	

Note: Obviously the Internet is missing from this chart since it rose to importance only in the 1990s. Heidi Hochenedel (2005) argues that the Net is tepid, sharing characteristics of both hot (basic text and photos) and cool (the use of e-mail, messages, and hypertext) media.

up of writing to repeatable print led to the religious wars of the sixteenth and seventeenth centuries as Protestants and Catholics could now read books explaining why they hated each other so much. Hot media create specialization and fragmentation, just as cool media create tribalism. Specialist exchanges of information in the age of print fragment tribal structures. Specialist media such as money and print speed up social exchanges and information flows. As Marx observed, under the influence of the callous cash nexus, all that's sacred melts into air. McLuhan says that a tribal and feudal hierarchy 'collapses quickly when it meets any hot medium of the mechanical, uniform, and repetitive kind' (McLuhan, 1994: 24). This isn't hard to believe— Western culture has definitely eroded the tribal, oral cultures it colonized in Africa, Asia, and the Americas through print and money, then later radio and TV. And as we'll see in the next chapter, the establishment of global financial markets is one of the main pillars of globalization, which is blamed by many critics for eroding local cultures.

Yet electricity speeds things up. McLuhan thinks it may restore a tribal pattern of intense involvement such as took place with the introduction of radio in Europe and later with television in America. He remarks that Hitler could only have come to power in a radio age: his speaking style and personality would have flopped on television. He raised the tribes of Germany for his quest for world domination thanks to the peculiar type of sensory involvement intrinsic to the hot medium of radio. It was their tribal drum. In short, McLuhan sees radio, film, and television as retribalizing us, as compelling us to get involved with others in our tribe in depth. Whether this is true is one of the main bones of contention between McLuhanites and their critics. For instance, are the chat-room junkies, fandom subcultures, and the many special interest groups spawned by the Net really separate electronic tribes or mere tributaries of a mightier common virtual river? This remains a hotly debated question among communications scholars.

McLuhan defines 'myth' as the instant vision of a complex process that really takes place over a long period of time. It's the perception of things in depth. In our own day the instant speed of electricity confers a mythic dimension on ordinary industrial and social action. Yet though we *live* mythically, we continue to think in fragments, on single planes (ibid., 25). We haven't caught up psychologically and socially with the technological realities of the global village. Today the new structure of life created by electric media encounters more and more frequently the old linear and fragmented patterns and procedures left over from the mechanical age (ibid., 26). We have seen this especially in education, where teachers try to convince students to read books and articles instead of watching TV or surfing the Net. McLuhan notes that traditional, non-industrial cultures adapt better to the electric age, since they're still in contact with their oral traditions, unlike the mechanical cultures of the West.

McLuhan partially places his tongue in his cheek when he argues that backward countries are cool, while modern industrial ones are hot; that the rustic hick is cool and impenetrable, while the 'city slicker' is hot. But as we move from the mechanical to the electronic age, we reverse the process, moving from a hot to a cool culture. McLuhan even thinks that hot and cool media could raise or lower the emotional climate of a country, e.g., if it's too high, then program a diet of TV to cool it down. Psychologically, this isn't all that crazy: it's like playing soothing music in a dentist's office to calm down nervous patients. Being playful, he also says that men aren't attracted to women with glasses because they fill in the feminine image too much— they're too high definition. But dark glasses are compelling since they're cool, creating an inscrutable, inaccessible image that compels the looker to want to participate (ibid., 31).

The ability of television to transmit images and information around the world quickly made McLuhan see the world as contracting into one big global village where everyone is involved with everyone else. Everything seems to happen at once, without clear order or sequence. The television medium brought about all sorts of changes in the US in the 1960s, McLuhan's heyday: it brought awareness of the civil rights movement to the whole country, not to mention the cruelties of the Vietnam War and the widespread domestic opposition to it. McLuhan noticed an ironic paradox about TV viewing: even though viewers were highly involved with the images shown on this medium, it minimized their response to them. It 'cooled down' their reactions to the events depicted. For example, John F. Kennedy's funeral involved viewers in depth, but didn't excite or agitate them. Television is a 'cool' medium in this respect—it cools down our responses to crises. Even live action reports from the wars in Vietnam and the Persian Gulf seem somehow less real when seen on TV, more like movies than real events. Many have even claimed that when they saw the television footage of the shocking events of 11 September 2001, the attacks looked like clips from a Hollywood thriller, not a real tragedy.

A television image is really just hundreds of dots of light projected onto a screen surrounded by empty space (at least in the case of cathode ray tubes). We have to connect the dots, close the mesh. McLuhan saw this as involving a sensuous participation in a tactile sense: it engages our sense of touch. McLuhan thinks that our tactile sense is affected by TV because the eye is so intensely engaged by the TV screen that it has the same effect as touching it (Gordon, 1997: 94). Television creates a new balance between our senses—just as it awakens our tactile sense, it also diminishes the visual sense that we relied on so much in a print culture. McLuhan warns that sensory closure can be a bad thing because it causes conformity to the pattern of experience presented by the medium (in our case, television). He thinks that the only way to defend oneself against the 'bacteria' of TV is to use the antidote of a related medium like print. We can't avoid all media, but we can choose the ones we want to extend ourselves with.

In the global village with its instant communications, people tend to become more conservative, more wrapped up in cool media like TV. The old, hot, mechanical age 'explodes', expanding across the globe through colonialism; the cool electric age implodes, conflicting with the older patterns. Our obsession with the older patterns of mechanical, one-way expansion from centres to margins is no longer relevant to our electronic world. Electricity decentralizes us, turning us into global villagers happy in our peripheries. The global village brings with it the renewed possibility of cottage industries (e.g., people with computers and modems can now work at home). There are no more centres: people can live and work at the margins, connected to each other electronically. This is especially true now, given the explosion of the World Wide Web. He even thinks that electronic technology will allow Quebec to separate, which was not possible in a railway economy (McLuhan, 1994: 36). Given the support for Quebec's separation from Canada in the referenda of 1980 and 1995, he wasn't far off the mark (though this support may bottom out in the years to come).

In the electric Age of Information, commodities assume more and more the character of information, especially because of ever-increasing advertising budgets. McLuhan chastises Marx for trying to impose a mechanical understanding on a society that was becoming electric, seeing Marxism as a product of a mechanical and print culture. There are 'break boundaries' between different stages of a socio-economic system, when one stage gives way to another. One example is how modern roads and transport have reversed the ancient pattern found in agricultural societies, making the country a place of leisure instead of work, with cities playing the opposite role (though obviously cities have lots of entertainment in them). One of the most common causes of these breaks is the cross-fertilization of media, e.g., radio added to silent films giving way to talkies. Today the printed word has become 'electrified', stored more and more in memory banks of computers. Books have become items with a handicraft character.

Sometimes changes in media cause people to become nostalgic about the past. McLuhan mentions how in the nineteenth century, the first great age of the machine, such British writers as Thomas Carlyle and John Ruskin idealized physical work as providing a bond of mystical social communion. This was despite the fact that the machines were taking over more and more of this work. Today, in the computer age, some academics hanker after the days when their students actually went to the library and read books instead of surfing the Internet to do research. Yet almost all of us are electronically connected, plugged in to global information and communication networks. The global village is here to stay, whether we like it or not.

HEATHER MENZIES ON THE GLOBAL VILLAGE TODAY

Road Kill on the Information Superhighway

Heather Menzies (1949–) is an independent scholar and political activist who has followed in the tradition of Harold Innis (1894–1952), Marshall McLuhan, and George Grant (1918–88), the trio of great Canadian theorists of technology and communications. Working on the fringes of academia as a part-time professor at Carleton University in Ottawa, she follows Innis and McLuhan in believing that media have a powerful effect in shaping our social and political lives. We'll look at two of her half-dozen books.[3] *Whose Brave New World? The Information Highway and the New Economy* (1996) focuses particularly on the computer and the communications networks it makes possible. Although this is not explicitly a treatise on McDonaldization, her critique of the plugged-in workplace parallels Ritzer's picture of the fastfoodization of our economy. She starts by recounting some of the details of the economic recession of the early and mid-1990s, and how this recession was connected to the tearing up of the old social contract between industrial workers and corporations that offered employment and a decent life based on mass consumption. Instead, the 1990s were a period of government deficit reduction, the downsizing of corporations, cutbacks, and layoffs. This was tied to the new wired economy, which creates mostly contract, short-term, and temporary workers, with telework—where people do information processing at home for poor pay—becoming the norm (Menzies, 1996: 76).[4]

Our high-tech economy is being increasingly dominated by McJobs, part-time or contract jobs that pay less and have fewer benefits than full-time ones. McJobs digitize the workplace either literally—when workers spend their days in front of computer screens—or by creating scripted routines: 'the system software controls and defines the work' (ibid., 36). The McJob is made possible and powered by machine intelligence. These McJobs cannot support a decent lifestyle for families, not even for singles a lot of the time. Families need two incomes, so they moonlight. Machine-based industrial economies are being replaced by global computerized postindustrial economies (ibid., 7). As we become more and more mired in our e-mail, cellphones, pagers, and voice mail, we become McLuhan's 'sex organs of the machine world' (ibid., 44). This McDonaldization, discussed in greater depth in Chapter 12, is by its very nature wired: it needs sophisticated machines to extend its domain throughout the globe.

The core of the new economy is the information highway, its centre lane the Internet. It has digitized our work lives. Sometimes we work directly on it; in addition, it supervises work, dispatches it to distant locations, and is a marketplace in itself (think of eBay and Amazon.com). This social transformation, according to Menzies, is on the level of the Industrial Revolution, which moved work from the home to factories. Now work is an extension of computerized management information systems—work is moving from the factory and field to the information highway. Our ability to connect to the economy is decentralized while that economy's control over us is simultaneously centralized (ibid., 77). In this process, people are being left behind.

Menzies echoes Marx, arguing that the computerized globalized economy is turning full-time jobs into part-time temporary McJobs, hollowing out the middle ranks of the white-collar workforce.

Computers now do our thinking and organizing for us. Society is slowly breaking up into two great camps: those who own and make the technology, on the one hand, and the working poor, the proletariat of the virtual age, on the other. People are becoming human post-it notes, extensions of computerized systems (ibid., 10). This is helped by the fact that unpaid consumers now do their own banking, pump their own gas, and prepare their own lunches at smorgasbords. The hope that techno-rogues would rule the new economy died when Internet entrepreneurs were bought up or pushed aside by Microsoft, Bell, and other big corporations in the 1990s, thus increasing the inequalities of the digital age. Society is splitting up into technological and economic over- and under-classes, into Eloi and Morlocks.[5] We are experiencing a cybernetic apartheid with a working class that is digitally alienated from its work, 'the "products" it produces, fellow workers, and human nature' (ibid., 128).

A *silicon curtain* has fallen in the Western world, between rich and poor, between those who control computers and those who merely work on them. The new tools of communication are becoming tools of production and control, tools of domination. This new economy exists in cyberspace. In this space, people become closed off, and Taylor-like systems of management can be used to train people to comply in a fully wired and programmed work environment. Behind this silicon curtain are the wizard-like virtual corporations that run the new economy. They have 'globally networked electronic infrastructures' that blur the borders between countries, individual industries, and even goods and services (ibid., 72–3). Goods become information as information becomes a valuable good in itself, with the ultimate good being disembodied digital code.

Menzies ties this into globalization, arguing that the neo-liberal/neo-conservative agenda aims to take apart the welfare state and the idea of the common good by reducing all social relations to bits of property, consumer service, and labour–management contracts. This destroys the idea that we are first and foremost citizens of dem-

ocratic societies (ibid., 41). Free trade, deregulation, government cutbacks, and the privatization of public services allow transnational corporations to operate globally, to 'boldly go throughout the cyberspace of the new economy, wherever a new market or investment opportunity beckons' (ibid., 78–9). The combination of computer technologies and neo-liberal policies has turned transnationals into freebooters attached to no home port, no native land: they are free to invest as they see fit.

Menzies believes that these wired work environments, with their electronic surveillance, raise vital questions about human rights and social justice. The Internet promises a 'rich ecology of reciprocal interactivity' where diverse communities could flower, but this is possible only if our vision of the Net stays democratic, inclusive, and participatory (ibid., 12). The danger is that this democratic vision of the Net will be corrupted by its conversion into an extension of a few corporate minds, thus turning freedom of expression into a limited series of corporate choices. Menzies fears that the information highway will close living human communities down, turning us into slaves of corporations speaking only in the language of economic efficiency. Democratic dialogue will be amputated. She sees a new machine at the heart the world: a computerized global financial market, a digitized hyperreal engine that drives the global division of labour, exploiting racial divisions and developing world poverty in its call for increased productivity. Marshall McLuhan predicted in the last article he ever published that in the 1980s man would live at the speed of light and be reduced to an item in a data bank, 'software only, easily forgotten' (ibid., 14). It took only one more decade before his prophecy was fulfilled.

Menzies argues that if we're going to fight the global technological restructuring of the economy, we have to oppose the ideology of the new technological class with an alternative vision of human communities. She talks about how the mass media select certain experts to put forward the 'official' view of the new digital economy, silencing others. It filters out lived experience and turns people from being subjects to objects in their own stories. Even left-wing experts like her learn to speak the new language of deficit-cutting, global competition, and productivity. They get sucked into talking about the globalized market economy as though this was the only reality. This is an example of Marx's view of how the ideology of the ruling class becomes the dominant ideology of the age—those who control the economy control the cultural ideas.

Moral and political debates become technologies of management. The 'newspeak' of the modern technocratic economy doesn't want people thinking for themselves—after all, freedom is slavery. Instead of being laid off or fired, one is 'downsized' or 're-engineered'. The techniques of advertising are used to turn us into the pawns of the new economy, the whole thing showed on the telescreens of public perception. We see experts on TV explain to us the need to tighten our belts in the new globalized marketplace while their masters are making record profits. The global village of today is a battleground of two ideologies: the dominant one of the corporate monoculture of the international financial system, and the fragmented diverse cultures of the Net anarchists and localists. Which one will win? At present the corporate monoculture definitely has the upper hand.

In the end Menzies offers two paradigms of the purpose of global communications: the *communitarian paradigm*, where we value face-to-face dialogue and personal participation, and the *commodity transmission paradigm*, whose aim is to sell products using fast, distance-spanning communication networks (ibid., 147). The latter is tied to the rise of the McJob, where we surrender control over our work environments to computerized systems. The core issue today is, as it always was, who controls the distribution of power in society (ibid., 151). Menzies wants the new social contract torn up, replacing it with one promising full employment and participation in the global political economy. She wants people to participate meaningfully in it as citizens, not just as consumers. Our choice is between real communities and a fast, efficient, predictable McWorld. Yet,

many of us don't have to time to think seriously about this choice, letting external systems make our decision for us.

No Time To Be Anywhere

In 2005 Heather Menzies published her provocative *No Time: Stress and the Crisis of Modern Life*, a book very much in line with the sped-up spirit of our times. In many ways it's an update of *Whose Brave New World?* Recall that English social theorist David Harvey sees a basic quality of the postmodern era as the compression of time and space due to modern means of travel and communication, work pressures, and technological advances. We can go from place to place in a fraction of the time it took our ancestors a century ago and can communicate around the world at the speed of light. Yet, according to Menzies, this speeding up of time and swallowing of space isn't all that it's chalked up to be. She notes how today more and more people complain about having 'no time' for the things they once upon a time enjoyed doing: having conversations, reading a book, going to a movie.

There are two principal culprits for this lack of time: modern technology—she mentions e-mail, cellphones, and the Internet—and modern work pressures created by employers and public institutions that expect more productivity out of workers in the same amount of time. As a result, life seems to have sped up, and more and more people are facing stress and burn out. The Internet is especially to blame for this because it annihilates distance and time: communication is instant, with no time lag between sending a message and the receiver receiving it (Menzies, 2005: 2). People are afraid to press their 'off' buttons: they leave their cellphones on in class and in cinemas, frenetically check their e-mail, compulsively finger their personal organizers.[6] This causes stress, headaches, insomnia, and a disconnection from the self.

Today the fast-paced, high-end lifestyle is cool. It's hip to live in the 24/7 environment—after all, no one brags about sitting in the backyard and reading poetry! Menzies argues, as a good

McLuhanite techno-skeptic, that the speeding up of life is inherent in modern technology, as is its tendency towards superficiality and human disconnection. Computer technology strips down ideas and feelings into symbolic codes that can be transmitted (ibid., 4). It creates a hypermedia environment where reality is divorced from engaged conversation and the complexities of real life. This process numbs the senses.

The Internet allows us to have many 'virtual selves' in different places. It's like the transporter on *Star Trek*: we 'beam' facsimile copies of ourselves to other places and people through the Net. When we do this, we make virtual demands on the receivers of our messages for almost instant replies. We can derive from Menzies's work two phenomenological categories: the being-there of *embodied presence*, the place where most of us are right now, and the being-somewhere-else of *virtual presence*, the type of being we experience in e-mailing, Net surfing, and cellphone chats. Embodied presence is physical, virtual presence mental. Virtual presence always involves being-somewhere-else—with the person at the other end of a cellphone conversation, or the facsimile presence of the writer of an e-mail. Embodied presence is real, while virtual presence is a pseudo-presence. This is the difference between what Menzies calls 'the living matrix' and hyper-reality (ibid., 5). We even think in terms of the virtual code when we're embodied, worrying about our unanswered e-mail or list of things to do on our Blackberries. Our everyday experience has become digitally encoded.

Menzies argues that dialogue roots us back in real space and time, in real bodies in the here and know. A healthy culture requires bridges between people as embodied presences, especially if those people are being educated to become technocrats: computer specialists, engineers, or bureaucrats. She wants students today to become full-bodied participants in the game of life. To do so, universities have to become slow zones, where talk trumps technology. She agrees with Manuel Castells that the world today is dominated by the 'space of flows' populated by transnational corpo-rations, logos, brand names, and digitized money (ibid., 27). Within this new space, things move quickly: we cut, paste, download, upload, mix and mash, whether it's money, music, texts, or web pages. We work with dematerialized pseudo-people who are turned into units of labour, consumption, or credit. Real places become empty portals for consumption (ibid., 43).

Menzies worries that modern life is leading to a profound disconnect from shared social reality (ibid., 8). In overworked environments and political life, people respond to the pseudo realities on the screen first. We lose touch with things that really matter. The point-and-click logic of computers infects business and government: think of those annoying help lines where you have to go through a series of menu choices—'Push 1 if you're slightly peeved; push 2 if you're very angry'—to get a simple question answered. She mentions how in 2001 an Ontario government agency let a baby starve to death as bureaucrats sent messages to each other about the case, and how President Bush's administration invented fictional weapons of mass destruction in Iraq to justify the 2003 Gulf War and the American media accepted his claim as fact. Yet our virtual social organization seems to make this inherently easier: think of how the Enron accountants cooked the books to create an imaginary profit. If everyone's lying and making stuff up, and people have short memories and can't understand complex issues anyway, why not get a piece of the action? The danger here is a lack of accountability, which is made a more serious problem because of the fictional worlds we live in made up of virtual friends, virtual interaction, and virtual profits. This is also accelerated by the fact that the media are our main source of reliable information. Governments are becoming more remote, ruled by technocrats interested more in statistics than the people they refer to.

Menzies mentions the May 2000 Walkerton, Ontario, tainted water tragedy as an example of the noisy silence that public life has become (ibid., 11). The residents didn't know how to respond to a local political problem, and seven died to pay for their silence. We feel a combination of hysteria and powerlessness when dealing with public issues. Stressed and scattered people feel a profound disconnect from social institutions. That's why many young people today are totally apathetic about politics—it's either a part of the old world of conversation and public debate, which bores them, or a media spectacle they have no power over and thus ignore.

Dialogue in the Virtual Schoolyard

Later in *No Time*, Menzies talks about how kids living in a virtual presence only are growing up without social skills. When they get to university they suffer from a cultural shock as they have to learn to express themselves in person. Her solution to the space-time compression and sense of alienation of modern life is dialogue, which returns us to embodied presence and active interaction with another living person. She takes the traditional humanist view that education is all about becoming engaged with one's students, an engagement that technology gets in the way of too often. This engagement comes in small groups like a university seminar, 'a small crucible of democratic practice' (ibid., 184). She hopes that universities can create engaged participants in a public culture, people willing to be present and accounted for in society. Yet from the 1990s on, Menzies, as well as many others, has noticed how students are feeling more disengaged due to the pressures of part-time work and the distractions of modern technology. As all university instructors today know, students seem motivated to attend class and do work only if it affects their grades. They've become shameless consequentialists—mark hogs.

Students today suffer from a memory deficit. This is caused by a number of factors:

- their reliance on computers as an external memory;
- their distraction by various technologies (laptops, cellphones, electronic organizers, portable digital music players);

- information overload;
- a sense of learning as assembling and downloading 'bits' of information without connecting everything together (ibid., 185).

Of course, this is a McLuhanesque point: our sense ratios are changed by the technologies that dominate our lives. Computers extend our memories externally, but also amputate them. Memory and dialogue go together. If you know nothing about history, politics, literature, philosophy, and art beyond bits and bites memorized for multiple-choice exams, you can't be an engaged citizen.

The great danger today, according to Menzies, is the wired university, itself linked to the cutbacks of the 1980s and 1990s, which promoted centralized businesslike decision-making as a survival strategy. Why hire 10 people to do registration when a computer can do it? Why hire full-time teachers if you can hire part-timers to prepare computer-based distance education packages that can be reused over and over? For the most part, academics go along with the computerization of the university: they enjoy being globally connected, doing research and publishing on line, posting course notes on websites, and preparing Power Point presentations. But the price they pay is more and more time spent on keeping up the virtual side of things instead of reading broadly and engaging in dialogue. As a result, even though universities have snazzy logos and glossy brochures, they are disintegrating as organic wholes.

Menzies bemoans the fact that increasing virtual presence leads to a decline in the embodied presence of professors with students. She interviewed an engineer who demanded that students come to talk to him, in part because doubt can only be taught in dialogue. A film studies professor tells her that students are in danger of losing the skills of interacting, as modern technology allows educators to turn people into things. For one thing, virtual communication misses all body language. Students are becoming mere processors of information. The film professor speaks of the lack of depth to students' readings due to an 'Internet' style of jumping around from text to text. Multi-tasking leads to intellectual schizophrenia.[7]

Menzies holds out some hope that people will be ethically responsible and stand up to excessive bureaucracy and out-of-control technology. She mentions the noted mid-twentieth-century political philosopher Hannah Arendt and her famous discussion of the banality of evil with respect to the Nazi war criminal Adolf Eichmann, who claimed at his trial that he was just an ordinary bureaucrat following orders—even though he helped to manage shipments of Jews to the death camps (ibid., 199). Arendt stressed how dialogue and ethical thinking go hand in hand. The danger of modern life is that we'll be like Eichmann and slip into mechanical ways of thinking and acting.

The most famous dialoguer in history was Socrates, who discussed matters philosophical with his students and fellow citizens in the marketplace of ancient Athens. He was a mentor for many, including Plato. Education is best when teachers can mentor students, as the philosopher of technology Ursula Franklin did for Menzies. Yet mentoring can't happen with only virtual presence. Menzies's students sometimes *do* conclude that they are in school to think critically. But the larger danger is that this part of education will disappear as it becomes more and more virtual, turning public discourse into an empty shell. Real people disappear, replaced with a virtual presence mediated by information systems that only care about speed and turnover. If this process is completed, the public space will become a desert of the real.

STUDY QUESTIONS

1. In what ways does Jessica McMillan plug into the global village? Is she typical of students in your own university or college? What are some of the negative effects of being constantly 'plugged in'?
2. What did McLuhan mean when he said 'the medium is the message'? What effect do media and technology have on human beings? Give a couple of examples of how contemporary media fit into McLuhan's general position.
3. What does McLuhan mean by 'hot' and 'cool' media? Give examples of each. Which category does the Internet fit into?
4. How, according to McLuhan, does television 'cool down' and 're-tribalize' our culture? Is the television of the cable and digital age as much a 'cool' medium as it was in McLuhan's heyday of the 1960s?
5. According to Menzies, how have computers and the Internet helped to promote the rise of McJobs and accentuated economic and social inequality in North America?
6. Why do people today think they have 'no time' for things they used to do? Is Menzies right that modern technology is largely to blame for this state of affairs?
7. What does Menzies mean by 'virtual' and 'embodied' presence? Is she right to criticize computers and cellphones for promoting virtual presence?
8. What are Menzies's criticisms of the 'wired university'? Is she right?

SHORT BIBLIOGRAPHY

Benedetti, Paul, and Nancy DeHart, eds. 1996. *Forward through the Rearview Mirror: Reflections on and by Marshall McLuhan*. Toronto: Prentice-Hall.
Gordon, Terrence W. 1997. *McLuhan for Beginners*, illus. Susan Willmarth. New York: Writers and Readers.
Hochenedel, Heidi. 2005. 'Love and War in the Global Village: A Techno-Pragmatic Perspective', in Douglas Mann and G. Elijah Dann, eds, *Philosophy: A New Introduction*. Belmont, Calif.: Wadsworth.
McCloud, Scott. 1994. *Understanding Comics: The Invisible Art*. New York: HarperCollins.

McLuhan, Marshall. 1994 [1964]. *Understanding Media: The Extensions of Man*, intro. Lawrence H. Lapham. Cambridge, Mass.: MIT Press.

———— and Quentin Fiore. 1967. *The Medium Is the Massage: An Inventory of Effects*. Toronto: Bantam Books.

Menzies, Heather. 1996. *Whose Brave New World? The Information Highway and the New Economy*. Toronto: Between the Lines.

————. 2005. *No Time: Stress and the Crisis of Modern Life*. Vancouver: Douglas & McIntyre.

CHAPTER 12 GLOBALIZATION, MCDONALDIZATION, AND CORPORATISM

A SHORT HISTORY OF THE GLOBAL POLITICAL ECONOMY

In this chapter we look at a trio of separate though interconnected social forces: globalization, McDonaldization, and corporatism. Though these forces have been the objects of intense theoretical speculation only since the late 1980s, they have come to dominate much of social, political, and cultural theory today. To understand them fully we must start with a quick history lesson.

From the Dawn of Industrialism to World War II

Before dealing with a panoply of issues in this chapter, it behooves us to examine in some detail the major events in global politics and economics over the last century or so and to see how these are linked. Let's start by turning the clock back to the days of Jane Austen and William Wordsworth and listen to the sound of the first locomotives as they puffed and clanked their way to the mills of Manchester and Birmingham. Industrial capitalism got started in England in the early nineteenth century and grew by leaps and bounds in the Western world up until the outbreak of World War I. Alongside this vast growth of capital was the parallel development of an impoverished working class—Marx's proletariat. Their lot was improved by the end of the nineteenth century by workplace safety laws, restrictions on the length of the workweek, and, most importantly, the demand for higher wages by increasingly powerful trade unions. The sun never set on the British Empire

and its networks of world trade in this period. Most British, as the world's greatest trading power, naturally favoured free access to markets around the globe. As Marx said, modern capitalism carried with it a tendency to constantly revolutionize the means of production and lend a 'cosmopolitan' character to economic activity wherever it dominated. In other words, capitalism has an inherent drive to spread its tentacles around the globe. It globalizes.

In this period the currencies of the great powers were on the gold standard: their value was backed by gold in their national vaults and fixed to a set exchange rate. If an economy imported too much, it had to export gold, which forced it to increase interest rates and reduce its supply of money. This put more workers on the breadline. If it suffered from inflation, it would be forced once again to reduce its money supply to keep it in line with its gold supply. As reasonable as this may sound, the classical gold standard created a cruel system where governments were in effect compelled to engineer unemployment to keep their money supply stable.

After World War I, some economies prospered while others declined. Germany, crippled by huge reparation payments to the Allied powers insisted on by France in the Treaty of Versailles, experienced rampant inflation—housewives took bushels of Deutschmarks to the market to buy a loaf of bread. This economic chaos led to a parallel political chaos where Nazis and Communists fought in the streets, and the demagogic street fighter Adolf Hitler learned how to manipulate the nation with anti-Semitic and anti-Bolshevik rhetoric.

In 1929 the American stock market crashed, leading to the Great Depression of the 1930s. Millions of workers in Western countries were jobless, without any welfare payments to fall back on. Shantytowns and dust bowls dominated the American imagination. The initial response by most countries to these hard times was to build tariff walls to keep out foreign imports, thus in theory allowing domestic manufacturers a greater opportunity to sell their products at home. The same countries played a 'beggar thy neighbour' game where they also devalued their own currencies to encourage consumers in other countries to buy their now cheaper products. But when everyone jumped on the bandwagon of tariff walls and devaluation, the net effect was to depress the Depression further.

To get out of this sticky economic wicket, English economist John Maynard Keynes (1883–1946) proposed that governments run deficits to spend money on public works and other projects to kick-start their ruined economies and reduce unemployment to a few percentage points. He also suggested that workers' incomes be raised to a reasonable level to stimulate consumer spending power and once again stimulate the economy. Keynes favoured relative freedom of trade but wanted controls on international capital so investors couldn't just pull their money out of a country overnight for political reasons. US President Franklin D. Roosevelt took Keynes at his word and started his 'New Deal' program after his election in 1932. FDR spent large sums on projects like the Tennessee Valley Authority to put Americans back to work. He also defended the idea that all men have a right to a decent job and standard of living, and created a social security system to help out the millions who still couldn't find work. Keynes and Roosevelt set the stage for the liberal welfare state of the post-war period.

World War II and Bretton Woods

More than Keynesian economic policies and Roosevelt's New Deal, World War II effectively ended the Depression. The main industrial nations—Britain, Germany, the US, Japan, France, and Canada—spent massive sums on guns, bombs, tanks, planes, and ships, thus creating full employment (to the point where large numbers of women went to work in factories to replace the men who had left to fight in the war). The forced Keynesianism of the 1939–45 period put questions of economic policy temporarily on hold.

As the war neared its end, the Allied leaders were determined to avoid the short-sighted protectionist policies of the 1930s and a new depression. This wasn't just for economic reasons—Roosevelt, Britain's Prime Minister Winston Churchill, and other Western leaders quite reasonably connected the rise of fascism in Germany and Italy and communism in Russia to unemployment and economic crises in those countries. They linked depression to war, prosperity to peace. In July 1944 the representatives of 44 Allied nations met in a hotel in Bretton Woods, New Hampshire, to negotiate the shape of the post-war economic order. The American position tended to dominate the negotiations, though Keynes had his fair say as one of the British delegates. The agreements they arrived at were later called the 'Bretton Woods system'. It regulated the political economy of the globe (outside of the Communist countries) from 1945 to 1971, with some of its elements still in force today.

First of all, the delegates agreed that the exchange rates between national currencies would be more or less fixed, pegged to the US dollar, which itself would be convertible to gold. This was due to the fact that when the war ended in 1945 the US was the dominant economic and political power in the world. The Americans had about 60 per cent of the world's gold in their vaults in Fort Knox and controlled over half the world's manufacturing output and investment capital, not to mention the only atomic weapons. Exchange rates could fluctuate by plus-or-minus 1 per cent, with local governments expected to prop up their own currencies by buying up US dollars if their value threatened to drop. The US dollar became, in effect, the world's currency, its value pegged to gold at the official rate of $35 dollars per ounce.

The Bretton Woods negotiations created the International Monetary Fund (IMF) along with the International Bank for Reconstruction and Development (IBRD), which later became the cornerstone of the World Bank. Both came into existence in 1945 and were funded by cash quotas from their members, at first dominated by American donations. The IMF had two jobs. First, it was to help countries to get over trade imbalances and currency problems with short-term loans. Second, if a country wished to revalue or devalue its currency outside the 1 per cent fluctuation mentioned above, it had to get IMF approval. Its purpose was to stabilize national currencies and thus avoid the temptation to return to the 'beggar thy neighbour' policies of the 1930s. The IBRD was charged with making loans to Western European nations trying to reconstruct their economies after the devastation of World War II. Later, as the World Bank, it was assigned the more general task of promoting economic development and protecting investment capital throughout the world. Both institutions were dominated by the US, with their headquarters in Washington, DC. The IMF and the World Bank became embroiled in controversy in the 1990s. They were seen by the left as fronts for transnational corporations' greedy attempt to milk the developing world for as much cash as they could grab. More on this later.

The Bretton Woods negotiations also led to the signing of the General Agreement on Tariffs and Trade (GATT) in 1947, a treaty that aimed to reduce tariffs and other barriers to world trade. GATT went through eight rounds of renegotiations between 1948 and 1993, culminating in the Uruguay Round in 1993 that created the World Trade Organization (WTO) to replace GATT. All signatories to GATT agreed to apply the 'most favoured nation' principle to each other: if your country extended the privilege of low tariffs to one member nation, you had to extend it to all the others, too. In other words, there would be no more playing favourites.

The general goal of the Bretton Woods accords was to 'liberalize' trade. Its signers wanted to minimize the barriers to international trade and investment, hoping this would bring global prosperity and peace by avoiding the protectionism of the 1930s. But they wanted to do this within a regulated world system where the value of national currencies was relatively stable. The American push for free trade made good sense in the 1940s and 1950s given their hegemonic position in the global economy. The system largely ignored the problems suffered by Third World economies, which came more and more to public notice in the 1950s and 1960s as the colonial empires of Britain, France, Holland, and Belgium were fragmented into a series of newly independent states.

The major problem with world capitalism in 1945 was that the economies of most of Europe and East Asia lay in ruins, notably those of Germany and Japan, which the Allies had bombed into submission. Communist parties in France, Italy, and Greece tried to exploit this economic hardship by winning power through the ballot box instead of revolution. The US had to do something to revive these economies, not only as markets for its burgeoning exports (thus preventing domestic depression), but also to save them from what the Americans saw as the evils of communism and the slippage of global power away from capitalist America to Stalin's Soviet Union. So, over the period 1947–58 the US spent billions in the Marshall Plan, giving generous grants to non-Communist European countries. Another problem was that there were too many US dollars floating around, given the Americans' trade surplus with the rest of the world. The Marshall Plan helped to cure this problem, flooding Europe with dollars and thereby reviving European economies. It worked. By the early 1960s Western Europe had fully recovered, and Germany and Japan were economic powerhouses. The US trade surplus became a deficit, as it remains today.

From 1965 to 1972 the Americans faced another problem: the billions of dollars they poured into that black hole called the Vietnam War and other military commitments abroad. This increased government deficits and weakened the dollar. The decline in the American economy vis-à-vis Western Europe and Japan made the status of the dollar as the world's unofficial currency and the fixed $35-per-ounce price of gold unrealistic. The official fixed exchange rates were used by speculators to make bundles of cash by selling weak currencies and buying stronger ones. The early seventies saw the beginning of a period of rampant inflation and oil shortages in America. To deal with this economic crisis, on 15 August 1971, US President Richard Nixon announced what later became known as the 'Nixon Shock': he ended the convertibility of the US dollar to gold to prevent its outflow to stronger economies, which quickly led to the end of fixed exchange rates. He also imposed price and wage controls to fight inflation.

By 1976 the values of all the major currencies in the world were floating, thus crumbling a major pillar of the Bretton Woods system. Speculative currency markets soon opened up, trading in dollars, pounds, francs, marks, and yen. This created instability in international financial circles, as exchange rates rose and fell with little connection to real national economic performance. Nixon's rash move also encouraged the globalization process in that national governments now had to take into account these unstable currency markets and the wishes of the conservative IMF in making economic policy. This ended the political autonomy of the welfare state. Currency speculators and transnational corporations are now in the driver's seat, at least in terms of taxation and spending policies.

Two Paradigms of the Global Economy

Ethan Kapstein argues that the Bretton Woods system involved a grand alliance between capital and labour, between a moderate globalization and the welfare state. The post-war global economy 'was a machine so perfect that for a generation it delivered both peace and prosperity to the members of the Western alliance' (Kapstein, 1998–9: 23). This 'social capitalism' brought growth and rising incomes to the masses in the West. But with the Nixon Shock, 'mobile capital finally broke the shackles that had held it down since the war, and now it was free to roam the planet' (ibid., 30).

Finance went from the periphery to the centre of the global economy, receiving a 'varnish of respectability' from neo-liberalism, which would shortly get the ear not only of corporate chieftains but of elected politicians as well.

In the late 1970s and 1980s conservative governments swept to power in the US (Ronald Reagan's Republicans), Britain (Margaret Thatcher's Conservatives), Canada (Brian Mulroney's Conservatives), and elsewhere in the Western world. These governments favoured free trade—Reagan and Mulroney were responsible for the Canada–US Free Trade Agreement, signed in 1989—along with deficit reduction and reduced taxes for the rich. Reagan's 'voodoo economics' proposed the rather odd idea that if rich people had a bit more money in their pockets they would rush out and invest it in job-creating enterprises, creating national wealth that would 'trickle down' to the poor. Needless to say, it didn't quite work out this way, though by the mid-1990s the American economy was booming again under Democratic President Bill Clinton.

This period saw the rise of the neo-liberal ideology as the dominant way of thinking about the global political economy in the US, Britain, and other Western countries. These 'new liberals' were arguing for a return to early nineteenth-century liberalism, with its support for unfettered free trade and laissez-faire capitalism.[1] They argued that governments must cut back on social spending to eliminate budget deficits, which brought with them inflation and economic inefficiency. Neo-liberals want to dismantle large pieces of the modern welfare state by privatizing as many government institutions as possible. Their naive (or Machiavellian) claim is that greater corporate profits will lead to greater wealth for everyone. Internationally, they believe that freed-up global financial markets will discipline governments that spend too much on social programs with a crack of the monetary whip: their currency will be deflated, forcing them to reduce now-expensive imports. Ian Robinson calls this aspect of the neo-liberal philosophy 'sado-monetarism' (Robinson, 1995: 380). It's based on the sadistic desire of big capital to inflict pain on governments that stray too far from the post-Cold War capitalist hegemony. Neo-liberal thinking dominated the IMF, World Bank, and WTO throughout the post-1991 period, causing a backlash from disadvantaged groups worldwide. It has developed what Gramsci would call an 'ideologically hegemonic' status due both to the economic troubles of the 1970s and 1980s and to the willingness of the mass media and politicians to act as its mouthpieces, thus deceiving the greater public into believing that its bitter medicine is the only one for sale in the global drugstore.

The opposing paradigm may be called 'social democratic'. Social democrats want to defend the welfare state and Keynesian economics in some form, and reject the notion that what is good for multinational business is good for the public as a whole. Globalized free trade has eroded the power of national governments to make decisions for their own peoples and has extended the grasp of unregulated capitalism throughout the world. The corporations, banks, and currency speculators that run the global political economy are responsible to no one other than their shareholders: they are profoundly undemocratic. Social democrats

have formed various labour, consumer, ecological, and other citizen groups to do battle with neo-liberalism, leading to showdowns such as the Battle in Seattle at the end of 1999. Table 12.1 summarizes the major differences between these two paradigms of the global political economy.[2]

From the Fall of the Berlin Wall to the Battle in Seattle and Beyond

In case you weren't paying attention, the period between 1991 and 2005 saw many changes in the global political economy, including a radical advance in economic globalization. When the Berlin Wall fell in November 1989 the days of the Soviet Communist empire were numbered. Two years later, on Christmas Day 1991, Soviet Premier Mikhail Gorbachev resigned, thus ending the USSR. The Cold War was over, and capitalism had won. The main economic powers of the capitalist world—the US, the European Community (led by Germany, France, and Britain), and Japan—set about writing new rules for the Bretton Woods system. Their main creation was the World Trade Organization in 1995, which replaced the GATT treaty. The WTO is a formal organization head-

Table 12.1 Paradigms of the Global Political Economy Today

	Neo-Liberal (Conservative) Paradigm	Social Democratic Paradigm
Main loyalty	Business corporations	The public good (civil society)
Economic ethic	Economic efficiency and corporate profits	High employment and economic equality
Favoured institutions	Transnational corporations, the IMF, the World Bank, the World Trade Organization	Democratically elected legislatures, citizen groups, labour unions, environmental organizations
Position on government intervention	'Night watchman' state: minimal government regulation of the economy; profits come first; skepticism about ecological concerns	Welfare state: moderate to high government regulation; Keynesian interventions when needed; social equality trumps corporate profits; ecological concerns real
Public services that should be run by the state	Police, armed forces, primary education, basic infrastructure (though not especially utilities)	Police, armed forces, water, gas, electricity, parks and nature preserves, health care, education, infrastructure (e.g., roads), some transportation (e.g., national airline), some communications (e.g., state-run television network), post office
Position on international trade and finance	Free trade; floating exchange rates; disciplining of weak economies by a 'free' market and stricter controls on deficit-spending governments by refusing World Bank/IMF assistance	Regulated trade: national tariffs and subsidies are acceptable; regulation or fixing of exchange rates; more consideration to be given to developing countries that fall behind on loan payments

quartered in Geneva, Switzerland, that binds 150 countries to about 30 economic and political agreements. It keeps in place the 'most favoured nation' provision of GATT, so that if a member country gives a trade concession to another WTO member it must extend the same concession to all other members (with some exceptions). The WTO aims to continue the GATT policy of lowering tariff and other barriers to trade, and to make those barriers remaining as predictable as possible. Unlike GATT, it has a formal organizational structure for resolving disputes. It can also enforce its decisions with trade sanctions should a member decide to not play ball. Since the WTO favours open markets, free trade, and a stable global capitalist system, it's very popular with transnational corporations and neo-liberal politicians.

At the same time that the WTO came into existence in January 1995, the General Agreement on Trade in Services (GATS) came into force. This aimed at extending free trade to services, including those often seen as partly under government control (such as railways, airlines, and broadcasters) or as provided entirely by the state (such as health and education). Under GATS a private corporation can in theory sue a government if it provides subsidies to local service providers or insists on providing the service itself. Maude Barlow of the Council of Canadians, a left-leaning citizen action group, argues that since the purpose of GATS is to liberalize trade in services, it paves the way for the privatization of health care, education, post offices, museums, and public transport (Barlow, 2001: 23). Under a liberalized trading regime governments won't be able to just say no to transnational corporations that want to set up McHospitals or McColleges to replace state-run institutions. Needless to say, Barlow is not McHappy about this possibility.

All three institutions—the IMF, the World Bank, and the WTO—have also been accused of being fronts for transnational corporations in that they usually defend neo-liberal policies such as free trade and free markets, allowing these corporations to exploit cheap Third World labour without unions to protect workers' rights and raise their wages above subsistence levels. The case against the new global economy is put admirably by Collingsworth, Goold, and Harvey:

> The clash between capitalism and communism is over, and the winners have set about making the world a safe and efficient place for business. The reality is plain enough. Nike is making its famously expensive athletic shoes in Indonesia, where its women workers labor long hours for a meager $38 a month. Wal-Mart, K-Mart and Sears, the great American retail icons, are having their shirts made in Bangladesh by culturally passive Islamic women toiling 60 hours a week and making less than $30 a month. . . . These examples illustrate how a global economy has allowed multinational companies to escape developed countries' hard-won labor standards. . . . Multinational companies have turned back the clock, transferring production to countries with labor conditions that resemble those in the early period of America's own industrialization. (Collingsworth et al., 1994: 8–9)

They argue that during the Depression, President Roosevelt and other New Dealers understood quite well that improved wages and working conditions turned workers from destitute survivors to willing consumers. Yet the export of blue-collar work to the Third World deprives the global economy of the very thing it needs the most: a broad base of consumer purchasing power (ibid., 11). Although the idea of moving industrial jobs away from the unionized West may be good for profits in the short run, in the longer term it will undermine the very prosperity that neo-liberals claim is a natural product of global free trade.[3]

Criticisms of the World Bank, the IMF, and the newly formed WTO accumulated rapidly in the 1990s. The World Bank has been accused of undermining national sovereignty of poorer nations by insisting that their governments pursue policies of free trade and deficit reduction before giving them money. Although it does loan money to developing countries to fight poverty, the money comes with strings attached. And corrupt dictators and petty potentates throughout Africa, Asia, and Latin America don't help things much: Africa is still an economic disaster zone almost a half-century after decolonization thanks in part to the greedy and incompetent rule of tinpot dictators like Robert Mugabe of Zimbabwe and Mobutu Sese Seko of Zaire. Although the Bank's defenders argue that no one is forced to borrow its money, the claim that its policies are ideologically motivated by neo-liberal premises was given yet more support in June 2005 when Paul Wolfowitz, the arch-conservative former George W. Bush adviser, was appointed as the Bank's president.

One of the major problems in the global political economy today is capital flight and the fear it causes in national governments. This has eroded the political will of governments to tax transnational corporations, which can simply pull up stakes and move to warmer fiscal climes if they don't want to pay their fair share of the national revenue. Agreements such as GATT, the North American Free Trade Agreement (NAFTA), and the WTO prevent governments from raising tariff barriers to protect local businesses or expropriating corporations that express a desire to leave their territory. The new rules of the global trading game give corporations the power to demand reductions in taxes from governments, thus devolving power from the democratic state to transnationals, whose main purpose is to make the rich richer (Robinson, 1995: 375). There is an asymmetry in bargaining power between fairly mobile corporations and immobile governments and labour unions, and this leads to a decrease in tax rates and wages even in developed countries like Canada and the US (ibid., 376). Transnational corporations are like pirate ships sailing the briny deep in search of booty, with neo-liberal economists sitting on the shoulders of their captains squawking their approval. Under Bretton Woods these pirates were more tied to their home bases (by higher tariff barriers and fixed exchange rates), their potential victims defended in part by domestic patrol ships (i.e., the welfare state and government control of key public services). Today they prowl the globe in search of gold largely unopposed, their sails billowing with the balmy breezes of neo-liberal ideological rhetoric.

The WTO has been accused by social democrats of giving itself legislative powers without being democratically elected. Tony Clarke argues that in the age of global capitalism, the 'corporate security state' has replaced the welfare state, the rights of corporations replacing the rights of citizens (Clarke, 2000: 12). He sees the WTO as the body that promotes those corporate rights internationally. Its constituency is not the public as a whole, but transnational corporations. It has no real interest in defending democratic rights and freedoms. Maude Barlow is more succinct: the WTO is a 'global policeman for the trading agenda of rich corporations', and has become 'the most powerful, secretive, and anti-democratic body on Earth', with the danger of becoming a de facto global government that no one actually voted for (Barlow, 2001: 40). Second, the WTO has been slammed for preventing countries from banning a product for precautionary reasons: under WTO rules, the government must prove that the product is unsafe first or it can be sanctioned for creating an unfair barrier to trade. The European ban on genetically modified foods is a reasonable precaution that could be challenged by the WTO. The World Bank and WTO have also been criticized for promoting ecological damage by pushing the governments of poor nations to maintain lax environmental safeguards in order to promote foreign investment.

Lastly, perhaps the liberalized global trade promoted by the WTO and the IMF simply fails to bring prosperity to the masses. It's more likely to line the pockets of the wealthy with further corporate profits. Social democrats argue that free trade only increases the gap between rich and poor: it drives a wedge between classes, increasing economic inequality.

Of great interest to Canadians is the coming into effect of NAFTA in January 1994. This pact between the US, Canada, and Mexico created a continental trading bloc within which many (though not all) restrictions on trade and investment were removed. Corporate intellectual property such as trademarks and copyrights was also protected by the agreement. NAFTA, like the WTO and World Bank, has been the object of much criticism. American and Canadian unions fear losing their jobs to cheaper Mexican labour. Some Canadians worry that sleeping too close to the American economic elephant is dangerous for the Canadian mouse, that Canada has become a branch-plant colony of the US and lost its freedom of economic action. Further, NAFTA hasn't helped Mexican workers: their wages have decreased in many sectors, and it spawned the Zapatista rebellion in the south of the country. In addition, the agreement could be an ecological nightmare since it allows a corporation to sue a federal government that passes environmental regulations if it sees these as restricting its trade (there have already been a few such suits).

Without the power to protect their economies with reasonable tariff barriers, and having the value of their currencies under the control of money changers in the virtual temple that is the global currency market, provincial, state, and national governments today are running scared. They worry that increased spending on health, education, welfare, or state-run businesses will increase taxes or deficits, thus offending transnational corporations that will leave the country and set up shop somewhere else. The post-Cold War global economy is one where capitalism rules supreme, where big money talks so loud that it drowns out most talk of economic fairness and equality.

These criticisms led activists to mobilize a wide variety of citizen groups to protest against neo-liberal policies and institutions. The moment of truth came in 1999 when the WTO met in Seattle, Washington, between 29 November and 3 December. About 50,000 protestors descended on the city to disrupt the meetings. The 'Battle in Seattle' pitted such groups as the Sierra Club, the AFL-CIO, the Direct Action Network, anarchists, defenders of animal rights, and women's organizations against local police and security services.

The dissident groups used mass marches, rallies, teach-ins, and civil disobedience to make their case against corporate greed. Many of those who were involved or who considered its aftermath saw it as a history-making event in that it broke the ideological consensus between neo-liberal political and economic elites and 'civil society', the public at large (Clarke, 2000: 8). Subsequent showdowns with the meetings of the World Bank and IMF in Washington, DC, in April 2000, with the Free Trade of the Americas summit in Quebec City in April 2001, and in several other cities showed that the slugfest between neo-liberalism and social democracy promised to go quite a few rounds. This game is still very much in play. Globalized capitalism shows no danger of disappearing any time soon. Nor does democracy, however diluted it has become by the influence of power elites. It's the match of the twenty-first century. Stay tuned.

McDONALDIZATION

You enter the swinging doors of the Burger Queen at 12:15 with less than an hour to eat lunch. Up to the counter you go where a chirpy teenager greets you with a 'How are you today, sir?' You ignore this standardized greeting, but smile at her royal purple uniform with a crown-shaped plastic badge on her lapel that reads 'Hi, My Name is Britney!' You order the Burger Royale with cheese, the king-sized fries, and an imperial gallon of cola. You strum your fingers on the counter absent-mindedly for two minutes as Britney smiles the same smile she's already smiled a hundred times today. Then your food magically arrives, sitting on a bright purple tray with a paper liner picturing the members of the Burger Queen family—the Queen herself, King Louis de French Fries, Prince Taco of Salsa, and Princess Chocolate Sundae, all of them equally yummy looking. You leave the lineup, Britney's attentions now turned to the customer behind you, but not before she says goodbye with a 'Have a nice day!' You sit down in a hard plastic seat at a clean white table. The restaurant is jammed for lunch. The décor is lively, loud, and garish. In the corner is a plastic statue of the Queen. Her body is a giant burger with glistening yellow eyes. Atop the burger body sits a golden crown; below is a long flowing plastic purple robe. Bemused children run up to the Queen and press a glowing red button that causes her to say in an upper-class English accent: 'Greetings children, I hope you are enjoying your time in my *rrroyal court!*' They giggle and return to their families. You gulp down the fatty calories in front of you, toss the empty wrappers into the trash, are back on the road by 12:45. You've just been McDonaldized.

George Ritzer on McDonaldization

One of the key theorists of both globalization and McDonaldization is George Ritzer (1940–), a professor at the University of Maryland who is also known for writing widely used textbooks in social theory. Ritzer's McDonaldization thesis, first sketched out in an article in 1983 but not given a full treatment until the first edition of *The McDonaldization of Society* in 1993, is simple enough: the principles of the fast-food restaurant are being applied to more and more sectors of modern society (Ritzer, 2000: 1). This includes not only business corporations such as McDonald's, Nike, and Starbucks, but education, health care, travel, politics, and religion, to name only the principal culprits. Ritzer notes that there were 320,000 franchised small businesses in the US in 2000, which, collectively, had $1 trillion in sales (ibid., 2). This includes everything from Pizza Hut and Taco Bell to The Gap, Home Depot, and a lot more in between. These are all McDonaldized institutions.

Ritzer argues that McDonaldizing institutions are part of modernity's general drive to rationalization. They share four dimensions. They aim to increase *efficiency, calculability, predictability*, and *control* in the production and consumption of goods and services. A few words on each. *Efficiency* is choosing the best, quickest, or least difficult means to a given end. If you can make a burger in five minutes with four simple physical movements, that's better than taking 10 minutes

and using a flurry of more complex movements. If you can eat lunch in 10 minutes instead of waiting a half-hour for a chef-prepared meal, you've saved 20 minutes to use in some other McDonaldized activity. It's more efficient for corporations to offload work onto consumers, for example, letting them do their banking via an ATM and networked computer system rather than lining up in front of a teller. Ritzer mentions the ultimate example of a McDonaldized experience: the Orgasmatron from Woody Allen's film *Sleeper* (1973), which provides citizens of the future with a worry-free sexual jolt without any need to touch each other.

Calculability is the emphasis on the quantitative aspects of the product being sold. The cheaper a product is, the better. The quicker you can deliver the product, the better: a pizza at your door in 20 minutes is far better than one that takes an hour. The bigger a portion is, the better: hence McDonald's 'super-sized' menu items. Calculability implies that costs should be kept down and that the customer be given as much product as can be pumped out for a given amount of money. Naturally, this reduces the role of quality in production. A McDonaldized society is one where lots of stuff is available, though much of it is of mediocre quality—though this is perhaps more true of foodstuffs and quickly replaceable consumer goods than expensive items like computers and cars.

Predictability involves the customer knowing what to expect from a given producer of goods or services. A given type of setting for consumption in Anytown, USA, looks pretty well the same as the same type of setting in Nowhere, Canada, or Rienville, France. Every Big Mac is more or less the same. A coffee at Starbucks will always have that bite to it. Subway sandwiches will always be the same size and shape. A given model of Compaq computer bought in Vancouver will be identical to one bought in Halifax. This also applies to interactions between customers and workers: McDonaldized businesses try to make their employees follow scripts that create the illusion that all customers are special. The whole idea of predictability has even spilled over into popular entertainment. The same character types, plot structures, and even jokes get repeated time and time again from one TV show to another. Hollywood churns out sequels of hit movies with the same characters, actors, and types of plots—think of the six *Star Wars* movies, the six *Rocky* movies, the three *Matrix* films, and the amazing ten *Friday the 13th* films. Sequels tend to be sure money-makers for the studios, while they're easier to process mentally for lazy consumers who want to switch their brains off for two hours and commune with their old friends Luke, Rocky, Neo, and Jason.[4]

Finally, *control* is important as a way of keeping a McDonaldized system working smoothly. Fast-food restaurants, stores, and offices don't run themselves: rigid rules and regulations along with the latest in labour-saving machines must be in place to keep things working at peak levels of efficiency and cost-effectiveness with predictable outcomes. Workers in McDonaldized businesses are expected to know how to do only a few things: they are programmed and controlled by technological systems (ibid., 15). The customer is also controlled: he or she has only a limited menu of options (think of those annoying computerized telephone help lines most major corporations now have), has to line up in a given place to receive the product, and is expected to stay for only 20 minutes or so, allowing new customers to take his or her place.

Ritzer admits that McDonaldization has a number of very concrete advantages:

- It can provide a wide variety of goods to lots of people.
- You don't have to worry about where you are in order to consume most McDonaldized products: for example, with Internet markets like www.amazon.com, all you need is a computer and modem.
- It provides products quickly (at least in theory).
- Its products are more uniform and affordable than in previous eras.
- It fits in very well with the fast-paced, 'no time' lifestyles of today.

- It offers a predictable, stable environment for consumption, sometimes providing safer products because of safety controls in the production process.
- It doesn't discriminate against racial minorities, women, or the working class: everyone can buy a Big Mac or go to the latest *Star Wars* film.
- It quickly diffuses products and technological innovations throughout the world (ibid., 16).

Yet having said this, Ritzer emphasizes the fact that McDonaldization is really a Siamese twin: only one-half is rational, while the other is deeply irrational. First and foremost, fast-food restaurants, chain stores, and mass-produced consumer goods create huge quantities of waste: discarded food, paper wrappers, Styrofoam cups, plastic containers, and obsolete products themselves, not to mention the waste connected to the actual agricultural systems used to produce the meat, vegetables, and other foodstuffs that feed the fast-food nation. This leads to pollution and degradation of the natural environment. A further degradation comes to the workplace itself, which becomes a dehumanized and over-patrolled environment for the McDonaldized worker. As work is increasingly standardized, made more routine, and sped up, workers become alienated, bored, or burned out. Also, more and more today consumers are duped into doing the work of McDonaldized corporations. We see this at ATM machines (you do your own banking), salad bars (you become your own salad chef), gas stations (you pump your own gas), and most Internet services (you research and order your own books, CDs, and DVDs on websites).

Ritzer admits that given the pace of life and rising numbers of human beings on the planet, we can't return en masse to the days of home-cooked meals and artisan-produced goods (ibid., 18). Yet we *can* use the technological advances that McDonaldized systems use in thoughtful and creative ways. And there are a few things that *are not* McDonaldized, such as locally owned restaurants and variety stores, bed-and-breakfast inns, and traditional pubs. Still, even if McDonald's itself were forced to close many of its outlets, as it has in some countries, the McDonaldization process is too deeply entrenched in retail, fast food, and other sectors of the economy to be stopped any time soon.

The spectacular growth of franchises in the last quarter of the twentieth century is proof positive of the power of the McDonaldization process. Go to any suburban mall and look around: you're likely to see the same stores and fast-food restaurants time and time again. In Canada you can have coffee at a Tim Horton's, lunch at a Wendy's or Burger King or Taco Bell, buy some electronic gadgets at the Source (formerly Radio Shack), your aspirin at Shopper's Drug Mart, household knick-knacks at Wal-Mart, clothes at Zeller's or Sears, a new computer at Future Shop. You can repeat a more or less identical version of this shopping spree in pretty well every city in the country, getting almost carbon copies of the same coffee, tacos, clothes, and computers as you can find in your own hometown.

McDonald's itself is a global icon of the success of American capitalism. Thousands lined up in Moscow and Beijing after the Cold War thawed and the golden arches finally appeared in these former capitals of the Communist empire (the Beijing location served 40,000 customers on its opening day in 1992). Yet McDonald's outlets in Europe and the Middle East have also been the targets of anti-American anger during the Gulf wars and at the hands of anti-globalization protestors. In America itself Ritzer notes that the wave of franchise-building has probably reached a saturation point. It's possible that McDonald's itself will at some point in the near future no longer be the main player in the fast-food game. But the McDonaldization process will continue apace even if its creator goes under since it's part and parcel of a larger, almost unstoppable modern trend: what Ritzer calls in a later book 'the globalization of nothing'.

Part of the efficiency and predictability of fast food comes from the use of standardized raw materials and packaging. Everything is established in advance: the size, shape, and quality of the meat, the buns, the frozen fries, even the pick-les. Everything is pre-ordered and pre-measured, its method of preparation rigidly prescribed by company rules. Fast-food outlets have swamped many previously sacrosanct public spaces in the last few decades: railway stations, airports, highways, hotels, and even university student centres. The latter look more and more like shopping mall food courts, with famous franchise names glistening on a dozen or more signs on any given campus in the country today. At my own university there are Tim Horton's, Pizza Pizza, Starbucks, Mr. Sub, and Pita Pit outlets, among others, and no one bats an eyelash. They serve students who grew up on fast food both as a form of nutrition and as a set of cultural icons.

So what drives McDonaldization? Here's Ritzer's short list:

- McDonaldized systems lower production costs and thus increase profits.
- People, especially Americans, like McDonaldization in and of itself. They like rationality and efficiency at whatever cost it comes.
- McDonaldization suits a changing society with more single-parent families where the parent has no time to shop or cook, where people are constantly on the move in their cars, and most importantly, where technology drives economic changes. Ritzer mentions in the latter regard computers, ATMs, supermarket scanners, credit cards, factory farms, CDs, and the microwave oven, among other things, as furthering the McDonaldization process.

In summary, for many people McDonaldization is profitable, desirable, and at the cutting edge of technological advances. It's an easy sell.

The Victories, Defeats, and Future of McDonaldization

Although Ray Kroc is famous for spreading the McDonald's brand throughout the US and later around the world in the 1950s and later, the roots of McDonaldization can be traced back to Frederick Taylor's principles of scientific management and Henry Ford's automobile assembly in the early twentieth century. Taylor tried to rationalize work by training 'efficiency experts' to conduct time-and-motion studies on workers. These experts timed each step in a work process with the goal of eliminating unnecessary movements and thus making work as efficient as possible. Taylor wanted to standardize tools and work processes, to rationalize work, even though his technology of control dehumanized it (ibid., 32). Taylor's principles of scientific management were put to work on Henry Ford's assembly lines. Ford's workers were trained to do simple tasks over and over again without any wasted movements or steps; machines moved the cars from one place to another; parts were shipped as short a distance as possible. This 'Fordist' method of production reduced the time and costs of production, giving Ford Motor Company a healthy profit. The assembly-line method of production was adapted by Mac and Dick McDonald in the original McDonald's restaurant in Pasadena, California, in 1937. It spread to other American franchises such as A&W, Dairy Queen, Burger King, and Kentucky Fried Chicken from the 1930s to the 1950s.

For North Americans, shopping malls are cathedrals of consumption, temples of capitalism. They provide homes for McDonaldized franchises. They are efficient: everything you need is under one roof. They are calculable: you can wander from store to store checking for the best deal, while the store owners are guaranteed an instant shopping crowd. They are predictable: the same franchises are found in most major malls in North America. And they offer both shopper and seller an enclosed, safe, controlled environment, even if you have to drive to get there. Malls have replaced downtowns as venues for consumerism, creating spaces where products and consumers can be processed with maximum efficiency.

McDonaldized travel can be found in package tours of distant lands where the traveller is protected from significant interaction with the locals. Walt Disney World provides simulacra of foreign locales to tourists who want predictability and calculability for their travel dollar.[5] Even campgrounds like KOA offer predictable, controlled experiences for city folk looking to get away from it all. These are the country equivalents of shopping malls, with the product being a sanitized version of nature.

Newspapers, radio, TV, and other forms of home entertainment have also become McDonaldized. *USA Today* is full of short stories with lots of photos and colourful graphics, being as much entertainment as news. Commercial radio stations are committed to playlists of music aimed at specific demographics: classic rock for baby boomers, hip-hop and pop for the 15–25-year-olds. TV sitcoms and dramas notoriously replay the same handful of themes, character types, and plot structures over and over again: think of *Friends*, *Will and Grace*, or *Everybody Loves Raymond*. People no longer need to go to cinemas to watch a film: they can rent a DVD at the local Blockbuster's—which guarantees a plentiful supply of new releases—or watch it on pay-per-view from their local cable company. Phone sex lines provide disembodied, fast, efficient encounters.

Even health care and education aren't immune. In universities and colleges, computers have allowed the widespread use of multiple-choice exams that can be machine-graded or marked by underpaid graduate students instead of time-consuming handwritten essays. Publishers produce customized textbooks that can be streamlined to fit a given course. Students expect to have lecture notes posted on-line and demand quick service from their professors in response to e-mailed questions. Logging on a website replaces actually going to class. Worst of all, some of the less scrupulous students purchase pirated papers on-line, with plagiarism becoming no more difficult than picking up a pizza at Domino's. Meanwhile, there are more and more cases of assembly-line procedures in clinics and hospitals such as in the increasingly popular walk-in clinics found in many Canadian cities.

At its core, McDonaldization is about the creation of illusions. As Jean Baudrillard said about modern culture as a whole, McDonaldized systems are deserts of the real. They populate their worlds with pseudo-events: the false friendliness of the Wal-Mart clerk, the manufactured fun of the McDonald's outlet, the phony camaraderie of the telemarketer. Ritzer explicitly mentions the phoniness of employees who say to customers 'have a nice day' as they leave: what they really mean is 'get lost' (ibid., 141). Then there's those annoying waiters who announce their presence with a 'Hi, my name is Billy, I'll be your server today' or variations thereon: their fraternization is nothing more than a pre-programmed script, as phony as a three-dollar bill, the mere illusion of intimacy.

This leads to a disenchantment of the world and the replacement of magic and surprise with efficiency and routine. The fantastic and the dreamy fade away. Even when mega-corporations like Disney try to artificially manufacture enchantment, it winds up becoming all too predictable: Mickey and Goofy stand-ins follow routines and scripts. In fact, Ritzer believes that the mass production of magic, fantasy, and dreams is guaranteed to 'undermine their enchanted qualities' (ibid., 144). In addition, McDonaldized systems threaten our health. The typical fast-food meal is loaded with unhealthy doses of salt, sugar, and fat. These are yet more irrational consequences of McDonaldization's attempt to rationalize the world.

So where does McDonaldization fit in terms of the three 'posts': post-industrialism, post-Fordism, and postmodernism? Daniel Bell's prediction of the coming of a post-industrial economy has come true in the sense that the service sector now employs more people than factories do. But some of Bell's other predictions, such as the dominance of creative knowledge workers, are still little more than utopian visions. Ritzer notes that low-status jobs are as important as they ever were, probably more so given the decline of industrial unionism. Further, McDonaldized systems are rigid hierarchies tightly bound by rules, not hotbeds of creativity. In the end, Ritzer believes that—although there are islands of creativity in our economy—McDonaldization and post-industrialization coexist, and they are by no means happy companions (ibid., 191).

Many social theorists have speculated about the rise of a 'post-Fordist' model of production to replace Henry Ford's assembly lines. While a Fordist method emphasizes the mass production of homogeneous products, standardized work routines, inflexible technologies, and mass markets, post-Fordism supposedly emphasizes more specialized products, shorter production runs, more flexible production methods, and more capable workers (ibid., 192–3). Yet as Ritzer rightly points out, the rumours of Fordism's death have been greatly exaggerated, as seen in the homogeneous foodstuffs offered by fast-food restaurants, the standardized work routines throughout most service industries, the replaceability of most workers, and attempts to quickly and efficiently process customers through McDonaldized environments (think of drive-through windows, ATMs, and Amazon.com). Yet as Starbucks coffee proves, Fordist methods don't *always* result in a poor quality product, even if most of the time they do.

Lastly, Ritzer argues convincingly that McDonaldization is both modern and postmodern at the same time. He agrees with David Harvey that an essential element of modernity, a process that accelerates in postmodernity, is space-time compression. Distances vanish as time speeds up. Fast-food restaurants and other businesses based on their model compress the time taken to produce their products while simultaneously compressing the geographic spaces between diverse cultures: we can get a 'little bit of Mexico' at our local Taco Bell, and pretty quickly to boot. Cable news networks like CNN offer instant transport to distant lands, as seen all too clearly during the TV coverage of Gulf War Parts I and II.

McDonaldization also fits fairly well into Frederic Jameson's picture of postmodernism as a stage of late capitalism. Its products are superficial and depthless, in the worst cases mere simulations: think of Chicken McNuggets, Disneyland, or the TV sitcom family. It's also a world without deep emotions, echoing Jameson's 'waning of affect': the store clerk's or waiter's friendly greeting is a mere simulation of personal warmth. People move from restaurant to restaurant or store to store with no particular attachment to any of them. In addition, we see a loss of any sense of historicity: past, present, and future are exploited equally in the décor and experiences offered by shopping malls, Disneyland, and Hollywood movies. And as Jameson claimed, productive technologies like the automobile assembly line are replaced by reproductive technologies like the TV and computer. These produce flattened, featureless products that are reproduced over and over (ibid., 199). Finally, McDonaldization takes place within hyperspaces that are difficult for people to map or orient themselves in since things are changing so rapidly. Examples include malls, casinos, cruise ships, and Las Vegas. In short, whether McDonaldization is connected to postmodernism depends largely on how one defines the latter: based on Harvey's and Jameson's definitions, it most definitely is.

As for the future, Ritzer offers some cautionary notes. The fast-food industry is saturated in the US. On a global scale, fast-food chains have been attacked for their connections to environmental degradation, unhealthy diets, unfair working conditions, Americanization, and the excesses of capitalism in general (ibid., 207). There are other counter-trends, for example, the attempt to build baseball stadiums that mimic the 'retro' feel of Boston's Fenway Park, with its fabled Green Monster in left field. Yet most importantly, there's the attempt to manufacture high-quality products using McDonaldized systems (e.g., Starbucks coffee), though Ritzer isn't so sure that this can be done with all products. Much of this is what he calls 'sneakerization', where a company like Nike produces a hundred or more varieties of a given product to create the illusion that its lines are customized for individual consumers. Another example of sneakerization is Dell's system of allowing each customer to specify what components he or she wants in a computer. This is just McDonaldization with a slightly less mechanized face.

In the end we can look at McDonaldization as one of three types of cages. It could be like Max Weber's *iron cage*—cold, hard, rational, and inescapable. At the other extreme, for more and more people McDonaldized systems are the only thing they know. For these sad folks they're a *velvet cage*: they represent automated, impersonal worlds without the need for any messy human interaction (except with other human robots). Everything is soft, comfy, and predictable, without any great need to think for oneself. For a third group, McDonaldized systems are a *rubber cage*. Rubber cages are still confining, but their bars can be stretched to allow for temporary escape. For the rubber-cagers McDonaldization is sometimes good, sometimes bad, and often escapable: one can go to a local grocery store instead of the mega-mart, to a locally owned restaurant instead of a Burger King or Wendy's. It's up to you. Yet one gets the feeling from Ritzer's *The Globalization of Nothing* that in the end the velvet cage will triumph, short of some environmental catastrophe that destroys the very material foundations of McDonaldization.

THEORIES OF GLOBALIZATION

Defining Globalization

Globalization defies any simple definition. In general, it is a shift from the dominance of economic, political, and cultural exchanges of a local or national nature to ones of a global nature, aided by the revolution in communication and information technologies of the last third of the twentieth century. To understand the diversity of the phenomenon of globalization we have to flesh out this simple definition with 10 specific trends of the global age we live in:

1. The coming of a global village of communication flows brought about mainly by television (in its cable and satellite modes) and the Internet. Everyone with fairly basic means can talk to everyone else at the speed of light, or see images of key events in distant corners of the globe the same day they happen.
2. The possibility of a 'global consciousness' brought about by the near instantaneity of

modern mass media. This doesn't mean everyone agrees, merely that local problems become 'front-page news' much more quickly than in the age of the telegraph, newspaper, and radio. In fact, inherent in this global consciousness is the danger of local political problems such as Islamic terrorism becoming world problems.

3. A relative freedom of travel and interaction, at least between developed countries, partially compromised recently by the political fallout from the 11 September 2001 terrorist attacks.

4. Multiculturalism—created in part due to the presence of large immigrant populations with distinct languages, religions, or social values—in Western countries such as the US, Britain, and Canada.

5. The commodification of the world by capitalism, including the invasion of pretty well all natural spaces by economic development (the 'end of nature'). This has especially been possible with the demise of communism as an alternative economic system.

6. The danger of local cultures being homogenized by global economic and cultural forces. The McDonaldization of global goods and services: Starbucks and McDonald's franchises in every major city; the threat of Americanization in both the economic and cultural realms.

7. The shift in sovereignty away from the nation-state towards transnational corporations and international political organizations.

8. The deliberate reduction of barriers to international trade among the major economic powers through GATT, the WTO, and regional trade blocs such as the European Community and NAFTA.

9. The creation of an electronic global financial market presided over by the IMF and liberated from the gold standard in 1971 by the 'Nixon Shock'.

10. The growing hegemony of neo-liberal economic ideas coupled with the declining legitimacy of the democratic welfare state and of trade unionism.

In short, the globalized world is one where global communications, transportation, financial, and trade networks rule, controlled by a coalition of nation-states, transnationals, and international political associations where the average citizen is little more than a private consumer. Yet globalization involves a lot more than this, as we'll see as we review the ideas of four prominent theorists on globalization.

Anthony Giddens's Runaway World

We start our tour of theorists of globalization with Anthony Giddens (of structuration theory fame), who situates globalization within a broader picture of a rapidly changing late modern world and how the self faces that world. Giddens's 1999 Reith lectures for the British Broadcasting Corporation, *Runaway World*, give us the rosiest picture of the new world order of the theorists we consider here. He optimistically paints a picture of a modern 'risk society' with its own unique challenges, advantages, and drawbacks. A few general remarks are in order before we look at the lectures themselves. Giddens sees us as living in a period of *late modernity* rather than postmodernity. The lessons of the Enlightenment—the value of rationality, science, and technological progress—still loom large over the West. What's really different about life at the turn of the millennium is that we have embarked on an irreversible course towards a *post-traditional order*. This is one where traditions and customs melt away, to be replaced by an intense 'reflexive' awareness of the fragile nature of our self-identity as individuals and as members of a given sex, religion, or nation. We create our own values and habits. We have to continually question, construct, and reconstruct our sense of personal identity, whether in terms of our economic roles (we might go through several careers), sexual status, family membership, or political commitments. We have to tell ourselves a story about who we are, a story that keeps changing. We 'must continually integrate events which occur in the external world, and sort them into an ongoing "story" about the self' (Giddens, 1991: 54). As

Goffman and Lasch also noted, this construction of the self is our greatest life project. Yet this also opens up the basic psychological problem of late modernity, the fear of personal meaninglessness, that one's life is inauthentic and phony (ibid., 9). Such an existential angst is unique to a post-traditional order where everyone has to choose his or her own social roles.

Modernity is the enemy of tradition and of a self defined by rigid social norms and roles. Our roles and actions are no longer justified by customs and traditions, but by a reflexive or active connection with various sources of information and values, not the least of which is the mass media. The self now has a 'puzzling diversity of options and possibilities' to choose from (ibid., 3). In this post-traditional order, the self feels compelled to opt for one or another 'lifestyle', a choice that medieval peasants or Russian serfs never had to worry about: 'Should I be a construction worker? File clerk? Doctor? Dentist? Have a family? Travel? Join the army?' Once it constructs itself, the self reflects this construction back onto its social relations with others. But this dialectic between the self and the ever-changing social practices (both local and global) it links up to in everyday life is increasingly disconnected from traditions. The abandonment of tradition is the sea change that Giddens sees as driving our runaway globalizing world towards an uncertain, risky future.

Giddens defines globalization as 'the intensification of world-wide relationships which link distant localities in such a way that local happenings are shaped by distant events and, in turn, distant events are shaped by local happenings' (Giddens, 2003).[6] It's a major consequence of modernity. In our late modern world, space, time, and geography cease to be significant constraints on social change as people begin to see the world as one thing instead of as a collection of nations. Late modernity reorganizes time and space through 'disembedding mechanisms' that rip social relations from specific times and places (Giddens, 1991: 2). Think of international jet travel, satellite TV, and the Internet, which allow the spanning of great chunks of space in less and less time. The world has become a single 'framework of experience' despite the considerable fragmentation we find within it.

This leads us into *Runaway World*, which is divided into five lectures on five distinct though connected topics. To start with, Giddens believes we're living through a 'major period of historical transition' that started back in the seventeenth and eighteenth centuries when science, technology, and rational thought started their ultimately successful battle with tradition and religious belief (Giddens, 2000: 19). As a result, we can control large parts of our world, making it more predictable; at the same time, this global control of nature has brought with it new risks and dangers such as global warming, mad cow disease, and environmental pollution. Our globalized world is driven by a haphazard collection of forces, not by a collective human will (ibid., 37).

In his first lecture, Giddens discusses globalization itself, noting how it has come out of nowhere to dominate political speech in the 1990s. There are two positions on the reality of globalization. The 'skeptics' argue that a global economy has existed for centuries and that globalization is nothing new, while the 'radicals' argue that globalization is all too real and has led to the decline and fall of the nation-state. Giddens is a radical. The global economy today is a new type of animal: for one thing, there's a global electronic economy of bankers, corporations, and currency speculators who trade a trillion dollars a day in global markets with the click of thousands of computer mouses (ibid., 28). Yet even the radicals miss the fact that globalization is not only economic, but simultaneously political, cultural, and technological. Commercial satellites have created a planetary communications network. The Internet took the developed world by storm in the 1990s. The traditional family structure is fading away. These and other developments have driven globalization, which not only creates a global culture, but leads to the revival of local ones such as those in Scotland and Quebec. Further, globalization creates local and transnational cultural-economic zones such as Hong Kong and Silicon Valley, California (ibid., 31). Globalization was responsible for the collapse of communism in the Soviet Union and Eastern Europe by the end of the eighties. The failure of the Soviet empire to computerize and join the global information age led to the decline of the socialist economies, the nail put in their coffin by the rise of global media leading up to the 'television revolutions' of 1989.

Globalization does create great poverty in parts of the world, yet to return to a protectionist policy would be disastrous for both rich and poor countries. The globalized die is cast. There's even some reverse colonization: the Latinizing of American culture, the rise of a large high-tech industry in India. Globalization has hollowed out what were once healthy institutions: the nation, the family, work, tradition, along with pushing nature into the background. Giddens calls these 'shell institutions' that can't do anymore what they once did.

In the second lecture Giddens raises a key issue in his theory of globalization: the notion that we live in a 'risk society', an idea he shares with Ulrich Beck, another important commentator on globalization. Late modernity has broken free of fate, destiny, and the gods as a result of its never-ending campaign to dominate nature. Humanity can control its own fate to a large degree. But some of this control brings with it great risks, e.g., the industrialization of the world and the environmental pollution it brings in its wake seem to have heated things up, creating global warming. Giddens notes that July 1998 was possibly the hottest month in the history of the world at the time he wrote the book (ibid., 38). What makes risk different from fate is that risk involves deliberately sailing into uncharted waters, going boldly where no society has gone before. Traditional societies certainly faced dangers and hazards, but not risk, a calculated attempt to break the chains of the past. Modern capitalism itself, as Weber pointed out long ago, is based on a regular calculation of risk, of profit and loss. The welfare state developed to manage such risks as unemployment, ill health, and accidents on the job (ibid., 42).

Risk can even be exciting, as seen in fast driving, gambling, promiscuous sex, and roller coasters (ibid., 41). It's the energy that drives the modern global economy. Giddens breaks risk down into two categories: *external risk*, which comes from nature and fixed traditions, and *manufactured risk*, which comes from the increased impact of science and technology on our world (ibid., 44). Annual floods fit in the former category, the Chernobyl explosion in the latter. We're living through a period where nature as a hostile external force is disappearing: as Jameson notes, the natural world is no longer a menacing Other. In this new climate of risk, politics bounces back and forth between scaremongering and cover-ups (ibid., 47). When a government is faced with a potential problem such as AIDS, mad cow disease, or global warming (or recently in Canada, SARS), what should it do? Scare the public to head off the problem? Or downplay it, and be accused of covering it up if the problem gets out of hand? Both approaches have been tried. Governments today have to actively engage scientific and technological problems brought on by the manufactured risks of our age: they can't avoid them. Yet Giddens doesn't see this challenge as entirely negative. After all, to risk is to dare, and risk is a vital part of a 'dynamic economy and innovative society' (ibid., 53).

In the third lecture, Giddens discusses how modernity is at odds with tradition. Of course, much of what we think of as 'tradition' is of fairly recent invention, e.g., the Scots' kilt, which in its present form was invented by tailors in the nineteenth century. Obviously, all societies have customs. Yet for Giddens the very notion of 'tradition' is the invention of modernity, specifically of the Enlightenment, with its attack on what it saw as irrational customs and beliefs. Medieval peasants didn't *have* traditions: they lived them. Traditions are invented and reinvented over time, and are held by groups and communities, not individuals (ibid., 58–9). A tradition isn't a tradition because it's been around for a long time; what's more important is the fact that the practice is *repeated* and is part of a *ritual*. Giddens gives the example of the British monarch's Christmas address, clearly a tradition—yet it dates back to only 1932.

Giddens claims that both Western and Third World societies are becoming 'detraditionalized'. In their place a global cosmopolitan society is emerging (ibid., 61). It's not that tradition has entirely disappeared. Instead, traditional societies find it harder and harder to justify their beliefs with internal claims to truth. Today science has a near-monopoly on such claims: if we want to establish whether the Shroud of Turin is the authentic burial cloth of Christ, we turn to X-ray technology, not faith. Yet Giddens thinks that we can't entirely abandon tradition in our globalized world. For one thing, the increase in personal freedom the decline of tradition brings in its wake leads to a bevy of addictions, which Giddens sees as 'enthralments' to the past: we replace tradition with addictions to work, food, exercise, and sex (ibid., 64–5). As Yeats poetically said of modernity as a whole, the centre cannot hold—so we replace it with some compulsion we hope will fill in that empty centre.

A major response to the decline of tradition is the rise of religious fundamentalism, which seeks to fight global cosmopolitanism and manage people's lives by returning to the literal meaning of sacred texts. Fundamentalism for Giddens is:

> . . . beleaguered tradition. It is tradition defended in the traditional way—by reference to ritual truth—in a globalising world that asks for reasons. . . . It has no time for ambiguity, multiple interpretation or multiple identity—it is a refusal of dialogue in a world whose peace and continuity depend on it. (Ibid., 67)

For Giddens fundamentalism includes not only Islamists like the Taliban, but also the Chinese Red Guards of the 1960s, with their slavish admiration for Chairman Mao's Little Red Book. The struggle between fundamentalism and cosmopolitanism will define the twenty-first century. Giddens sees the former, with its intolerance and openness to violence, as 'problematic'. Yet we can't live entirely without the sacred, which must be integrated into a passionate appreciation of an open cosmopolitan order (ibid., 68). Values can be universal and still worth dying for.

Our late modern risk society has called into question the traditional notion of the family, the subject of Giddens's fourth lecture. Not that there ever really was a single 'traditional' family structure for angry conservatives to demand a return to: the idealized nuclear family of the 1950s, where Dad was the breadwinner, Mom stayed home, and the obedient kids went to school during the day and curled up in front of the TV at night, lasted little more than a decade. Everywhere in the world—outside of authoritarian regimes that repress it—an active debate about sexual equality and the changing nature of the family is taking place. Recently in Canada, for example, the legality of gay marriage has been upheld by the Supreme Court. For Giddens the traditional family was an economic thing where women and children were the property of their husbands or fathers, where the double standard of male sexual freedom and female chastity was enforced to guarantee that family lineage and inheritances were passed from father to son (ibid., 72). This double standard about sex was not just a Victorian invention: it pervades all traditional societies. Only in the late modern age, where birth control allows the separation of sex from reproduction, could this duplicity be abandoned. This led naturally to the fading of fears concerning homosexuality, which by its very nature separates sex from reproduction: gays cannot have babies without some help from science or straights.

Marriage has become a shell institution. Only a minority of people in the West now live in a fifties-style nuclear family. This has been replaced by 'coupledom', a relationship defined by emotional intimacy. For Giddens, the ideal type of connection between people today is the 'pure relationship' defined by emotional communication, whether the connection is between friends, lovers, or parents and children (ibid., 79). Such a pure relationship is ideally between equals who communicate, respect, and trust each other and refrain from coercion and violence. Not too coincidently, the qualities of the pure relationship—equality, dialogue, trust, non-violence—also happen to be the qualities of the best democracies (ibid., 80). A democratic approach to coupledom and parent–child relationships results in what Giddens calls a 'democracy of emotions', a central feature of the growing cosmopolitanism today and anathema to fundamentalists, who want nothing to do with sexual equality and the freedom of women.

Finally, Giddens connects globalization to democracy. He witnessed first-hand the fall of the Berlin Wall in November 1989, where it was crystal clear that the Eastern European anti-Communist revolutions of the day were made possible by the advance of global communications, especially television (ibid., 86). Giddens defines democracy in a fairly commonsensical way: political parties, free and fair elections open to all adults, and civil liberties such as freedom of speech and assembly. Although almost everyone supports democracy today, only in the early twentieth century did democracy in its modern form really develop. As late as the 1970s, it was basically a European, North American, and Australasian thing. But then in the 1970s Spain, Greece, and Portugal democratized, followed by much of Latin America in the 1980s and Eastern Europe from 1989 on. This post-sixties expansion of democracy is striking, especially given what Giddens calls 'the paradox of democracy': the fact that just as democratic systems are all the rage outside their traditional homes, in those homes—Europe, North America, and Australia—a deep disillusionment with politics has set in. Corruption scandals are rife as many have lost their trust in politicians, seeing many of them as corrupt; as a result, fewer and fewer people vote, especially among the young. Giddens's explanation of this simultaneous alienation from politics in the West and celebration of democracy in the East and South is that hierarchical power based on a top-down economic system or a monopoly on information could not survive in the coming of the global information age (ibid., 90–1). There are too many leaks, too many holes in the wall. Once both Western democratic politicians and Soviet commissars had to appear on TV to explain their actions (and later were held up to ridicule by bloggers and unfriendly web pages), old-fashioned horse-trading and sleazy backroom politics were held up to the bright light of the media. The result wasn't too pretty.

To get the rubes back in the tent of democracy in the West, Giddens argues that we have to *democratize democracy*. He's a bit vague on specifics, though greater openness by politicians, constitutional reform, and the devolution of power to regions (as Tony Blair did in Britain by finishing the process of granting local autonomy to Scotland and Wales) are on the menu. The major element of this process will be the recreation of a strong civic culture, a bolstering of civil society, which Giddens defines as that part of society between the state and the marketplace. The state cannot generate political commitment by itself, while the capitalist market isn't the place to build democracy. Democracy is like a three-legged stool: it's held up by the state, the free-market economy, and civil society (ibid., 96). All three legs must be in good shape for democracy to stand straight. The mass media have a major role to play here—they're a democratizing force, but they also tend to destroy the public spaces where political discussions used to take place. Now people drink their coffees not in public cafés but in front of their TVs: a revitalized democracy must try to correct this. Since nation-states have lost some of their sovereignty, democracy must be built across state borders through transnational organizations like the European Union, which uses some of the sovereignty given it by member states to build democracy within those states. Giddens concludes that since the expansion of democracy is directly tied to the globalization process, we need stronger democratic institutions if this new global democracy is to take root (ibid., 100).

Elsewhere, Giddens has defended a 'Third Way' approach to modern democracy, one between the individual and the community, between the new right and the old left. His ideas on the subject got the ear of British Prime Minister Tony Blair, whose Labour Party attempted to implement them in the 1990s and later. Giddens sees the Third Way as an attempt to revitalize social democracy and the left in the face of the changes brought about by globalization. The Third Way takes a positive attitude towards globalization while trying to respond to the changing nature of inequality (Giddens, 2003). Giddens has a love/hate relationship with the old-fashioned welfare state—it solves some social and economic problems while creating others. He prefers what he calls a more 'active welfare' and reform of the labour market and welfare state (ibid.). In other words, he wants a redefinition of the relationship between the democratic state and global capitalism.

As sensible as Giddens's picture of the runaway world is, a few criticisms of his views are obvious. For one thing, the cosmopolitan global order he speaks of, with its free flows of capital and communications, is very much a bourgeois, capitalist order where only those with the cash are truly mobile (we'll see this critique in the next section from Zygmunt Bauman). Those taking the risks and reaping the benefits of playing in the global financial casino are once again the wealthy, while the lower classes experience these risks as external impacts on their lives. Giddens pays lip service to class differences, but seems rather blithe about the degree to which it often relegates the majority of people in the world to economic fates not of their choosing. Third, as Ethan Kapstein notes (1999: 31), any 'third way' policy must deal with the fact that however much the welfare state is reformed, something must be done to even out the imbalance between mobile capital and immobile labour. Workers, generally speaking, can't just pack up their kit bags to follow corporations that decide to leave town in search of softer tax policies or slacker environmental regulations. Lastly, at least in *Runaway World*, Giddens fails to consider the degree to which globalization is bound up with McDonaldization and the slow eradication of local cultural diversity. His runaway world seems to be running in fewer and fewer cultural paths, with unique languages and cultures disappearing as fast as animal species in the Amazonian rain forest.

Zygmunt Bauman's Globalized World

Zygmunt Bauman (1925–) is an important social theorist who has written on British socialism, modernity, consumerism, globalization, postmodern ethics, and the Holocaust, to name just his principal interests. He was born in Poland, fought in a pro-Soviet Polish army unit in World War II, and then studied sociology in Poland and England. He taught in Warsaw from the mid-fifties until 1968, when he was sacked for being Jewish; he eventually found his way to the University of Leeds in England, where he taught from 1971 to 1990. After his retirement, Bauman became an incredibly prolific writer, publishing over a book a year to date.

His *Globalization: The Human Consequences* (1998) is more passionate, poetic, and critical of globalization than Giddens's rosily optimistic *Runaway World*. For Bauman, we're all being globalized—it's our fate (1998: 1). The key factor in our globalized world is mobility: this is what stratifies our societies, what separates the winners (the mobile) from the losers (the stuck-in-place). Our economic, political, and academic elites can fly from place to place at the drop of a pin; they may have apartments or houses on several continents; they're sure to be fully integrated into the global web of communications via the Internet, cellphones, TV, and other modern electronics. They're the players of the global world, so he calls them the 'globals'. In contrast, the 'locals' are the unemployed, those with temporary jobs or who work full-time in the service industry in the West or in sweatshops in the Third World, the great unwashed masses who would *like* to be more mobile but are stuck where they are. They move when they *have* to, in search of work, when their rent goes up too much, or when family conflicts make life at home unbearable. They're part of the global web only tangentially, as passive spectators, watching the spectacle of the lives of the rich nightly on their TV screens. Class is alive and well in the globalized 'utopia'.

A key event in the history of globalization is the 'Great War of Independence from Space' waged by corporations (ibid., 8). No longer tied to a specific territory, investors are free to move their investments from one place to another in the blink of a computer's virtual eye. This 'free-floating' capital can now run away from the consequences of its actions, from any obligation to employees thrown out of work, to governments needing tax money for infrastructure, or to a despoiled environment (ibid., 9). These 'absentee landlords' can simply leave if local conditions are too unfriendly.

For Bauman, space is a social product of the means of transportation in place in a given era. All national borders and continental divides are the 'conceptual derivatives' of speed limits (ibid., 12). With relatively primitive means of transport— e.g., walking, horses, and sailing ships—France and Germany are big places; they get a bit smaller with railways and steamships; they can be traversed in an hour or two in a jet plane. The nation-state is made less viable in part because of our much higher speed limits today. Modern history has seen a constant improvement in the means of transportation, including the transportation of information. Old-fashioned local communities were formed around the capacities of ordinary human bodies: how far you can walk or ride in a day or so, how far you can see, how many people you can talk to. This original sort of space was replaced by an engineered, modern space that was 'tough, solid, permanent and non-negotiable', made up of the steel of railway tracks and the concrete of highways (ibid., 17). The state was the manager of this modern space, whose centre was the urban metropolis. The third type of space is the cyberspace of the global information web, which is simultaneously everywhere and nowhere. This type of space needs neither a physical community nor a nation-state to manage its affairs.

All this new speed doesn't make people more and more the same, as some globalization theorists suggest. Instead, it *polarizes* people into a mobile elite and an immobile mass. In all eras, borders have been considerably more porous to the wealthy: they could move from country to coun-

try with cosmopolitan abandon, spending the spring in Venice, the summer in Scotland, the fall in New York. Now the global elites are free to move from place to place while being attached to no local community at all. They are *extra-territorial*, their power bodiless, non-physical. They rule by proxy the billions of locals who are very much tied to their bodies and their territories. The globals work in cyberspace, which in its ethereal and disembodied nature is akin to the Christian picture of heaven (ibid., 19). Ironically, even though the globals become deterritorialized, they still need somewhere to live (or at least spend the night), so local territories are structured so that there are isolated and secure 'safe zones' such as American gated communities or multinational-managed luxury hotel chains for the elite to retreat to. They are surrounded by the late modern equivalent of medieval moats and turrets: security guards, concrete walls, mega-freeways. The elites like isolation and are willing to pay for it. In contrast, there are fewer and fewer public agoras where the ordinary citizen can meet for some face-to-face meetings and casual conversation. These agoras have been privatized into places of consumption: Socrates now eats at the mall food court.[7]

For the locals on the other side of the fence, territoriality feels like a prison, especially given the fact that they can watch the wonderfully mobile lives of the rich and famous every night in regularly televised broadcasts of heaven (ibid., 23, 54). They feel cheated. The public spaces today aren't constructed for 'wetware' (i.e., physical brains and bodies) but software. Shopping malls aren't made for casual conversation and debate, but to keep people moving, shopping, buying. The old meeting places were where norms and values were created, where communities were forged. But a territory without such spaces is unlikely to offer any place for meaningful debate of morals and politics outside of the elite opinions offered by mass media pundits (ibid., 25). Localities are losing their ability to create meaning. There are no local opinion leaders because there is no local opinion.

We're all on the move today, whether it's in jet planes or on our couches surfing a hundred satellite channels. Space and borders aren't obstacles to our movement. Nothing is fixed, including our desires and needs. This is as it should be in a consumer society, which aims to produce a continual series of attractions and temptations luring us siren-like to the rocky shoals of the shopping mall and big-box store. Yet when we give in to these desires to consume, just as we give in to desire in general, they disappear like puffs of smoke, only to be replaced by new ones (ibid., 79). This endless wheel of temptation creates a consumer psychology where nothing should be embraced fully. Satisfaction is but an instant in a long series of instants. The best consumer is one who suffers from a severe attention deficit, one whose desires are fleeting, who is (like Lasch's narcissist) impatient, impetuous, and easily bored (ibid., 81). The promise of satisfaction is even more exciting if attached to some unfamiliar good or experience, to a 'brand-new' product one didn't even think existed. The consumer is a restless collector of sensations more than things; his or her real horror is to live in a world where there's nothing left to desire (ibid., 83). Consumers *travel hopefully*, seeking that final buzz of ultimate pleasure from some future act of consumption. Yet it's not all the corporations' fault: the consumer must want to be seduced by the promise of new joys. This seduction is wrapped up in the illusion that the consumer is consuming by an act of free will. They really can't stop and smell the roses, no more than the chain smoker can take a week off tobacco.

Yet not everyone has the physical and financial mobility to be a good consumer. Though everyone may want to wander, some do it out of choice and find some pleasure in the act, while others are compelled to do so. The former wanderers, made up of the global elite, Bauman calls 'tourists'. The wanderers by compulsion, made up of the great mass of humanity in the lower classes, he calls 'vagabonds'. The tourists live on the good side of the tracks, the vagabonds on the side with the filth and squalor. Bauman mentions Washington, DC, Chicago, and Baltimore as examples of divided cities with clear borders between these two worlds. Just as space has shrunk for the

tourist, time has also faded away: one lives in a perpetual present, always busy, always short of time (more so with the invention of the Blackberry, I might add). On the other side of the tracks, the vagabonds are weighed down by redundant and useless time they have to 'kill': they don't punch the factory clock like their fathers and grandfathers, but just 'hang out'. Their only timetable is the *TV Guide*. The tourists travel at will, living in time but ignoring space. The vagabonds live in heavy, brooding spaces that burden them with time beyond their control.

The tourist is very much in touch with globalization: it's geared to her lifestyle and dreams (ibid., 93). She jets from New York to London to Tokyo, feeling at ease in the bar of the Hilton hotel in each city. She feels the reality of postmodern freedom. Sure, she may be a bit homesick, but that's the price of all that mobility. Yet not everyone moves around so freely and pleasurably. The immobile masses are stuck in one place:

> These are the *vagabonds*; dark vagrant moons reflecting the shine of bright tourist suns and following placidly the planet's orbit; the mutants of postmodern evolution, the monster rejects of the brave new species. The vagabonds are the waste of the world which has dedicated itself to tourist services. . . . The tourists travel because *they want to*; the vagabonds because *they have no other bearable choice*. (Ibid., 92–3)

The vagabonds look up to the tourists, admiring their power to create their own lives, to pick and choose between careers, romantic partners, houses, and cars. Yet it's not the rich themselves who are admired, but their wealth, their ability to consume endlessly unrelated to the pursuit of any sort of work ethic. The vagabond is a flawed consumer, without the means to live the mobile lifestyle of the latter. For the tourists the vagabonds are a nightmare of what they might descend to if their luck changes, so they exorcise the vagabond demon by banning beggars and the homeless, by making sure that even the working vagabond is confined to a separate part of their shared cities (ibid., 96–7). Yet the vagabond is the alter ego of the tourist, someone to look down upon in order to make the hardships of their touristic freedom more bearable. There's precious little communication between the vagabond and tourist classes. The tourists live the postmodernist story of a privatized consumer paradise where they're free to trot the globe in style. The vagabonds are stuck in that world's peripheries and no-go zones, slaving away to make sure the tourists get their perks.[8]

Bauman repeats the familiar (but nonetheless true) argument that, given the capacity of capital to rove the globe at the speed of mouse clicks and electronic signals, money is no longer tied in any meaningful fashion to territory. The nation-state is withering away, no longer able to balance the books of national profits and losses. Nation-states can no longer be purposeful and rational actors in an economy run by de-territorialized transnational corporations. The coming of this new world disorder was covered up for a while by the Great Schism of the Cold War from the late 1940s to 1989, when the world was divided into two great power blocs, which made it all seem like one total, organized system (ibid., 58). Every little European state and African petty potentate had a meaningful place in the world order of things. Now that that great division of the globe is history and the Communist bogeyman has faded to black, we face a disordered world controlled by no single issue.

This lack of central control is reflected in the very meaning of the term 'globalization', which is all about things that happen to us—global *effects*—rather than anything we plan to do, any global undertaking (ibid., 60). From roughly the Renaissance to the middle of the twentieth century, a people's power was defined by its ability to win and control a state. In this period the state had to do three things to maintain order: defend its territory against enemies, balance the economic books, and manage its cultural resources well enough so that its citizens saw it as having a distinct identity (ibid., 62). The global scene was one where states challenged or recognized each other's power while trying to erase a few sovereignty

'dead zones', blank spots on the map where no single state could claim clear jurisdiction. The Cold War brought many of these nation-states into one or the other of the two great power blocs, creating groups of states that co-operated with each other to oppose their capitalist or Communist enemy. Non-aligned states such as India and Egypt were seen as no man's lands for Russia and America to fight over by all means fair and foul.

In the post-Cold War globalized era all three legs of the state's 'sovereignty tripod' have broken: its exclusive military, economic, and cultural power over its own people and land is gone (ibid., 64). Now states almost beg to have part of their sovereignty taken away, as seen in most members of NATO and the European Community. Once able to use tax and tariff policies to control their internal markets and how these meshed with world trade, now governments have become the servants of economic forces over which they have little control. Due to free trade and the free movement of money in a global financial market, national politicians have become little more than administrators of the interests of transnational corporations and banks. If they tried to cause a ruckus and reassert control over the national books in the public interest, the markets would punish them promptly: the national currency would fall, loans would be called, and those new Japanese car plants wouldn't be built. Ironically, the global era has seen a proliferation of 'feeble and impotent' sovereign states filling the corridors of the United Nations. But this political fragmentation is no contradiction. These weak states, especially underdeveloped ones, are perfect fodder for the new world order. Having no power to say 'no' to the global economy, they act as the equivalent of local police precincts, guaranteeing that minimum of local order required by transnational businesses setting up sweatshops in them (ibid., 68). And besides, while it may be hard to bribe the Premier of France, it's not so hard to do so with the President of the Seychelles or Burundi. Political fragmentation greases the wheels of the economic side of globalization— they are allies.[9]

Globalization creates a new class structure in the world, restratifying it to create new structures of poverty and wealth, of impotence and power. Those at the top of the pyramid have a far greater freedom of mobility and action. And the wealthy are getting wealthier: Bauman quotes from a UN report the fact that the total income of 358 global billionaires was as great as that of the 2.3 billion poorest people in the world (ibid., 70). This wealth does not trickle down from the rich to the poor. The most astonishing thing about the new economic elite is that their efforts at wealth creation are largely insulated from the reality of 'making things, processing materials, creating jobs and managing people' (ibid., 72). It's done in the virtual reality of corporate boardrooms and the Internet. The old rich needed the poor to make money; the new rich don't. This poverty is covered up by the media, which focus on the hunger, wars, drugs, diseases, and refugees in the impoverished parts of the world, creating an image of a 'gangland, an alien, subhuman world beyond ethics and beyond salvation' (ibid., 75). The Western viewer, sickened by the sight of so much pointless violence and death, tunes out these human consequences of globalization. In the end, the globalized world is really two worlds, or a world within a world, that of an elite of global tourists surrounded by a mass of local vagabonds. Bauman's description of the human consequences of globalization, based on spatial, temporal, and power differences connected to class, is quite convincing.

Douglas Kellner on Technocapitalism

Douglas Kellner (1943–), a prominent contemporary critical theorist, is a professor in the graduate faculty of the philosophy of education at the University of California at Los Angeles (UCLA). Kellner's attempt to understand the globalized world today owes a lot to the Frankfurt School and a little to Jean Baudrillard's postmodernism, although he thinks Baudrillard is too enraptured by modern technology. In his 2002 article 'Theorizing Globalization', he outlines a theory that sees globalization as the product of two forces: a techno-

logical revolution and the global restructuring of capitalism (Kellner, 2002: 285). Kellner sees globalization much as I've outlined it at the beginning of this section, as a complex series of both mutually reinforcing *and* warring forces. There's an ever-flowing dialectic between the power of globalization to liberate and to oppress us. In fact, globalization (following Castells) is dominated by flows: of goods, services, technology, ideas, and people. Yet, this multi-faceted technological, economic, political, and cultural phenomenon cannot be reduced to a simple formula.

Having said this, the globalized world *is* a capitalist world, one where money, products, technology, cultural forms, and people flow relatively freely (ibid., 287). The Internet and global computer networks form the foundation of the new world economy: they are the matrix through which capital flows, just as blood flows through our veins and arteries. Kellner has nothing but scorn for technological determinists—whether optimists like Microsoft's Bill Gates or pessimists like the German philosopher Martin Heidegger—who treat high technology as an independent and unstoppable force. Similarly, he also attacks economic determinists who see globalization as nothing but the triumph of free-market capitalism throughout the world. Both determinisms fail to see how capitalist restructuring and the technological revolution are dialectically linked. Instead, Kellner suggests that what we see today is the triumph of technocapitalism. This is a system where a capitalist economy manages the production, distribution, and consumption of goods and services by using the machines and networks provided by modern technology.

Technocapitalism has a number of cultural and political effects, most notably the dominance of neo-liberal ideas about how the state should manage the economy. This leads to a partial abandonment of public goods and the public sphere, as most other theorists of globalization have also pointed out. It leads to a greater homogenization and standardization of cultures, at the same time creating some heterogeneity and local hybrids (as we'll see in greater detail when we examine once again the ideas of George Ritzer) (ibid., 292). Yet technocapitalism also creates hostility and resentment against this process of cultural standardization. The 2001 terrorist attacks on the World Trade Center could be an example of the destruction and violence opened up by the 'objective ambiguity' of globalization, though these could also be seen as having more to do with a conflict between a backward-looking Islamic fundamentalism and the Bush administration's 'Wild West militarism' (ibid., 291).

Being a critical theorist, Kellner is concerned about whether we can do anything about the negative side of globalization. He urges us not to become despondent determinists: the technological and economic forces driving globalization can be opposed. Sometimes globalization promotes democracy, sometimes it doesn't. Parts of globalization are progressive: Kellner mentions the Internet in this regard, which was used to organize protests in Seattle against the WTO in 1999. Global communication and media networks allow movements against capitalist globalization, specifically against the WTO, the IMF, and the worst transnational corporations, to spring up. Cyberactivists create networks of solidarity and share ideas with those opposed to the capitalist globalization from 'above', from transnational corporations (ibid., 297). These movements try to promote human rights, labour regulations, social justice, and ecological health (ibid., 293). They are part of a 'globalization from below' where marginalized people can resist the negative effects of globalization by using the very instruments of mass communication employed by governments and big business to create a global political economy to promote democracy instead. Yet the Internet has also been used by Hamas, the Tamil Tigers, and al-Qaeda to promote terrorism, and more generally by capitalist consumer society to promote commodity fetishism (ibid., 299). Thus, like globalization as a whole, the Net is an ambivalent power: it offers knowledge and information to many, yet widens the field for the domination of capitalism.

Globalization isn't just about the triumph of capitalism—it opens up new fields of struggle between capitalism and democracy. Politics today is deeply mediated by radio, TV, and the Internet, so some of this struggle isn't in the streets, but on the airwaves and in cyberspace. In the end, Kellner returns to Marx and Engels's *The Communist Manifesto* of 1848, where they picture capitalism as both a progressive force for change that swept away obsolete feudal structures in favour of a global cosmopolitanism and at the same time a 'major disaster' for the human race (ibid., 300). For Kellner, globalization is such a progressive/regressive thing. To get the state and corporations to distribute the benefits of the globalized information economy, a vigorous 'globalization from below' is needed to insist on more equality, more democracy, and more action to defend the environment (ibid., 302). Thus Kellner calls for a radicalized version of Giddens's civil society as a check on the power of transnational corporations and their servants, neo-liberal politicians.

George Ritzer on the Globalization of Nothing

George Ritzer's *The Globalization of Nothing* (2004) presents a sophisticated argument about the nature of globalization in terms of the consumption of goods and services. He sees globalization as taking place in many different fields: politics, business, markets, technology, religion, sports, music, and terrorism, to mention only a few obvious ones. He defines it as involving a worldwide diffusion of practices, relations, and forms of social organization and the growth of a global consciousness (Ritzer, 2004: 72).

Ritzer's key concept here is 'nothing', which he sees as '*a social form that is generally centrally conceived, controlled and comparatively devoid of distinctive substantive content*' (ibid., 3). In other words, 'nothing' is an organization or product with little original content that is controlled from afar, such as a McDonaldized franchise. Ritzer's grand narrative is the idea that nothing is getting bigger and bigger, like those spreading black ink blots on maps of Europe in World War II propaganda films depicting the Nazi campaign of conquest. The opposite of nothing is 'something', a locally conceived and controlled social form that is *comparatively rich in distinctive substantive content*' as well as being fairly unique (ibid., 7). He sets up a scale or continuum between nothing and something: a fast-food restaurant would probably be near the nothing end, a small bakery near the something end.

Ritzer warns us that both nothing and something are Weberian ideal types, like the rest of his central concepts: we might never meet them in their unrefined forms in the real world. No phenomenon is purely 'nothing', a hollow empty form designed and controlled by a central body: even the humblest McDonald's franchise might have a few local touches. The same goes for pure 'somethings': such a strange bird exists only in social theory textbooks. Further, both 'nothing' and 'something' are *social constructions* in the sense that a given place, thing, or service only becomes what it is by the actions of human beings (ibid., 13–14). For instance, no physical space is inherently a 'non-place'. A building that served as a Taco Bell restaurant could be bought by a local restaurateur and turned into a funky café oozing local colour. Lastly, Ritzer concentrates on consumption and thus on Western consumer societies. He's fully aware that 'nothing' is also *produced*, not just consumed, the former process often taking place in underdeveloped countries where workers toil for paltry wages and can only stare in envy at the piles of Nike sneakers they've just sewed and glued together.

'Nothing' is increasingly coming to dominate the world, though Ritzer claims that this dominance isn't *always* bad, just as the more substantial 'somethings' aren't always good. For one thing, centrally designed and manufactured products can be quite a bit cheaper and more readily available than highly specialized or handmade products. There are four types of nothing, which Ritzer calls the four 'nullities' (ibid., xi):

- Non-places like shopping malls and drive-through windows.
- Non-things like name-brand T-shirts.
- Non-people like McDonald's employees.
- Non-services like ATMs and Internet markets.

A non-place is a largely empty social form, centrally conceived and controlled, that sells non-things or non-services and is staffed by non-people (more on these later). The four nullities operate in a vicious circle, mutually supporting each other—non-people sell non-things and offer non-services in non-places, e.g., McDonald's employees peddling Big Macs over the counter in a McDonald's restaurant, while underpaid adjunct professors offer 'distance education' courses through Internet universities. Once the golden arches appear on a highway strip, one is quite sure that minimum-wage dehumanized workers offering empty smiles and corporate-designed standardized foodstuffs will follow in their wake.

All the types of nothing exist on a continuum: some things are more 'nothing' than others. Yet overall, globalization and nothing—the proliferation of centrally controlled but empty social forms—go hand in hand. It's easier to globalize an empty form like a shopping mall than a fuller one such as traditional folk music. Admittedly, consumers often try to turn nothing into something, to take the empty forms offered them by modern capitalism and add some personal or local flavour to them (just as office employees stick pictures and notes on their computers). Yet more and more those who seek a substantial something over the more generic nothing are seen as abnormal outsiders, even freakishly strange in some cases, e.g., customers who expect detailed technical knowledge of electronics from McDonaldized sales clerks at big-box stores like Future Shop or Best Buy. That's what the Internet is for!

It's helpful at this point to chart Ritzer's various categories and distinctions (Table 12.2). Ritzer spends a couple of chapters outlining in great detail the subcontinua and subtypes of both nothing and something, offering a number of counter-examples to his categorical distinctions. The places, things, people, and services of 'something' tend to be unique or one-of-a-kind, have local geographic ties, are connected to a specific time

Table 12.2 Ritzer on the Main Existential Categories of Globalization

	Something	Nothing
Main processes of diffusion	Glocalization Local Traditions	Grobalization (the dominant globalizing force today)
Subtypes (with examples)	Place (local café) Thing (home-cooked meal) Person (gourmet chef) Service (local handyman)	Non-place (Internet university) Non-thing (Big Mac) Non-person (Tim Horton's server) Non-service (ATM)
Subcontinua (qualities of nothing and something)	Unique Local geographic ties Temporally specific Humanized Enchanted	Generic No local ties Timeless (free-floating) Dehumanized Disenchanted

Source: Adapted from Ritzer (2004: esp. 10, 20).

period, and are non-alienating or humanized and enchanted. Conversely, non-places, non-things, non-people, and non-services are rationalized and centrally controlled; hence they are generic, have few local ties, lack a connection to a given time period, and are alienating and disenchanted.

The five subcontinua tend to cluster together: unique places, things, people, and services are usually also tied to a specific geographic place and time, are human, and enchanted, and vice versa for generic ones. To illustrate the unique/generic distinction, Ritzer compares a gourmet meal with a visit to a fast-food restaurant: the former experience is a highly individual one, the latter like a race car refuelling at the pit stop. One Big Mac is pretty well the same as all the others. As for geographic ties, he compares handmade Mexican pottery, with its ties to the town or province where it was made, to its mass-produced cousin. The hand-painted ceramic cat I have on my bookcase, with its bright blues, yellows, and reds, is a unique product of a journey to specific place—St Miguel de Allende, in the central Mexican highlands—while the ceramic cat one might buy at Wal-Mart could have been made anywhere in the world. Ritzer compares the temporally rich case of certain types of cars—the 1969 Pontiac Firebird and the 1938 Volkswagen Beetle—to generic models such as the Dodge Neon and all of Hyundai's and Kia's products, which are soulless mass-produced designs that are forgotten a few years after they're

made. Fourth, Ritzer juxtaposes the relatively humanized environment of a small teaching college, with its strong ties to a particular place and time and sense of identification by both students and faculty, to Internet universities like the University of Phoenix, places through which information flows, all contacts are fleeting, and deep human relationships are impossible (ibid., 33). Finally, he compares the enchantment of a well-cooked homemade meal with the disenchantment of a Domino's delivery boy at the front door.

As for the nullities, Ritzer offers more examples to illustrate his basic distinctions. He spends the most time dealing with places and non-places, the sites of the other three subtypes of both something and nothing. He compares his notion of places and non-places with Manuel Castells's 'spaces of places' and 'spaces of flows' (ibid., 40). Real places tend to contain 'something', while 'nothing' is usually found in spaces through which things are constantly flowing: a drive-through fast-food window, an Internet market, or, to use Ritzer's own example, a planned suburban community. This leads him to embrace Ray Oldenburg's notion of a 'great good place', such as an English pub, café, local bookshop, or diner, where people gather informally in a place they see as a comfortable 'third setting' for their lives away from home and work (ibid., 42). In such places, to borrow from *Cheers*, 'everyone knows your name' and people feel welcome in a safe haven. Of course, great good places cannot be McDonaldized or globalized very effectively, so they tend to be one-of-a-kind places that pay for their human and magic qualities with being very localized in time and space. Every town and city—except perhaps soulless suburban pseudo-communities—has them, even if they're under constant threat from franchises and strip malls.

Ritzer contrasts the diner (something) to the fast-food restaurant (nothing) as archetypal places and non-places. Young people who grew up in a McDonaldized and globalized era tend to favour the latter, while older people like the former (ibid., 47). The fast-food restaurant is a non-place where things are produced efficiently and predictably in standardized architectural structures with little if any local flavour. They're ephemeral places through which an endless line of eaters and drinkers flow every day. These eaters and drinkers really don't care about the décor of the restaurant or having a meaningful dialogue with its servers: they just want to get their food quickly and cheaply. In contrast, a diner welcomes its regulars for a time in a place where human relationships can develop, where the customers can get a taste of some local magic. They can be places where enchantment slows down for awhile the overall modern drive to economic rationality.

As one would suspect, non-things are centrally controlled and conceived, yet lack distinctive substance (ibid., 56). More and more non-things are being sold today, not only in non-places like a McDonald's restaurant, but in *places* too. Our North American lives are immersed in non-things. Ritzer compares an Italian Culatella ham—a thing tied to rich historical traditions—to a Big Mac, which is an ephemeral product of a highly rationalized fast-food business. Naturally, non-places are staffed by non-people who act like scripted robots rather than human beings when interacting with customers. Ritzer compares a bartender, who displays a specific character in a specific place for a limited period of time, with the workers who don Mickey Mouse, Goofy, and Snow White costumes at Disney World, who are generic and interchangeable

(even if the actual Disney characters do have a certain permanent quality). The bartender's job is obviously much more humanized than that of playing an ersatz Mickey, not to mention the fact that Disney's 'magic' is mass-produced and simulated—Disney World is Baudrillard's perfect simulacrum. Lastly, non-services are those done by scripted performers following corporate guidelines in places of flows without distinctive substance. These four nullities are spread by the globalization of nothing.

Ritzer's most interesting argument is that what most theorists refer to as 'globalization' is really two different processes that aren't usually in sync: 'grobalization' and 'glocalization'. Glocalization is the relatively benign process where the interaction of the global and the local produces a new social form that combines both (ibid., xiii). Glocalization is closest to the 'something' end of things—though there are exceptions—since it aims to create cultural hybrids. It creates variety, heterogeneity.

Grobalization is where nations, transnational corporations, and other international bodies seek to increase their power and profits by expanding globally, imposing themselves on local cultures. It's the imperialistic form of globalization, the form that causes radicals in Paris to trash McDonald's outlets. Grobalizers want to spread their organization's influence over greater and greater areas. In the realm of consumption, corporations search for ever-greater markets to sell more and more products. Grobalization seeks to impose homogeneous practices on the spaces under its sway: it aims to absorb the local into its global networks. Since the four nullities lack specific local content, they're easier to create centrally, to mass-produce and export throughout the world. Although there's no law-like or causal relationship between the presence of grobalization and nothing, there is an 'elective affinity' between the two forces (ibid., 101). The search for new markets is driven by capitalist firms producing vast quantities of relatively cheap products that can be sold almost anywhere: great heaps of nothing.

Ritzer (ibid., 77) lists four essential elements of each process. First glocalization:

1. The world is becoming more and more plural, or as the French say, *vive la différence!*
2. The glocal person can be creative and innovative and has cultural room to manoeuvre.
3. Social processes are flexible and can feed back into the system and change globalization.
4. Consumer goods and the mass media aren't seen as *entirely* coercive, but can be used to enhance personal growth and group solidarity.

As for grobalization, it creates a world where:

1. Things are more and more the same everywhere.
2. Larger forces overwhelm the power of people to adapt and innovate in ways that preserve their autonomy.
3. Social processes are coercive, determining the nature of local communities, which have little room to manoeuvre.
4. Consumer goods and the media are key forces that largely dictate the nature of the self and the groups a person joins.

The glocalization process, as we've seen, involves greater heterogeneity. It leads to hybrids that combine elements of two or more cultures, which can also be called *creolization*, the combination of two languages to produce a third, as in Haitian French. The world is now going through a profound process of globalization where the grobal and the glocal struggle with each other. Ritzer foresees a death of the local as a part of this struggle, and the coming of a state of affairs where 'globalization will reign supreme throughout much of the world' (ibid., xiii). He wonders whether local culture, politics, and economics could be revived, perhaps as a result of frustration and alienation felt by globalization's losers. His conclusion is that any such revival is likely to be swept up in the currents of grobalization, especially if it's successful economically (ibid., 170).

Another important theme of Ritzer's book is the idea of having lost something amid monumental material abundance: things and experiences that are locally created and controlled. Less

and less of our everyday lives are tied to the purely local, whether where we eat, the media we watch and listen to, or the consumer goods we buy and use. Think about how and where you shop, eat out, and enjoy recreation: if you're a typical North American, most of what you consume fits comfortably within Ritzer's definition of nothing.

Ritzer argues that grobalization involves three motor forces: capitalism, McDonaldization, and Americanization. We've already looked in detail at McDonaldization, so we'll concentrate on the other two forces here. Capitalism is the main motor force for grobalization, as Marx and Engels saw as early as 1848 in their *Communist Manifesto*, where they predicted that capitalist expansion would melt all that's local into air and create a more 'cosmopolitan' world order. During the Cold War the Soviet and Chinese Communist blocs acted as serious barriers to the expansion of capitalism throughout the world. But now that Stalin, Khrushchev, and Mao are little more than mischievous ghosts, capitalism is 'free to roam the world in search of both cheap production facilities and labour as well as new markets for its products' (ibid., 81). And McDonaldization, with its drive to proliferate a formal model of production and consumption largely devoid of specific cultural content, is the perfect partner for capitalism today. So Ritzer sees grobalization as part of a political economy that features economic forces on the one side—capitalist expansion and McDonaldization—and political and cultural on the other—Americanization backed by US military and political power.

Ritzer sees capitalism as favouring the globalization of nothing since this makes the selling of products over larger expanses of time and space easier. Capitalism proliferates non-places, non-things, non-services, and non-people, all backed up by nudges both gentle and nasty from the massive US military machine. A major thrust in grobalization is the desire by American corporations to rake in greater profits and the related drive by American institutions to exert more and more cultural hegemony over the rest of the world (ibid., 74). Both are backed by American diplomacy and military might, which support democracy in the name of capitalism and capitalism in the name of democracy.

Americanization, like McDonaldization, is another happy partner for grobalization. In its train it brings a familiar series of products and icons: Hollywood films and stars, Coca-Cola, the NFL and NBA, blue jeans, Microsoft Windows, the American soldier, Wal-Mart, The Gap, fast food, the cowboy, Mickey Mouse, and Marlboro cigarettes, to mention just a few. Some of these have become so ingrained in local cultures that children growing up in them don't know they're American: Ritzer speaks of a Japanese Boy Scout visiting Chicago being surprised to find an outlet of the 'Japanese' restaurant McDonald's there (ibid., 91). Americanization also involves what Ritzer calls 'new means of consumption', new ways and places for buying stuff—this includes franchises, mega-malls, superstores, home shopping networks, cyber-shopping, theme parks, and cruise ships (ibid., 87). These new means are part of the Americanization process for four reasons:

- America is still the world leader in consumption, and Americans are hyperconsumers who invented many of the massive empty forms of grobalized consumption.
- America is a mobile culture. Americans are addicted to the automobile, and to a lesser degree to flying. These new means are tied intimately to this love of being on the move (think of airport food courts and highway mini-malls). This love is symbolized in 'road movies' like *Easy Rider* and *U Turn*.
- Americans are so affluent that they, of all peoples, can best afford to 'descend in droves on meccas of consumption' such as Las Vegas, a Minnesota mega-mall, or superstores like Wal-Mart (ibid., 88).
- Americans love huge things—the bigger, the better, whether it's 'cathedrals of consumption' such as mega-malls and superstores or super-sized tabernacles of kitsch culture such as Disney World or the Vegas strip.

Summing up, capitalism finds it easier to export 'nothing' than 'something', since the former has less content that will conflict with local cultures. The same goes for McDonaldized systems: local people don't have to change their ways much before a Coca-Cola or Taco Bell can set up shop in their country. Americanization doesn't fit quite as easily with the globalization of nothing, yet since many aspects of American culture have become of late almost universal—think of Hollywood movies and their effect on filmmaking worldwide—it's not such a hard sell most of the time.

As for the future, Ritzer does note that all three of the motor forces of grobalization—capitalism, McDonaldization, and Americanization—have come under attack since the 1990s. The most stunning example of such an attack is obviously al-Quaeda's 9/11 assault on the twin towers of American grobal capitalism. Ritzer sees the attacks on the World Trade Center, the Pentagon, and the abortive attack on the White House as assaults on symbols of America's economic, military, and political grobal reach (ibid., 171). At least in part, 9/11 was the result of resentments felt in the Islamic world to the triple threat of capitalism, McDonaldization, and Americanization. These and many other lesser attacks—including the Battle in Seattle in 1999—have made it seem that it's becoming increasingly difficult to distinguish between these three motor forces. If a McDonald's outlet is firebombed in France or Iraq, what's being attacked: the globalization of fast food, capitalism as a whole, or the United States? It's difficult to say.

Yet Ritzer doesn't think that such attacks signal the beginning of the end of these three processes or of the globalization of nothing. Quite the contrary. For one thing, capitalism is friskily on the march in the wake of the collapse of its communist alternative. Second, any anti-Americanism in the world is more than countered by American political and economic power along with a genuine fondness for American culture in most nations. Third, whether or not McDonald's itself declines and falls, the McDonaldization process is too big a part of economic rationalization for it to disappear any time soon. Finally, grobalization is such an important process that most nations have little choice but to jump on the grobal bandwagon (ibid., 94–5).

Ritzer makes things more complex by noting that there can also be a grobalization of something and a glocalization of nothing. An example of the grobalization of something is an exhibit of a major artist like Van Gogh that tours from city to city all over the world over the course of a year: the 'product' is one-of-a-kind (i.e., there's only one genuine copy of each of Van Gogh's paintings) and is presented by knowledgeable guides, not bored teenagers schlepping shakes and burgers (ibid., 99). On the other side, we see the glocalization of nothing in souvenir shops that sell mass-produced trinkets with some local flavour. Imagine buying a snow globe in Toronto containing a plastic Mountie and a picture of Niagara Falls: when you turn it over, you see a 'Made in China' sticker on its base. Yet these two counter-processes are comparatively rare. Further, in some cases the grobalization of nothing pisses the locals off, and they return to native traditions. To respond to this, grobal companies from time to time create products that appeal to a 'wilful nostalgia' for some aspect of a local culture, for instance, French chocolates or McDonald's *kampong* burgers in Singapore. Although such products may appear to be local, they are just empty forms given a local sheen by grobalizing corporations. In the end, Ritzer seems to believe that the globalization of nothing is almost unstoppable.

As for criticisms, Ritzer himself forestalls the notion that his categories of 'nothing' and 'something', the four nullities, grobalization, and globalization are too abstract and static by insisting that they're all ideal types not found in their pure forms in the real world. Further, his distinctions are in real-life *continua*: unlike being pregnant, which at last report was an all-or-nothing proposition, a given product or place *can* be just a little bit 'nothing'. The most stinging critique one could make of his book is that it lacks Adorno-style anger at a phenomenon he clearly finds troubling: globalization. He ends his book by telling

his readers that it's up to them to decide if his analysis is valid and whether they should do anything about the problems associated with globalization (ibid., 216). After 200 pages of clear-headed analysis, this is hardly the call to action one would have liked to hear from a major critic of the globalized world.

CORPORATISM

'Corporatism' has a number of definitions, two of which dominate. In the narrow sense it means the domination of a society by business corporations, along with the excessive loyalty of large numbers of people to the goals and values of those corporations. We'll have a look at two theorists who discuss corporatism from this angle later in this section: Joel Bakan and Naomi Klein. In a broader sense, corporatism is the organization of a society in terms of the loyalty of its citizens to formal groups, usually of an occupational or professional nature, instead of to their individual goals and interests or to the nation as a whole. John Ralston Saul focuses on corporatism in this second sense, tracing it back to the work of Émile Durkheim and to Italian fascism in the 1920s. Under such a corporatist system, each group represents the interests of its members to the state, which then manages conflicts between them. Individual interests, rights, and the public interest as a whole are largely ignored. The theorists discussed here all argue that in our globalized age industrial societies have, sadly, become all too corporatist.

John Ralston Saul on Our Unconscious Civilization

John Ralston Saul (1947–) was born in Ottawa and has had a varied career as an economist, world traveller, novelist, philosopher, and cultural critic. He was educated at McGill University and at the University of London, where he received his Ph.D. in 1972, though he didn't use it as a ticket into academe, spending the 1970s travelling, writing novels, and working for Petro-Canada instead. Later in his career Saul turned to writing non-fiction, following in the footsteps of Enlightenment philosophers like Voltaire, Hume, and Adam Smith, aiming his books at an educated public instead of just academics. His wit and suspicion towards the powers that be can be seen in his 1992 book, *Voltaire's Bastards: The Dictatorship of Reason in the West*, which discusses how an excessive love of abstract reason has been used by the Western power elites to create institutions that are bureaucratic nightmares. His mock dictionary *The Doubter's Companion: A Dictionary of Aggressive Common Sense* (1994) offers witty and ironic definitions of key terms in political and economic rhetoric today, once again with the aim of taking the piss out of the power elite. Saul went on to publish *On Equilibrium* (2002), which argues that we must balance common sense, ethics, imagination, intuition, memory, and reason to achieve individual and social wisdom, and *The Fall of Globalism* (2005), which argues that globalization, though all the rage a few decades ago, is being slowly dismantled by national leaders. Our central concern here is Saul's attack on corporatism and related structures in *The Unconscious Civilization*.

The Rule of Corporatism

Saul's *The Unconscious Civilization* (1995) came out of a series of five Massey lectures for CBC radio in 1995, and has since won the Governor-General's award for non-fiction. In it he presents a model of modern Western civilization as a dangerously unconscious one, one that's hooked on the ideology of corporatism. Saul is a combination of Enlightenment *philosophe* and critical theorist. He sees social structure as important, but places almost all responsibility for social decisions on the individual level. We can't say 'society made me do it': this is a cop out. He tries to be a Socrates for the modern age, asking us to examine critically the main social forces that drive us today. Among these social forces the main culprit is corporatism.

Saul starts with a voice from the distant past: medieval thinker John of Salisbury thought that only self-knowledge makes life worth living (Saul, 1995: 1). To see individualism as at its core self-

ish is a hijacking of Western civilization. Saul summarizes his views in speaking of a society addicted to ideologies, especially the ideology of corporatism, which holds modern culture in a tight grip:

> The acceptance of corporatism causes us to deny and undermine the legitimacy of the individual as a citizen in a democracy. The result of such a denial is a growing imbalance which leads to our adoration of self-interest and our denial of the public good. Corporatism is an ideology which claims rationality as its central quality. The overall effects on the individual are passivity and conformity in areas that matter and non-conformism in those that don't. (Ibid., 2)

For Saul, a corporation is any formal collective body with an economic or political purpose. Business corporations count, but so do special interest groups, government ministries, and university departments. Under corporatism, we tend to owe our primary loyalty as citizens not to society as a whole, but to the corporation we belong to. Only the corporation has real legitimacy. Corporatism promotes narrow bands of specialist information, with each corporation having its own special dialect, its own way of thinking and speaking. Against the skeptical doubters of the world, our huge, specialized, technocratic elites 'are shielded by a childlike certainty' (ibid., 5). The reaction of sophisticated elites to criticism is to build a wall between themselves and reality and thus to create an artificial sense of well-being on the inside, thereby shielding themselves from outside critique (ibid., 8–9). Managerial elites manage, but crises require active thought. We teach people how to manage, not how to think; indeed, we actually punish thought as unprofessional. Saul thinks we live in a clinical state of unconsciousness where people are limited to a narrow area of knowledge, and operate with the naïveté of a child elsewhere (ibid., 15). We've become a society of specialists, not citizens.

This results in social structures of highly specialized bureaucracies, where the people on the lower rungs of the ladder must kiss up to the higher-level managers. The educated, specialized technocratic elites that make up about a third of our population are 'caught in structures which require of them courtier-like behaviour' (ibid., 26). They have to kowtow to bosses, managers, department heads, and chairs to get ahead. Being critical and thinking outside the box are rarely rewarded—outside of Hollywood movies, that is.

Language: Ideology vs Reality

In our corporatist society, we deny reality. We have an addictive weakness for large illusions, for *ideology* (which he sees as the worship of all-inclusive truths and utopias). This weakness is getting worse. Marxism, fascism, and the neo-conservative (i.e., neo-liberal) worship of the marketplace are all similar: they're hooked on corporatist structures and technology as their golden calves (ibid., 18). To live in utopia is to live 'no place', nowhere, to live in a void where the illusion of reality is 'usually created by highly sophisticated rational constructs' (ibid., 28). So Saul also believes that ideologies pervert reason to their own ends. They are oversimplifications of the world, easy ways out. The great leap backwards is into the unconscious state of the subject who, as a function of belonging to a corporation, gives up his or her personal, disinterested responsibility for the shape of the society in exchange for the easy certainties offered by ideology (ibid., 35). The opposite of ideology is doubt, which is essential in a healthy democratic society.

Saul sees two types of language in corporatist societies: the Public, which is enormous, rich, and varied, but mostly powerless; and the Corporatist, which is attached to power and action. Corporatist language is made up of rhetoric, propaganda, and dialects (ibid., 46). Rhetoric is the use of emotionally charged language to convince someone to think or do something he or she cannot rationally be convinced to think or do. It sometimes creates abstract notions to obscure real events: the Nazis were among the first to do this, using business and engineering terms for unpleasant actions, e.g., the killing off of 'inferior' racial groups such as the Jews

was called 'special treatment'. This sort of abstraction is the natural outcome of a society broken down into interest groups—it's now rare in public debate to hear from someone who's not the official voice of an organization (ibid., 61). Most public debate today is between the mouthpieces of concerned interest groups. We can see an example of this in a TV news report of a burning public issue, which usually consists of a statement of the issue under debate by a representative for the 'pro' and the 'anti' groups, an analysis of the situation by an 'expert' (often a university professor), then maybe a comment from the man or woman in the street. Underlying it is the assumption that concerned groups will settle the problem themselves without the couch potatoes getting involved.

As for political propaganda, its selling device is essentially the same as advertising. Political propaganda was fully developed under fascism in Italy and Germany in the 1930s and 1940s. The basic idea in both propaganda and advertising is to replace words or ideas with images and music, as seen in TV commercials, music videos, and Nazi propaganda films such as *The Triumph of the Will*, which Saul identifies as an early piece of brilliant propaganda. The drums beating in MTV music videos are only a slight remove from those pounding at the Nuremberg Nazi Party rally seen in Leni Reifenstahl's 1935 film extolling the virtues of *der Führer* and his henchmen.

The University as Corporatist Handmaiden

Like Lasch, Saul ties in a critique of university life with his critique of the 'unconscious civilization'. Within a corporatist society, most people in positions of responsibility are rewarded for controlling language. Saul thinks that the universities have become to a great extent the handmaidens of the corporatist system (ibid., 67). In them, knowledge is power: 'Knowledge is owned and controlled, bought and sold, in a corporatist society—knowledge which matters, that is' (ibid., 42). This is due to impenetrable academic dialects—read just about any academic journal for proof of this—and the betrayal of higher education's wider mission, the humanist tradition. Saul sees university academics as sinking deeper and deeper into a form of medieval scholasticism that speaks in these obscure dialects. They act as gatekeepers barring entrance to outsiders—if you can't speak the lingo, you can't play the game.

The university community doesn't teach elites to rise above self-interest and the narrow view of things because it has slipped into these views, so natural in a world of professional corporations (ibid., 68). University departments and faculties see themselves as corporate entities, not as serving a greater public good. This is especially true of academic philosophy. Saul says that the 'great philosophical voice of humanist decency' has vacated public debate. Why? Because the members of the corporation of philosophy are 'caught up in the complexities of philosophical professionalism—a world of narrow specializations and impenetrable dialect.' They have abandoned the field of public debate to more cynical forces, thinking that such debate is no longer worthwhile (ibid., 161–2). It's far safer to while away the hours solving problems in logic. The result of this abdication of critical thought in the universities is a 'crisis of conformity' where academics hide under the umbrellas of their separate specializations free from any attempt to examine society critically, allowing market forces to run the system as a whole (ibid., 70).

Saul bemoans the eagerness with which liberal and social democratic governments embrace 'restructured' schools that act as a direct channel to the managerial economy. These changes won't help people in the workplace, but they will help to prepare young people to accept the structures of corporatism (ibid., 163). The German philosopher Friedrich Nietzsche echoed this skepticism about higher education over a century ago, saying that the meaning of all higher education is to tame the beast of prey in man. Citizens feel as though their professional thinkers have abandoned them, becoming specialized gatekeepers of isolated dialects rather than active critics of society (ibid., 174). Overall, universities teach the lesson of conformity to corporatist structures rather than creating free-thinking and disinterested citizens.

The False Fable of the Economic Origin of Democracy

Saul attacks the false belief that democracy was born of economics, that it was a product of capitalism and the Industrial Revolution. In reality, it was born long before this, in ancient Greece. The received wisdom is that the heart and soul of our 2,500-year-old civilization is economics. But every key aspect of individualism and democracy is more than a thousand years old, and are the *causes*, not the *effects*, of the rise of capitalism and other important economic events of the last few centuries (ibid., 3). Today we have both poor democracies and prosperous authoritarian regimes: no hard-and-fast relationship exists between the degree of democracy in a society and its economic well-being.

In the last 25 years, economics has been spectacularly unsuccessful in its attempts to apply its models and theories to the reality of our civilization. If economists were doctors, they would be mired in malpractice suits (ibid., 4). Note that Saul studied economics at the doctoral level, so he's not just talking nonsense here. The management of business and the consulting industries, not the expansion of government services, keep the economy in depression. There are just too many managers. *They* are the cause of corporate inefficiency.[10] Saul thinks that most business leaders who preach about personal initiative, risk, and free markets are bureaucratic managers, not true capitalists. Their obsession with efficiency, which brings in its train 'downsizing' and pointless mergers, creates conservative corporate thinking and stymies growth (ibid., 123–4).

Saul attacks the neo-conservatives, who argue for deep cuts to government services and a less regulated marketplace and believe that the free market by itself will solve all of our social and economic problems. They are the courtiers of corporatism, their agitation for laissez-faire capitalism filled with the bitterness and cynicism typical of lackeys scrambling for crumbs at the table of power (ibid., 17). The neo-conservatives create an oppressive air of conformity that tells everyone to embrace the globalization of our economy, and that cutting government spending to kill the debt is the only way to revive the economy. These notions aren't facts, but the products of ideologies.

There was no role for economics in the Renaissance, the Protestant Reformation, or the English Civil War, the historical cornerstones of modern society. In general, democracy and individualism have advanced in spite of and often against specific economic interests, requiring financial sacrifice, not gain (ibid., 83). Saul thinks that the citizenry and democracy have, over the centuries, forced the economic machine into a socially acceptable and reasonably stable shape (ibid., 117). For example, labour unions over the last century and a half have managed to extract decent wages and working conditions from employers. There's no money in a corporatist system for the public good because our society is based too much on self-interest. Corporatism is a friend to conformity and an enemy to democracy: it encourages citizens to retreat to the cozy confines of whatever professional or interest group they occupy.

Politics is often separate from economics, contrary to what the neo-conservatives tell us. The corporatist and market theorists share a religious devotion to the market and an inability to see government as the justifiable force of the citizen. Their inability to see human beings driven by anything other than the market makes it impossible for them to imagine that 'pool of disinterest called the public good' (ibid., 84). Markets don't learn from the past, as we've seen in the countless economic booms and busts, upswings and recessions, over the last two centuries. The idea that market forces will automatically deliver prosperity has been refuted time and time again. Although a good way of conducting business (given proper regulations), the market doesn't create or encourage democracy (ibid., 134). How could a crucible of self-interest magically transform itself into a central pillar of the public good?

Saul considers the stripping of public assets by cost-cutting governments to be a form of religious self-flagellation. The fiscal crisis that motivated the cost-cutting was caused by steady reductions in the tax rate for corporations (ibid., 105–6). Similar to other critics of globalization discussed earlier in this chapter, Saul bemoans the fact that globalization has created a situation where if government tries to tax a transnational corporation above the 'going rate', the company just packs up and leaves. Yet none of this is part of destiny or fate; governments committed to the public good *can* come to international agreements to stop this corporate game if pushed to do so by their citizens. After all, most corporations have a lot of managerial fat to start with. Their cries for greater efficiency all too often come from executives with multi-million-dollar salaries.

The Critical Life and the Public Good

The source of political legitimacy is at the heart of all civilizations. There have been four distinct sources for this legitimacy in Western history: God, the king, groups, individuals. The first three forms reduce the individual citizen to a subject, while political individualism requires participation. Important decisions in our society today are made by negotiations between relevant groups. We live in a corporatist society that merely pretends to be a democracy. Power is slipping every day from individuals to groups. In fact, we know that expressions of too much individualism are often punished, and that the 'active, outspoken citizen is unlikely to have a successful professional career' (ibid., 31–2). Those in power don't like whistle-blowers and social critics, and are unlikely to offer them jobs.

Saul emphasizes the notion of the public good or 'common weal', which dates at least to the Enlightenment, if not the seventeenth century. This is the idea that a social or political good transcends all our individual self-interests. Hence the American colonies, such as Massachusetts, were often called 'commonwealths' to reflect this notion of working together for a common goal, in this case, carving out a home in the wilderness of the New Land. The concept of the public good is in direct contradiction to the view of neo-conservatives, who see the role of government as refereeing the conflict between the individual self-interests they see as making up society. Saul says that we can reassert a citizen-based society only by rediscovering the simple concepts of disinterest and participation, to protect ourselves against the seemingly unconscious desire to take refuge in ideology (ibid., 33).

Saul concludes that the very core of individualism is the refusal to mind your own business. He hearkens back to Socrates, who saw himself as a gadfly stinging the lazy beast of the *polis* (city-state), the citizens of Athens, to wake up and get involved. This critical life isn't a particularly pleasant or easy one:

> It often consists of being persistently annoying to others as well as being stubborn and repetitive. . . . Criticism is perhaps the citizen's primary weapon in the exercise of her legitimacy. That is why, in this corporatist society, conformism, loyalty and silence are so admired and rewarded; why criticism is so punished and marginalized. Who has not experienced this conflict? (Ibid., 165)

He concludes that corporatism depends on a citizen's desire for inner comfort. Our political participation consists of voting every few years and doing a bit of volunteering here and there. But being a critical and committed citizen of a democracy involves doing much more. A greater sense of equilibrium would depend on our recognition of reality (as opposed to ideology) and our acceptance of permanent discomfort, which is the acceptance of consciousness (ibid., 190). We have to wake our civilization up from a passive worship of ideologies, which today are dominated by those singing the praises of abstract reason, technology, the free market, globalization, and corporatism.

The Corporation

In this section we'll break with tradition and have a look at a film and its companion book, *The Corporation*. This Canadian film from 2003 is a doc-umentary by Mark Achbar, Jennifer Abbott, and Joel Bakan, the 2004 book of the same name by Bakan alone. They offer a critical history and analysis of the modern business corporation that fits in well with our theme of corporatism in this section. We'll start by looking at Part I of the film, 'The Pathology of Commerce', then move on to two key chapters in Bakan's book, those on externalities and democracy.

The film starts by contrasting the power of modern corporations to generate great wealth with their enormous ability to inflict harm on society. Enron and other corrupt corporations of the new millennium are compared by media pundits to a 'few bad apples' in the capitalist barrel. The film questions whether bad corporate behaviour is really just an anomaly, as the 'bad apple' explanation suggests. But what is the most appropriate metaphor for the corporation? The CEOs and intellectuals interviewed early in the film give us a few:

- A sports team.
- A family.
- The telephone system.
- People pulling together.
- A noble eagle.
- A monster like Godzilla devouring profit.
- A two-headed person.
- A beehive.
- A big machine.

This is obviously a very mixed bag of metaphors. Ultimately, a corporation is a group of individuals working together to make profits by legal means. Yet it's also a legal 'person'. Back in the seventeenth and eighteenth centuries chartered corporations had limited goals, e.g., building a bridge. They were liable for their legal misdeeds and could not own each other. Yet as the American economy took off after the Civil War (which ended in 1865), lawyers looked for a way to protect big business. They found it in the Fourteenth Amendment, which declared that no one could deprive a person of life, liberty, or property. It was meant to protect former slaves. But lawyers convinced the courts that corporations were persons too: they were 'legal' persons who, likewise, couldn't be deprived of their property. That way a corporation could buy and sell property, including other corporations, and could go bankrupt without the owners being liable for debts. The problem is that these so-called 'persons' don't have a conscience: their purpose is to make a profit. In fact, they're legally bound to put the interests of their stockholders first. Corporations always want to offload costs to someone else. These costs are called 'externalities', e.g., roads, power sources, unemployment insurance, environmental cleanup. Just as sharks are killing machines, corporations are externalizing machines. More on this later.

The core of Part I of *The Corporation* is a diagnosis of the corporate legal person as a psychopath as defined by the Personality Diagnostic Checklist in the World Health Organization's *Manual of Mental Disorders*. There are six points on the checklist, all of which apply to corporations. The film gives evidence for each psychopathic trait:

1. *Callous unconcern for the feelings of others.* The evidence here is the use by major corporations of sweatshops in the Third World. Activist Charles Kernaghan of the US National Labor Committee shows how a $15 shirt included only 3 cents of labour in its cost and recounts his visit to workers in a Honduran clothes factory where conditions were horrible. Michael Walker of the Fraser Institute—a Canadian pro-business think-tank—defends this practice, saying that when Nike sets up a plant in the Third World the locals see it as a godsend, even if the plant pays only 10 cents an hour.

2. *Incapacity to maintain enduring relationships.* Here the evidence given is the way that corporations set up factories in the Third World to employ desperate people, and then leave as soon as they become comfortable and demand higher wages. Naomi Klein discusses how Third World nations create free trade zones and then compete against each other by keeping labour costs and taxes at a minimum.

3. *Reckless disregard for the safety of others.* Here the examples are toxic waste, pollution, and the promotion of illness. Samuel Epstein, a med-

ical doctor, speaks of an epidemic of cancer and birth defects caused by synthetic petrochemicals from 1940 on.

4. *Deceitfulness: repeated lying and conning others for profit.* Here the example is Monsanto's promotion of Posilac, an artificial growth hormone for cows that increases milk production but causes the animals to suffer and allows antibiotics and pus to leak into the milk produced. Monsanto lied about the effects of this harmful drug.

5. *Incapacity to experience guilt.* The first evidence here is the use of Agent Orange by the American military in Vietnam, which caused thousands of birth defects and cancers. Monsanto was sued by American soldiers, lost, paid $80 million, but never admitted guilt. Other examples of environmental damage include the clear-cutting of forests, nuclear waste, CO_2 emissions leading to global warming, and massively polluted rivers.

6. *Failure to conform to social norms with respect to lawful behaviours.* Here Carlton Brown, a broker, notes that commodities traders ignore the social effects of their trading. Since clean air and water are not tradable commodities, they don't care about them. The film lists a long series of corporations that were fined large amounts in the 1990s, including Exxon (which was fined $125 million), GE, Chevron, Kodak, IBM, Sears, Pfizer, and Roche.

Corporations only obey the law if it's cost-effective. Ray Anderson of Interface, the world's largest commercial carpet manufacturer, fears that corporations are leaving behind a terrible legacy of a diminished environment for their grandchildren. He calls it an 'inter-generational tyranny'. Yet the problem is not the morality of individual CEOs but the stated purpose of corporations—to make money. Noam Chomsky, the noted linguist, author, and activist for peace and social change, talks in the film about how individual slave owners might have been very charming gentlemen while supporting a morally monstrous institution. We see the former head of Royal Dutch Shell, Sir Mark Moody-Stuart, charming some protestors at his house with tea and conversation, despite the fact that Shell has major investments in Nigeria, where the company indirectly promotes terrible pollution and the murder of dissidents. Part I ends with some examples of the corporate mindset: seeds genetically engineered to produce only one crop; Phil Knight of Nike refusing to visit his sweatshop factories in Indonesia; Ray Anderson's deploring of the corporation's role as a plunderer of the environment; Carlton Brown's excitement over the 9/11 attacks and war in Iraq for the profit-making opportunities they presented. The film concludes that the corporate person is indeed a psychopath.

Externalities

In his book, *The Corporation: The Pathological Pursuit of Profit and Power* (2004), Joel Bakan doesn't hesitate to lay his cards on the table:

> As a psychopathic creature, the corporation can neither recognize nor act upon moral reasons to refrain from harming others. Nothing in its legal makeup limits what it can do to others in pursuit of selfish ends, and it is compelled to cause harm when the benefits of doing so outweigh the costs. Only pragmatic concern for its own interests and the laws of the land constrain the corporation's predatory instincts, and often that is not enough to stop it from destroying lives, damaging communities, and endangering the planet as a whole. (Bakan, 2004: 60)

The modern corporation is forced by its very nature to 'externalize' as many of the costs of doing business as it can, to turn them into other people's problems. The most famous externality is, of course, environmental pollution. Yet Bakan also mentions how corporations try to offload their legal and moral responsibilities for injuries and deaths caused by their products to the public. He describes a legal suit involving the tendency of the 1979 Chevrolet Malibu to blow up real good when hit from behind in an accident. General Motors executives used a 'formula' to determine the cost of making safety improvements to the car as opposed to the costs involved in lawsuits con-

nected to fatalities their shoddy products caused. In the case of the Malibu, the cost of improved fuel tanks was $8.59 per car, while the estimated cost of legal actions against them was $2.40 per automobile, so naturally GM left the design of the car stand (ibid., 63). A cost-benefit analysis has nothing to do with moral responsibility and everything to do with the corporation's nature as an amoral externalizing machine.

A second example Bakan cites is the investigation by Charles Kernaghan of the use of Third World sweatshop labour by American corporations. Thanks to liberal trade laws in our globalized era, the practice has become common. Kernaghan went through a garbage dump in the Dominican Republic and found some Nike internal documents related to one of the company's local sweatshops. It contained a list of the time required to do each step in the process of making a shirt down to a ten-thousandth of a second: he calculates that Nike paid its local workers 8 cents per $23 shirt (ibid., 66). This exploitation burns out the lives of the young women working in the factories, who usually quit by the age of 25. Kernaghan also uncovered the use of sweatshop labour under terrible conditions to produce the Kathie Lee Gifford clothing line in Honduras. He and a young Honduran worker named Wendy Díaz contacted Gifford, who, once she realized the exploitation that was going on in her name, signed an agreement to stop using the sweatshops. The moral of the story is that corporations are psychopathic personalities that will use cheap labour working long hours in dreadful conditions to make a profit if they can get away with it (ibid., 69). By its very nature, the corporation tries to externalize its costs.

The more enlightened business leaders realize that in creating the corporation as a legal person whose purpose is only to seek wealth, we may have created a monster that will destroy us. Ray Anderson of Interface, seen in the film a number of times, believes that corporations are 'driving the biosphere to destruction' due to their false belief that nature has no limits as a source of raw materials and is a bottomless sink into which to dump our poisons and waste (ibid., 71–2). Yet the corporation is both programmed and legally compelled to externalize its costs even if this hurts people and nature (ibid., 73). Added to this is the fact that corporations regularly break the law and pay hefty fines when they are caught: Bakan lists four pages of convicted major corporate lawbreakers for the 1990s. Yet we shouldn't be surprised, for those who own and operate corporations are protected by law from any personal responsibility for corporate misdeeds. Corporations have no moral responsibility to do anything other than make a profit. If the money a company can make by doing something prohibited by law is greater than the costs of getting caught, then it goes ahead and does it (ibid., 80). In fact, the corporation's mandate, in a manner of speaking, *forces* it to break the law when there's money to be had. In the corporate world, nice guys finish last.

Democracy

In his chapter on corporations and democracy, Bakan argues that corporations use lobbying, political contributions, and public relations campaigns to influence government in a way that erodes democracy and takes away the average citizens' power to influence their representatives for the public good (ibid., 85). As pyschopaths, they are amoral: they have no feeling of any moral obligation to support democracy. In other words, capitalism and democracy are at odds with each other due to the very nature of the corporation, an entity whose purpose is to make money for its owners or stockholders.

In the 1930s corporations proved this to be true. Fascism was on the march in Europe—in Italy Mussolini had already seized power, while in Germany Adolf Hitler became Chancellor in 1933. American capitalism was in ruins due to the Depression. Franklin Delano Roosevelt became President in 1933, and he promptly put into place the New Deal, a series of reforms and regulations meant to put an end to the unfettered operation of the invisible hand of the free market, which had caused the stock market crash in the first place.

Naturally, the bankers and corporate chiefs were not pleased. They had no problem with working with fascism in Europe. Subsidiaries of GM and Ford produced trucks for the Nazi army in Germany, while IBM made punch-card machines to aid in the Nazis' mass extermination programs in the concentration camps (ibid., 88). Corporations were (and still are) amoral. Alfred Sloan, the chairman of General Motors, said in 1939 he didn't want to interfere in Germany's internal affairs by shutting down their profitable Opel plants.

Back in the States, representatives of several major companies—J.P. Morgan, Goodyear, Anaconda Copper, E.F. Hutton, Rockefeller Associates—tried to recruit a former Marine Corps general and war hero, Smedley Darlington Butler, to raise an army of veterans to march on Washington and impose himself as a sort of 'assistant president' who would overthrow Roosevelt if he didn't 'play ball' (ibid., 92). They wanted Butler to become a fascist dictator who would guarantee that their interests would be served by the US government. They offered Butler millions of dollars to put the plan into effect. The plan failed because Butler, who had led American interventions in Nicaragua, the Dominican Republic, and Cuba, was tired of being a 'racketeer for capitalism'. He revealed the plot to Congress and it fell apart. Now, long afterwards, big corporations no longer plan to install a fascist dictator in power. Instead, they use their substantial financial resources to buy control of the US government and get what they really want: freedom from democratic control of their activities (ibid., 95).

The main way that corporations try to get that freedom is by championing deregulation. Bakan mentions President George W. Bush's cutting the budget of the Mine Safety Bureau, which led to fewer inspections and an inability to enforce mine safety rules. This may have resulted in a potential mine disaster in 2002, when mines were flooded with water by drilling in the wrong place. Other than funding cuts to regulatory agencies, a second way that deregulation happens is by rolling back laws that protect the public interest. The most notorious case of this was the Enron debacle.

Enron, a large American energy corporation, spent big bucks lobbying and bribing Congress and federal bureaucrats to get rid of the regulation forcing energy companies to disclose their commodity trades to a federal agency (the Commodity Futures Trading Corporation) and the law requiring regulated auctions. Corrupt bureaucrats and lawmakers co-operated, and in 1993 and 2000 the disclosure regulation and auction law disappeared (ibid., 99). Enron was now able to make whatever energy deals it wanted without government scrutiny. The company manufactured an artificial electricity shortage in California, leading to 38 power blackouts in six months and much higher prices for electricity. Enron made huge profits. The wife of the senator who pushed the deregulation bill, Phil Gramm, was on Enron's board of directors. But when the US federal government imposed price controls on California's energy markets in June 2001, Enron's little scheme fell apart. It began to lose a lot of money and filed for bankruptcy. Yet Bakan does not blame corporations entirely for their attempt to buy influence over government: the job of a CEO isn't to protect democracy but to protect the corporation's profits.

Corporate lobbyists in Washington are paid huge amounts of money to either stop the government from introducing new regulations or reduce those already in place. This has especially been the case from the 1970s on, as corporations reacted to all the new social legislation coming out of the 1960s. All major corporations now have offices in Washington whose goal is to lobby for favourable laws and regulations. The second major way that corporations influence government is by means of campaign contributions, which the US Supreme Court protects. It's hard for a legislator to say no to a corporation that wants a certain law passed or jettisoned if he or she has taken thousands of dollars from that firm. Bakan gives several examples of these contributions from the coal industry, energy companies like Enron, and drug companies. In the wake of the 2003 Iraq War, critics have accused the Bush administration of being in the pocket of big oil companies and have noted that Halliburton, Vice-President Dick

Cheney's former firm, has unethically profited from government contracts to rebuild Iraq.

So corporations spend large sums of money on lobbying, campaign contributions, and public relations campaigns to get government policies changed in their favour. This is so much true that there is a real danger of the US government (and maybe all Western governments) being co-opted by big business. The rhetoric used by influence-peddling lobbyists includes phrases like 'helping government to understand the issues', 'sharing points of view', and establishing a 'symbiotic relationship' between two partners. Yet there are no powerful countervailing citizens' rights lobbies in America to oppose these corporate lobbyists (ibid., 106–7).

The idea that governments and corporations are equal partners sounds nice, but it is not democratic. In a true democracy, the people and their representatives have sovereignty over the actions of corporations. Talk of partnership means abdication of part of our democratic control over corporations (ibid., 108). It would be like walking up to random strangers on the street and offering to be their 'partner' in helping them to spend their money and manage their family affairs. We wouldn't put up with such effrontery in our personal lives—yet governments today put up with it from big business. In addition, how can the ordinary citizen stand up against a huge corporation? Only through the state. Some corporate representatives say that corporations, as partners, should be free to regulate themselves. Bakan argues that the idea of corporate social responsibility is a contradiction. Deregulation assumes that corporations will be socially and environmentally responsible without laws forcing them to be so. Yet we wouldn't want to repeal the laws against theft and murder in the hope that people could regulate themselves. Why should we think that institutional psychopaths—i.e., corporations—will regulate themselves?

The picture of corporatism in its narrow sense—the economic, political, and moral hegemony of business corporations—presented by Bakan is a dark one to say the least. Without sufficient taming and caging, the corporation is a ferocious predator one is best advised to avoid having in one's backyard. It's always hungry, and it's not picky about who it eats.

Naomi Klein on Branded Culture

Naomi Klein (1970–) is a Canadian journalist, cultural commentator, and activist. Her book *No Logo: Taking Aim at the Brand Bullies* (2000) is a sort of critical diary of the effects of corporatism (in its narrower sense) on the culture of the 1990s. In it she tells the story of how multinational corporations have come to dominate public life by selling brands and logos instead of products to the masses, thus commodifying both our outer physical and inner spiritual lives. More and more of us worship at the altar of Nike's swoosh, Starbucks' New Age mermaid, or Ralph Lauren's polo player. This has gutted public space and replaced the public square with shopping malls as the centre of a degraded public discourse. To paraphrase Descartes, too many of us today are only certain of our existence because we can say, 'I am branded, therefore I am.'[11]

Branding

Klein's central thesis about corporatism is that, in North America and Europe, we've moved from an economy that produces goods to one that sells *concepts* of those goods, brands:

> The astronomical growth in the wealth and cultural influence of multi-national corporations over the last fifteen years can arguably be traced back to a single, seemingly innocuous idea developed by management theorists in the mid-1980s: that successful corporations must primarily produce brands, as opposed to products. (Klein, 2000: 3)

At the start of the 1990s, corporate marketing types saw their world as filled with too many people and things and not enough concepts. They wanted to sell images of their companies and let overseas contractors deal with the messy business of actually producing the products their companies sell. The core meaning of the modern corporation—whether Nike, Ikea, The Gap, Body Shop, or AOL—is its brand, which is sold to the world via advertising (ibid., 5). This new paradigm associates a spiritual quality with the brand independent of any practical considerations of the quality of the products it represents: the Nike swoosh becomes for impressionable youth today what the Christian cross was a century ago. Corporations seek to free themselves from the corporeal world of commodities as part of a series of New Age vision quests headed up by high-profile CEOs such as Phil Knight of Nike and Richard Branson of Virgin (ibid., 22). They want to exist on another plane, to deindustrialize the West in terms of production while recommodifying it in terms of branding. In the extreme but increasingly common case, the corporate brand is like a celebrity's autograph. Tommy Hilfiger merely signs his name to his shirts and paraphernalia: his company doesn't directly manufacture any of them (ibid., 24).

Klein outlines a number of key events in the rise of the superbrands. This rise could be said to really have begun in 1988, when Philip Morris (the tobacco giant) bought Kraft for $12.6 billion, six times what it was worth (ibid., 8). They weren't just buying a lot of Kraft Dinner, but the Kraft name and logo. As branding replaced production as the key economic activity for major corporations in the Western world, advertising spending has steadily climbed. Yet a moment of panic came on 2 April 1993, when Phillip Morris announced it would cut the price of a pack of Marlboros by 20 per cent to compete with bargain brands (ibid., 12). Was marketing dead? Was advertising pointless in the face of cost-conscious consumers? Not at all. In the 1990s savvy 'attitude' brands like Nike and The Gap rewrote the book on how to advertise to the hot new demographic of 15–35-year-olds, while big-box stores such as Wal-Mart sucked up the retail bargain market like giant vacuum cleaners. A third option was seen in the 'organic' advertising of Starbucks, which avoided direct advertising but spread like a virus into the community through a variety of channels: cultural sponsorships, in-store cross promotions of other products, even political controversy (ibid., 20). Ad agencies began to see themselves not as corporate shills hocking patent medicines but as 'brand stewards' creating cultural and lifestyle images associated with the use of a company's products and services.

Logos Swallow Up Space

Of course, all brands are symbolized by logos. Back in the seventies, the company logo was usually discretely placed on a tag inside an article of clothing, perhaps reflecting a holdover of the anti-corporate feeling of the peace-and-love generation. But in the eighties, when being preppy and bourgeois became all the rage, Ralph Lauren's polo player and Izod Lacoste's alligator moved from the country club to the campus and the street (ibid., 28). By the 1990s, logo inflation was galloping ahead: we now see kids proudly wearing walking billboards for Nike or Tommy Hilfiger. Klein sees this logo inflation as part of a broader movement where popular (and in some cases even high) culture has been so soaked up by corporate sponsorships and direct sellouts to become a mere extension of corporate brands. The logo is the central focus of branding, the corporate equivalent of a religious icon. Mind you, ads always associated corporations' products with good cultural and social experiences. But today they seek to make these associations not through some sort of indirect connection—e.g., if I drink Molson's maybe pretty women will like me—but a lived reality—drinking Molson's in and of itself is cool, hip, a party (ibid., 29). It's true that there's no mythic brand-free past. The problem today is that the balance has tipped so far to what I've called 'corporatism' that there's a very real danger of our culture being stripped of any inherent value apart from the selling of corporate images (ibid., 39). In short, corporate advertising and sponsorships have created a 'third culture' beyond advertising and non-corporate everyday life: 'a self-enclosed

universe of brand-name people, brand-name products and brand-name media' (ibid., 60). Like the steers of yesteryear, most of us have been branded by our corporate masters.

Due to this integration between ads and art, brands and culture, Klein is concerned that unmarketed cultural space is fast closing up (ibid., 45). Walking down a busy street in any modern city would seem to confirm this fear. Klein isn't rabidly anti-corporation: she argues that culture has always been a compromise between the public good and the business ambitions of the rich and powerful (ibid., 34). Yet the problem in the 1990s was that brands didn't just sponsor culture—in many cases they *became* the culture. Celebrities like basketball star Michael Jordan rushed out to co-brand themselves with major corporations. In the wake of government cutbacks, schools, museums, and libraries actively seek corporate money to maintain their levels of service. At my own university, the University of Western Ontario, some of the buildings have corporate monikers: the Kresge Building, the 3M Centre, Labatt's Hall. Yet no one complains.

All of this leads to the loss of public space. Buses, streetcars, and taxis whiz by sporting moving billboards. Entire towns are branded by major corporations, the most famous being Disney's Celebration, Florida. Beer and alcohol companies sponsor or create rock music tours, making their brand, not the band and singers, the real stars. Even the bands themselves are marketed as brands, not artists: think of all those nineties stars who are slowly fading from memory—N'Sync, the Backstreet Boys, the Spice Girls. Big-budget Hollywood films are regularly marketed as 'branded media properties' with cross-promotions in fast-food restaurants (*Star Wars* placemats at McDonald's), toys (Batman and Catwoman action figures), on television (*Entertainment Tonight* and its many clones), and in bookstores (novelizations and comic-book treatments of the film). Klein mentions how the *Star Wars* franchise is co-promoted by Pepsi, Pizza Hut, and KFC (ibid., 44–5).[12] MTV, the purveyor of music videos and skin cleansers for teenagers, is a marketing tool not only for the products it advertises, but for itself as well. It shamelessly and continuously promotes itself. This is the thin end of the wedge for a new type of branded media outlet, one that makes no pretense of being independent from its corporate owners or place in the media market.

Perhaps more extreme as an example of corporate brands leading culture was The Gap's 1998 TV ad campaign for khaki pants featuring fresh-faced teenagers dancing to the swing music of their grandparents (ibid., 45). These ads didn't piggyback on a swing revival—in essence, they created one. The Gap was now in the culture-creation business. Although Klein doesn't mention it, her argument here parallels Jean Baudrillard's idea of the 'precession of simulacra', his tale of a society where simulacra of people and events *precede* their real-world equivalents (e.g., a nuclear disaster movie precedes Chernobyl). In many cases, brand-based culture now precedes general culture—which admittedly is produced for a profit, but not especially just to promote a corporation or product. Branded culture becomes a simulacrum of real culture. We also see this sort of thing on the Internet, where the line between editorial content and ads is blurred: newspaper websites have links selling the books they're reviewing, pop cultural commentaries are linked to amazon.com pages where the reader can buy the CD or DVD being commented on. Further, corporations have become 'content providers', creating branded media outlets on the Net (ibid., 43).

All of this has led to a situation where the creativity and congregation that make up culture are now seen as no longer possible without the largesse of corporate sponsorship or control (ibid., 35). There may be an itching sense of a loss of authenticity and alienation in consumers who witness this branding of culture. But a few sarcastic yawns won't stop the logo machine. Klein believes that today the very idea of unbranded space is unthinkable: brands and culture have merged (ibid., 59). And this is a fairly recent phenomenon. In the spring of 2006 CBC television rebroadcast the final game of the Edmonton Oilers' first Stanley Cup triumph from 1984. As I watched Gretzky bob and weave and Messier crash the net, I had a nagging sense that something was missing. I quickly realized what it was—they were playing in an unbranded hockey rink called Northlands Coliseum, and there were no ads on the ice, boards, or jerseys. Now advertising saturates pro sports—logos are everywhere. Culture isn't just owned by corporations: it's saturated with their self-images.

The Selling Out of Alternative Culture

What about alternative culture? Did it survive the brand explosion? Klein discusses the differences between the famous 1969 Woodstock music festival and its 1994 doppelgänger. Despite her obvious hostility to the 'baby boomers' who attended the original festival, she admits at least that their event was part of a meaningful generational self-definition whereas the 1994 event was sold to kids as a prepackaged good shaped by marketing hype. John Roberts, a promoter of Woodstock 1994, claims with some merit that without merchandise to buy, the kids would go out of their minds, and that selling out is 'considered hip'. The moral of the story for Klein is that the 1990s saw a colonization of both physical and mental space by corporate brands (ibid., 64–5). As a young woman, she felt a lack of space—all the archetypes had become empty and hackneyed, even that of the trendy black-clad intellectual. This led her generation to feel a deep craving for metaphorical space apart from consumer and branded culture, as expressed in the nineties in a renewed interest in the occult (think of the popularity of the TV show *The X-Files*), raves, extreme sports, even road hockey (ibid., 63–4).

The problem, from Klein's point of view, is that the youth subcultures of the 1970s and 1980s (e.g., punk and early rap) were largely ignored by marketers in favour of more merchandisable commodities such as disco and heavy metal. As late as the mid-eighties there was no Internet, no corporate rock tours, no mass-produced alternative culture such as Lilith Fair. Klein argues that a marketing paradigm shift happened in the late

1980s and early 1990s. Until then, consumerism was aimed at the 'consumption-crazed yuppies' of the Woodstock Nation (ibid., 67).[13] Then marketers realized that they were targeting the wrong demographic; instead, they decided that the kids were, indeed, all right, and used subtle forms of advertising-induced peer pressure to herd youth to the shopping mall. Corporations now embraced nineties cool: the new music, the new styles, even the new (largely ironic) politics. The transcendent brand companies all wanted to be alternative, young, and hip, as that most ephemeral of all social qualities— 'cool'—became the touchstone of branding (ibid., 70). As all high schoolers know, the quest for cool is riddled with self-doubt. Yet it has come to dominate the modern marketplace. Ad writers, art directors, and CEOs became 'turbo-powered teenagers' who asked themselves over and over, Hamlet-like, 'do the kids think I'm cool?' (ibid., 69).

To help them answer this question, they hired 'cool hunters' to search out pockets of cutting-edge lifestyles to turn into branded products (ibid., 72). Their favourite place to look for these lifestyles was among young black Americans, from whom they borrowed both a sense of identity and a justification for turning ball caps, baggy jeans, and Nike sneakers into consumer fetishes. Klein dates this to 1986, when the rap group Run-DMC penned a homage to their favourite sneakers, 'My Adidas'. A year later, the rappers and the shoe company were doing cross-promotions. Later, Nike enthusiastically jumped on the bandwagon, borrowing heavily from black urban youth, especially the hip-hop culture of the 1990s. In return they swooshed inner-city basketball courts and sports programs. The previously preppy Tommy Hilfinger even joined in, changing its marketing style to feed off the alienation of the American racial divide by selling white suburban youth a fetishized version of black culture—baggy jeans and hoodies—and black youth a fetishized version of white wealth—what used to be seen as skiing, golfing, and boating gear (ibid., 76).

One alternative to the fetishizing of black culture is being an 'in-between', ironically consuming things *knowing* that you're doing so, especially kitschy culture that has previously been branded 'uncool'. Klein mentions karaoke bars and such bad movies as *Showgirls* in this regard (ibid., 77–8). Of course, the cozy, self-referential niche that irony represents doesn't disguise the fact that the ironist is still consuming *something*, still buying a brand. A third tentacle of branding, other than the co-optation of street styles and ironic detachment, is the revival of some largely forgotten past pop cultural phenomenon—for example, Hollywood films of old TV shows such as *Lost in Space*, *Starsky and Hutch*, *Charlie's Angels*, and *The Dukes of Hazzard* (ibid., 79). In all cases, street style and youth culture have become marketable commodities, with street snitches in the 'hood' and brand shills on campus helping interpret this culture for the corporations. Yet the real rock stars today are the superstar CEOs like Phil Knight and Richard Branson, professional teenagers without the homework and chores.

For Klein, all of this has exposed the impotence of all other forms of political resistance to the status quo except anti-corporate resistance embodied in taking on specific marketing trends (ibid., 81). Yet, as she admits later, the danger of anti-brand activism is that it becomes a mirror image of brand culture—the activist wears a Greenpeace symbol instead of a Nike swoosh on her T-shirt. Cool and anti-cool just trade places, both equally branded. Klein senses part of the futility her own generation of activists feel when discussing that great failed subculture of the early 1990s, the Seattle music scene centred on bands such as Nirvana, Pearl Jam, and Soundgarden. These Seattle heroes couldn't express a single solid political position, being trapped in the 'headlights of irony' their music fostered (ibid., 83). When you're trying to be 'in-between' mainstream consumerism and activist chic, it's hard to ignore the 800-pound culture industry gorilla sitting on the couch beside you trying to sell you boy band CDs, Gap shirts, and Nike sneakers. Being campy isn't possible in a consumer culture where most participate ironically, not taking their acts of consumption entirely seriously. In the end Klein's acid test of alternative politics and culture is simple enough: if a movement is a fad affected by events in the fashion and advertising industries, it doesn't really challenge the structures of economic and political power (ibid., 85). She should have continued this thought by asking, 'What movement since the late eighties *has not* been affected by trends in fashion and advertising?'

No Choice

Just as the first part of Klein's book is entitled 'No Space', recounting the decline of unbranded physical and cultural space in the 1990s, the second part is titled 'No Choice', telling the story of how corporations have reduced our consumer and cultural choices. This assault on choice is a three-pronged attack:

- Structurally, in terms of corporate mergers, company buy-outs, and the evolution of 'synergy' (which is basically one corporate structure selling different but related products, e.g., a film studio selling DVDs, branded clothes, and comic books).
- Locally, as superbrands like Wal-Mart and Ikea swallow up local businesses.
- Legally, as corporations protect their trademarks and copyrights through lawsuits and by criminally punishing samplers and downloaders (ibid., 130).

Klein sees parallels between the privatization of language and cultural discourse brought about by copyright bullying and other measures aimed at protecting corporate property and the privatization of space, which has come from the erection of superstores, theme-park malls, and branded villages. These private branded enclaves become de facto town squares, pseudo public–private spaces where only consumer chatter is allowed. Community discussions, political rallies, and protests are strictly verboten: only a few tastes from the ice-cream barrel of pop culture are allowed (ibid., 182–3). More and more, we live, we gather, and we shop in corporate-controlled spaces where our choices are limited. Carnival on the outside, a solidification of the corporate control of culture and the economy on the inside.

Multinational corporations don't want real diversity; instead, they want armies of teen clones marching in uniform to the global mall (ibid., 129). National habits and regional quirks are their enemies. 'Brand bombing' is their chosen attack strategy, which uses several distinct tactics. First, Wal-Mart uses the blanket bombing approach, blanketing an area with stores while it sets up a regional distribution centre. This has helped it to become the largest retailer on the continent. Its huge windowless stores sit like Leibniz's monads on cheap land on the dark edges of town where the taxes are low. These retail monads then lure shoppers to the suburbs with their gargantuan selection and cheap prices, sucking the life out of the community and of competing small businesses, which eventually close up shop. Downtowns are hollowed out, while the suburbs become a 'geography of nowhere' accessible only by cars (and for students and the underclass, crowded buses) (ibid., 130). Selection comes to dominate choice. Sure, upscale neighbourhoods still have their trendy boutiques; but the masses do their shopping at the self-replicating clones of Wal-Mart, Future Shop, Starbucks, Ikea, The Gap, and other megastores. These expand like identical pieces of a Lego set, snapping on one new piece at a time. As a result, public space is redefined: open public spaces, unbranded alternatives, and uncensored art are all disappearing (ibid., 131). Life takes place at the mall, in the aisle of Wal-Mart, or on-line in the virtual aisles of amazon.com or bestbuy.ca.

The second brand-bombing tactic—Starbucks' cluster bombing of franchises in one select area after another—is a bit more subtle than Wal-Mart's blanket approach. Starbucks saturates an area with its cafés, often buying up other cafés or chains, and in a few cases even poaching leases from competitors (ibid., 136–7). One day there's no Starbucks in town; a year later a half-dozen or more franchises. The domination of cityscapes by strip malls and big-box stores has led to a hunger for the old-fashioned town square, which

Starbucks and megastores such as those built by Virgin, Chapters, and Barnes and Noble attempt to simulate (ibid., 135). Book signings, concerts, and talks now take place in these private branded spaces instead of in libraries and real town squares. In all these franchises, whether they are mammoth big boxes or intimate cafés, shoppers become brand-obsessed, adopting an almost fetishistic approach to buying (ibid., 141). The brand name has become a talisman, with generic products being reserved for the poor and uneducated.

As the attempts at censorship of the Internet by the AOL thought police have shown, meaningful opportunities to speak loud enough to break through commercial noise are fast disappearing (ibid., 185). Do we live in a fascist state where we all salute the logo, with no opportunity for criticism of corporate interests? Klein admits that there are still some exceptions to corporate censorship, her own book being one, Michael Moore's 1997 anti-corporate film, *The Big One*, which was distributed by Disney-owned Miramax, another (ibid., 187).[14] Yet, clearly, we're losing space where the non-corporate mind can flourish. Perhaps it's not a question of having 'no choice', but of our choices quickly closing down.

Discarded Production

Following quite logically from her section on 'No Choice', the third part of Klein's book is titled 'No Jobs'. It outlines how good manufacturing jobs have left North America and Europe for points east and south to help pay for all that corporate branding and advertising in the nineties. Products are made in factories, but it's the brands that First World consumers buy. Branding has allowed corporations to create wondrous new souls. Yet the Faustian bargain they had to make for these branded souls was to rid themselves of their cumbersome bodies, weighed down by the massive costs of corporate mergers, marketing, and advertising, so they moved most production from high-wage Europe and North America to the low-wage Third World (ibid., 196). Labour costs are a shrinking part of corporate budgets, as the people

who actually make the products sold by corporations become chaff thrown to the wind. In some cases corporations 'outsource' all of their production—Nike, for example, doesn't actually own any factories. They are a simulacrum of a manufacturing corporation. The 1990s saw a series of massive layoffs and factory closures in North America and Europe, despite healthy corporate profits. These jobs didn't disappear: they rematerialized in factories in China, the Philippines, Indonesia, Vietnam, Mexico, and other places where governments were willing to enforce low wages, poor working conditions, and a no-union rule with the policeman's baton.

Branded corporations are like shoppers searching for cheap labour in a global industrial supermarket—and they don't care *why* the labour they buy is so cheap (ibid., 202). One way this is done is by the creation of hundreds of 'free-trade zones', sometimes called 'export processing zones' (EPZs), throughout the poorer half of the world, most of them concentrated in East Asia and Central America. Those just across the Rio Grande in northern Mexico are called *maquiladoras*—they have prospered since NAFTA was signed. Klein discusses in detail one such EPZ called Cavite, located in the city of Rosario in the Philippines, where a hodge-podge of Nike, The Gap, IBM, Old Navy, and other products are assembled. The Cavite workers live in a tax-free miniature military state, working long hours for paltry pay for contractors filling orders for North American and European companies. There are at least 850 EPZs in 70 countries around the world employing about 27 million workers, with 124 zones in China alone (ibid., 205). Manufacturing is concentrated in the zones like toxic waste. In them we find abusive supervisors, subsistence or lower wages, low-skill tedious work, and a refusal to commit to the local community.[15] Workers and politicians are in constant fear of these industrial 'swallows' flying the coop, taking with them their order sheets and jobs. So contractors are lured by Third World governments to the zones with zero taxes, low minimum wages, lax workplace regulations, squads of military goons ready to enforce order, and a militant anti-union policy. This is zero-risk globalization (ibid., 207). Yet there is no permanent development: the workers in the zones can't afford the products they make, and if they unionize to raise their wages the swallows take flight for warmer fiscal climes. The contractors producing goods in the zones are economic tourists who aim to reproduce in the Third World the industrial slums that populated the cities of the early Industrial Revolution in Europe. There's no trickle-down of benefits.

The rules for workers in the free-trade zones are simple: no unions, no strikes, forced overtime, no job security, you have to work to get paid (i.e., no long-term guarantee of steady work hours), and if you get pregnant you're gone. The zone workers are mostly contract employees or part-timers, and are often young women from small towns or villages who are fired when they reach their mid-twenties (ibid., 221). The zones have created a radical shift in the nature of work: their workforce is largely 'footloose' young childless women. The factories themselves are mobile, fleeing rising wages and environmental regulations, as contractors did from South Korea and Taiwan in the late 1980s when unions demanded more than dollar-a-day wages (ibid., 224). Yet this is not the classic Marxist division between workers and owners, since multinational corporations have divested themselves of the 'means of production' to contractors, allowing them to advertise their brands and play merger and divestment games back home. Overall, we see the corporate divestment from the world of work in the creation of the free-trade zones. This is reflected in the drive to hire more and more temps, part-timers, and freelancers in North America and Europe (ibid., 229).

Temp Nation

Continuing on with the theme of 'no jobs', Klein discusses the winds of impermanence blowing through the workforce in North America and Europe: temporary, contract, retail, and fast-food jobs now greatly outweigh high-paying, permanent factory and office jobs. As we have seen in discussing the postmodern economy, the service sector houses about 75 per cent of jobs in North America. This enforced 'casualization' of labour has come from corporations that want a fluid reserve of part-timers and freelancers to ride the rising and falling waves of the marketplace and thereby maximize profits. Offering full-time work with benefits and security is out of economic fashion (ibid., 231). Yet retail clerks are still needed to sell all those products made in China, Mexico, and the Philippines. To keep profits high, corporations have become artful at dodging commitments to their service-industry employees, infantilizing their jobs, treating them as little more than hobbies with tips (ibid., 232). Most service workers buy into this paradigm, all those Starbucks baristas, Chapters clerks, and Wal-Mart checkout girls seeing their jobs as temporary, as a springboard to something better that in some cases never comes. In fact, brand-name clothing and fast-food companies actively encourage the idea that their clerking jobs are disposable temporary employment for teenagers and twenty-somethings, and by no means real careers. Thus wages are kept at or near legal minimums, with corporations using their profits to open up new franchises—despite the fact that our consumer economy needs a large base of consumers being paid more than poverty-line wages to prosper. After all, minimum-wage video store clerks don't buy too many $25,000 Fords or $2,000 computer packages (ibid., 238).

So in both the export processing zones of the Third World and the cafés and food courts of the West, corporations have managed to avoid paying a living wage to their employees (ibid., 237).[16] The branded chains usually fight unionization, sometimes closing down outlets after successful union drives and always suggesting to potential union members that they might be gambling away their jobs. Added to this is the fact that the number of part-time workers in North America is way up over the last generation: in Canada from 1975 to 1997, three times as many part-time as full-time jobs were created (ibid., 242). Almost all Starbucks baristas are part-time, reflecting a general trend throughout the retail sector. Further, Klein points out that Starbucks, Wal-Mart, and other major players in the service industry purposely give their employees just less than 40 hours a week in shifts, thus avoiding the full-time cutoff that brings with it overtime pay, benefits, and a higher wage scale (ibid., 244).[17] Even worse than this rise of part-time labour is the use of unpaid workers as interns and apprentices in the cultural industries: at magazines, MTV and Much Music, TV network news, and other broadcast outlets. Here the young and the naive slave away for nothing in the hope that one day they'll be the next star VJ or *Sex and the City*-style columnist. In addition, there has been a massive increase in the use of temporary workers in the economy. These people who shuttle from job to job, assigned by Manpower Temporary Services and similar firms from week to week to corporations who need no-commitment short-term staff. The use of temps in the US was up 400 per cent between 1982 and 2000; Klein estimates that there are now 36 million temporary workers in America and Europe (ibid., 247–8).

Yet won't the high-tech industry save us? What about the 'shimmering digital mecca' of Silicon Valley and its clones elsewhere, with their promise of silicon gold? As Klein points out, the digital gold rush is long over, the richest streams already panned out. Now even Microsoft is trying to shed itself of employees by outsourcing divisions, hiring freelance programmers and technologists, and making their products in factories owned by contractors (ibid., 249). The company now relies more and more on 'permatemps' who have none of the generous stock options or job security of the original microserfs, and who aren't even welcome at the midnight pizza parties. The company has also amputated entire divisions and contracted out such internal functions as the mailroom, photocopying, and even the company store (ibid., 252). In short, Bill Gates won't save us.

Some erstwhile futurists talk about self-incorporation and of the coming of a Free Agent Nation full of 'extreme self-employers' as ways to deal with the rise of part-time and contract work. Not everyone, however, can be a freelance writer

working in a trendy downtown loft, making oodles of cash; most 'casualized' or temporary workers work for low wages and without benefits or security (ibid., 254). This is in sharp contrast to the temp CEOs who work a few years at a given firm, make kamikaze cuts to the company workforce, and then exit stage right with multi-million dollar 'golden handshakes' in their back pockets. Klein mentions several examples, with George Fisher, CEO of Eastman Kodak in 1997, standing out: he cut 20,100 jobs and got a US $60 million bonus for his efforts (ibid., 256). That bonus by itself is the equivalent of 3,000 jobs at $20,000 a year. In the post-industrial West, corporate profits have been unplugged from job creation.

Brand-based Politics and Its Limitations

In the final section of *No Logo*, Klein discusses in detail culture jamming, the Situationist-inspired 'reclaim the streets' movement, and other forms anti-brand and anti-corporate activism. Since we have already looked at culture jamming and Situationism in Chapter 4 on critical theory, we'll skip over most of this material and head straight to her conclusions. The questionable ethics of modern multinational corporations in relation to Third World sweatshops, the destruction of the natural environment, union busting, and the denial of workers' rights are connected to a broader global economic system aimed at reducing all barriers to trade. The big question for anti-corporatist activists is how to assault this system. One way is to attack one logo or brand at a time—this seems to be a practical tactic that empowers the often powerless people making the attacks. Since the multinationals are the 'celebrity face of global capitalism', when one of them comes under close public scrutiny, the whole system is put under a microscope (ibid., 421). Yet this tactic lets all the other corporate villains off the hook—it shines the ethical spotlight on a single corporation at a time, leaving the rest in moral darkness. Individual companies respond by writing their own codes of conduct or by signing on to those created by industry associations.

This leads to a situation where companies adhere to ethical standards of conduct in a haphazard and piecemeal way, with no universal code of corporate behaviour in the offing.

Brand-based activism lets resource companies off hook, too, since most aren't 'branded' and don't care about their public image. Their conduct can only be challenged by secondary boycotts of their products, e.g., old-growth logging in British Columbia was challenged by a boycott of companies such as 3M, Kinko's, and Home Depot that used the wood and paper coming from the harvested trees. Second, in our Age of Shopping, it's hard to make people feel guilty about going to the mall. Third, if we really need the 'glittering presence' of celebrity logos like those of Nike and McDonald's to create a sense of shared humanity and collective responsibility, maybe brand-based activism is the ultimate triumph of branding (ibid., 428). The danger is that brand-based campaigns will degenerate into ethical shopping guides with their own snazzy logos and T-shirts.

Klein follows Saul in arguing that we need democratically elected governments writing laws and treaties and ordinary citizens working through unions and human rights groups to compel corporations to pay workers fair wages, create fair working conditions, and protect the environment. The key to improving the condition of the workers in the free-trade zones of China, the Philippines, Central America, and elsewhere is to provide guarantees that unions can be formed and bargain freely without the fear of government bullying or capital flight (ibid., 436). Corporate codes of conduct aren't democratic. When we let corporations regulate themselves, we've given up on a basic democratic principle—that government represents and regulates *all* of us. We need public political solutions to the abuse of corporate power, not promises from corporations that they will be good if we leave them alone. Klein ends her book on an optimistic note. At the end of the 1990s, she saw a broad citizen-based movement against the excesses of globalization made up of culture jammers, Situationists, service industry union organizers, human rights watchdogs, and anti-corporate fighters coming into being. It uses some of the technology of globalization to help create a co-ordinated global network to resist the growing power of corporatism (ibid., 446). This struggle between corporations and ordinary citizens is an ongoing affair, one sure to make the nightly news now and again in the years to come.

STUDY QUESTIONS

1. What changes to Western economic policies did John Maynard Keynes propose? How did Franklin D. Roosevelt respond to the Depression? How did each affect post-World War II policies of Western governments?

2. What were the Bretton Woods agreements? What new internal organizations did they create? What events in the 1960s and 1970s led to a partial collapse of these agreements?

3. What are the neo-liberal and social democratic approaches to the global economy today? Defend one of them in detail.

4. What are NAFTA and the WTO? What effects on globalization did they have? Were these effects positive or negative?

5. What are Ritzer's four categories of McDonaldization? Give examples for each category based on franchises and institutions in your hometown.

6. What forces drive McDonaldization? What are its advantages? Are these advantages worth the negative effects of McDonaldization that Ritzer outlines?

7. How has McDonaldization affected the mass media, travel, and education? How has life at your university been 'McDonaldized'?

8. Outline three or four of the 10 major aspects of globalization, giving examples from your own experience of how globalization has affected your life.
9. What does Giddens mean when he says we live in a 'risk' society? How is this related to his view of late modernity as a post-traditional order?
10. What is Giddens's attitude towards globalization? Compare this to the view of Bauman, Kellner, or Ritzer, defending one theorist's position.
11. How does Giddens think that globalization has affected family life and democracy? Has this effect been positive or negative?
12. How does Bauman connect globalization to changes in human mobility and perceptions of space? What aspects of the way you view space today would be radically different from those of a person of the same age, sex, and class living in 1900?
13. What does Bauman mean by 'tourists' and 'vagabonds'? Is this a good way of dividing classes in the new global economy?
14. How, according to both Giddens and Bauman, has globalization affected the nation-state? Evaluate these effects: do we live in a more democratic world today than a generation ago?
15. What, for Kellner, are the two main components of 'technocapitalism'? What are its political effects? How does his article criticize other theories of globalization?
16. What does Ritzer mean by 'nothing', 'something', and 'the globalization of nothing'? What are his four 'nullities'? Give an example or two of each nullity from your own everyday life.
17. How does Ritzer define 'grobalization' and 'glocalization'? Give examples of each.
18. How does Ritzer connect globalization to capitalism, McDonaldization, and Americanization? Do any of these forces conflict with globalization, or do they all support it?
19. How does Saul define corporatism? What sorts of language does a corporatist society promote? What's wrong with these types of language according to Saul? Evaluate his position.
20. What does Saul think is the relationship between democracy and capitalism? Why does he think the neo-conservatives have misunderstood this?
21. Is Saul right when he says that living a critical life in a corporatist society is very difficult?
22. Outline the argument made by the film *The Corporation* that business corporations are psychopaths. Have the filmmakers overstated their case or is it valid? Explain your position.
23. Outline Bakan's argument that corporations, by their very nature, undermine democracy.
24. Why does Klein think that we are now living in a branded society? How has the attitude of corporations to production and workers changed over the last 20 years? What effect did this change have on corporate priorities?
25. How did alternative culture sell out to corporations in the 1990s? Do you think this was entirely the corporations' fault, or did young people co-operate in this sell out?
26. How does the 'outsourcing' of production to the Third World tie into Klein's general critique of branded culture and corporatism? What do you think of the conservative argument that providing *any* industrial jobs to countries like the Philippines and Indonesia is better than nothing?
27. Is Klein right that we live more and more in an economy dominated by temporary and part-time non-union labour? Is this an inevitable product of globalization or simply an attempt by greedy capitalists to extract more surplus value from the working class?

SHORT BIBLIOGRAPHY

Bakan, Joel. 2004. *The Corporation: The Pathological Pursuit of Profit and Power.* New York: Free Press.
Barlow, Maude. 2001. 'The Last Frontier', *The Ecologist* 31 (Feb.): 38–43.
Baudrillard, Jean. 2002. *The Spirit of Terrorism and Requiem for the Twin Towers*, trans. Chris Turner. London: Verso.
Bauman, Zygmunt. 1998. *Globalization: The Human Consequences.* Cambridge: Polity Press.

Beck, Ulrich. 2000. *What Is Globalization?*, trans. Patrick Camiller. Cambridge: Polity Press.

Bell, Daniel. 1960. *The End of Ideology: On the Exhaustion of Political Ideas in the Fifties.* Glencoe, Ill.: Free Press.

Bleyer, Peter. 2000. 'The Other Battle in Seattle', *Studies in Political Economy* 62 (Summer): 25–34.

Clarke, Tony. 2000. 'Taking on the WTO: Lessons from the Battle of Seattle', *Studies in Political Economy* 62 (Summer): 7–16.

Collingsworth, Terry, J. William Goold, and Pharis J. Harvey. 1994. 'Labor and Free Trade: Time for a Global New Deal', *Foreign Affairs* 73 (Jan.–Feb.): 8–13.

Gates, Bill. 1995. *The Road Ahead.* New York: Viking.

Giddens, Anthony. 1991. *Modernity and Self-Identity: Self and Society in the Late Modern Age.* Stanford, Calif.: Stanford University Press.

———. 1999. *Runaway World.* Cambridge: Polity Press. Reith Lectures for the BBC. Also at <www.lse.ac.uk/Giddens/RunawayWorldPR.htm>. Cited from web version.

———. 2000. *Runaway World: How Globalization Is Reshaping Our Lives.* New York: Routledge.

———. 2003. 'The Director's Home Page', London School of Economics, at: <www.lse.ac.uk/Giddens>.

Hardt, Michael, and Antonio Negri. 2000. *Empire.* Cambridge, Mass.: Harvard University Press.

Helleiner, Eric. 1994. 'From Bretton Woods to Global Finance: A World Turned Upside Down', in Richard Stubbs and Geoffrey R.D. Underhill, eds, *Political Economy and the Changing Global Order.* Toronto: McClelland & Stewart.

Huntington, Samuel P. 1993. 'The Clash of Civilizations?', *Foreign Affairs* 72: 22–49.

———. 1996. *The Clash of Civilizations and the Remaking of the World Order.* New York: Simon & Schuster.

Kapstein, Ethan B. 1998–9. 'A Global Third Way: Social Justice and the World Economy', *World Policy Journal* 15 (Winter): 23–35.

Kellner, Douglas. 2002. 'Theorizing Globalization', *Sociological Theory* 20, 3: 285–305.

Klein, Naomi. 2000. *No Logo: Taking Aim at the Brand Bullies.* Toronto: Vintage.

Lash, Scott, and John Urry. 1994. *Economies of Signs and Spaces.* London: Sage.

McQuaig, Linda. 1998. *The Cult of Impotence: Selling the Myth of Powerlessness in the Global Economy.* Toronto: Viking.

———. 2001. *All You Can Eat: Greed, Lust and New Capitalism.* Toronto: Viking.

Nichols, John. 2000. 'Now What? Seattle Is Just a Start', *The Progressive* 64 (Jan.): 16–21.

Peet, Richard. 1999. *Theories of Development.* London: Guilford Press.

Pieterse, Jan Nederveen. 2000. 'After Post-Development', *Third World Quarterly* 21 (Apr.): 175–92.

Ritzer, George. 2000. *The McDonaldization of Society*, revised New Century edn. Thousand Oaks, Calif.: Pine Forge Press.

———. 2004. *The Globalization of Nothing.* Thousand Oaks, Calif.: Pine Forge Press.

Robinson, Ian. 1995. 'Globalisation and Democracy', *Dissent* (Summer): 373–80.

Saul, John Ralston. 1995. *The Unconscious Civilization.* Concord, Ont.: Anansi.

Sklair, Leslie. 2001. *The Transnational Capitalist Class.* Cambridge: Blackwell.

Steil, Benn. 1994. '"Social Correctness" Is the New Protectionism', *Foreign Affairs* 73 (Jan.–Feb.): 14–20.

Urry, John. 2000. *Sociology beyond Societies: Mobilities for the Twenty-first Century.* London: Routledge.

Wikipedia articles on Bretton Woods, the World Bank, GATT, NAFTA, and the WTO, at: <en.wikipedia.org>.

Film

The Corporation. 2003. A film by Jennifer Abbott, Mark Achbar, and Joel Bakan.

NOTES

CHAPTER 1

1. I follow Glover (1960), Chitnis (1976), and Swingewood (1970) in the following pages.
2. Scotland and England were united by the Act of Union of 1707 as Great Britain, a union the Scottish elites of the day were quite enthusiastic about due to the economic progress it promised.
3. Arthur Herman, in his *How the Scots Invented the Modern World: The True Story of How Western Europe's Poorest Nation Created Our World and Everything in It* (New York: Crown, 2001), gives the Scots credit for all of modernity. This is perhaps an exaggeration, though certainly no worse a position than that taken by those who entirely ignore the role of the Scottish Enlightenment in founding the modern social sciences, assuming that their birth was the work of French and English theorists.
4. Later in his life, after a tragic love affair with Clothide de Vaux, Comte embraced a 'religion' of humanity based on the idea of universal love as an adjunct to his positivism. This line of thought was largely contrary to the contributions he made earlier and will not be examined here.
5. To confuse things even further, 'modern' sociological theory usually refers to works produced after World War I (1918) or after Weber's death (1920). This makes almost all of the theorists discussed in depth in this book 'modern', excluding the classical triad of Marx, Durkheim, and Weber and the transitional figures G.H. Mead and Sigmund Freud.
6. A sizable literature by scientific 'realists' of various stripes calls into question the assumptions behind Kuhn's paradigmatic concept.

CHAPTER 2

1. John Boorman's 1974 film *Zardoz* fits Dahrendorf's model of utopias perfectly.
2. In the Sonoran Desert just outside Tucson, Arizona, the US military maintains an airplane graveyard where 4,000 obsolete aircraft sit parked, waiting to be cannibalized for their spare parts or used as target drones. Assuming a nominal cost of $15 million per plane (the price of an F-111 fighter/bomber in 1973), this 'boneyard' of dead planes represents at least $60 billion of military spending, or about $200 billion in 2004 dollars. The entire Canadian military budget in 2004 was $12.9 billion.
3. John Porter's *The Vertical Mosaic* (1965) makes a similar argument in regard to Canada.
4. During World War II, the Germans in their propaganda films and posters depicted the Jews, Russians, and other enemies as animalistic, as did the Americans in their depiction of the Japanese enemy. American comic books of the 1942–5 period, for example, show the same reduction of an enemy to subhuman status.

CHAPTER 3

1. This little story is fictional, yet could easily be true. Its purpose is to illustrate some of Marx's central ideas.
2. Of course, this begs the question of how bourgeois intellectuals like Marx and Engels could penetrate the ideological veil surrounding their own class biases and develop the theory of historical materialism in the first place.
3. It should be noted that even the brief sketch of Marx's materialism offered in this section is highly contentious. Scholars of Marxism usually distinguish between the 'young Marx' of the 1840s, a somewhat romantic philosophical rebel still under the spell of Hegel who was very much aware of the human capacity to change the environments we live in, and the 'mature Marx' of the 1850s and later

who was more interested in economic statistics, the mechanics of the capitalist economy, and the 'iron laws' of history. We find most of the language of economic determinism in the mature Marx.

4. To be fair, however, Marx himself rejected the possibilities of a purely 'local' communism and a successful proletarian revolution in Russia, which in the nineteenth century was still a backward peasant society ruled by an autocratic Czar.

5. To be more accurate, Marx said that the value of a commodity was the 'socially necessary labour time' required to make it, not especially the *actual* amount of labour put into it. The former is the amount of time an average worker must expend making the product given current levels of technology and industrial organization.

6. Czar Alexander II had liberated the serfs in 1861 and gave the Russian peasantry some control over their local village affairs, though their situation was still a miserable one.

7. Phenomenologists study human experience free from moral or psychological prejudices. They do things like focusing on a single experience of colour or sound, or a single emotion, seeing these things as distinct 'phenomena' (hence 'phenomenology') that can be understood without bringing in physical science, moral codes, or religious ideas. Husserl called this freeing of ourselves of moral and other forms of judgement the 'phenomenological reduction' of experience.

8. Granted, books, music, and art have a material component, yet their 'essence' consists of ideas, sounds, and visual images, respectively.

9. In fact, Bourdieu says that one doesn't have to be a Machiavellian schemer to win the game of social distinction—it's better if you really believe in the superiority of cultural capital your class sees as sacrosanct (Bourdieu, 1986: 257). Yet the concept of 'habitus' seems to contain an inherent cynicism about culture—for Bourdieu, one cannot appreciate cultural objects in themselves but only as members of a given class.

10. I am relying mostly on the excerpts from these early works found in *Jean Baudrillard: Selected Writings* (2001) edited by Mark Poster. Unless otherwise indicated, all Baudrillard references in this chapter come from this book.

11. This idea was revived by President George W. Bush after the 11 September 2001 terrorist attacks when he urged his fellow US citizens to go out and shop to keep America strong.

12. This isn't to deny the obvious fact that hammers are quite useful, but instead to point out that in capitalist societies the hammer's use value is swallowed up by its exchange value. Besides, how many hammers does one have to buy in a lifetime? If the answer is only 'one', then the hammer industry is in trouble.

13. This despite the fact that European countries such as Germany, Sweden, and Norway have mixed economies with strong public sectors and some Latin American countries, such as Fidel Castro's Cuba and Hugo Chavez's Venezuela, are ruled by socialist parties.

14. Except as ironic consumer images or to advertise products like Revolution Soda.

CHAPTER 4

1. Older translations render the German as 'the real is rational, and the rational is real', which gives one a livelier picture of his holistic view of things, though confusing what Hegel meant by 'actuality' and 'reality'.

2. My example is a negative one; in most cases, Hegel's philosophy of history is the story of progress.

3. Karl Popper and others have argued that when Hegel said that Spirit's culmination can be found only within the state, he meant specifically the Prussian state of his own day, making his philosophy of history a massive justification of the status quo. This is an oversimplification, but it is based on some reasonable inferences from what Hegel actually says.

4. One way out of this fuzziness is to claim that all Hegel meant by the 'cunning of reason' is that everything that happens in history does so for a reason. Yet this claim is so vague as to be useless. Besides, it does not seem to be what Hegel, a strong believer in teleology, meant. It can also be seen as a much stronger version of what later became known as 'unintended consequences'.

5. Unlike Adorno, Benjamin celebrated the cinema as a popular medium, arguing that ordinary people could go to films and be their own critics. This was contrary to 'high art' like painting and sculpture, which was displayed in galleries and required a refined taste to be appreciated.

6. movies.yahoo.com/mv/boxoffice/weekend/

7. www.rottentomatoes.com/m/boogeyman/
8. We actually see this sort of thing in the 1985 film *Back to the Future*, where Michael J. Fox plays a time traveller who visits a 1955 high school prom. He plays guitar first in the style of Chuck Berry, then Jimi Hendrix, the latter causing the teenage dancers to stare at him in astonishment, their mouths agape. Yet Hendrix was only a dozen years in the future!
9. Debord's book is divided into 221 numbered sections. All references to *The Society of the Spectacle* are to sections, not pages.
10. References to Vaneigem are to chapters rather than pages because the Internet version of his work is more accessible than the printed book.

CHAPTER 5

1. I'm simplifying Collingwood's language a bit here.
2. This despite the fact that some commentators see it as a very important part of social theory. Wallace and Wolf (1999) devote a 74-page chapter to it in their popular textbook.
3. See my *Structural Idealism: A Theory of Social and Historical Explanation* (Waterloo, Ont.: Wilfrid Laurier University Press, 2002) for an attempt to grapple with Giddens's duality of structure and related problems in the social theory of Weber, Collingwood, and Winch.

CHAPTER 6

1. The solar metaphor is mine, the levels are from Schutz.
2. The opposite point of view is that millennia of biological and cultural evolution have inculcated in us a strong sense that some things are better to eat than others, for example, tomatoes are better than tree bark, and thus such choices aren't solely social constructs. The same goes for our choices of sexual partners.
3. Note that these breaching experiments are considered unethical by many people since their subjects have not given their consent to the trouble being made. Of course, if they *had* given such consent, they would probably have also been told what the experiment's goals were, thus making the breach of everyday expectations rather pointless. In the example just given, telling the students that 'this is just a sociological experiment' would explain the professor's behaviour, therefore precluding the need to account for it in some other way.

CHAPTER 7

1. Freud isn't *just* a structuralist, though there is undoubtedly a structuralist element in his work. Similarly, Louis Althusser read Marx in structuralist terms, though not all Marxists are structuralists.
2. Note that some folklorists and anthropologists have considered the Jungian archetypal myth, as popularized by Campbell, to be more psychobabble than serious theory, and have pointed out that the common motifs and story-types of ancient myths have spread about the world by simple processes of transmission and diffusion.
3. Joel and Ethan Coen, who wrote and directed *Oh Brother*, explicitly acknowledge Homer's *Odyssey* as the inspiration for their film. The fact that the hero's name is 'Ulysses' makes this connection obvious.
4. I refer to the hero as male to reflect the fact that almost all mythical heroes were men.
5. These four modes of the symbolic construction of subcultural style were introduced by Phil Cohen in 1972 in a working paper written for the CCCS.
6. In March of 2005, after a lecture on subcultural theory, I asked a number of male undergraduates what was the cultural meaning of the baseball caps most of them were wearing. None gave a coherent answer.
7. I rely to no small degree in this section on Rosenau's excellent summary of postmodernism in her *Post-Modernism and the Social Sciences*.
8. Foucault would seem to be obviously wrong about the bourgeois origins of authorship: the ancient Greeks had a healthy sense of the self and a pride in what they wrote. Read Heraclitus, Herodotus, Thucydides, or Plato for evidence of this.
9. What he actually said was '*Il n'y a pas de hors-texte*', which translates more directly as 'there is no outside-text.'
10. This is according to Derrida. At least in the English-speaking world, cultural anthropology dates back well into the nineteenth century, the heyday of European imperialism, not its last gasp.
11. 'Episteme' is an ancient Greek word meaning 'knowledge' and is the root of the English word 'epistemology', the theory of knowledge.
12. Volume III of Foucault's *History of Sexuality* goes on to discuss sexuality in ancient Rome.

CHAPTER 8

1. Taylorism refers to the principles of the scientific management of work developed by Frederick W. Taylor in the early twentieth century. Taylor treated the individual worker as a machine that can perform a given number of motions in a given amount of time, the goal being to minimize labour costs.
2. Of course, designating these as 'mega-cities' based purely on their population is a crude judgement of their significance. It would be more useful to follow other theorists who use the term 'world city' to describe the economic, political, and cultural importance of certain urban centres. Under such a designation, Paris beats Mexico City and Washington beats Osaka because of the cultural and political clout of the French and American capitals.
3. Sometime around 1995 I remember putting a 'for sale' ad on a user-group web board at my university. A student responded to it; when I failed to acknowledge the response in a three- or four-hour period—I was busy with the 'real' world—he sent a second angry and hostile message rebuking me for failing to answer! Time has indeed been compressed in the Information Age.

CHAPTER 9

1. As I write this in the summer of 2005, mediocre remakes of two very average films from the 1970s are being shown in local cinemas—*The Longest Yard* and *Bad News Bears*—as well as a fair remake of the classic 1953 science fiction film *The War of the Worlds*. The many film remakes of recent years provide evidence that a waning sense even of film history has been promoted by postmodern culture, to the point where millions of North Americans attend screenings of revamped versions of earlier simulacra without complaint.
2. I am extending Jameson's analysis a bit here and adding some more recent examples.
3. Baudrillard is wrong on this: Walt Disney's cryogenic suspension is an urban myth!
4. Note that Baudrillard really seems to be predicting a trend here, not observing one. In the mid-1980s we were still 15 years away from the likes of *Survivor*, *Joe Millionaire*, and *Big Brother*.
5. Baudrillard's analysis makes more sense when applied to the middle and upper classes, for surely America is no utopia to the urban poor working

for minimum wage without health insurance or decent living conditions.
6. Of course, it was certainly a lot more 'real' to the Iraqis than to the Americans.
7. I loosely follow Dominic Strinati's (1995) list of the elements of postmodern culture here, redefining and expanding on some of his categories and using more current examples. Also see Jameson (1991) and Harvey (1989) for more comments on postmodern popular culture.
8. I refer to Barnet Newman's *Voice of Fire*, 1967, which hangs in the National Gallery in Ottawa. See <kentasy.net/Images/VoiceOfFire.JPG>.
9. Note that Borgmann's 'postmodern realism' is a far cry from the information society of Lyotard and Castells and from Baudrillard's third order of simulacra, which more closely match what Borgmann calls 'hypermodernism'.

CHAPTER 10

1. Interestingly, in Canada, Quebec was the laggard, with women having to wait until 1940 for the right to vote in provincial elections.
2. Some might date the beginning of second-wave feminism to Simone de Beauvoir's *Le Deuxième Sexe* (1949). Although influential, Beauvoir's work was largely a lone feminist cry in the wilderness, especially in North America.
3. Though it might not be evident from the theorists covered in this chapter, Foucault's theories of power/knowledge and sexuality have been tremendously influential on radical and postmodern feminist theorists from the mid-1980s to today. Foucault emphasizes the notion that we live continually under the malevolent and controlling gaze of powerful and partially hidden figures, just as radical feminism posits of patriarchy.
4. However, Wolf engaged in a bit of backsliding when in February 2004 she publicly accused the prominent Yale literary critic Harold Bloom of groping her in 1983 when she invited him to her apartment for some dinner, wine, and poetry. Wolf says that his advance caused her to vomit, whereupon Bloom left. She claimed in her *New York* magazine article of 1 March 2004 that the event undermined Yale's credibility. Critics, including feminists of various ideological stripes, almost unanimously condemned her for 'crying wolf' two decades after the fact and for painting herself as a

helpless victim who couldn't stand up to the 'powerful' Bloom. For Wolf's side of the story, see: <www.newyorkmetro.com/nymetro/news/features/n_9932/>.

5. In 2003 this number had risen to 77 per cent in the US, or about 80 per cent if one corrects for occupation, race, and experience. See <www.sfgate.com/cgi-bin/article.cgi?file=/chronicle/archive/2005/01/09/CMGLHABABH1.DTL>.

6. Of course, this opens up a potentially ugly debate over whether married workers would be paid half of the standard wage for their positions, or the same as single workers with a whole 'extra' salary going to their partners. In the latter case, single workers would be justifiably irate.

7. This proposal could act as a great disincentive to overtime work or career ambitions, since the man's income would be taxed twice: 30 per cent or more by the state, and then another 50 per cent by his former partner.

8. This section is loosely based on my 'Carol Gilligan on the Different Voice of Women', in Douglas Mann and G. Elijah Dann, eds, *Philosophy: A New Introduction* (Belmont, Calif.: Wadsworth, 2005), 587–9.

9. Of course, one needs no Marxist ghost to tell us this. Note that Karl Mannheim's sociology of knowledge also considerably predates feminist standpoint theory.

10. 'Cartesian' refers to the seventeenth-century French philosopher René Descartes (1595–1650), who used the famous quip 'I think therefore I am' to summarize his argument that the one thing he could be certain of was that he existed as a thinking thing (*ego cogitans* in his original Latin), a rational ego. Descartes didn't trust the reality of his bodily senses, which he saw as regularly deceiving him.

11. In philosophy this is called the 'genetic fallacy'. Suppose a scientist who discovered the cure for the common cold cheated on his wife, while another scientist who was faithful to his spouse proposed that smoking cigarettes would cure a cold. Most philosophers say that the genesis of the cure in the mind of an unfaithful scientist has no effect on its validity. Similarly, the 'good' husband isn't necessarily a good scientist. Harding seems to be saying the opposite: if a theoretical idea comes from an immoral source, it becomes suspect.

12. The ancient Rosetta stone featured the same text in Egyptian hieroglyphics, demotic Egyptian, and ancient Greek. It was discovered by French troops in 1799 and allowed François Champollion to decipher the meaning of Egyptian hieroglyphics in 1822 by reading back from the Greek.

13. Paglia makes the interesting point in *Vamps and Tramps* that at all the elite schools in the US in the 1990s, there was only one sixties radical in a tenured position, Todd Gitlin. In other words, the most critical elements of the 1960s and 1970s generation simply dropped out of higher education, leaving it to 'conformist clones'. From my experience, this is equally true of Canadian universities: excessive specialization and conformity are actively rewarded in arts and social science departments.

14. As Paglia herself has noted, feminist critics have twisted this argument into the notion that 'Paglia thinks rape is OK!', a wilful distortion of her views that I have heard several times myself from undergraduate students repeating comments made by feminist professors.

CHAPTER 11

1. In fact, a number of other Canadian theorists have painted striking pictures of the effects of modern communication technologies on social life, including 'classical' theorists such as Harold Innis and George Grant, and contemporary theorists such as Arthur Kroker and Mark Kingwell.

2. Watch David Cronenberg's 1982 film, *Videodrome*, for a visceral picture of a character being absorbed by television in a literal and very sexual way.

3. Also worth mentioning are two of Menzies's earlier works, *Computers on the Job* (1982) and *Fast Forward and Out of Control* (1989).

4. If I might be allowed a personal note, I wrote this book as an 'adjunct' or contract professor. In some university departments contract instructors teach half or more of all first- and second-year courses.

5. I refer to H.G. Wells's classic, *The Time Machine* (1895), in which our hero travels to a sinister future society.

6. In my view, chronic cellphone users are in danger of losing their inner dialogue in the constant babble produced by their virtual network of friends and family. The bus rider listens to her messages instead of reading a book; the walker gabs to a friend instead of thinking about her day or fantasizing about alternate realities. Literacy and imagination suffer little microwaved deaths.

7. In my own recent experience in teaching sociology, I have found that many students are very good at memorizing lecture notes; but as soon as they are asked to explain a theoretical concept in their own words they fall apart, having become far too accustomed to merely parroting data back to their professors.

CHAPTER 12

1. Political terminology here is rather confusing. Speaking in economic terms, a modern American 'liberal' is someone on the left who favours government intervention in the economy and greater economic equality (in Canada we would call many of these liberals 'social democrats'), while a 'conservative' favours more limited government, low taxes, and free trade. To further complicate things, we have to distinguish 'fiscal' from 'social' conservatives. The former confine themselves to economic matters, namely reducing taxes and government spending; the latter defend religious and family values against threats such as abortion, illicit drugs, divorce, homosexuality, and secular society as a whole. In the US most conservatives are both social and fiscal; in Canada, most are merely fiscal.

2. Not included in Table 12.1, but discussed later in the chapter, is the 'Third Way' defended by Tony Blair and Anthony Giddens, which seeks to steer a middle course between neo-liberalism and social democracy.

3. To be fair, some conservatives argue that the left's insistence that firm labour regulations, a minimum wage, and a social security system should be tied to globalized trade is a sort of 'social correctness' that cynically protects the economies of the countries where these leftists live (Steil, 1994: 14). Yet even if this is partly true, in some cases conservative intellectuals themselves are in the pay of transnational corporations (e.g., through right-wing think-tanks like the Fraser Institute in Canada), or are at least dependent on big business for their livelihoods (e.g., business schools at universities).

4. Although the idea of movie sequels goes back at least the 1930s, as with the *Tarzan* and *Sherlock Holmes* series of films.

5. A Canadian example of a McDonaldized pseudo-travel experience can be seen in the West Edmon-ton Mall, with its replica of one of Columbus's ships, wave pool, dolphin tank, skating rink, and *faux* Latin Quarter.

6. Of course, even in the ancient Roman Empire distant events such as the assassination of a Caesar could affect local ones. It's a question of degree.

7. On a personal note, I visit a large shopping mall in the south end of London, Ontario, from time to time. Almost every visit I notice a group of conservatively dressed elderly Italian gentlemen sitting at a table in the food court chatting, probably for hours. This is their piazza; there is nowhere else to go—no sidewalk cafés, no public square. The spectre of a mall food court as the true agora of the city is a sad one, to say the least, hardly a replacement for the public places of Roma, Napoli, or Firenze.

8. One might note at this point that Bauman's tourist/vagabond distinction is rather extreme. Many people are part vagabond and part tourist. He concedes this at a few points. It is perhaps better to see his distinction as a pair of ideal types where a minority of people (at least in the industrialized West) fit entirely into either stereotype. In the Third World, however, this distinction is more real than ideal: there are plenty of actual vagabonds and not a few tourists there.

9. As I write this in May 2006, I hear on the radio that Montenegro has just voted in a referendum to break free of Serbia, thus putting the last nail in the coffin of the Yugoslav federal republic. Montenegro's area is 13,812 square kilometres, about one-quarter the size of Nova Scotia. It will need 'help' from nations much larger than itself to prosper politically and economically.

10. The recent Enron scandal, where the company's executives reaped huge profits from shady manipulations of the energy markets, seems to prove Saul right on this point. Saul argues that the modern business corporation isn't a hotbed of risk and innovation, except when buying up smaller, more creative firms. He further thinks that Canadian business schools are impediments to prosperity, turning out cautious conformists instead of risk-takers, and should be removed from universities (Saul, 1995: 131).

11. Needless to say, in 2007 the logo still rules supreme. One could argue that the height of anti-corporate activism came in 1998–2001, around when Klein wrote her book, and has declined considerably

since then, perhaps a result of a chilly political climate following 9/11. Thus, the first part of her book, in which she diagnoses the disease of brand worship, is even more relevant today. On the other hand, her hope that culture jamming will reduce this brand worship now seems a bit utopian.

12. However, this marketing synergy does not always work, as witnessed by the massive promotion for the 1998 remake of *Godzilla*, which flopped at the box office due to poor word-of-mouth reviews.

13. Klein is being a bit narcissistic here. Even though she acknowledges that teenage narcissists falsely believe that the world only came into existence the moment when the teen in question was born, she ignores the rather obvious fact that we have lived in a youth-obsessed culture at least since the mid-1960s. This certainly was not invented in 1990. TV ads for cars, beer, and soda pop from the 1960s and 1970s demonstrate direct marketing to youth. Perhaps the marketing shift she outlines is more a matter of the removal of certain moral and political barriers to the selling of alternative culture to kids—it is no longer associated with 'dangerous' politics such as opposition to the Vietnam War or the fight for civil rights and social equality—rather

than any sudden revelation that corporations had a 'new' age group to sell commodities to.

14. Yet Moore's 2002 film, *Bowling for Columbine*, had to use money from the relatively small Canadian production company Salter Street Films and a patchwork of distributors to get onto North America's screens.

15. Klein found one Chinese factory that paid a wage of just 13 cents an hour, much less than the 87 cents estimated to be the minimum cost of living in China at the end of the nineties.

16. For example, a Wal-Mart clerk being paid $7.50 an hour working for 40 hours a week, 50 weeks a year, will earn $15,000. Of course, she is likely to be allowed to work only 28 hours a week, reducing her yearly salary to about $11,000, hardly a living wage.

17. Although Klein does not mention this, the ratio of part-time to full-time faculty on North American university campuses has climbed steadily since the early nineties, with the predictable negative effect on the morale and quality of research of these contract instructors. This is something I am intimately familiar with, having taught in 10 different departments at three universities and two colleges.

INDEX

Note: Figures in **bold type** indicate illustrations or tables.